JUVENILE JUSTICE IN CANADA

A Theoretical and Analytical Assessment

Raymond R. Corrado
Nicholas Bala
Rick Linden
Marc Le Blanc

Butterworths
Toronto and Vancouver

Juvenile Justice in Canada: A Theoretical and Analytical Assessment

© Butterworths Canada Ltd. 1992

Printed and bound in Canada

The Butterworth Group of Companies

Canada
> Butterworths Canada Ltd., 75 Clegg Road, MARKHAM, Ont. L6G 1A1 and 409 Granville St., Ste. 1455, VANCOUVER, B.C. V6C 1T2

Australia
> Butterworths Pty. Ltd., SYDNEY, MELBOURNE, BRISBANE, ADELAIDE, PERTH, CANBERRA and HOBART

Ireland
> Butterworth (Ireland) Ltd., DUBLIN

New Zealand
> Butterworths of New Zealand Ltd., WELLINGTON and AUCKLAND

Puerto Rico
> Equity de Puerto Rico, Inc., HATO REY

Singapore
> Butterworth ASIA, SINGAPORE

United Kingdom
> Butterworth & Co. (Publishers) Ltd., LONDON and EDINBURGH

United States
> Butterworth Legal Publishers, AUSTIN, Texas; BOSTON, Massachusetts; CLEARWATER, Florida (D & S Publishers); ORFORD, New Hampshire (Equity Publishing); ST. PAUL, Minnesota; and SEATTLE, Washington

Canadian Cataloguing in Publication Data

Main entry under title:

Juvenile justice in Canada

Includes bibliographical references.
ISBN 0-409-88886-9

1. Juvenile justice, Administration of — Canada.
2. Canada. Young Offenders Act. I. Corrado, Raymond.

KE9445.J88 1992   345.71'08   C92-094331-4

Project Editor: Alexander Schultz
Cover Design: Valerie Cooke
Production: Marlene Roopsingh

Juvenile Justice in Canada

ACKNOWLEDGMENTS

Marc Le Blanc, Rick Linden, and I originated the idea for this volume as a follow-up to *Current Issues in Juvenile Justice* published in 1983. This book dealt with various topics leading up to the passage of the *Young Offenders Act*. We felt sufficient time had passed to assess the impact of the *YOA* on juvenile justice in Canada. Nicholas Bala was invited to join us as a co-editor because he had contributed significantly to the design of the proposed volume. Alan Markwart has also been vitally important in structuring most of the chapters in Part One. He should be considered a co-editor as well.

Research assistants, Garth Davies, Suzanne Noble, Terri Jarvis, and Mike Young were involved with bibliographic work and certain table and figure constructions in Part One. We appreciate their efforts. We would also like to thank the external reviewers of the manuscript for their input, particularly Robert Silverman whose comments were most valuable. Finally, we are all grateful for the support and assistance from various members of the team at Butterworths. We owe a special thanks to Sandra Magico for her early encouragement. We are deeply saddened by her death.

Raymond R. Corrado

CONTRIBUTORS

Don Andrews
Department of Psychology
Carleton University

Nicholas Bala
Queen's University Law School

Hélène Beaumont
Groupe de recherche sur l'inadaption
psycho-sociale chez l'enfant
Université de Montréal

Raymond R. Corrado
School of Criminology
Simon Fraser University

Paul Gendreau
Department of Psychology
University of New Brunswick
Saint John

Peter G. Jaffe
London Family Court Clinic

Rod Kueneman
Department of Sociology
University of Manitoba

Marc Le Blanc
École de psycho-éducation
Université de Montréal

Alan W. Leschied
London Family Court Clinic

Rick Linden
Department of Sociology
University of Manitoba

Alan Markwart
British Columbia Ministry of
Attorney General

Heather A. Milne
Prairie Research Associates
Winnipeg

Susan D. Turnbull
Department of Psychology
Simon Fraser University

CONTENTS

Contents

CHAPTER 1

INTRODUCTION

Raymond R. Corrado

The *Young Offenders Act (YOA)* was enacted by the Canadian Parliament in 1982 and came into force in 1984,[1] replacing the *Juvenile Delinquents Act (JDA)* of 1908.[2] The *YOA* establishes the legal principles for juvenile justice in Canada for young persons between 12 and 18 years of age, although each province has the constitutional responsibility to establish its own administrative structures to implement the *YOA*. The *YOA* has been in effect for approximately seven years, and sufficient time has now passed to assess its impact on the provincial and territorial juvenile justice systems. This book provides the beginnings of this much-needed evaluation of the *YOA* from the perspective of a number of different authors. The primary objectives of this book are: (1) to describe the legal structure of the *YOA* and how young persons are processed under the Act; and (2) to analyse the changes in how young offenders are dealt with under the *YOA* as compared to the *JDA*.

Changes in the administration of juvenile justice were expected, because the *JDA* and the *YOA* reflect fundamentally different philosophies about how to structure juvenile justice systems. The *JDA* was based on the positivist philosophy that children and adolescents engage in deviant and criminal behaviour due to problems involving their families, peers, education, poverty, cultural values and other factors affecting their socialization. Accordingly, the juvenile justice system based on this philosophy was designed to rehabilitate misguided or inadequately socialized delinquents using informal legal procedures and indeterminate, treatment-oriented sentences.

In contrast, the *YOA* is based in significant measure (although not fully, as will

---

[1] S.C. 1980-81-82-83, c. 110 [now R.S.C. 1985, c. Y-1].

[2] S.C. 1908, c. 40.

1

become clear in this book) on the neo-classical philosophy[3] that adolescents wilfully engage in criminal behaviour and, therefore, should be held responsible and accountable for their actions. A juvenile justice system based solely on a philosophy of accountability would be organized similarly to the existing Canadian adult criminal system, which focuses on criminal offences, procedural fairness, and determinate sentences based on the severity of the offence and the prior record of the offender.

Different conceptualizations of the reasons underlying adolescents' deviant and/or criminal behaviour provide the theoretical models of juvenile justice and have enormous practical implications. A brief outline of these different models of juvenile justice is therefore in order.

MODELS OF JUVENILE JUSTICE

Historically, three main approaches to juvenile justice have been articulated. These are the positivist and neo-classical traditions, described above, and a third position which emphasizes protection of society over offender-related concerns. In turn, each of these theoretical orientations has given rise to a specific model of juvenile justice. Thus, proponents of the positivist tradition espouse a Welfare Model of juvenile justice, which is primarily concerned with the rehabilitation of offenders. Neo-classicists champion a Justice Model, which focuses on due process[4] and the assignment of punishment proportionate to the crime. Finally, those who consider protection of the community to be paramount are associated with a Crime Control Model of juvenile justice, which emphasizes incarceration

---

[3] The neo-classical philosophy of crime emerged in the 19th century. It challenged the rigidity of the central proposition of the classical philosophy; that is, all criminal behaviour was wilful and rationally calculated. The neo-classicists modified this proposition by asserting that there are personal factors, such as age and maturity, that can mitigate the degree to which individuals are responsible for their behaviour. (See Vold & Bernard, 1979 for a review of theories of crime.)

[4] Due process is a legal doctrine reflected in both the Canadian and American constitutions premised on the notion that individuals are to be treated in accordance with the law and afforded a full set of legal rights. In a criminal law context, it refers to the rights afforded an individual, beginning with the police investigation stage through to final appeal stage in the criminal justice system. For example, a person cannot be jailed beyond a very short period without being formally charged and brought before a judge for a hearing. In the Canadian legal context, these due process rights are included in the concept of principles of "fundamental justice" under ss. 7 to 13 of the *Canadian Charter of Rights and Freedoms*. These rights are also protected in various sections of the *YOA*. (See Chapter 2 by Bala.)

of offenders, particularly repetitive and violent offenders, with objectives of both punitiveness and societal protection.

These models may be considered to lie on a continuum loosely based on scope of concern for the offender, with the offender-focused Welfare Model at one end and the more broadly focused community-protection Crime Control Model at the other. This continuum is theoretical, and in practice there is some overlap of approach, procedures and outcomes under the different models. For example, those who are successfully rehabilitated under the Welfare Model pose a reduced risk to the public, a result consonant with the goals of the Crime Control Model. This continuum will be addressed more fully below.

In practice, no juvenile justice system exists in one of these three pure forms. While juvenile justice systems may be classified according to the models, actual systems are based on some combination of philosophical rationales. In addition, logistical and administrative concerns intrude upon the theory to modify the application of any juvenile justice model. Pratt has recently formulated one mixed model, which he calls the Corporatist Model.[5] Emphasis in this model is on the diversion of young offenders, both from the formalized juvenile justice system and from custody, and an administrative system is constructed to achieve this purpose. Because of its focus on offenders, the Corporatist Model may be located near the Welfare Model end of the continuum. The specific characteristics of each of these models, along with their location on the continuum, are presented in Figure 1.

A fifth model also included in Figure 1 is the Modified Justice Model. This model retains many of the features of the Justice Model, but has been altered in some respects to reflect welfare concerns. Because this model has been developed by this author and is newly introduced in this book, it will be elaborated upon in some detail below. It argues that the *YOA* is best conceptualized as a representative of the Modified Justice Model of juvenile justice.

There are several advantages in employing these models to understand the impact of legislation such as the *YOA* on juvenile justice. First, they reduce the complex legislation and diverse juvenile justice agencies to essential sets of characteristics. In effect, models facilitate an understanding of complex phenomena by simplifying them. Second, the models facilitate comparisons. It is extremely unwieldy and cumbersome to compare detailed legislation such as the *YOA* and the *JDA* section by section, rather than comparing a small set of essential principles. It is even more daunting to compare the highly diverse provincial juvenile justice systems, particularly in light of the considerable variations which exist *within* provinces.[6]

---

[5] Pratt, "Corporatism: The Third Model of Juvenile Justice" (1989) 29(3) *British Journal of Criminology* pp. 236–53.

[6] Bala and Corrado, "Juvenile Justice: A Comparative Study" (Ottawa: Ministry of Solicitor General, 1985).

Figure 1
Continuum of Juvenile Justice Models

Focus on offender ←————————————————————→ *Focus on protection of society*

Characteristics	Welfare[1,2]	Corporatism[1]	Modified Justice[1]	Justice[1]	Crime Control[2]
General Features	Informality Generic referrals Individualized sentencing Indeterminate sentencing	Administrative decision-making Offending Diversion from court/custody programmes Alternative to care/custody programmes	Due Process informality Criminal offences Bifurcation: soft offenders diverted, hard offenders punished Determinate sentences	Due process Criminal offences Least restrictive alternative Determinate sentences	Due process/discretion Offending/status offences Punishment Determinate sentences
Key Personnel	Childcare experts	Juvenile justice specialists	Lawyers/childcare experts	Lawyers	Lawyers/criminal justice actors
Key Agency	Social work	Interagency structure	Law/social work	Law	Law
Tasks	Diagnosis	Systems intervention	Diagnosis/punishment	Punishment	Incarceration/punishment
Understanding of Client Behaviour	Pathology/environmentally determined	Unsocialized	Diminished individual responsibility	Individual responsibility	Responsibility/accountability
Purpose of Intervention	Provide treatment (*Parens Patriae*)	Retrain	Sanction behaviour/provide treatment	Sanction behaviour	Protection of society/retribution/deterrence
Objectives	Respond to individual needs/rehabilitation	Implementation of policy	Respect individual rights/respond to "special" needs	Respect individual rights/punish	Order maintenance

[1] Pratt, "Corporatism: The Third Model of Juvenile Justice (1989) 29(3) *Br. J.C.* pp. 236–53.
[2] Reid and Reitsma-Street "Assumptions and Implications of New Canadian Legislation for Young Offenders" (1984) 17(1) *C.C.F.* pp. 334–52.

These problems in comparative analysis are compounded when cross-national perspectives are attempted. Unique historical and cultural differences between countries make the use of models very helpful in identifying similarities and differences in juvenile justice experiences. A comparative perspective is important because it provides valuable information for those attempting to profit from the experiences of other jurisdictions. For example, juvenile justice trends in other countries which have already implemented *YOA*-type legislation can be evaluated to assist in predicting and understanding similar trends in Canada. Further, countries that have employed radically different juvenile justice legislation provide additional information on the advantages of dissimilar approaches.

A third reason for employing models is that they are used extensively in the empirical and theoretical literature on juvenile justice. As will be discussed below, senior federal bureaucrats responsible for drafting the *YOA*, and their provincial counterparts, referred to this literature in drafting the *YOA* and preparing for its implementation.

There is little doubt that the Welfare and Justice Model constructs are particularly important in understanding the historical debate over the appropriate form of juvenile justice. According to one of the foremost American scholars of juvenile justice, Malcolm Klein:

> This seemingly inevitable tug of war between Welfare and Justice Models, between paternalism and legalism, may provide the single most pivotal dimension along which to array and assess different juvenile justice systems.[7]

Similarly, David Farrington maintains that

> English scholars have usually classified methods of dealing with juvenile delinquents into extreme stereotypes, termed 'justice and welfare'.[8]

In sum, at least a minimal understanding of these models is beneficial in attempting to evaluate the *YOA*. What follows is a brief review of the historical context in which the *YOA* developed. This will contribute to an appreciation of the impact of this legislation, and of the ways the legislation itself was influenced by the theoretical models just discussed.

HISTORICAL CONTEXT OF THE *YOA*

Within a span of five years beginning in 1977, major juvenile justice reforms were enacted in England and Wales, in several states in the U.S., and in Canada. Generally, these reforms can be characterized as having moved juvenile justice

---

[7] Klein, *Western Systems of Juvenile Justice* (Beverly Hills, Calif.: Sage Publications, 1984), p. 13.

[8] Farrington, "England and Wales," in Klein, ed., *Western Systems of Juvenile Justice* (Beverly Hills, Calif.: Sage Publications, 1984), p. 71.

systems from the Welfare Model end of the continuum toward the Justice Model (see Figure 1). This movement from juvenile justice systems characterized in the ideal form by informal processes and an emphasis on rehabilitation of delinquents, to systems requiring due process and focusing primarily on the offence and prior record of the offender to determine severity of sentence, has stirred controversy among scholars and social commentators. Proponents claim that these changes resulted in benefits to society that include greater protection from youth crime (and later adult crime), as well as greater protection for youth from arbitrary and usually ineffective intervention by government agencies. Critics of the Justice Model reforms claim that they resulted in greater punishment of young offenders without deterring future offending. They also maintain that these reforms led to greater substantive injustices by minimizing or ignoring the environmental context — that is, poverty, race and other factors associated with youth crime.[9]

Disagreements over the most appropriate type of juvenile justice system date back to the late 19th century, when reformers in several Western industrial countries sought.to create separate juvenile justice systems, distinct from the existing adult justice systems. From the beginning, there was controversy over the absence of due process in the Welfare Model approach. Despite the controversy, proponents of the Welfare Model largely succeeded in completely implementing this system in Canada and the U.S. by the early 1900s.

In Britain, on the other hand, from 1908 until the mid-1980s there was a mixed model which could be characterized as a Modified Justice Model. In Britain during this time, summary criminal procedures identical to those in the adult criminal court prevailed for juveniles, while the child's welfare, the offence, and

---

[9] See, for example:

Asquith, *Children and Justice: Decision-Making in Children's Hearings and Juvenile Courts* (Edinburgh: Edinburgh University Press, 1983).

Bortner, *Delinquency and Justice: An Age of Crisis* (New York: McGraw-Hill, 1988).

Clarke, "Whose Justice? The Politics of Juvenile Control" (1985) 13 *Int'l. J. Soc. L.* pp. 407–21.

Faust and Brantingham, *Juvenile Justice Philosophy: Readings, Cases and Comments* (St. Paul, Minn.: West Publishing, 1979).

Hackler, *The Great Stumble Forward: The Reinvention of Youthful Crime* (Toronto: Methuen, 1978).

Morris, "Revolution in the Juvenile Court" (1978) (September) Crim. L. Rev. pp. 529–39.

Morris and Giller, *Understanding Juvenile Justice* (London: Groom Helm, 1987).

Wilson and Hernstein, *Crime and Nature* (New York: Simon and Schuster, 1985).

the child's prior record were considered in sentencing. Until the 1970s, most attempts to reform British juvenile justice involved proposed shifts towards the more welfare oriented U.S. and Canadian approaches. The Scottish had achieved a shift to a pure Welfare Model by 1968. England and Wales, on the other hand, began swinging back towards a Justice Model during the early 1980s, and by the end of that decade had settled on a Corporatist Model — still a mixed model — for their juvenile justice system.[10]

The contemporary juvenile justice reform movement in Western countries began in earnest in the 1960s, with Canada among the first to initiate a formal review. In 1961, the federal Department of Justice appointed an advisory committee to examine why the juvenile justice system was apparently unable to stem the perceived growing number of young adult offenders.

This was a federally appointed justice committee, because, according to the *Constitution Act of 1867*,[11] the federal government had sole jurisdiction over criminal law legislation, while the provincial governments were responsible for the administration of both justice and child welfare services. The rationale for this division of constitutional authority was that a national criminal law legislation would enhance uniformity and equality of treatment before the criminal law, while each province could adapt the administration of justice — that is, specific agencies such as police and court structures — to the distinctive needs of the province. Since the creation and reform of a juvenile justice system involves changing criminal law to take account of age and other considerations, the federal government alone can enact juvenile justice law. However, the provinces have jurisdiction over not only the administration of juvenile justice, but also the enactment of legislation and provision of services in the fields of child welfare, health, mental health and education.

The *JDA* promoted direct contact between juvenile justice agencies and the agencies representing the latter areas. Therefore, the provinces had the major influence in adapting, and even modifying, the *JDA* principles through legislation and practices. This constitutional division of power is critical in understanding the history of juvenile justice reform, and it is discussed in detail in Chapter 4 by Corrado and Markwart.

The Department of Justice advisory committee published its highly critical findings and recommendations in the 1965 *Juvenile Delinquency In Canada* report. Criticisms focused on the lack of juvenile offender rights under the *JDA* and the inadequate resources that had been available to achieve its rehabilitative ideals. This report resulted in the drafting of the *Children and Young Persons Act* in 1967, which retained the rehabilitative objectives of the Welfare Model, but with the protection of legal rights. This draft statute was not enacted because of concerns of provincial bureaucrats and politicians about both the Act's proposed

---

[10] Pratt, *supra*, note 5.

[11] (U.K.), 30 & 31 Vict., c. 3.

jurisdiction over provincial statutes and municipal by-law violations and about the issue of federal/provincial cost-sharing.

The next reform attempt, Bill C-192, the *Young Offenders Act*, was introduced in 1970 with the above criticisms in mind. However, it too was rejected, primarily because treatment-oriented interest groups such as the Canadian Mental Health Association condemned this as moving too far toward an overtly legalistic and punitive model of juvenile justice.

The *Young Persons in Conflict with Law Act* was drafted in 1975 and it continued the trend away from the Welfare Model by emphasizing the legal rights of juveniles as well as the new theme of responsibility and accountability for criminal behaviour. The Bill failed when some provinces opposed the costs of moving toward a uniform maximum age and the proposed mandatory (diversion) screening agency.

The Conservative government introduced another series of legislative reform proposals in 1979 which retained the protection of the legal rights of juveniles and met most of the provincial jurisdictional and cost concerns while introducing another objective — the protection of society. Before the reforms could be enacted, the Conservative government was defeated and the newly elected Liberal Party in 1981 quickly reintroduced nearly identical legislation, Bill C-61, the *Young Offenders Act*. The adoption of the *Canadian Charter of Rights and Freedoms*[12] in 1982 provided significant impetus for repeal of the *JDA*. The Charter's emphasis on due process required more protection of legal rights of juveniles than afforded under the *JDA*. The Charter's guarantees of equal treatment were widely believed to require a uniform national age jurisdiction for juvenile courts. The *Charter* acceded to a uniform maximum age of 18.

It is important to understand that, while it required over 20 years for the federal government to enact the juvenile justice reform legislation, many provincial governments throughout the 1970s had introduced their own reforms, restructuring the administration of juvenile justice. The provincial constitutional authority over the administration of justice (in contrast to the federal authority over criminal and juvenile justice law) and the vague principles of the *JDA* allowed for substantial reforms. By 1981, it was evident that provinces such as Quebec and British Columbia had moved dramatically away from traditional *JDA* practices. Also, in most major urban centres, many of the proposed *YOA* policies had already been in effect.[13] Why these changes took place and a detailed description of them are presented by Corrado and Markwart in Chapter 4.

All of the authors of this book have been involved in some way in policy research for federal or provincial ministries, and several were also involved in a research project entitled the National Study of the Functioning of the Juvenile

---

[12] Part I of the *Constitution Act, 1982*, being Schedule B of the *Canada Act 1982* (U.K.), 1982, c. 11.

[13] Bala and Corrado, *supra*, note 6.

Court,[14] begun in 1980 and initiated, directed and funded by the federal Ministry of the Solicitor General. This research was not designed to affect the then proposed *YOA*, since the *YOA* was to become law before the research results became available but rather gathered information about the functioning of the juvenile justice system under the *JDA*. However, other research, mainly from the U.K. and the U.S., was influential in drafting the *YOA* and its unsuccessful predecessors. Research from other countries substantially contributed to a general consensus that the Welfare Model on which the *JDA* was based was a fundamentally flawed approach to juvenile justice.[15]

It was in this historical context that the *Young Offenders Act* became law in 1982. When initially introduced in Parliament in 1979, the *YOA* was hailed by Conservative Solicitor General Allen Lawrence as the "most progressive piece of social justice legislation in the last several decades." In 1982, it was unanimously passed by all political parties in the House of Commons.

---

[14] Researchers, mainly from universities across Canada, were invited to join in conducting a research project that would describe how juvenile courts operated in six urban areas (Vancouver, Edmonton, Winnipeg, Toronto, Montreal and Halifax), several non-metropolitan sites (for example, Kelowna, British Columbia), and selected rural areas in Alberta and Quebec. Through observations of court processes, from file information, and through survey interviews of juvenile justice personnel (from police through to judges), baseline data were obtained which would permit a future comparison with juvenile courts operating under the proposed *YOA* (see Bala and Corrado, 1985).

[15] Critics claimed that the Welfare Model ideals or objectives were rarely achieved in practice. Most importantly, there was little evidence that rehabilitation programs were effective (Martinson *et al.*, 1976; Hackler, 1978). They also argued that juvenile justice systems based on this model, like the *JDA*, had far too broad a jurisdiction over young people's lives; virtually any deviant behaviour was potentially delinquent. Status offences, in particular, were opposed by these critics because they in essence officially sanctioned behaviour such as "immorality" and "incorrigibility", for which adults could not be charged. Juvenile justice officials, child welfare authorities, teachers, and health representatives had few limits on their power to intervene in families and in the lives of delinquents as long as these officials acted, as the key *JDA* principle stipulated, "in the best interests" of the young person. With neither procedural safeguards enforced by judges, nor clearly and narrowly defined sentencing criteria, the Welfare Model facilitated arbitrary decisions which some critics asserted to be a denial of the fundamental right of every citizen to be treated fairly and predictably by government representatives. Other criticisms were that intervention programs to help delinquents and their families were vastly underfunded and that too many "helping professionals", such as probation officers and social workers, were inadequately trained and were preoccupied with bureaucratic politics.

THE *YOA* AS AN EXEMPLAR OF THE MODIFIED JUSTICE MODEL

Judge Omar Archambault, who played an important role in the drafting of the *YOA*, asserted that the *JDA* was based on the 19th-century positivist philosophy which emphasized treatment and rehabilitation of delinquent children as the primary method to protect the public from juvenile crimes. He noted that this approach minimized the accountability or responsibility of perpetrators. Furthermore, due process was largely ignored under this system because extensive intervention and informal processes were deemed necessary to further the "best interests" of "delinquents" (a non-criminal concept). Archambault asserts that this positivist philosophical basis was not only invalid but also inconsistent with contemporary cultural values regarding criminal justice. In contrast, the *YOA*:

> . . . is based on a new set of fundamental assumptions reflecting [cultural] evolution and inspired, as well, by extensive research and a more sophisticated knowledge of human behaviour generally, and the moral and psychological development of children in particular.[16]

For Archambault, one of the most important advances is the understanding that adolescents, even though they are in transition between childhood and adulthood, are capable of taking some responsibility for their criminal behaviour, although they are not necessarily as responsible as mature adults. This belief, along with the view that rehabilitation had been insufficiently (or not at all) effective in protecting society from youth crime, was critical in constructing the four key principles of the *YOA*.

These first two principles, according to Archambault, are the young offenders' responsibility and the protection of society. Although these two principles appear to blur the distinction between the juvenile and adult justice systems, the other two central principles — mitigated accountability and the "special needs" of young offenders — are what distinguish the adult and juvenile systems. Less severe sanctions, for example, limit the punitiveness of the juvenile justice system compared to the adult system. The greater use of medical and psychological

---

Another set of criticisms focused on the Welfare Model philosophy that delinquents are not responsible for their criminal behaviour and, therefore, should not be held accountable as adults are in terms of being subject to punitive sentencing. Police critics, for example, argued that Welfare Model systems promoted crime because delinquents did not fear punishment and respected neither this law nor the police. (See Bala and Corrado, 1985 and Chapter 3 by Corrado for a detailed discussion of the problems with the Welfare Model.).

[16] Archambault, "Young Offenders Act: Philosophy and Principles" in Silverman and Teevan, eds., *Crime in Canadian Society*, 3rd ed. (Toronto: Butterworths, 1986), p. 45.

assessments of young offenders, and the extensive monitoring and review of dispositions, not only by judges but also by the young offender, parents and Crown counsel, are seen as promoting the individual needs of young offenders. According to Archambault, other "progressive" principles include the guarantee of both young offenders' and parents' legal rights, restricted age and offence jurisdiction, treatment-oriented programs, and community involvement in crime prevention. There are additional principles and related sections in the *YOA* that will be examined in detail by Bala in Chapter 2.

The clear intent of the *YOA* is to protect society, to minimize the amount of interference in the lives of young people and their parents, and to ensure that due process is observed. Thus, the use of intrusive secure custody options is available only for those cases where the offence or prior record dictates their use, and placement in a treatment facility is available only to those young offenders who consent to this placement.

This mixture of principles and policies associated with the Justice, Welfare, and Crime Control Models makes it difficult to categorize the *YOA* according to the classic Welfare Model and Justice Model dichotomy. Hence, I would argue that the *YOA* can be best described as a Modified Justice Model.

The Modified Justice Model as an "ideal type" lacks the distinctiveness of the other models in Figure 1, partly because it has a mixture of characteristics from all these models. As outlined in Figure 1, the Modified Justice Model is located midway along a continuum that focuses on offender characteristics (for example, problems such as dysfunctional families and negative peer group influences) and treatment at one end, and the offence and prior record as well as protection of the public via custodial sentences at the other end. This continuum is helpful in understanding the evolution of diverse and complex types of juvenile justice systems, not only in the Canadian context, but also in other countries. (Corrado provides an analysis of the British and U.S. experiences in Chapter 3.)

By the late 1970s, legislative and policy reforms in some provinces, such as British Columbia, had resulted in certain juvenile court systems moving away from the Welfare Model toward the Justice Model. By 1980, despite the traditional characterization of the Canadian juvenile justice system as epitomizing the Welfare Model, there was no doubt that this categorization did not accurately describe the enormous variation in the types of juvenile justice systems across and within the provinces and territories.[17]

The Modified Justice Model is introduced in this book primarily because of difficulties in categorizing much of the juvenile justice reform legislation and practices of the last two decades in Canada, the U.S. and Britain. Scholars in the U.S., such as Faust and Brantingham[18] and Bortner,[19] have employed a variety of

---

[17] Bala and Corrado, *supra*, note 6.
[18] Faust and Brantingham, *supra*, note 9.
[19] Bortner, *supra*, note 9.

other mixed model constructs such as the "Janus Justice System" to describe changes among the diverse juvenile justice systems in that country. Similarly, scholars in the U.K. such as Bottoms[20] and Pratt[21] have attempted to categorize the evolution of justice systems in England and Wales with constructs such as "individualized criminal court" and "corporatism".

Since the trend in recent national juvenile justice reforms, with the notable exception of Scotland, has been toward the Justice Model end of the continuum (that is, a focus on offence, due process and proportionality of sentence to offence), the Modified Justice Model seems best to capture the nature of many recently legislated systems. The Modified Justice Model designation appears conceptually appropriate where the emphasis at the pre-adjudication stage of juvenile justice is on adult criminal procedure criteria, or due process, while sentencing criteria include a mixture of offence considerations (severity of offence and prior record), and offender considerations (special needs). This model is well suited to describe the *YOA*. Archambault would probably concur. He regards this law as a repudiation of the traditional Welfare Model, yet he maintains that the *YOA* does not reflect the Justice Model:

> What parliament has intended, in my view, is a system of juvenile justice which is neither exclusively treatment-based nor which subscribes primarily to deterrence and punishment; nor is it exclusively welfare or justice oriented.[22]

Archambault goes on to reject definitively the critical view that the Justice Model and Crime Control Model characteristics of the *YOA* (see Figure 1) essentially negate the need for a distinctive juvenile justice system. Archambault claims that there are numerous special procedures and measures which

> . . . clearly refute the thesis that the *Young Offenders Act* merely rubber-stamps a mini-adult system. The fact remains that a specialized juvenile justice system will continue to emphasize and cater to rehabilitation and reformation ideals, which many say are dead in the adult system. It is essential to continue the special juvenile justice system in order to capitalize on the opportunity to positively influence young persons while they are still malleable and receptive to change. A strengthened and effective juvenile justice system is still, in the long term, the best crime prevention measure. It is an investment in the future and in our young people. Even the increased emphasis on responsibility and public protection can, in most instances, be met by proper programs and effective measures to promote the self-improvement of young offenders. That is the spirit of the *Young Offenders Act*. While it allows the taking of adequate measures to protect society from dangerous offenders, let us not fall into the trap of equating public protection with harsh treatment or looking at responsibility only in terms of punishment. Such a narrow approach would not only

---

[20] Bottoms, "Justice for Juveniles Seventy-Five Years On" in Howath, ed., *Seventy-Five Years of Law at Sheffield 1909–1984* (Sheffield: University of Sheffield Press, 1984), pp. 95–116.

[21] Pratt, *supra*, note 5.

[22] Archambault, *supra*, note 16, at p. 51.

be contrary to the spirit of the *Young Offenders Act*, it would be a perversion thereof. Let me suggest that if such a narrow approach were to prevail, we would collectively have to accept responsibility for the failure to properly apply this legislation. I hasten to add, however, that I am fully confident that with a little good will, plenty of understanding and compassion and persistent efforts, we can and will achieve a measure of social justice, equal to none, for our young people.[23]

Archambault then approvingly quotes what can be viewed as a Modified Justice Model trend in the U.S., summarized by Faust and Brantingham as follows:

. . . a new system of juvenile justice is emerging — a system which preserves the socialized philosophy to the extent that advancements in behavioral sciences can be utilized in the treatment of troubled and troublesome youth, but only within a legal system of justice that protects the individual rights of such youth and precludes authoritative intervention in their lives without a crucially important reason for doing so.[24]

PROBLEMS WITH THE MODIFIED JUSTICE MODEL AND THE *YOA*

The conception of a Modified Justice Model is useful in understanding not only the *YOA*, but also the variety of provincial juvenile justice systems that could be found under the *JDA* by the late 1970s. These systems were not purely reflective of either the Welfare, Justice or Crime Control Models. Use of the Modified Justice Model also facilitates a cross-national comparative perspective on juvenile justice reform trends and their related problems and successes. In Chapter 3, for example, Corrado argues that the British 1908 *Criminal Justice Act* did not reflect the Welfare Model and was fundamentally different from the 1908 *JDA*. Nevertheless, both Acts had some key Welfare Model characteristics at the sentencing stage, such as the relevance of the offender's family and educational situation. Furthermore, because British juvenile justice followed a Modified Justice Model, it resulted in considerably more controversy historically than did the Welfare Model *JDA* in Canada.

The Modified Justice Model construct can be used to explain the complex and controversial juvenile justice policy trends in Canada since the *YOA* was implemented. A major theme developed by Markwart in Chapter 5 is that this model describes the implementation of diverse and often contradictory policies. For example, in sentencing, despite the *YOA*'s stated principle of least interference, the use of custody generally has increased more than can be readily justified by the principles of responsibility and protection of society. Most of these custodial sentences are not directed at either violent offenders or major property offenders, as would be expected on the basis of responsibility and protection of the public.

---

[23] Archambault, *supra*, note 16, at p. 51.
[24] Archambault, *supra*, note 16, at p. 51.

Some *YOA* critics, such as Reid and Reitsma-Street[25] and Hackler,[26] have argued that because this law contains principles from all the major models of juvenile justice, it fails to provide the clear direction that juvenile justice decision-makers or practitioners need in order to avoid inappropriate punitive consequences. Congruent with this position, Leschied *et al.* argue in Chapter 7 that the *YOA* emphasis on the offence and the adversarial process results in the increase in use of custody sentences as opposed to community or treatment options.

The Modified Justice Model construct is consistent with one of the dominant themes of contemporary juvenile justice reforms. This theme, developed most elaborately by Stanley Cohen in his classic book *Visions of Social Control*,[27] is that new juvenile justice laws, formal and informal government policies and juvenile justice practices, reveal, to varying degrees, a mixture of all the models of juvenile justice described in Figure 1. Cohen argues quite convincingly that *YOA*-type legislation is common throughout Western industrial countries, in part because it permits all of the vested interest groups — including governments, private agencies, politicians, and community groups — to be involved in juvenile justice. This theme will be developed more fully in Chapter 3.

Contradictory policies are only one problem arising out of the *YOA*. There are other controversial issues that have emerged since the *YOA* was implemented which can be better understood in light of the Modified Justice Model. Since most of these problems are considered at length in subsequent chapters, they will only be briefly discussed here in order to examine their link with the Modified Justice Model. Before examining these problems, though, it is important to point out that the Modified Justice Model construct is only explicitly used in the four chapters authored or co-authored by Corrado and Markwart. It is important to stress that the Modified Justice Model itself must be considered only an ideal type and that not all scholars subscribe to its use.

The use of juvenile justice models to analyse laws such as the *YOA* is often controversial because distinctive sets of problems have been identified with each model. Thus, the Welfare Model is associated in some critics' opinion with arbitrary, punitive and ineffective interventions. The Justice Model is considered by other critics too procedurally oriented while minimizing "substantive justice". The mixed models are regarded as too confusing and too easily co-opted by crime-control-oriented practitioners, and the Crime Control Model may be viewed as unfairly punitive and cynical, particularly toward less-advantaged young offenders.

---

[25] Reid and Reitsma-Street, "Assumptions and Implications of New Canadian Legislation for Young Offenders" (1984) 17(1) Can. Crim. Forum pp. 334–52.

[26] Hackler, *supra*, note 9.

[27] Cohen, *Visions of Social Control: Crime, Punishment and Classification* (New York: Basil Blackwell, 1985).

LeBlanc and Beaumont object in Chapter 6 to the view that mixed models are inherently confusing and punitive; they disagree that the practical problems of the *YOA* reflect this model's particular philosophical principles and assumptions. These authors maintain that since the enactment of the 1977 Quebec *Youth Protection Act*, modified slightly by the *YOA*, the Quebec juvenile justice system has been progressive and effective.[28] In other words, LeBlanc and Beaumont agree with Archambault that the law's mixed model objectives can be achieved if the *YOA* is properly implemented.

While LeBlanc and other prominent Canadian scholars such as Anthony Doob[29] are proponents of the *YOA*, none of them deny that there are significant problems associated with this law. The disagreement among most scholars is whether these problems reflect inherent flaws in the theoretical principles of the *YOA*, improper administrative and judicial implementation, or economic factors associated with advanced industrial economies. This theoretical debate will be touched upon to varying degrees in several chapters of this book, and is the major focus of Chapter 3.

One set of problems associated with the *YOA* consists of jurisdictional issues. Paradoxically, it is in the jurisdictional area that the *YOA* can be viewed as most progressive. First, the Act reflects the view that status offences (offences that adults cannot be charged with, such as truancy and incorrigibility) should not be responded to by criminal procedure and sanctions. Second, uniform minimum and maximum ages are essential to implement a truly national juvenile justice system. Third, the *JDA* minimum age of seven was considered too young for involvement with a formal criminal justice system. Finally, the enormous variations in juvenile court jurisdictions between provinces under the *JDA*, along with similar differences in availability of financing and programs, resulted in serious discrepancies in the way young people were dealt with by local juvenile justice systems.

Not all scholars concur that the *YOA* has resolved all jurisdictional problems. Canadian law professor, Larry Wilson, for example, has noted that:

> . . . the unequal treatment of young offenders is much more widespread than is generally recognized. This is a direct result of the transfer of jurisdiction [of provincial statute offences] to the provinces which occurred with the passage of the *Young Offenders Act*. More particularly, these differences in treatment flow from the changes to the minimum and maximum ages and the new offence jurisdiction of the youth court described above. Today, when young persons are prosecuted for provincial and territorial offences, the minimum age of responsibility may be seven, twelve or fourteen, and the maximum age for specialized young offender legislation may be either sixteen or eighteen. Furthermore, the availability and form of

---

[28] S.Q. 1977, c. 20.

[29] Doob, ''Disposition Under the Young Offenders Act: Issues without Answers?'' in Beaulieu, ed., *Young Offender Dispositions: Perspectives on Principles and Practice* (Toronto: Wall and Thompson, 1989).

additional protections such as provisions for notice to parents and an expanded right to counsel are largely a function of residence. It is important to remember that the number of offences, prosecutions and convictions pursuant to provincial and territorial legislation far surpasses the numbers under federal legislation.[30]

Caputo and Bracken have also argued that even for federal offences the province and locality where the offence took place may be more important than the offence itself in determining treatment or sentencing, as local facilities, programs, policies and attitudes may be crucial to the handling of a case.[31]

Jurisdictional issues are also the target of intense criticisms by Crime Control Model proponents who argue that the new minimum age allows ten- and eleven-year-olds to commit crimes, including violent offences, with impunity. For these critics, the primary consideration is the protection of society through incapacitation, punishment and deterrence, and they feel that these objectives have not been met by establishing an arbitrarily high minimum age for imposing criminal sanctions.

Another set of concerns about the YOA are raised by police and other advocates of law and order. The essence of police criticism here is that excessive concern with the protection of due process rights makes police crime control and protection functions decidedly more difficult than under the JDA. In particular, police feel that the requirements that they must immediately advise young suspects of their legal rights before initiating questioning, and that they must secure a written waiver or ensure the presence of a parent or lawyer prior to seeking a confession, seriously impede their investigations. In addition, some police are critical of the role of defence counsel and of the adversarial process which can appear to young offenders like a game in which factual guilt and legal guilt are not appropriately related. In effect, police critics maintain that young offenders learn to avoid responsibility for their crimes by taking advantage of their legal rights. Police tasks become especially difficult and frustrating when dealing with repeat young offenders and youth gang members who learn the necessary "due process tricks" through experience.

Increased legal representation has led to increased numbers of hearings and subsequent court delays in several jurisdictions. Other than increased custodial sentences, however, there appears to have been no discernible impact on the profile of court outcomes (on percentages of guilty pleas, acquittals and stays of proceedings). The question has arisen whether the YOA has increased the time and cost required to dispense juvenile justice without concomitant visible benefits to the young persons brought into this system. An original assumption had been that

[30] Wilson, "Changes to Federal Jurisdiction Over Young Offenders: The Provincial Response" (1990) 8(2) Can. J. Fam. L. pp. 342–3.

[31] Caputo and Bracken, "Custodial Dispositions and the Young Offenders Act" in Hudson, Hornick, and Burrows, eds., *Justice and the Young Offender* (Toronto: Wall and Thompson, 1989).

defence counsel would, via plea bargaining, trials and speaking to sentence, reduce the arbitrary and often unwarranted punitive interventions that were believed to have occurred under the *JDA*.[32] There is little evidence to support the view that this objective has been met (see Chapters 4 and 5).

Controversy has also arisen over disparities between provinces in the number of young offenders transferred to adult courts and the criteria employed in determining their transfer. In addition, there are disparities in sentences throughout the youth courts (see Chapter 2). Again, the issue is the disparity of treatment young offenders receive across and within the provinces and territories.

A major criticism of the *JDA* was that there were far too many arbitrary sentencing decisions made in the absence of uniform sentencing criteria. This flaw was viewed as inherent in Welfare Model legislation because a consideration of offender characteristics is incompatible with systematic sentencing criteria. In contrast, Justice Model criteria consisting primarily of the severity of offence and prior record should lead to more uniform sentencing outcomes than Welfare Model-based sentences, which reflect the recommendations and diagnoses of such "experts" as probation officers, social workers, psychologists and psychiatrists.

The *YOA* actually mixes sentencing criteria not only from the Justice and Welfare Models, but also considers the Crime Control Model's guiding principle, the protection of society. The question that has excited a good deal of controversy is whether this mixture of criteria is too confusing and allows too much judicial discretion to facilitate equitable and uniform sentencing. There is significant evidence of very substantial variation in sentencing patterns under the *YOA* (see Chapter 5 by Markwart).

Another issue related to sentencing criteria, alluded to earlier, involves the unintended and substantial increase in the custody dispositions in most provinces (see Chapter 5). A critical question is whether it is possible to clarify and structure custodial sentencing criteria in a manner that will reduce the use of custody.[33] Recent English juvenile justice sentencing reforms reflecting a similar concern over excessive use of custody have provided some reason for optimism that lower custody rates can be achieved within a Modified Justice Model (see Chapter 3).

The availability and variability of program resources, including institutional and community treatment facilities, is another major issue under the *YOA*. One concern is that some provinces and territories have reduced their resources for young offenders in response to their interpretation of the *YOA* as legislation that requires fewer resources than the Welfare Model *JDA*. Specifically, the critics argue that the *YOA* provision of requiring the consent of a young person before a residential treatment order sentence can be given has shifted the decision about

---

[32] Corrado and Markwart, "Is the Young Offender Act More Punitive?" in Beaulieu, ed., *Young Offender Dispositions: Perspectives and Practice* (Toronto: Wall and Thompson, 1989).

[33] Doob, *supra*, note 29.

treatment from judges, psychologists and psychiatrists to the young offender, and may have resulted in fewer resources for treatment. In addition, some *YOA* critics assert that the new emphasis on protecting society has allowed budget-conscious government officials to reduce the availability of offender treatment programs. Thus, many young offenders are essentially "warehoused" in custodial institutions and subjected to inadequate treatment resources there and in the community (see Chapter 7 by Leschied *et al.*).

This trend of reducing treatment programs is seen as negatively affecting the morale of the various "helping professionals" involved in working with young offenders. Further, the *YOA* has restructured the relationships between the juvenile court and probation officers, and between the juvenile justice system and members of agencies from the related ministries involving child protection, health (including mental health) and education. The *YOA* has augmented the roles of both Crown and defence counsels at the expense of the police and probation officers. In particular, some probation officers have felt that their once broad *JDA* decision-making functions have been reduced to servicing Crown counsel through diversion screening reports, advising judges through predisposition reports and monitoring probation orders.

The *YOA* has also limited the jurisdiction of the Youth Court to criminal offences removing such "status offences" as "sexual immorality" and precluding the *JDA* "sentence" of placement in the care of a children's aid society. As a result, therefore, with the exception of Quebec, there is no longer a direct connection between those who work in the juvenile justice end and to the other professionals concerned with services to young people. Some probation officers and other helping professionals believe that young offenders are in a poorer position without the availability of these direct, immediate, and integrated services. Particularly during the recent period of fiscal conservatism, social service ministries appear to be concerned with limiting access to such services to "problem" young offenders in order to stay within budget restrictions.[34]

Finally, there is a growing clamour among politicians and the general public about violent youth, especially in the major metropolitan areas of Vancouver, Toronto and Montreal. The media regularly publish lurid accounts of incidents involving youth murderers, gang shootings and vicious "swarming" attacks on innocent victims by "street kids". This issue, discussed in Chapter 4 by Corrado and Markwart, raises the Crime Control Model concern that the *YOA* is inadequate to deal with violent young offenders and, therefore, must be amended to provide greater protection to the public through custodial sentences longer than the current three-year maximum and more transfers to adult court. Forthcoming amendments to the *YOA* dealing with transfer to adult court and sentencing of young offenders for murder (Bill C-12) are discussed by Bala in Chapter 2.

---

[34] Cohen, *Visions of Social Control: Crime, Punishment and Classification* (New York: Basil Blackwell, 1985).

OVERVIEW OF THE CHAPTERS IN THIS BOOK

The remaining seven chapters in this book are organized into two parts. The chapters in Part 1 are conceptually integrated and set out the main themes discussed in this introductory chapter. In Chapter 2 by Bala, the legal structure of the *YOA* is described in detail, including the legal principles and related sections of the *YOA*. Case law regarding most of the controversial issues briefly described above is also discussed in some detail. As well, the amendments to the *YOA*, contained in Bill C-12 and dealing with transfer and sentencing for murder, are described and critically analysed with respect to their likely impact on juvenile justice policies and practices. The analysis of the *YOA* in Chapter 2, while criticizing disparities in transfer and sentencing practices, does not constitute a fundamental critique and rejection of the *YOA*. Essentially, Bala regards the *YOA* as progressive but in need of reform in order both to protect society more effectively and to provide more fully for the needs of youth. In effect, the Modified Justice Model, although it is not explicitly referred to in Chapter 2, is endorsed because the criticisms of the *YOA* and the proposed reforms do not amount to advocating a radical shift toward one of the other models.

Chapter 3 by Corrado and Turnbull is a comparative chapter and advances three themes. First, the British experience with a form of the Modified Justice Model and, more recently, with the Corporatist Model, is described. Second, a review and critical discussion of the major theoretical perspectives that can be employed to explain changes in British juvenile justice is provided. And third, a description and brief theoretical analysis of recent juvenile justice reforms in the U.S. is addressed. These comparative, historical and theoretical perspectives are relevent to understanding many of the controversial issues surrounding the *YOA*, especially whether Modified Justice Model-based legislation can be reformed to avoid such unintended consequences in juvenile justice practices as the excessive use of custodial sentences. Because Chapter 3 is divided into three distinct parts, it is possible to gain an understanding of how the British and American experiences are relevant to explaining juvenile justice trends in Canada, without necessarily having to read the more complex theoretical analysis provided in the second section of the chapter. This analysis is important, however, for students who want to understand the intense and diverse theoretical debates that engage scholars who have attempted to explain juvenile justice reform trends.

Chapter 4 by Corrado and Markwart examines the historical evolution of the *YOA* and its implementation over the last seven years. Many of the theoretical themes discussed in the previous chapters are re-examined in light of Canadian data and employing the models as a framework. Controversial issues such as whether violent juvenile crime is increasing and whether the offence profiles of those young people appearing in Youth Court reflect actual crime trends or only police charging practices are also addressed. The final sections of the chapter are concerned with detailing the impact of the *YOA* on the provincial organizational structures of the various juvenile justice agencies and related government departments, and on the roles of key juvenile justice personnel such as the police, Crown counsel, defence counsel, probation officers and judges.

Chapter 5 by Markwart provides an empirical and analytical examination of one of the most controversial and important issues associated with the *YOA* — the use of custodial sanctions. Markwart's position is that the use of custody has increased substantially in most provinces and that this cannot be attributed primarily to increases in the numbers of violent or serious property offenders. Issues related to custody such as the exercise of open versus secure custody options, and the impact of the uniform maximum age limit of 18 years are also examined. Alternative explanations for current custody trends are discussed, with an emphasis on the Modified Justice Model mixture of various sentencing criteria with the "protection of society" principle.

The chapters constituting Part 2 examine in more detail some of the critical themes and issues raised in Part 1. Chapter 6 by LeBlanc and Beaumont provides a description and empirical evaluation of the use of diversion in the Quebec juvenile justice system under the *YOA*. Since the passage of the *Quebec Youth Protection Act (YPA)*[35] in 1977, Quebec has developed the most distinctive juvenile justice system in Canada. It is the only provincial system that can be considered as integrating, to any substantial degree, key elements of the Corporatist Model and the Modified Justice Model.[36] LeBlanc and Beaumont argue in this chapter that the *YOA* is a progressive law that had been anticipated by the provincial *YPA* and that, when the *YOA* finally came into effect, Quebec's juvenile justice system had only to undertake a few modifications to adapt to the new federal law.

Chapter 7 by Linden *et al.* explores the various roles, such as advocate or guardian, that defence counsel employ under the *YOA*. An interesting case study of defence counsel in the Winnipeg Youth Court provides in-depth personal survey data to describe these variations in roles and the explanations lawyers provide for choosing a particular role. In many respects, the variation in roles adopted by defence counsel reflects the controversy over the appropriate model for juvenile justice.

Finally, Chapter 8 by Leschied *et al.* explores the hypothesis that the key *YOA* principles of due process and protection of the public have predominated over the treatment principle in the actual implementation of policy. It is argued that this outcome is unfortunate because it does not reflect current research which demonstrates the greater effectiveness of treatment over simple incarceration in responding to youth crime.

---

[35] S.Q. 1977, c. 20.

[36] LeBlanc identifies this new model as the Socio-legal Model or the Differentiative Model because of the following characteristics in relation to Figure 1: due process and administrative decision making, diversion from court and bifurcation, alternative to care and determinate sentences, lawyers and juvenile justice specialist, system intervention and diagnosis, retrain and sanction behaviour, respect of individual rights/respond to special needs. Since this model is unique to Quebec, it is not included in Figure 1.

PART I

THE YOUNG OFFENDERS ACT: THEORY AND PRACTICE

CHAPTER 2

THE YOUNG OFFENDERS ACT: THE LEGAL STRUCTURE

Nicholas Bala

HISTORICAL BACKGROUND

From the beginning of legal history, there were special rules for dealing with young persons who violated the law. Under English common law, the *doli incapax* (Latin for incapacity to do wrong) defence developed. A child under the age of seven was deemed incapable of committing a criminal act. For children between the ages of seven to thirteen inclusive, there was a presumption of incapacity, but this could be rebutted if there was evidence to establish that the child had sufficient intelligence and experience to "know the nature and consequences of the conduct and to appreciate that it was wrong".[1] While the *doli incapax* defence afforded certain protections to children, those children who were convicted faced the same penalties as adult offenders, including hanging or incarceration in such places as Kingston Penitentiary.

In the latter part of the 19th century, social movements which sought to promote better treatment of children developed in Britain, the United States and Canada. These movements led to such reforms as the establishment of child welfare agencies, and the creation of juvenile justice systems which had distinct philosophies and which provided facilities separate from adult systems.

The reformers of that era considered their paramount objective to be "saving wayward children" from a life of crime and destitution. They did not draw a clear distinction between neglected and criminal children. One of the principal drafters of Canada's early delinquency legislation stated:

---

[1] *Criminal Code*, R.S.C. 1970, c. C-34, s. 13; repealed as of April 1, 1984 by s. 72 of the *Young Offenders Act*, S.C. 1980-81-82-83, c. 110 (now R.S.C. 1985, c. Y-1) (*YOA*).

there should be no hard and fast distinction between neglected and delinquent children, but . . . all should be . . . dealt with with a view to serving the best interests of the child.[2]

The efforts of these early reformers culminated with the enactment of the *Juvenile Delinquents Act (JDA)* in 1908.[3] This federal legislation provided that children were to be dealt with by a court and corrections system separate from the adult system. At least in theory, the *JDA* had a child welfare (or *parens patriae*[4]) philosophy which was reflected in s. 38:

> . . . the care and custody and discipline of a juvenile delinquent shall approximate as nearly as may be that which should be given by his parents, and . . . as far as practicable every juvenile delinquent shall be treated, not as a criminal, but as a misguided and misdirected child . . . needing aid, encouragement, help and assistance.

The *JDA* created a highly discretionary system, which gave enormous power to police, judges and probation officers, to do whatever they considered in a child's "best interests". There were no legislative guidelines governing judicial sentencing, and youths who were sent to training school (reformatory) were generally subject to indeterminate committals. Release from reformatory occurred when correctional officials felt that rehabilitation had been effected.

Under the *JDA*, youths could be subject to "delinquency proceedings" for violation of any federal, provincial or municipal law, or for the status offence of "sexual immorality or any similar form of vice". Although this latter status offence was not an offence for adults, it was felt that the welfare of children could be promoted if they could be subjected to the juvenile court jurisdiction to obtain appropriate "treatment" for commiting such vaguely worded offences.

While the system created by the *JDA* in 1908 marked a very substantial improvement in the treatment of children and adolescents over earlier times, there were many serious, interrelated problems. By the 1960's juvenile justice in Canada was subject to criticism from different sources, and a process of reform began.

One major criticism of the *JDA* was that it created a system which tended to ignore the legal rights of children. This was true to such an extent that there were occasions when guilt seemed to be presumed so that "treatment" would not be delayed by "unnecessary formalities". In many parts of Canada lawyers rarely represented youths charged in Juvenile Court, and many of the judges in Juvenile Court lacked legal training. Critics charged that despite its articulated policy of promoting the welfare of children, the juvenile justice system was unfair and unduly harsh with some youths. Other critics pointed out that certain judges

---

[2] W.L. Scott, quoted in Archambault, "Young Offenders Act: Philosophy and Principles, Prov. Judges J. 7(2):pp. 1-7 (1983).

[3] S.C. 1908, c. 40.

[4] The Latin term *parens patriae* literally means "father (or parent) of the country", but it has come to mean a philosophy of state intervention based on an assessment of a child's best interests.

exercised their discretionary powers to promote their perceptions of the best interests of children in such a way that sentences were too lenient and failed to adequately protect society.

The substantial discretion which the *JDA* gave to juvenile judges and correctional officers was not the only reason for criticism. The Act also vested very significant authority for the system in the hands of provincial administrators. As a consequence, there were enormous disparities across Canada in how juveniles were dealt with.[5] The *JDA* allowed for the maximum age of juvenile jurisdiction to vary from province to province, ranging from the 16th to the 18th birthday. Provincial policies and legislation resulted in the minimum age varying from seven to fourteen; children under the minimum age in each province were dealt with exclusively in the child welfare system. There were also great disparties in respect of diversion from the formal juvenile justice system, access to legal representation and use of community-based sentencing options.

Beyond concerns about the specific legislative provisions, there was a more basic questioning of the implementation of the rehabilitative ideals of the *JDA*. In too many cases juveniles in correctional facilities were victims of physical or sexual abuse at the hands of staff, or of the corrupting influences of other offenders. Even in well-run facilities, many juveniles who were incarcerated under the *JDA* were not being rehabilitated and reoffended after their release.[6] This resulted in a questioning of the fundamental premises of the *JDA* and of whether a juvenile justice system should be based solely on the principle of promoting the "best interests" of the child offender.

The constitutional entrenchment of the *Canadian Charter of Rights and Freedoms* in 1982 provided a strong impetus to federal reform efforts. Many of the provisions of the *JDA* appeared to ignore the legal rights guaranteed in the Charter. Further the provincial disparities in juvenile justice invited challenge under s. 15 of the *Charter*, which guarantees equality rights. In 1982, with the support of all political parties, the *Young Offenders Act(YOA)*[7] received Parliamentary approval, and came into force on April 2, 1984.

The most controversial issue among politicans at the time of enactment of the *YOA* concerned the maximum age for youth court jurisdiction. There was opposition to establishing a maximum age jurisdiction running to the 18th birthday. Some of the provinces required to raise their age jurisdiction were concerned about the costs and administrative difficulties associated with this change. There was also a widespread view that 16 and 17 year-olds should be held more fully accountable and dealt with in the adult system; this view is still

---

[5] N. Bala and R. Corrado, *Juvenile Justice in Canada: A Comparative Study* (1985), Ministry of the Solicitor General of Canada.

[6] See, e.g., S.J. Shamsie, "Antisocial Adolescents: All Treatments Do Not Work — Where Do We Go From Here," (1981) 26 Canadian Journal of Psychiatry, 357-64.

[7] S.C. 1980-81-82-83, c. 110 (now R.S.C. 1985, c. Y-1).

expressed by some observers. The proclamation of the uniform maximum age provision of the *YOA* was delayed until April 1, 1985, to allow all jurisdictions sufficient time to adapt.

There has also been significant controversy over the minimum age of youth court jurisdiction, which was raised from seven to 12 by the *YOA*. At the time of enactment of the new law, it was considered inappropriate to deal with the younger group under the *YOA*, with its greater emphasis on a more formal court governed by due process and accountability.

Under the new regime, children under the age of 12 who commit what would otherwise be criminal offences can only be dealt with under child protection legislation. While some provinces have specific programs and legislation directed at the law-breaking activities of children under 12, in others child protection agencies have displayed little commitment to dealing with the problem, much to the frustration of police and victims. Some provinces and police forces continue to be of the view that the minimum age of 12 is too high. The debate over minimum age continues and some argue it should be lowered to ten, or perhaps even back to seven, with some form of judicial or prosecutorial control to ensure that only the most serious cases or repeat offenders under the age of 12 would be subjected to a criminal response.[8] To date, the federal government has resisted the pressures to raise the minimum age.

In 1986 several technical amendments were enacted to respond to some issues connected with implementation of the Act. Matters such as record keeping, breach of probation orders and publication of identifying information about dangerous young persons at large were also dealt with in the 1986 amendments. These did not alter the philosophy or basic provisions of the Act, but did facilitate the implementation of the Act by police and correctional officials.[9]

In the late 1980's the *YOA* became the centre of enormous public criticism, directed primarily at the perceived inadequacy of a maximum three-year sentence for dealing with violent offenders, especially those convicted of murder, and at the difficulty in transferring youths into the adult system where they may face much longer sentences. This criticism reflects broader public perceptions of increased violence and drug use among young persons.

In the summer of 1989 the federal government announced that it was considering a range of options for amendment of the *YOA*, and issued its *Consultation Document*,[10] which reviewed a number of areas of concern. In December 1989, the government introduced a bill to amend the provisions of the *YOA* dealing with

---

[8] See, e.g., L. Wilson, "Changes to Federal Jurisdiction Over Young Offenders: The Provincial Response", 8 Can. Journal of Family Law 306-18 (1990).

[9] Bill C-106, S.C. 1986, c. 32 (now R.S.C. 1985, c. 24 (2nd Supp.)) in force September 1, 1986 and November 1, 1986.

[10] Department of Justice, Canada, *Consultation Document - The Young Offenders Act Proposals for Reform* (Ottawa, July 21, 1989).

transfer to adult court and sentencing for murder. This Bill[11] was studied by a Parliamentary Committee in the fall of 1990, and was approved by the House of Commons late in 1991.

These legislative amendments and some proposals for reform of the *YOA* are discussed in this chapter.

PRINCIPLES OF THE YOUNG OFFENDERS ACT

The *YOA* constitutes a clear departure from the *JDA*. There is a uniform national age jurisdiction of 12 through 17 (as of the date of the offence), and the *YOA* is unmistakably criminal law, not child welfare legislation. The discretion of police, judges and correctional staff is clearly more circumscribed by the *YOA* then it was under the *JDA*. The only justification for state intervention under the *YOA* is the violation of criminal legislation, and this must be established by due process of law. Society is entitled to protection from young offenders, and young offenders are to be held accountable for their acts.

However, the *YOA* is not simply a "Kiddies' Criminal Code". Rather, the Act establishes a youth justice system which is separate from the adult criminal justice system and distinctive in several critical respects. First, while it recognizes that young persons must be held accountable for criminal acts, they need not always be held accountable in the same manner or to the same extent as adults. Secondly, the *YOA* extends rights and safeguards to youth that go beyond those enjoyed by adults. Perhaps most importantly, the Act recognizes that youth, by virtue of their adolescence, have special needs and circumstances which must be considered when any decision is made pursuant to the *YOA*.

The policy which is to govern where young persons come into conflict with the law is set out in the Act's "Declaration of Principle", found in s. 3 of the *YOA*. These principles are to guide the interpretation and implementation of the Act:

> 3(1) It is hereby recognized and declared that
> (*a*) while young persons should not in all instances be held accountable in the same manner or suffer the same consequences for their behaviour as adults, young persons who commit offences should nonetheless bear responsibility for their contraventions;
> (*b*) society must, although it has the responsibility to take reasonable measures to prevent criminal conduct by young persons, be afforded the necessary protection from illegal behaviour;
> (*c*) young persons who commit offences require supervision, discipline and control, but, because of their state of dependency and level of development and maturity, they also have special needs and require guidance and assistance;
> (*d*) where it is not inconsistent with the protection of society, taking no measures or taking measures other than judicial proceedings under this Act should be considered for dealing with young persons who have committed offences;

[11] Bill C-12, 3rd Session, 34th Parliament, Third Reading, November 25, 1991.

(e) young persons have rights and freedoms in their own right, including those stated in the *Canadian Charter of Rights and Freedoms* or in the *Canadian Bill of Rights*, and in particular a right to be heard in the course of, and to participate in, the processes that lead to decisions that affect them, and young persons should have special guarantees of their rights and freedoms;

(f) in the application of this Act, the rights and freedoms of young persons include a right to the least possible interference with freedom that is consistent with the protection of society, having regard to the needs of young persons and the interests of their families;

(g) young persons have the right, in every instance where they have rights or freedoms that may be affected by this Act, to be informed as to what those rights and freedoms are; and

(h) parents have responsibility for the care and supervision of their children, and, for that reason, young persons should be removed from parental supervision either partly or entirely only when measures that provide for continuing parental supervision are inappropriate.

Accountability: s. 3(1)(a)

The principle of accountability (or responsibility) is one that has historical roots as one of the foundations of criminal law. Those who violate the rules of society should in some way be held accountable to society, and subject to punishment or social retribution. With respect to young persons, accountability is premised on the assumption that adolescents are capable of a degree of independent thought and judgment. Accordingly, where a youth accepts responsibility for an offence, or is found guilty of it, the youth is expected to be accountable to society generally and, where appropriate, to the victim.

The principle of accountability is, however, tempered by a recognition that it is a limited accountability, that young persons should not normally be held accountable in the same manner and to the same extent as would adults. The concept of limited accountability is premised on the belief that young persons lack the judgment, foresight and responsibility of adults because of their immaturity. This is clearly reflected in the maximum disposition under the *YOA*, which is normally three years in custody, compared to life imprisonment which an adult may face. Limited accountability is especially important when sentencing youth or when deciding whether to divert a young person from the formal juvenile justice system to alternative measures.

The transfer provisions (s. 16 of the *YOA*) allow for a marked departure from the principle of limited adolescent accountability, permitting adult accountability for young persons. A transferred youth is dealt with in the adult justice system and may be subjected to the same sentences as an adult, up to and including life imprisonment.

The principle of accountability must be balanced against other principles in the *YOA*, most notably recognizing the special needs of young offenders (s. 3(1)(c)). For the majority of youth between the ages of 12 and 17 years, the existence of a condition such as a learning disability may assist in explaining behaviour, but does not excuse it. There are, however, situations in which a young person should not be dealt with in the juvenile system at all, but rather dealt with under provincial child welfare, education or mental health legislation. Where the illegal behaviour is of secondary importance in relation to the other difficulties facing the youth and protection of the public can be adequately addressed outside the juvenile justice system, use of the *YOA* may not be necessary or appropriate. The use of measures other than the *YOA*, in appropriate cases, is also specifically endorsed in s. 3(1)(*d*).

Another exception to a youth being made to assume responsibility for illegal acts arises if the youth is found to be not guilty by reason of insanity. If a youth is found to be not guilty by reason of insanity, the youth will be committed to a mental health facility for an indeterminate period, with periodic review to ascertain whether the mental illness has been cured, and provisions for eventual release.

Protection of Society: s. 3(1)(b)

A second major principle of the *YOA* is that society must be afforded the necessary protection from the illegal behaviour of young persons. It is this author's view that the principle of the protection of society should not be interpreted in a narrow sense, but rather speaks to the responsibility of the juvenile justice system to meet Canadian society's long-term interests in the reduction of crime by youth and the rehabilitation of young offenders, as well as the more immediate need for protection from crime for communities.

It is apparent however, that some youth court judges emphasize the principles of accountability and the protection of society as a justification for imposing sentences that are essentially punitive in nature, and not intended to have a direct rehabilitative value. These judges hope that these sentences will have a deterrent effect, though many social scientists question whether increasing the severity of juvenile sentences has a deterrent effect on the behaviour of young offenders.[12]

Special Needs of Youth: s. 3(1)(c)

While the *YOA* is clearly criminal legislation, it is different from the law applicable to adults because of its recognition that adolescents have special needs. The Declaration of Principle requires that the limited maturity and dependency of

---

[12] A. Leschied and L. Vark, "A Summary of Literature Related to the Young Offenders Act", in *Assessing Outcome of Special Needs Young Offenders*, London Family Court (1989) at 5-7. One of the causes of adolescent offending is the lack of capacity of young persons to appreciate the likely consequences of their behaviour, and increasing the severity of sanctions may not have any effect. However, increasing the likelihood of their being apprehended (i.e., increasing the efficiency of police enforcement efforts) may have some effect on youthful criminality.

youth be taken into account, and that decisions made about youth reflect their "special needs".

Canada's juvenile justice system is, in part, premised on a fundamental assumption that young persons have special needs by virtue of their adolescence. These needs will vary depending on a youth's level of biological, psychological and social development. The term "special needs" includes the needs of youth to form positive peer relationships, to develop appropriate self-esteem, and to establish an independent identity; it also extends to their health, educational and spiritual needs. Over and above the needs of and developmental challenges facing all adolescents, the Act recognizes the importance of identifying the additional needs of youth who may be suffering from such problems as a "physical or mental illness or disorder, a psychological disorder, an emotional disturbance, a learning disability or mental retardation" (s. 13(1)(e)).

For many youths appearing before the youth courts, their criminal behaviour constitutes an isolated and often not very serious act. For these youth such safeguards in the Act as limits on dispositions (s. 20), involvement of parents (ss. 9, 10, 20), bans on publication of identity (s. 38) and restrictions on use of records (ss. 40 to 46) are adequate to meet their needs. For some youths, however, their criminal behaviour is part of a pattern of more serious difficulties. A pre-disposition report (s. 14) or a medical or psychological assessment (s. 13) may be ordered by a youth court to better learn of the needs of an individual youth.

There are situations where the special needs of a young person would indicate that provincial child protection, education or mental health legislation should be used rather than or concurrently with the *YOA*. It must be recognized that the needs of some troubled youths will be on-going and may fall outside the mandate of the criminal justice system.

It is the view of most Canadian judges that the concept of "special needs" should not be used to justify intervention under the *YOA* which is not commensurate with the offence.[13] Thus if a youth commits a relatively minor offence, this should not be used as a justification for a very severe disposition, even if this would afford "treatment". The principle of least possible interference (s. 3(1)(f)) requires that other means, less intrusive than the criminal law and more appropriate, given the minor nature of the offence, be used to gain access to the needed treatment.

The making of various decisions about the young person, in particular in regard to sentencing, requires a balancing of the principles of accountability and protection of society with the special needs of youth. Sometimes this is not a difficult decision, and it is possible to impose a disposition which recognizes

---

[13] As discussed later in this chapter, most Canadian youth court judges appear to accept this proposition, but it is apparent that some judges do impose long custodial sentences with the intent of providing access to rehabilitative services; see, e.g., *R. v. B. (S.A.)* (1990), 56 C.C.C. (3d) 317 (N.S.C.A.) where a sentence of six months, open custody was imposed for two offences involving

"treatment" needs. For example, it may be best for the youth and society to have a probation term imposed, with a condition that the youth attend substance abuse counselling. In some situations, a residential or custodial disposition may be made which also involves treatment.

Other decisions are much more difficult. Perhaps the clearest choice between the protection of society and the needs of a young person has been when consideration is given to transfer to adult court pursuant to s. 16 of the *YOA*. Conflicting views on the appropriate balance in transfer cases are more fully discussed later in this chapter.

Alternative Measures and No Measures: s. 3(1)(d)

The *YOA* allows for young offenders to be dealt with outside the formal court system through the means of "alternative measures". Alternative measures are governed by s. 4 of the *YOA*. Use of such a program is generally restricted to relatively minor first offences. These programs have the advantage of being expeditious and informal, and they tend to minimize the stigmatizing effects of an appearance in youth court.

Section 3(1)(*d*) is intended to provide some guidance to police and Crown Attorneys who are considering whether to refer a youth to alternative measures, emphasizing that the protection of society is a primary consideration. It also indicates that in the case of less serious offences, there may be situations where it is appropriate to "take no measures", that is to lay no charges. This serves as a formal endorsement of a traditionally exercised police discretion not to commence criminal proceedings.[14]

In *R. v. T. (V.)*[15] a girl living in a group home was charged with offences relating to verbal abuse and throwing things at a staff member. The lower court held that under s. 3(1)(*d*), a youth court judge has "ultimate responsibility" and may dismiss the charges. However, the Supreme Court of Canada ruled that s. 3(1)(*d*) gives no authority to a judge to determine whether a person in a "parent like role" (i.e., a group home staff member) is misusing the court system by laying charges for "minor disciplinary infractions." Only the police and Crown prosecutor have a discretion about laying charges: a judge's views about the inappropriateness of a charge may only affect disposition.

---

violation of the curfew provision of a previous probation order and use of vulgar and threatening language to a school principal. The court emphasized the "needs and rehabilitation" of the youth in imposing this long sentence for two relatively minor offences.

[14] It is clear that police charging practices for young offenders vary substantially from one locale to another; see J. Hackler and D. Cossins, *Police Screening Patterns in Five Western Canadian Cities: Looking at Data in a Different Way*, Discussion Paper 20, Centre for Criminological Research, University of Alberta.

[15] [1992] S.C.J. 29, revg. (1991), 64 C.C.C. (3d) 40 (B.C.C.A.).

Rights of Young Persons: s. 3(1)(e) and (g)

The Declaration of Principle recognizes that young persons have "rights and freedoms in their own right" and, additionally, "that they should have special guarantees of their rights and freedoms". One of the special rights of young persons is to have counsel provided by the state if they are unable to obtain or afford a lawyer (s. 11). Adults only have the right to retain counsel, but if they cannot afford to do so they are forced to rely on the discretion of the legal aid authorities as to whether counsel will be provided.

Another important special protection for young persons is found in s. 56 of the *YOA*, which excludes from a trial any statement made by a youth, unless special warnings are provided, most notably a warning of the right to remain silent and of the right to have a parent or lawyer present when a statement is made to the police. It was felt by Parliament that these types of special protections are essential because young persons may not fully understand their rights and may not be able to fully exercise them without special assistance.

Some have argued that these special rights unduly restrict police and Crown Attorneys. The justification for these rights for young persons has been questioned by some who believe that they are inconsistent with the principles of protection of the public and responsibility for criminal behaviour. This debate is not new to criminal justice, and certainly is not restricted to juvenile justice. However, in the context of youth court proceedings, the debate takes on an added poignancy as it is sometimes argued that the exercise of legal rights may serve to defeat the needs of a young person.

The prominent Canadian defence lawyer, Edward Greenspan, acknowledged the "dilemma of due process".

> Due process is a costly, time consuming process and the procedural safeguards which make up "due process" are not always self-evident. . . . In ordinary circumstances, the child is urged to tell the truth and confess; under due process, the young person may be acquitted even though he has acknowledged responsibility to his lawyer. The dilemma of due process results in "some young people receiving the wrong message as to the appropriateness of their behaviour and the values underlying our system of justice".
>
> Due process has undoubted benefits for the child, who is now "entitled to protection from arbitrary or well meaning but mistaken government". The young person can no longer be removed from his/her home unless there has been "a scrupulous determination of the facts". At the same time, the "costs" of due process suggest the need to devise ways of avoiding the formal system.[16]

Despite concerns about the costs of due process for young offenders, it is clear that Canada has become a "rights-based society", as is both reflected by and

---

[16] *Y.O.A. Dispositions: Challenges and Choices* Ontario Social Development Council, (Toronto: 1988) at 14.

reinforced through the *Canadian Charter of Rights and Freedoms*. While the granting of rights always involves some costs, it also has benefits for the individuals affected and for society as a whole. Women, employees, tenants, consumers, aboriginal peoples, the disabled and others have increasingly asserted legal rights and seen those rights recognized in the courts. It would be anomalous and surprising to find that while everyone else in society is receiving increasing legal rights, young persons were receiving fewer rights. In the present social climate, those who work with children and adolescents will likely have to accept that there is unlikely to be any significant retrenchment of due process rights.[17]

Minimal Interference: s. 3(1)(f)

The principle of least possible interference requires that decision makers take the least intrusive measures, though this notion is considerably qualified by requiring that action must be consistent with the protection of society and the needs of young persons and their families.

In some situations the principle of least possible interference will justify alternative measures or taking no measures. This principle should also affect decisions about pre-trial detention, disposition and disposition review. It is the author's view that this principle requires that at the sentencing stage the *YOA* should not be used as a vehicle for imposing a disposition on a youth which is more severe than warranted by the offence but which could be justifiable on the grounds of treatment.

Parental Involvement: s. 3(1)(h)

The *YOA* recognizes that parents have an important responsibility for their children, and that young persons can often be best helped in a familial context. The underlying problems of young offenders are often most likely to be effectively resolved if parents are involved in any treatment or dispositional plan. Most young offenders will remain with or return to their families after involvement with the justice system is completed.

Section 3(1)(*h*) requires that decisions about pre-trial detention and disposition be made taking into consideration the desirability of parental supervision. The *YOA* requires that parents be notified of the arrest of their child (s. 8) and of youth court proceedings (s. 9). In certain cases, parents may be ordered to attend court (s. 10).

Parents also have the right to make submissions prior to a decision being made about disposition or transfer. It is important, however, to appreciate that parents are not parties to a *YOA* proceeding. It is only the young person who can instruct counsel; parents are sometimes confused about this matter and want to be involved in directing a case.

The old *JDA* provided that parents could be fined if their children committed

---

[17] For further discussion of the tension between due process and promotion of the needs of young offenders, see Chapter 8.

criminal acts. The *YOA* eliminated this. The *YOA* requires that young persons alone should be responsible for their illegal acts, but recognizes that parents can have an important role in their rehabilitation. In some situations, parents may also have a role in the protection of the legal rights of their children.

It is important, however, not to "romanticize" the role of parents in the lives of their children. Involvement in the youth justice system may reflect problems with the parent-child relationship. Some young offenders have been victims of physical, emotional or sexual abuse at the hands of their parents, and some youths have ceased to have meaningful relationships with their parents before they are involved in the youth court system. The fact that a youth is charged with a criminal offence often strains the relationship with parents, and those involved in dealing with young offenders need to be realistic about the role that parents are likely to play in their children's lives.

THE PRINCIPLES OF THE YOA: AN ASSESSMENT

Some commentators have suggested that the principles articulated in s. 3 are inconsistent and hence offer no real guidance for the implementation of the *YOA*. Others have been critical of the lack of legislative priorization among the principles articulated. One youth court judge commented that s. 3 reflects, "if not inconsistency, then at least ambivalence about what approaches should be taken with young offenders."[18]

The ambivalence found in the *YOA* probably reflects a level of societal ambivalence in Canada about the appropriate response to young offenders. On the one hand, there is a feeling that adolescents who violate the criminal law need help to enable them to grow into productive, law-abiding citizens. This view is frequently reflected in media stories about inadequate facilities for rehabilitating young offenders. On the other hand, there is a widespread public concern about the need to control youthful criminality and to protect society. This view is reflected in media stories and editorials commenting on the perceived inadequacy of the dispositions which can be applied to young offenders, a particular public concern in regard to those youths who commit serious or violent offences.

It is also important to appreciate that the Declaration of Principle represents an attempt to achieve an appropriate balance for dealing with a very complex social problem. Unlike the *JDA*, with its articulated child welfare philosophy, the *YOA* does not rest upon one single, unifying philosophy, for there is no single, simple principle which can deal with all situations in which young persons violate the criminal law.

---

[18] G. Thomson, Commentary on the *Young Offenders Act*, Prov. Judges J. (1982) at 24. See also *R. v. M. (S.H.)* (1987), 35 C.C.C. (3d) 515 (Alta. C.A.); affd. 50 C.C.C. (3d) 503 (S.C.C.), where Justice Laycraft stated (at 524-25): "Section 3 contains some statements which directly conflict with other declarations of principle in the same section. The balance between these conflicting principles is, in the individual case, not easy."

While the Declaration as a whole defines new parameters for juvenile justice in Canada, each principle is not necessarily relevant to every situation. The weight to be attached to a particular principle will be determined in large measure by the nature of the decision being made and the specific provisions of the *YOA* which govern the situation, as well as the views of the decision-maker. There are situations in which there is a need to balance competing principles, but this is a challenge in cases in the adult system as well as the juvenile system.

When contrasted with the child welfare oriented philosophy of the *JDA*, the *YOA* emphasizes the accountability of young offenders, due process, the protection of society, and limited discretion. In comparison to the *Criminal Code*,[19] however, the *YOA* emphasizes special needs and the limited accountability of young persons.

There is a fundamental tension in the *YOA* between such competing ideals as due process and treatment; in most situations the Act gives precedence to due process, though in exceptional circumstance special needs may be emphasized at the expense of due process.[20] The underlying philosophical tensions in the *YOA* reflect the very complex nature of youthful criminality. There is no single, simple philosophy and no single type of program which will "solve" the problem of youthful criminality. Judges and the other professionals who work with young persons who violate the criminal law inevitably require a complex and balanced set of principles like those found in the *YOA*.

However, it must be recognized that the existence of a "Declaration of Principle" with different, and in some respects inconsistent principles, without any priorization, gives individual decision-makers very substantial discretion to emphasize the principles they consider most important in any particular situation. Inevitably different individuals exercise their discretion in different ways, and there is substantial variation in how the *YOA* is interpreted and applied.

The rest of this chapter is devoted to a consideration of the substantive provisions of the *YOA*, with a discussion of how they reflect the principles found in s. 3 of the Act and of how the courts have interpreted these principles in different contexts, as well as considering some of the areas of continuing professional and public controversy in regard to the *YOA*.

ARREST AND POLICE QUESTIONING

In addition to those rights guaranteed to all under the *Charter*, the *YOA* affords special rights and protections to young persons who are arrested. Some of these

---

[19] R.S.C. 1985, c. C-46.

[20] There is only one provision of the *YOA* which clearly gives precedence to needs over due process. Subsection 13(6)(*a*) allows a judge to withhold all or part of a medical or psychological report from a young person if the judge is satisfied that "disclosure . . . would be likely to be detrimental to the treatment or recovery of the young person. . .". It may be argued that in some situations the application of this section could violate the *Charter*.

provisions are premised on the notion that many young persons lack the maturity and sophistication to fully appreciate their situation and, hence, require special legal rights. Other provisions are intended to involve parents in the process, both to protect the rights of their children and to recognize their supportive role.

The *Charter* provides:

> 8. Everyone has the right to be secure against unreasonable search or seizure.
> 9. Everyone has the right not to be arbitrarily detained or imprisoned.
> 10. Everyone has the right on arrest or detention
>   (*a*) to be informed promptly of the reason therefor;
>   (*b*) to retain and instruct counsel without delay and to be informed of that right; and
>   (*c*) to have the validity of the detention determined . . . and to be released if the detention is not lawful.

The rights which are guaranteed to all under the *Charter* may be of special significance to young persons, as they are particularly vulnerable to police supervision.

In *R. v. V. (I.C.)* a police officer observed a 15-year-old girl chatting quietly on a street corner in a place known by the officer to have an

> . . . almost magnetic appeal for children who have run from home, some of whom have become the so-called "street kids" and acts as a focal point for many persons involved in prostitution and drug trafficking.[21]

The officer believed that she was either "loitering" (not a criminal offence) "or possibly a runaway", and purported to "arrest" her under provincial child welfare legislation. A struggle ensued and the girl was charged with assaulting the police officer. In acquitting the girl of this charge, the judge observed:

> . . . the evidence presented . . . is more than sufficient to find that Christina V.'s rights were infringed under ss. 8 and 9 of the Charter and denied under para. 10(*b*) of the Charter. In regard to the latter, although she was advised of her right to retain and instruct counsel without delay, there is no evidence that she was provided with the opportunity and means to do so. In advance of that, she was deprived of her liberty, the security of her person was invaded, her property was unjustly seized and searched and she was arbitrarily detained and imprisoned. These gross violations of her fundamental rights were totally out of proportion with the situation and prescribed nowhere by law. Even if the law had provided for such interference, it would be unreasonable to find that such was demonstrably justified in a free and democratic society.
>
>   . . . .
>
> The phenomenon of the runaway child is, in the first instance, a social problem. Left unaddressed, it too often escalates into a legal issue involving either or both child welfare authorities and law enforcement officers. The magnitude of the problem as it relates to downtown Toronto . . . requires an urgent response.

---

[21] (1985), Young Offenders Service 85-106, at 7212 (Ont. Prov. Ct., Fam. Div.), *per* Main Prov. J. The location was the Yonge and Dundas St. corner of the Eaton Centre in Toronto.

Undoubtedly, as a result of pressure from concerned parents, politicians and business people in the area, the Metropolitan Toronto Police Department has felt obliged to provide that response. Unfortunately, the standard law enforcement approach to the problem is woefully inadequate as well as improper.

As was exhibited in this case, good faith and a sense of duty on the part of the police falls far short of adequately addressing the situation. The runaway child who has been reported missing but has not committed any criminal offence, *may* indeed be a child at risk. That is the issue which must be addressed first and it can only be accomplished in a competent and caring fashion by trained child care workers.[22]

In addition to the protections afforded under the *Charter*, special provisions found in s. 56 of the *YOA* are intended to ensure that there is no improper questioning of young persons by police and other persons in authority:

56(2) No oral or written statement given by a young person to a peace officer or other person who is, in law, a person in authority is admissible against the young person unless

(*a*) the statement was voluntary;

(*b*) the person to whom the statement was given has, before the statement was made, clearly explained to the young person, in language appropriate to his age and understanding, that

   (i) the young person is under no obligation to give a statement,

   (ii) any statement given by him may be used as evidence in proceedings against him,

   (iii) the young person has the right to consult another person in accordance with paragraph (*c*), and

   (iv) any statement made by the young person is required to be made in the presence of the person consulted, unless the young person desires otherwise;

(*c*) the young person has, before the statement was made, been given a reasonable opportunity to consult with counsel or a parent, or in the absence of a parent, an adult relative, or in the absence of a parent and an adult relative, any other appropriate adult chosen by the young person; and

(*d*) where the young person consults any person pursuant to paragraph (*c*), the young person has been given a reasonable opportunity to make the statement in the presence of that person.

Section 56 is based on the recognition that young persons may lack the sophistication and maturity to fully appreciate their legal rights or the consequences of making a statement, and so require special protections when being questioned by police.[23] It is also premised on the understanding that some youths can be easily intimidated by adult authority figures, and might make statements which they believe those authority figures expect to hear, even if the statements

---

[22] *Ibid.*

[23] W.S. Bailey and S. Soderling, "Born to Lose-Waiver of Fifth and Sixth Amendment Rights by Juvenile Suspects", 15 Clearinghouse Review 127-34 (1981) report on a number of American empirical studies that indicate most juveniles lack the intellectual capacity to knowingly and intelligently waive their constitutional rights, and that over 90 per cent of juveniles questioned by the police give a statement, despite being advised of their right to silence.

are false. Parliament felt that consultation with a parent[24] or lawyer should serve to protect the legal rights of young persons, and may prevent the making of such false statements.

Section 56 has been frequently invoked by the courts to exclude statements made by young persons. In *R. v. M.(M.A.)*,[25] a 16-year-old youth with a learning disability was charged with gross indecency. The police officer who arrested the youth purported to inform him of his rights by reading from a form which recited the words used in s. 56. As permitted in s. 56(4), the young person then signed a statement in which he waived his right to have a lawyer or parent present. In ruling the statements inadmissible, the British Columbia Court of Appeal wrote:

> . . . it appears . . . that the learned trial judge was confronted with the requirements of s. 56 and concluded that having the contents of the two forms read to him, the young person did not know what to do in the circumstances and did not know why a lawyer would be necessary. . . .
>
> . . . .
>
> . . . In my opinion, the course followed by the police officer in the present case did not meet the requirements of s. 56 of the *Young Offenders Act*. The forms themselves appear to be clear, but Parliament indicated the requirement that before the statement was made there must be a clear explanation to the young person. I am not persuaded that reading the contents of those two forms met the requirements imposed by Parliament before the statement could be taken from the young person.
>
> . . . .
>
> Parliament has paid special attention to the needs of young people for protective advice and has called on the police to provide it. There should be a genuine endeavour by the person in authority to describe the function of the lawyer and the benefits to the young person of having a lawyer, or parents, or relatives, or an adult friend present. That endeavour should be designed to lead to an appreciation on the part of the young person of the consequences of the choices that he makes.
>
> Even had this young person been a person without any learning disability, the

---

[24] While a lawyer who is advising a youth will emphasize the importance of legal rights, in particular, in the context of police questioning, the right to silence, there are real questions about the role that parents play when called to the police station. Although some parents will protect the legal rights of their children, others may pressure their children into making a confession. While s. 56(6) creates a presumption that an adult consulted pursuant to s. 56(2)(c) is not a person in authority, there may be circumstances in which a parent becomes a "member of the investigating team in attempting to elicit the truth out of the accused", in which case the threats or inducements of the parent may result in the statement being excluded. See *R. v. L. (S.)*, *Young Offenders Service* 84-020 (Ont. Prov. Ct., Fam. Div.) *per* Goulard Prov. J. where the parent's role in questioning a juvenile was a factor contributing to the court's conclusion that the statement was involuntary and, hence, inadmissible.

[25] (1986), 32 C.C.C. (3d) 566 (B.C.C.A.).

mere reading over of these two statements and then asking the young person to sign them, without any explanation to him whatsoever, would not, in my opinion, have been compliance with s-s. (2)(*b*) and (*c*) of s. 56 of the *Young Offenders Act*.[26]

The importance of full compliance with s. 56 was emphasized in a 1990 Supreme Court of Canada decision where the confession of a 17-year-old youth to the brutal sexual assault and murder of a three-year-old child was excluded, with the Supreme Court ruling that under the circumstances the remaining admissible evidence would only permit him to be tried for manslaughter, and not murder. In *R. v. J.(T.J.)*,[27] the police invited the youth to come to the police station for questioning, without charging him. At that time the police suspected the youth, but lacked the evidence to lay charges. After several hours of questioning, the youth made a statement in which he implicated himself. The police then charged him, and advised him of his right to consult an adult relative and a lawyer, which he did. After the lawyer left, the police again asked the youth whether he wanted to make a statement, to which he responded: "No. She [the lawyer] told me not to." The police divulged some of the evidence that they had obtained and asked further questions, which the youth answered. However, prior to resumption of questioning the police failed to advise him of his right to again consult and have present an adult and a lawyer; after the statement was made and the youth refused to sign a written waiver of his right of consultation.

The Supreme Court of Canada ruled these statements inadmissible, with Justice Cory writing:

> By its enactment of s. 56, Parliament has recognized the problems and difficulties that beset young people when confronted with authority. It may seem unnecessary and frustrating to the police and society that a worldly wise, smug 17-year-old with apparent anti-social tendencies should receive the benefit of this section. Yet it must be remembered that the section is to protect *all* young people of 17 years or less. A young person is usually far more easily impressed and influenced by authoritarian figures. No matter what the bravado and braggadocio that young people may display, it is unlikely that they will appreciate their legal rights in a general sense or the consequences of oral statements made to persons in authority; certainly they would not appreciate the nature of their rights to the same extent as would most adults. Teenagers may also be more susceptible to subtle threats arising from their surroundings and the presence of persons in authority. A young person may be more inclined to make a statement, even though it is false, in order to please an authoritarian figure. It was no doubt in recognition of the additional pressures and problems faced by young people that led Parliament to enact this code of procedure.

. . . .

---

[26] *Ibid*, at 571 and 573 (B.C.C.A.). There a strong argument that when advising a youth of the right to consult with a lawyer prior to making a statement, police should specifically mention that if a youth is unable to afford a lawyer, one can be obtained through Legal Air or by order of a court; see *R. v. Brydges* (1990), 53 C.C.C. (3d) 330 (S.C.C.).

[27] (1990), 79 C.R. (3d) 219 (S.C.C.).

Section 56 itself exists to protect all young people, particularly the shy and the frightened, the nervous and the naive. Yet justice demands that the law be applied uniformly in all cases. The requirements of s. 56 must be complied with whether the authorities are dealing with the nervous and naive or the street-smart and wordly wise. The statutory pre-conditions for the admission of a statement made by a young person cannot be bent or relaxed because the authorities are convinced, on the basis of what they believe to be cogent evidence, of the guilt of the suspect. As soon as the requirements are relaxed because of a belief in the almost certain guilt of a young person, they will next be relaxed in the case of those who the authorities believe are probably guilty, and thereafter in the case of a suspect who might possibly be guilty but whose past conduct, in the opinion of those in authority, is such that he or she should be found guilty of something for the general protection of society. Principles of fairness require that the section be applied uniformly to all without regard to the characteristics of the particular young person.[28]

One controversial issue which the Supreme Court of Canada decision has not fully resolved is whether a statement made to the police by a youth who is not charged with an offence at the time that the statement is made, must satisfy the section. In *R. v. J.(J.)*[29] a 14 year old girl reported to a social worker and a police officer that she had been sexually abused. She was warned about the seriousness of her allegation, but not advised of her rights under s. 56 of the *YOA*, which was not surprising, since she was viewed as a victim at that time. The statement proved to be false and the girl was later charged with mischief for making a false statement to the police. The statement was held admissible by the Ontario Court of Appeal, with Justice Cory concluding that s. 56(2) ''must refer to young persons *accused* of committing offences''[30] and not to statements of young persons not charged with an offence.

On the other hand, in *R. v. J.(T.J.)*,[31] the Supreme Court of Canada held that a statement made to the police by the youth prior to his being charged, was inadmissible due to s. 56. One could interpret this decision as requiring that s. 56(2) applies to any statements of a young person, regardless of the circumstances. In *J.(T.J.)* the youth had been ''invited'' to the police station to make a statement, and may have felt obliged to do so; he may not have appreciated the consequences of making a statement in these circumstances. As the Supreme Court observed, by the time the statement was made the youth ''was obviously a suspect, if not the prime suspect'' and the police could easily have complied with s. 56. However, in the Ontario case, *R. v. J.(J.)*, the youth had sought out the authorities, evidently with the very purpose of making a false statement. It would have been highly unusual, and indeed quite upsetting, to warn a self-described victim, of the legal rights afforded under s. 56.

Although not explicitly discussed by the Supreme Court in *R. v. J.(T.J.)*, it is

---

[28] *Ibid.*, at 242-43 (S.C.C.).

[29] (1988), 65 C.R. (3d) 371 (Ont. C.A.).

[30] *Ibid.*, at 383. See also the accompanying Annotation by N. Bala at 372, which compares the Ontario and Manitoba judgments.

[31] *Supra*, note 27.

apparent from the decision that the *YOA* cannot be used to exclude physical evidence obtained by the police as a result of a statement made by a youth which is inadmissible because of the failure to comply with s. 56. In *J.(T.J.)* the youth took the police to the scene of the crime and showed them a concrete block; the block was admissible as physical evidence, but the statement that the youth made at the time it was located was not admissible, because s. 56 was violated.

Similarly, in *R. v. C.(S.A.)*[32] the Alberta Court of Appeal held that a knife and clothing used in a robbery, and discovered by police as a result of statements of a young person, were admissible in evidence, despite the failure of the police to comply with s. 56. The court observed that the words of s. 56 applied only to "oral or written statements". At common law, courts have always displayed a greater concern with excluding improperly obtained statements, which are the product of self-incrimination and have the potential to be false, than in regard to physical evidence. However, if physical evidence is obtained in violation of a young person's rights under the *Charter*, it may still be excluded if "the admission of it . . . would bring the administration of justice into disrepute".[33]

Another interesting and difficult issue which has arisen is the extent to which individuals, such as school teachers, principals or social workers may be "agents of the state" and hence expected to comply with the requirements of the *Charter* and s. 56 of the *YOA*. In *R. v. H.*[34] a 13-year-old boy was charged with theft and the prosecutor wanted to have the court hear statements made by the youth to his teacher and the school principal. Prior to the statements being made, the teacher had promised that if the money was returned, nothing further would happen. Not surprisingly, neither the teacher nor the principal complied with the *Charter* or s. 56 of the *YOA* prior to the statements being made. The court ruled the statements inadmissible because of the violation of the *YOA* and s. 10 of the *Charter*. *R. v. H.* does not require school personnel to afford young persons the right to counsel in all situations, but it does indicate that if this right is not afforded a youth prior to questioning, statements which are made may later be ruled inadmissible in youth court proceedings.

A different outcome occurred in *R. v. G.(J.M.)*,[35] where a 14-year-old boy was charged with possession of a small amount of marijuana that had been discovered by his school principal after a search of the youth. The Ontario Court of Appeal emphasized that the search was carried out in the context of the principal's normal duties of maintaining discipline in the school, and hence did not constitute a violation of the *Charter*. The court recognized that while the relationship between student and principal was not like that of policeman and citizen, "there may come

---

[32] (1989), 47 C.C.C. (3d) 76 (Alta. C.A.).

[33] *Charter*, s. 24(2); see *R. v. Collins*, [1987] 1 S.C.R. 265, 56 C.R. (3d) 193.

[34] (1985), 43 Alta. R. (2d) 250, Young Offenders Service, 86-029, at 4140 (Prov. Ct. — Yth. Div.). *per* Russell Prov. J.

[35] (1986), 56 O.R. (2d) 705 (Ont. C.A.); leave to appeal to S.C.C. refused 59 O.R. (2d) 286*n*.

a time when such [significant legal] consequences are inevitable and the principal becomes an agent of the police in detecting crime".[36]

In such a situation a school principal or teacher might be expected to strictly comply with the warning requirements of the *Charter. R. v. H.* and *R. v. G.(J.M.)* illustrate that the courts will closely scrutinize each situation to determine the extent to which a principal or other person should be treated as an "agent of the state". It may also be significant that *R. v. G.(J.M.)* involved the seizure of physical evidence, which was clearly probative of the fact that the crime in question had been committed, while *R. v. H.* only involved a statement and the *YOA* has special provisions in regard to statements.

The federal government's 1989 *Consultation Document*[37] identified the amendment of s. 56 as a possible area for Parliamentary action. One of the options for reform included the repeal of s. 56(2), thereby giving youths no greater rights than adults. Other, less drastic proposals were to amend s. 56(4), to allow youths to waive their rights orally, rather then necessarily requiring a written waiver, or to give courts a discretion to admit a statement taken in violation of s. 56(2), if this would be in the interests of the administration of justice.

The impetus for these proposals came from police forces and Crown Attorneys, who are concerned that confessions are often excluded because of a failure to meet the strict requirements of s. 56, and that this may give youths a "bad message" about the justice system. Similar proposals were made at the time of the 1986 *YOA* amendments, but were dropped due to opposition from the defence bar and advocates for youth, who argued that a strict exclusionary rule is the best way to ensure police recognition of the rights of youth. It seems that concern about the controversial nature of amendments to s. 56 prompted the federal government to again postpone action to amend the section, despite the fact that at their June 1989 meeting in Charlottetown the provincial Attorneys-General unanimously favoured changes to facilitate the admissibility of statements of young persons.

In view of the fact that a violation of an adult's rights under the *Charter* does not lead to an automatic exclusion of evidence but only gives a court the discretion to exclude the evidence if "the admission of it . . . would bring the administration of justice into disrepute", it may be difficult to justify an absolute prohibition of the exclusion of evidence for even relatively minor violations of the more exacting standards of s. 56 of the *YOA*.

NOTIFICATION OF PARENTS

Section 9 of the *YOA* provides that if a young person is arrested or detained, a parent must be notifed "as soon as possible" of the place of detention and the

---

[36] *Ibid.*, at 712.

[37] Department of Justice, Canada, *Consultation Document — The Young Offenders Act: Proposals for Reform* (Ottawa, July 21, 1989).

reason for the arrest. This is to inform parents of what had happened to their children, and allow them to take steps to assist or visit them.

A parent must also be notified in writing of any youth court hearings. If a parent is not available, notice may be given to an adult relative or other appropriate adult. The Act also allows a youth court to order that a parent attend any proceedings if such attendance is considered "necessary or in the best interests of the young person". While parents are not parties to youth court proceedings, they have a statutory right to address the court prior to disposition, disposition review or possible transfer to adult court.

The Declaration of Principle, s. 3(1)(*h*), recognizes the role of parents in the lives of their children, and ss. 9 and 56 ensure that parents have notice of arrest, detention and youth court proceedings. These provisions are premised on the notion that parents will normally provide emotional support and ensure that a youth's legal rights are protected. It should be emphasized that under s. 56(2) it is the youth who has the right to decide whether or not a parent will be present during police questioning. Some youths may be unwilling to have parental involvement, and there may be cases where such involvement is clearly not appropriate. Parents will normally not be considered "persons in authority", and statements made to them by their children will usually be admissible, despite the absence of any form of caution.[38]

There may, however, be cases in which parental involvement in questioning will amount to duress, and a statement in such circumstances could be ruled inadmissible. In *R. v. L.(S.)*,[39] the judge felt that a father who became actively involved with the police in the questioning of his son about a suspected homicide became a "member of the investigation team". The court ruled the youth's confession inadmissible, saying:

> There is no doubt that most well-thinking parents in a situation involving the death of a youngster would be anxious to co-operate in finding the truth, but when that involves co-operating with the police and obtaining some incriminating evidence against their own child, and without being made aware of all the information that the police had against the child, it is, I feel, not a rightful situation and can constitute an abuse of the very special relationship of authority and influence that a parent has on his child.[40]

---

[38] *R. v. B. (A.)* (1986), 50 C.R. (3d) 247 (Ont. C.A.); leave to appeal to S.C.C. refused [1986] 1 S.C.R. v; see also *YOA*, s. 56(6).

[39] (1984), Young Offenders Service 84-020 (Ont. Prov. Ct. — Fam. Div.). Subsection 56(5) of the *YOA* provides that a statement made to a person who is not in law "a person in authority" may nevertheless be ruled inadmissible if the youth establishes that it was made as a result of "duress".

[40] *Ibid.*, at 4085.

PRE-TRIAL DETENTION AND RESTRICTIONS

Youths who are arrested for relatively minor charges are normally released pending a hearing, but those charged with more serious offences, or who have long records of prior convictions, or who might not appear for trial, may be detained pursuant to the order of a youth court judge or a justice of the peace. Section 7 of the *YOA* specifies that such detention will normally be separate from adults. The *YOA* allows for detention with adults only if a court is satisfied that this is necessary for the safety of the youth or others, or if the youth is in a remote location and no youth detention facilities are available within a reasonable distance. While pre-trial detention is normally separate from adults, youths who are awaiting trial are often kept in the same facilities as young offenders who have been convicted or who are serving sentences in custody.

At least in theory, the decision to order a youth's detention, pending trial, is to be made on the same legal basis as that applicable to adults, and is governed by s. 515(10) of the *Criminal Code*. This section provides that detention is justified only:

> (a) on the primary ground that . . . detention is necessary to ensure . . . attendance in court . . . and
>
> (b) on the secondary ground that . . . detention is necessary in the public interest or for the protection or safety of the public, having regard to all the circumstances including any substantial likelihood that accused will, if he is released from custody, commit a criminal offence or an interference with the administration of justice [for example by threatening a witness].

Despite s. 515(10), some youth court judges seem to be taking "social factors" into account, and ordering pre-trial detention if it is, for example, felt that the youth does not have adequate housing or the parents are unwilling to have the youth reside with them.[41]

Parliament recognizes that pre-trial detention has the potential of being extremely disruptive to a young person, as it may result in sudden removal from familiar surroundings and placement in an often intimidating, institutional environment. Such detention will usually interfere with schooling or employment, and with familial and peer relationships. Further, it is highly intrusive since it occurs without any finding of guilt, and in some ways pre-trial detention is inconsistent with the presumption of innocence.

---

[41] There has been a significant increase in the use of pre-trial detention in Canada in recent years. J. Kenewell, P. Colfer & N. Bala, "Young Offenders". In B. Barnhorst and L. Johnson, eds., *The State of the Child in Ontario* (Toronto: Oxford University Press, 1991), at 172, report an increase in the average number of youths in pre-trial detention from 685 in 1986-87 to 812 in 1989-90, with the greatest increase in Ontario, from 294 to 397. It is at least possible that some judges may be influenced by punitive considerations in using pre-trial detention, though clearly this is not consistent with the *Criminal Code* or *Charter*.

To attempt to minimize the possibility of such disruption, s. 7.1 of the *YOA* allows a judge to order that a young person who would otherwise be detained be placed under the care and control of a "responsible person"; a "responsible person" would normally be a parent or other adult who is respected by the youth. This will only be done if the "responsible person" undertakes in writing to exercise control over the youth and satisfy such other conditions as may be imposed, for example, ensuring that the youth refrain from consuming alcohol pending trial. A "responsible person" who "wilfully fails" to comply with the undertaking may be charged with an offence under s. 7.2 of the *YOA*. Section 7.1 has not been used frequently, since if the court feels that detention is appropriate, it is usually reluctant to permit an adult in the community to supervise a youth pending trial. However, in a few localities innovative programs have been established to allow supervision by professionals in the community of youths released pending trial.

The *YOA* provides in s. 13 that if there is a quesiton about a young person's mental capacity to stand trial (*e.g.*, to understand the nature of the proceedings), or if there is an application for transfer of the case to adult court, the youth court may order a medical, psychological or psychiatric assessment prior to trial. In other situations, there is no jurisdiction for a court-ordered pre-trial assessment. Assessments and transfer applications are discussed more fully below.

Consistent with the presumption of innocence and the restrictions on pre-trial detention, is *Re Peel Board of Education and B.*[42] Justice Reid of the Ontario High Court of Justice held that male students facing serious charges involving alleged sexual assaults on a female student at another school could not be suspended or expelled pending judicial resolution of the charges. The decision in part rested on the prohibition in s. 38 of the *YOA* on "publication" of identifying information about a young person appearing in youth court, since the effect of expulsion of the students would inevitably be to identify the students within their school. The court observed: "Rumour and gossip to the effect that the students have been expelled and must therefore be guilty of the offences with which they have been charged are . . . the almost inevitable consequences of expulsion".[43]

The judge also said that the expulsion of the students prior to resolution of the charges "comes distressingly close to condemnation without trial. . . . That is wholly contrary to the fundamental principle of our system of justice."[44] The judge further indicated that even if the youths were convicted of these offences, it might not, in itself, be grounds for expulsion. Arguably, the outcome in this case might have been different if the charges involved offences alleged to have occurred on school property, or involved an alleged victim attending the same school. In this situation the allegations might have been sufficient to satisfy the criteria of s. 22(3) of the *Education Act*, namely, that the student has engaged in "conduct . . . so refractory that his presence is injurious to other pupils".

---

[42] (1987), 59 O.R. (2d) 654 (H.C.J.).

[43] *Ibid.*, at 659-60.

[44] *Ibid.*, at 661.

ALTERNATIVE MEASURES

Section 3(1)(d) of the Declaration of Principle recognizes the value of "taking measures other than judicial proceedings" under the *YOA*. Section 4 of the *YOA* creates a legislative framework for "alternative measures", that is to say, for dealing with young persons outside the formal youth court process.

Alternative measures are a form of diversion from the court process and are typically used for first time offenders charged with relatively minor offences, though some provinces, most notably Quebec, allow youths facing more serious charges to be considered for alternative measures. An alternative measures program allows a youth to be dealt with in a relatively expeditious, informal fashion and enables a youth to avoid a formal record of conviction.[45] It is felt that some youths may be unnecessarily harmed by being "labelled" as "young offenders" through the formal court process, and that they may benefit from relatively informal treatment. Use of alternative measures is also consistent with the principle of "least possible interference", which is articulated in s. 3(1)(f) of the *YOA*. Further, alternative measures programs may increase the scope for involvement of parents, victims and the community, which may be especially valuable in such localities as aboriginal communities. Such programs may also be less expensive to operate than the formal youth court system.

The process for invoking alternative measures varies from one jurisdiciton to another. In some localities it may occur without charges being laid (pre-charge), but in others charges must be laid (post-charge). Generally, an initial decision is made by prosecutor (or police) about whether a case should be considered for alternative measures, and then the person or agency responsible for the program meets with the youth to ensure that suitable alternative measures are appropriate and available, and are acceptable to the youth.

Section 4(1)(b) of the *YOA* specifies that the initial decision about whether a case is suitable for alternative measures is to take account of whether this would be "appropriate, having regard to the needs of the young person and the interests of society". Further, in accordance with s. 3(1)(d), the use of alternative measures must not be "inconsistent" with the protection of society. The prosecutor must also be satisfied that sufficient evidence exists to take the case to court, as cases where there is insufficient evidence should not be dealt with by the legal system.

In some provinces, responsibility for supervision of alternative measures is given to a community agency with a paid staff or volunteers, while in other

---

[45] While a youth who participates in alternative measures receives no formal record of a conviction, there is a record of participation in alternative measures that may be considered if a later offence occurs and the youth is sentenced in youth court: see *YOA*, s. 14(2)(iv). If a youth is not convicted of any offence within two years of agreeing to participate in alternative measures, the record of participation is no longer to be used for any purpose: see *YOA*, s. 45(1)(d).

provinces government social workers or juvenile probation staff are responsible.[46]

If the case is eligible for alternative measures and the youth is willing to participate, the program administrator meets with the young person and proposes some form of "alternative measures" which might involve, for example, an apology, restitution, some form of work for a community organization or a charitable donation. Youths must "fully and freely consent" to participating in the specific measures proposed. The young person always has the option of having the charge dealt with in youth court.

To participate in alternative measures the youth must also "accept responsibility" for the offence alleged to have been committed. If the young person denies responsibility, the matter must go to court for a judicial finding of guilt or innocence. The young person must be advised of the right to consultation with a lawyer prior to consenting to participation.

If a young person agrees to participate and successfully completes the alternative measures agreed to, the charges must be dropped. Whether or not there is successful completion, no statement made by a youth in the process of consideration of whether alternative measures should be imposed may be used in later court proceedings. If there is only partial completion of alternative measures, there is a discretion as to whether the matter can be brought back to court.

While there is controversy over the efficacy of alternative measures as opposed to court in terms of reducing the likelihood of the commission of future offences,[47] every province, except Ontario, implemented s. 4 of the *YOA* soon after it came into force in 1984. It was generally felt that alternative measures represented a socially useful experiment for dealing with first time offenders in a humane, expeditious and relatively inexpensive fashion.

The decision in Ontario not to implement s. 4 of the *YOA* was challenged as a violation of the Equality Rights provisions guaranteed by s. 15 of the *Charter of Rights*. In 1988 in *R. v. S. (S.)*[48] the Ontario Court of Appeal held that the absence of such programs in Ontario constituted a "denial of equal benefit and protection of the law" on the basis of place of residence and hence, was in violation of s. 15

---

[46] P. Rabinovitch, "Diversion Under Section 4: Is There a Future For It In Ontario?" (1986) Young Offenders Service 7533-42. Canadian Centre for Justice Statistics (1990) "National Summary of Alternative Measures Services for Young Persons", 10 Juristat 2.

[47] See, e.g., Moyer, *Diversion from the Juvenile Justice System and Its Impact on Children: A Review of the Literature* (Ministry of the Solicitor General of Canada, 1980).

[48] (1988), 26 O.A.C. 285 (C.A.); revd. see note 50, *infra*. There is also some concern that use of alternative measures may result in "net widening" with youths, who in the past would have been dealt with informally by the police, being formally charged so that they can be dealt with by alternative measures. There is some evidence that this might have happened in Ontario in 1988: see Kenewell, Bala and Colfer, *supra*, note 41, at 165.

of the *Charter*. The Government of Ontario responded to the Court of Appeal decision by establishing alternative measures programs across the province, albeit on an "interim basis",[49] but also appealed the decision to the Supreme Court of Canada.

In June 1990 the Supreme Court of Canada reversed the Ontario Court of Appeal decision in *S. (S.)* and ruled that the delegation of authority to the provinces to decide whether or not to have alternative measures was constitutionally valid.[50] The Supreme Court ruled that under Canada's federal system it is not a violation of the *Charter* to have youths in one province denied access to alternative measures, even if youths elsewhere have access to such programs. Despite the Supreme Court decision the Ontario government continued its "interim" program. With the election of a new Ontario government in September 1990 and growing concerns about overcrowding in the courts, there is increased interest in continuing and even expanding alternative measures in Ontario.

YOUTH COURT

Proceeding under the *YOA* are conducted in a specially designated "youth court". In a number of provinces, the Family Court, which is responsible for such matters as child protection and adoption, has been selected to be the youth court. In other jurisdictions it is the Provincial Court, which deals with most adult criminal charges, that has been designated as the youth court, although the proceedings must be held at a separate time from those involving adults.

Ontario and Nova Scotia adopted a "two tier" youth court model. As was the practice under the *JDA*, 12 to 15-year-olds are dealt with in Family Court, while 16 and 17-year-olds are proceeded with in the adult Provincial Court, albeit with adult court judges nominally sitting as youth court judges. Critics argued that Ontario and Nova Scotia simply acted in an expedient fashion and failed to implement the spirit of the *YOA* by maintaining the court jurisdiction in effect under the *JDA*.[51] It has also been suggested that older youths may be subjected to harsher dispositions and have less access to certain kinds of rehabilitative services

---

[49] The Ontario government's policy establishing offence criteria for eligibility for the program were considerably narrower than the guidelines in other provinces.

Further, the Ontario "interim" scheme is the most procedurally complex scheme in Canada, since it requires at least one court appearance by the young person before the case is referred to alternative measures. This defeats one of the prime purposes of alternative measures, as the youth may feel stigmatized by that court appearance, as well as needlessly utilizing scarce judicial resources.

[50] (1990), 77 C.R. (3d) 273 (S.C.C.).

[51] N. Bala, "Annotation to *R. v. Robert C.*", Young Offenders Service 7353-3 to 7353-6 (1987); D. Stuart, "Annotation to *R. v. C. (R.)*" (1987), 56 C.R. (3d) 185-86.

than the younger age group, though it must be recognized that the division has the advantage of encouraging the development of age appropriate programs and facilities.[52] The courts have ruled that the two-tier implementation model is permitted under the *YOA* and does not violate the *Charter*.[53]

In 1990 the Ontario government began to transfer responsibility for all young offenders cases to the Family Court. This process is proceeding slowly and, in many localities, it may be some time before 16 and 17-year-olds are all dealt with in Family Court. This change is part of a plan for restructuring the Ontario judicial system and is a response to the problem of overcrowding in the courts. It may not represent a fundamental change in philosophy, as Ontario has retained a division of ministerial responsibility for young offenders, with 12 to 15-year-olds dealt with by the Ministry of Community and Social Services, but 16 and 17-year-olds are the responsibility of the Ministry of Correctional Services, a ministry with a reputation for placing less emphasis on treatment and rehabilitation.

THE TRIAL PROCESS

In s. 52, the *YOA* stipulates that proceedings in youth court are to be similar to those governing "summary conviction offences" in adult court. This means that the proceedings are less complex and more expeditious than those applicable to the more serious adult "indictable offences". There are no preliminary inquiries, and all trials are conducted by a judge alone. There are no jury trials in youth court.

It is important for young persons to have the expeditious resolution of their cases available through summary procedures, without the more complex and time consuming procedures available to adults. The courts have held that the failure to afford young persons an opportunity for trial by jury does not violate the provisions of the *Charter*, which guarantee equality and the right to a jury trial to persons facing imprisonment of five years or more. In *R. v. L. (R.)*,[54] the Ontario Court of Appeal denied the right to a jury trial, emphasizing that the maximum penalty under the *YOA* is three years, as opposed to the life sentence an adult may face for certain serious offences. Justice Morden wrote:

---

[52] *Y.O.A. Dispositions Challenges and Choices* (Toronto: Ontario Social Development Council, 1988), at 99.

[53] *R. v. C. (R.)* (1987), 56 C.R. (3d) 185, Young Offenders Service 87-052, at 7353 (Ont. C.A). See, however, *R. v. Richard B.* (1986), Young Offenders Service 86-134, at 7353-6 (Ont. Yth. Ct.) which invoked s. 15 of the *Charter* to place a 16-year-old youth in local open custody facility designated for 12 to 15-year-olds. The failure to have an open custody facility near the youth's home was held to violate the *Charter*. It may well be that individual youths who can clearly establish detrimental treatment because of the two tiers can continue to invoke the *Charter* to obtain an appropriate remedy.

[54] (1986), 52 C.R. (3d) 209 (Ont. C.A.).

> . . . the Young Offenders Act is intended to provide a comprehensive system for dealing with young persons who are alleged to be in conflict with the law which is separate and distinct from the adult criminal justice system. While the new system is more like the adult system than was that under the Juvenile Delinquents Act it nonetheless is a different system. As far as the aftermath of a finding of guilt is concerned, the general thrust of the Young Offenders Act is to provide for less severe consequences than those relating to an adult offender. . . .

> . . . .

> . . . the establishment of the legal regime . . . for dealing with young persons, which is separate and distinct from the adult criminal justice system, is of sufficient importance to warrant the overriding of the equality right alleged to be infringed in this proceeding . . .[55]

While a young person being tried in youth court is denied the opportunity to a preliminary inquiry and a jury, a youth is afforded all of the procedural protections which are given to an adult who faces a summary charge. Indeed, in *R. v. M. (G.C.)*[56] the Ontario Court of Appeal indicated that the right of an accused person to a trial "within a reasonable time", guaranteed by s. 11(*b*) of the *Charter*, has special significance for young persons.

The Supreme Court of Canada in *R. v. Askov*[57] held that a court should consider four factors in assessing whether there has been an unreasonable delay in bringing a person to trial:

- the duration of the delay;
- the explanation for the delay;
- waiver by the accused; and
- prejudice to the accused.

The Ontario Court of Appeal in *M. (G.C.)*[58] declined to impose a fixed judicial "limitation period" within which youth court proceedings need to be completed and stated that youths are "not . . . entitled to a special constitutional guarantee to trial within a reasonable time". However, Justice Osborne stated:

> There is a particular need to conclude youth court proceedings without unreasonable delay, consistent with the goals of the *Young Offenders Act* . . . . it seems to me that, as a general proposition, youth court proceedings should proceed to a conclusion more quickly than those in the adult criminal justice system. Delay, which may be

[55] *Ibid.*, at 219 and 225; to the same effect, see *R. v. B. (S.)* (1989), 50 C.C.C. (3d) 34 (Sask. C.A.).
[56] (1991), 3 O.R. (3d) 223, [1991] O.J. 885. "Processing Time in Youth Courts", 11 Juristat 4, Canadian Centre for Justice Statistics (1991) reported that in 1989-90 33 per cent of young offender cases were resolved on first appearance (80 per cent were guilty pleas), 70 per cent of cases were resolved in two months or less, with a median time resolution of 23 days, an increase of two days from 1986-87. Ontario is *not* included in the data from Statistics Canada.
[57] (1990), 59 C.C.C. (3d) 449 (S.C.C.).
[58] *Supra*, note 56.

reasonable in the adult criminal justice system, may not be reasonable in the youth court. There are sound reasons for this. They include the well established fact that the ability of a young person to appreciate the connection between behaviour and its consequences is less developed than an adult's. For young persons, the effect of time may be distorted. If treatment is required and is to be made part of the *Young Offenders Act* disposition process, it is best begun with as little delay as is possible.

From a conceptual standpoint, the basis of the need to try young persons with reasonable dispatch is best analyzed and understood if it is viewed as a part of the consideration of prejudice, one of the four factors referred to is *Askov*. These four factors have to be balanced in each case to determine if an accused, young or old, has been brought to trial within a reasonable time.[59]

Justice Osborne went on to suggest that as an "administrative guideline", youth court cases should be brought to trial within five to six months of the time that a youth appears in court with a lawyer ready to enter a plea and set a trial date.

While the issue of the application of *Askov* remains contentious, steps are being taken to ensure that charges are not stayed by the courts as a result of a violation of s. 11(*b*) of the *Charter*.

Young persons facing trial have a constitutionally guaranteed presumption of innocence,[60] with the onus upon the prosecution to prove its case. If a not guilty plea is entered, the Crown must call witnesses to establish its case and each witness will be subject to cross-examination. The youth is entitled to call witnesses and to testify, subject to the Crown's right of cross-examination, but there is no obligation upon the accused to adduce any evidence or testify. After all the witnesses are called, there may be submissions (or arguments) and the judge then renders a verdict.

If the judge is satisfied, beyond a reasonable doubt, that the offence as charged has occurred, a conviction is entered, and the case proceeds to disposition under the *YOA*. Otherwise, an acquittal is entered and this ends the *YOA* proceeding, though in appropriate cases the youth might still be dealt with under provincial child welfare or mental health legislation.

Most cases under the *YOA* do not in fact result in trials, but rather are resolved by guilty pleas. Frequently the youth recognizes that an offence has occurred and wishes to plead guilty. If a guilty plea is entered, the Crown Attorney will read a summary of the evidence against the youth. Section 19 of the *YOA* has a special provision requiring a judge in youth court to be satisfied that the facts read by the Crown at the time of a guilty plea support the charge. If they do not, the judge must enter a plea of not guilty and conduct a trial. This provision recognizes that a youth may not appreciate the significance of a guilty plea as fully as an adult.

It is not uncommon in youth court for a guilty plea to be the product of a "plea bargain". A "plea bargain" is typically the result of informal discussions between the Crown Attorney and the lawyer representing the youth.[61] There is an

---

[59] *Ibid.*, at 230-31.

[60] *Canadian Charter of Rights and Freedoms*, s. 11(*d*).

[61] An important aspect of court preparation for counsel for an accused person is obtaining "full disclosure" from the Crown prosecutor of all evidence relevant

agreement to plead guilty to certain charges in exchange for dropping of other charges, or for a request by the Crown to the court for a particular disposition. Though considered controversial by some, "plea bargaining" is not unethical or illegal. It should be noted that if there is a plea bargain, the judge is not bound to impose the disposition agreed to by counsel, though the court usually accepts it.

The *YOA* affords very important rights in regard to the provision of legal representation. Section 11 requires that as soon as a young person is arrested or appears in youth court, the youth is to be advised of the right to counsel. If the young person is "unable" to obtain counsel, the youth court judge shall "direct" that legal representation be provided. While adults have the right to retain counsel, if they are unable to afford a lawyer, they must rely on legal aid, which has fairly stringent criteria for deciding whether to provide representation for adults. The *YOA* guarantees that whenever a youth is "unable" to obtain counsel, it will be provided. It has been held that when assessing financial ability to retain counsel, the court should not have regard to parental resources.[62] In practice this means that most youths are represented by lawyers who are paid by the government since few young people have significant financial resources. In most localities in Canada, such representation is provided by lawyers in private practice, though in some places, especially in Quebec, there are clinics that specialize in representing youths.

While a youth is not obliged to be represented by a lawyer and may choose to appear unrepresented or assisted by some other adult, like a parent, the effect of the *YOA* has been to ensure that most youths are represented by counsel. This has proven controversial to some observers, who have argued that securing legal representation often results in unnecessary delays and that lawyers often fail to promote the "best interests" of adolescent clients.[63] Some observers have expressed a concern that as a result of increased legal representation, it may be more difficult for a judge to engage a youth in dialogue, and the potential for the court appearance to have a positive impact may thereby be reduced.

The *YOA*, however, is clearly criminal law and it is understandable that those subject to potential punishment by the state are entitled to full legal representation.

---

to the guilt or innocence of the accused. This disclosure usually occurs at a meeting between the Crown prosecutor and defence counsel, at which copies of documents and statements will be given the defence. It is common for plea bargaining to occur at such meetings. In *R. v. B. (S.)* (1990), 75 O.R. (2d) 646 (Prov. Ct. — Fam. Div.) a mistrial was declared when it was discovered that the Crown had inadvertently failed to give complete disclosure; the case provides a description of disclosure practices and policies.

[62] *R. v. Ronald H.* (1984), Young Offenders Service 3319 (Alta. Prov. Ct.); *R. v. M.* (1985), Young Offenders Service 3322 (Ont. Prov. Ct. — Fam. Div.).

[63] A. Leschied and P. Jaffe, "Impact of the *Young Offenders Act* on Court Dispositions: A Comparative Analysis" (1987) 30 Can. Journal of Criminology 428.

Young persons without lawyers are rarely in a position to appreciate the significance of their involvement in the legal system or to protect their rights. It is apparent that in some localities administrative difficulties have resulted in delays in obtaining legal counsel, and that some lawyers involved in the representation of young persons lack the training and sensitivity to provide truly adequate legal services. However, denial of access of access to counsel does not seem an appropriate strategy for dealing with these problems; rather administrative changes to eliminate delays and increased training for lawyers would be desirable.

The *YOA* has a number of provisions intended to protect the privacy of young persons involved in the youth court process and to minimize the stigmatization they may face. Section 38 provides that the media cannot publish identifying information about a young person, though in 1985 a special exception was added to the *YOA*, at the request of the police.[64] If a youth is at large, the police may seek an order from a youth court judge allowing publication of identifying information; the judge must be satisfied that there is reason to believe that the youth is "dangerous to others" and that publication is necessary to assist in the youth's apprehension. A judge may also permit publication of identifying information at the request of a youth, if satisfied that doing so "would not be contrary to the best interests" of the youth.

Section 39 stipulates that while youth court proceedings are generally open to the public, the judge may make an order excluding some or all members of the public, if their presence "would be seriously injurious or seriously prejudicial" to the young person.

Sections 40 to 46 govern records; access to records of youths involved with the court system is generally restricted.[65] While police may fingerprint and photograph youths charged with indictable offences, the central records of the Royal Canadian Mounted Police must be destroyed five years after the completion of any sentence for an indictable offence, provided the youth commits no further offences in that five-year period. Local police forces and others who have records related to young offenders are not obliged to destroy their records, but their use is severely restricted after the five years have passed. Section 36 of the *YOA* prohibits employers governed by federal law from asking whether a potential employee has ever been convicted of an offence under the *YOA*. These provisions

---

[64] Bill C-106, S.C. 1986, c. 32 (now R.S.C. 1985, c. 24 (2nd Supp.)). See s. 38(1.2) of the *YOA*

[65] The importance of complying with the non-disclosure provisions of the *YOA* was demonstrated in *O. (Y.) v. Begbie* (1991), 3 O.R. (3d) 261, where a municipality and local police commission were held liable for $2,500 in damages to a youth whose young offenders' record was revealed by the police to the municipality, resulting in the youth losing a summer employment opportunity. The court held that a consent that the youth signed to a "police check" was not binding, since there was no proof that the youth "knowingly and voluntarily intended to waive his rights to privacy".

recognize the "limited accountability" of young persons and are intended to afford a "second chance" to those who are convicted under the *YOA* and do not commit further crimes for a specified period.

DISPOSITION

Young persons convicted of offences pursuant to the *YOA* receive a "disposition" (or sentence) pursuant to s. 20 of the Act. The available dispositions in youth court are:

- an absolute discharge;
- a fine of up to $1,000;
- restitution or compensation;
- up to 240 hours of community service;
- up to two years' probation;
- detention for purposes of treatment for up to two years;
- open or secure custody for up to three years, and as a result of Bill C-12, up to five years in custody for murder.

For relatively minor offences, a court may make a disposition immediately after a finding of quilt. In more serious situations, however, the court will normally adjourn to allow preparation of a report to assist the court. Commonly the youth court will request a "pre-disposition" report, sometimes called a social history, which is prepared by a youth court worker. The worker will interview the youth, the youth's parents, the victim and any other significant individuals, and will summarize the youth's background and provide information about the offence. Frequently the report will include a recommendation about disposition. Although not binding on the court, these recommendations are usually influential. The youth has the right to challenge the report, and may introduce independent evidence about disposition. Parents also have the right to make submisisons prior to disposition.

In more serious cases, or cases where there is particular concern about a young person, the court may make an order under s. 13 of the *YOA* for a psychiatric, medical or psychological assessment to assist in arriving at an appropriate disposition. A s. 13 report would seem appropriate whenever the circumstances of the youth or of the offence suggest that more information is needed to enable the court to make a disposition which is responsive to the youth's "special needs". Some commentators argue that, at least in certain localities, insufficient use is being made of s. 13 reports.[66]

Following the enactment of the *YOA*, appellate courts in different Canadian provinces have gradually articulated a dispositional philosophy for young offenders. In *R. v. I. (R.)*,[67] the Ontario Court of Appeal acknowledged that in

---

[66] Leschied and Jaffe, *supra*, note 63. See also Chapter 8.
[67] (1985), 17 C.C.C. (3d) 523 (Ont. C.A.).

comparison to sentencing adults "the task of arriving at the 'right' disposition may be a considerably more difficult and complex one, given the special needs of young persons and the kind of guidance and assistance they may require."

In *R. v. F.*,[68] Justice Morden of the Ontario Court of Appeal considered the appropriate balance between the principles of accountability, protection of society and recognition of special needs, and wrote:

> While undoubtedly the proteciton of society is a central principle of the Act. . . it is one that has to be reconciled with other considerations, such as the needs of young persons and, in any event, it is not a principle which must inevitably be reflected in a severe disposition. In many cases, unless the degree of seriousness of the offence and the circumstances in which it was committed militate otherwise, it is best given effect to by a disposition which gives emphasis to the factors of individual deterrence and rehabilitation. We do not agree that it put the matter correctly to say the whole purpose of the Act is to give a degree of paramountcy to the protection of society — with the implicaiton that this is to overbear the needs and interests of the young person and must result in a severe disposition.[69]

One controversial issue is whether courts making dispositions under the *YOA* should take into account the principle of general deterrence. In *R. v. K. (G.)*[70] the Alberta Court of Appeal declined to impose a custodial disposition on a youth without a prior record who was convicted of armed robbery, emphasizing that a psychiatric report indicated that there was no likelihood of a recurrence of delinquent acts. Justice Stevenson wrote:

> We . . . reject the suggestion that the young offender's sentence should be modelled on the sentence that would be imposed on an adult offender. If a custodial sentence is warranted then it ought not to be in lengthier than that which would be imposed on an adult. . . .
> In any event, deterrence to others does not, in my view, have any place in the sentencing of young offenders. It is not one of the principles enumerated . . . in s. 3 of the Act which declares the policy for young offenders in Canada.[71]

However, most other appellate courts have held that general deterrence may play a role in the sentencing of young offenders. The approach of the Alberta Court of Appeal in *R. v. K. (G.)* was specifically rejected by the Ontario Court of Appeal in *R. v. O.*:

> The principles under s. 3 of the *Young Offenders Act* . . . do not sweep away the principle of general deterrence. The principles under that section enshrine the principle of the protection of society and this subsumes general and specific deterrence. It is perhaps sufficient to say that . . . the principles of general deterrence

---

[68] (1985), 11 O.A.C. 302.

[69] *Ibid.*, at 304.

[70] (1985), 21 C.C.C. (3d) 558 (Alta. C.A.).

[71] *Ibid.*, at 560. To a similar effect see *R. v. L. (C.J.)* (1986), 29 C.C.C. (3d) 123 (Nfld. C.A.); *R. v. S. (R.C.)* (1986), 27 C.C.C. (3d) 239 (N.B.C.A.); leave to appeal to the S.C.C. refused 69 N.R. 239*n*.

must be considered but it has diminished importance in determining the appropriate disposition in the case of a youthful offender.[72]

Another controversial issue is the extent to which courts should consider the promotion of the welfare of a youth as a basis for imposing a custodial sentence. In *R. v. R.*[73] the Nova Scotia Court of Appeal upheld a sentence of five months open custody imposed on a 14-year-old youth, without a prior record, who was convicted of the theft of a skateboard. The court felt the youth "desperately requires strict controls and constant supervision."[74] The commission of the offence was considered a justification for imposing needed care, even though the sentence was grossly disproportionate to the offence and far in excess of what an adult would have received for the same offence.

A more common approach, however, has been to reject the use of the *YOA* as a route for providing treatment, if this results in a sentence disproportionate to the offence; this accords with the principle of least possible interference, set out in s. 3(1)(f) of the *YOA*. In *R. v. B. (M.)*[75] the Ontario Court of Appeal overturned an order for five months' open custody imposed upon a youth who committed a relatively minor assault and had no prior record. The trial judge had been concerned that the boy was suicidal and neither his family nor the mental health facility he had been staying in wanted to accept him. Justice Brooke concluded that incarceration under the *YOA* "was not a sentence that was responsive to the offence, but in reality was what seemed at the time a sensible way of dealing with a youth who had a personality problem and needed a place to go."[76] The Court of Appeal suggested that "involuntary mental commitment was the appropriate route to follow; in fact this had occurred by the time the case came before that court.

As a result of the *YOA*'s distinctive dispositional philosophy and reflecting the fact that many youths involved in the criminal justice system have not committed serious offences, most convicted young offenders receive dispositions which keep them in their communities. The *YOA*, s. 20(1)(a) allows the imposition of an absolute discharge if the court considers "it to be in the best interests of the young person and not contrary to the public interest". This disposition is reserved for minor first offenders and results in no real sanction being imposed, other than the fact of conviction. An absolute discharge will rarely be given to a youth who has previously participated in alternative measures. Restitution, community service and fines allow the court to impose a real penalty on the youth, without unduly restricting freedom. In appropriate cases, victims may be compensated by restitution.

---

[72] (1986), 27 C.C.C. (3d) 376 at 377 (Ont. C.A.); see also *R. v. W. (M.Y.)* (1986), 26 C.C.C. (3d) 328 (B.C.C.A.).

[73] (1986), 17 W.C.B. 109, Young Offenders Service 86-091 (N.S. C.A.).

[74] *Ibid.*

[75] (1987), 36 C.C.C. (3d) 573 (Ont. C.A.).

[76] *Ibid.*, at 574.

The most frequently imposed disposition under the *YOA* is probation.[77] The nature of a probation order depends on the circumstances and various conditions may be imposed. Typical conditions might be that a youth maintain a curfew, attend school, or reside with parents.[78] Probation may also entail regular reporting to a probation officer, and can even be used to require a youth to live in a group home or with a suitable adult person.[79]

One of the most controversial dispositional provisions of the *YOA* deals with "treatment orders," which allow a youth to be "detained for treatment" in a psychiatric hospital or other "treatment facility" instead of in custody. Such orders may only be made on the recommendation of a medical, psychiatric or psychological report, prepared pursuant to s. 13 of the *YOA*, and only if the youth and the facility consent; normally parents must also consent to such an order being made, though there is provision for dispensing with parental consent.

The statutory requirement that the youth consent to a treatment order, found in s. 22, has been criticized by some mental health professionals. Very few treatment orders have been made and it has been argued that relatively few youths are prepared to admit that they need treatment, even if they are highly disturbed. Indeed, it is argued that mental and emotional disturbance both cause criminal behaviour and affect the capacity to appreciate problems. As a result, some mental health professionals have advocated removal of the requirement for a youth's consent to such a treatment order, although they acknowledge that "the efficacy of compulsory treatment for young offenders is an area laden with considerable debate".[80]

In considering the issue of "treatment orders", it should be appreciated that rehabilitative services can be provided in custody facilities without a court order

---

[77] "Dispositions Under the *Young Offenders Act*", 11 Juristat 5, Canadian Centre for Justice Statistics (1991) reported that for 1989-90 there were 43,711 young offenders cases with findings of guilt, for which the most serious dispositions were: absolute discharge 4 per cent; fine 13 per cent; community service and restitution 8 per cent; probation 48 per cent; open custody 14 per cent; secure custody 12 per cent; other 1 per cent (including 17 treatment orders).

[78] Youth court judges disagree about the legal propriety of imposing as a term of probation that the youth "obey curfew and house rules" set by parents, or a probation officer. For example, Judge Felstiner in *R. v. L. (A.)* [summarized at (1988), 5 W.C.B. (2d) 423 (Ont. Prov. Ct. — Fam. Div.)] felt that delegating such responsibility was consistent with the *YOA*'s recognition of the importance of parental supervision. However, Judge Nasmith in *R. v. F. (A.)* (1990), 74 O.R. (2d) 107 (Prov. Ct. — Fam. Div.) considered such a term to be an improper delegation of the judicial function and refused to convict a youth for breach of a probation term that involved violation of the curfew set by his mother.

[79] *R. v. G. (W.)* (1985), 23 C.C.C. (3d) 93 (B.C.C.A.).

[80] Leschied and Jaffe, *supra*, note 63 at 427. See also Chapter 8.

for "treatment". Further, without their consent, young offenders are sometimes place on probation with a requirement that they attend counselling or participate in a special program (for example for drug or alcohol abuse, or for adolescent sexual offenders).[81] The *YOA* s. 22 requires that a youth consent to being "*detained* for treatment", where such an order is made *instead* of placing a youth in custody, though it should be noted that provincial laws generally require that young persons in custody, like adults, give informed consent to the provision of mental health services.

In cases involving severely disturbed youths, the insanity provisions of the *Criminal Code* or provincial mental legislation may be invoked to require that a youth be involuntarily confined in a mental health facility. Some youths who commit relatively minor offences are diverted in order to receive assistance for their "special needs" through the mental health, education or child protection systems. It would seem that in many situations the failure of young offenders to receive appropriate treatment and rehabilitation is not a result of inadequacies in the law, but rather reflects a lack of resources or suitable facilities.

The 1989 federal *Consultation Document* on possible legislative reforms suggests various options intended to ensure that young offenders receive appropriate "treatment" for their "special needs".[82] This is a complex issue since it involves an interaction of provincial mental health laws and young offenders legislation, as well as the relationship of mental health and young offenders facilities. In view of the complexity and lack of consensus about these issues, it is not surprising that the federal government decided to postpone immediate action in this area.

It may be that there is a need to amend the *YOA* to ensure that young offenders in custody receive counselling and therapy,[83] even if they do not technically

---

[81] In a recent decision, *R. v. Rogers*, [1990] B.C.J. 2752 (B.C.C.A.) the British Columbia Court of Appeal held that it was a violation of s. 7 of the *Charter*, which guarantees that deprivations of "liberty and security of the person" are to be in accordance with "the principles of fundamental justice", to order that an adult on probation be required to undergo psychiatric treatment or medication without his consent. However, the court did indicate that depending upon the threat to public safety the failure to consent "might very well" lead a judge to conclude that the protection of the public would require custody instead of probation. *Rogers* indicates that probation orders for young offenders requiring treatment should only be made on consent. The decision raises obvious constitutional concerns about amending the *YOA* to require involuntary treatment for offenders.

[82] Department of Justice, Canada, *Consultation Document — The Young Offenders Act Proposals for Reform* (Ottawa, July 21, 1989).

[83] It may also be desirable to amend the *YOA*, s. 22(1) to clarify that once a youth consents to the making of an order under s. 20(1)(*i*), a subsequent withdrawal of that consent does not result in the youth being released from the mental health

"consent" to this, although it must be appreciated that most forms of therapy require the co-operation of a young person to be effective. However, there also should be legislative provisions to ensure that young offenders are not subjected to such intrusive procedures as electroshock therapy or drug treatment without their consent. Otherwise there may be a temptation to simply sedate young offenders rather than dealing with their problems.

The most effective means of successfully engaging a young offender in therapy or counselling will usually involve offering early review and release from custody as an incentive to participation; it makes some sense to offer early release to a youth who has successfully undergone treatment. It may be helpful to amend the *YOA* to ensure that involvement in treatment is appropriately taken into account in making review decisions.[84]

The most serious disposition which can be ordered under s. 20 of the *YOA* is placement in a custodial facility. For most offences the maximum custodial disposition is two years, but for offences for which an adult may receive life imprisonment the maximum is three years, and Bill C-12 permits for up to five years in custody for youths convicted of murder and sentenced in youth court. The *YOA* requires a judge, placing a youth in custody, to specify whether the sentence will be served in "open custody" or "secure custody".

Section 24.1 of the *YOA* specifies that an open custody facility means a "community residential centre, group home, child care institution, or forest or wilderness camp, or any other like place of facility" designated as "open" by the provincial government, while "secure custody" means a place "for the secure containment or restraint" of young persons which is designated as secure by the provincial government. The intention of the Act is that judges should have control over the level of restraint imposed on a youth. Provincial governments also retain significant control because they are able to designate the level of specific facilities. The courts have indicated, however, that they will review provincial designations which are obviously inappropriate.

In one case,[85] a Prince Edward Island court held that one floor of a building which had formerly served as an adult jail and which was then serving as a secure

---

facility. A reading of the present provisions clearly suggest that there only needs to be a consent at the time the order is made, and there are no reported cases of young offenders being released due to withdrawal of consent. However, concern over this issue may be making some courts and professionals reluctant to have these orders made, and the legislation might be more usefully clarified to specify that a youth who withdraws consent may be returned to court for resentencing, which might involve custody instead of treatment.

[84] At present, s. 28(4)(*c*) specifies that a ground for review is that "the young person has made sufficient progress to justify a change in disposition". While this arguably should make progress in treatment relevant to a review decision, in practice it is not always interpreted this way.

[85] *Re F. (L.H.)* (1985), 57 Nfld. & P.E.I.R. 44 (P.E.I.S.C.).

custody facility could not simply be designated a place of open custody. The judge stated:

> Undoubtedly the physical characteristics are not the only things to be looked at. Other factors which make a place suitable for open custody would include the security that is in place, the number of staff, the qualifications of the staff, bearing in mind that one of their primary functions is to teach young offenders how to better achieve in society. Additionally, a place of open custody will have a program set up for the benefit of the offenders.[86]

Section 24.1 stipulates that secure custody can only be used if a youth is convicted of a more serious offence, or where there is a history of prior offences. In *R. v. H. (S.R.)*[87] the Ontario Court of Appeal stated:

> The courts have never doubted that they had power to impose a period of secure custody to act as a deterrent or to reflect the community's abhorrence of a particular crime. . . .
>
> . . . .
>
> . . . when deciding whether a young person should be committed to open or secure custody, is required to consider a number of factors. Without intending to compose an exhaustive list, some of those factors would be the following. The first and most obvious factor would be whether or not secure custody is necessary to prevent escape, further misconduct or violence by the young person. The next factor would be the effect upon the rehabilitation of the young person. The next, keeping in mind the caveat . . . of their diminished importance in the case of youthful offenders, would be the factors of general and specific deterrence and the expression of society's abhorrence of certain crimes.
>
> . . . .
>
> The factors of general and specific deterrence and the abhorrence of society of certain crimes must be taken into account by the youth court both when deciding whether there should be a period of custody and when deciding whether that custody should be open or secure or a combination of both.[88]

In this case, the Court of Appeal specifically approved of use of:

> . . . a short, sharp period of secure custody as a deterrent to a particular young person who was becoming a recidivist but who was not a security risk. In such a case, a youth court may think that the only way in which the youthful offender can be brought to his senses is by the imposition of a short period of secure custody.[89]

Since the *YOA* came into force, in most provinces there has been an increase in the number of custodial dispositions for young persons who have violated the

---

[86] *Ibid.*, at 46. For a case illustrating the reluctance of courts to overrule provincial designations of "open" or "secure" custody, see *F. (C.) v. R. et al.*, [1985] 2 W.W.R. 379 (Man. C.A.).

[87] (1990), 56 C.C.C. (3d) 46 (Ont. C.A.).

[88] *Ibid.*, at 48-51.

[89] *Ibid.*, at 50.

criminal law.[90] However, to a significant extent, youths who are being sentenced to custody under the *YOA* are serving shorter periods of time in custody than those sent to training school under the *JDA*. In some provinces the shorter sentences have actually resulted in a decline in populations residing in juvenile custody facilities in comparison to under the *JDA*, even though larger numbers of youths are receiving custodial sentences.

These trends may, in part, be attributed to the attitudes of some youth court judges, who appear to have emphasized the protection of society and the youth's responsibility over the recognition of special needs and limited accountability.[91] It would seem that there has, for example, been an increase in the use of the "short sharp shock" type of sentence (e.g., under three months) which is unlikely to serve much theraputic value, but is regarded by the courts as serving accountability or deterrent functions.[92] Although the case has yet to be convincingly made, it may be that some of the increase in use of custody may be attributed to changing patterns of criminality, and, in particular, an increase in violent crime by young persons.[93]

It may also be that in those province where the age jurisdiction was raised, older

---

[90] See Chapter 5 in this book.

[91] See P. Gabor, I. Greene and P. McCormick, "The *Young Offenders Act*: The Alberta Youth Court Experience in the First Year", 5(2) Can. J. Fam. L. 301-19 (1986) and D.K. Hanscomb, *The Dynamics of Disposition in Youth Court* (unpublished L.L.M. Thesis, University of Toronto, 1988) for surveys of youth court judges in Alberta and Ontario which demonstrate that many youth judges have placed a greater emphasis on accountability since the *Y.O.A.* came into force.

[92] There is considerable doubt as to whether, in reality, increased sentences have a deterrent effect on juvenile criminality; A. Leschied and L. Vark, "A Summary of Literature Related to the Young Offenders Act", *Assessing Outcome of Special Needs Young Offenders* (London Family Court Clinic, 1989). However, youth courts generally appear to act on the assumption that there is a deterrence effect from increased severity of sanctions. See *R. v. H. (S.R.)*, *supra*, note 87.

[93] It would require an analysis of offence and disposition patterns to establish whether the increased use of custody reflects an increase in criminal activity. Presumably, it would also be necessary to compare changes over time in provinces where there has been an increase in the use of custody, and provinces where there has not been an increase. Comparisons with pre-*YOA* data are difficult because of changes in age jurisdiction and methods of collecting data. Further, it must be appreciated that official statistics represent police charges and not actual offences, and may be effected by charging policies.

It is, however, interesting to note that in Canada in 1990-91 there were 9,013 cases involving young persons with violence as a principal charge, a 34 per cent increase since 1986-87: non-violent youth court case load increased only 11 per

youths who had been appearing in adult court as "first time offenders" (their juvenile records being ignored), were appearing in youth court with long records of prior offences.

Further, it seems that some youth court judges have been making extensive use of open custody as a "middle option" for youths who have not committed serious offences, but who "need some help". Prior to the enactment of the *YOA*, many of these youths were placed in residential facilities under child welfare legislation. At least in some jurisdictions, the enactment of the *YOA* has been accompanied by a shift in resources from the child welfare and mental health systems towards the juvenile justice system. Professionals who work with young persons might wish to use other types of resources, but the only available facilities for troubled adolescents may be young offender custody facilities and, hence, these professionals become involved in recommending their use for troubled young persons who have committed offences.

It must be appreciated that use of custody has not increased in all provinces since the enactment of the *YOA*. Most notably in Saskatchewan the rate of custody use marginally decline between 1984 and 1989 and, in Quebec, the rate of custodial dispositions has not changed appreciably since the *YOA* came into force. Quebec has a more extensive child welfare system for dealing with troubled adolescents than other Canadian jurisdictions, and it is apparent that youths who might be in custody under the *YOA* in other provinces are in child welfare facilities in Quebec.[94] It is apparent that there are very significant differences in sentencing patterns in different jurisdictions under the *YOA*.

It remains to be seen whether this trend to increased use of custody will continue. In most provinces, the appellate courts have rendered decisions which reduce the length of custodial dispositions for young offenders, and emphasize limited accountability and the recognition of special needs of young persons. As originally enacted, the *YOA* placed certain restrictions on the use of custody, requiring a pre-dispostion report before any custodial disposition was made, and restricting the use of secure custody to cases where a more serious offence occurred or where there was a record of prior offences. In amending s. 24(1) of the *YOA* in 1986, Parliament provided that a youth court should not place a young offender in open *or* secure custody unless this was considered "necessary for the protection of society having regard to the seriousness of the offence and . . . the needs and circumstances of the young person". Under the original legislation this consideration only applied to secure custody.

In addition to these signals from the appellate courts and Parliament on the

---

cent in the same period (Ontario is not included in this data.) (Canadian Centre for Justice Statistics (1991) "Violent Offence Cases Heard in Youth Courts, 1990-91", 11 Juristat 16. This would suggest that there has been an increase in violent crime by young persons, and the increase in the use of custody may partially be a response to this.

[94] See Chapters 5 and 6.

possible over-use of custody, the 1989 and 1991[95] federal *Consultation Documents* suggested various options to amend some of the sentencing provisions of the *YOA* with the objective of ensuring that custody is not used inappropriately. One option is to eliminate the statutory distinction between open and secure custody, in the belief that some judges may be inappropriately using open custody in situations where they would not make an order just for "custody". Another option discussed in the federal discussion papers was to add specific offence criteria which must be satisfied before an order is made for open custody, similar to those found in subss. 24.1(3) and (4) which now restrict use of secure custody.

There are other possible reforms which are being considered. Should there be an amendment to s. 3 for example to provide that the long-term interest and protection of society would be best served by the rehabilitation of young offenders?[96] Would such a charge have any effect on the actual sentencing practices of the courts? Or should there be more explicit sentencing guidelines for youth courts, as have been proposed for adult offenders by the Canadian Sentencing Commission?[97]

The federal government decided not to bring forward any proposals for the amendment of the dispositional provisions of the *YOA* in its 1989-1992 statutory reforms, other than those governing sentencing for murder, which are discussed below.

In view of the lack of sound empirical data on the causes of the increase in the use of custody, or even data on the extent to which it has occurred in differnet provinces, it seems appropriate to avoid precipitous legislative reform which may have uncertain or unintended effects. However, given the critical importance of sentencing to the young offenders system and the disturbing increase in the use of custody, there is clearly a need for careful study and appropriate action to ensure that custody is only being used to the extent necessary to protect society. This will probably require amendments to the *YOA*; it will almost certainly necessitate changes to provincial policies and programs.

DISPOSITION REVIEW

When a youth is ordered into custody, provincial correctional officials have significant control over the youth's placement. While the youth court specifies the level of custody, correctional officials select the specific facility a youth will reside in and can move the offender from one facility in that level to another. Provincial officials may also permit the temporary release of the youth from

---

[95] Canada, Department of Justice. *Consultation Document on the Custody and Review Provisions of the Young Offenders Act.* (Ottawa, 1991)

[96] *Brief in Response to Bill C-58: Proposed Amendments to the Young Offenders Act* (Ottawa: Canadian Council on Children and Youth, 1990).

[97] Brodeur, "Some Comments on Sentencing Guidelines", L.A. Beaulieu ed., *Young Offenders Dispositions* (Toronto: Wall and Thompson, 1989).

custody, either to engage in employment, education or other activities, or to return home for a specified period of time. Additionally, correctional officials have the authority under the *YOA* to transfer a youth from an open to a secure custody facility for up to 15 days, if there has been an escape or attempted escape, or if, in their opinion, this is "necessary for the safety" of the young person or others in the open custody facility.

The *YOA* provides that once a disposition has been imposed on a young offender, the youth court retains the authority to conduct a review hearing to ensure that the disposition remains suitable to the needs of the youth, and in appropriate cases release the youth from custody. For youths placed in custody, there is a mandatory review hearing by the court after one year, with the possibility of an earlier review, but there is no automatic sentence remission for young offenders. Correctional officials may release a youth from custody onto probation or may transfer a youth from secure to open custody, but these decisions are subject to the approval of a youth court judge; normally these processes can be carried out without a hearing, though sometimes one is required. There continues to be controversy over the effectiveness of the review process. In certain localities there are delays in conducting review hearings and some judges seem reluctant to reduce originally imposed dispositions.[98]

At a review hearing, the youth court cannot increase the level of security which was specified in the original disposition. However, if there has been a wilful failure to comply with a disposition, for example a breach of probation or an escape from custody, this would constitute an offence for which a new disposition may be imposed.

The 1989 and 1991 federal *Consultation Documents*[99] contained a range of proposals intended to facilitate the review process, and ensure that young offenders are transferred to less secure settings as early as possible. Legislative action concerning disposition reviews doubtless will have to await amendments to the legislative provisions dealing with disposition.

TRANSFER TO THE ADULT SYSTEM

The most serious decision to be made regarding a young person charged with an offence is transfer to the adult system. Such a transfer can only occur after a youth court hearing, which must be held prior to any adjudication of guilt or innocence. If a youth court judge orders transfer, there will be a trial in adult court. If there is a conviction in an adult court, sentencing will in significant measure be in accordance with the law applicable to adults. If a transfer order is made, adult laws relating to disclosure of records and trial publicity will also apply.

Although it is theoretically possible for a youth to seek transfer, for example in order to have the benefit of a jury trial, it is usually the Crown that makes an

---

[98] *Y.O.A. Dispositions: Challenges and Choices* (Toronto: Ontario Social Development Council, 1988) at 39.

[99] *Supra*, notes 82 and 95.

application for transfer in order to subject the young person to the much more severe maximum penalties which can be imposed in adult court. Transfer applications are generally made if the Crown considers the maximum custodial disposition under the *YOA* inadequate for the protection of the public or in terms of social accountability or, in some situations, because the security afforded by youth custody facilities is considered inadequate.

Under s. 16 of the *YOA* an application for transfer can be made in regard to any serious indictable offence alleged to have been committed by a young person 14 years or older at the time of the alleged offence. Under the provisions originally reached in the *YOA*, transfer was only to be ordered if the youth court "was of the opinion that, in the interest of society and having regard to the needs of the young person" it was appropriate. In deciding whether to transfer a case, s. 16(2) instructs the courts to consider: the seriousness of the alleged offence; the age, character and prior record of the youth; the adequacy of the *YOA* as opposed to the *Criminal Code* for dealing with the case; the availability of treatment or correctional resources, and any other relevant factors.

Transfer hearings are adversarial in nature, but they are not formal criminal trials. The rules of evidence are greatly relaxed, and the court can receive hearsay evidence about the youth's background and the circumstances of the alleged offence. The court need not be satisfied beyond a reasonable doubt that an offence occurred, but rather decides what is the appropriate forum for the trial and disposition of the charge in question.[100] Witnesses are often called to describe the differences between the fate of the youth if placed in custody under the *YOA* as opposed to incarceration pursuant to the *Criminal Code*.

A pre-disposition report must be presented at a transfer hearing and there is often a s. 13 psychiatric report prepared as well. Typically, two of the most important issues in a transfer hearing are the amenability of the youth to rehabilitation within the period prescribed as the maximum *YOA* disposition, and the availability of resources appropriate for achieving this goal; the reports and other expert testimony often focus on these issues.

There has been substantial disagreement between provincial appellate courts in Canada about the appropriate interpretation of the standard for transfer as originally set out in s. 16(1) of the *YOA*, "the interest of society . . . having regard to the needs of the young person". The courts have compared this to the standard articulated under s. 9 of the *JDA* — that transfer was to occur only if "the good of the child and the interest of the community demand it".

Justice Monnin of the Manitoba Court of Appeal wrote:

> The test under this Act [the *YOA*] is different than that under the old Juvenile Delinquents Act. . . . In the new test there is at least a slight emphasis on the interest of society having regard to the needs of the young person.[101]

---

[100] *R. v. H. (S.J.)* (1986), 76 N.S.R. (2d) 163 (N.S.S.C.).

[101] *R. v. M. (C.J.)* (1985), 49 C.R. (3d) 226 at 229 (Man. C.A.).

Another Manitoba decision commented:

> With the advent of the *Young Offenders Act* the transfer provisions ensure a more realistic approach to transfer. The fact that transfer exists in certain cases for those over the age of fourteen, by implication, considers that in some instances those youths will face a period of adult incarceration. While the primary concern has now shifted so that the interests of society would appear to be of primary importance, the needs of the young person are still to be addressed and these needs might well be so addressed with the treatment available in an adult institution. [102]

This emphasis on the protection of society was most apparent in Manitoba and Alberta, and led to a relatively high transfer rate in those jurisdictions, especially for murder and attempted murder. While some of the variation in transfer rates may have reflected differences in judicial perceptions of the adequacy and security of the youth corrections system in different provinces, it was also apparent that there was significant disagreement as to the appropriate interpretation of s. 16.

The approach of the Manitoba and Alberta courts can be contrasted with the more restrictive approach to transfer taken in Quebec, Ontario and Saskatchewan courts. In *R. v. Z. (M.A.)*[103] the Ontario Court of Appeal refused to transfer a youth who, at the age of 15, shot and killed his mother and sister. Justice Mackinnon observed that "a charge of murder does not automatically remove a youth from the youth court." The judge stressed the amenability of this youth to treatment and wrote:

> In light of s. 3 [of the *YOA*] I do not think that the interests of society or the needs and interests of the young person are to be given greater importance one over the other. They are to be weighed against each other having regard to the matters directed to be considered in s. 16(2). [104]

In September 1989 the Supreme Court of Canada rendered judgments on two transfer appeals from Alberta, *R. v. M. (S.H.)*[105] and *R. v. L. (J.E.)*[106] The Supreme Court affirmed the decision of the Alberta Court of Appeal[107] to transfer the youths to the adult system; the youths were 17 at the time of the alleged offence and charged with the brutal murder of an unconscious man. The majority of the court stated that it was inappropriate to say that the Crown faced a "heavy onus" or had to demonstrate that the circumstances were "exceptional", though the Supreme Court recognized the "seriousness of the decision".

At first glance, it would seem that the effect of these decisions should be to

---

[102] *R. v. J. (J.T.)* (1986), Young Offenders Service 3409-31, at 3409-32 (Man. Prov. Ct. — Fam. Div.).

[103] (1987), 35 C.C.C. (3d) 144 (Ont. C.A.); leave to appeal to S.C.C. refused 70 N.R. 398*n*.

[104] *Ibid.*, at 162. To a similar effect see also *R. v. B. (N.)* (1985), 21 C.C.C. (3d) 374 (Que. C.A.); and *R. v. H. (E.E.)* (1987), 35 C.C.C. (3d) 67 (Sask. C.A.).

[105] (1989), 71 C.R. (3d) 257 (S.C.C.).

[106] (1989), 50 C.C.C. (3d) 385 (S.C.C.).

[107] (1987), 35 C.C.C. (3d) 515 (Alta. C.A.).

make it easier for the Crown to succeed in having youths transferred to adult court,[108] especially for murder charges, since the Supreme Court stated that the Crown did *not* face a heavy onus, and upheld decisions of an appellate court which has tended to transfer cases and has taken a relatively broad interpretation of s. 16. However, there remains some doubt about the full effect of the Supreme Court of Canada decisions. The majority judgments failed to directly address the fact that different appellate courts have taken conflicting approaches to the interpretation of s. 16. The Supreme Court also emphasized that its role was limited to correcting an "error of principle", and that the legislation gave the trial courts and provincial appeal courts a "discretion" to decide cases. Madam Justice McLachlin wrote:

> It is inevitable that in the course of the review, some factors will assume greater importance than others, depending on the nature of the case and the *viewpoint of the tribunal in question*. The Act does not require that all factors be given equal weight, but only that each be considered.[109]

In fact the Supreme Court decisions may have given lower courts relatively little real direction as to the proper interpretation of s. 16, and that different courts have continued to take somewhat different interpretations of this critical legislative provision.

The lack of direction provided by the Supreme Court of Canada was remarked upon by Justice Locke of the British Columbia Court of Appeal in *Re T. (E.) and I. (L.R.)* [110] He quoted the passage from the judgment of Justice McLachlin set out above, and stated: "This provides little specific guidance. It appears to leave an almost completely free hand".

In view of the limited guidance provided by the Supreme Court of Canada, there has continued to be injustice as youths in different jurisdictions received very different treatment. This has heightened the need for legislative reform, though it remains to be seen whether the reforms in Bill C-12 will produce greater uniformity.[111]

---

[108] See *R. v. S. (G.)* (1989), 9 W.C.B. (2d) 119 (Ont. C.A.) where the Ontario Court of Appeal decided to transfer a youth who was 16 at the time of the alleged murder. The decision of Justice Sirois rendered before the Supreme Court of Canada decisions, was reversed by the Court of Appeal and the youth was transferred to adult court.

[109] *Supra*, note 105, at 305. Emphasis added.

[110] (1989), 53 C.C.C. (3d) 209, at 235 (B.C.C.A.); leave to appeal to S.C.C. refused 107 N.R. 233*n*. The B.C. Court of Appeal refused to transfer three youths charged with first degree murder.

[111] Introduced as Bill C-58, December 20, 1989, 2nd Session, 34th Parliament. Reintroduced on May 29, 1991 in 3rd Session, 34th Parliament as Bill C-12, with minor amendments from Bill C-58.

AMENDMENT OF THE TRANSFER AND MURDER PROVISIONS: BILL C-12

Judges and correctional experts recognized the inadequacies of the provisions of the *YOA*, as originally enacted, governing transfer, especially as they are applied in cases of murder. In a transfer application involving a charge of first degree murder, a youth court was faced with choosing between the three-year maximum disposition under the *YOA* and the possibility of life imprisonment with no opportunity for parole for at least 25 years. Quite frequently, neither extreme was appropriate; one was too short and the other too long.

In *R. v. Z. (M.A.)*, the Ontario Court of Appeal refused to transfer a youth facing a first degree murder charge, with Justice MacKinnon stating:

> Put bluntly, three years for murder appears totally inadequate to express society's revulsion for and repudiation of this most heinous of crimes. . . . This is obviously an area for consideration and possible amendment by those responsible for the Act.[112]

A leading juvenile forensic psychiatrist, Dr. Clive Chamberlain, supported the view that for homicides, judges acting under the *YOA* should be able to impose sentences of longer than three years, noting that for a few highly disturbed youths it may be necessary to have up to 10 years of treatment in a secure setting. Dr. Chamberlain commented on the problem with the *YOA*'s three-year maximum disposition, saying that it

> . . . puts pressure on the Crown to move these kids into the adult court, where a 25 year murder sentence is available. As a result some of them will wind up in the adult prison population, where there is no treatment for them and where they just get worse. . . . Society would be better served, I believe, if the three-year maximum term of the youth system — of which the greater part involves counselling — were extended in the rare cases where kids kill somebody.[113]

There was also an enormous amount of public and media concern expressed about the inadequacy of the provisions of the *YOA* for dealing with violent offences, particularly with murder. Much of this was directed towards the judicial reluctance, at least in provinces like Ontario, Saskatchewan and Quebec, in transferring youths, and the perceived inadequacy of a three-year sentence for certain offences, most notably murder. As discussed above, some of the judicial reluctance to transfer, even in murder cases, reflected the enormity of the consequences of transfer, both in terms of length of sentence and the place where the sentence was served.

In Bill C-12, originally introduced into Parliament in December 1989, the federal government set out its proposals for the amendment of the transfer and murder sentencing provisions of the *YOA*. This Bill was studied by a House of

---

[112] *Supra*, note 103 at 162.

[113] Quoted in G. Bagley, "'Oh, what a good boy am I': Killer angels chose when friends die", *The Medical Post*, December 8, 1987 at 61.

Commons Committee in the autumn of 1990, passed by the Commons in November of 1991 and sent to the Senate for approval early in 1992.

For young persons convicted in youth court of first or second degree murder, the maximum disposition is altered from three years in custody to five years less a day,[114] which shall consist of not more than three years in custody plus a period of "conditional supervision".

At the time scheduled for release under conditional supervision the youth court may order that a young offender not be released "if it is satisfied that there are reasonable grounds to believe that the young person is likely to commit an offence causing the death of or serious harm to another person prior to the expiration" of the period of the total disposition that the youth is serving (s. 26.1). Otherwise, a youth court judge will set conditions prior to the release, establishing the terms on which the youth will reside in the community. The released youth may be apprehended for a breach of a condition to serve out the balance of the disposition in custody, subject to further court "review". Thus Bill C-12 will permit a maximum period in custody for youths convicted of murder in youth court of five years less a day, though young offenders convicted of this offence, and dealt with under the *YOA*, should normally serve shorter sentences in custody.

For young persons who are charged with first or second degree murder and have been transferred to adult court and convicted, Bill C-12 provides that the sentence shall be life imprisonment just as for an adult. However, unlike at present, where transferred youths must serve the same 10 to 25 years as adults before being eligible for parole, the sentencing judge in adult court will set a parole eligibility date of five to ten years. In establishing the parole eligibility date, the sentencing judge shall have "regard to the age and character of the offender, the nature of the offence and the circumstances surrounding its commission",[115] and as well as to the recommendation of the jury.

For all offences where a youth court is considering transfer, not just murder, Bill C-12, proposes a change in the test for transfer. The new s. 16(1.1) stipulates that "in making the determination" whether to transfer a case

> 16(1.1) . . . the youth court shall consider the interest of society, which includes the objectives of affording protection to the public and rehabilitation of the young person, and determine whether those objectives can be reconciled by the youth remaining under the jurisdiction of the youth court, and if the court is of the opinion that those objectives cannot be so reconciled, protection of the public shall be paramount and the court shall order that the young person be proceeded against in

---

[114] The maximum total disposition that a youth court may impose is five years less a day. Thus young persons tried in youth court are *not* entitled to a jury trial under s. 11(*f*) of the *Charter*.

[115] Section 744.1 of the *Criminal Code*, as enacted by Bill C-12.

ordinary court in accordance with the law ordinarily applicable to an adult charged with the offence.[116]

Just before final approval by the House of Commons, provision was added to the Bill dealing with the confinement of young persons who have been subjected to transfer. If an order is made to transfer a youth, and the youth is in custody pending trial (which is usually the case) there is a presumption that a youth under 18 will remain in a youth detention facility; for youths over 18 by the time a transfer order is made, there is a presumption of detention with adults following transfer.

If there is a conviction at trial following transfer, the sentencing judge shall determine whether the youth should be detained in a youth custody facility, in a provincial adult correctional facility, or in a federal adult penitentiary, having regard to such factors as the safety of the youth and others, as well as whether the youth "could have a detrimental influence on other young persons" if held in a youth custody facility. The order made regarding the place of custody may be reviewed, and one would normally expect that at the latest by the age of 20, any person serving a long sentence for an offence committed while a young offender would be transferred into an adult facility.[117]

ASSESSMENT OF BILL C-12[118]

Bill C-12 will provide more flexibility for dealing with young persons convicted of murder, and should reduce the disparity in treatment between youths convicted of murder in different provinces. The Bill does raise the spectre of a significant increase in the transfer rate for a wide range of offences, not just murder, though whether this occurs will depend upon how the courts interpret the new provisions.

Bill C-12 clearly provides more flexibility for dealing with youth who commit murder. In particular, for first degree murder, judges will no longer be forced to choose between three years, which may often seem too short, and life imprisonment with no parole for 25 years, which will often be too harsh. The increased flexibility is desirable, as it will allow the courts to impose a sentence more appropriate to the circumstances of the offence and offender. Further, this increased flexibility should go some way to reducing the enormous interprovincial disparities which have arisen under the present legislation. At least in part, these disparities reflected a situation where judges were forced to choose between two extreme positions. While it is likely that there will be differences in how the new

---

[116] The Committee Report to the House, December 20, 1990, substituted "rehabilitation of the young person", for the vaguer concept of "serving the needs of the young person".

[117] Section 16.1.

[118] The analysis of Bill C-12 which is offered here is more fully developed in N. Bala, "Dealing With Violent Young Offenders: Transfer to Adult Court and Bill C-58", (1990) 9 Can. J. Fam. L. 1.

provisions are interpreted and applied, the consequences of any disparities in approach will be reduced.

Reducing the parole eligibility date for youths convicted of murder in adult court is desirable, and reflects the principle of limited accountability of young offenders, as well as the fact that many of them are amenable to rehabilitation. The introduction of the concept of "conditional supervision" for young offenders who stay in the youth system has considerable value, and recognizes that youths often require supervision and support after their release from custody. It remains to be seen how conditional supervision will operate in practice. It is important that these provisions not simply result in two more years being added to custodial sentences, and that adequate resources are provided to ensure meaningful supervision after release.

Similarly, the new flexibility about the placement of youths subject to transfer in youth or adult facilities, as appropriate for the particular youth, is most welcome. Under the *YOA* as originally enacted a young person who was the subject of a transfer order was automatically transferred before trial to an adult detention facility, and once sentenced was generally in an adult correctional facility. While the long sentences permitted by transfer may be justified, placement of youths under the age of 18 with adult offenders is rarely, if ever, justified.

It seems likely that the proposed amendments concerning the consequences of transfer will in themselves result in more transfers for youths facing murder charges, particularly in provinces where the courts have thus far demonstrated reluctance to transfer. While the possibility of somewhat longer sentences in youth court may cause some judges to keep some youths charged with murder in the youth system, it seems that it was the prospect of very long periods of incarceration that made many judges reluctant to transfer. A period of five to ten years before parole eligibility may seem more appropriate and will tend to diminish the reluctance some judges have demonstrated in deciding whether to transfer.

The tendency of Bill C-12 to increase the likelihood of transfer in cases involving murder is demonstrated in a recent decision of Ewaschuk J., where two youths were facing first degree murder charges based on offences alleged to have been committed when they were 16 years of age. The judge noted that the new law would likely be in force by the time of any sentencing in adult court.[119]

> In my opinion, [Bill C-12] and the social climate which produced it, provides an answer to the submission that it is unthinkable to subject young person to imprisonment for periods of more than three years.

The impact of Bill C-12 for murder cases, at least in part, will be determined by the new sentencing provisions, and its impact seems relatively clear. However, the effect of the new law on other offences may be less certain, and will turn on the interpretation of the new s. 16(1.1).

---

[119] *R. v. B. (B.A.),* Lawyers Weekly, February 2, 1990, at 9, full text 937-005 (Ont. H.C.J.), *per* Ewaschuk J.

As originally enacted, the *YOA* stipulated (in s. 16(1)) that the court should be of "the opinion that, in the interests of society and having regard to the needs of the young person" the young person required transfer. The test set out in Bill C-12, s. 16(1.1) requires the court to consider "the interest of society, which includes the objectives of affording protection to the public and rehabilitation of the young person, and determine whether those objectives can be reconciled" in the youth system, and only if these objectives cannot be reconciled in the youth system, "protection of the public shall be paramount and the court shall order" that the youth be transferred.

It seems likely that there will again be a period of uncertainty as the courts begin to interpret the new transfer provision. While the enumerated factors set out in s. 16(2) of the *YOA* will continue to be relevant, it seems that with the change in wording in the primary test the pre-Bill C-12 transfer jurisprudence will be of limited relevance. It seems inevitable that the question of the interpretation of s. 16 will ultimately have to be brought back to the Supreme Court of Canada, though it is to be hoped that the court will provide clearer direction on this issue than it has in the past.

It could be argued that in enacting s. 16(1.1) Parliament is signalling a desire to increase the number of cases transferred, and that it is preferring the approach to transfer adopted by the courts in Alberta and Manitoba. These courts emphasize the "interests of society", which they have been regarded as being served by longer sentences vor violent offenders.

While some observers believe that the new test will increase the willingness of courts to transfer cases, it is submitted that if Parliament wished to achieve this objective, it should have emphasized "social accountability" (or vengeance or punishment), as opposed to simply placing the "protection of society" in a paramount position.

It would seem that if, under the new test, a youth is charged with a serious offence which might merit a longer sentence than three years (or five years for muder) in terms of social accountability, then transfer may be considered. If in this situation a youth court is of the opinion that a youth cannot be rehabilitated by a sentence of three years in the youth system (or five years less a day for murder), then the youth should be transferred to the adult system, where the youth will be incarcerated for a longer period and society afforded protection during the period of incarceration. On the other hand, if the young person appears amenable to rehabilitation within the youth system, then the youth should not be transferred. While it might be argued that society's protection is enhanced by giving youths convicted of violent offences longer sentences for purposes of deterrence, there is significant evidence that increasing the severity of sentences has no real deterrent effect on violent young offenders.[120]

---

[120] A. Leschied and L. Vark, "A Summary of Literature Related to the Young Offenders Act", *Assessing Outcome of Special Needs Young Offenders*, (London Family Court Clinic, 1989) at 5-7. Indeed, one of the main causes of

It is also significant to note that, when applying s. 16(1.1) to a murder charge, Parliament has specifically extended the maximum disposition that a youth court can impose for a conviction of this offence. This clearly indicates that in enacting Bill C-12 Parliament does *not* intend that all youths facing murder charges should be transferred.

The words of s. 16(1.1) require that the youth court give paramountcy to the protection of society only if the objectives of the "protection of the public" and "the needs of the young person" "cannot be . . . reconciled" in the youth system. It is thus apparent that under the new provision there will continue to be an onus on the applicant, invariably the Crown, to satisfy the youth court of the need to transfer the case. However, in practical terms, in cases involving very serious acts of violence or a prior history of violence, there may well be a tactical onus on the young person to satisfy the youth court that rehabilitation is likely to occur within the sentencing provided under the *YOA* and, hence, that the protection of society can be secured without transferring the youth.[121] In other words, placing the protection of society in a paramount position would seem to require that in situations where a young person has demonstrated a capacity for violence, the court must be satisfied that a sentence of three years in the youth system (or five years less a day for murder) will be adequate to rehabilitate the youth and hence protect society.

From a legal realist perspective one can question whether judges actually place significant emphasis on the exact verbal test for transfer. The test under the old *JDA* seemed almost impossible to satisfy; the Crown had to establish that both the "good of the child and the interest of the community demand[ed] transfer",[122] yet in practice there were more cases transferred under the *JDA* than under the *YOA*. It seems that in reality judges are more heavily influenced by their own biases and by the consequences of transferring a youth, or not doing so, than by merely considering the verbal test.

It thus remains to be seen whether altering the verbal formula will in itself result in more transfers. If it does, this will be most apparent and important in regard to offences other than murder, for in regard to murder the change in the sentencing and parole provisions is likely to be more important than the change in the verbal test. It would be most unfortunate if there is a significant increase in the extent to cases which non-murder cases are transferred, since for the vast majority of youths a maximum three-year sentence in a youth facility is more than adequate

---

the violence of many young offenders is their incapacity to consider the consequences of their acts, and increasing the severity of the consequences may not have any impact on their behaviour, though increasing the likelihood of their being apprehended may have some effect on youthful criminality.

[121] It would seem that under the present provisions counsel for young persons have been regularly adducing this type of evidence in transfer hearings, so it is not clear that there will be a significant practical change in this regard.

[122] *JDA*, s. 9(1).

for either rehabilitation or punishment, and the consequences of transfer to the youth may be quite detrimental, especially if the youth is placed in an adult facility. If there is an increase in transfers, it will be critically important that adult correctional authorities develop appropriate programs and services.

CONCLUSION

The *JDA* came into force at the start of the 20th century, and by the 1980's major reforms were inevitable. The *YOA* created a more uniform, national scheme for dealing with adolescents who violate the criminal law. While these youths are no longer afforded a child welfare approach, neither are they subject to the full rigours of the adult criminal justice system. The Act has achieved certain objectives, most notably protecting the legal rights of young persons and decreasing some of the variation in how young offenders in different parts of Canada are dealt with.

The *YOA* is still a relatively new piece of legislation. The process of adjustment and implementation has not been easy. Some involved in the juvenile justice system continue to view the new legislation with a degree of skepticism and even hostility. Some may be reluctant to accept change and continue to hope for a return to the child welfare approach of the old *JDA*. Some reject the possibility for meeting the special needs of youth without abandoning their legal rights. Some struggle with the principles of accountability and special needs, believing that punishment and rehabilitation are mutually exclusive objectives. But for others, an initial period of frustration that accompanies any major change is slowly giving way to growing acceptance of the new legislation.

Attempts to modify our youth justice system must focus on the source of difficulties: the Declaration of Principle (s. 3) or other specific provisions of the *YOA*, provincial implementation of the Act or judicial interpretation. Any assessment of the juvenile justice system must examine the interrelationship of that system with the health, education and child welfare systems.

There are a number of issues which must be addressed by the responsible authorities. This chapter has identified some of the sections of the *YOA* which are creating controversy and may need to be amended.

Many observers continue to express concern about the adequacy of facilities, programs and resources devoted to dealing with young offenders.[123] These concerns must be addressed by provincial governments, and cannot be directly addressed by amending the *YOA*, although the federal government has an important role in terms of providing funding.

Dispositional practices must be carefully monitored. Of particular concern has been the increase in the use of custody and pre-trial detention, and the apparent

---

[123] Of particular concern are the lack of appropriate programs and facilities for dealing with aboriginal youth, who have special needs and are disproportionately represented in the youth justice system. See C. Laprairie "The

disparities in dispositional practices. As discussed in this chapter, it may be necessary to consider further legislative changes, or even amendments to the Declaration of Principle or the creation of sentencing guidelines, in order to ensure that custody is not used inappropriately or excessively.

More fundamentally, it must be appreciated that the law is a blunt social tool, and can only have a limited effect on a complex problem like youthful criminality. The public is understandably concerned about the apparent increase in violence in our society, in particular among young persons. However, legislation or changes to legislation can only have a limited impact on offence patterns of adolescents.

Significant changes in offence patterns will require more than mere legislative changes. A reduction in the rate of youthful criminality will require significant social changes. There have to be improvements in our youth corrections system as well as more fundamental social changes. Our mental health, education and welfare systems must be made more responsive to the needs of youth. We need improvements in how we deal with such problems as drug and alcohol abuse, adolescents with learning disabilities, and with the integration of young persons into meaningful jobs in the labour force. We need a society that more fully recognizes the special problems of aboriginal and visible minority youth. Most basically, we must have a society that values its youth and recognizes their need for a nurturing environment.

Young Offenders Act and Aboriginal Youth'', J. Hudson, J. Hornick and B. Burrows eds., *Justice and The Young Offender in Canada* (Wall & Thompson, 1988). It would be appropriate to have a statement in the Act's ''Declaration of Principle'' (s. 3) that ''facilities and programs are to be provided in a manner that recognizes the cultural and linguistic diversity of Canada, and in particular recognizes the special needs of aboriginal youth''. See *Brief in Response to Bill C-58: Proposed Amendments to the Young Offenders Act* (Ottawa: Canadian Council on Children and Youth, 1990).

CHAPTER 3

A COMPARATIVE EXAMINATION OF THE MODIFIED JUSTICE MODEL IN THE UNITED KINGDOM AND THE UNITED STATES

Raymond R. Corrado
and
Susan D. Turnbull

Developments in juvenile justice in the United Kingdom and the United States parallel many of the trends and controversies discussed in the previous chapter. Canada, however, has much in common with the U.K. and the U.S. beyond shared Common Law and juvenile justice traditions. Numerous political, economic and social structures and events in Canada have been historically intertwined with those in the U.K. and the U.S., reflecting Canada's colonial ties and its shared border, respectively. Canadian parliamentary principles, for example, obviously continue to reflect to a considerable extent British political traditions, while the Canadian federal/provincial structures mirror much of the U.S. federal/state system. Economically, Canada has evolved through agrarian and industrial stages similar to those in the U.K. and the U.S., and currently all three countries are among the ten most advanced economies in the world. Many social traditions are common due to the founding role of the British culture in creating both Canada and the U.S., and due to the continued preeminence of the English language and continual multi-media exchanges such as television, movies and newspapers. These numerous and intricate ties between Canada, the U.K. and the U.S. largely explain why the history of juvenile justice in the latter two countries are so potentially relevant to understanding contemporary juvenile justice issues in Canada.

   The major question that will be addressed in this chapter is what changes occurred in juvenile justice in the U.K. and the U.S. during the same historical period that included the evolution and implementation of the *YOA* in Canada. Specifically, did custody rates change in the former countries when laws and policies shifted from the Welfare Model toward the Justice Model end of the continuum? Also, to what extent have Crime Control and Corporatist Model policies been implemented in the U.K. and the U.S.? (See Figure 1, Chapter 1.) In attempting to answer these questions, it will be possible to address similar issues, about changes brought about by the *YOA* which are described in the previous chapter and in more detail in the next two chapters.

The U.K. will be examined first and more elaborately than the U.S. for two main reasons. First, juvenile justice in the U.K. evolved differently than in Canada and the U.S. The Welfare Model was fully adopted initially in the latter countries, while, it will be argued, the Welfare Model was never completely implemented in the U.K. It was only briefly in the late 1960s and early 1970s that Welfare Model principles influenced juvenile justice legislation in the U.K. to the same degree that they have for over 60 years in Canada and the U.S. Second, it is less difficult to generalize about juvenile justice trends in the U.K. than in the U.S. In the U.S. federal system, there are 50 legislatively distinct state juvenile justice systems, while in the U.K. there are only three legislatively distinct regions — England and Wales, Scotland, and Northern Ireland. For the contemporary period beginning in the 1960s, our focus will be on England and Wales, with only a brief discussion of Scotland's radical shift in abolishing its juvenile court in 1968.

Before describing the inception of juvenile justice in the U.K., it is necessary to return to our discussion of the models of juvenile justice introduced in Chapter 1. It will be argued that until the 1960s, juvenile justice in the U.K. could be identified most closely with Modified Justice Model characteristics. This model is distinguished from the Justice Model in the U.K. context for two essential reasons: first, there is less formality in the role of magistrates in the due process summary procedures used to determine guilt; and second, Welfare Model principles are important in sentencing (i.e., consideration is given to the welfare of the young person in terms of his or her rehabilitation). In turn, the Modified Justice Model differs from the Welfare Model because there is more emphasis on the rules, principles and procedures designed to protect the rights of the individual. An additional difference is the Modified Justice Model emphasis on personal responsibility for illegal behaviour versus the Welfare Model focus on social, economic and developmental explanations for such behaviour. Of course, it is critical to keep in mind that these models are "ideal types" and that when analytically applying these models to actual juvenile justice systems it is most useful to view them as differing in degrees rather than absolute or nominal terms. This caution is particularly important in understanding juvenile justice in the U.K., since from the passage of the *Children's Act* in 1908[1] (which finalized the 19th-century evolution of a juvenile justice system which functioned completely separately from the adult system) until the 1970s, most of the policy debates and related theoretical controversies have concentrated on the movement toward or

---

[1] (U.K.) 8 Edw. 7, c. 67.

away from either the Justice Model or the Welfare Model. Since the 1970s, the Crime Control and Corporatist Models have more commonly been utilized to analyse changes and reforms in juvenile justice in the U.K. The Crime Control Model policies are characterized as enhancing the abilities: of the police to investigate and arrest young offenders; of the courts to speedily process and sentence them according to incapacitation and punishment/deterrence principles; and of corrections personnel to enforce rigorous physical discipline and personal responsibility in custodial institutions. The Corporatist Model emphasizes not the role of police (according to the Crime Control Model), nor the role of lawyers (according to the Justice Model), nor the role of social workers and other helping professions (according to the Welfare Model), but rather the roles of *all* of these groups acting in an interagency structure which efficiently diverts minor offenders, requires less serious property offenders and violent offenders to participate in attendance programs and sentences the few serious offenders to custodial institutions.[2]

The major theoretical issue of concern in this chapter is whether the problems in contemporary juvenile justice in Canada — problems such as the difficulties the police have in investigating and charging young offenders, increased court delays and costs and increased use of custody — are linked to the Modified Justice Model principles incorporated in the *YOA*. Since certain juvenile justice legislation in both the U.K. and the U.S. can be characterized as reflecting Modified Justice Model principles, it is useful to ascertain whether similar problems took place after these legislative changes occurred in these other countries. In other words, we can attempt to evaluate the degree to which current difficulties in Canadian juvenile justice are attributable to the theoretical shortcomings of the model upon which the system is based. Equally important, we can examine the U.K. and the U.S. to determine whether Modified Justice Model legislaiton has been successfully amended in these countries to eliminate or reduce problems, as Bala has suggested in Chapter 2, and consider potential applications of this to the *YOA*.

The present chapter is divided into three parts, beginning with the history of the development of juvenile justice in the United Kingdom. The focus will be on shifts in legislation and practices between the Welfare Model and Justice Model ends of the continuum. The second part consists of a discussion and critique of the major competing theoretical perspectives that attempt to explain the course of juvenile justice in the U.K. Part 3 includes a brief history of contemporary juvenile justice trends in the U.S. and a review of some of the theoretical accounts of these trends.

---

[2] Pratt, "Corporatism: The Third Model of Juvenile Justice" (1989) 29(3) *British Journal of Criminology* pp. 236–54.

PART 1: AN HISTORICAL OVERVIEW OF JUVENILE JUSTICE IN ENGLAND AND WALES

1800–1908: The Beginning of Juvenile Justice in the United Kingdom

Juvenile justice in the U.K. originated with the movement in the early 19th century to develop separate post-prison release facilities for young people. Once released, the young person stayed in the Philanthropic Society's house of refuge for 12 to 18 months. The first juvenile prison, Parkhurst, opened in 1838. Deterrence, rather than reform, was the main policy objective of the Parkhurst model. Combining adults and juveniles was opposed because it hampered deterrence. At the same time, industrial schools were created to provide education and training for dependent and neglected children and for those who were seen as either pre-delinquent or unmanageable by their parents. Reformatories were to provide middle-class family and religious values to young people up to age 16 who had been sentenced to prison terms or to penal servitude.

A separate juvenile court began to take form in 1847 with the passage of the *Juvenile Offenders Act*.[3] Children under age 14 charged with larcenies and thefts had their cases committed to magistrates in Petty Sessions. By 1879, most indictable offences could be tried summarily for those under 16 years of age.

The *Children's Act* of 1908 created separate juvenile courts throughout England and Wales which were closed to the public. This Act introduced a Modified Justice Model system, as the juvenile courts were to operate as criminal courts with summary trial procedures similar to those in adult courts. The seriousness of the offence and the interests of the public were to influence sentencing, as were the "special needs" of the juvenile offender.[4]

---

[3] (U.K.), 10 & 11 Vict., c. 82.

[4] John Pratt, who has written extensively about juvenile justice trends in England and Wales, disagrees that the 1908 *Children's Act* can be categorized as legislation based on a Modified Justice Model. He claims that Garland's (1985) historical research convincingly demonstrates that this act represented a decisive shift toward Welfare Model principles. By the end of the 19th century, the neo-classical theory of crime (i.e., that free will or conscious choice explained crime) was being successfully challenged by positivist theories (i.e., that predetermined factors such as heredity, poverty, family problems, and mental disorders explained crime). Garland maintains that penal policies began to include welfare objectives. Pratt asserts, then, that the creation of a distinctive juvenile justice system, with probation officers, industrial schools and borstals (a form of reform schools for delinquents between the ages of 16 and 23) indicated decisive emphasis on the Welfare Model end of the continuum (personal conversation with, and critical review comments by, John Pratt,

Lay persons, usually of respectable middle-class backgrounds, were appointed to serve as magistrates on a part-time basis in a judicial panel format. While summary procedures in court were to be consistent with the common law adversarial tradition, sentencing criteria reflected prevailing theoretical explanations concerning the causes of delinquency. Family corruption and the degenerative influences of the city, it was argued, had combined to produce the "dangerous criminal classes" which, if left unchecked, could infect the respectable working class and create uncontrollable mobs. For youthful offenders, the appropriate response was to subject them to the discipline and moral training necessary to reintegrate them into respectable working-class occupations and family traditions. Personal rejuvenation through the state's promotion and enforcement of middle-class family norms and structures was the underlying theoretical perspective for the consideration of the "special needs" of juvenile delinquents at sentencing. Reformatories and industrial schools, and later borstals, emphasized discipline through work.

The influence of the Welfare Model was further evident in that the *Children's Act* also provided magistrates with a variety of sentencing options, including primarily probation, which marked a shift toward less intrusive and punitive interventions within the community. This shift reflected the increasing political concern for the declining birthrate and the poor physical state of the British working class in a period of economic and social uncertainty. As Morris and Giller observed, "(t)he 1908 *Children's Act* reflected concern for the future; juveniles' health and well-being was one of the nation's greatest assets".[5] From the beginning then, macro-level factors appeared to push the British juvenile justice system increasingly toward Welfare Model considerations, even though it would not be until the 1930s that these considerations would gather a steady momentum. In contrast to the ebb and flow of the influence of the Welfare Model reforms in the U.K., this model was adopted in its entirety in the U.S. In the U.S. juvenile courts, offenders were viewed as fundamentally different from adults and therefore as requiring completely different procedures based on the Welfare Model principles, while:

> (t)he English juvenile courts, on the other hand, viewed the juvenile offender as a miniature adult who had to be protected by the due process of law and its accompanying procedures and safeguards. They were part of the general system of criminal justice.[6]

December 1990). However, as argued above, certain fearures of this act appear to be more consistent with a Modified Justice Model influence than with a Welfare Model.

[5] Morris and Giller, *Understanding Juvenile Justice* (London: Groom Helm, 1987), p. 31.

[6] *Ibid.*, at p. 67.

1908–1960: The Early Challenge of the Welfare Model

The Welfare Model juvenile justice systems in the U.S. and Canada received considerable publicity in the U.K. Given the apparent advantages of a juvenile court system that eschewed criminal procedure completely in order to concentrate on rehabilitating young people, the inevitable issue was whether to abandon the Modified Justice Model and move completely to the Welfare Model.

In 1927, a Departmental Committee on the Treatment of Young Offenders (the Molony Committee) explored this possibility and rejected it. Its rationale was that the key principles of responsibility for crimes and respect for the law would be fundamentally weakened by a welfare tribunal. Nevertheless, while the Molony Committee accepted the neo-classical view that juvenile delinquents were largely responsible for their criminal acts and therefore should be subject to formal court procedures, there was also recognition of the social and psychological factors that influenced them. To accommodate this dual image of delinquency, the Molony Committee explicitly recommended that magistrates be required to consider the social welfare of a young person in sentencing. This key recommendation was enacted in the *Children and Young Persons Act* of 1933.[7] This law, however, did not make the welfare of the child the major goal of the juvenile court but instead reinforced the principle that juvenile courts would remain criminal courts.

After World War II, an important parallel development to the evolution of the juvenile justice system occurred with the establishment of Children's Departments in each local authority (in towns and cities throughout Great Britain) with the power to assume the duties of parents for children "in need of care or protection". This development was important since a significant proportion of juvenile delinquents would now effectively be wards of the state, and eventually the distinction between these two statuses, and the organizations dealing with them, would be blurred. As we will see, this blending would lead to considerable confusion and controversy.

The ambivalent attitude toward juvenile justice policy in the U.K. was further revealed in the *Criminal Justice Act* of 1948.[8] The Act abolished corporal punishment as a sentence and set a maximum age of under 17 for imprisonment in a juvenile facility, while at the same time introducing detention and attendance centres. The former were designed for short stays, while the latter were for even shorter periods such as weekends. Both institutions were to incorporate tough and punitive regimens, along with education programs, according to the proposition that "toughness deters and education reforms".[9]

In response to growing concern about the perceived increase in juvenile crime throughout the 1950s, the Home Office established the Ingleby Committee to explore ways to improve the juvenile court. Again, the major issue that emerged

---

[7] (U.K.), 23 & 24 Geo. 5, c. 12.

[8] (U.K.), 11 & 12 Geo. 6, c. 58.

[9] Morris and Giller, *supra*, note 5, at p. 72.

was the conflict between the court's justice and welfare functions. Despite the absence of social workers on the Ingleby Committee, its members identified family problems as the most important factor in juvenile delinquency. Yet, the juvenile court was primarily concerned with trying offences and only secondarily in dealing with personal, family and social considerations. As with the Molony and other previous committees, the Ingleby Committee did not explicitly recommend the adoption of social welfare principles or the Welfare Model but instead prompted a further move toward it. The fact that no major changes in juvenile court procedures resulted from this committee was not surprising, given the policy dilemmas that characterized its investigation.

1960–1980: Welfare Model Reforms and Ideological Debates

In the 1960s, the debate over juvenile justice took a more explicitly ideological turn when, partly in response to its critical view of the Ingleby Committee report, the Labour Party established the Longford Committee. The Longford Committee advocated the radical step of abolishing the juvenile courts. Criminal procedures, the Longford Committee argued, were totally inappropriate for juveniles whose delinquent acts were caused by inadequate family circumstances. The proposed alternative was a family service structure where the child, family and social worker together could identify specific problems and resolve them. Only when an offence was denied or an agreement could not be reached would a case go to family court.

As one would expect, when the Longford Committee report became the basis of the Labour government's 1965 White Paper, Justice Model supporters vehemently opposed it, claiming that the legal rights of juveniles would no longer be protected. Opposition arose primarily from Justice Model-oriented interest groups, including the probation service, justices' clerks and magistrates.[10] Given the controversial nature of this White Paper and the opposition within the Home Office, the Labour government appeared unwilling to risk its small majority position in Parliament by introducing legislative reform. Instead, a second White Paper was produced in 1968 which recommended a variety of ways to reduce the number of cases going to juvenile court and which favoured civil proceedings and informal action. To accomplish these goals, the role of social workers in processing young persons would be substantially increased at the direct expense of the existing functions of probation officers, the police and magistrates. As one would expect, these juvenile court functionaries opposed the proposed reduction in their roles and sought the support of the Conservative Party opposition in Parliament when the 1969 *Children and Young Persons Act* was introduced.[11] However, the retention of the central role of the juvenile court mitigated some of

---

[10] Bottoms, "On the Decriminalization of the English Juvenile Courts" in Hood, ed. *Crime Criminology and Public Policy* (London: Heinemann, 1974).

[11] (U.K.), 1969, c. 54.

the opposition of these key interest groups to the proposed law. In effect, the 1969 Act was another compromise between the Welfare and Justice Models, and the consequent dissatisfaction of proponents of both models ensured that further conflict would be inevitable.

Partial Implementation of the 1969 **Children and Young Persons Act**

Prior to the complete implementation of the 1969 Act, the Labour government was defeated in 1970 by the Conservative Party, led by Edward Heath. The new Conservative government failed to proclaim into law several critical sections of the 1969 Act which would have shifted the juvenile justice system much further toward the Welfare Model. As a consequence, magistrates simply continued their practices as before despite the introduction of an expanded role for social workers. Nonetheless, a backlash against the 1969 Act occurred. According to one magistrate's clerk, this Act had fundamental flaws; most important was the breakdown of law and order which had occurred by the early 1970s. This clerk claimed that this absence of effective control of young criminals resulted in a:

> . . . fast-approaching state of anarchy and the public seems totally unable to protect itself. The courts are impotent, the police seem dazed and the local authority social workers appear to relish their new-found power to over-rule the so-called reaction-ary ideas of the magistry.[12]

This vitriolic attack had little substance since, according to government research conducted by the Department of Health and Social Security (D.H.S.S.) in 1981, the Act was working well and social workers were not acting in a manner that could be construed as defying the sentencing objectives of magistrates.

Additional research also failed to substantiate a decline in the role and powers of the juvenile court. For example, despite the presence of diversion programs, there was an increase in the volume of cases going to the juvenile court. Morris and Giller have observed that, in fact, "the opposite to that intended by the 1969 Act occurred — sentencing had become more penal than welfare oriented".[13] To substantiate this observation, they point out that in 1965 one in 800 boys between 14 and 17 years of age appearing before magistrates was sentenced to a detention centre or borstal, while in 1979 the rates had changed dramatically to one in every 180 boys receiving custodial sentences. Only a small fraction (one-sixth) of this increased use of custody could be attributed to changes in offences.[14]

For Morris and Giller, both strong proponents of the Justice Model, there is little doubt that the opposition of many magistrates to the 1969 Act's attempt to shift juvenile justice toward the Welfare Model was largely based on their lack of confidence that social workers would make the "tough" decisions to remove juveniles from their homes. They were especially concerned about the hardened recidivists who, they feared, would otherwise openly flout the authority of the

---

[12] Morris and Giller, *supra*, note 5, at p. 94.

[13] *Ibid.*, at p. 97.

[14] *Ibid*, at p. 98.

juvenile courts. In effect, depriving magistrates of their exclusive and key decision-making power to remove juveniles from their homes under the new "care order" would, according to many magistrates, result in a "powerless" juvenile court and unprotected public.

Again, however, these perceptions were not supported by the 1981 D.H.S.S. findings, which revealed an increase, not a decline, in custodial penalties. Equally important, social workers during the 1970s appeared to have adapted to their new "crime control" roles and were not at all reluctant to recommend custodial and other intrusive orders in their social inquiry reports.[15] While there appeared to be initial ambivalence and confusion over their new roles in juvenile justice, social workers generally appear to have made decisions similar to those made by probation officers prior to the legislation, albeit for somewhat different reasons. For example, recommendations for intrusive care orders for minor property or first offenders resulted in a substantial number of juveniles being subjected to the next stage in the sentencing tariff — a custodial order. It seems that where social workers did not believe they could work effectively with a juvenile, they were likely to resort to a secure and/or custodial placement without having exhausted all other alternatives.[16] Organizationally, it appears that the enhanced role of social workers in juvenile justice likely influenced their social inquiry recommendations to coincide more with the expectations of magistrates. After 1979, additional funding was more likely to be provided by the Thatcher government for social workers in their new crime control roles than in their traditional care roles.[17]

1980 — Present: A Shift to Modified Justice Principles with the *Criminal Justice Act* of 1982

The 1969 Act was blamed for the failure of the juvenile justice system to prevent delinquency, reduce recidivism and control street hooligans, despite both the government's own research showing that the 1969 Act had not diminished custodial orders, and the fact that social workers had adapted rather quickly to the organizational and political imperatives of their juvenile justice crime control roles. The criticism came from interest groups such as magistrates who complained about their lack of power and "get tough" options.

In 1974, a subcommittee of the House of Commons Expenditure Committee reviewed the 1969 Act. According to Morris and Giller, the interest groups that appeared before this committee represented four different models of juvenile justice:

---

[15] Harris and Webb, *Welfare, Power and Juvenile Justice: The Social Control of Delinquent Youth* (London: Tavistock, 1987).

[16] Cawson and Martell, *Children Referred to Closed Units*, D.H.S.S. Research Report No. 5 (London: H.M.S.O., 1979).

[17] Harris and Webb, *supra*, note 15.

> . . . the "radical view" that the Act did not go far enough; the "crime control" view that the Act was based on unsound principles; the "child care" view which accepted the broad principles of the Act and called for full implementation; and the "crime control/child care view" which suggested that some juvenile offenders were susceptible to welfare measures, but that others required penal measures.[18]

Not surprisingly, the Committee report recommended measures that would deal both with children in need of care through a welfare approach and with the small percentage of children who they believed needed control and punishment in a correctional setting. As Bottoms has argued, this "bifurcation" of juvenile justice was the obvious and politically expedient decision since it attempted to combine both welfare and crime control approaches.[19] Given the moral panic over violent and "hard core" juvenile offenders in the 1970s, such a compromise was intended to mollify the British electorate, who in 1979 were being subjected to an intensive and vehement "law and order" media campaign by the soon-to-be-elected Conservative Party government led by Margaret Thatcher. The crime control theme was central to her appeal, not only to the traditional Conservative Party supporters among the middle- and upper-income groups, but also to a critical number of traditional Labour supporters among the lower-income groups.

It did not seem to matter that key Welfare Model measures in the 1969 Act either were not implemented or were blunted by the magistrates and police, or that government research revealed an (apparent) increase in custody orders.[20] According-ing to Farrington, the Conservative government ignored available research and proceeded with its 1980 White Paper, "Young Offenders", which was intended to shift juvenile justice toward a mixed Justice/Crime Control Model.[21] This was evident in the recommendations that diversion should be increased through expanded police cautions while giving magistrates more direct authority to impose various custody options, such as new, shorter custodial sentences. Also, magistrates were to be given the option of fining the parents rather than the juvenile.

While many of the 1980 White Paper proposals were enacted in the *Criminal Justice Act* of 1982,[22] other provisions were introduced later. As a result, the British juvenile justice system at this time could still be more accurately charac-terized as a continuation of the Modified Justice Model system than as reflecting a significant shift to the Crime Control Model so strongly identified with the Thatcher government's electoral and media images of what this system should

---

[18] Morris and Giller, *supra*, note 5, at p. 108.

[19] Bottoms, *supra*, note 10.

[20] As will be discussed below, more recent government custody statistics since 1979 indicate no increase during this time period.

[21] Farrington, "England and Wales" in Klein, ed., *Western Systems of Juvenile Justice* (Beverly Hills, Calif.: Sage Publications, 1984).

[22] (U.K.), 1982, c. 48.

be.[23] There were several reasons why the anticipated switch to the Crime Control Model did not occur. Most importantly, Morris and Giller maintain that the ''justice for children'' movement had strong proponents both in academia and among Liberal MPs.[24] Pratt claims further that even among social workers there was support for this movement.[25] In addition, the ''justice for children'' movement was central in the intense debates in the United States and Canada over the failure of the Welfare Model to provide either due process or rehabilitation. Along with the influence of U.S. publications advocating a ''return to justice'', the Black Committee had proposed that many of the Justice Model principles be the basis for revamping the juvenile justice system in Northern Ireland.[26]

Justice Model advocates maintained that there must be proportionality between the seriousness of the crime and the sentence, and that the least restrictive sentence should be applied. In effect, custody should be a sentence restricted to the most serious offence. This principle was seen as critical because the apparent increase in custody sentences worried Justice Model advocates. They believed that more rigorous sentencing guidelines needed to be imposed to reverse this punitive and inintended consequence of the 1969 Act. The success of the Justice Model advocates was evident in the 1982 Act, and in the subsequent 1988 *Criminal Justice Act*, previously both of which specified new and more restrictive criteria for the use of care and custodial orders as well as for the use of harsher placements. A custody order could only be imposed if non-custodial penalties had previously been attempted, if there was a perceived need to protect the public or if the crime was particularly heinous. In addition, the new legislation required social inquiry reports to be obtained to decide if these criteria were met, and specified that legal representation be offered to the juvenile. The 1982 Act also specified that sanctions be determinate and proportional to the seriousness of the offence. Finally, the shift toward Justice Model criteria was evident in the recognition that court proceedings should be more adversarial.

The reversal away from the Welfare Model trends that had been so prominent from the mid-1930s to the mid-1970s, and toward Justice Model reforms, was also influenced by similar reforms in the U.S. Scholars such as Paul Tappan initiated the critique of the Welfare Model-based U.S. juvenile justice system, and by the 1960s the U.S. Supreme Court had, in landmark decisions such as *Re Gault*,[27] provided the main impetus for a partial shift toward a Justice Model in many of the state juvenile justice systems. Labelling theorists such as the U.S.

---

[23] Tutt and Giller, *The Criminal Justice Act 1982* (Lancaster: Information Systems, 1983).

[24] Morris and Giller, *supra*, note 5.

[25] Pratt, J. (1987) ''A Revisionist History of Intermediate Treatment'', 17 *British Journal of Social Work*, pp. 417–36.

[26] Black Committee, *Report of the Children and Young Persons Review Group* (Belfast: H.M.S.O., 1979).

[27] 387 U.S. 1 (1967).

scholar Edwin Lemert[28] also added to the growing criticisms of the Welfare
Model. During the 1970s, the "return to justice" movement in the United States
had developed into a broadly based alliance of appellate judges, scholars and legal
professionals. They provided further documentation of the fundamental problems
and abuses of the welfare approach, but also provided elaborately conceived
alternative Justice Models. The Justice Standards Project of the Institute of
Judicial Administration (IJA) and the American Bar Association (ABA) provided
a report that supported Justice Model criteria and procedures in 1977. In the same
year, Washington State enacted legislation that established the first juvenile
justice system to incorporate many of the Justice Model principles.

Morris and Giller claim that these events in the U.S. influenced scholars and
policy-makers in Britain.[29] Morris, in particular, became a strong proponent of
the "return to justice" movement in Britain.[30] In addition to being a magistrate in
the juvenile court in Cambridge, England, Morris has examined various welfare-
based systems, including those in the United States and Scotland. She has argued
forcefully that the Justice Model is the most effective way to avoid many of the
problems inherent in attempts to control and process youth crime.

The Debated Consequences of the *Criminal Justice Act* of 1982

Two key objectives of the 1982 Act were to establish sentencing criteria that
would reduce custodial sentences in general, and to reduce the frequency of longer
forms of custody in particular. According to some British scholars, neither of
these objectives were attained. Andrew Rutherford[31] reviewed custody trends
before and after the 1982 Act and concluded that custody trends became more
punitive following the legislative change. Other researchers, including Burney,[32]
Reynolds,[33] and Whitehead and MacMillan[34] examined various English courts'
sentencing patterns and concluded that custody orders had increased even though
these sentences were not associated with more frequent serious offences. In

---

[28] Lemert, *Instead of Court: Diversion in Juvenile Justice* (Chevy Chase, Md.:
National Institute of Mental Health, 1971).

[29] Morris and Giller, *Understanding Juvenile Justice* (London: Groom Helm,
1987).

[30] Morris, "Revolution in the Juvenile Court" (1978) (September) Crim. L. Rev.
529–39.

[31] Rutherford, *Growing Out of Crime* (Harmondsworth: Penguin, 1986).

[32] Burney, "All Things to All Men: Justifying Custody Under the 1982 Act"
(1985) (May) Crim. L. Rev. 284–93; *Sentencing Young People* (Aldershot,
U.K.: Gower, 1985).

[33] Reynolds, "Magistrates' Justifications for Making Custodial Orders on Juvenile Offenders" (1985) (May) Crim. L. Rev. 244–98; *A Lack of Principles*
(Oxford: Oxford University Department of Social and Administrative Studies,
1985).

[34] Whitehead and MacMillan, "Checks or Blank Cheque?" (1985) 32 Probation
87–9.

reviewing these data, Morris and Giller state that "the statutory [sentencing] criteria to restrict the use of custody by juvenile court magistrates were commonly misused or ignored".[35] In most cases, magistrates ignored probation officer recommendations for non-custodial dispositions.[36] For these scholars, the fact that some magistrates personally favoured a more punitive approach at least partially explains why the clear intention of the 1982 Act to use the least restrictive sentencing option was not being followed. Prior to the 1982 Act, Crown court judges reviewed borstal or long-term custody sentences handed down by magistrates, and one-quarter of these recommendations were rejected by the appellate courts. However, the 1982 Act empowered magistrates to directly sentence youth to long-term custody without this routine higher court review.

Pratt, however, disagrees with this initial analysis of the 1982 *Criminal Justice Act*.[37] He maintains that custody rates have remained stable throughout the 1980s at approximately 12 percent of all juvenile court dispositions (see Table 1). While there has been a slight increase in the longer youth custody sentences, there has been an approximate proportionate decline in detention centre sentences. In effect, the 1982 *Criminal Justice Act* was not more Crime Control-oriented than previous legislation and, further, juvenile justice policy-makers under the Thatcher government continued to restrict magistrates' abilities to resort to custody by providing more explicit and stringent criteria for its use in the *Criminal Justice Act* of 1988. Pratt's view of what has occurred since the height of the influence of Welfare Model proponents (with the passage of the 1969 Act) and their subsequent demise with the Justice Model-oriented 1982 and 1988 Criminal Justice Acts[38] is that these two models do not adequately explain what in fact has

---

[35] Morris and Giller, *supra*, note 29, at p. 127.

[36] Whitehead and MacMillan, *supra*, note 34.

[37] Pratt "Corporatism: The Third Model of Juvenile Justice" (1989) 29 *British Journal of Criminology* pp. 236–54.

[38] With respect to juvenile justice, the *Criminal Justice Act* of 1988 is an attempt to address the issues that arise with the detention of young persons convicted of a criminal offence. Under s. 123(3) of the Act, magistrates are more restricted when assessing a disposition for a young person. This section of the Act provides that a court may not sentence a young person to custody for life unless it is satisfied, "[t]hat the circumstances, including the nature of the offence, are such that if the offender were aged 21 or over the court would pass a sentence of imprisonment. Furthermore, the young person must qualify for a custodial sentence under this section of the Act. The Act specifies three qualifications. First, the young offender". . . (h)as a history of failure to respond to non-custodial penalties and is unable or unwilling to respond to them: or (second) only a custodial sentence would be adequate to protect the public from serious harm: or (third) the offence of which he has been convicted or found guilty was so serious that a non-custodial sentence for it cannot be justified".

occurred over the last 20-year period. He argues that a Corporatist Model (see Figure 1.1) best describes the long-term trends in juvenile justice in England and Wales. This model will be discussed in the section on macro perspectives in Part 2 of this chapter.

It is important to note that there is no consensus among scholars in the U.K. either about which model is best represented by the juvenile justice system or about the theories purporting to explain why juvenile justice changes have taken place. As mentioned in the introduction, there is a lively and insightful theoretical debate about juvenile justice trends among scholars in the U.K. which is relevant to understanding these trends in Canada. To reiterate, custody trends are a controversial issue among scholars in Canada, as are related questions about whether the YOA philosophically is more punitive because it is too Justice Model- and Crime Control Model-oriented; whether the ''special needs'' of young offenders are being provided for in both community and custodial institutions; whether the juvenile justice and related social, health and educational agencies are more concerned with preserving their functions and budgets in the face of fiscal restraint than in genuinely servicing young offenders; and whether the YOA is a progressive law designed to protect young persons' due process rights or whether it was designed to meet the needs of powerful interest groups such as capitalists, government bureaucrats and lawyers. These issues are addressed in Part 2, where the major theoretical perspectives will be divided into macro-level, middle- (or organizational) level and micro- (or individual) level theories.

PART 2: THEORETICAL PERSPECTIVES ON CONTEMPORARY TRENDS IN JUVENILE JUSTICE IN ENGLAND AND WALES

Macro theories focus on society-wide structures and processes such as those involved with the economy and politics. Given this broad scope, these theories are complex and somewhat difficult to understand. Yet, there can be little doubt that macro theories are important in understanding juvenile justice. As was evident in Part 1, the political process is critical to the passage of juvenile justice legislation and the structure of funding of all the relevant bureaucracies in England and Wales. It is equally obvious that bureaucracies and agencies are the administrative focal point of juvenile justice. It is within government and private organizational contexts that individuals as professionals relate to young people. Middle-range or organizational-level theories are, therefore, central to explaining juvenile justice trends. Finally, individual-level theory involving the role of ideology will be discussed because, within any organization or agency, individuals vary in the way they view their job functions, and consequently they vary in how they act.

Conceptualizing influences on juvenile justice trends as originating from different levels is an analytic abstraction which is helpful in disentangling the complexity of juvenile justice systems. In the final analysis, our concern is to try to explain what happens to young persons involved in juvenile justice. While all of the theories discussed below address this concern, they differ in terms of which level they suggest is a most appropriate focus for examining the issue.

Macro-Level Perspectives

Macro-level perspectives will be discussed first. Included here are Marxist theories and the theory developed by Michel Focault. It is important to keep in mind the major limitation of these perspectives — they are overly deterministic and minimize or deny the influence of either individual-level factors (especially ideological elements such as humanitarianism and altruism) or organizational-level factors (such as the structure and role of juvenile courts). The Marxist perspectives, however, do provide critical insight about the importance of contradictions in the relationships between capitalist economies on the one hand, and the welfare state and political pluralism on the other.

Marxist Perspectives

There is no doubt that the Thatcher government viewed its restructuring of the economy toward classic capitalist criteria as the only response to the major British economic problems of poor, annual Gross National Product growth trends; inflation; major budget deficits; investment capital flight; low productivity; devalued currency; foreign trade deficits; outdated extractive and manufacturing industries and one of the world's worst labour strike rates. Thatcher's policies blatantly were designed to increase profits and capital. Denationalization or privatization of numerous industries has taken place at an unprecedented rate, and the tax rate has been reduced from one of the highest among advanced industrial countries to one of the lowest. The economic and political position of unions has been systematically and dramatically diminished through both anti-union legislation and business incentive packages. The welfare state has been another target. Severe budget restraints resulted in a sharp curtailment of a wide range of government-funded programs designed to assist those in need. The near half-century trend of building a mixed economy of private and state-capitalized industries has been fundamentally reversed. The division of wealth and opportunity are left increasingly to market forces, with the result that the southeast of Britain (including London) has a prosperous middle- and upper-class while lower-income individuals and the rest of the country are experiencing recession and even depression-level economies. For Thatcher, the solution to poverty was not the welfare state but the enhancement of competition and private capital. The crisis in capitalism that Spitzer[39] and others have noted has shifted political power and economic advantage to those favouring individual responsibility in all facets of life. Thatcher's ''get tough'' crime control juvenile justice philosophy embodied the political reaction of the Conservative Party to its perception that the Labour Party's experiment in social welfare had failed.

---

[39] Spitzer, ''Toward a Marxian Theory of Deviance'' (1974) 22 *Social Problems* pp. 641–51.

In effect, by the late 1970s a crisis had emerged in the traditional consensual politics that had dominated most of the post-World War II period and which had allowed for the development of the welfare state (including the *Children and Young Persons Act* of 1969) and moderate or "middle of the road" government policies. From a Gramscian Marxist perspective[40], these consensual politics were critical in maintaining the ruling class hegemony. Under both Labour and Conservative governments, international capitalists effectively controlled the British economy and, indirectly, politics, by using the benefits of a mixed (publicly and privately owned enterprises) economy to fund the welfare state, thereby producing consensus within the electorate. Until Thatcher, Liberals, (Red) Conservatives and social democrats, including many Labour Party members, and later all Social Democratic/Liberal Party members, had dominated British political institutions. The "crisis in hegemony" occurred in the 1970s when traditional Keynesian[41] fiscal and budget policies failed to stem Britain's precipitous economic decline because of "stagflation" (i.e., inflation and unemployment escalated while GNP grew marginally and, consequently, government budget deficits and interest rates rose sharply). The so-called moderate Keynesian policies gave way to the harsh monetarist and privatization policies of allowing market forces to decide both interest rates and currency values, and which businesses, including newly privatized industries, could survive in the ever-increasing international competition.

Taylor has utilized this Gramscian Marxist perspective in explaining the shift to "Thatcherism" in economics and other policies, including juvenile justice:

> A developed crisis of hegemony of the kind identified by Hall et al. for Britain requires a displacement of the fundamental character of the crisis in the contradictions of international capitalist competition in declining markets, in conditions of energy shortages and inequalities in technological capability onto the heavily "commonsensical" terrain of authority, discipline and control, in the specific sense

---

[40] Gramscian Marxists differ from other Marxists in that they emphasize that political structures can be directed by the elite to convince the masses that there are no viable alternatives to existing societal structures, while traditional Marxists believe that class conflicts are unavoidable and are ultimately reflected in political structures.

[41] Keynesian fiscal and budgetary policies are based on two principles. The first is that governments should intervene in the economy during a recession or depression by stimulating growth through: (1) lowering interest rates to make captial easier to borrow for businesses and individuals; and (2) increasing spending through budget deficits, which increases demands for services and products and consequently keeps businesses operating and workers employed. The second principle is that during times of inflation, governments should restrict demand for capital, services and products by raising interest rates and decreasing government spending.

of enabling otherwise potentially electorally-unpopular political forces to move into hegemonic domination of the state.[42]

While Marxist perspectives do provide considerable insight into the relationship between broad macro-level economic and political factors and changes in juvenile justice, there are far too many juvenile justice policies and trends within Great Britain that are not adequately or convincingly explained by any of the Marxist perspectives. Specifically, despite the unequivocal crime control rhetoric of Thatcherism, the *Criminal Justice Act* of 1982 and other juvenile justice policies have resulted neither in the demise of traditional Welfare Model themes, nor in a radical shift to crime control policies. The 1982 Act did reinforce the dominant position of magistrates, but it did not remove social workers from the judicial process. Also, while magistrates were given more direct access to Crime Control Model-type custodial sentencing options, the 1982 Act explicitedly identified custody sentences as either a last resort option, or immediately appropriate only for severe offences. Diversion remained the favoured policy for initial and trivial offences. Even with Thatcher's severe budget slashing, Welfare Model treatment programs were not dismantled. On the contrary, Intermediate Treatment (I.T.) programs were introduced with a substantial budget. These programs were divided into "low intensity" I.T. community work schemes such as youth employment plans for at risk youth, and "heavy-end" I.T. programs involving intense social worker surveillance and residential stays as an alternative to custody. Numerous I.T. programs have been developed, all sharing some degree of preventive social work.[43]

Foucaultian Perspective

Both Foucault[44] and Donzelot[45] have a different macro theoretical perspective about the course of juvenile justice in Western society than do the Marxist scholars. For these authors, the explanatory focus is not economic imperatives and the repression of working-class youth; it is the broadest dynamic of social control which consists of a universal network of interventions dedicated to disciplining all behaviour. Since the early 19th century, numerous professions have evolved within industrial/urban society which are ultimately dedicated to their own particular sphere of specialized knowledge or expertise. These professionals or experts have been located in institutions of discipline such as prisons, work houses, asylums, schools and universities and, more recently, in non-

---

[42] Taylor, *Law and Order: Arguments for Socialism* (London: MacMillan, 1981), p. 8.

[43] Pratt, "Juvenile Justice, Social Work and Social Control. The Need for Positive Thinking" (1985) 15 *British Journal of Social Work* pp. 1–25.

[44] Foucault, *Discipline and Punish: The Birth of Prison* (London: Allen Lane, 1977).

[45] Donzelot, *The Policing of Families* (London: Hutchinson, 1979).

judicial tribunal institutions such as workers' compensation boards, community juvenile court committees and community diversion committees. In conjunction with the formal judicial institutions of discipline, community groups form an all-inclusive disciplinary network far more powerful than the traditional family and religious agents of norm-setting and social control which dominated the pre-19th-century period. For Foucault, each knowledge/expert sphere operates as an autonomous power unit with no single economic or political imperative as the underlying cohesive dynamic. While there are interconnections between health care institutions, juvenile courts, social welfare organizations, community diversion groups, the police and schools, they are not ultimately bound together to enhance the overarching controlling position of capitalists or any other societal unit. Donzelot, on the other hand, does maintain that there are hierarchical patterns in the broad juvenile justice disciplinary network. The numerous government agencies, community organizations and professionals involved in processing youth can be arranged along a continuum of intervention or decision-making power. According to Donzelot:

> . . . the court has become the overseer of this continuum: it co-exists with a number of other sites (such as pre-court tribunals and diversion schemes) in the decision-making process, to be brought into play when these have failed or are thought to be inappropriate — while at the same presiding over and existing as the ultimate arbiter in the inter-locking channels of communication and referral.[46]

From Foucault's and Donzelot's combined perspectives, the political and theoretical debate among proponents of the Justice, Crime Control and Welfare Models is misplaced because such debate is focused not on qualitative differences in what is done to youth, but on quantitative differences in (or degrees of) intervention. In effect, whether administrative decisions are made by social workers, probation and police officers or by judges, the intervention outcome is the same — social control. The common objective for all these decision-makers is to force youth into conforming. Thus, to focus on judicial and quasi-judicial judges is too narrow. Foucault has written that ''(t)he judges of normality are present everywhere. We are in the society of the teacher-judge, the doctor-judge, the education-judge, the 'social worker'-judge''.[47]

Foucault also provides an insightful theoretical account of the resilience of all the juvenile justice agencies in spite of no evidence of successful interventions or, even worse, evidence of counter-productive interventions (for example, causing crime such as delinquency by the labelling effect resulting from official judicial processing of youth). Foucault's contention is that the realm of the bureaucrat and expert involves knowledge that is inaccessible to outsiders. This knowledge is a powerful political tool because experts routinely utilize it, ironically, not only to justify their continued existence despite program failures, but also to expand their

---

[46] As quoted in Pratt, *supra*, note 43, at p. 3.
[47] Foucault, *supra*, note 44, at p. 304.

power by adding new programs and institutions with a new nexus of experts, knowledge and power. This explanatory perspective was used by Harris and Webb to describe British juvenile justice evolution and expansion:

> . . . (We) can certainly see too that the failure of the separate and silent [penal] systems to prevent [inmate] contamination in the 1850s came to justify the development of the reformatories; the failure of the reformatories to do the same led to the placing of the youngest thieves in the industrial schools; the failure of the prisons led to the Borstal and probation systems, to the development of discharge on licence and hence to the increasing penetration of power into the lives and families of the criminal. It is when the boy persists in his petty thefts in the face of parental admonition that are summoned in, simultaneously or consecutively, teacher, doctor, clergyman, psychologist, psychiatrist, psychotherapist, youth leader, agony aunt, social worker, probation officer, policeman, magistrate, residential worker, and prison officer. Each expert offers a different perspective and cure involving perhaps, the deep treatment of the boy, the broad treatment of his family and friends, or both. And the boy's failure or refusal to succumb to the best efforts of these experts comes to justify each successive penetration.[48]

Foucault's perspective has been utilized routinely and extensively by scholars such as Harris and Webb, Cohen,[49] Pratt[50] and Ignatieff,[51] who have examined the British criminal and juvenile justice systems. With a few exceptions, this perspective does not adequately answer several key issues about the roles of altruism and humanitarianism, or about the constraints on continued expansion of state power and the image of the state as a smooth running machine.[52] An inherent difficulty with macro theoretical perspectives is that individual-level factors such as personality and ideology are ignored, assumed irrelevant or asserted to be of less explanatory power than macro-level variables. It is not surprising that theoreticians such as Cohen, who are personally familiar with experts and bureaucrats, view Foucault's perspective as uninformed about the variation in individual-level factors which may account for differences in individual-organizational-and macro-level outcomes in juvenile justice.

Such differences are as obvious to systematic observers as are the commonalities. Within the United Kingdom, for example, the Scottish juvenile justice system is fundamentally different from the English system in that there is no juvenile court in Scotland. These different systems are characterized not only by differences in modes of processing youth, but also in types of social control

---

[48] Harris and Webb, *Welfare, Power and Juvenile Justice: The Social Control of Delinquent Youth* (London: Tavistock, 1987), p. 64.

[49] Cohen, *Visions of Social Control* (New York: Polity Press, 1985).

[50] Pratt, *supra*, note 43.

[51] Ignatieff, "State, Civil Society, and Total Institutions: A Critique of Recent Social Histories of Punishment" in Tonry and Morris, eds., *Crime and Justice* (Chicago: Chicago University Press, 1981).

[52] *Ibid.*

outcomes such as the frequency of custody sentences.[53] There are also enormous variations within the English systems themselves,[54] even in the same metropolitan area.[55] Finally, there are enough attitudinal studies of police, magistrates, probation officers and social workers within the same court indicating ideological variations to suggest that, at the micro level of decision-making, uniform notions of social control are problematic. Importantly, these ideological variations are associated to some degree with differences in sentencing outcomes.[56]

Bottoms has raised several fundamental issues about Foucault's inability to account for the substantial limits of expansion of state power in terms of direct surveillance of juveniles despite the significant rise in crime rates.[57] For Bottoms, the expansion of weaker disciplinary options such as fines and diversion are not to be considered the simple disciplinary equivalent of custodial sentencing. It is evident that ideological constraints within bureaucracies, political parties and governments restrain the inexorable expansion of state power. As mentioned above, for example, Thatcher's obsession with monetarist fiscal and budgetary principles precluded an open-ended commitment to financing the expansion of juvenile justice crime control institutions and programs.

To summarize, Foucault, like those from the Marxist perspectives, provides considerable insight into why the Modified Justice Model evolved in England and Wales. Yet, each leaves far too many issues unresolved; especially the issue of why so many differences, some fundamental, exist within the same system. Rothman points out the direction that Foucault missed or ignored: "Foucault's analysis never enters into the everyday world of criminal justice . . . . There is much more room for maneuver than a Foucault could ever imagine to allow."[58]

Middle-Level Perspectives

Given the overwhelming evidence of the impact of Thatcherism on British

---

[53] Asquith, *Children and Justice: Decision-making in Children's Hearings and Juvenile Courts* (Edinburgh: Edinburgh University Press, 1983); Martin, Fox and Murray, *Children Out of Court* (Edinburgh: Scottish Academic Press, 1981).

[54] Anderson, *Representation in Juvenile Court* (London: Routledge and Kegan Paul, 1978).

[55] Parker, Casburn and Turnbull, *Receiving Juvenile Justice* (Oxford: Blackwell, 1981).

[56] Asquith, *supra*, note 53; Harris and Webb, *supra*, note 48; Morris and Giller, *Understanding Juvenile Justice* (London: Groom Helm, 1987).

[57] Bottoms, "Neglected Features of Contemporary Penal Systems" in Garland and Young, eds., *The Power to Punish* (London: Heinemann, 1983).

[58] Rothman, *Conscience and Convenience* (Boston: Little Brown & Co., 1980), p. 11.

society, Cohen,[59] Harris and Webb[60] and most other British scholars are in agreement that macro-level economic and political factors directly affect the course of contemporary British juvenile justice. There is less consensus, however, on the extent of the impact of these factors. Tutt and Giller maintain that macro factors are substantially modified by local or specific juvenile court contexts.[61] They effectively deny that any uniform juvenile justice system exists in England and Wales. Local political authorities and bureaucrats along with juvenile justice personnel make the daily decisions, and they do so under enormously varied economic, ethnic and political conditions. Thus, an increase in custody sentences in one locality might reflect a crime control value, while in another, even adjacent, locality, it might reflect a fiscal decision to shift certain juvenile justice costs to the national government.

Rutherford has identified confusion on the part of local authorities over their role in administering the provisions of the *Children and Young Persons Act* of 1969 as another critical factor in the lack of uniform policy application.[62] He claims that during the decade following this Act, the confusion and uncertainty at the central government level about responsibility for young offenders created parallel confusion at the local government level. New social service departments were being created at the local level at the same time as local authority boundaries were being redrawn. Social workers and probation officers had to establish functional jurisdictions because of their divided responsibilities under the 1969 Act, while at the national level the Department of Health and Social Services and the Home Office were engaged in a similar territorial dispute. According to Rutherford, the outcome of the struggle at the local level was not uniform: "The split has remained very uneven across the country, but, nationally, probation has retained primary responsibility."[63]

It is also important to reiterate that the so-called Thatcher economic revolution resulted in massive regional disparities in unemployment and growth. Pratt argues that because structural unemployment disproportionately affected lower income youth, especially those outside southeastern England, young adults and older adolescents were directly affected by the economic changes.[64] In turn, the

---

[59] Cohen, *supra*, note 49.

[60] Harris and Webb, *supra*, note 48.

[61] Tutt and Giller, *The Criminal Justice Act 1982* (Lancaster: Information Systems, 1983).

[62] Rutherford, "A Statute Backfires: The Escalation of Youth Incarceration in England During the 1970s" in Doing, ed., *Criminal Corrections: Ideals and Realities* (Toronto: Lexington Books, 1983).

[63] *Ibid.*, at p. 83. By the late 1980s, however, the role of probation officers in juvenile justice generally had been reduced substantially.

[64] Pratt, "Crime, Time, Youth and Punishment" (1990) *Contemporary Crisis* pp. 219–42.

development of the novel Intermediate Treatment Programs varied sharply by region and city in terms of their specific functions or program resources available. According to Pratt, some of these programs focused on problems of youth unemployment while others were more narrowly oriented towards monitoring problem youth.[65]

To understand the controversies surrounding the Modified Justice Model system in England and Wales, it is necessary to examine the relationships among the key legislative Acts (the *Children and Young Persons Act* of 1969 and the *Criminal Justice Act* of 1982), the organizational dynamics of juvenile justice agencies and the individual decision-makers. It is clearly beyond the scope of this chapter to describe these relationships in detail, and it would also be somewhat redundant since several excellent publications exist which address these issues. (See, for example, Harris and Webb,[66] and Morris and Giller[67].) Therefore, only a brief summary will be provided here.

The organizational structure of the English and Welsh juvenile justice system essentially consists of five elements. First, the police hold power of investigation and power of arrest or discretionary release of youth by way of a recorded caution;[68] second, probation officers and social workers share responsibility both for preparing reports which contain sentencing recommendations and for supervision orders; third, the defence counsel and prosecutor maintain adversarial roles in attempting to influence adjudication and sentencing decisions; fourth, the magistrates perform the actual adjudication and sentencing functions; and fifth, institutions and programs are operated through the local authorities (for example, Intermediate Treatment Programs) and in conjunction with the (national) Department of Social Services and Housing and the Home Office (the Ministry responsible for probation officers).

The role of police in juvenile justice is substantial and at times controversial (for example, such as when they voiced strong opposition to the *Children and Young Persons Act* of 1969). In addition, defence counsel and prosecutorial roles are important because of due process requirements and the "speaking to sentence" input they provide to magistrates. Their adversarial roles are central to the Justice Model. Although the juvenile court was abolished in Scotland, protecting the procedural rights of youth has been a long-standing principle in British juvenile justice. While the police and lawyers are critical in juvenile justice, however, the focus of much of the theoretical concern in this area has been on the

---

[65] Pratt, "A Revisionist History of Intermediate Treatment" (1987) 17 *British Journal of Social Work* pp. 417–36.

[66] Harris and Webb, *Welfare, Power and Juvenile Justice: The Social Control of Delinquent Youth* (London: Tavistock, 1987).

[67] Morris and Giller, *supra*, note 56.

[68] Farrington and Bennett, "Police Cautioning of Juveniles in London" (1981) 21(2) *British Journal of Criminology* pp. 123–35.

policies, roles and decision-making of magistrates, probation officers and social workers.

Magistrates make a collective decision concerning culpability for crime according to the traditional common law criteria of legal guilt, and they are likely to favour Justice Model criteria — seriousness of offence and prior offence record — for sentencing decisions.[69] Since the failure of the *Children and Young Persons Act* of 1969, magistrates under the *Criminal Justice Acts* of 1982 and 1988 remain in the pivotal decision-making role. It is evident that mitigating and aggravating circumstances influence magistrates' decisions, as does the availability of sentencing resources. Social workers provide this additional information in their reports to the magistrates. Other experts are also involved on a case basis, depending upon the type of problem identified as a relevant mitigating or aggravating factor. Psychologists, psychiatrists and teachers are only a few of the experts who can be called upon to assist the social worker and probation officer in making the diagnoses and recommendations magistrates seek. It is at this juncture that the Modified Justice Model can interact with organizational role dynamics and ideologies to produce negative consequences.

Despite Thatcher's Crime Control Model media rhetoric, it is possible for magistrates to interpret the *Criminal Justice Act* of 1982 differently. Instead of relying on the "get tough" direct custody options, magistrates could infer that the Justice Model "least intervention" principle in this Act predominates and choose alternative sanctions. Magistrates may avail themselves of numerous Welfare Model policies including care orders (although these are infrequently used) and Intermediate Treatment programs. In effect, the absence of a pure Justice Model law places magistrates in the position of having to decide what type of sentencing (Crime Control, Justice, Welfare or Mixed Model) to apply in each case. One would predict that the inherent tendency, given this range of options, would be to bifurcate cases according to serious and non-serious criteria and then to resort to crime control sentencing options for the former and other models for the latter.[70] Yet, it is evident from the sentencing patterns since both the 1969 and 1982 Acts that no simple bifurcation decision-making process has taken place. Custody orders have not been systematically associated with seriousness of cases.[71] While there can be little doubt that seriousness of the offence and prior offence history

---

[69] Asquith, *Children and Justice: Decision-making in Children's Hearings and Juvenile Courts* (Edinburgh: Edinburgh University Press, 1983).

[70] Bottoms, "Justice for Juveniles 75 Years On" in Hoath, ed., *75 Years of Law at Sheffield 1909–1984* (Sheffield: Sheffield University Press, 1985), pp. 95–111; Cohen, *Visions of Social Control* (New York: Polity Press, 1985).

[71] Harris and Webb, *Welfare, Power and Juvenile Justice: The Social Control of Delinquent Youth* (Cambridge: Cambridge University Press, 1987); Morris and Giller, *supra*, note 56.

are important considerations, there must be other mitigating factors in a substantial number of cases.

Magistrates rely on social workers as well as other experts for information on family, education, mental health and social relationships. These experts usually function within organizations and, therefore, are governed to varying degrees by formal and informal policies developed through a hierarchical administrative structure. As well, professional ideologies are learned through formal education, job training and experience. These experts bring their organizational imperatives and professional ideologies into the courtroom context where magistrates are in the dominant decision-making position. Among these experts, however, social workers routinely exercise some autonomy with their ability to initiate breach and care proceedings. Their investigative, supervisory and welfare functions involve more diverse knowledge needs than either the police, teachers or psychologists. Probation officers and social workers often are the intermediaries between these other experts and the magistrates, as well as between youth and the magistrates. According to Harris and Webb, occupational uncertainties characterize the social workers' functioning because it is a "more weakly framed activity, characterized less by coherence than by the necessary but conceptually unclear function of plugging gaps left by the more strongly framed activities of other professionals".[72] Harris and Webb further contend that social workers and probation officers are exposed to a diversity of theories, educational experiences and profoundly difficult social and psychological problems which compound their occupational uncertainty. While there is, for example, consensus among experts that family dynamics is a critical factor in understanding delinquency, social workers and probation officers have to incorporate numerous problem-solving theories and expert advice in providing specific recommendations to magistrates. The absence of a dominant theory and/or "successful" family intervention program explains to some degree the considerable variation in individual case decision-making among the experts. The net result of all of this ambiguity and uncertainty is that it is not uncommon to observe social workers and probation officers making recommendations that encompass principles from either Crime Control, Justice, Welfare or mixed Models.

Harris and Webb maintain that juvenile justice experts in England and Wales lack occupational coherency because of fragmented and internally inconsistent ideas at the individual or case level. They note that:

> . . . the sum effect of all these fragmented interpretations, these personal syntheses, is paradoxically to create yet further uncertainties: the professional co-existence of such incompatible beliefs and purposes, lacking as some of them do even the most basic agreement about the core of the job can have no other effect.[73]

Pratt, on the other hand, maintains that by the end of the 1980s, there was considerable coherence among juvenile justice agencies in promoting common

---

[72] Harris and Webb, *supra*, note 71 at p. 107.
[73] *Ibid.*, at p. 109.

objectives.[74] He believes that even social workers had adapted their "helping" ideology to their juvenile court roles and their monitoring functions within Intermediate Treatment programs. In effect, he believes that the corporatist structure which he suggests evolved in earnest in the 1980s had overcome, to a considerable extent, the disorganization and confusion that appeared to characterize the period between 1969 and 1982.

The Corporatist Perspective

Corporatism is essentially a descriptive or conceptual perspective in comparison to the explicitly theoretical Marxist perspective. The major focus of Corporatism is the organizational structure of a society's institutions, be they economic, political, social or even more specific, such as the juvenile justice system. A Corporatist organizational structure is reflected in the Corporatist Model described in Chapter 1 (see Figure 1). It is hierarchical and integrative; coordinated policies are disseminated from a central institution such as a Parliament or a Cabinet to specific agencies with such diverse functions as police, courts, schools, welfare and mental health agencies. This structure facilitates efficient implementation of complex policies from the national level down to the local level. While Corporatism is primarily a descriptive construct, Pratt maintains that it also includes a theoretical dimension,[75] and it is for this reason that it is discussed here not only as a model of juvenile justice structure but also as a theoretical perspective. Theorists such as Cohen[76] explain that Corporatist structures have emerged from various industrial and post-industrial economic, political and social trends and are included in various (often competing) theoretical perspectives such as Marxist, Focaultian and Humanist/Reform theories. Cohen, as will be discussed below, argues, for example, that both fiscal crises and the desire to continue Humanist (i.e., rehabilitative) policies toward most delinquent youth have contributed to the evolving Corporatist juvenile justice systems in contemporary post-industrial countries such as Canada and the U.K. In effect, the Corporatist theoretical perspective is based on an eclectic or diverse set of hypotheses about organizational trends in post-industrial society. This perspective, consequently, lacks the explicit theoretical integration of hypotheses and explanations provided, for example, by a Marxist theory of juvenile justice reform. However, Pratt asserts that the Corporatist perspective best describes what has occurred in England,[77] and LeBlanc (see Chapter 1) similarly argues for a Corporatist-type account of recent reforms in juvenile justice in Quebec. Therefore, we turn now to an examination of the Corporatist view of juvenile justice in the U.K.

---

[74] Pratt, "Corporatism: The Third Model of Juvenile Justice" (1989) 29 *British Journal of Criminology* pp. 236–54.

[75] Pratt, *supra*, note 64.

[76] Cohen, *supra*, note 70.

[77] Pratt, *supra*, note 64.

As noted in Chapter 1, Pratt has taken the view that many of the contemporary trends evident in juvenile justice in England and Wales do not represent the struggle and confusion resulting from policy shifts from the Justice Model end of the continuum to the Welfare end and *vice versa*.[78] He maintains that these two models were relevant in understanding trends and controversies until the early 1970s, but since then, despite the ideological dominance of the Justice Model and Thatcher's political rhetoric regarding the Crime Control Model, the most appropriate description of juvenile justice trends in England and Wales is found in the Corporatist Model. Pratt maintains that the following characteristics define this model:

> . . . an increase in administrative decision-making, greater sentencing diversity, centralization of authority, and coordination of policy, growing involvement of non-juridical agencies, and high levels of containment and control in some sentencing programmes.[79]

Justice Model proponents would argue that the policy objectives of the 1982 and 1988 Criminal Justice Acts involved a distinctive shift toward Justice Model principles away from the Welfare Model-oriented 1969 *Children and Young Persons Act* and that, therefore, juvenile justice practices inconsistent with the former model are anomalies or unintended consequences. Pratt, however, argues that fundamental organizational and policy changes have occurred and are being entrenched in a manner which suggests a coherent long-term commitment by bureaucrats and politicians.

He points first to the dramatic increase in administrative discretion involving diversion programs; police cautions, for example, are currently the predominant sanction for juvenile offenders, having risen nearly threefold to 99,000 in 1984 from 33,702 in 1968. And in the North Hampton Local authority area, for example, over 1,000 referrals were made to the (administrative) interagency Juvenile Liaison Bureau, while there were only 101 court referrals.[80] The second change involves the growth of interagency cooperation at the local level, with a focus on more efficient and effective sentencing policies and the creation of crime prevention programs. The third trend consists of the evolution of alternatives to care/custody programs under the Intermediate Treatment policy set forth in the 1969 *Children and Young Persons Act*. The fourth change is the decline in the autonomy of juvenile justice agencies, most importantly in the judiciary and for social workers. The 1982 and 1988 Criminal Justice Acts have narrowed the discretionary sentencing power of the judiciary and more fully integrated social workers into the judicial process in their referral and monitoring functions. The fifth trend is marked by the increased role of the volunteer sector, primarily in the provision of Intermediate Treatment programs. Private agencies have experienced a substantial growth in funding since 1983. The sixth change involves the

---

[78] Pratt, *supra*, note 74.
[79] *Ibid.*, at p. 245.
[80] *Ibid*, at p. 241.

introduction of computer and information technology in the administration of juvenile justice. This trend has also brought in more of the private sector and, as well, has required the greater assistance of social workers in administrative services. These developments have had the impact of increasing interagency cooperation. The seventh change is the bifurcation of offenders into serious and non-serious categories, with custodial sentences reserved for the former. As mentioned earlier, Pratt maintains that during the 1980s, despite Thatcher's Crime Control Model rhetoric, epitomized by the introduction of the "short, sharp, shock" punishment of young offenders, custody rates remained consistent at approximately 12 percent of the total number sentenced in juvenile court.[81] Thus, to summarize, the major policy themes of the Corporatist Model are efficiency and coordination in monitoring the majority of young offenders within the community (and outside the expensive and time-consuming court process and custodial institutions).

These themes are consistent with Cohen's perspective that, while the Welfare Model juvenile justice systems in many countries have been sharply criticized by both liberals and conservatives for failing to rehabilitate young offenders, most reforms continue to attempt to change youth (albeit by controlling behaviour) while maintaining the "soft-core" or minor offender within the community, and reserving more punitive custodial sanctions for the minority of "hard-core" or violent offenders.[82] Cohen seems to view contemporary policy reforms as eclectically reflecting principles from all the models of juvenile justice. In extending Cohen's position, Pratt's Corporatist Model apparently could explain, for example, the increased presence in the 1980s of Crown counsel and the routine provision of defence counsel, through legal aid schemes, for the small proportion of cases that proceed to the juvenile court, a change normally viewed as consistent with Justice Model reforms. Under a Corporatist system, a "true" adversarial process involving a not guilty plea and a trial is limited to a small fraction of young offenders whose lawyers are not able to negotiate a plea bargain with Crown counsel. In effect, there are political and organizational pressures to move cases quickly to completion, and counsel help to facilitate this process.

While Pratt acknowledges that Justice Model reforms have occurred, he believes that the most substantial changes are found not in the juvenile court processes themselves, but in the administrative processes which include police, social workers and Intermediate Treatment programs.[83] The dominant policy objectives are monitoring minor young offenders and changing the behaviour of these individuals without removing them from the community.

---

[81] Home Office, "Observations on the 11th Report from the Expenditure Committee" (Cmrd 6494) (London: H.M.S.O., 1976).

[82] Cohen, *supra*, note 70.

[83] Pratt, *supra*, note 74.

Micro-Level Perspectives

According to Cohen, there is no paradigm or controlling organizational theoretical perspective among juvenile justice personnel in other common law countries.[84] Consequently, ideologies become critical in understanding diversity in decision-making. In effect, while political and economic variables, juvenile justice laws and organizational dynamics explain some of the variation in decision-making in juvenile justice, conflicting ideologies of experts probably account for the enormous inconsistencies and unintended consequences of many of the remaining decisions. Out of a mixture of theories and juvenile justice histories, Cohen has identified five ideological categories: pragmatists, disillusioned liberals, neo-conservatives, anti-professionals and sentimental anarchists.[85] It is this range of conflicting ideologies among experts in England and Wales that likely precludes them from being guided directly and uniformly by the 1969 Act and the subsequent amendments effected by the 1982 and 1988 Acts. When organizational-level factors are considered, the link is further confounded. Taken together, the two Acts convey the mixed messages that have characterized the Modified Justice Model approach since its inception — while experts are to

---

[84] Cohen, *supra*, note 70.

[85] Cohen, *supra*, note 70, at pp. 128–30 defines these categories as follows:
Pragmatists cite "minor case" clogging and a lack of practical discretion as crucial problems with a demonstrably inefficient centralized juvenile justice system. Inefficency is seen as compromising expediency and serving to discredit perceptions of justice. Pragmatists argue that minor case bifurcation is a necessary perquisite to the proper allocations of resources (i.e. toward crime control considerations).
Disillusioned Liberals distrust the benevolence espoused and embodied by liberal reformers and moral entrepreneurs. They reject the "needs" rhetoric of "do good" paternalism which resulted in civil and human rights abuses. In opposing closed institutions and the ideology of treatment, D.L.s instead advocate a return to due process and "justice" considerations.
Neo-Conservatives (New Right) share the same disillusionment as the D.L.s, except that they see the failure of the "welfare" orientation as inevitable. N.C.s propose reality and practicality, with an emphasis on "hard" cases.
Anti-Professionals challenge the system power monopolies which have developed from the myth of professional expertise. Social workers, in particular, are seen merely as disguised agents of social control. A.P.s de-emphasize the importance of schools, medical professionals and psychology. (Presumably, these theorists represent the antithesis of Pratt's Corporatist model).
Sentimental Anarchists espouse radical non-intervention by the juvenile justice system in order to avoid creating crime (i.e., they believe that secondary deviance is created through court processing and labelling of widespread temporary adolescent [primary] deviant behaviour).

follow due process and to consider the seriousness of the offence and prior record for sentencing, welfare considerations are also to be given weight. It appears that Crime Control Model politicians and the media interpret the Modified Justice Model as serving the primary purpose of getting tough with or punishing young criminals. Given the periodic media sensationalism about youth crime in Britain, it should not be surprising that some juvenile justice experts, especially police and magistrates, are affected by crime control principles. However, there is little evidence that crime control-oriented experts predominate throughout juvenile justice.

What appears to emerge at the operational level of juvenile justice, where daily decisions are made, is not at all what either Modified Justice Model theoreticians, policy-makers, politicians, or Marxist critics expected. Unintended outcomes, such as an increase in the use of custody by a particular court, might better be explained by Harris and Webb's description of what they observed in their research:

> . . . in practice as we have seen, it has not worked so neatly. Reality is more erratic, even anarchic, and we have begun to understand why. The experts' tasks are self-constraining, riddled with paradox, irony, ambivalence; their relationship with the court is varied and unpredictable: certainly they are locked into no cosy conspiracy with the court to control ever more penetration, but supposing that too fails, as often it must? What do we derive from such failures but unread dossiers, identified but unmet needs, known but unpunished infractions?[86]

This pessimistic view of the English juvenile justice system is consistent with other scholarly perspectives such as Cohen[87] and Foucault,[88] but not with the more recent perspective developed by Pratt,[89] and it also runs counter to Millham's[90] encouraging assessment of the impact of reforms.

Summary of the British Experience

Before examining the United States experience, it is important to reiterate the fundamental problem of the current English Modified Justice Model-based juvenile justice system. Rutherford identifies the key policy flaw as "the attempt to straddle the contradictory aims of reducing the use of custodial sanctions and increasing the flexibility of the courts in their sentencing task".[91] Morris and

---

[86] Harris and Webb, *supra*, note 71, at p. 86.

[87] Cohen, *supra*, note 70.

[88] Foucault, *Discipline and Punish: The Birth of Prison* (London: Allen Lane, 1977).

[89] Pratt, *supra*, note 74.

[90] Millham, *Juvenile Justice and Child Care in England* (Ann Arbor, Mich.: Center for the Study of Youth Policy, 1991).

[91] Quoted in Harris, "Towards Just Welfare" (1985) 25(1) *British Journal of Criminology* p. 37.

Giller, whose theoretical analysis and empirical review of the English juvenile justice system is both thorough and insightful, are concerned that the modification and movement toward the Justice Model has resulted in unintended negative consequences as well as desired outcomes:

> This realignment of the decision-making basis in the juvenile court which gives centrality to the offence may turn out to be a major factor in promoting feelings of justice and fairness among juveniles and their parents. But the juvenile court's decision alone, coming as it does at the end of a process of discretionary and often 'hidden' decisions will not necessarily promote substantive justice.[92]

Proponents of Welfare, Justice and Corporatist Models agree that the English experience to date has not resulted in substantive justice, although this consensus is based on conflicting theoretical rationales. There is, therefore, no obvious or simple explanation for the problems of the English juvenile justice system. It remains an open question whether problems such as the lack of substantive justice and "net-widening" (broader social control) can be attributed to the apparent shift toward the Justice Model. It is also important to keep in mind Pratt's contention that the major shift in juvenile justice has been toward a Corporatist Model.

Further comparative cross-national analysis, however, can add to our understanding of juvenile justice trends in Britain and Canada. While there may be problems with comparability, there is evidence, for example, that the Welfare Model system in Scotland is characterized by drastically lower custody rates. Custody rates in England and Wales were approximately twice as high as in Scotland between 1972 and 1982 and, in several years, nearly four times as high (see Figure 1). Pratt has also compared the English justice system with the system in Norway (which is based on a pure Welfare Model) and concluded that in Norway high custody rates and other intrusive interventions have been avoided.[93]

Whether one accepts that the movement of juvenile justice in England and Wales toward the Justice Model (or the Corporatist Model) end of the continuum is more punitive or not, it is likely that the debate will continue, at least among scholars, about the advantages and disadvantages of this shift. The arguments will also likely remain the same. For the Justice Model proponents, any Welfare Model substitute is fraught with fundamental problems. Most importantly, executive decisions made by welfare experts are considered as intrusive as judicial decisions and result in unintended negative consequences. For Justice Model proponents, the radical Scottish solution of abolishing the juvenile court and replacing it with a non-judicial lay penal system is not a significant advantage over the English system. And, for Morris and Giller, the Scottish welfare system may

---

[92] Morris and Giller, *Understanding Juvenile Justice* (London: Groom Helm, 1987), p. 232.

[93] Pratt, "A Comparative Analysis of Two Different Systems of Juvenile Justice: Some Implications for England and Wales". Unpublished paper, Institute of Criminology; Cambridge University, 1985.

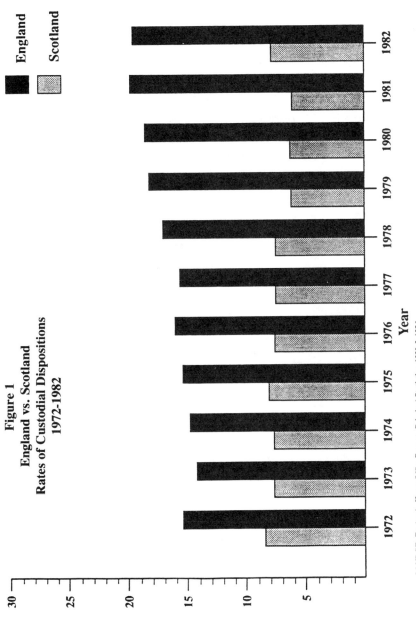

Figure 1
England vs. Scotland
Rates of Custodial Dispositions
1972-1982

England

Scotland

Year

Percentage of Cases Resulting
in a Custodial Disposition*

SOURCE: England - Home Office Report, Criminal Statistics, 1980 & 1986.
Scotland - Scottish Home & Health Department Report, Scottish Crime Statistics, 1984.

*Custodial Disposition was taken to include Attendance Centre Orders, Detention Centre Orders, Borstal Training, and Imprisonment.

Table 1

Custody Rates in England and Wales 1978–1988

Persons aged 14 and under 17 sentenced for indictable offences by sex and type of sen**or order including percentages**

Sex & Year	Total number of persons sentenced	%	Absolute or conditional discharge	%	Supervision order	%	Fine	%	Community service order
Males									
1978	60.5	100	11.4	19	8.6	14	23.5	39	•
1979	56.3	100	9.8	17	9.0	16	20.9	37	•
1980	63.2	100	11.3	18	10.4	16	22.4	35	•
1981	62.0	100	11.9	19	10.4	17	19.9	32	•
1982	59.2	100	11.9	20	9.6	16	18.5	31	•
1983	54.4	100	11.7	21	8.9	16	15.7	29	0.5
1984	52.8	100	11.5	22	8.9	17	14.1	27	1.7
1985	47.9	100	10.7	22	8.4	17	12.0	25	1.9
1986	37.7	100	9.1	24	6.8	18	9.2	24	1.5
1987	34.2	100	8.4	24	6.3	18	7.3	23	1.6
1988	26.9	100	7.4	25	5.4	18	6.6	22	1.4
Females									
1978	8.0	100	2.3	29	1.8	22	3.2	40	•
1979	7.1	100	1.9	27	1.7	25	2.8	39	•
1980	7.8	100	2.2	28	1.9	25	2.8	36	•
1981	7.4	100	2.3	31	1.9	25	2.4	32	•
1982	7.0	100	2.3	33	1.6	23	2.3	33	•
1983	6.1	100	2.1	35	1.3	21	1.9	31	-(1)
1984	5.4	100	2.0	37	1.1	21	1.5	28	0.1
1985	5.0	100	1.9	37	1.0	21	1.4	28	0.1
1986	3.7	100	1.6	42	0.7	19	0.9	26	0.1
1987	3.1	100	1.3	43	0.6	20	0.7	24	0.1
1988	2.9	100	1.4	48	0.5	18	0.6	21	0.1

(1) Less than 50
(2) Less than 0.5 percent
(3) Includes borstal training (abolished May 1983), detention centre orders and youth custody (both abolished October 1988)
• Not applicable

Source: Home Office.

Table 1 (Cont'd.)

Custody Rates in England and Wales 1978–1988

rsons aged 14 and under 17 sentenced for indictable offences by sex and type of sentence or order including percentages

Attendance centre order	%	Care order	%	Young offenders (3) institution	%	Otherwise dealt with	%	Total immediate custody	%
6.9	11	2.6	4	7.3	12	0.3	1	---	---
7.1	13	2.2	4	6.9	12	0.3	1	6.9	12
9.0	14	2.3	4	7.4	12	0.4	1	7.4	12
9.6	16	2.1	3	7.7	12	0.4	1	7.7	12
9.8	16	1.9	3	7.1	12	0.4	1	7.1	12
9.4	17	1.2	2	6.7	12	0.5	1	6.7	12
8.6	16	1.0	2	6.6	12	0.4	1	6.5	12
5.8	16	0.8	2	5.9	12	0.5	1	5.9	12
5.8	15	0.6	2	4.3	11	0.4	1	4.3	11
5.3	16	0.5	1	3.9	11	0.5	1	3.9	11
4.7	16	0.3	1	3.2	11	0.5	2	3.2	11
•	•	0.6	8	0.1	1	-(1)	-(2)	0.1	1
0.1	1	0.5	6	0.1	1	-(1)	-(2)	0.1	1
0.3	4	0.5	6	0.1	1	-(1)	1	0.1	1
0.4	5	0.4	6	-(1)	1	-(1)	1	-(1)	1
0.4	6	0.3	5	-(1)	1	-(1)	-(2)	-(1)	1
0.4	7	0.2	4	0.1	1	-(1)	1	-(1)	1
0.4	7	0.2	3	0.1	2	0.1	1	0.1	2
0.3	7	0.1	3	0.1	2	-(1)	1	0.1	2
0.2	7	0.1	2	0.1	2	-(1)	1	0.1	2
0.2	6	0.1	2	0.1	2	-(1)	1	0.1	2
0.2	5	0.1	2	-(1)	2	-(1)	1	-(1)	2

be even worse than the British one, since it lacks due process, while its decisions are punitive and include offence and prior offence record considerations.[94] These scholars maintain that the Modified Justice Model in England and Wales, despite both its limited co-optation by crime control experts and politicians, and contro-versies over custody rates, still has distinctive advantages over any Welfare Model. In the absence of empirical evidence of the effectiveness of treatment programs, they argue that the Modified Justice Model is less intrusive and more protective of youth rights. However, proponents of Welfare Model principles, such as Clarke,[95] dispute the assertion that the Justice Model is at least equitable in the processing and sentencing of youth and that no treatment programs work. Their first criticism is that youth differ substantially in terms of income, status, education, ethnicity and family support, and that the less fortunate are more likely to be processed and punished. Their second criticism is that Welfare Model approaches are not as inherently intrusive and punitive as Justice Model process-ing without benefit. They assert that the Scottish Welfare juvenile justice system introduced in 1970 is a success for the following reasons: a large proportion of cases are handled without any penetration beyond the police report to the reporter; custody has been reduced; the negative effects of labelling are minimized; young people, the family, community representatives and social workers are involved in addressing youth crime; and there has not been an increase in youth crime.

This debate has continued in the U.K. for virtually the entire 20th century, albeit with varied degrees of intensity and controversy. It will likely be reviewed vigorously if and when a Labour government is elected. A similar debate in the United States has a much more limited history; however, the U.S. experience more closely parallels the Canadian shift toward the Justice Model.

PART 3: MODIFIED JUSTICE MODEL TRENDS IN THE UNITED STATES

There is no single juvenile justice system in the United States. Each state has the constitutional responsibility to legislate, implement and operate its own juvenile justice system. However, the Supreme Court of the United States has sought to mandate certain common principles through case law. Also, the federal govern-ment has attempted to influence state juvenile justice practices by enacting legislation that provides financial and related organizational incentives if states implement federally mandated policies. Despite these national imperatives, there remains an enormous diversity in juvenile justice practices at both state and local levels. States differ in their maximum age of juvenile court jurisdiction (17 to 18-

---

[94] Morris and Giller, *supra*, note 92.
[95] Clarke, ''Whose Justice? The Politics of Juvenile Control'' (1985) 13 Int'l J. Soc. L. 407–21.

years-old), the minimum age (7 to 10-years-old) and the inclusion of certain violent felony crimes such as murder and rape. In several states, 15- or 16-year-old youths charged with these violent felonies are automatically raised to adult criminal court. In Georgia and Florida, for example, youths are punishable by death or life imprisonment for first degree murder. It is evident through both state legislation and juvenile court practices that major differences exist in terms of adherence to either the Modified Justice Model or the Welfare Model.[96] In addition, state corrections policies vary radicaly. Florida and Texas have adopted crime control policies with an emphasis on incapacitation and punishment, while Massachusetts and Utah have closed large scale youth prisons and limited the number of available spaces by utilizing small service units spread throughout their states. Considerable differences also exist in juvenile court jurisdictions involving status offences and dependent or neglected children. Finally, state juvenile statutes have been characterized as ambiguous and vague while encompassing an enormous array of diverse types of youth misbehaviour. Bortner concludes in her review of juvenile justice in the United States that:

> One of the major characteristics of our national system of juvenile justice is a remarkable variation in decision-making, a situation that produces widespread inconsistencies when the system is examined nationwide. There are hundreds of separate juvenile court jurisdictions within the United States, and each has considerable flexibility and leeway to create a unique brand of juvenile justice.[97]

The Constitutional Context and the Introduction of the Welfare Model

Despite the diversity of juvenile justice practices in the United States, the same policy and theoretical controversies evident in England, Wales and Canada have occurred in most states and within successive federal governments, particularly since the 1960s. The focus of the criticisms are the ineffectiveness of the Welfare Model in controlling juvenile crime, and the violation of due process which this system allows. While the ineffectiveness criticism is more recent, due process or "constitutionalist" critics have attacked the Welfare Model since its inception at the turn of the 19th century. While similar criticisms simultaneously were voiced in Canada, it can be argued that the U.S. critics were on more fundamental political and legal grounds. The U.S. constitution defines the cornerstone of justice as procedural regularity and respect for individual rights. For the constitutionalists, the procedural informality of the Welfare Model — based on the principle of "the best (welfare) interests" of young people and a drastic reduction in the role of lawyers — were seen as an untenable denial of justice. These critics

---

[96] Stapleton, Aday and Ito, "An Empirical Typology of American Metropolitan Juvenile Courts" (1982) 88 *American Journal of Sociology*, pp. 549–64.

[97] Bortner, *Delinquency and Justice: An Age of Crisis* (New York: McGraw-Hill, 1988), p. 125.

were also skeptical of a Welfare Model system's ability to correctly diagnose social and psychological problems of delinquents, let alone to rehabilitate them. Despite the Constitution and the Bill of Rights, the "child savers" in the U.S. had little, if any, more difficulty than the Canadian child-savers in persuading state legislatures and the U.S. Supreme Court to adopt the Welfare Model. The child-saving movement was as effective in the U.S. as it was in Canada despite constitutional differences. This success depended largely on the common cultural assumption that young people are not able to form the same measure of rational intent as adults and, therefore, they cannot be held as culpable. Accordingly, young people and society would benefit more from welfare or rehabilitation-based judicial procedures than from Justice Model procedures.

Problems and Initial Criticisms of the Welfare Model

The goal of rehabilitation became the major focus of the criticisms in the U.K., Canada and the U.S. by the 1970s. In the U.S., fundamental problems with the Welfare Model arose very quickly. Urban juvenile court resources were overwhelmed by the enormous volume of cases. Ten-minute hearings occurred, probation officer caseloads were staggering and supervision declined. Reforms focused on theoretical innovations concerning individualized treatment plans. Freudian psychology and social, medical, physical and anthropometric diagnostic measures were introduced to locate the "disease" causes of delinquency. Between World War II and the mid-1960s, additional problems, most importantly adolescent drug use and urban youth gangs, confronted the juvenile courts in the U.S. Minority youth also increasingly dominated the major urban courts, while poverty and related social problems further strained already limited court resources.[98]

The major challenges to the Welfare Model began with the soaring juvenile crime rate and the attendant media publicity in the late 1960s, along with a series of U.S. Supreme Court decisions. Politically conservative critics accused juvenile court officials of being overly lenient with violent and serious offenders. In the absence of retribution and punishment, delinquents were seen as not being held responsible for their crimes and, consequently, the moral force of the law and deterrence was undermined, and society was left unprotected.[99] Criticisms were also raised about the inherent problems of sending dependent and neglected youth to the same institutions used to house hard-core offenders.[100] Civil libertarians and other reformers opposed court jurisdiction over status offenders, and were

---

[98] Krisberg, " Juvenile Justice: The Vision and the Constant Star" in Schwartz, I. and Gilgun, J. eds. *Rethinking Child Welfare* (Lincoln Nebr.: University of Nebraska Press, 1991).

[99] van den Haag, *Punishing Criminals* (New York: Basic Books, 1975).

[100] Silberman, *Criminal Violence, Criminal Justice* (New York: Vintage Books, 1978).

particularly upset by the disproportionate punitiveness evident toward female status offenders.[101] By the mid-1970s, Martinson *et al.*'s "nothing works" thesis,[102] which was based on a largely negative evaluation of rehabilitation programs, had precipitated a sharp controversy over the efficiency of juvenile justice systems premised on Welfare Model principles. Lemert[103] and Becker[104] added to the chorus of criticisms by asserting an even more radical thesis. It was their view that the juvenile court actually contributes to juvenile criminality because of the labelling process. In many states these criticisms resulted in the decline of Welfare Model programs and policies, and the introduction of Justice Model reforms and experiments. Before discussing these changes, however, it is necessary to review the impact of certain U.S. Supreme Court decisions which were also instrumental in the development of the Modified Justice Model.

United States Supreme Court Decisions and Justice Model Reforms

In one of the most frequently cited cases, *Kent v. U.S.*,[105] the Supreme Court warned juvenile court judges about arbitrary procedures while, in *Re Gault*,[106] it identified a specific list of due process rights that had to be accorded to juveniles. Discretion in juvenile corrections was also limited in *Morales v. Terman*,[107] which specified the rights of incarcerated juveniles. In other cases, such as *Re Winship*[108] and *Schall v. Martin*,[109] however, it became evident that the intention was not the total dismantling of the Welfare Model. In these cases, the majority of the Supreme Court approved certain key Welfare Model principles, including broad discretion to promote the best interests of youth through preventive detention and maintaining a lesser degree of formality in juvenile court procedures than in the adult criminal court. In effect, the Supreme Court under three successive Chief Justices — Warren, Berger and Rehnquist — has delivered a mixed message concerning the constitutional interpretation of the Welfare and Justice Models of juvenile justice. Essentially, as long as a minimum degree of due process is available, then other welfare-based principles are still appropriate.

---

[101] Chesney-Lind, "Girls in Jail" (1988) 34(2) *Criminal Delinquency* 150–68.

[102] Martinson and Palm, *Rehabilitation, Recidivism and Research* (Haskensack, NJ: National Council on Crime and Delinquency, 1976).

[103] Lemert, *Instead of Court: Diversion in Juvenile Justice* (Chevy Chase, Md: National Institute of Mental Health, 1971).

[104] Becker, *Outsiders: Studies in the Sociology of Deviance* (New York: Free Press, 1963).

[105] 383 U.S. 541 (1966).

[106] 387 U.S. 1 (1967).

[107] 383 F. Supp. 53 (1974).

[108] 397 U.S. 358 (1970).

[109] 476 U.S. 253 (1984).

Currently, the Rehnquist-led Supreme Court has adopted a laissez-faire approach, allowing state Supreme Courts and legislatures wide latitude in juvenile justice. The cumulative effect of these Supreme Court rulings has led to a shift in juvenile court practices toward the Justice Model. It must be reiterated that this trend has not occurred in a uniform or consistent manner. Numerous factors, beginning with the constitutional prerogatives of states to enact juvenile justice legislation and the legal authority given to counties and cities to operate their juvenile courts in a relatively autonomous manner, have contributed to this trend. Organizational exigencies, ideologies and the offence profile of cases processed by individual courts are among the other important factors that have influenced the degree to which individual juvenile justice systems have adopted Modified Justice Model practices.

With this caveat in mind, it appears that considerable controversy has arisen nationally as a result of the U.S. Supreme Court decision to unite "the procedural rigor of due process and the informality and discretion of individualized treatment".[110] The attempt to combine the two divergent models of juvenile justice — the treatment model and the post-*Gault* legalistic model[111] — has resulted in practical problems involving the discrepancy between the (supposedly) rigid due process procedures used to determine guilt and the lack of uniform and equitable sentencing standards. In effect, the Modified Justice Model appears to have been extremely difficult to implement because, while due process principles involve a relatively straightforward set of practices, the traditional rehabilitation principle remains an ambiguous basis for sentencing. Sentencing practices are further compounded by the Crime Control principles which became increasingly popular particularly during the Reagan administration (1980–1988). Sharp increases in punitive sentencing indicate that incapacitation, retribution and deterrence principles have had an effect on sentencing practices.

For our purposes, the central question is whether there is a link between the implementation of Modified Justice Model practices and increased punitive sentencing in the U.S. Unfortunately, no U.S. scholar has systematically addressed this question, although there has been discussion both about the impact of crime control policies and the feasibility or potential success of the Modified Justice Model. According to Bortner, "(a)nalysts are divided in their assessment of whether such a synthesis (i.e., Modified Justice Model) is possible and their assessment of the resulting impact on juveniles' experiences within the system."[112] Interestingly, Bortner bases her statement partly on research from Scotland and England, which suggests that there is insufficient U.S. data to assess the diverse American experience with the Modified Justice Model. A major difficulty in forming a generalization about this recent historical period involves

---

[110] Bortner, *Delinquency and Justice: An Age of Crisis* (New York: McGraw-Hill, 1988), p. 68.

[111] See p. 111

[112] Bortner, *supra*, note 110, at p. 70.

the shifting ideological positions on juvenile justice which have characterized federal policies.

Divergent Federal Policies Toward Juvenile Justice

Until the passage of the *Juvenile Delinquency and Youth Offender Act* of 1961, U.S. law did not directly address juvenile justice. New Deal legislation[113] beginning in 1933 involved the federal government in an indirect and incremental manner with juvenile justice. The National Youth Administration (1935) employed high school students, and the *Social Security Act* (1935) provided states with federal grants-in-aid for dependent mothers and their children and for potentially delinquent youth. Technical advice and policy guidelines were also provided to the states during the post-World War II period. More direct federal involvement occurred during the 1960s when ''alarming juvenile justice statistics indicated incremental federal commitment was not enough''.[114] Numerous legislative acts were passed, especially by the Democratic administration of Lyndon Johnson, dealing not only with employment and educational needs of youth, but also with problems of delinquency. The latter was addressed by the *Juvenile Delinquency Prevention and Control Act* of 1968 which provided funds for coordinating federal youth development programs and grants-in-aid to state and local delinquency programs. While these laws established new federal obligations in juvenile justice, they were not based on any coherent philosophy or model. According to Olson-Raymer, this deficiency resulted in organizational and policy confusion and paved ''the road for yet another era of fragmented public responses''.[115]

Thus, by the early 1970s juvenile justice practices were, despite the above federal reform policies, controversial. In a 1973 report the National Advisory Commission on Criminal Justice Standards and Goals concluded that ''(t)he failure of major juvenile and youth institutions to reduce crime is incontestable.''[116] A broader indictment of juvenile justice was made by then-Senator Birch Bayh, who engineered the next federal reform phase with enactment of the *Juvenile Justice and Delinquency Prevention Act* of 1974:

---

[113] New Deal was the phrase used by President Franklin Roosevelt in 1933 to characterize a broad array of legislation he proposed in order to overcome many of the economic and social problems created by the collapse of the stock market.

[114] Olsen-Raymer, ''National Juvenile Justice Policy: Myth or Reality'' in Decker, ed., *Juvenile Justice Policy: Analyzing Trends and Outcomes* (Beverly Hills, Calif.: Sage Publications, 1984), p. 33.

[115] *Ibid.*, at p. 33.

[116] As quoted in Schwartz, *(In) Justice for Juveniles: Rethinking the Best Interests of the Child* (Lexington, Mass.: Lexington Books, 1989), p. 6.

. . . [the 1974 Act recognized] that our present system of juvenile justice [was] failingly miserably. [This Act] was . . . designed specifically to prevent young people from entering our failing juvenile justice system and to assist communities in developing more sensible and economic approaches for youngsters already in the juvenile justice system.[117]

The 1974 Act directed the federal Office of Juvenile Justice and Delinquency Prevention to coordinate policy and program initiatives and incentives to assist states and local officials in removing status offenders, dependent, abused and neglected youth from adult jails, detention centres and training schools. A second objective was to stop the common practice of placing adult and youth offenders in the same detention facilities. A third objective involved the development of community-based programs in place of institutions for non-violent and non-dangerous delinquent youths. Decriminalization, diversion and deinstitutionalization objectives were contractually linked to state receipt of federal funds. Although participation of states was voluntary, the financial incentives were designed to gain cooperation.

While most states responded positively to the 1974 Act, there was considerable variation among the 50 states in terms of reducing custody rates. Massachusetts took radical steps to deinstitutionalize two years before this Act when Jerry Miller, as Commissioner of the Department of Youth Services, closed all of the large training schools and replaced them with 12 smaller facilities (15–20 beds) located throughout the state. Private, non-profit organizations have played a central role in the development and operation of highly structured community-based services and programs in this state.

Emerging Crime Control Model Trends

Despite the novel federal agenda and the innovative Massachusetts corrections policy, the trend in nearly half of the states focused on "get tough" crime control changes in juvenile justice. Specifically, these states passed legislation that either made it easier to prosecute serious juvenile offenders in adult courts, lowered the minimum age for waiver, or mandated minimum custodial terms. The expected results occurred since, between 1977 and 1985, juvenile detention rates in pre-trial holding facilities increased by more than 50 percent on any given day, while training school rates rose more than 16 percent.[118] One of the reasons for this increase was the growing popularity among judges of committing youth to short-term detention centre stays as a way of maintaining the "credibility response" of the juvenile justice system and making youth accountable for criminal behaviour.

Schwartz is highly critical of this sentencing practice because he maintains it generally involves youth who have committed minor offences. He is similarly critical of the movement to give adult courts initial jurisdiction over 13- to 15-year-olds for extremely violent crimes:

---

[117] *Ibid.*, at p. 4.
[118] Schwartz, *supra*, note 116, at p. 7.

Although the stampede to change state laws to allow juveniles to be treated as harshly as adults has not had the desired effect in some jurisdictions, the impact in many states has been unmistakable. Juveniles have been propelled into adult prisons in record numbers. There were 1,445 persons under the age of 18 admitted to state prisons in 1981. By 1982, the number had skyrocketed to an estimated 2,834. Florida, a state where prosecutors have broad discretion in trying juveniles in adult courts, accounted for 769, or 28 percent of these admissions.[119]

Schwartz and other researchers, such as Krisberg,[120] are troubled not simply by this enormous increase but rather by research that indicates most youth waived to adult courts are involved with property and public order offences, while less than one-quarter are waived for violent offences.[121]

Another disturbing finding is the racial composition of the growing custodial population. By 1985, racial minorities constituted half of detention centre one-day inmate counts, up from 43 percent in 1977. This change was not attributable to demographic changes.[122] In his review of these incarceration trends, Schwartz specifically attacked the politicians who benefited politically from the implementation of "get tough" measures, but who "failed to appropriate the necessary funds to ensure that the incarcerated youth are treated and housed safely and humanely".[123] He claims that there has been "a wholesale retreat from sound professional standards and practices, deteriorating physical plants, increased reports of abuse, scandals and lawsuits. Solitary confinement was used excessively."[124]

As a former Administrator in the Office of Juvenile Justice and Delinquency Prevention during the Carter presidency, Schwartz was disappointed that the 1974 Act failed in its attempt to direct juvenile justice policies in the states toward the desired reforms. While several states such as Massachusetts and Utah introduced innovative measures to drastically reduce the number of youth in custody, Crime Control Model policies appeared to be the dominant response to the perceived failure of the Welfare Model juvenile justice system to stem young, and especially violent young, offenders.

Justice Model policies were also encouraged by the U.S. Supreme Court decisions discussed earlier and by the efforts of nationally influential interest groups such as the Institute of Judicial Administration and the American Bar Association Joint Committee. This latter group produced the 1973 detailed report

---

[119] *Ibid.*, at p. 10.

[120] Krisberg, "Juvenile Justice: The Vision and Constant Star" in Schwartz and Gilgan, eds., *Rethinking Child Welfare* (Lincoln, Nebr.: University of Nebraska Press).

[121] U.S. Department of Justice, *Major Issues of Juvenile Justice Information and Training* (Washington, D.C.: U.S. Government Printing Office, 1982).

[122] Schwartz, *supra*, note 116, at p. 9.

[123] *Ibid.*, at p. 11.

[124] *Ibid.*

mentioned above which outlined the complete reform of the Welfare Model juvenile court and replaced it with Justice Model principles.

In 1977, Washington State introduced the most radical Justice Model legislation in the country. This legislation theoretically was designed to reduce both the sentencing discretion of judges and the number of status offenders appearing in juvenile court. A formal sentencing model was created based on the seriousness of the offence, prior record, and mitigating and aggravating factors. Probation officers complete the sentencing grid information and judges are expected to impose sentences within the legislatively specified ranges, although they may choose to deviate from the guidelines, in which case they must stipulate their reasons in writing. According to Ann Schneider (personal correspondence), who has monitored the impact of the new law since its inception, this discretionary option has resulted in the unintended consequence of increasing custody rates beyond that expected, based on legislative guidelines. Thus, it appears that some judges have employed even more punitive Crime Control criteria than those outlined in the new law.

The issue of the association between Justice Model reforms and increased custody rates will be examined in greater detail later, but there is little doubt that the Reagan administration viewed the Washington State Justice Model legislation as consistent with its crime control approach and promoted it as a model reform to other states. We will return to Reagan-era reforms below.

It is important to reiterate that states have the sole constitutional responsibility for juvenile justice legislation. Further, despite federal legislative and financial initiatives involving either Justice or Crime Control Model principles, several reform trends emerged. This precludes any single description of juvenile justice in the United States. Those states that retained the Welfare Model juvenile justice system had to modify processing procedures in order to comply with Supreme Court decisions requiring due process for juvenile offenders. In addition, politicians and juvenile justice practitioners were influenced by media and interest group pressures to "get tough" with violent and/or career delinquents. In some states, systems became increasingly bifurcated according to seriousness of offence and prior record. Young people involved in property crimes, or other less serious offences — in other words, the majority of young offenders — were diverted out of the system and into diversionary and rehabilitative programs, while the more serious and violent offenders were subject to due process provisions, and the inevitable imposition of more severe sentences. In California, major Justice Model reforms were not introduced, at least initially. California Youth Authority spokesman Ted Palmer maintained that rehabilitation remained an important principle;[125] nonetheless, the state legislature introduced several crime control measures, including relaxed criteria for transfer into adult court and

---

[125] Palmer, *Correctional Intervention and Research* (Lexington, Mass.: Lexington Books, 1978).

increased use of custodial facilities. Between 1974 and 1987, one-day detention centre populations increased by 51 percent.

The net result of this complex picture is that no simple correlation between Welfare Model or Justice Model states and increased custody rates can be found in the United States. It is likely that the media-induced fear of youth crime within the public and the influence of crime control politicians affects juvenile justice decision-makers (including police, probation officers, judges and corrections personnel) in an increasingly similar crime control orientation: incapacitate and punish. However, it may be the case that Justice Model reforms have accentuated the custodial trend. Before examining this issue further, it is important to explore whether youth crime has escalated as dramatically as the media and conservative politicians portray.

Youth Crime Trends

For a brief period in the late 1960s and early 1970s, the rate of serious juvenile crime increased significantly. However, rates stabilized in 1979 and then decreased over the subsequent five-year period. This trend was reversed in 1985 when the serious juvenile crime rate again rose.[126] There can be little doubt that the recent resurgence of youth gangs in metropolitan areas such as Los Angeles and the spread of crack cocaine, particularly in urban ghettos, are both associated with the dramatic increase in homicides and other violence involving youths.

It is reasonable to conclude that despite the public's tendency to overstate the problem (often referred to as moral panic), there is evidence in at least some cities of a serious problem. The number of homicides which took place during 1990 in Washington, D.C. (483), with its population of approximately three-quarters of a million people, approached the number of murders (653) occurring in all of Canada during the same year. Many of the deaths are a result of youths and adults fighting over control of the immensely profitable crack cocaine business. While the media sensationalizes the violence, politicians generally acknowledge both that they cannot build prisons fast enough to incapacitate all of the young offenders, and that a crime control response alone is insufficient.

While in many urban contexts in the United States local juvenile justice systems appear to be overwhelmed by youth crime problems, at the aggregate state level there appears to be little or no relationship between the rates of serious juvenile crime and incarceration rates.[127] While youth gang problems overwhelmingly involve minority youth, according to Huizingar and Elliot these minorities do not commit a substantially disproportionate amount of serious crime.[128] In their

---

[126] Schwartz, *supra*, note 116, at p. 26.

[127] Krisberg, Litsky and Schwartz, "Youth Confinement: Justice by Geography" (1984) 21(2) *Journal of Research in Crime and Delinquency*, pp. 1–25.

[128] Huizingar and Elliot, "Juvenile Offenders: Prevalence, Offender Incidence and Arrest Rates by Race (1987) 33(2) *Criminal Delinquency*, 206–23.

analysis of data from the National Youth Survey, Huizingar and Elliot claim that white youth who commit serious crimes are at less risk of being arrested and charged with serious crimes than minority youth. However, it is also evident that a small proportation of those arrested for a violent crime account for a disproportionate amount of subsequent violent crime.[129] While Huizingar and Elliot would probably disagree, it seems probable that these violent recidivists are likely representative of youth involved in gang activities.

These data present a complex image of serious and violent crime in the United States. Not only are there enormous variations among states, but there is also substantial variation within states, metropolitan and city areas. There are numerous factors that confound any simple interpretation of juvenile justice data at any of these aggregate levels. Bortner[130] and other researchers[131] have described the intricate operations that occur within a juvenile court, including its processing links to the police, probation, corrections, social services, mental health and education. Equally importantly, and as discussed above, juvenile court judges and other decision-makers have personal views about appropriate decisions and, therefore, ideology or individual theories of juvenile justice are likely to be critically important in explaining why youths are treated so differently, even though the law is the same.

The Reagan Administration Crime Control Ideology

Despite the considerable state diversity in juvenile justice policies and practices, there nonetheless is the national influence of the Congress and the presidency. Olsen-Raymer asserts that federal policies can be categorized historically in terms of distinct reform policy phases.[132] A general expansion of Welfare Model policies occurred throughout the 1960s and '70s, while in the early 1980s the Reagan administration attempted to eliminate the Federal Office of Juvenile Justice and Delinquency Prevention (OJJDP) and return management of social and health service programs related to juvenile justice back to the individual states.

This attempt to radically shift away from the federal initiative was partially blocked by a coalition of interest groups, academics and congressmen who

---

[129] Hamparian, Davis, Jacobson *et al.*, "The Young Criminal Years of the Violent Few" in Schwartz, ed., *(In) Justice for Juveniles: Rethinking the Best Interests of the Child* (Lexington, Mass.: Lexington Books, 1989).

[130] Bortner, *Inside a Juvenile Court: The Tarnished Ideal of Individualized Justice* (New York: New York University Press, 1982).

[131] Cicourel, *The Social Organization of Juvenile Justice* (London: John Wiley and Sons, 1968); Emerson, *Judging Delinquents: Contexts and Process in Juvenile Courtroom* (Chicago: Aldine Press, 1969).

[132] Olsen-Raymer, *supra*, note 114.

favoured a continued federal role. The Reagan administration, however, succeeded in politicizing the OJJDP by appointing an administrator, Alfred S.
Regnery, to replace Ira Schwartz. Regnery, with no prior experience in juvenile
justice, was to implement a new policy which viewed the *Juvenile Justice and
Deliquency Prevention Act* of 1974 as anti-family and not sufficiently tough on
youth criminals. Schwartz, not unexpectedly, is scathing in his view of what then
occurred:

> In their zeal to implement this new agenda, Reagan administration officials turned
> their backs on the need for reform, put out inaccurate and misleading information,
> and either ignored or tried to influence research findings that didn't support their
> policies or point of view. [133]

Schwartz, citing a 1986 *Wall Street Journal* story, accuses Regnery of creating a
moral panic or pseudo crisis by claiming that federal polices favouring deinstitutionalization of status offenders undermined parents' ability to control unruly
children, and that this anti-family policy resulted in an estimated more than one
million children running away from home. These runaways, Regnery further
asserted, were being murdered or kidnapped and sexually exploited. Schwartz
cites the Pulitzer Prize-winning *Denver Post* series of articles in May of 1985 as
crucial in uncovering these gross exaggerations. The *Denver Post* stories stated
that separated and divorced parents kidnap the overwhelming majority of children
and that most children killed are victims of parents and other family members or
acquaintances. Equally contradictory was the discovery that only 200 unidentified
youth are buried in the U.S. by the police every year, not the figure of 2,000
published by Regnery.

Competing Interest Groups and Perspectives on Juvenile Justice Reforms

Child advocates and researchers who support the Welfare Model, including
former juvenile court judge and noted author Ted Rubin and professor Rosemary
Sarri, were opposed to the conservative views of the OJJDP and of the National
Council of Juvenile and Family Court Judges. Schwartz claims that this latter
interest group and others were dependent upon, and influenced by, federal
juvenile justice funds at the state and national levels; consequently, they have
"been indifferent, resisted and attempted to undermine many of the needed
changes in the juvenile justice system".[134]

It is not possible to summarize juvenile justice trends in the United States as
simply as in England and Wales. Child advocates support the due process
protection of the Justice Model while they also support rehabilitation programs
identified with the Welfare Model. Krisberg, who is extremely critical of the

---

[133] Schwartz, *supra*, note 129, at p. 118.
[134] *Ibid.*, at p. 104.

Crime Control Model, maintains that those states with greater due process incarcerate fewer youth. He maintains that youth justice systems should reflect a blending of Justice and Welfare Model policies:

> The concerns for the 'best interests of the child' need not mean a return to the excessive discretion that has plagued the juvenile court. It is time to recognize that due process and equal protection are in the best interests of children. The excellent work of the standards project to the American Bar Association and the Institute for Judicial Administration provides a blueprint for court proceedings that are completely consistent with a humane vision of justice for youth. Jurisdictions possessing the richest treatment resources for youth are often those that also pay careful attention to protecting the legal rights of children.[135]

Feld, who has written numerous insightful critiques of the Welfare Model, argues that due process or Justice Model reforms are crucial even though juvenile courts continue to resist them.[136] And Schwartz concludes his excellent book, *Justice for Juveniles*, with seven recommedations which embody most of the principles of Canada's *Young Offenders Act*. In contrast, Rubin wants to avoid the replication of the adult criminal justice process in the juvenile court.[137] He claims that "justice" is hardly the routine outcome in the current adult court and, therefore, that Justice Model reforms of the juvenile court might simply result in similar problems.

A review of U.S. juvenile justice textbooks confirms the image that criticisms of the Welfare Model are widespread and fundamental. However, there is no consensus about reforms beyond the desire to see increased due process rights for youth. It appears that most academic observers support reforms based on the Modified Justice Model. There appears to be little support for radical solutions such as either abolishing the juvenile court or implementing the Washington State Justice Model. Several states, including Utah and Oklahoma, have followed the Massachusetts example of replacing large training schools with a limited number of small, secure custody institutions. Reformers such as Jerome Miller and researchers such as Barry Krisberg, Ira Schwartz and Rosemary Sarri have provided convincing evidence that reducing the availability of custodial placements is the most direct way to both limit the incarceration of non-violent youth and to avoid excessively punitive custody.

Reforms continue to be pushed by child advocates, yet little attention is paid to the inherent problems of the Modified Justice Model. Discourse on this issue is muted at best, even though Feld has confirmed comparative research findings that

---

[135] Krisberg, "Juvenile Justice: The Vision and the Constant Star" in Schwartz, I. and Gilgun, J. eds. *Rethinking Child Welfare* (Lincoln Nebr.: University of Nebraska Press, 1991) at p. 18.

[136] Feld, "Criminalizing Juvenile Justice: Rules of Procedure for the Juvenile Court" (1984) 69(2) Minn. L. Rev. 141–276.

[137] Rubin, "The Emergence of Prosecutor Dominance of the Juvenile Court Intake Process" (1980) 26(3) *Criminal Delinquency* 299–318.

the presence of defence counsel is associated with more severe sentencing outcomes and that waiver or transfer reforms for more serious offences have resulted in confusing and unintended consequences.[138] While Schwartz and Krisberg, for example, are scathing in their criticisms of crime control politicians, bureaucrats and interest groups for ending or stalling the reform period policies of decriminalization and deinstitutionalization, they too have avoided the question of whether the Justice Model, when implemented, is likely to be co-opted by Crime Control interests, and lead to an inevitable increase in custodial sentencing.

There are a few scholars, such as Zimring,[139] Rubin,[140] and Faust and Brantingham,[141] who have cautioned against completely rejecting the admittedly flawed Welfare Model. However, the focus of the debate is between Modified Justice Model advocates and Crime Control advocates such as Wilson and Hernstein.[142]

A Conflict Theoretical Perspective on Reform

Conflict scholars raise fundamental questions about the functions of any form of juvenile court. For example, ignoring the philosophical rhetoric, is the purpose of juvenile courts in advanced industrial societies to coerce deviant youth into embracing an efficient and profit-driven consumer society? While this question appears to reflect an extreme theoretical perspective, there are other and more immediate insights that conflicting scholars have provided about juvenile justice in the U.S. Most important of these is the apparent contradiction, or at least inconsistency, involved in the continuation of certain Welfare Model practices along with the introduction of certain Justice Model and Crime Control practices.

Bortner, in her textbook *Delinquency and Justice: An Age of Crisis*, maintains that these juvenile justice trends represent an attempt to deal with the crisis of legitimacy concerning the efficiency and effectiveness of juvenile justice in the U.S. According to Bortner, the media, Crime Control politicians and certain academics have popularized the view that violent young criminals are neither punished, deterred nor rehabilitated by the traditional Welfare Model.[143] This negative image of the traditional juvenile justice system approach, if not coun-

---

[138] Feld, *supra*, note 136.

[139] Zimring, ''Pursuing Juvenile Justice: Comments on Some Recent Reform Proposals'' (1978) 53 J. Urb. L. 631–45.

[140] Rubin, *supra*, note 137.

[141] Faust and Brantingham, *Juvenile Justice Phiolsophy: Readings, Cases and Comments*, 2nd ed., Criminal Justice Series (St. Paul, Minn.: West Publishing Co., 1980).

[142] Wilson and Herstein, *Crime and Human Nature* (New York: Simon and Schuster, 1985).

[143] Bortner, *Delinquency and Justice: An Age of Crisis* (New York: McGraw-Hill, 1988).

tered through contrary information and reforms, can threaten the survival of the complex bureaucracies that comprise this system. Unless a substantial portion of the public and politicians believe that juvenile justice deters youth crime and protects society through a combination of rehabilitation, incapacitation and punishment, then a loss of legitimacy occurs followed by political decisions to reduce or to eliminate juvenile justice programs and organizations. Essentially, the public is faced with two scenarios: either Justice Model and Crime Control Model critics are wrong and youth are being rehabilitated and society is being protected; or Justice Model-oriented reforms will prove more effective than the current system. In other words, the Welfare Model can be successfully modified to eliminate due process abuses and at the same time both incapacitate and punish violent and career youth criminals and rehabilitate non-serious delinquents.

For Bortner, the numerous juvenile justice systems throughout the United States are responding to political pressures to alter the processing of deviant youth in a manner that is consistent with the current dominant ideological view of such youth. She claims that this view includes two types of youths: those who fit "the traditional U.S. image of adolescents — innocent, unsophisticated, vulnerable and 'the hope of the future' ", and those who "are relegated to a semi-monster status of non-juveniles . . . as a dangerous threat to society . . . threatening aliens".[144] Traditional Welfare Model practices, focused within the community and treatment-oriented, are reserved for the first type, who comprise the vast majority, while imprisonment and punishment await the second type. Due process, while not inappropriate for either type, is usually viewed as imperative for those requiring incarceration. Bortner asserts that this bifurcation of deviant youth is resulting in the:

> . . . emergence of a Janus system of juvenile justice, that is, a system of justice that may be likened to the Roman god possessing a head with two opposing faces. While they are joined in a unified juvenile justice system, these two components or subsystems differ greatly.[145]

Despite her excellent review of current trends in U.S. juvenile justice and related empirical research, Bortner could identify no simple variable or set of variables which appear adequately to account for the trend of increased punitiveness apparent in the U.S. The substantial increase in the average length of detention which occurred in the 1980s has been attributed to more frequent use of detention as a precursor to probation and to the Modified Justice Model itself (i.e., with its increased formality of processing and greater punitiveness). Bortner acknowledges that the decision to incarcerate cannot be interpreted as simply reflecting the desire of juvenile justice personnel to incapacitate and punish. She maintains that diverse and often contradictory objectives co-exist, including public protection, punishment and rehabilitation. Because of these mixed objectives, political pressures, and major differences in the "organizational interests"

---

[144] *Ibid.*, at p. 351.
[145] Bortner, *supra*, note 143, at p. 364.

of individual juvenile justice systems among and within states, incarceration policies vary enormously in the U.S.

Krisberg *et al.* found that only the organizational variable of available bed spaces was associated with variance in detention admission rates among the states. This variable explained 77 percent of the variance, while the combination of major property offence rates, violent arrest rates and unemployment rates accounted for only four percent of the variation in detention rates.[146] Bortner, nonetheless, concludes that the trend toward increased punitiveness in the U.S. is associated with the Modified Justice Model and Crime Control Model reforms.[147] She argues that these reforms do not address the fundamental causes of youth deviance and criminality, but they do constitute an effective symbolic response to the negative view of much of the public, media and politicians toward the traditional Welfare Model of juvenile justice. While Bortner, along with other conflict theorists, is critical of the traditional model, she maintains that, at least symbolically, it focused on the total lifestyle problems of youth. Bortner's fear about the Modified Justice, or ''Janus'', Model is that in emphasizing the formal, legalistic aspect of justice reform, attention is diverted away from substantive justice reforms in areas such as education, health and employment. This shift, however, also accentuates the problems that characterize the Welfare Model — troubled middle- and upper-class youth can be induced to conform, given the potential lifestyle rewards of adulthood, yet many poor and especially minority youth are unlikely to benefit from individual treatment programs which do not deal with the ''grave structural ills such as poverty, racism and sexism'' which affect them.[148]

Bortner argues that, in effect, Modified Justice Model and Crime Control Model reforms, effectively directed at the lower-income minority youth who predominate among those processed for serious property and violent charges, continue to ignore the above fundamental structural problems and that, worse, these reforms increase the likelihood that minority youth will experience an even more destructive incarceration experience before being released back to the same troubled communities, and lifestyles marked by hopelessness.[149]

---

[146] Krisberg, Lisky and Schwartz, ''The Watershed of Juvenile Justice Reform'' (Minneapolis, Minn.: University of Minnesota, Hubert H. Humphery Institute of Public Affairs, 1985).

[147] Bortner, *supra*, note 143.

[148] *Ibid.*, at p. 369.

[149] Bartolas, Miller, Dinitz *et al.*, *Juvenile Victimization: The Institutional Paradox* (New York: John Wiley and Sons, 1976); Hamparian, Davis, Jacobson *et al.*, ''The Young Criminal Years of the Violent Few'' in Schwartz, ed., *(In) Justice for Juveniles: Rethinking the Best Interests of the Child* (Lexington, Mass.: Lexington Books, 1989).

Confounding Variables Affecting Custody Rates

Despite Bortner's pessimistic assessment of the Modified Justice Model, there is no research in the U.S. which directly examines this model's association with increased custody rates. Barry Krisberg and Ira Schwartz are among the foremost critics of punitive trends in the U.S., but they are both supportive of Justice Model protections of youth rights. In other words, there is no theoretical or empirical consensus about the impact of the Justice Model reforms on custody trends. As was the situation in England, Justice Model and Crime Control policies are confounded at every decision-making point (arrest, charge, prosecution, sentence and release) in juvenile justice. Justice Model proponents argue that increased custody rates are not attributable to their reforms, but that they occur because of the subversive effect of Crime Control ideologies held by a substantial number of police, probation officers and judges.[150] These decision-makers are not guided by key Justice Model principles defined by state laws specifying proportionality between offence and sentence; instead, they engage in policies reflecting Crime Control principles such as "short, sharp, shock" custody sentences for non-serious property crimes.

Another major confounding factor involves the organizational interests which have been mentioned several times throughout this chapter. Essentially, this umbrella concept describes policies and decisions that are based primarily on the preservation and/or expansion of juvenile justice agencies. In a situation where a youth detention facility has a surplus of bed spaces, a probation officer (as a member of the correctional community) may respond to such an organizational need by recommending custody to the court. Obviously, a Crime Control-oriented judge would likely view such a recommendation more favourably than a judge who adhered to either Justice Model or Welfare Model ideologies. Conversely, a custodial disposition will be less likely if court staff know that custodial facilities are full. These organizational imperatives are very complex in the U.S. because while day-to-day decision-making occurs at the local level (i.e., town, city, suburb), there are executive legislative and senior bureaucratic decision-makers at higher levels (i.e., county, state and federal).[151] At these higher levels, major political policy and financial determinations are made which affect the juvenile justice agencies and program operations at the local level. Partly because this elaborate multi-level juvenile justice system reflects a similar multi-level political

---

[150] Morris and Giller, *Understanding Juvenile Justice* (London: Groom Helm, 1987).

[151] Becker, "Book Review of A. Cicourel's *The Social Organization of Juvenile Justice* (1968) 160 *Science* p. 644; Cicourel, *The Social Organization of Juvenile Justice* (London: John Wiley and Sons, 1968); Emerson, *Judging Delinquents: Contexts and Process in Juvenile Courtroom* (Chicago: Aldine Press, 1969); Sarri and Hasenfeld, Brought to Justice? *Juveniles, the Courts, and the Law* (Ann Arbor, Mich.: University of Michigan, 1976).

party and interest group profile with elected officers at each level, it is possible to maintain that juvenile justice in the U.S. is more politicized than in Canada or the U.K.

Police chiefs, prosecutors and judges in many states are elected officials. Interest groups representing juvenile justice professions, religious organizations and political parties along with the local media are likely to be influential in affecting elected officials at the local level. Immediate public opinion might have more of an impact on juvenile justice decision-makers in the U.S. than in Canada and the U.K., where provincial and national influences are stronger. As a result, state juvenile justice laws and federal initiatives are likely modified by local political pressures.

Finally, individual or local juvenile justice systems differ fundamentally in terms of their environments and demographic contexts. These differences exist both between and within states and include numerous variables such as population density, racial configuration, family profiles and income distribution.

Analysis of State Custody Trends

The complexity and diversity of juvenile justice systems in the U.S. partly explains why it is difficult to explain theoretically and to assess empirically the relationship between the Modified Justice Model reforms and changes in juvenile justice practices, including custody rates. Validity issues become paramount when state level aggregate data are used to examine this relationship. Unless the array of multi-level variables (i.e., individual, local, state and national) discussed above are statistically controlled, it will remain the case that researchers can make only tentative inferences about the impact of Modified Justice Model reforms on juvenile justice. Another research limitation in conducting such analyses involves the classification of states along the Welfare Model-Justice Model continuum because, with few exceptions, such as Washington State, assigning states is problematic. As mentioned above, Bortner concluded in her review of the literature on state juvenile justice legislation that these laws are extremely ambiguous.[152]

Ideally, it would enhance the accuracy of classifying states if they could be assigned interval scores representing the exact degree to which they differed along the Welfare Model-Justice Model continuum. The few classification studies to date, however, have used only a limited number of indicators related to these two models and, consequently, only nominal classifications (i.e., state laws are identified either as Welfare or Justice Model in type), are available. It would be particularly helpful had at least ordinal scaling been used in these studies to classify states as either Welfare Model, Modified Justice Model, Justice Model or Justice/Crime Control hybrid. Such a scheme could test the prediction that

---

[152] Bortner, *Deliquency and Justice: An Age of Crisis* (New York: McGraw-Hill, 1988).

punitiveness, as measured by the frequency of custodial sentencing, increases from the Welfare Model across to the Justice/Crime Control Hybrid Model end of the continuum. Even had this more sophisticated classification been available, it is unlikely that equally valid measures would be used for all the remaining multi-level variables mentioned above. Because it is not possible to make confident inferences about the relationship between type of state law and custody rates, it is important to keep in mind the major validity limitations of the training school and detention[153] data presented in Tables 2 and 3. The classification of states in Tables 2 and 3 is based on research by Krisberg *et al.* for the year 1974[154] King for the year 1979,[155] and Schwartz for the years 1982 and 1987.[156]

Among the ten states with the highest rates of remand to training schools, no substantial differences exist in terms of whether Welfare Model or Justice Model systems are in place. It is important to mention that classification schemes were available only for the last three periods studied. Dramatic increases in custody rates were evident in both Welfare and Justice Model states.[157] In Oregon, for example, which has a Welfare Model system, the rate rose from 152 per 100,000 in 1979 to 640 in 1987, while the rate during the same period in Delaware, a Justice Model state, increased from 213 to 368. California and Minnesota, which introduced Justice Model reforms in the 1980s, appeared in the top ten for the first time in 1987, with rates of 318 and 367 respectively, compared to rates below 157 for the previous three periods (see Table 3). While the largest rate increases took place in Welfare Model states, Justice Model states constituted the majority (six) of the top ten states for the first time in 1987.

In the absence of an in-depth examination of each state, which is beyond the scope of this chapter, it is not possible to explain why rate increases occurred. Certain demographic patterns, however, are evident. Montana, Nevada, Wyoming and the District of Columbia (D.C.) appear in all four periods, with D.C. always having the highest or second highest rate. Noteworthy here is the fact that the U.S. capital has a higher proportion of blacks than any of the 50 states. (Recall our earlier discussion of minority statistics.) Half of the states that appear three or

---

[153] Training schools are generally reserved for serious offenders serving lengthy sentences, while detention centres provide pre-trial holding facilities and are also used for the incarceration of short-term and minor offenders.

[154] Krisberg, Schwartz, Litsky *et al.*, "The Watershed of Juvenile Justice Reform" (1986) 32(1) *Criminal Delinquency* 25–38.

[155] King, *A Comparative Analysis of Juvenile Codes* (Washington, D.C.: Government Printing Office, 1979), prepared by the Community Research Forum, University of Illinois.

[156] Schwartz, *(In) Justice for Juveniles: Rethinking the Best Interests of the Child* (Lexington, Mass.: Lexington Books, 1989).

[157] It is estimated that in 1979, 46 percent of states were classified as "Justice Model" states. By 1982, that figure had risen to 52 percent.

Top 10 States in Rate of Incarceration to Detention Centres
Justice vs. Welfare Model
1974, 1979, 1982 & 1987

Rank	1974 State	1974 Model*	1974 Rate per 100,000	1979 State	1979 Model	1979 Rate per 100,000	1982 State	1982 Model	1982 Rate per 100,000	1987 State	1987 Model	1987 Rate per 100,000
1	California		127	California	Justice	113	California	Justice	157	D.C.	Justice	321
2	Nevada		81	Michigan	Justice	70	Nevada	Justice**	125	California	Justice	192
3	Michigan		64	Nevada	Welfare	67	Washington	Justice	94	Nevada	Justice	182
4	Georgia		60	Washington	Justice	59	Florida	Justice	87	Florida	Justice	121
5	Florida		56	Florida	Justice	57	Georgia	Justice	67	Washington	Justice	100
6	Utah		55	Arizona	Justice	54	Michigan	Justice	61	Georgia	Justice	88
7	Washington		54	Georgia	Justice	50	Ohio	Justice**	58	Arizona	Justice	82
8	Arizona		51	Virginia	Welfare	49	Alaska	Justice	57	New Jersey	Justice	78
9	Kansas		48	Utah	Welfare	46	Arizona	Justice	55	Michigan	Justice	72
10	Delaware		43	Ohio	Welfare	43	Delaware	Justice	55	Ohio	Justice	68

SOURCE: 1974, 1979, 1982 - U.S. Department of Census, Children in Custody Series.
1987 - From Ira Schwartz's data on Detention Centre Populations.

These data are based on one-day counts and age-eligible youth population in state.

MODEL CLASSIFICATION:

1979 - J. King, *A Comparative Analysis of Juvenile Codes.*
1982, 1987 - I. Schwartz

* No model classification was available for 1974.
** The model classifications for these states changed between 1979 and 1987.

Note: It is estimated that in 1979, 46% of states were classified as "Justice Model" states. By 1982, that figure had risen to 52%.

Table 3

Top 10 States in Rate of Incarceration to Training Schools
Justice vs. Welfare Model
1974, 1979, 1982 & 1987

Rank	1974 State	1974 Model*	1974 Rate per 100,000	1979 State	1979 Model	1979 Rate per 100,000	1982 State	1982 Model	1982 Rate per 100,000	1987 State	1987 Model	1987 Rate per 100,000
1	D.C.		597	D.C.	Justice	408	D.C.	Justice	484	Oregon	Welfare	640
2	Nevada		303	Nevada	Welfare	261	Delaware	Justice	262	D.C.	Justice	580
3	Wyoming		210	Wyoming	Welfare	256	Wyoming	Welfare	248	Arizona	Justice	518
4	New Hampshire		190	Alaska	Welfare	248	Alaska	Welfare	235	Montana	Welfare	461
5	Alaska		190	Delaware	Justice	213	Nevada	Justice**	225	Wyoming	Welfare	456
6	Vermont		187	Oregon	Welfare	176	Louisiana	Welfare	205	Delaware	Justice	368
7	Louisiana		176	Kansas	Welfare	171	Montana	Welfare	157	Minnesota	Justice	367
8	N. Carolina		166	Louisiana	Justice	160	Kansas	Welfare	154	Nevada	Justice	347
9	S. Carolina		161	New Hampshire	Justice	146	Oregon	Welfare	152	Tennessee	Welfare	335
10	Montana		157	Montana	Welfare	143	Maryland	Welfare	143	California	Justice	318

SOURCE: 1974, 1979, 1982 - U.S. Department of Census, Children in Custody Series.

1987 - From Ira Schwartz's data on Detention Centre Populations.

These data are based on one-day counts and age-eligible youth population in state.

MODEL CLASSIFICATION:

1979 - J. King, *A Comparative Analysis of Juvenile Codes.*

1982, 1987 - I. Schwartz

* No model classification was available for 1974.

** The model classifications for these states changed between 1979 and 1987.

more times in the top ten are western states, and this area predominated (six) in the most recent period.

When all 50 states are examined during the initial three periods, it is not possible to find consistent trends among Welfare and Justice Model states.[158] Ira Schwartz and his colleagues at the Center for the Study of Youth Policy are currently analysing the complete Children in Custody dataset for 1987. These analyses might uncover demographic and policy patterns associated with the variation in training school incarceration rates. Yet it may be that differences between Justice and Welfare Model states are not to be anticipated because both models consider it appropriate to sentence violent and serious offenders to training schools, although the reasons are different. It is possible that training schools in Welfare Model states have more treatment programs and indefinite sentencing than Justice Model states. According to the latter model, mandatory treatment programs are unacceptable; they involve too many discretionary or arbitrary decisions by non-judicial personnel, and there is little evidence that treatment is effective.

It is also critical to examine state correctional policies. Recall that, according to Krisberg *et al*, ''available bed space'' was by far the strongest correlate of custody rates in the earlier Children in Custody data,[159] and thus it is imperative to control for the ever-increasing number of states that have followed the Massachusetts deinstitutionalization policies. Utah is one of the states which has most recently closed its large training schools and reduced the number of spaces available to a limited number of small, secure units. Under these circumstances, probation officers, prosecutors and judges are constrained by correctional policy on custody options. The net result is that neither Justice, Welfare nor Crime Control ideologies can result in low-risk and non-violent youth being sent in substantial numbers to training schools.

A more distinctive pattern is evident in Table 2, which provides a comparison of detention centre (pre-trial and short-term sentence) incarceration rates in Justice and Welfare Model states. Again, classification of states by model was available only for 1979, 1982 and 1987. However, for some states there is little ambiguity before 1979. For example, there is no difficulty in identifying Washington as a Welfare Model state in 1974. California, on the other hand, had introduced several Justice Model reforms by this time. There were four welfare states in the top ten in 1979, but by 1982 there were none. Several Justice Model states more than doubled their detention rates. Between 1974 and 1987, the Florida rate changed by 112 percent, while California, Georgia, and Washington state rates changed by 70 percent or more. Nevada showed a dramatic 172 percent increase. With the exceptions of Nevada and possibly Arizona, the top ten states all have major urban areas with substantial racial minorities. Unlike the top ten

---

[158] Krisberg, *supra*, note 146.

[159] *Ibid*.

training-school states, western states do not comprise the majority of top ten detention states.

It is possible to maintain that detention centre rates are more representative of punitive custodial ends than training schools (see Table 2). Recall that, while the latter usually are reserved for more serious property and personal offences, detention centres serve pre-trial custody options and short-term and split sentences (30 to 40-day sentences plus a probation period). Clearly, these sentences can be seen as reflecting ''short, sharp, shock'' punishment/deterrence policy. Krisberg *et al.* have noted with alarm the increased popularity of this policy among legislators and the judiciary and the dramatic increase in its use from 4,800 short-term admissions in 1977 to 21,000 in 1982.[160] The confounding effect of the Crime Control (particularly in transferring juveniles to adult court) and Justice Model reforms on these detention rates is summarized by Bortner:

> . . . (T)he process has become more formal and penalties have become more severe. A greater proportion of cases referred to the juvenile courts are being handled through the formal process, including formal petition. This, coupled with the fact that punishments are getting harsher, has lead to a greater number of contested court proceedings, that is, more official hearings (''trials'') with more adversarial fights between prosecution and defense. The adjudicatory, guilt-finding portion of the process is lengthened, and those juveniles detained during this process have increased stays. Juveniles transferred to adult court also contribute to these statistics because they usually wait in juvenile detention centres until their transfers are completed.[161]

Notwithstanding the unintended consequences likely resulting from the co-optation of the Justice Model by some Crime Control-oriented practitioners, especially judges, Justice Model proponents maintain that this model can lower inappropriately high custody rates. Anne L. Schneider (personal communication), who conducted much of the research on the implementation of Washington State's innovative Justice Model approach, is not pessimistic after more than a decade of experience with this model. While she admits that some judges may have overused their discretion to impose custody sentences despite the less intrusive options specified by the legislated sentencing grid formula, the current custody trend is encouraging (see Figure 2). According to Schneider, during the initial approximately four-year period the average daily residential population increased, but it has declined since 1982 and has now nearly returned to the 1979 level low point. The expectation was that custody rates would drop with the introduction of Justice Model legislation, because status offenders would no longer constitute a substantial proportion of Washington state's residential population. It is hoped, as Schneider's research continues, additional data and explanations will be available to address the relationship between increased custody reates and the Justice Model.

---

[160] *Ibid.*

[161] Bortner, *supra*, note 152, at p. 334.

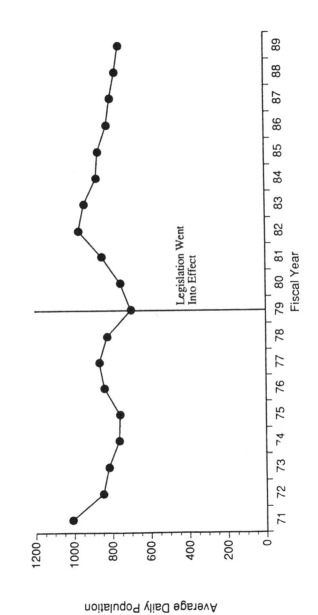

Figure 2
Washington State Residential Population:
Average Daily Population

Average Daily Population

Fiscal Year

Legislation Went
Into Effect

71 72 73 ⁊4 75 76 77 78 79 80 81 82 83 84 85 86 87 88 89

1200 1000 800 600 400 200 0

From: Anne L. Schneider
Arizona State University

Summary of U.S. Trends

As has been stated several times, it is not possible to generalize with any confidence about the U.S. experience with the Modified Justice Model. As in Canada, there appears to be a consensus in the U.S. that the traditional Welfare Model has fundamental flaws, but responding reforms have been more varied in the U.S. Given the constitutional responsibility of individual states to enact and to implement juvenile justice legislation, this diversity in reforms is to be expected. In this field, the role of the U.S. federal government is neither as direct nor as powerful as the Canadian federal government. However, it is also true that the U.S. Supreme Court and various federal laws have had a profound impact on juvenile justice trends. Equally important, crime control issues are far more politically sensitive in the U.S. than in Canada. Urban violence, drug abuse, youth gangs, racial divisions, and poverty are daily media issues.

Under politically conservative administrations — including those of Presidents Nixon, Reagan and Bush — crime control values have had a substantial effect on federal policies and initiatives directed towards the 50 states and the District of Columbia. There is little doubt that juvenile justice decision-makers are influenced to some degree by their own frustrations with Justice Model due process principles and the apparent ineffectiveness of Welfare Model treatment programs. Crime Control solutions are obvious alternatives: incapacitate to protect society and punish to gain retribution and to deter. Yet, despite this "get tough" scenario, there are several cases, even in traditionally conservative states such as Utah, where reforms have sought to limit the use of the custodial response to youth crime. Not all such program reforms can be identified directly with Justice Model reforms; however, youth advocates such as Ira Schwartz believe that this model is critical to the progressive reforms needed to reduce unnecessary and inappropriate punishment of youth.

CONCLUSION

A comparative perspective is useful in answering questions about the impact of the *YOA* on juvenile justice systems in Canada. The most controversial issue is whether these systems have become more punitively or custodially oriented. It is assumed that custodial sentences are inherently more punitive than the remaining sentencing alternatives such as probation and community service. It is also overwhelmingly evident that custody rates in most provinces have increased dramatically since the implementation of the *YOA*. Since the offence profile has not changed proportionately, it appears that the *YOA* has affected sentencing patterns independently of the youth crime profile (see Chapter 5). However, we cannot conclude that the YOA has caused this increased punitiveness without a systematic attempt to examine alternative explanations. Other changes might have occurred in Canada that have resulted in a more punitive juvenile justice system. The economy, ideologies, racial and ethnic composition, age profile, leisure time, family structures and suburbanization are among the structural factors which may have an influence on deviant behaviour and on the way it is defined and socially controlled. A cross-national comparative perspective allows us to examine parallel events which can assist in controlling for alternative explanations to juvenile justice changes.

Juvenile justice in Great Britian provided a useful case study of a Modified Justice Model system, since some of the legislative principles and juvenile justice procedures found in the *YOA* had been in place there since 1908. During the contemporary period from the 1960s, juvenile justice in Britian divided into several patterns, each of which has considerable theoretical relevance. In Scotland, the Modified Justice Model was abolished, while in England and Wales the movement toward the Welfare Model was reversed by Justice Model and Corporatist Model reforms. Custody rates have been substantially lower in Scotland than in England and Wales. While the Scottish system of institutionalized diversion and community-based lay panels employing Welfare Model criteria has been criticized for the absence of due process, there has been considerably more controversy in England and Wales. Complaints here focused initially on the assertion that there was an unintended increase in custody rates. Despite national policy attempts to curtail the use of custody by introducing stricter Justice Model proportionality and least interference criteria, both Welfare Model and Justice Model proponents felt that too many magistrates were resorting to Crime Control sentences, including punishment and deterrence through "short, sharp, shock" detention centre sentences.

There was no shortage of spectacular media stories of violent and uncontrollable hooligans terrorizing the populace, not only in British cities but also in Continental European cities during international soccer matches. The sense of "moral panic", citizen outrage and Thatcherite political reaction appears to have influenced some magistrates to employ Crime Control sentencing criteria. In England and Wales, it is difficult to avoid the conclusion that the Justice Model lends itself to co-optation by Crime Control-oriented decision-makers. This ideological perspective seems particularly attractive during periods of major economic and social changes and uncertainties. There is little doubt that Thatcher's Crime Control rhetoric, particularly evident during her three successful election campaigns, appeals to those juvenile justice decision-makers who fear the breakdown of traditional social control values and processes. The Modified Justice Model in England and Wales has appeared to emphasize the decision-making power of magistrates. Magistrates in Britian are predominantly middle-class and locally prominent individuals. Judicial discretion regarding daily sentencing was not monitored closely by the appellate courts, Home Office or any other national ministry, and thus magistrates had considerable sentencing latitude (at least until the 1988 *Criminal Justice Act*). As an interest group, magistrates have been successful in avoiding any fundamental weakening of their traditional authority and, with three successive Thatcher governments, they have had a powerful ally in maintaining their power. In effect, those magistrates who incorporate Crime Control Model criteria in their juvenile justice ideology have avoided the custody-reducing Justice Model criteria emphasized in the 1982 *Criminal Justice Act*, just as they ignored the key Welfare Model reforms introduced by the 1969 *Children and Young Persons Act*.

A somewhat different interpretation is offered by Pratt, who persuasively argues that custody rates have changed little and that there is sparce evidence that a more punitive system has emerged.[162] Pratt further claims that the current trends in juvenile justice are best understood by the Corporatist Model which eschews the Welfare Model focus on rehabilitation, the Justice Model focus on due process and the Crime Control focus on incapacitation. Instead, the emphasis is on administrative efficiency and the monitoring of less serious offenders in community-based programs. For Pratt, both the 1982 and 1988 Criminal Justice Acts reduced the discretion of magistrates while enhancing the functions of administrative agencies.[163] In effect, senior bureaucrats in the Home Office Ministry have been successful in drafting and implementing legislation that by the late 1980s had introduced certain Justice Model reforms such as increasing the role of Crown prosecutors and defence counsel in the adversarial process, while at the same time ensuring that Corporatist Model policies became the basis of dominant juvenile justice reforms.

In the United States, the experience with a Modified Justice Model is much more recent and, therefore, it is more difficult to discern distinctive patterns of punitiveness. Nonetheless, there are sentencing trends that indicate an increased use of short-term detention for non-major offences. Again, the Crime Control ideology appears critical because punitiveness and deterrence rather than rehabilitation seems to provide the rationale for custodial sentences for minor offences.

Like Britian, the U.S. has experienced considerable urban turmoil predominantly involving racial minorities. The U.S. media graphically portrays the violence that undeniably exists. Youth gangs, in particular, with their "drive by" shootings of rival gang members and bystanders, their involvement with crack cocaine sales and their increasing numbers in both juvenile and adult prisons, contribute to the image that lawlessness is rampant in many urban areas. The Reagan administration, so strongly identified with the Crime Control Model, clearly sought to steer national policies away from the traditional Welfare Model. Equally important, it is possible to argue that his key law enforcement officials promoted the co-optation of the Justice Model by Crime Control-oriented juvenile justice decision-makers.

This co-optation explanation is plausible, given the expectation that custody rates in Justice Model states should be lower than when they operated under the Welfare Model due to the removal of status offenders from juvenile court

---

[162] Pratt, "Corporatism: The Third Model of Juvenile Justice" (1989) 29 *British Journal of Criminology* pp. 236–54.
[163] *Ibid.*

jurisdiction, and due to the proportionality and least interference principles. Yet, this reduction has not occurred. Washington State provides an important illustration of this unintended custodial trend while, theoretically having the most complete Justice Model legislation and, according to the Reagan administration, was an exemplary model of juvenile justice reform. It experienced an increase in custody over the decade after 1974 despite a substantial drop in the number of youth in the state.

Co-optation of the Justice Model by Crime Control proponents may also explain the increased youth custody rates, even though many Modified Justice Model and Welfare Model states have passed bifurcation legislation directed toward transferring violent or career young offenders to the adult criminal justice system. If it is assumed that the more serious offenders are transferred, and yet juvenile court custody rates have not declined proportionately, then it is plausible to infer that juvenile court judges are resorting to custodial sentences for non-serious offenders. This is consistent with Crime Control values such as "short, sharp, shock" reactions to control minor acts of deviance.

This process may also be facilitated by due process rights. The adversarial process may result in judges reacting more punitively at sentencing. It may be that judicial ideologies are similar between the juvenile and adult courts: an immediate admission of guilt is rewarded with a more lenient sentence, while playing the adversarial "game" and "losing" entails a more punitive custodial sentence.

Finally, the Modified Justice Model might itself facilitate increased punitiveness because its sentencing principles are too ambiguous, inconsistent and contradictory. According to this model, the key decisions are made by prosecutors, who have discretion on how to proceed (such as whether to divert, to seek a transfer to adult court or to remain at the juvenile court level), and by judges, who usually determine legal guilt and sentence. Both these decision-makers are supposedly guided by the Modified Justice Model goals of protecting society; holding youth responsible for criminal acts, subject to maturity level; proportionality of offence and sentence; least interference from official interventions; and providing resources voluntarily to meet the special needs of youth. Given this broad mandate, and decision making criteria which are difficult to operationalize, it is quite likely that prosecutors and judges resort more to their own ideologies in making decisions than they otherwise would. In effect, Crime Control-oriented decision-makers are permitted to bias their sentencing toward protecting society through incapacitation, punishment and deterrence, while ignoring the proportionality and least interference principles.

It is important to reiterate that there is no theoretical consensus among British and U.S. scholars about juvenile justice trends in their countries. As stated several times throughout this chapter, the available data are too tentative to assess with any confidence the validity of the different and complex multi-level theories discussed above. The major purpose of employing a comparative perspective at this time is to identify empirical trends and related theoretical accounts which can assist in understanding parallel events in Canada. Chapter 4 will take the initial step in detailing how the *YOA* appears to have affected key juvenile justice institutions and roles. In addition, Chapter 5 will provide an in-depth examination of the most controversial impact of the *YOA* — the increased use of custodial sanctions.

CHAPTER 4

THE EVOLUTION AND IMPLEMENTATION
OF A NEW ERA OF JUVENILE JUSTICE
IN CANADA

Raymond R. Corrado
Alan Markwart[1]

A NEW ERA IN CANADIAN JUVENILE JUSTICE

Just as the year 1984 marked the tenth anniversary of one of the most dramatic symbols of the reform of juvenile justice in the United States and, as well, the beginnings of a "watershed period" in the reform process in that country,[2] so too did the Canadian juvenile justice system enter its own watershed period with the proclamation of the *Young Offenders Act*[3] (*YOA*) in that same year. Heralded in Parliament (no less than by the Opposition party justice critic) as the first major "social justice bill" to come before Parliament in three decades[4] and, later, as an exemplary model of juvenile justice at United Nations conferences,[5] the Act promised a "new era" in juvenile justice in Canada.[6]

---

[1] Alan Markwart is a Program Analyst with the British Columbia Ministry of Attorney General. Raymond Corrado is a Professor of Criminology at Simon Fraser University. The opinions expressed are entirely those of the authors and do not reflect the views of the British Columbia Ministry of Attorney General.

[2] Krisberg, Schwartz, Litsky and Austin, "The Watershed of Juvenile Justice Reform" (1986) (32) (1) Crime and Delinq. pp. 5-38.

[3] *Young Offenders Act*, S.C. 1980-81-82-83, c. 30 [now R.S. 1985, c. Y-1].

[4] House of Commons, *Debates*, First session of the Thirty-Second Parliament. Ottawa: House of Commons, p. 9494.

[5] Kaye, "There Oughta Be a Law". (1990) (15) (11) *Can. Liv.* pp. 83-89.

[6] Bala, "The Young Offenders Act: A New Era in Juvenile Justice?" in B. Landau, ed., *Children's Rights in the Practice of Family Law* (Toronto:

The *YOA* has certainly delivered on its promise of this new era; there is no doubt that the new Act, as detailed in this chapter, has radically transformed the juvenile justice systems of most provinces, although Quebec seems to be a notable exception.[7] The critical question, however, is whether these changes represent a substantial improvement in the juvenile justice process and its outcomes or, at least, a step forward. We have previously been critical of, in particular, the substantial increases in rates of committals to custody and in court delays evidently brought about by the new Act.[8] In this chapter, we will continue this critical examination of the *YOA*, analysing the evolution of the legislation, including recent and pending legislative changes; the organizational changes prompted by the new Act; concerns about increasing juvenile crime, particularly crimes of violence; and the effects of implementation of the new Act on the roles of key actors in the juvenile justice process.

It should be said from the outset that while we continue to be critical of the *YOA* and its implementation, we do not take the view that the Act has been without (some) benefits, nor that a (modified) "Justice Model" approach necessarily must (but unfortunately, often does) lead to undesirable outcomes. The standardization of age jurisdiction across Canada, the abolition of status offences (in federal law, at least), the raising of the minimum age of criminal responsibility, determinate sentencing, and the stimulation of the development of new diversion and community service programs are a few examples of positive changes brought about by the new Act. But do these few benefits offset the significant disadvantages of the Act? We do not think so. Any major change in social legislation can, of course, suffer flaws in conception, in implementation, or in both. The flaws in the *YOA* have not, however, been minor; rather, it is our view that the "mixed model" of the Act is fundamentally flawed in conception and has been uneven and inadequate in its implementation.

Carswell, 1986); Caputo, "The Young Offenders Act: Children's Rights, Children's Wrongs" (1987) (13) (2) Can. Pub. Pol. pp. 125-143.

[7] LeBlanc and Beaumont, "The Quebec Perspective on the Young Offenders Act: Implementation Before Adoption" in Hudson, Hornick and Burrows, eds., *Justice and the Young Offender in Canada* (Toronto: Wall and Thompson, 1988).

[8] Corrado and Markwart, "The Prices of Rights and Responsibilities: An Examination of the Impacts of the *Young Offenders Act* in British Columbia"; Markwart and Corrado, "Is the Young Offenders Act More Punitive?" in Beaulieu, ed., *Young Offender Dispositions: Perspectives on Principles and Practice* (Toronto: Wall and Thompson, 1989).

BACKGROUND TO THE REFORM OF CANADIAN JUVENILE JUSTICE

Any understanding in the *YOA* and the present state of affairs of Canadian juvenile justice would be incomplete without first addressing the historical forces and circumstances leading up to proclamation of the new legislation. While the period leading up to the passage of the Act in 1982 has received some critical attention, [9] there has not, to date, been an adequate explanation of how Canada came to the point of adopting the Modified Justice Model of the *YOA*.

As Corrado and Turnbull discuss in Chapter 3, the process of reform leading to the passage of Modified Justice Model legislation in England and several American states was — as well as being affected by the emergence of civil rights and due process concerns, and by criminological theory and research — heavily influenced by partisan politics and political ideology bolstered, in part, by "moral panics" about (ostensibly) rising juvenile crime rates. In these countries, the debate about the direction of juvenile justice was very public, political and sometimes heated. For example, the British Labour government introduced radical changes with its 1969 *Children and Young Persons Act*,[10] which was designed to shift the English juvenile justice system toward the Welfare Model. The vehement reaction of supporters of the existing Modified Justice Model such as judges, magistrates, lawyers and the police, and, most importantly, the election of a Conservative government in 1971, resulted in a severe blunting of the 1969 Act. Interest group opposition appears to have contributed to the hesitation of the subsequently re-elected Labour government to implement all of the provisions of the 1969 Act. Juvenile justice reforms were a bitter electoral issue in the British parliamentary election of 1979.[11] The election that year of Margaret Thatcher and the Conservatives resulted in a decisive move back toward a Justice Model with

---

[9] See, for example, Cousineau and Veevers, "Juvenile Justice: An Analysis of the Young Offenders Act" in Boydell, Grindstaff, and Whitehead, eds. *Deviant Behaviour and Societal Reaction* (Toronto: Holt, Rinehart and Winston, 1972; Leon, "New and Old Themes in Canadian Juvenile Justice: The Origins of Delinquency Legislation and the Prospects for Recognition of Children's Rights" in Berkeley, Gaffield and West, eds., *Children's Rights: Legal and Educational Issues* (Toronto: The Ontario Institute for Studies in Education, 1978); West, *Young Offenders and the State: A Canadian Perspective on Delinquency* (Toronto: Butterworths, 1984); Havemann, "From child saving to child blaming: The political economy of the Young Offenders Act, 1908-1984" in Brickey and Comack, eds., *The Social Basis of the Law* (Toronto: Garamond Press, 1986); Caputo, *supra*, note 6.

[10] *Children and Young Persons Act*, (U.K.), 1969, c. 54.

[11] Taylor, *Law and Order: Arguments for Socialism* (London: MacMillan, 1981); Morris and Giller, *Understanding Juvenile Justice* (London: Groom Helm, 1987).

the 1982 *Criminal Justice Act*[12] and the much publicized policy of "short, sharp shock" detention orders. Similarly, in the United States the Reagan presidency marked a turning point in federal juvenile justice policy — through both severe budget cuts and financial grants to certain states, the Reagan government promoted its conservative combination of Crime Control and Justice Model policy to state and urban governments.[13]

In reviewing the 20-year process leading to the passage of the *YOA*, and subsequent amendments to the Act, we will attempt to demonstrate that the Canadian experience has been decidedly different. While it is clear that juvenile justice reform has been a politically partisan (or ideological) and public issue in England and the United States, and therefore has the potential to be so in Canada, this has clearly not been the case in the development of the *YOA*, although it seems, as will be discussed later, that politically partisan and public interest in the reform of the *YOA* appear to have become more prominent factors in the late 1980s and early 1990s. Although Canadian juvenile justice reform was by no means completely free of these political influences, the effects were decidedly muted. Rather, the Canadian debate about juvenile justice policy has (until, perhaps, very recently) taken place well outside of the public limelight and has been largely free of partisan political interests. As discussed in more detail later, the *YOA* was (broadly speaking) endorsed in principle by a divergent range of interest groups and was unanimously passed by all three political parties in the House of Commons. The Canadian public, and the media, appeared to be remarkably disinterested during this process (at least until after the Act was implemented). It will be argued that the key factors in juvenile justice reform in Canada during this period have been, not political ideology, public concerns or the media, but rather the dynamic interplay of federal and provincial politics arising from Canada's unique constitutional arrangements; the role of senior federal and provincial civil servants, who in turn were influenced by criminological/legal theory and research; and, to a lesser extent, professional interest groups.

Canada's constitutional arrangements respecting the justice system are unique: the federal government has sole jurisdiction over the formulation of criminal legislation, but the provinces are responsible for the administration of that legislation. Further, the provinces have exclusive jurisdiction (i.e., both the law and its administration) over child welfare and mental health services, systems which can have a critical connection to the juvenile justice system. As well, the federal government has the capacity to — and, of course, does — enter into cost-sharing of justice, child welfare and health services administered by the

---

[12] *Criminal Justice Act*, (U.K.), 1982, c. 48.

[13] Krisberg, Schwartz, Litsky and Austin, "The Watershed of Juvenile Justice Reform" (1986) (32) (1) *Crim. Delinq.*, pp. 5–38; Olsen-Raymer, "National Juvenile Justice Policy: Myth or Reality?" in Deeker, ed., *Juvenile Justice Policy: Analyzing Trends and Outcomes* (Beverly Hills, Calif.: Sage Publications, 1984).

provinces. This constitutional division of powers between the federal and provincial governments may, in part, account for the apparent diminished role of political influences in Canadian juvenile justice reform. Since there is no single level of government solely responsible for juvenile justice, the political responsibility for the same, unlike Britain and American states, is much more diffused. In fact, the constitutional division of powers can act as a kind of political safety valve, enabling governments to "get off the hook" when complaints about the juvenile justice system arise; i.e., they can point fingers at their federal or provincial counterparts.

While the federal government could, theoretically, enact juvenile justice legislation without consultation and negotiation with the provinces, this would be politically unacceptable. As a result, the process of reform necessarily involves negotiation and accommodation with the provinces which, of course, are represented by different political parties. Within the provinces, different government departments — typically, Attorney General, Solicitor General and Social Services (child welfare) departments, all of which have vested interests in and sometimes competing views about juvenile justice policy — must consult and negotiate a common provincial policy position. It is inevitable in this convoluted (and time-consuming) federal/provincial structure of consultation and negotiation that compromise and the search for consensus would be the result. Key actors in this process are senior bureaucrats who are (largely) apolitical and not ideologues, and who engage in a process of identifying and assessing various policy options — filtering out unacceptable options for eventual presentation to their political masters. This is not to say that these bureaucrats do not second-guess the ideological interests (if any) of their political masters, nor ignore the influence of interest groups, but rather that the role of these bureaucrats and the nature of the process is, again, one that necessarily leads to compromise — the moderate and "saleable" option. Given this process, it should come as no surprise that, at the end of the day, the resulting *YOA* would prove to be, while emphasizing Justice Model principles, really an amalgam of four theoretical models of juvenile justice.[14] In this sense, the *YOA* can be construed as a masterful political document insofar as it appeals to a divergent range of interest groups.[15]

There is no question that the *YOA* is based on a "Modified Justice Model"; that is, an approach which incorporates the key principles of the Justice Model, but also includes some key elements of other approaches to juvenile justice. It is not pure Justice Model legislation akin to what has been established in, for example, Washington State.[16] The modification of the *YOA*'s Justice Model really becomes

---

[14] Reid and Reitsma-Street, "Assumptions and Implications of New Canadian Legislation for Young Offenders (1984) (7)(1) Can. Crim. Forum pp. 1-19.

[15] Corrado and Markwart, *supra*, note 8.

[16] See, for example, Trépanier, "Trends in Juvenile Justice: Washington State" in Corrado, LeBlanc and Trépanier, eds., *Current Issues in Juvenile Justice* (Toronto: Butterworths, 1982).

apparent if one looks separately at the "front" and "back" ends of the processes established by the Act; i.e., pre- and post-adjudication. At the front end, the *YOA* adopts an almost pure Justice Model approach in establishing restraint in the application of criminal law (for example, reduced jurisdiction, diversion), in ensuring rights and due process (for example, guaranteed right of counsel, restrictions on the admissibility of statements, bail rights), and in focusing on the offence. It is at the back end — sentencing — where the modification (and confusion) arises: here, we see the mixture of the Justice Model principles of responsibility and accountability, the Crime Control principle of protection of society and the Welfare Model orientation of the "special needs" considerations — all combined with a significant degree of discretion.[17]

Theoretical Considerations

Before discussing the process of Canadian juvenile justice reform in more detail, we should first address the competing theoretical explanations of the role of macro-level political and economic factors in the passage of the *YOA*. A similar debate arose with the *YOA*'s Welfare Model predecessor, the *Juvenile Delinquents Act*[18] (*JDA*), which was proclaimed in 1908. The key theoretical debate over the *JDA* has involved the humanistic-reform perspective versus the conflict-Marxist perspective. The empirical issue is whether the individuals behind the "child saving" movement,[19] which was the driving force behind the *JDA*, were motivated by altruism and a real commitment to improving the lives of delinquent youth, or whether their motivation was really prompted by professional self-interest and/or the manipulative influences of capitalist forces which had vested interests in promoting capital accumulation in a rapidly changing economy. Hagen and Leon have provided some convincing empirical evidence that the latter theoretical perspective is suspect in Canada.[20] Nonetheless, there is considerable consensus that political and economic factors affected the emergence of the *JDA*. The change from a rural/agrarian to an urban/industrial society, particularly in central Canada, and the major influx of immigrants from both Europe and the rural areas within the provinces, resulted in a fundamental restructuring of Canadian society. The control of young people became one of the many social control issues that emerged in this changing urban context. The relevance of political economy is further evident in the emergence of identical social control issues in the United States and western Europe. It is unlikely, therefore, that similar juvenile justice

---

[17] See Chapter 5 and Doob, "Dispositions Under the Young Offenders Act: Issues Without Answers?" in Beaulieu, ed., *Young Offenders Dispositions: Perspectives on Principles and Practice* (Toronto: Wall and Thompson, 1989).

[18] *Juvenile Delinquents Act*, R.S.C. 1970, c. J-3.

[19] Platt, *The Child Savers: The Invention of Delinquency* (Chicago: University of Chicago Press, 1977).

[20] Hagan and Leon, "Rediscovering Delinquency: Social History, Political Ideology and the Sociology of Law" (1977) (42) (3) *Am. Soc. Rev.* pp. 587-98.

law reforms in most Western industrialized countries, at about the same time at the turn of the century, were merely coincidental and unaffected by these common political and economic factors.

A similar argument has been advanced for the influence of macro-level political and economic factors in the emergence of Justice Model reforms in several Western countries in recent decades as these societies made the transition to post-industrial economies. From a neo-Marxist perspective, corporate interests are served by the *YOA* because it allows the political elite to continue to legitimize the "neo-liberal ideology" that is essential to the accumulation of corporate capital in the current neo-competitive phase of the Canadian economy. This hypothesized relationship between the *YOA* and corporate capital is complex and requires an elaboration of political economy theories which are beyond the scope of this chapter. In brief, however, the essence of this hypothesized relationship is that, although the Canadian public wants to feel protected from youth crime, Canadians also want the rights of youths to be protected. At the same time, corporations of the post-industrial economy need young people to be managed and controlled in a manner in keeping with their corporate interests so that this population can be used both for cheap labour and as a market for their products. To accomplish these convoluted objectives, the state has to create the impression that it has the right, or even the obligation, to liberate young people from parental tyranny; i.e., youth have the right to work and purchase what they want. Therefore, the state has increasingly been assuming the role of the family regarding young people. The state has to legitimize this radical intrusion into the role of the family by maintaining that the protection of society requires governments to treat certain criminal youths in an adult-like manner in terms of rights, responsibilities and punishment, while other less serious criminal youth can be processed, and increasingly controlled, by less intrusive "alternative measures".

For Gordon West the *YOA* represents little more than the extension of state control serving the interests of the corporate sector:

> Basically it seems that Canadian governments have less concern with justice and the prevention of delinquency than with maintaining control and legitimacy by managing youth . . . The extension of the delinquency legislation to include all sixteen and seventeen year olds extends the state's control over this age group and raises the age of total non-citizens from seven to twelve. The cutting of costs in response to delinquency, while increasing the net through cheaper measures such as diversion and community corrections helps to meet the fiscal crisis of the state. In all these ways . . . it would seem that the recent policy decisions would be basically in the interests of the Canadian Corporate sector. . . . Certainly neither working class populations nor the young were involved in formulating these reforms.[21]

West's arguments simply do not stand up to a critical analysis. Sixteen- and seventeen-year-olds were already subject to state control prior to the *YOA* either

---

[21] West, *Young Offenders and the State: A Canadian Perspective on Delinquency* (Toronto: Butterworths, 1984) at p. 218.

(depending on the province) under the auspices of the *JDA* or the *Criminal Code*. It can hardly be said that the rights of children under 12 years of age, who were rarely prosecuted under the *JDA*, were rigorously protected; moreover, while this population was subject to both criminal law (*JDA*) or child welfare jurisdiction prior to the *YOA*, the state's control has now been limited by removing criminal jurisdiction. The *YOA* did not cut costs; in fact, it substantially increased costs to both the federal and provincial governments (largely as a result of the uniform maximum age) and it was, as then-Solicitor General Robert Kaplan readily acknowledged,[22] well known that this would be the case when the Bill was before Parliament. The fact that this decision to knowingly and substantially increase juvenile justice costs was taken in the midst of the worst recession since the Great Depression, in this case at least, hardly supports the views of radical critics such as West and Scull[23] that recent justice system reforms are necessarily shaped by the alleged fiscal crisis of the capitalist state.

In a similar neo-Marxist analysis, Currie argues that the *YOA* is a radical departure from the *JDA* because the latter was designed to promote the role of the family in controlling youth, while the former law enhanced the role of the state at the expense of the family.[24] Nonetheless, both Acts have served and reflect the prevailing capitalist interests and conditions of these different times. In the case of the *YOA*, the ultimate aim is to serve corporate capital interests by according the state, rather than the family, a stronger hand in shaping the role of youth in the contemporary economy. The *YOA* then is just one law among many directed at Canadian youth with the objective of integrating them into the economy in a manner that enhances corporate profit and capital. This integration, however, is far from beneficial to certain youth, particularly those from the working class, because these young persons are often "marginal" to the work force; i.e., they hold part-time, low-paying jobs with few benefits and little security, and this is immensely profitable for corporations.

There is no obvious and direct empirical evidence supporting this neo-Marxist perspective of the *YOA*. It remains to be empirically demonstrated how conditions which benefit capitalist interests directly, or even indirectly, accrue from the *YOA*. Even assuming such a linkage were plausible and demonstrable, it also remains to be demonstrated whether and how these political economic forces generally, and corporate capitalist interests particularly, have at a practical level played a direct or indirect role — either through politicans, senior bureaucrats or

---

[22] House of Commons, *Minutes of the Proceedings and Evidence of the Standing Committee on Justice and Legal Affairs* (Ottawa: House of Commons, 1980-81-82).

[23] Scull, *Decarceration: Community Treatment and the Deviant — A Radical View* (Englewood Cliffs, N.J.: Prentice-Hall, 1977).

[24] Currie, "The Transformation of Juvenile Justice in Canada: A Study of Bill C-61" in Maclean, ed., *The Political Economy of Crime* (Scarborough, Ont.: Prentice-Hall, 1986.

interest groups — in the actual formulation of the *YOA*. Cohen describes the implausibility of this linkage nicely:

> Even if apologists for the system are only apologists, they cannot be consigned to represent historical forces. It is unreasonable to assume that the reformers were propelled by class interests beyond their understanding, and then only afterward drew on a plausible vocabulary of legitimization.[25]

As well, the neo-Marxist analysis has not adequately explained why, if juvenile justice policy is shaped by these capitalist political economic forces, different juvenile Justice Models are in place across (and within) Western industrialized countries. Arguably, the exigencies of similar post-industrial political economic conditions should have brought about a more common international response in these countries, as was the case with the Welfare Model reforms at the turn of the century. But this is not the case. For example, while England, many American states, Canada and Australia have moved toward Justice and Crime Control Models, Scotland and Western Continental European countries have continued with Welfare Models. Similarly, within the U.S. — i.e., within the same capitalist economic system — a variety and range (for example, the states of Massachusetts and Washington) of juvenile Justice Models have been embraced and the Welfare Model still prevails in many states.

This is not to say that there may be no validity at all to the neo-Marxist view that changing economic conditions for the accumulation of capital have had an impact on the structure of the family, which is associated with youth deviance and crime, and with how the state responds. This theoretical perspective remains, however, narrowly focused and suspect, and has yet to be empirically justified. A more plausible approach, as Cohen points out, to explaining juvenile justice reform may be found in recognizing that these reforms have arisen from a multiplicity of factors; he argues, for example, that progressive ideals or motives, partisan politics, inter-organizational dynamics, contemporary theory and research and intra-bureaucratic imperatives are important factors in justice reforms.[26] We will explore these and other factors in the Canadian context.

The Process of Reform

It is widely agreed that the reform of Canadian juvenile justice began with the appointment in 1961 of an Advisory Committee of the Department of Justice, which in 1965 formally reported its findings and recommendations in *Juvenile Delinquency in Canada*.[27] The appointment of the Committee seems not to have arisen in response to political, ideological or public concerns, nor interest group

---

[25] Cohen, *Visions of Social Control: Crime, Punishment and Classification* (Newark, N.J.: Basil Blackwell, 1985).

[26] *Ibid.*

[27] Department of Justice, *Juvenile Delinquency in Canada: The Report of the Department of Justice Committee* (Ottawa: Queen's Printer, 1965).

lobbying, but rather as a result of a bureaucratic initiative, the report of a 1960 Correctional Planning Committee of the Department of Justice. This Planning Committee report recommended that the best way of "stopping the flow of an ever increasing number of young *adult* offenders through the criminal courts and into Canadian prisons" was to prevent crime through an organized, integrated approach to the problem of delinquency.[28] There was also another link here with previous efforts to reform the adult correctional system. The 1956 Fauteux Commission had recommended a careful examination of the whole legislative framework (including the *JDA*) of the Canadian correctional system. Interestingly, the senior Departmental advisor to the Fauteux Commission — Allen MacLeod, a lawyer and bureaucrat — would later become chairman of the Juvenile Delinquency Committee.

The Department of Justice's Committee inquiries were broad, considering, for example, briefs from a diverse range of organizations and interest groups in Canada; international proposals such as England's Ingleby Committee report and Scotland's Kilbrandon Committee report; American and European trends and practices; and academic critics such as Matza.[29]

The Committee's 1965 report was critical of both the *JDA* itself and the inadequate resources made available to the juvenile justice system to implement the rehabilitative ideals of the Act. In many respects, the recommendations of the Committee's report, broadly speaking, established the procedural framework of the *YOA* that was eventually to be proclaimed nearly 20 years later, particularly with respect to the legal rights of juvenile offenders. For example, the Committee recommended abolition of the omnibus offence of delinquency and of status offences from the federal Act; definite custodial sentences to a maximum of three years, with annual reviews and judicially authorized early release; embodiment of the concept of imposing institutional confinement only as a last resort; procedural safeguards respecting the taking of statements (confessions) from youth by the police; limitations on the use of pre-trial and pre-adjudication detention; provisions that the accused be informed of his or her right to counsel and of the right to have counsel appointed at public expense; procedural regularization of "informal adjustment" (diversion) practices; broadened appeal rights; a raised minimum age and uniform maximum age; and equality in the operation of law and provision of services throughout Canada. It is clear that the Committee's concern about the rights of juvenile offenders was prompted by a recognition of the inherent dangers of the Welfare Model:

> It does not follow, of course, that acceptance of what has been called the "rehabilitative ideal" means that the question of civil liberties can be safely ignored. So beguiling, in fact, is the language of therapy that all the more care must be taken to ensure the protection of these liberties.[30]

---

[28] *Ibid.*, at p. 1.

[29] Matza, *Delinquency and Drift* (New York: John Wiley & Sons, 1964).

[30] *Supra*, note 27, at p. 88.

It should be noted that, while the Committee's report was produced at about the same time as civil rights concerns were in the forefront in the United States, it nonetheless pre-dated key U.S. Supreme Court decisions — *Kent* (1966), *Gault* (1967) and *Winship* (1970)[31] — and the *U.S. President's Task Force Report on Juvenile Delinquency and Youth Crime*,[32] which would shake the foundations of the *parens patriae* doctrine of the juvenile court and provide a major impetus for juvenile justice reform in that country. Given that the rights and due process orientation of the Committee's report had already been officially "made in Canada" prior to the above-noted American events, it cannot be said that these milestones in American juvenile justice reform directly prompted Canadian reform. Still, these American events and trends undoubtedly spilled over and influenced the Canadian move to a legal rights orientation in the sense that they affirmed the direction already signalled by the Committee. Moreover, stinging American academic critiques of the legal rights abuses of the *parens patriae* juvenile court had considerably pre-dated[33] the American *Kent*, *Gault* and *Winship* decisions and were likely well known to the committee.[34]

The Committee, ironically, did not receive a brief from the Canadian Bar Association or from any provincial Bar Association. Still, the rights and due process orientation of the Committee's recommendations should not be surprising — four of the five Committee members were lawyers (who were also civil servants). Moreover, emerging Canadian concerns about civil rights had already been signalled by Parliament's passage of the Canadian *Bill of Rights* in 1960[35] (although this law would later prove to be largely ineffectual) and by Canada being a signatory to the first United Nations Declaration on the Rights of the Child in 1959.

While the rights and due process orientation of the Committee report set the stage for the *YOA* that was eventually to emerge many years later, it differed in one key respect — the Committee endorsed the welfare/treatment philosophy of the existing *JDA* wherein juvenile offenders would continue to be dealt with "not as a criminal, but as a misdirected and misguided child, and one needing aid, encouragement, help, and assistance".[36] In effect, the "responsibility" aspect of

---

[31] *Kent v. U.S.* 383 U.S. 541 (1966); *Re Gault* 387 U.S. 1 (1967); *In the Matter of Samuel Winship* 397 U.S. 358 (1970).

[32] President's Commission on Law Enforcement and Administration of Justice, *Task Force Report: Juvenile Delinquency and Youth Crime* (Washington, D.C.: U.S. Government Printing Office, 1967).

[33] For example, see Tappan, "Treatment Without Trial?" (24) (3) *Social Problems* pp. 306-11.

[34] For discussions of the emergence of the children's rights movements from a political economic perspective, see Currie, *supra*, note 28 and Havemann, *supra*, note 10.

[35] *Canadian Bill of Rights*, S.C. 1960, c. 44, Part I.

[36] *Juvenile Delinquents Act*, *supra*, note 18, s. 38.

the *YOA*'s "rights and responsibilities" model[37] had yet to emerge. In this regard, the Committee did indicate that in 1961 Canadians knew that there was a problem of juvenile delinquency in Canada, cited "alarming" increases in delinquency in recent years (which, considering population increases, were hardly alarming), and warned of more "alarming" increases to come with the emergence of the "baby boom" generation into adolescence.[38] Nonetheless, these concerns did not appear to be in reaction to or prompt moral panic,[39] nor a Crime Control response. With its embrace of the rights of juvenile offenders and a welfare philosophy, coupled with sharp criticism of the inadequacy of resources, the Committee seemed to be saying that a Welfare Model, circumscribed by a due regard for legal rights, was still the proper course if only the juvenile justice system could be given the resources to implement the idealistic goals of rehabilitation. In effect, rehabilitation had not been given a chance.

The 1965 report of the Department of Justice Committee resulted in the development of a draft *Children and Young Persons Act* in 1967.[40] The draft act, which was discussed at a federal/provincial conference in 1968, was rejected, however, as a result of provincial objections arising from Canada's unique constitutional arrangements for justice. The provinces objected to the Bill's proposed jurisdiction over provincial statute and municipal by-law violations, regarded by the provinces as a federal intrusion into provincial jurisdiction, and were concerned about federal cost-sharing of provincially operated programs.

The then-Liberal government, led by Prime Minister Pierre Trudeau in his quest for a "just society", followed with the introduction of Bill C-192, the *Young Offenders Act*, into Parliament in 1970. While this Bill restricted the jurisdiction of the proposed Act to federal criminal offences in order to appease provincial concerns, it nonetheless generally adhered to the approach and substantive proposals recommended by the 1965 committee; i.e., a mixed model of legal rights superimposed over a welfare/treatment philosophy. One would have expected that this Bill, which seems to have been designed to placate both provincial jurisdictional concerns and the legal rights and treatment/welfare constituencies, would have been met with approval, but this did not materialize. While the Bill was endorsed by the Canadian Bar Association, it was condemned as too legalistic and punitive — a "criminal code for children" — by welfare/treatment interest groups, notably the Canadian Mental Health Association, and

---

[37] Solicitor General Canada, *Young Offenders Act, 1982, Highlights* (Ottawa, Minister of Supply and Services Canada, 1982).

[38] Department of Justice, *supra*, note 27 at p. 7. "The Young Offenders Act: Children's Rights, Children's Wrongs" (1987) (13) (2) Can. Pub. Pol. pp. 125-143.

[39] Caputo, however, seems to have a different view, suggesting that concerns about rising delinquency rates did, in part, prompt the reform process.

[40] This draft Act was not, however, tabled in the House of Commons.

many juvenile court officials and academics.[41] As a result of this opposition by interest groups — as well as resistance from the provinces, and the combined opposition of the politically polarized (left wing) New Democratic and (right wing) Conservative parties in Parliament — the Bill was allowed to die on the Order Paper in 1972.

The failure of Bill C-192 obviously indicates that the Welfare Model constituency remained influential in 1970 in Canada. It is also an example of how interest groups played a key role in (stifling) juvenile justice policy reform. As Cousineau and Veevers put it, the debate about a simple but basic issue had not yet been decided in 1970: should the societal response to delinquents be formulated primarily in terms of their legal rights, or should it be oriented mainly in terms of their social and psychological needs?[42] The Bill's failure is also somewhat ironic, given that it endorsed a welfare philosophy (albeit in legalistic trappings). The *YOA* that was eventually passed by Parliament in 1982 would retain a legal rights orientation, but the welfare philosophy of the 1970 Bill would be largely abandoned in the new (1982) *YOA* and replaced by a philosophy which gives greater prominence to the Crime Control and Justice Model principles of public protection, responsibility and accountability. This begs two key questions: What accounts, a decade later, for the muted influence — even silent voices — of proponents of the Welfare Model? And, what accounts for the emergence and acceptance of the Crime Control/Justice Model principles of the present day *YOA*?

In response to the failure of Bill C-192, the federal Solicitor General in 1973 established a committee of nine persons, again largely comprised of senior federal civil servants who were also lawyers, to review developments that had taken place in the field. Part of this Committee's mandate was to consider the deliberations of a Federal/Provincial Joint Review Group, established at a 1973 Conference of Corrections Ministers and largely comprised of senior provincial bureaucrats. This latter group issued a report in 1974 which, among other recommendations, included a statement of principles intended to guide new federal legislation. This set of principles, although ill-defined, remained infused with the Welfare Model orientation of the earlier reform proposals. This would not prove to be the case, however, with the federal Committee's report and draft legislation, entitled *Young Persons in Conflict with the Law (YPICL)*, in 1975. While the draft *YPICL* was similar in thrust to its predecessor proposals — i.e., a legal rights orientation — the draft's Preamble, which was a statement of philosophy and principles intended to guide the interpretation and operation of the proposed Act, marked a substantial turn in direction. The Preamble was, in many respects, similar to the present

---

[41] For example, see Cousineau and Veevers, *supra*, note 9, and MacDonald "Critique of Bill C-192: The Young Offenders Act" (1971) (13) (1) Can. J. Crim. and Corr. pp. 166-180.

[42] Cousineau and Veevers, "Juvenile Justice: An Analysis of the Young Offenders Act" in Boydell, Grindstaff and Whitehead, eds., *Deviant Behaviour and Societal Reaction* (Toronto: Holt, Rinehart and Winston, 1972) at p. 244.

YOA's Declaration of Principle[43] insofar as it retained some vestiges (for example, special needs) of the Welfare Model, but this was subordinated in a philosophy which emphasized the legal rights of juveniles and, importantly, the new concept of responsibility and (diminished) accountability. The principle of public protection was, however, not reflected in the Preamble. This mixing of various elements of competing theoretical and philosophical positions in these new reform proposals appears to be the product of an effort to arrive at a politically acceptable compromise which could be acceptable to various interest groups.[44]

The *YPICL* report was again subject to academic critiques and provincial opposition, the latter arising largely as a result of the arcane Canadian constitutional division of powers between the federal government and the provinces: provinces were, among other things, opposed to the costs of the proposed uniform maximum age of 18 years as well as the proposal for a mandatory screening agency, which was regarded as a federal intrusion into provincial jurisdiction over the administration of justice.

The Liberal federal government of the day developed further proposals in 1977[45] but a federal election intervened, resulting in a Conservative government taking power. The new Conservative federal government mollified earlier provincial concerns with new proposals,[46] which provided for a flexible maximum age (16 to 18 years, at the province's discretion) and abandonment of the notion of a mandatory screening agency. It is at this time that we see the completion of the shift away from a Welfare to a Justice/Crime Control Model philosophy first signalled by the *YPICL* report; this 1979 outline of legislative proposals incorporated the philosophical thrust — accountability, responsibility and legal rights — of *YPICL*, but extended it further by incorporating the Crime Control notion of the "protection of society" as a key consideration in its proposed statement of principles. Indeed, this statement of principles is virtually identical to what would eventually emerge in the 1982 *YOA*.

The delay between these 1979 proposals, which were tabled in the House of Commons by the Conservative minority government, and the introduction of the *YOA* (Bill C-61) in the House of Commons in early 1981 by the Liberal government seems to be attributable to political developments unrelated to the debate about the appropriate direction of juvenile justice reform; i.e., the interruption brought about by another federal election and the defeat of the Conservative government of Joe Clark. In fact, as the former Solicitor General (Allan Lawrence) for the Clark government acknowledged when the *YOA* was brought before Parliament by the Liberal government in 1981, his Conservative government had

---

[43] R.S.C. 1985, c. Y-1, s. 3.

[44] Caputo, *supra*, note 39 at pp. 126-143.

[45] Solicitor General Canada. *Highlights of the Proposed New Legislation for Young Offenders* (Ottawa: Queen's Printer, 1977).

[46] Solicitor General Canada. *Legislative Proposals to Replace the Juvenile Delinquents Act* (Ottawa: unpublished, 1979).

intended to push forward with almost identical legislation in 1980, but the government was defeated before it was able to do so.[47] No wonder that Lawrence — by then Opposition Critic — hailed the new legislation as the "first major social justice bill to come before this House in over three decades".[48] More importantly, a political consensus about the fundamental direction of juvenile justice reform had been achieved among the two dominant political parties. The socialist-oriented New Democratic party might have been expected to lament the demise of a welfare/treatment approach. But, while criticizing the Bill as a "pint-sized *Criminal Code*"[49] and advocating a greater emphasis on crime prevention through social measures and on the rights of juveniles, the NDP was still relatively restrained in its criticism of the philosophical direction of the Act. The Bill eventually passed with the unanimous approval of all three political parties.

Even though this political consensus emerged, the Bill — unlike the *JDA*, which in 1908 was subject to less than one hour's debate in the House of Commons[50] — was the subject of extensive study and debate in Parliament. More than 40 interest groups made representations to the parliamentary subcommittee studying the Bill. These groups — as diverse as the Canadian Foundation for Children and the Law (a child advocacy group) and the Canadian Association of Chiefs of Police — were, though critical of particular aspects of the Bill, still generally supportive of the proposed legislation. The Canadian and Ontario Psychological Associations offered only muted criticisms. The Toronto Viking Houses organization, which provided treatment services to delinquents, expressed philosophical opposition,[51] but obviously to no avail. In fact, the philosophical direction of the proposed legislation, in sharp contrast to the failed 1970 *YOA*, was hardly debated at all. The legal rights orientation of the Bill went virtually unchallenged; what was really at issue in this regard was, not rights *per se*, but nuances respecting these legal rights.

Similarly, the almost complete abandonment of the Welfare Model philosophy went almost entirely unchallenged. This may, to some extent, have been attributable to the mixed model and inconsistent nature of the proposed legislation which enabled then-Solicitor General Robert Kaplan, responsible for shepherding the Bill through Parliament, to embrace and placate diverse interest groups by offering such rationalizations as . . .

---

[47] House of Commons, *Debates*, First Session of the Thirty-Second Parliament (Ottawa: House of Commons, 1980-81-82) at p. 9494.

[48] *Ibid.*,

[49] House of Commons. *Minutes of the Proceedings and Evidence of the Standing Committee on Justice and Legal Affairs*, Issue 61 (Ottawa: House of Commons 1981-82-83) at p. 21.

[50] Wilson, *Juvenile Courts in Canada* (Toronto: Carswell, 1982).

[51] Senate of Canada, *Proceedings of the Standing Senate Committee on Legal and Constitutional Affairs* (Hull, Quebec: Canadian Government Publishing Centre, 1980-81-82).

> . . . the opportunity of rehabilitating young offenders will be greater. I think also
> that the opportunity of punishing young offenders will be greater than under the
> present system . . .[52]

Nonetheless, Kaplan went largely unchallenged in stating his views about the
fundamental shift in direction of the new legislation, which would, as he put it,
"toughen the kiddie-court image of the juvenile court".[53] Perhaps nothing
captures this better, and illustrates the startling contrast to the *JDA* philosophy,
than Kaplan's justification for saying that the first principle of the *YOA*'s
Declaration of Principle — responsibility and accountability — should be
regarded as the most important of all the principles:

> . . . I prefer the first priority being given to the responsibility of the young person.
> After all, if the home has failed the young offender badly, if he comes from a family
> of criminals or a negligent family, he is still responsible for what he does; and the
> whole philosophy of this bill in comparison with the act which it is to replace is the
> increasing emphasis on the individual and his direct and personal responsibility and
> accountability for his offences. . . . A bad family is no defence.[54]

Further, in his final substantive statement to the House of Commons Committee
on Justice and Legal Affairs, Kaplan also signalled his intentions that the new
legislation be criminally focused and tough:

> . . . criminal responsibility is attributed in this act . . . . So to pussyfoot around by
> suggesting they are not criminally responsible for their acts takes us away from some
> of the purposes that we intend in this tougher approach to crime commited by young
> people . . .[55]

While Kaplan observed that the Bill enjoyed a large degree of support from all
sectors, including the media, the spirit of "national consensus" was, as the
Saskatchewan submission put it, broken at the federal/provincial level principally
as a result of substantive amendments the federal government introduced between
First and Third Readings in the House of Commons. These changes were many,
but those arousing most provincial opposition included: the uniform maximum
age of 18 years, regarded by several provinces as imposing unacceptable costs,
and the open/secure custody provisions, regarded by several provinces as an
unacceptable jurisdictional transfer of powers from the executive arm of (provincial) governments to the courts.

The need for a uniform maximum age was prompted by the adoption of the
Canadian Charter of Rights and Freedoms in 1982[56] and the pending (1985)
advent of the "equality" provisions of the *Charter*, which (it was argued) could

---

[52] House of Commons, *Minutes, supra*, note 49, Issue 67, at p. 15.

[53] *Ibid.*, at p. 81.

[54] *Ibid.*, Issue 69, at p. 8.

[55] *Ibid.*, Issue 71, at p. 107.

[56] *Canadian Charter of Rights and Freedoms*, Part I of the *Constitution Act, 1982*,
being Schedule B of the *Canada Act 1982* (U.K.), 1982, c. 11.

no longer tolerate different maximum ages set by the provinces. Kaplan acknowledged that the chosen maximum age of 18 years would be more costly, was arbitrary and that he had not been pressured by Quebec and Manitoba (which already had that age in effect) to choose the age of 18 years. It seems the selected age was very much a personal (ideological) decision; he simply thought it was "best" and the "proper way".[57] The origins of the open/secure custody provisions are less clear; these provisions are consistent with Justice Model principles — i.e., reduced administrative discretion — and are believed to have been prompted by private lobbying by the judiciary.

As well, provincial governments expressed concerns about a variety of matters, but foremost about unresolved cost-sharing formulas, the cost of the right to counsel provisions, anticipated costs and administrative difficulties implementing the records provisions of the Act, and the limited (initially two years) custodial sentence length available to the court. It was these themes, rather than the fundamental direction of the Act, that dominated the House of Commons Debates and which continued long after the Bill was passed by Parliament, leading to provincial opposition to proclamation and, once proclaimed, subsequent provincial lobbying for amendments.

To explain the sharp contrast between the consensus that emerged with the successful 1982 Act and the political and interest group divisions prompted by the failed 1970 Bill — and particularly the obviously waned influence of Welfare Model advocates in the intervening years — requires us to step back to examine trends that had emerged before and during this period. The 1960s and 1970s were a period during which the juvenile (and adult) justice and correctional systems became the subject of critical examination by legal scholars, academic theoreticians and social science researchers. These critics increasingly challenged discrepancies between the ideals and apparent realities of the juvenile justice system generally and, in particular, the bedrock of the Welfare Model — the assumed effectiveness of treatment.

During the 1960s, labelling theory[58] emerged; this theory postulated the notion of secondary deviance and argued that the juvenile justice system actually fosters further delinquency; i.e., the system itself is criminogenic. Simply put, the theory argues that when adolescents who engage in what many self-report studies confirm are normal mischievous and illegal behaviours are officially processed by the juvenile justice system, they may subsequently behave in keeping with their new-found official identity of being a delinquent. Labelling theory (however misunderstood and co-opted) quickly became widely accepted among senior bureaucrats and practitioners in the juvenile justice system and, arguably, has

---

[57] House of Commons, *Minutes, supra*, note 49, Issue 68, at p. 15-17.

[58] Becker, *Outsiders: Studies in the Sociology of Deviance* (New York: Free Press, 1963); Lemert, *Human Deviance, Social Problems and Social Control* (Englewood Cliffs, N.J.: Prentice-Hall, 1967).

even been widely accepted by the lay public. Labelling theories culminated in the
call for "radical non-intervention"[59] and laid the theoretical foundations for the
diversion and decriminalization movements of the 1970s in both Canada and the
United States. These theories were widely accepted by bureaucratic policy-
makers. The influences of labelling theories are legislatively reflected in the
YOA's abolition of (federal) status offences and its provisions for alternative
measures (diversion), as well as its endorsement of "taking no measures".[60]

In fact, the diversion and decriminalization implications of labelling theories
had already been translated into practice by some provinces well before the
YOA.[61] For example, during the early 1970s British Columbia instituted a
legislatively required scheme of universal consideration of all *Criminal Code* and
federal statute offenders for diversion,[62] while in 1977 Quebec's *Youth Protection
Act*[63] legislatively mandated an extensive system of diversion.[64] More modest
diversion schemes were also established in Manitoba and, to a lesser extent, other
provinces. Similarly, in the mid-1970s, initiatives were taken by some provinces
to abolish or at least limit the penalties for status offences. For example, British
Columbia, by policy, prohibited the prosecution of status offences and later
repealed the provincial statute offence of unmanageability, while Ontario's
Training Schools Act[65] was amended to prohibit direct committals to training
schools for status offences.

An arguably even more profound influence than labelling theory on juvenile
justice policy, however, would arise somewhat later with social scientific research
on the effectiveness of correctional treatment programs. By the time of the failure
of Bill C-192 in 1972, early critiques of the effectiveness of delinquency
prevention[66] and correctional treatment programs in the United States[67] and

---

[59] Schur, *Radical Nonintervention: Rethinking the Delinquency Problem*
(Englewood Cliffs, N.J.: Prentice-Hall, 1973).
[60] *Supra*, note 43.
[61] Osborne, "Juvenile Justice Policy in Canada: The Transfer of the Initiative"
(1979) (2) (1) Can. J. Fam. L. pp. 7-32.
[62] *Correction Act*, R.S.B.C. 1970, c. 10, s. 6 [now R.S.B.C. 1979, c. 70, s. 5].
[63] *Youth Protection Act*, S.Q. 1977, c. 20.
[64] Trepanier, "The Quebec Youth Protection Act: Institutionalized Diversion" in
Corrado, LeBlanc and Trépanier, eds., *Current Issues in Juvenile Justice*
(Toronto: Butterworths, 1982).
[65] *The Training Schools Amendment Act*, S.O. 1975, c. 21.
[66] For example, see Witmer and Tufts, The Effectiveness of Delinquency Prevention Programs (Washington, D.C.: U.S. Department of Health, Education, and
Welfare, Government Printing Office, 1954).
[67] For example, see Bailey, "Correctional Outcome: An Evaluation of 100
Reports" (1966) (57) (2) *J. Crim. Law, Criminol. and Pol. Science*, pp.
153-60.

Canada[68] were not well publicized and were little known outside academic circles. This would change, however, with the well-known and devastating "nothing works" critique of correctional treatment programs by Martinson[69] and Lipton, Martinson and Wilks.[70] The impact of this new research and the consequent decline of the rehabilitative ideal throughout the 1970s has been extensively detailed by Allen.[71] While the "nothing works" doctrine was eventually recanted to some degree by Martinson and challenged with some success by critics such as Palmer[72] and Ross and Gendreau,[73] welfare proponents nonetheless could no longer uncritically claim the success of their rehabilitation programs. The attack went far beyond a mere challenge to effectiveness. If rehabilitation programs did not work, or could not be shown to work, then the care and treatment administered to delinquents really amounted to a kind of misguided benevolence that masked real punishment. As well, because of the vast amount of discretion available in the Welfare Model system, treatment resulted in intolerable coercion, injustices and disparities. Moreover, a Welfare system that could not deliver on its promise of rehabilitation did not protect the public.

The impact of this critical questioning of rehabilitation programs profoundly influenced policy-makers in Canada and elsewhere. Disillusionment set in.[74] The extent of this disillusionment with the Welfare Model is reflected by then-Solicitor General Robert Kaplan in the parliamentary debates: "even the most critical briefs expressed satisfaction that the *JDA* is about to be put into history".[75] If the juvenile justice system could not "do good", it could at least "do justice". As a result, many abandoned the Welfare Model, and a new kind of "child saver" emerged — the Justice Model advocate — this time trying to save delinquents from the very system that was originally designed to help them. As Cohen puts it:

---

[68] Outerbridge, "The Tyranny of Treatment. . .?" (1968) (10) (2) *Can. J. Corr.* pp. 378-387.

[69] Martinson, "What Works?: Questions and Answers About Prison Reform" (1974) (35) (1) *The Public Interest*, pp. 22-51.

[70] Lipton, Martinson and Wilks, *The Effectiveness of Correctional Treatment: A Survey of Treatment Evaluations* (New York: Praeger, 1975)

[71] Allen, *The Decline of the Rehabilitative Ideal* (New Haven, Conn.: Yale University Press, 1981).

[72] Palmer, *Correctional Intervention and Research* (Toronto: Heath, 1978).

[73] See: Gendreau and Ross, "Revivification of rehabilitation: Evidence from the 1980's" (1987) (4) (3) Justice Q. pp. 349-408 and Ross and Gendreau, *Effective Correctional Treatment* (Toronto: Butterworths, 1980).

[74] Corrado, "Introduction", in Corrado, LeBlanc and Trépanier, eds., *Current Issues in Juvenile Justice* (Toronto: Butterworths, 1983).

[75] House of Commons. *Minutes of the Proceedings and Evidence of the Standing Committee on Justice and Legal Affairs*, Issue 61 (Ottawa: House of Commons, 1981-82-83) at p. 5.

The liberal left "capitulated", thinking that if the state could not be trusted to do good and if doing good anyway had ambiguous results, then we should, at least, let the system be fair, just, open and safe from abuse. So came the birth of the "Justice Model" or the "back to justice" movement.[76]

Given this tidal change in thinking, it should come as no surprise that the almost total abandonment of the Welfare Model and the emergence of the principles of responsibility and accountability arose in the Canadian legislative reform proposals of the mid-and late 1970s. After all, the various committees, federal/provincial forums and reports were staffed and fashioned by senior civil servants who were, generally speaking, well aware of the recent critical research and new thinking (and, accordingly, would advise or influence their political masters). Nor, too, should one be surprised at the obviously diminished voices and influence of Welfare Model advocates — contrasting sharply with the 1970 experience — in the parliamentary debates of 1982.

This is not to say that the transformation of Canadian juvenile justice legislation has necessarily followed a simple "progress model" — the belief that reform is simply a function of advances in knowledge.[77] It matters little whether these advances in knowledge are indeed "advances" (i.e., correct or not). But in the bureaucratic and political environment in which legislative reform is fashioned, it matters a great deal what the key actors — senior bureaucrats and legislators — believe and, accordingly, what weight is given to the views of various interest groups.

Although the virtual abandonment of the Welfare Model seems explainable, the emergence of the protection of society principle in the 1979 proposals and the often-times tough rhetoric of the parliamentary debates, which smack more of a Crime Control orientation, are more difficult to explain. The protection of society, of course, is traditionally a central principle of criminal justice. Its emergence during a Conservative federal government administration should therefore not be surprising. As well, the sometimes blurred boundaries and linkages between the Justice and Crime Control Models may also account for this more conservative posturing. In this regard, the Justice Model advocates not only the principles of the restraint of the criminal law, rights and due process, but also embraces punishment (albeit fair and proportionate). Once punishment is embraced, however, it takes little to move beyond this to the advocacy of public protection through, for example, general deterrence, "short, sharp, shocks" and incapacitation. (And it is this kind of potential slippage — as well as its preoccupation with process — that is perhaps our primary concern about the Justice Model.)

As well, it is likely that broader social events, which led to a shift to greater public and political conservatism in Canada (and elsewhere) in the later 1970s and early 1980s, had some influence on the direction of juvenile justice reform. These

---

[76] Cohen, *Visions of Social Control: Crime, Punishment and Classification* (Newark, N.J.: Basil Blackwell, 1985) at p. 288.
[77] *Ibid.*

broader influences, for example, included ongoing economic difficulties such as "stagflation" and severe recession; increasing questioning of the role and effectiveness (and costs) of the welfare state generally; the emergence and increasing visibility of "victim rights" and similar "law and order" interest groups; the emergence of Reaganism in the United States and Thatcherism in Britain; and lingering public concerns about rebellious youth cultures. While these economic, political, and social changes undoubtedly influenced the social and political climate in which the new Canadian juvenile justice reforms were fashioned and enacted, a direct linkage between these changes and the more conservative aspects of the *YOA* cannot be made. For example, in spite of these social changes, there still was not a public outcry for, nor ideologically inspired political or media intrusion into, the reform process, which remained a largely publicly invisible debate among senior bureaucrats and professional interest groups. Rather than directly affecting the reform process, these changing social circumstances likely fostered a social and political climate in which tougher criminal legislation and tougher political rhetoric would be more likely to flourish.

Osborne has argued that because of the long delays in achieving the reform of Canadian juvenile justice legislation, the initiative for reform during the 1970s shifted from the federal government to the provinces.[78] While modest changes were made in several provinces, the key provinces of British Columbia and Quebec underwent the most radical changes.

British Columbia's experience appears to be one of the few (if only) examples of a "top down" (i.e., politically initiated) juvenile justice reform process in Canada.[79] British Columbia's transformation (largely) began with the election of Dave Barrett's (socialist-oriented) New Democratic Party in 1972. Barrett, a former prison social worker, and other key Cabinet ministers had an ideological interest in radical deinstitutionalization and transformation of the juvenile justice system. As a result, all sentenced secure custody programs were abolished in the province. As well, a universal diversion system, community-based alternatives to custody, and bureaucratic constraints on transfers to adult court and prosecutions of status offences were introduced.[80] However, with the defeat of the Barrett government and subsequent election of the (conservative) Social Credit party in 1975, as well as public outcries about juvenile offenders running amuck in the

---

[78] Osborne, *supra*, note 61.
[79] Ekstedt, "History of Juvenile Containment Policy in British Columbia in Corrado, LeBlanc and Trépanier, eds., *Current Issues in British Columbia* (Toronto: Butterworths, 1982).
[80] See, for example, Ekstedt, *Ibid.*; Markwart, "Youth Containment in British Columbia, paper presented to the Canadian Sociology and Anthropology Association, Learned Societies Conference, Halifax, Nova Scotia, May 1982; and MacDonald, "Juvenile Training Schools and Juvenile Justice Policy in British Columbia (1978) (20) (3) Can. J. Crim. pp. 418-36.

community, a new "containment" (secure custody) program was introduced in 1977. The new system became very much oriented along the lines of Justice Model principles — the focus shifted to the offence and the control and containment, without any accompanying rehabilitation rhetoric, of "hard-core" young offenders. As well, the administration of juvenile correctional services was severed from child welfare services.

In the late 1970s, Quebec, with its *Youth Protection Act*, also radically transformed its juvenile justice system, limiting the prosecution of juveniles under 14 years of age, introducing an extensive screening and diversion system, and introducing new procedural measures to better safeguard the rights of young persons. Most importantly, however, the Quebec juvenile justice service system remained integrated at the administrative and service delivery level with the child welfare system, maintaining and even strengthening the treatment focus and rehabilitative goals of the system.[81]

It is true then that these key provinces did take the initiative in juvenile justice reform, but they moved in decidedly different directions. Although there was a commonality between the two provinces in terms of the extensive use of diversion and in limiting the range of juveniles who could be prosecuted, British Columbia's offence-based containment system administered by correctional authorities stands in sharp contrast to Quebec's integrated treatment-oriented system administered by social service personnel. It has been argued that Quebec had largely implemented the *YOA* well before it became law;[82] interestingly, the same view prevails in British Columbia. As we will observe in our discussion of the organizational response to the *YOA*, it seems, however, that other provinces have tended to follow British Columbia's pre-*YOA* lead in implementation of the new Act.

Given these differences in direction taken by the provinces, it cannot be said that the provinces actually took the lead and therefore prompted changes in federal legislation. Further, with the exception of British Columbia's early experiment with deinstitutionalization, most of the substantive provincial changes arose in the latter part of the 1970s; i.e., at a time when the direction of change at the federal level had already crystalized. Indeed, it could be argued that the provinces, with their persistent concerns about jurisdictional and cost-sharing matters, were significant obstacles to federal reform.

In summary, the long process of juvenile justice reform in Canada has been influenced by a variety of factors, but critical among these have been the role of senior bureaucrats, federal/provincial relationships and interests, professional

---

[81] See, for example, Trépanier, *supra*, note 64, and LeBlanc and Beaumont, "The Quebec Perspective on the Young Offenders Act: Implementation Before Adoption" in Hudson, Hornick and Burrows in *Justice and the Young Offender in Canada* (Toronto: Wall and Thompson, 1988).
[82] LeBlanc and Beaumont, *ibid*.

interest groups and the influence of criminological/legal theory and research. Largely absent from this reform process were political ideology and public concerns. There are signs, however, that the process of reform in the post-*YOA* era may be beginning to change.

Amending the Act: A Drift to Crime Control?

Since the *YOA* was proclaimed into force on April 2, 1984, there has been considerable provincial opposition to various aspects of the Act and, generally, increasing public concern.

The resistance of several provincial governments, largely based on unresolved cost-sharing concerns and the need for further time to adjust administrative and service delivery systems, initially delayed the new law from coming into force. Once proclaimed, intense lobbying by several provincial governments continued during the first implementation year (1984) to delay or alter the coming into force of the costly uniform maximum age provisions on April 1, 1985, but to no avail. Even though the Conservative Party, while in opposition in 1982, was very critical of the Liberal government's selected age of 18 years, it was the Conservative Party, elected in 1984, which decided to let the maximum age provision come into force without change on April 1, 1985. It seems there was little choice. With the equality provisions of the *Canadian Charter of Rights and Freedoms* scheduled to come into force in April 1985, it was commonly accepted that a uniform age needed to be established. The only other choice would have been to bring a Bill before Parliament and lower the maximum age, a change which could possibly have alienated the province of Quebec, which was an ardent supporter of the new law and already had long established a maximum age of 18 years under the *JDA*. Quebec, of course, is a powerful influence in the Canadian confederation and also at the time was a principal source of federal Conservative Party political power.

Lobbying by several provinces to amend the other provisions of the Act also continued from the outset of implementation. Several of these provincial proposals reflected concerns carried over from the parliamentary debates noted earlier (for example, open/secure custody), and ongoing federal/provincial forums were established to address these.[83] Ontario and British Columbia, two of the three most powerful voices (along with Quebec), took the lead at these forums.[84]

Eventually, these federal/provincial conferences resulted in a first round of amendments passed by Parliament in 1986 (Bill C-106),[85] a second round of

[83] Coflin, "The Federal Government's Role in Implementing the Young Offenders Act" in Hudson, Hornick and Burrows, eds., *Justice and the Young Offender in Canada* (Toronto: Wall and Thompson, 1988).

[84] Alan Markwart was a direct participant in these federal/provincial forums.

[85] *An Act to Amend the Young Offenders Act, the Criminal Code, the Penitentiary Act and the Prison and Reformatories Act* (Bill C-106), S.C. 1984-85-86, c. 32.

amendments initiated by Bill C-12 (formerly Bill C-58[86]), tabled in late 1989, and a planned third round of public consultations and amendments scheduled for late 1991 and 1992. What is notable about these amendments is that they have virtually all concerned matters of enforcement and public safety. This is not to say that these amendments have been, by any means, Draconian in nature — they have, in fact, been modest — but they do seem to reflect a continuing shift along the spectrum to Crime Control considerations. The provinces, often strongly influenced by Crown counsel and police interests, have certainly been very instrumental in shaping the amendment agenda. What is also notable, however, is the role the public and media have played in bringing political pressure to bear to amend the Act, especially with respect to Bill C-12, which addresses the provisions for transfer to adult court and the maximum penalties for juvenile murderers.

Bortner describes "moral panic" as the ability of the media to create fear among the public by presenting images of rampant and ever-escalating juvenile crime, even though this is not necessarily substantiated by official statistics.[87] Youth crime is presented as a phenomenon out of control and the public as unable to protect itself. There is certainly strong evidence that the Canadian public of the late 1980s and early 1990s substantially misperceives, not with young offenders specifically but with crime in general, the extent and treatment of crime. In a review of previous public surveys and current surveys of its own, the Canadian Sentencing Commission found that the public: believes crime rates are higher than they are; over-estimates the degree of recidivism of offenders; underestimates the maximum prescribed sentencing penalties; and underestimates the severity of actual sentencing penalties.[88] Critically, the Commission also found that 95 percent of the survey respondents cited their sources of information as the news media. A content analysis of newspaper crime stories found that crimes of violence were the most common subjects and were represented far in excess of the proportion these types of crimes comprise of actual crimes in general. As well, earlier studies of public perceptions have indicated that Canadians grossly over-estimate the amount of crime involving violence.[89]

Since the proclamation of the YOA, young offenders have attracted a great deal of attention in the news media as a result of a number of sensational incidents, notably in Ontario (but also in other provinces) and particularly concerning juvenile gangs and murderers. While the sensational incidents that have been

---

[86] An Act to Amend the Young Offenders Act and the Criminal Code (Bill C-12), 3rd Session 34th Parliament, 1990.

[87] Bortner, Delinquency and Justice: An Age of Crisis (Toronto: McGraw-Hill, 1988).

[88] The Canadian Sentencing Commission, Sentencing Reform: A Canadian Approach (Ottawa: Minister of Supply and Services Canada, 1987).

[89] Doob and Roberts, Crime and the Official Response to Crime: The View of the Canadian Public (Ottawa: Department of Justice, 1987).

widely reported are too numerous to cite, a few examples include: the escape of a dangerous young offender in Orangeville, Ontario, causing public alarm because publication restrictions precluded warning of the public; a 14-year-old Ontario youth who murdered three members of his family and received the maximum penalty of three years' youth custody; the murder of a group home worker by a female young offender in Midland, Ontario; a mass escape from a Toronto detention centre culminating in the deaths of several of the escapees in an accident arising from a police chase; the hatchet murder of a foster family by two adolescents in a Vancouver suburb; and the murder of a younger child by a 13-year-old in a Vancouver suburb that was not discovered for several months even though many of his adolescent associates (allegedly) were aware of the crime. In Manitoba the initially successful appeals of convictions in the case of a young offender who had sexually assaulted and murdered a three-year-old child led to the formation of a citizen's group to petition the federal government to amend the Act. In Toronto, one newspaper printed coupons that the public could complete and mail to the federal Minister of Justice in support of amendments to the Act.

As well, media reports have tended to focus on the emergence of youth gangs, crack cocaine and associated violence, such as "swarming" and "drive-by" shootings, in the major metropolitan centres of Toronto, Vancouver and Montreal. In a review of the stories published in *The Toronto Star* in the first week of December 1990, we found at least one article relating to youth crime every day. Several of these were sensational — for example, the shooting of a senior citizen in the eye; a Toronto Police Commission hearing being told that seniors increasingly live in fear of violence and that a war on drugs should be proclaimed; and claims of an epidemic of violence in the popular media, decreased compassion amongst young people, and increased levels of violence in high schools. In March 1991, *Maclean's Magazine* (the Canadian equivalent to *Time Magazine*) joined in the media attention with a cover story on youth gangs entitled "Terror in the Streets".

In general, these kinds of media stories have fostered impressions among the public (shared by many in the justice community) that violent juvenile crime is extensive and increasing, and that the Act is "soft" on juvenile offenders. These impressions have the cumulative effect of increasing public and political pressures to address the problem. The possible effects of these media impressions may be evident in an early 1992 Gallup poll which found that the fundamental premise of the juvenile justice system — special provisions for young offenders — is now questioned by the Canadian public: 48 percent of respondents indicated that young offenders should be tried in courts in the same way as adults versus 47 percent who believed there should be special provisions for accused young offenders. In Ontario and the four Western provinces a majority of respondents believed young offenders should be tried in the same way as adults, but this was not the case in Quebec and the Atlantic provinces.[90] The Crime Control constituency — the

---

[90] The Canadian Press, "Poll Finds Draw on Special Court for the Young." *Times-Colonist*, January 6, 1992.

police, Crown counsel and the increasingly influential "victim rights" groups, naturally capitalize on these forces, and provincial politicans, eager to foist the problem on the federal government, consequently urge amendments to federal legislation.

It is evident that these conservative influences were reflected in the 1986 amendments to the Act, virtually all of which (putting aside technical matters) addressed issues of enforcement and public safety. They included the creation of the new section 26 offence of breach of a community disposition and the application of the *Criminal Code* escape custody provisions; alteration of the publication prohibitions to permit the public identification of dangerous young offenders; allowing a consecutive custodial sentence beyond the three-year limit to be imposed in certain specified circumstances; creating a new offence in the *Criminal Code* of counselling children under 12 years of age to commit a crime; providing that the record of a young offender acquitted by reason of insanity be able to be retained; and relaxing the records provisions such that only non-disclosure rather than destruction of records is required. One exception to this conservative trend in 1986 was, in response to provincial concerns about increasing custody rates, a change in the sentencing criteria for open custody (section 24) in an effort to restrain the use of this sanction. This, however, proved to be, as is discussed in Chapter 5, a weak and ineffectual change.

Similar shifts are evident in the 1989 Bill C-12 (formerly Bill C-58) passed by the House of Commons in November 1991 which is designed to address the problem of juvenile murderers. This Bill provides that: the criteria for transfer to adult court be changed such that the protection of society becomes the paramount consideration when the court cannot reconcile the (competing) interests of society and the rehabilitation of the young person; that the youth disposition for murder (if not transferred to adult court) be increased to five years less a day (including a period of conditional supervision which may be "gated"); and, if transferred to adult court, that a young person convicted of murder, while still receiving life imprisonment, will be eligible for an earlier release on parole than would an adult. While the latter proposal may seem to be a move in the other direction, it may in fact result in an increased number of transfers to adult court since, with a more moderate penalty available in the adult system, judges will be more inclined to transfer alleged juvenile murderers to adult court.

Other amendments which address enforcement and public safety also appear to be in the offing. For example, in 1989 provincial Attorneys General unanimously resolved that the strict provisions (section 56) in the Act governing the admissibility of a young person's statements (confessions) to the police should be relaxed to some degree. They also resolved that, where the court authorizes an early release from custody, that this release be in the form of "conditional supervision" (like parole), which would enhance enforcement capability.[91] Mea-

---

[91] Department of Justice, *The Young Offenders Act: Proposals for Amendment* (Consultation Document) (Ottawa: Department of Justice, 1989).

sures to address violent young offenders other than murderers also remain on the longer-term federal/provincial agenda. As well, Ontario and British Columbia have urged amendments to permit the prosecution of offenders under the age of 12 years.

In detailing these actual and proposed amendments, it is not necessarily suggested that these changes are unnecessary or inappropriate, but only to observe that there has been a decided movement toward Crime Control concerns. Nor can it be said that these actual and proposed amendments have been harsh. The proposed Canadian penalties for juvenile murderers, for example, stand in stark contrast to the many juvenile murderers waiting on Death Row in several American states. The political need to seek accommodations — arising from the give-and-take nature of federal/provincial negotiations and from federal consultations with interest groups with often divergent points of view — militates against resorting to extreme measures in Canadian juvenile justice reform.

While there seems to have been a drift toward Crime Control concerns in national juvenile justice policy in the late 1980s and early 1990s, it is entirely unclear whether this will continue to be the case. Demographic trends such as increasing immigration and a growing adolescent population (the "echo boom") during the 1990s, along with an aging and likely more conservative population, all suggest that Crime Control concerns may well continue. Competing interests are, however, also at work. For example, public consultations on federal proposals to introduce much stricter legislative criteria for custody, lengthened temporary absences from custody and more effective court review (early release) mechanisms began in 1991. While these reform efforts, largely urged by provincial correctional authorities and child advocacy groups, may well be resisted by Crime Control advocates (and, perhaps, the judiciary), the voices of child advocacy and affiliated groups, several of which are represented at the "*YOA* Table",[92] still remain influential in juvenile justice policy formulation. Further, political considerations such as the recent election of left wing New Democratic Party governments — apparently more sympathetic to child advocacy concerns — in Ontario, British Columbia and Saskatchewan as well as the withdrawal of Quebec from all federal/provincial negotiations (in response to the failure of the Meech Lake Accord), will likely change the landscape of federal/provincial negotiations.

OFFICIAL DELINQUENCY IN CANADA: IS VIOLENT JUVENILE CRIME INCREASING?

As discussed previously, there has been a significant amount of public and media concern about a perceived increasing degree of juvenile crime, particularly violent crime, in recent years. These concerns seem to have been, in part at least, instrumental in prompting complaints about the inadequacies of the new legislation and consequently have been influential in bringing about amendments that

---

[92] Coflin, *supra*, note 83.

have been almost entirely oriented to public safety and enforcement matters. Are these concerns justified? This section examines available official delinquency statistics with a view to ascertaining the extent of reported and processed juvenile crime and the types of those crimes, particularly focusing on the extent and proportion of violent juvenile crime.

This analysis is necessarily limited to "official" delinquency statistics reported in Canada through police crime, the Youth Court Survey and other provincial correctional and court data sources. These data do not, of course, describe the actual extent and nature of juvenile crime in Canada. In this regard, numerous self-report studies have consistently indicated that the vast majority of adolescents have been involved in delinquencies. It is also well established that the extent of official crime reported and processed is significantly affected by a variety of factors, including, among others, the willingness of victims to report crimes and the discretion exercised in screening offenders throughout the system — for example, police discretion to charge, prosecutional discretion and alternative measures. This limitation is, however, of little consequence since the interest here is in how the system established by the *YOA* affects the way in which juvenile offenders are processed. Since the jurisdiction of the *YOA* is limited to *Criminal Code* and other federal statute offences, so too is the data used in the analysis.

Unfortunately, there is no comparable data available which can establish long-term trends concerning the extent of juvenile crime across Canada because police crime statistics (the Uniform Crime Reporting Survey) do not categorize young offenders by age. The implementation of the uniform maximum age (UMA) of (under) 18 years in 1985, and consequent great increases in the number of young people falling under the jurisdiction of the new Act in most provinces, therefore, confounds time series comparisons before and after the UMA. Such comparisons would, in jurisdictions where the former age limit was (under) 16 years, indicate a more than doubling of juvenile crime, but this is precisely because (as youth court statistics confirm) 16- and 17-year-olds comprise a substantial majority of those processed by the juvenile justice system. For example, in Ontario the Phase I (under 16 years of age) youth court system accounts for less than one-half (46 percent) of the total number of juveniles processed by the court in that province.[93] In short, these apparent "increases" in juvenile crime are an artifact of the re-definition of the age jurisdiction of the Act.

There are, however, comparable police crime data available for the period from 1986[94] to 1988, as presented in Table 1. This table indicates, unsurprisingly, that

---

[93] Moyer, "*A Description of the Application of Dispositions Under the Young Offenders Act by the Ministry of Community and Social Services of Ontario.* (Toronto: Department of Justice, 1989).

[94] Because police data is reported on a calendar year basis and the UMA was implemented partway through (April) the 1985 calendar year, 1985 cannot be used as a base year.

TABLE 1

Number of Young Persons Charged by
the Police, by Offence Type,
Canada, 1986 to 1988

Total Accused

Type of Offence	*1986* Number (%)	*1987* Number (%)	*1988* Number (%)
Crimes of Violence	9,275 (8.2%)	10,165 (9.1%)	11,385 (10.0%)
Property Crimes	78,862 (69.8%)	74,769 (66.9%)	74,285 (65.1%)
Other Criminal Code	20,869 (18.5%)	22,764 (20.4%)	24,165 (21.2%)
Drugs	3,568 (3.1%)	3,265 (2.9%)	3,273 (2.9%)
Other Federal Statutes	453 (0.4%)	768 (0.7%)	923 (0.8%)
TOTAL	113,027	111,731	114,035

Source: Statistics Canada, Canadian Centre for Justice Statistics, Uniform Crime Reports, 1986, 1987, 1988.

property offences remain the staple of juvenile offenders, comprising two-thirds of all juvenile charges. Other *Criminal Code* offences account for about 20 percent of the total, followed by crimes of violence[95] at about 10 percent and drug offences at about 3 percent. In terms of types of property offences (not shown in the table), theft under $1,000 accounts for nearly one-third of all criminal offences and breaking and entering nearly one-quarter.[96] Across provinces (not shown), there was little variation in the proportion of these types of offences.

While the time period presented in Table 1 is much too short to establish consistent trends over time, it nonetheless indicates that the total number of juveniles charged remained stable over the three-year period. Among offence categories, however, the volume of juveniles charged with crimes of violence increased by a sizeable amount — 19 percent. While this increase may suggest some support for those who are concerned about increasing violent crime by juveniles, it should be put into context. "Crimes of violence" here include: homicide, attempted murder, sexual assault, non-sexual assaults, other sexual offences, robbery and related offences. In 1988, nearly three-quarters of these crimes of violence were non-sexual assaults, the majority of which were common assaults. Whether these can be considered, qualitatively, real "crimes of violence" — or the kinds of crimes the public is alarmed about — is seriously open to question. Putting these non-sexual assaults aside, in 1988 juveniles charged with homicides accounted for 0.04 percent of the total, attempted murder 0.05 percent sexual assaults 1.1 percent, other sexual offences 0.1 percent and robbery 1.5 percent — all miniscule proportions.

One would expect that, because of their serious nature, violent offences are more likely to be prosecuted (as opposed to diverted) than non-violent offences. Similarly, one would expect that violent offences are more likely to attract a custodial disposition or result in a transfer to adult court. Therefore, it would be expected that violent offences would comprise a larger proportion of prosecuted juvenile court cases, custodial committals, and transfers to adult court than would arise with police charges. Court and correctional data do confirm that this is the case. Nonetheless, violent offences still comprise a relatively small proportion of court and custodial cases, and even transfer cases. In this regard, Table 2 describes the number of cases heard in youth courts by most serious type of offence from 1986–87 to 1988–89.[97] (Again, 1986–87 is used as a base year to account for the implementation of the UMA in 1985 and its transitional effects). This table indicates that violent offences accounted for only 13.5 percent of youth court cases in 1988–89, while property offences accounted for 60 percent of

---

[95] These offences include categories such as mischief, obstruction of a peace officer, prostitution, arson, gaming and betting and so forth.

[96] Statistics Canada, "Youth Crime in Canada, 1986-88" (1990) (10)(2) *Juristat Services Bulletin* (Ottawa: Canadian Centre for Justice Statistics).

[97] Ontario does not report data to the Youth Court Survey.

TABLE 2

Number and Proportion of Cases Heard in Youth Courts by Type of Most Serious Offence, 1986–87 to 1988–89

Offence Type	1986–87 Number (%)	1987–88 Number (%)	1988–89 Number (%)
Violent	6,619 (12.7%)	6,654 (12.2%)	7,256 (13.5%)
Property	35,070 (67.4%)	33,444 (61.3%)	32,416 (60.2%)
Other Criminal Code	6,481 (12.5%)	7,400 (13.6%)	7,118 (13.2%)
Drugs	2,269 (4.4%)	2,087 (3.8%)	1,840 (3.4%)
Other Federal Statutes	1,574 (3.0%)	5,003 (9.2%)	5,189 (9.6%)
TOTAL	52,013	54,588	53,819

Source: Statistics Canada, Canadian Centre for Justice Statistics, Youth Court Survey, 1986–87, 1987–88, 1988–89.

cases. In terms of changes over time, the total volume of cases remained stable, while the volume of violent offences increased modestly (9 percent) from 1987–88 to 1988–89. Here too, though, the time frame is too short to establish a trend.[98] Common assaults alone comprised more than one-third of the "violent" offences in 1988–89, whereas the general category of non-sexual assaults comprised 65 percent of all violent offences. The relative lack of seriousness of these supposedly violent non-sexual assault cases is, perhaps, reflected in the fact that nearly 80 percent resulted in a non-custodial disposition in 1988–89.[99] Further, it would be expected that violent offences would account for the vast majority of transfers to adult court, but this is not the case: more than two-thirds of transfer cases do not involve a violent offence.[100]

Turning to custodial committals, data from the Youth Court Survey for 1987–88 indicates that in Canada as a whole (Ontario not reporting) only 15 percent of secure custody and 12 percent of open custody committals were for violent offences — i.e., the vast majority of young offenders are committed to custody for non-violent crimes, again largely (approximately three-fifths) for property offences (see Chapter 5). Separate data for the Ontario youth custody population (Phase I) in 1987–88 indicates a somewhat higher proportion of admissions are for violent offences — 23.6 percent of the secure custody population, and 17.5 percent of the open custody population.[101] In contrast, in British Columbia only 13.6 percent of secure custody admissions and 13 percent of open custody admissions in 1988–89 were for violent offences.[102]

It was earlier indicated that, given the effects of the UMA, reliable time series comparisons of Canadian police data could not be made. Some comparisons can be made with two provinces, however — specifically Quebec and Manitoba — since these provinces were unaffected by the UMA. In this regard, Table 3 describes the volume of violent and non-violent juvenile offences dealt with by the police in these two provinces from 1980 to 1988. As this table indicates, juvenile offences in total in these provinces have not increased; rather, the volume has remained relatively stable in Manitoba and has declined markedly in Quebec. Interestingly, this change in Quebec is solely attributable to a decline in non-

---

[98] One significant change is the sharp rise in the volume of other federal statute offences, largely s. 26 *YOA* offences from 1986-87 to 1987-88. This was attributable to the s. 26 *YOA* amendment, proclaimed partway through 1986-87.

[99] Statistics Canada, "Violent Offences by Young Offenders, 1986-87 to 1988-89 (1990) (10) (15) *Juristat Services Bulletin* (Ottawa: Canadian Centre for Justice Statistics).

[100] Department of Justice, *supra*, note 91.

[101] Moyer, *supra*, note 93.

[102] Markwart, *A Description of the Application of Dispositions Under the Young Offenders Act in the Province of British Columbia* (Ottawa: Canadian Centre for Justice Statistics, 1989).

TABLE 3

Young Offenders Dealt with By the Police,[1] by Offence Type
1980 to 1988

Year	Quebec			Manitoba		
	Violent	Non-Violent Criminal Code	Total	Violent	Non-Violent Criminal Code	Total
1980	2,417 (6%)	38,442	40,859	586 (6%)	9,317	9,903
1981	2,433 (6%)	39,501	41,934	633 (6%)	9,989	10,622
1982	2,348 (6%)	35,717	38,244	536 (6%)	8,113	8,818
1983	2,173 (6%)	36,365	38,538	724 (7%)	8,939	9,663
1984	1,883 (7%)	26,201	28,084	768 (8%)	8,371	9,139
1985	2,084 (7%)	27,324	29,408	819 (8%)	8,864	9,863
1986	1,890 (7%)	24,512	26,402	891 (8%)	9,846	10,737
1987	2,190 (9%)	22,495	24,685	756 (9%)	7,397	8,153
1988	2,600 (10%)	22,169	24,769	976 (10%)	8,327	9,303

Source: Statistics Canada, Canadian Centre for Justice Statistics Uniform Crime Reports, 1980 to 1988.

[1]Refers to juveniles both charged or dealt with informally by the police.

violent offences coinciding with proclamation of the *YOA* in 1984. This change may be attributable to police reaction to the new Act, a matter we will discuss later.

With respect to types of offences, non-violent offences, of course, are most common, comprising 90 percent or more of offences in each year in both provinces. In Quebec, the volume of violent offences generally declined from 1980 to 1986, but then reached a peak in 1988. A one-year peak, of course, does not indicate a trend. This is not the case in Manitoba, however, where there has been a more consistent and substantial increase in violent offences in recent years. For example, the volume of violent offences in the 1986–88 period represents a 49 percent increase over the 1980–82 period (and when one considers that the adolescent population diminished during this period, then the increase in rate is even greater). These patterns are generally confirmed by the data in Table 4, which describes the volume of young persons appearing in youth courts by most serious offence type in Quebec and Manitoba during the *YOA* years 1984–85 to 1988–89, but there is one notable exception — the number of young persons appearing in Manitoba youth courts for violent offences in 1988–89 declined quite markedly. Given this, the evidence respecting violent offences in Manitoba is somewhat inconsistent.

With respect to homicides committed by persons under 18 years of age — a matter that has captured a great deal of public attention — an analysis by Silverman for the period from 1974 to 1986 indicates that there has been no increase during this time; in fact, the trend has been slightly downward.[103] A more recent report on homicides in Canada in 1989 indicates that juveniles under 18 years of age accounted for only 9 percent of all homicides, a proportion fairly close to the average for the previous 10 years.[104]

In summary, then — and although there are some inconsistencies — there does indeed appear to be some evidence to suggest that there have been some increases in officially reported and processed violent offences committed by juveniles in recent years. Notwithstanding this, crimes of violence account for only a small proportion and small volume of offences processed by the juvenile justice system under the *YOA* (and, if one considers provincial and municipal statute offences processed under provincial legislation, an even smaller proportion). A significant proportion of crimes of "violence" are, in fact, common assault charges and therefore many likely do not result in substantial harm to the victim. As well, it is adult offenders, not juveniles, who account for the overwhelming majority of crimes of violence in Canada: adults accounted for 88 percent of the violent crimes processed by the police in 1989.[105]

---

[103] Silverman, "Trends in Canadian youth justice: Some unanticipated consequences of a change in law." (1990) (32) (4) Can. J. Crim.

[104] Statistics Canada, "Homicide in Canada" (1990) (10) (14) *Juristat Services Bulletin* (Ottawa: Canadian Centre for Justice Statistics).

[105] Statistics Canada, "Violent Crime in Canada" (1990) (10) (15) *Juristat Services Bulletin* (Ottawa: Canadian Centre for Justice Statistics).

TABLE 4

Number of Young Persons Appearing in Youth Court by Type of Principal Charge 1984–85 to 1988–89

Year	Quebec			Manitoba		
	Violent	Non-Violent	Total	Violent	Non-Violent	Total
1984-85	990 (19%)	4,088	5,078	698 (18%)	3,259	3,955
1985-86	1,222 (20%)	4,747	5,969	832 (21%)	3,128	3,960
1986–87	1,233 (21%)	4,536	5,769	928 (24%)	2,895	3,823
1987–88	1,206 (23%)	4,106	5,312	943 (22%)	3,328	4,271
1988–89	1,484 (28%)	3,826	5,310	726 (21%)	2,789	3,515

Source: Statistics Canada, Canadian Centre for Justice Statistics Youth Court Survey, 1984–85 to 1988–89.

This is not to say that violent crimes committed by juveniles, and their apparent increasing rate, are not cause for concern. Of course, they are. Rather, the obvious point is that, as under the *JDA*, the juvenile justice system under the *YOA* continues to be overwhelmingly occupied with the processing of non-violent crimes no matter which component of the system is examined — police charges, youth court cases and even custody committals and transfers to adult court. Certainly, increases in violent crimes cannot account for the apparently great increases in committals to custody in several provinces under the *YOA* discussed by Markwart in Chapter 5: the vast majority of young persons committed to custody under the *YOA* continue to be non-violent offenders. It seems, however, that media-fostered concerns about violent crimes by juveniles have hardened attitudes toward juvenile crime generally among the public and key juvenile justice decision-makers. The great increase in public and political concern does not appear to be warranted by the relatively small volumes and proportions of violent crimes attributed to juveniles, and the relatively modest increases in violence. Moreover, other significant concerns — increased custody and court delays, for example — have tended to be obscured by this public and political preoccuption with violent juvenile crime.

Before leaving this section, it should be noted that there are substantial variations in officially reported crime rates across the provinces, as described in Table 5. This table indicates that crime rates are lowest in the Atlantic provinces and Quebec, the Ontario crime rate approximates the Canadian average, and crime rates are highest in the prairie provinces and British Columbia. The crime rate in the western provinces is nearly double that of the Atlantic provinces. One would, perhaps, expect that higher crime rates would be associated with higher rates of incarceration, but this does not appear to be the case. For example, while British Columbia's per capita crime rate is substantially greater than Ontario's, British Columbia's per capita rate of use of custody is nonetheless substantially lower than Ontario's.[106]

ORGANIZATIONAL IMPACTS: THE CRIMINALIZATION OF SERVICE DELIVERY?

The proclamation of the *YOA* has brought about significant changes in the organization of juvenile justice services, most notably in the provincial government departmental (or subdepartmental) responsibility for dispositional services; that is, probation and custody. Given Canada's constitutional division of powers, wherein the federal government is responsible for the formulation of uniform criminal law and the provinces are independently responsible for the administration of that law, it cannot be said that the organizational changes that accompanied the implementation of the Act were legally required. The provinces are constitu-

---

[106] Derived from Moyer, *supra*, note 93, Markwart, *supra*, note 102 and annual reports of the Ontario Ministry of Correctional Services.

TABLE 5

Number of Criminal Code and Other Federal Statute Offences Per 10,000 Youths Population by Province, 1988

Jurisdiction	Rate/10,000 Youths	(Rank)
Newfoundland	330	(10)
Prince Edward Island	377	(9)
Nova Scotia	448	(6)
New Brunswick	418	(7)
Quebec	399	(8)
Ontario	497	(5)
Manitoba	726	(2)
Saskatchewan	771	(1)
Alberta	649	(3)
British Columbia	636	(4)
Canada	518	

Source: Statistics Canada, Canadian Centre for Justice Statistics, Uniform Crime Reports Survey, 1988.

tionally free to organize juvenile justice services in any manner they choose. Nonetheless, significant organizational changes were clearly prompted by the new Act. These changes reflect not merely provincial government adaptation to the new law, but also the perceptions and attitudes of key political and senior bureaucratic figures in the provinces about what the Act intends and how it should be implemented. These changes — which generally, but not exclusively, reveal a marked shift toward a justice (correctional services) approach to the delivery of services, and a concurrent separation of juvenile justice and child welfare services — tend to belie the suggestion that the *YOA* is not a Justice Model.[107] There is little doubt that these changes have signalled a movement toward the greater criminalization — and adultification — of juvenile justice services.

Although the police and prosecutors (Crown counsel) have, as we will discuss later, experienced significant changes in their roles under the *YOA*, there has been little change at the provincial departmental level. Nor should such organizational change have been expected, precisely because police and prosecutional services in the juvenile system were already organizationally integrated with the corresponding adult police and prosecutional services prior to the *YOA*.

Some changes in organizational responsibility did, in fact, occur in the late

---

[107] Archambault, ''Young Offenders Act: Philosophy and Principles'' in Silverman and Teevan, eds., *Crime in Canadian Society* (Toronto: Butterworths, 1986).

1980s in British Columbia, Nova Scotia[108] and New Brunswick, where police and prosecutional functions, formerly overseen by a single department (Attorney General or Justice) were divided into separate government departments with the creation of new departments of the Solicitor General, which are responsible for police and correctional services. These organizational changes do not appear, however, to be directly related to the *YOA* itself, but rather to broader criminal justice concerns connected to ensuring a greater independence of Crown counsel and the courts from the police. These changes, while likely not significantly affecting day-to-day operations, can have an effect on future juvenile justice policy. In this regard, provincial departments of Justice (or Attorney General), typically staffed by lawyers (prosecutors), tend to have greater status and influence at both national and provincial levels than do Solicitor General departments, which are typically represented in juvenile justice matters by correctional officials. This imbalance in status and influence can have an effect on the development and negotiation of policy where there are divergent special interests: on the one hand, the greater justice and Crime Control orientation of the prosecutional community and, on the other hand, the fiscal and philosophical interests of correctional departments in constraining custody rates. It should also be noted that shortly after the proclamation of the new Act, the responsibility for the *YOA* was shifted at the federal government level from Solicitor General to Justice. Considering these organizational changes at both the federal and provincial levels, it seems that the influence of the legal, and particularly the prosecutional community, has been somewhat enhanced in federal/provincial discussions of juvenile justice policy.

Under the *JDA*, the provincial court systems (being summary conviction courts) were largely responsible for hearing juvenile matters in most provinces, except in Saskatchewan, New Brunswick and Prince Edward Island, where superior courts heard juvenile matters. With proclamation of the *YOA*, only New Brunswick persisted with a superior court being designated as the youth court; however, as a result of a superior court decision in 1985, jurisdiction was given to the provincial court in New Brunswick.[109]

Under the *JDA*, Ontario and Nova Scotia had established separate juvenile (or family) court systems. These were specialized courts which dealt with juvenile delinquency, child welfare and family matters. With these family court systems hearing the cases of juveniles under 16 years of age, Ontario and Nova Scotia were faced with a dilemma about how to manage the influx of a vast number of new youth cases arising from the uniform maximum age provisions coming into

---

[108] In 1991, however, British Columbia re-integrated its two justice-related departments into a single justice department, but due to organizational changes, correctional authorities still have less influence than formerly.

[109] Komar and Platt, *Young Offender Service* (Markham, Ont.: Butterworths, 1984).

effect in 1985. These provinces elected, primarily due to the substantial reorganization that necessarily would have arisen otherwise, to effectively stay with the status quo: "two-tiered" or "split jurisdiction" court systems were established with the family courts continuing to hear cases involving youths under 16 years of age (Phase I), and the criminal divisions of the provincial court system hearing *YOA* cases involving those 16 years or older (Phase II). These, of course, are examples, not of organizational change, but of organizational resistance to change.

The two-tiered court (and correctional) system in Ontario, although not completely without some supporters, has been controversial and roundly criticized on several grounds. Critics argue that it is an inequitable system; that Phase II courts deal with young offenders more harshly; that Phase I judges have greater knowledge of available community and agency resources for young people; and that it is a makeshift arrangement which is contrary to the intent of Parliament.[110] Nonetheless, when challenged on constitutional grounds, the Ontario Court of Appeal held that the two-tiered system was not contrary to the equality provisions of the *Canadian Charter of Rights and Freedoms* in *R. v. C.(R.)* (1987).[111]

Although the two-tiered system has been the target of much criticism, there is little in the way of convincing evidence that young offenders in Ontario are treated in systematically different ways by the two courts that could not otherwise be explained by the age differences in the youths being dealt with. Harsher treatment — i.e., more frequent use of custody — of older young offenders in Phase II Ontario courts is to be expected, given the differences in maturity and the time available for the accused appearing before these courts to acquire a record of previous offences. Custodial rates increasing as a function of age, for example, also occurs in British Columbia, where there is not a two-tiered court system.[112]

In response to these criticisms, and to the recommendations of a report recommending the reform of the entire Ontario court system,[113] there are plans to eventually merge the Ontario family court with the adult criminal division of the provincial court. However, in 1990, the Ontario government, rather than merging these courts, began to transfer responsibility for all young offender cases to the family court, but it appears that it will be a fairly lengthy period before this slow transfer of cases will be complete. As well, with the 1990 election of the New

---

[110] Ontario Social Development Council, *Proceedings of the Conference on YOA Dispositions: Challenges and Choices* (Toronto: Ontario Social Development Council, 1987).

[111] *R. v. C.(R.)* (1987), 56 C.R. (3) 185 (Ont. C.A.). Leave to appeal to S.C.C. refused (1987), 23 O.A.C. 397n, 83 N.R. 80n (S.C.C.).

[112] Corrado and Markwart, "The Prices of Rights and Responsibilities: An Examination of the Impacts of the Young Offenders Act in British Columbia" (1988) (7) (1) Can. J. Fam. L. pp. 93-115.

[113] Zuber, *Report of the Ontario Courts Inquiry* (Toronto: Queen's Printer, 1987).

Democratic Party government, the status of the plans for eventual merger of the two court systems is unclear. As well, the Ontario adult criminal courts have for several years now been severely backlogged with heavy caseloads, resulting in such extraordinary case delays that the Canadian Supreme Court found in 1990 that this violated an accused's right to be tried within a reasonable time.[114] The transfer of jurisdiction for all young offender cases to the family court may be viewed as a partial, pragmatic response to the overcrowding in the criminal division of the provincial court. How this change in the court system in Ontario will affect the processing of young offender cases is not entirely clear, but there could potentially be significant effects. For example, dealing with an increased volume of 16- and 17-year-old cases in the family court may lead to more backlogs and delays in the young offender system. As well, if there have been true differences between the way in which the criminal division and the family court have treated their respective young offender populations, then the transfer of all cases to the family court system may result in, for example, an alteration in sentencing patterns, but also more consistency of treatment.

While the police, prosecutional and court systems have undergone some organizational changes under the *YOA*, the greatest changes, by far, have been in the provincial social services and the correctional systems responsible for the administration of court orders such as probation and custody. Under the *JDA*, provincial social services departments were responsible for the delivery of these services in 10 of the 12 (including the 2 territories) jurisdictions (see Chart 1). The only exceptions to this were British Columbia and New Brunswick, where correctional branches that also administered adult correctional services and were integrated under a single justice ministry were responsible for these services. As Chart 1 illustrates, every Canadian jurisdiction, except British Columbia and Quebec, has undergone organizational change at the departmental or subdepartmental level since the *YOA* came into force. These organizational changes reflect three themes: the emergence of correctional departments in the delivery of services (at the expense of social service departments), the development of distinct young offender branches or divisions within those social services departments that retain responsibility for young offenders, and the operational separation of child welfare and young offender services.

Alberta and Prince Edward Island underwent the most radical organizational change, completely transferring responsibilities for young offender services from social services departments to correctional organizations that are also responsible for adult correctional services. In the case of Alberta, one apparent reason for the change was that the Department of the Solicitor General was already experienced

---

[114] *R. v. Askov*, [1990] 2 S.C.R. 1199, 75 O.R. (2d) 673, 59 C.C.C. (3d) 449, 79 C.R. (3d) 273, 49 C.R.R. 1, 74 D.L.R. (4th) 355, 113 N.R. 241, 42 O.A.C. 81.

in dealing with the older (16- and 17-year-old) young offender group;[115] costs and the stronger orientation of correctional services toward public protection were other considerations. Under the *JDA*, Prince Edward Island transferred training school committals to other Maritime provinces, since this small province had no local facilities. With the transfer of service responsibility to the correctional services division of the Department of Justice under the *YOA*, custodial facilities were developed within the province. As well, young offender services in the Northwest Territories are now administered by the same division responsible for adult correctional services.

Although Manitoba's transfer of service responsibility to the Department of Justice did not occur until several years after proclamation of the *YOA*, significant organizational and policy changes were actually implemented from the outset of the new legislation. For example, under the *JDA* the Manitoba Youth Centre, the province's largest secure youth custody facility, was roughly equally populated by young offenders and child welfare wards. With the advent of the *YOA*, however, a policy decision — seen to be philosophically consistent with the intent of the new legislation — was implemented to completely separate young offenders and child welfare services at the operational level so that these two populations would no longer be mixed in the same programs. As Chart 1 indicates, the separation of young offender and child welfare youth into separate programs — achieved either through the transfer of departmental responsibilities, the creation of the distinct young offender branches within social services departments or simply by policy and operational changes — is a consistent trend across several provinces. In fact, in stark contrast to the widespread co-mingling of delinquents and child welfare wards in the same institutional resources in several provinces under the *JDA*, now only Quebec (to any significant degree) places these two populations in the same secure facilities, while only Quebec, Ontario (Phase I) and Nova Scotia (Phase I) operate mixed open custody/child welfare programs. These organizational changes *vis-à-vis* young offender and child welfare services were also encouraged by federal changes in cost-sharing arrangements.[116] It is likely that the separation of provincial child welfare and young offender services was an unstated policy objective of the federal government.

Since young offender services in British Columbia and New Brunswick were already organized under the auspices of correctional departments, and were separate from child welfare services under the *JDA*, there was no need to re-organize services in these provinces. In fact, New Brunswick does contract open custody services through the province's social services department, but child

---

[115] Mason, ''Implementing the Young Offenders Act: An Alberta Perspective'' in Hudson, Hornick and Burrows, eds., *Justice and the Young Offender in Canada* (Toronto: Wall and Thompson (1988).

[116] See Coflin, ''The Federal Government's Role in Implementing the Young Offenders Act'' in Hudson, Hornick and Burrows, *Justice and the Young Offender in Canada* (Toronto: Wall and Thompson, 1988).

CHART 1

Organizational Responsibility for Dispositional Services

Province	JDA	YOA	Sub-Departmental/Changes
Newfoundland	social services	social services	separate young offenders branch; separation of young offender and child welfare cases
Nova Scotia	social services	social services/ corrections (split jurisdiction)	separation of young offender and child welfare cases (social services)
New Brunswick	corrections	corrections	open custody contracted to social services
P.E.I.	social services	corrections/justice	—
Quebec	social services	social services	—
Ontario	social services	social services/ corrections (split jurisdiction)	—
Manitoba	social services	justice/corrections (1988)	separation of young offender and child welfare cases
Saskatchewan	social services	social services	separate young offender branch; separation of young offenders and child welfare cases

CHART 1

Organizational Responsibility for Dispositional Services

Province	JDA	YOA	Sub-Departmental/Changes
Alberta	social services	corrections	—
British Columbia	corrections	corrections	—
Yukon	social services	social services	separate young offender branch
N.W.T.	social services	social services	integrated with adult corrections administration

welfare and young offender cases are nonetheless kept separated in different facilities.

Quebec also did not undergo any significant organizational change, maintaining an integrated child welfare and young offender system with a clear focus on rehabilitation goals. One could argue that by maintaining its pre-*YOA* organizational structures and goals Quebec has simply gone its own way in interpreting the Act but, at the same time, this does demonstrate that the Act is sufficiently flexible (or confused) in its apparent intent to accommodate very different approaches.

As with their court systems, Ontario and Nova Scotia established two-tiered systems for youth correctional services, with social services departments maintaining responsibility for youth under 16 years of age (Phase I) and correctional departments handling those 16 years or older (Phase II). (In Nova Scotia, however, secure custody services for juvenile males of all ages are operated by the correctional department). This again can be regarded as an example of organizational resistance and has been the subject of much criticism in Ontario.[117] There can be vast differences in Ontario in the types of services provided to the two young offender populations. For example, youths committed to secure custody in the Phase I system are held in small, well-staffed facilities with a far greater care and treatment orientation, whereas similarly committed Phase II youths are largely held in former adult jails (or portions thereof), with leaner resources and an adult-like correctional orientation. Also, since the age for child welfare jurisdiction in Ontario is under 16 years, many Phase I young offenders are able to be provided (concurrent or after-care) child welfare services. These services are not, however, available to the older Phase II young offenders.

The two-tiered court and correctional systems in Ontario, as well as that province's refusal to implement alternative measures programs (until compelled to do so by the courts in 1988), have led some to argue that Ontario has strongly resisted implementation of the *YOA*. A reorganization, however, would have led to a massive relocation of resources and personnel; for example, there are more than 1,000 Phase II young offenders in custody on any given day. As well, shifting the responsibility for young offender services to the Social Services Department (COMSOC) might well, given the disparity between the maximum ages of the *YOA* and provincial child welfare jurisdiction, have led to pressures to extend the child welfare age, an enormously costly prospect. Still, political factors may come into play in Ontario in the future as a result of the 1990 election of the left wing New Democratic Party, which has been critical of the previous government's young offenders policy. Given this, there is the potential for significant change in that province.

In general terms, then, there have been significant organizational changes in several provinces, the key trends being the increasing emergence of correctional

---

[117] For example, see Ontario Social Development Council, *supra*, note 110.

departments in the provision of young offender services and the organizational or functional separation of child welfare and young offender services. These changes amount to far more than a simple changing of bureaucratic faces, but rather have had, and will continue to have, profound implications. In those provinces where correctional departments have responsibility for young offender services, the adult correctional components of those organizations are, by far, the largest. As a result, adult correctional thinking and practices tend to be imposed on, or permeate through to, the youth correctional systems. Correctional systems are decidedly different from child welfare systems: there tends to be far less emphasis on care and treatment, or rehabilitation, and far more emphasis on containment, control and public protection. In short, there is a greater emphasis on criminalization. These philosophical differences tend, as well, to be reflected in the fewer staffing and treatment resources that are available in youth correctional systems.

Under the *JDA*, there was a direct link between the juvenile courts and child welfare systems — in law, organizationally and operationally. With the removal of the legal jurisdiction under the *JDA* to commit delinquents to the care of child welfare authorities, the *YOA* has severed the youth court's relationship with the child welfare system in law, and this has been carried further, organizationally and operationally, in the implementation of the Act. It is well established that a substantial proportion of young offenders have been, are, or could be the recipients of child welfare services.[118] However, with the legal, organizational and operational interfaces no longer available in many provinces, the youth courts and probation officers can no longer depend, to the same degree, on intervention and assistance from child welfare authorities, who now have greater discretion about whether to provide child welfare services to young offenders. Inter- or intra-departmental disputes about who has the "mandate" for services tend to ensue, each department wanting to foist the responsibility on the other. Without these linkages, child welfare authorities, attempting to cope with a rising tide of child sexual abuse reports amidst limited resources, tend to be less likely to provide services. Many young offenders then tend to "fall between the (bureaucratic) gaps" and either not receive services at all, or find themselves committed to the youth justice system surrogate of the child welfare system — open custody.

The *YOA* has also prompted further organizational changes in terms of the creation of new programs and services and the increasing involvement of the private sector in the youth justice system. While British Columbia, Quebec, and, to a lesser extent, Manitoba had well-established diversion systems in place well before the *YOA*, the alternative measures (diversion) provisions of the new legislation have prompted the development of many new diversion systems and

---

[118] For example, see Thompson, "The Young Offender, Child Welfare and Mental Health Caseload Communalities" (1988) (30) (2) Can. J. Crim. pp. 135–144.

programs,[119] particularly in the Prairie and Atlantic provinces.[120] While some provinces such as British Columbia had universally available community service programs prior to the YOA,[121] Ontario[122] and other provinces did not. These programs have proliferated under the YOA in these provinces. Further, most provinces operated larger, centralized training school facilities under the JDA, but with the creation of the new disposition of open custody new resources were required. As well as these new types of services, the sheer volume of services available was greatly increased in the eight provinces affected by the uniform maximum age. In most provinces, these new and expanded diversion, community service and open custody programs are largely contracted to non-profit agencies and, in some instances, for-profit companies. The net effect has been a significant increase in involvement in the youth justice system by the private sector,[123] and, accordingly, a greater degree of professional and economic investment in the new system. As well, at least one province, Manitoba, has actively promoted the involvement of community members in the system through the widespread development of youth justice committees.[124] This increased involvement by private agencies, which tend to be less constrained than public servants in voicing criticism and in advocating for their professional views (and interests), may lead to these agencies having an increasing influence on juvenile justice policy and resource allocation.

---

[119] For example, see Statistics Canada, "National Summary of Alternative Measures Services for Young Persons" (1990) (10) (11) *Juristat Services Bulletin* (Ottawa: Canadian Centre for Justice Statistics).

[120] Ontario stood alone in refusing to implement the alternative measures provision of the Act, but was legally required to do so in 1988 as a result of an Ontario Court of Appeal decision which found that this failure contravened the equality rights provisions of the *Charter (R. v. Sheldon S.,* (1988), 16 O.A.C. 285, 63 C.R. (3d) 64 (Ont. C.A.). As a result, an interim program of "minimal compliance" was established. While this court decision was eventually overturned by the Canadian Supreme Court, Ontario has maintained its program and is likely to continue to do so, and perhaps expand it, under the New Democratic Party government in Ontario.

[121] Markwart, *supra,* note 102.

[122] Moyer, *A Description of the Application of Dispositions Under the Young Offenders Act by the Ministry of Community and Social Services of Ontario* (Toronto: Department of Justice, 1989).

[123] See Weiler and Ward, "The Voluntary Sector Response to the Young Offenders Act" in Hudson, Hornick and Burrows, eds., *Justice and the Young Offender in Canada* (Toronto: Wall and Thompson, 1988).

[124] Ryant and Heinrick, "Youth Court Committees in Manitoba" in Hudson, Hornick and Burrows, eds., *Justice and the Young Offender in Canada* (Toronto: Wall and Thompson, 1988).

Before leaving this section, some comments should be made about whether there are signs of a new model of juvenile justice — "corporatism" — emerging in Canada, as Pratt suggests has taken place in England and Wales.[125] Corporatism is, in our view, hardly a new "model" of juvenile justice insofar as, unlike the Welfare or Justice Models, it lacks a theoretical foundation and systems of intervention that logically flow from that foundation. Corporatism really represents more of a technocratic organizational approach to the implementation of juvenile justice policy objectives. It is a tendency toward centralization of policy, increased government intervention, the co-operation of various professional and interest groups into a collective whole with homogeneous aims and objectives, and the legal process assuming the form of "bureaucratic-administrative law".[126] This has been manifested in Britain, for example, with the emergence of pre-court tribunals as the primary mechanism for the dispensation of justice, increased administrative discretion, the enhanced role of intermediate sanctions (for example, attendance programs), enhanced involvement of the private sector and enhanced inter-agency co-operation.

While it is difficult to speak of the disparate provincial juvenile justice systems as a whole, we see, generally speaking, little evidence of the emergence of corporatism in Canada, although some elements are evident generally (for example, private sector involvement) and in specific provinces (for example, intermediate sanctions in British Columbia). For example, although diversion programs have emerged across Canada, informal police discretion not to charge and appearances in court remain, by far (except, perhaps, in Quebec), the primary mechanisms for processing juvenile cases, not diversion. The *YOA* has, as well, reduced rather than enhanced administrative discretion. Further, given our earlier discussion about the general trend toward the separation of young offender and child welfare services, it can hardly be said that enhanced inter-agency co-operation has been the order of the day, with the possible exceptions of Quebec, and to a lesser extent Ontario (Phase I).

THE IMPACT OF THE *YOA* ON JUVENILE JUSTICE ROLES

A central question in assessing the impact of the *YOA*[127] on juvenile justice is whether the attitudes and behaviour of key decision-makers such as police and judges have changed. Change was anticipated, since the *YOA* includes numerous sections that, in varying degrees, define the altered roles for each set of juvenile justice personnel. Probation officer functions, for example, are partly outlined in section 14 of the Act, which specifies the new criteria for the generation of

---

[125] Pratt, "Corporatism: The Third Model of Juvenile Justice" (1989) (29) (3) *Brit. J. Criminol.* pp. 236-53.

[126] *Ibid.*

[127] R.S.C. 1985, c. Y-1.

predisposition reports to assist judges in sentencing, and in section 37, which prescribes the duties and functions of youth workers. Similarly, police functions are directly affected by several sections: as examples, section 11(2) concerning the right to counsel, and section 56 concerning the taking of statements, as well as section 44, which addresses fingerprinting, all directly impinge on police procedures. Other sections indirectly prescribe role functions.

It is quite possible that role changes influence attitudes toward the *YOA*. Arguably, those decision-makers whose roles have been augmented by the *YOA* would tend to regard the Act more positively than those who have had their roles circumscribed. A less positive view of the *YOA* may be associated with decision-making or behaviour that results in consequences unintended by the Act. If, as will be discussed in detail in the next section, the police, for example, believe that the *YOA* inhibits their ability to extract confessions from young people, they might then restrict their efforts to pursue offences, such as break and enter, where confessions are often critical to a successful prosecution.

Even when, however, role changes brought about by the *YOA* are regarded positively by a key group, unintended consequences still might occur. Defence counsel, for example, are central to court proceedings under the *YOA* and they, with few exceptions, are strongly supportive of this law,[128] yet it appears that their routine presence in court is associated with longer and more hearings as well as stiffer sentences.[129]

The impact of the *YOA* on the police role in juvenile justice will be examined first because the police are critical to the investigation and charge procedures which initiate a young person's involvement with the criminal justice system.

Police: A Crime Control Perspective Critical of the YOA

Police officers, police chiefs and other senior police personnel, as well as provincial Attorneys General, have consistently been among the most critical opponents of some of the Justice Model aspects of the *YOA*. In essence, these critics are opposed to those sections that they perceive as limiting their Crime Control functions. Among the most important (perceived) handicaps to Crime Control are the strict codification (section 56) of procedures for informing young persons of their legal rights and observance of those rights. These include the right to have their rights explained in language appropriate to their age and understanding, to remain silent, to consult and be provided with legal counsel, to have counsel or another adult present during questioning by the police, and the

---

[128] Moyer and Carrington, *The Attitudes of Canadian Juvenile Justice Professionals Toward The Young Offenders Act* (Ottawa: Ministry of Solicitor General Canada, 1985).

[129] See Chapter 5 and Corrado and Markwart, "The Prices of Rights and Responsibilities: An Examination of the Impacts of the Young Offenders Act in British Columbia" (1988) (7) (1) Can. J. Fam. L. pp. 93-115.

necessity of a written waiver of rights. The criticisms of these provisions have been sharp, even strident, from the outset. For example, in a formal submission to the Canadian Senate in 1982, British Columbia, although supportive of the general thrust of the proposed Act, warned that these new rights would create in Canada a "Miranda-type" of phenomenon[130] which, it was argued, had contributed to great public disenchantment with the administration of justice in the United States.[131]

Another issue that stirred controversy, especially in Ontario and to a lesser extent in British Columbia, is the 12-year-old minimum age jurisdiction of the new Act. The Metropolitan Toronto Police Chief, for example, has complained of the police's hands being tied in dealing with hundreds of serious offences committed by under-age children which could not be pursued under the *YOA* or any other criminal proceedings.[132] For police critics, there is no deterrent or effective control of these under-age child offenders, since provincial child welfare programs are the only recourse. Child welfare authorities, however, are often reluctant to get involved or, if they do become involved, are, from the police perspective, often found wanting in the type of intervention taken. For the police, the answer to these perceived failures of the child welfare system is resort to the criminal law again. Hence, they have lobbied to have the Act amended. They have persisted in these efforts despite the relative infrequency of crimes by children under 12, and despite the known infrequency of prosecutions of under 12s under the *JDA*. For example, in 1983 children under 12 comprised only 1.6 percent of the juveniles found delinquent in *JDA* courts.[133] Still, critics in Ontario and British Columbia, including the Attorneys General of those provinces, have urged amendment of the *YOA* to allow for either a lowering of the minimum age or a judicial process to allow youth court proceedings for certain under-age offenders. A related reform did occur with the 1986 amendment to the *Criminal Code*, arising from Bill C-106, that made it a criminal offence to aid and abet under-12s in committing a crime.

Police also have been severely critical of the three-year maximum sentence under the *YOA*. Since not all young persons 14 years of age and older who have

---

[130] The *Miranda* case was a U.S. Supreme Court decision requiring the police to promptly inform arrested persons of their legal rights (eg. remain silent, retain counsel). Law and order constituencies in the U.S. have complained that technicalities arising out of this decision, and other decisions which followed, have compromised law enforcement efforts in that country.

[131] Vogel and Robinson, *Bill C-61, The Young Offenders Act: Submission to the Standing Senate Committee on Constitutional and Legal Affairs* (Victoria: Ministry of Attorney General, 1982).

[132] Caputo, "The Young Offenders Act: Children's Rights, Children's Wrongs" (1987) (13) (2) Can. Pub. Pol. pp. 125-143.

[133] Statistics Canada, *Juvenile Delinquents, 1983* (Ottawa: Supply and Services Canada, 1984).

been charged with serious violent crimes, including murder, are transferred to adult court, police again argue that a three-year custody sentence is grossly insufficient to deter heinous crimes. As discussed previously, the control of violent young offenders has become a major public and media issue, especially in the three largest metropolitan areas of Canada: Vancouver, Toronto and Montreal. In Vancouver, violent youth gang activity has increased dramatically (although most youth gang members are, in fact, young adults). "Drive-by" shootings of rival gang members, executions of suspected police informants, assaults on non-gang members on school grounds, extortions in the Chinese business district by Asian-born gang members and violent clashes between rival gangs in restaurants and other public places have resulted in the creation and rapid growth of special police gang units working together with specially dedicated Crown counsel.[134] In Toronto, violence among "street kids", "swarming" (the random mass assault of individuals in public places by groups of young persons), "skin-head" (fascist-garbed young people) attacks on visible minority individuals, random beatings in schools and violence by Asian-born youth gang members are almost routinely reported in newspapers such as *The Toronto Star*. Again, the image that emerges is that of a growing epidemic of youth violence. Similarly, in Montreal, youth violence against the public, including taxi and bus drivers, especially by Haitian-born youths, appears to have increased both the fear of crime among the public and the pressure on the police to prevent violent youth crime.

While police representatives do not point to the *YOA* as the only thing responsible for their perceived inability to protect the public in major metropolitan centres, they commonly do argue that effective Crime Control requires a more speedy and less legally constrained criminal justice system which can offer more certain punishment and incapacitation. For these critics, the *YOA* is seen as far too concerned with due process for violent and recidivist youth, at the expense of the protection of the public. This Crime Control perspective was evident before the *YOA* became law in 1984. A survey sample of 745 police officers (representing a 73 percent response rate) from Vancouver, Edmonton, Winnipeg, Toronto, Montreal, Halifax and several smaller communities in six provinces were asked about their views on the then-proposed *YOA*. Compared to similar sample profile of other juvenile justice personnel (including judges, Crown counsel, defence counsel and probation officers), the police were the least supportive of the *YOA* philosophy. More specifically, most police officers were opposed to the provision for special guarantees of rights and freedoms for young offenders.[135] Similarly, at

---

[134] As a result, law and order, including crackdowns on youth gangs, become a key plank in the (conservative) Social Credit government's 1991 bid for re-election in British Columbia.

[135] Interestingly, police officers' responses from Montreal (from those affiliated with the youth squad) were as supportive of the *YOA* principle of limited youth accountability as Quebec defence counsel and probation officers. As noted

least 80 percent of the police officers (as well as Crown counsel) did not agree with
the three-year maximum for ''life offences'' and at least half were opposed to the
two-year maximum for other offences.[136]

In summarizing the police perspective on the *YOA* compared with other
juvenile justice personnel, Moyer and Carrington concluded that the ''police
sampled had the most negative reactions to the *YOA*''.[137] Police fears that the
Justice Model principles incorporated into the *YOA* would make their Crime
Control functions more difficult is a theme that continued to emerge soon after the
Act was implemented. Writing in 1985, Provincial Court Judge John F. Bennett
stated:

> What I am seeing now are charges 'coming down the chute' against kids who are
> easy to identify and who generally will plead guilty without a lawyer. The real
> criminal types cover their tracks better and cause problems with investigations.
> When charged they know their rights including the right to counsel 'at every stage of
> the proceedings' and they cause bottlenecks in the system.[138]

Pressures from the police and other Crime Control advocates such as Crown
counsel resulted in a failed attempt to amend the provisions of section 56 in 1986,
but the pressure has continued unabated and a consensus among provincial justice
representatives has been achieved: in 1989 Canadian provincial attorneys general
unanimously resolved that section 56 should be amended to permit the
admissibility of voluntary statements, notwithstanding a technical breach of the
section, providing that the administration of justice is not brought into disrepute
by such judicial action.[139]

Unfortunately, there has been no systematic research to assess the police
concern that the *YOA* has made their Crime Control roles more difficult. However,
an attempt was made to examine the change in the number of charges brought
forward by the police in three Vancouver suburbs.[140] RCMP Constable Bill
Dingwell, who conducted the study, wanted to examine the hypothesis that, after
proclamation of the *YOA*, there would be a significant reduction in the number of
young persons charged with certain offences such as break and enter, thefts and
property damage as a result of the new constraints on the taking of statements from

---

above in the section on provincial organization of juvenile justice, Quebec
prior to (and after the *YOA*) was closer to the Welfare Model end of the
continuum than any province.

[136] Moyer and Carrington, *supra*, note 128.

[137] *Ibid.*, at p. 109.

[138] Bennett, ''Concerns About the Young Offenders Act'' (1985) (8) (4) Prov.
Judges J. pp. 17-18, at p. 18.

[139] Department of Justice Canada, *The Young Offenders Act: Proposals for
Amendment* (Ottawa: Deparment of Justice, 1989).

[140] Dingwell, ''The Impact of the Young Offenders Act on Policing in Two
Suburban Communities'', unpublished paper, Simon Fraser University, Burnaby, B.C., 1987.

suspect juveniles. For offences of this sort, a confession (statement) by the accused to the police is often crucial to proceeding with a charge. In contrast, Dingwell expected no significant reduction in charges for offences such as assault and possession of stolen property. For these sorts of offences, corroborating and incriminating evidence is more likely to come from sources other than the accused's statement — that is, from witness, fingerprint or material evidence.

Given the limits of the research design and the difficulty in compiling the appropriate statistics, the data used in Dingwell's research to assess the above hypotheses have several validity limitations which make any inferences tentative. Because of low frequencies for most offence categories in two of the three suburbs, only the data from Burnaby, British Columbia (population 210,000), are presented in Tables 6, 7 and 8.

Table 6 indicates the number of youths charged with break and enter of business establishments declined from 39 in 1982, when the *JDA* was in effect, to 30 in 1986 under the *YOA*, whereas the number of youth not charged for this offence increased to 19 in 1986 from 2 in 1983. A more inconsistent pattern, however, is evident in Table 7 for residential break and enter. Moreover, combining Tables 6 and 7 indicates the charge rate for all break and enter offences declined only modestly from 1983 (*JDA*) to 1986 (*YOA*) — from 87 percent to 80 percent.

Since 17-year-olds were under the jurisdiction of the *YOA* by 1986, and based on Dingwell's estimate that at least one-third of those charged under the *YOA* were 17-year-olds,[141] it was expected, all other factors being equal, that the number of charges would increase proportionate to the inclusion of 17-year-old offenders. This did not, however, occur with break and enter cases. In contrast, charges for assaults in Burnaby increased nearly three-fold between 1982 and 1986; albeit the volumes not charged with assault also increased considerably (see Table 8).

These data lend some equivocal support to the police criticism that under the *YOA* it is more difficult to gather sufficient (confession) evidence to support certain property crimes, but that with offences such as assault, where confessions are not necessarily crucial to the prosecution's case, there has been no apparent inhibiting effect from the *YOA* on the police capacity to gather evidence and charge. (An ironic implication not noted by Dingwell, however, is that police complaints about the *YOA* inhibiting the police capacity to gather evidence in cases of crimes of violence — possibly excepting murder — do not appear to be supported by his data.)

Dingwell also conducted a sample survey of the 55 RCMP officers of the Maple Ridge, British Columbia, detachment to assess their views about policing under the *YOA* compared to the *JDA*.[142] Thirty-seven officers completed the question-naires (a 67 percent response rate). Three-quarters of the officers indicated they

---

[141] This figure approximates the average percentage of 17-year-olds charged under the *JDA* in Montreal and Winnipeg in 1980 (see Bala & Corrado, 1985). The *JDA* age limit in British Columbia was under 17 years.

[142] Dingwell, *supra*, note 140.

TABLE 6

Charge Profile for Business Break and Enter in Burnaby, B.C., Under *JDA* (1982–83) and *YOA* (1985–86)

Year	Number of Youth Charged	Number of Youth Not Charged
1982	39	not available
1983	30	2
1985	26	7
1986	30	17

Source: Dingwell, 1987.

TABLE 7

Charge Profile of Residential Break and Enter in Burnaby, B.C., Under *JDA* (1982–83) and *YOA* (1985–86)

Year	Number of Youth Charged	Number of Youth Not Charged
1982	102	not available
1983	62	12
1985	110	4
1986	106	16

Source: Dingwell, 1987.

TABLE 8

Charge Profile for Assault in Burnaby, B.C., Under *JDA* (1982–83) and *YOA* (1985–86)

Year	Number of Youth Charged	Number of Youth Not Charged
1982	12	2
1983	10	1
1985	31	12
1986	34	29

Source: Dingwell, 1987.

wanted the minimum age of the Act to be reduced to 10 years and the maximum age reduced to 17 years (nearly two-thirds favoured a further age reduction to 6 years). These responses reflected the consistent police perception that the majority of criminal acts were committed by this older adolescent age group and, by inference, that dealing with them under the *Criminal Code*, rather than the *YOA*, would enhance Crime Control.

Regarding the key controversy about the difficulty of charging sophisticated or experienced offenders, the police respondents were overwhelmingly more critical of the *YOA* than the *JDA*. Virtually all the officers (91 percent) either moderately or strongly agreed that it was difficult to charge this offender type under the *YOA*, compared to 72 percent who felt there were similar difficulties with the *JDA*. This response pattern was repeated for several more specific questions about charging experiences and Crime Control functions. For example, two-thirds of the respondents believed young offenders' knowledge and methods of committing crime had increased since the *YOA*, while a similar percentage of young offenders were perceived to have increased their understanding of their due process rights. Nearly three-quarters (73 percent) of the police maintained that it was now more difficult to gather evidence and charge a young offender than an adult offender. Also, the vast majority of officers (86 percent) believed their ability to protect the public had decreased, while three-quarters felt their enthusiasm for policing had declined under the *YOA*.

With regard to police frustration in dealing with young offenders under the two laws, Dingwell found that the gap was not extreme: 70 percent felt frustrated under the *JDA* compared to 82 percent under the *YOA*. This latter finding of widespread dissatisfaction with both legal schemes suggests, perhaps, that this disenchantment may be connected to factors common to both legislative schemes — the perception of lenient sentencing outcomes, for example — or to intra-organizational factors. In this latter regard, the investigation of juvenile offences can be associated with low status, even ridicule, within police departments.[143] Given this, it is likely that any juvenile legislation, and particularly legislation which establishes impediments to police investigations, will be regarded unfavourably.

Finally, Dingwell asked the police about their perceptions of the effectiveness of youth courts in deterring crime through sentencing. Approximately half of the respondents (51.4 percent) felt the *JDA* juvenile courts were effective sometimes, while 37 percent regarded them as not effective. In contrast, only 21.6 percent believed the *YOA* youth courts were sometimes effective, and nearly three-quarters (73 percent) regarded these courts as not effective. This was the case even though, apparently unbeknownst to these officers, the rate of admissions to custody, controlling for the uniform maximum age, has risen substantially in

---

[143] Moyer, *Diversion from the Juvenile Justice System and Its Impact on Children: A Review of the Literature* (Ottawa: Ministry of Solicitor General, 1980).

British Columbia under the *YOA* (see Chapter 5). As expected, an approximately similar number (71 percent) maintained that custody sentences were too short.

There is little doubt that the above data reflect a Crime Control perspective of the impact of the *YOA*. Constable Dingwell's concluding remarks about his research findings succinctly summarize this theoretical perspective:

> The police are just not able to collect the crucial information required for prosecution and those young offenders appearing in court are for the most part the first time offenders. The repeat offenders are almost untouchable. They are more aware of their rights, and as indicated in this study, most officers adopt the conservative response which suggests they are well aware of the gains to be made and consequences risked and the lack of certainty and severity of punishment reinforces criminal activity. Succinctly, the losers are society. They must endure increased criminal activity at their expense. As it is now many young offenders are running rampant and are not subjected to any form of intervention. The system response to juvenile delinquency is insufficient and unacceptable and a revamping of philosophy appears to be in order.[144]

As well as being critical, Dingwell acknowledges several positive Crime Control changes initiated by the *YOA*, such as fingerprinting and the capacity to issue police process (for example, appearance notices). Police authority was enhanced because the police were given the explicit legal capacity in the *YOA* (section 44) to employ adult criteria for fingerprinting and photographing alleged young offenders. In British Columbia, for example, the proportion of young persons fingerprinted has increased since the *YOA*,[145] and this is likely also the case in other provinces. When this is taken in conjunction with the additional authority given to the police to initiate a young offender's appearance in court by directly issuing processes such as appearance notices, which require an offender to appear in court on a fixed date, it is easy to see that the police have been able to exert considerable influence in maintaining and even enhancing both their identification function and "gatekeeper" role in processsing cases.[146] Under the *JDA*, the police could not directly compel a juvenile to appear in court, except by way of arrest and detention; otherwise, non-detained cases could only be summonsed to court after the laying of a charge. In this situation, Crown counsel decided whether to proceed with the charge and, unless the juvenile was charged, no fingerprinting could take place without the juvenile's consent.

While Crown counsel still retain this critical screening function for charge approval in key provinces such as British Columbia and Quebec, police can partly circumvent it when they issue process (for example, an appearance notice) with a fixed date for court appearance. Once this occurs, fingerprinting is allowed without an information (formal charge) being sworn. Crown counsel can only stop the case from proceeding through a formal and time-consuming process of de-notification. Even if the de-notification is processed before the court appearance,

---

[144] Dingwell, *supra*, note 140 at p. 54.
[145] Corrado and Markwart, *supra*, note 129.
[146] *Ibid.*

or if Crown counsel withdraws or stays the charges, or resorts to alternative measures (diversion), the police can still use the fingerprints for one year. As we have noted elsewhere, this police option is a significant Crime Control device: "police authorities acknowledged that their motivations for adopting this new practice were to 'ensure appropriate action is taken', i.e., to enhance the likelihood of the case being proceeded to court, and to facilitate the taking of fingerprints."[147]

Even in other major jurisdictions such as Ontario and the Prairie provinces, where there is not a pre-court Crown counsel charge approval screening system in place and the police have the capacity to lay an information (charge) directly, the police can still readily obtain fingerprints by issuing police process or by way of summons, even though the Crown may withdraw or stay the case once in court. As we shall see later, withdrawals and stays of charges arise quite frequently in several jurisdictions.

The validity limitations of the Dingwell project preclude agreement with his conclusions about the impact of the *YOA* on policing youth. Nonetheless, his research does reveal the extent of the negative perception of the *YOA* among the police in several Vancouver suburbs and, quite likely, throughout many other police forces in Canada. The lobbying efforts of the Canadian Association of Police Chiefs to amend the Act attest to the dissatisfaction many police feel toward the Justice Model/due process provisions of the *YOA*.

This opposition was also evident among Crown counsel before the *YOA* and has continued since, as is evident by official Crown counsel representatives joining forces with the police in lobbying for amendments to the (section 56) provisions concerning confession evidence. Despite the enhanced role of Crown counsel under the *YOA*, it will be argued that their criticisms, like those of the police, reflect their Crime Control values.

Crown Counsel: The New "Gate-keepers" of the Youth Justice System

During most of the history of the *JDA*, Crown counsel was not central to the juvenile court process. In fact, until the 1960s and 1970s, Crown counsel only infrequently appeared in juvenile court in most provinces; police prosecutors and probation officers were largely responsible for presenting cases to the court. The *JDA* instead enhanced the roles of probation officers, social workers and judges. In the less adversarial proceedings of *JDA* courts, Crown counsel (and defence counsel) necessarily had limited functions. The juvenile court process largely concentrated on "fact finding", in the context of sentencing, to address the question of how a judge could best deal with a juvenile's social/psychological problems. Primary Crime Control Model objectives concerned with protecting the public were not unimportant in the investigative tasks of probation officers in preparing either their pre-court enquiry reports for Crown counsel and their pre-

---

[147] *Ibid.* at p. 100.

disposition reports for judges. However, rehabilitation was supposed to be a guiding principle for both probation officer recommendations and judicial decision-making.

By the later 1970s, juvenile courts in urban areas in Canada had already made significant shifts in procedures away from the Welfare Model toward the Justice Model. As a consequence, the role of Crown counsel in these jurisdictions was enhanced considerably; both due process and adversarial procedures became more evident, and with Crown counsel becoming more regularly involved with the decision to proceed with a charge, prosecuting cases and ''speaking to sentence'' (or stating their position about the appropriate sentence to the deciding judge).

The extent of Crown counsel involvement in the *JDA* juvenile court process varied according to metropolitan and non-metropolitan courts and by province. Crown counsel played a major role, for example, in the Vancouver juvenile court, compared to a minor role in the non-metropolitan Kelowna court in the Interior of British Columbia. In Quebec, Crown counsel's role, generally, was limited to those cases that had not already been diverted by Welfare Model-oriented intervention assessment teams. In Ontario, Alberta and Nova Scotia, roughly two-thirds of first appearances, bail hearing and uncontested guilty pleas were dealt with, not by Crown counsel, but by police officers acting as Crown agents.[148] Under the *YOA*, Crown counsel's role in these provinces has been enhanced considerably since police prosecutions are now uncommon. For example, Milner reports that under the *JDA* 65 percent of cases in the Edmonton court were dealt with by police prosecutors, but this had dwindled under the *YOA* to only 0.2 percent by 1985.[149] Under the *JDA* in Ontario, police officers acted as prosecutors in many family courts but, with the advent of the *YOA*, Crown counsel assumed this role in all *YOA* matters.[150]

As a result of these variations in Crown counsel's role, it was expected the *YOA* would have a differential impact depending on how prominent Crown counsel's role was before the *YOA*. Little change, for example, was expected in key metropolitan centres, where Crown and defence counsel already played prominent roles and more adversarial proceedings tended to be the rule, but more change was likely in non-metropolitan courts, where Crown counsel appeared far less commonly. Similarly, relatively little change was likely to occur in British Columbia, where all cases were handled by legally trained Crown counsel under

[148] Bala and Corrado, *Juvenile Justice in Canada: A Comparative Study* (Ottawa: Ministry of Solicitor General Canada, 1985).

[149] Milner, ''The New Juvenile Justice: The Impact of the Young Offenders Act in The Edmonton Juvenile Court'' (Ph.D. thesis, University of Alberta, Department of Sociology, 1991).

[150] Moyer, *A Description of the Application of Dispositions Under the Young Offenders Act by the Ministry of Community and Social Services of Ontario* (Toronto: Department of Justice, 1989).

the *JDA*, compared to Ontario and Alberta, for example, where police prosecutions were common under the *JDA*.

Despite these role variations under the *JDA*, it is possible to characterize Crown counsels' position on the *YOA* prior to its implementation by referring to their views expressed in the National Study of the Functioning of the Juvenile Court Project (NSFJC).[151] On several key *YOA* principles, such as the provision of special guarantees of rights and freedoms to young persons and minimal interference[152] with freedom, most Crown counsel responded negatively. Crown counsel, like the police, also were more approving of the emphasis on the protection of society principle than other juvenile justice personnel. For many of the remaining *YOA* principles, the association between police and Crown counsel responses was not an uncommon pattern. Crown counsel opposition also paralleled the police opposition to several substantive and procedural provisions of the Act, including the sections restricting fingerprinting for summary offences, the raising of the minimum age limit and the limitations on disposition lengths.[153] Crime Control Model criticisms of the *YOA* appeared, therefore, to characterize Crown counsel's perspective. Protecting society and assisting the police in identifying, processing and incapacitating young offenders quite likely remain common values among Crown counsel.

As mentioned above, Crown counsel representatives have consistently sought to soften the legal admissibility criteria for voluntary confessions made by young persons to the police. They would prefer that violations of narrow technical aspects of section 56 be allowed to occur as long as the administration of justice is not brought into disrepute. This position has been promoted despite the situation in British Columbia and Quebec where, for example, Crown counsel screen all or most charges for sufficiency of evidence before a charge is laid. In British Columbia, it has been estimated that a softening of the secion 56 provisions would lead to a substantial, and consequently costly, increase in approved charges since many cases are presently screened out by Crown counsel because of the strict limitations on admissibility of statements. Similar effects may even result in other provinces where there is not a Crown counsel screening system — that is, where the police lay charges directly. In these provinces, many cases that, once in court, are now stayed or withdrawn by the Crown due to weakly grounded statement evidence could, under more lenient regulations, proceed to trial or result in convictions and sentencing. These potential increases in court processing would have major repercussions for case delays and court backlog.

---

[151] Moyer and Carrington, *supra*, note 128.

[152] Moyer and Carrington (1985) note that the survey question dealing with the minimal interference principle did not include the s. 3(1)(f) qualifier "consistent with the protection of society".

[153] Moyer and Carrington, *The Attitudes of Canadian Juvenile Justice Professionals Towards the Young Offenders Act* (Ottawa: Ministry of Solicitor General Canada, 1985).

It is likely that part of the initial opposition by Crown counsel to the Justice Model principles of the *YOA* was based on their concern that, not only would it be more difficult to proceed with certain charges, but also that court delays would occur. While the evidence concerning impediments to charging presented in the previous section on the police are either equivocal or impressionistic, the evidence on court delays in British Columbia is decidedly more convincing. In this regard, Table 9 demonstrates that, compared to the *JDA*, the functioning of the youth courts in British Columbia has been characterized by dramatic increases in cases delayed for more than 90 days and in the volume of cases backlogged in court.

TABLE 9

Changes in Youth Court Processing in British Columbia for 83–84 to 88–89

	Cases Delayed >90 Days	Minutes Per Case	Court Backlog (Cases)
FY 83/84			
(*JDA*)	2.5%	17	1,034
FY 84/85	28.2%	24	1,121
FY 85/86	40.1%	25	1,877
FY 86/87	41.0%	23	2,177
FY 87/88	38.0%	23	2,056
FY 88/89	38.0%	25	2,067

Source: Court Activity Summary Reports, Court Services Branch, B.C., Ministry of Attorney General, 1983-84 to 1988/89.

Concerns about substantially increased court delays and backlogs have been reported in other provinces as well and, while no systematic studies are currently available, it is widely accepted among juvenile justice officials in these provinces that similar increases have arisen there.

There is, however, some conflicting evidence from Alberta. Although Gabor *et al.* reported that three-quarters of the Alberta youth court judges they surveyed indicated an increase under the *YOA* in the average time per case,[154] Milner, in a comparison of court processing measures under the *JDA* and *YOA* in the Edmonton youth court, found no differences in case delays in spite of very substantial increases in Crown counsel (rather than police) prosecutions, defence counsel representing cases, adjournments for plea and adjournments to obtain social

---

[154] Gabor, Greene and McCormick, ''The Young Offenders Act: The Alberta Youth Court Experience in the First Year (1986) (5) (2) Can. J. Fam. L. pp. 301-319.

reports.[155] Milner attributes this lack of increase in court delays to a procedural innovation instituted under the *YOA* (related to the appointment of counsel), yet this very same innovation was also established in British Columbia, where case delays (province-wide) have been documented. Alternative explanations are that Milner's sample measures were taken early (1985) in the implementation of the Act and that, as she documents, most judges at that time ignored several procedures required under the new Act.

Since all juvenile court cases in British Columbia were already prosecuted by Crown counsel under the *JDA* — that is, there was no change with the advent of the *YOA* in that province — and there were still marked increases in court delays and backlogs, these delays and backlogs cannot be attributed to Crown counsel. This suggests that these delays and backlogs are attributable to other factors, even in other provinces where there were changes in roles from police to Crown counsel prosecutors. It is likely that these delays and backlogs were attributable to a variety of factors: principally, the increased presence of defence counsel and consequent enhancement in the adversarial nature of the proceedings; increased *voir dires* and trials related to technical arguments about the admissibility of confession evidence; delays related to the procedures for appointment of counsel; the increased formality of bail hearings; the provisions requiring pre-disposition reports to be in writing; and the very complex procedures governing the judicial review of disposition.[156]

The impact of the *YOA* on Crown counsel's role in juvenile justice is paradoxical: On the one hand, they have become central to many of the key decision-making junctures, including what offence to charge, whether to proceed or to use alternative measures and in speaking to sentence. On the other hand, it is their enhanced adversarial function that requires the due process provisions which are associated with court backlogs, more and longer hearings, and possible difficulties both in charging and obtaining guilty verdicts for certain types of property crimes. The problems associated with this paradox have not, however, evidently diminished Crown counsel's ability to obtain guilty pleas from most of those cases brought to court. In this regard, Table 10, derived from the Youth Court Survey,[157] describes the most significant decisions[158] in cases dealt with by the

---

[155] Milner, *supra*, note 149.

[156] Corrado and Markwart, "The Prices of Rights and Responsibilities: An Examination of the Impacts of the Young Offenders Act in British Columbia" (1988) (7) (1) Can. J. Fam. L. pp. 93-115.

[157] Statistics Canada, *Youth Court Statistics, Preliminary Data, 1988-89* (Ottawa: Canadian Centre for Justice Statistics, 1990).

[158] A case can involve more than one charge. When different findings are rendered on different charges, only the more significant decision is counted; for example, a finding of guilty on one charge and dismissed on another charge in the same case would be counted as a guilty finding.

TABLE 10

Most Significant Decisions in Cases Dealt with by Youth Courts, by Province, 1989–90

Province	Guilty	Not Guilty/ Dismissed	Decision Stayed/ Withdrawn	Other	Actual Guilty Rate
Newfoundland	87.2%	3.5%	9.2%	0.1%	96.2%
P.E.I.	92.9%	1.0%	6.9%	0.0%	99.0%
Nova Scotia	79.8%	9.7%	10.1%	0.4%	89.1%
New Brunswick	91.3%	1.8%	6.9%	0.0%	98.0%
Quebec	83.0%	8.2%	8.6%	0.3%	91.0%
Manitoba	58.3%	1.7%	40.0%	0.0%	97.2%
Saskatchewan	74.1%	6.5%	19.3%	0.1%	91.9%
Alberta	78.1%	4.2%	17.6%	0.1%	94.9%
B.C.	70.6%	3.9%	25.4%	0.1%	94.8%
Total	75.7%	4.8%	19.4%	0.1%	94.1%

Source: Statistics Canada, Canadian Centre for Justice Statistics, Youth Court Survey, 1989-90.

youth courts in nine provinces[159] in 1988–89. This Table indicates a marked variation in the proportion of cases resulting in a guilty finding, but these proportions are affected by equally marked variations in the proportions of cases resulting in stays of proceedings or withdrawals, particularly in the Western provinces. The varying proportions of stays and withdrawals may be related to different practices. For example, in screening for alternative measures after the laying of an information (charge) or, where the police lay charges directly, Crown counsel may enter stays/withdrawals in court when the evidence is reviewed and considered too weak to proceed.[160] By eliminating stays/withdrawals and "other" cases, and considering only those cases where the court has decided the case on the basis of the evidence or a guilty plea — i.e., guilty findings and not guilty findings/dismissals — an "actual guilty rate" can be calculated (right-hand column). These guilty rates indicate Crown counsel are remarkably successful in securing guilty findings: the Canadian average guilty rate is 94 percent, with provincial rates varying from a low of 89 percent to a high of 99 percent.

---

[159] Ontario does not report data to the Youth Court Survey.

[160] Stays of proceedings/withdrawals on "included" offences cannot account for the relatively high proportions of these decisions in some provinces; for example, where a youth is found guilty on theft on one charge (in the same case) and the possession of stolen property charge is stayed, the case would only be counted as guilty.

While Ontario does not report data to the Youth Court Survey, Hanscomb's survey of Ontario Phase I (12- to 15-year-olds) youth court judges suggests that Ontario Crown Counsel are similarly successful — 86 percent of cases are estimated to involve guilty pleas.[161] In addition, the custody rate data presented in Chapter 5 suggests that Crown counsel have apparently been able to secure this disposition far more frequently than under the *JDA*, in provinces where comparable data is available, and with increasing frequency since the proclamation of the *YOA* in most provinces.

The enhanced role of Crown counsel is likely to be affected by many of the organizational dynamics that have characterized Crown counsel functions in the adult criminal justice system. Because of relatively low salaries (compared to private legal practice), the increase in temporary contracts, large case loads (in metropolitan courts) and limited preparation time per case, Crown counsel positions tend to attract younger and inexperienced lawyers who often regard their jobs as a valuable though transitory training experience for entry into a more financially lucrative private law practice. In contrast to adult court, Crown counsel in youth court are exposed to a more limited range of cases in terms of charges and the type of proceedings (for example, the absence of jury trials). Youth court experience, as well, (and like the police) generally does not carry the same professional status as adult court experience.

One of the few studies to examine the performance of Crown counsel under the *YOA* involved assessments by Ontario Provincial Court (Family Division) judges.[162] In her study, Hanscomb distributed questionnaires to 77 judges throughout Ontario; 67 were completed, for an 88 percent response rate. A key hypothesis she wanted to assess in an exploratory manner was that increased custody rates under the *YOA* had occurred, despite the legislation's apparent emphasis on relying on alternative programs and the least interference sentencing principle, because judges were not given sufficient background information about the offender, the offence and alternative programs. Hanscomb maintained that Crown counsel had a responsibility (jointly with defence counsel and probation officers) to provide judges with this information at sentencing, but she found that the Ontario judges' experiences in youth court had led them to assess the performance of Crown counsel (and others) in a critical manner: at least half (54 percent) of the responding judges claimed they "almost never" received a detailed disposition plan from the Crown, even though 63 percent of these judges believed these plans to be "very" or "quite" important. As an example of the judges' critical views, one judge responded that:

---

[161] Hanscomb, *The Dynamics in Youth Court: A Report on a Survey of Youth Court Judges on Matters Affecting Disposition*, (LL.M. Thesis, University of Toronto, 1988).

[162] *Ibid.*

> Crown usually know little (if anything) about cases they present. They are handed
> the briefs on the way into court. They read the PDR [Predisposition Report] the same
> as everyone else but really know little about disposition.[163]

Generally, judges in this study were not favourably impressed with the
performance of Crown counsel at the dispositional stage of proceedings, even
though there was overwhelming approval by these judges of the increased
presence of Crown counsels in their youth courts under the *YOA*.

Hanscomb also sought judges' feedback about the critical relationship between
Crown counsel and defence counsel in serving certain key Justice Model principles included in the *YOA*. Hanscomb's summary statement and concluding
assessment is critical of Crown counsels' contribution, as well as defence
counsels' efforts:

> The responses of the judges to this series of questions about the role and performance
> of lawyers in Youth Court amounts to an indictment of their competency. The
> responses fully support the hypothesis that judges are not adequately served at
> disposition by these professionals whose job it is, as adversaries, to ferret out and
> provide the information needed to base a fair and just disposition. . . . (R)eliance
> placed on the probation officer to fill this void fails to serve the interests of the
> Defence and indeed may contribute to the overuse of custodial disposition.[164]

Obviously, the generalizability of Hanscomb's findings and inferences about
Crown (and defence) counsel's role under the *YOA* are limited to the pool of
Ontario Provincial Court (Family Division) judges surveyed. Yet, it is plausible
that the judicial dissatisfaction with Crown counsel in Ontario may be similarly
felt elsewhere in Canada if part of the explanation for their inadequate performance is based on the limited organizational resources that have characterized
Crown counsel offices in both the adult and youth justice systems. Considering
their relatively low salaries and heavy case loads, involving primarily property
and non-serious assault cases, it is possible that Crown counsel are neither very
experienced, nor are they given adequate time and other resources to prepare for
their routine youth court cases. These resource limitations appear evident in adult
provincial courts as well, where junior Crown counsel are often assigned to
process the less serious property and personal offences. In contrast, more
experienced Crown counsel are more likely to be assigned the high profile cases
involving, for example, murder charges, and to be given more substantial
resources to process these cases, including case preparation time and police and
forensic investigative assistance. Since few high-profile cases are tried in the
youth courts, less experienced Crown counsel are more likely to be assigned
there, and often for limited time periods, while they await their turn to move to the
senior court levels in the adult system. It is likely then that, although the *YOA* has
necessarily enhanced the role of Crown counsel in order to implement key Justice
Model principles involving due process and adversarial functions, structural or

---

[163] *Ibid.* at p. 22.
[164] *Ibid.* at p. 24 and 26.

organizational factors may significantly restrict the extent to which Crown counsel are able to fully satisfy the new and greater demands of this enhanced role.

Hanscomb's contention that inadequate Crown counsel performances contribute to judges resorting too frequently to custody, as opposed to alternate sentences or less punitive sentences, is not entirely convincing. As her own survey responses indicate, judges use a variety of sentencing principles. Other research confirms the lack of uniform judicial sentencing philosophies under the *YOA*.[165] It is questionable, therefore, whether judges routinely, or in any systematic manner, sentence youths to custody because Crown counsel (in conjunction with defence counsel) have not provided sufficient information about the most appropriate, i.e., least interfering, sentence. It seems more plausible that judges are aware of the inability (for whatever reason) of Crown counsel to provide more complete information. As one judge commented: "Except in unusual circumstances, most lawyers just 'wing it' and most Crowns just 'wing it' and *nothing* will change that approach".[166] Given this cynical view of Crown counsel's ability to function, it is more likely that individual judicial ideologies, probation officer predisposition reports and the availability (or lack thereof) of community-based sentencing options better explain why custodial sentences are so unexpectedly frequent under the *YOA*.

Another potentially important factor is that some Crown counsel probably place much greater weight on the Act's key principles of protection of society, responsibility and accountability. Consequently, they would be more likely to support custodial sentences to incapacitate, punish and deter even relatively minor offenders. Crime Control-oriented Crown counsel also might view any additional efforts on their part in routine cases as a waste of resources as long as the protection of society is enhanced (even temporarily) through custodial sentences.

It is also somewhat doubtful that many Crown counsel would necessarily concur with Hanscomb's suppositions about their prescribed roles at disposition — i.e., assisting in presenting detailed disposition submissions to the court. In a descriptive study of Crown counsel practices in British Columbia, Markwart reported that Crown counsel varied in the extent to which they would make submissions at sentencing, except with (perceived) more serious cases, in which cases they virtually always made sentencing submissions.[167] This would suggest Crown counsel can be quite selective. They may be more likely to defer to defence

---

[165] For example, see Doob, "Dispositions Under the Young Offenders Act: Issues Without Answers?" in Beaulieu, ed., *Young Offender Dispositions: Perspectives on Principles and Practice* (Toronto: Wall and Thompson, 1989).

[166] Hanscomb, *supra*, note 161, at p. 23.

[167] Markwart, "Crown Counsel Services in British Columbia" in *A Description of the Youth Justice Process Under the Young Offenders Act* (Ottawa: Canadian Centre for Justice Statistics, 1986).

counsel and probation officer submissions in more routine cases, but then more uniformly assume an adversarial role and put on their Crime Control hats in more serious cases. As well, most Crown counsel probably believe that their primary functions are to screen cases and to present evidence in contested cases; accordingly, their role at disposition is likely to be regarded as a lower priority and therefore attracts less attention.

The opposition to several Justice Model principles by a considerable proportion of Crown counsel prior to the implementation of the *YOA*, the recent lobbying efforts to mitigate some of the related sections of this legislation, and Hanscomb's survey results all suggest that the role of Crown counsel under the *YOA* is somewhat ambiguous. Their gate-keeping function — i.e., charge approval and alternative measures screening — and their adversarial role clearly add up to a more entrenched and critical decision-making function, yet due process provisions likely put greater demands on their limited organizational resources and therefore make it more difficult to satisfy the demands of their enhanced roles.

Impact of the *YOA* on Defence Counsel: Enhanced Role Perspective Versus Nothing Really Has Changed Perspective

Of all the juvenile justice roles, defence counsel is the most difficult to assess and to generalize about when considering the effects of the *YOA*. There is little systematic research, especially in Canada, focusing on the role of defence counsel. In Chapter 6, Linden *et al.* review this limited literature and examine the key hypothesis that the defence counsel role is most likely to be characterized by two styles or ideal types — the advocate and the guardian. The authors used data from the National Study of the Functioning of the Juvenile Court (NSFJC) survey and from a 1986 in-depth personal interview survey of 15 lawyers in youth court. In both studies, few defence counsel could be categorized as fitting neatly into either an advocate or guardian role. Instead, a mixture, consisting of combinations of the two types, was most common.

Evidently, there are complex multi-level factors that are associated with how defence counsel have adapted to the *YOA*. Provincial variations, for example, in the organization and roles of defence counsel were observed in the 1982 NSFJC project: public defenders — i.e., full-time salaried employees paid by the Quebec government — operated in the Montreal juvenile court, while in the Vancouver court private defence counsel selected by the juvenile were usually paid by Legal Aid Services (a non-profit society funded mainly by the British Columbia government) on a fee-for-services basis.[168] These different arrangements continue in these two provinces under the *YOA*. Another related variation involved defence counsel who were privately retained counsel, although these rarely appeared in juvenile court (and, given the appointment of counsel at public expense under the *YOA*, probably appear even less commonly now). Defence counsel do not form a homogeneous group. They vary in years of experience; in the proportion of adult

---

[168] Bala and Corrado, *supra*, note 148.

versus youth clients they serve; in the number of criminal versus civil cases they carry; in the formative articling and initial law practice experiences; and, as mentioned above, in their personal role definitions as well.

Partly because of the more entrenched role of defence counsel anticipated under the *YOA*, it was expected that they would be the most supportive of the new legislation. The NSFJC survey data confirmed this expectation, yet defence counsel disapproval was evident for two of the Crime Control Model aspects of the Act: fingerprinting and photographing of youths charged with indictable offences and the proposition that the protection of society should be given priority over the needs of the young person when these two principles could not be reconciled.[169] Defence counsel opposition to these aspects of the Act was not, of course, unexpected, since these provisions would give advantages to the police at the investigative stage and to Crown counsel at the sentencing stage, and therefore would make it more difficult for defence counsel to get the best outcome for their clients.

The *YOA* substantially enhances the role of defence counsel by virtue of several provisions, but particularly by section 11, which establishes a guaranteed right to counsel once a young person is charged and appears in court — i.e., if the young person is ineligible for Legal Aid and requests counsel, the court is legally obliged to appoint counsel at public expense. There is considerable evidence that these rights, which go far beyond what is accorded adult accused, have significantly increased the presence of defence counsel in Canadian juvenile courts. In Ontario, Moyer reports that young offenders are almost always represented in Phase I youth courts and that this represents an increase over the *JDA*, particularly in non-metropolitan courts.[170] In her study of the Edmonton youth court, Milner reports an increase in legal representation from 58 percent under the *JDA* to 72 percent by the beginning of the second *YOA* year.[171] It is likely that the degree of representation in the Edmonton youth court has increased further from this early *YOA* data, since there is also evidence that representation has increased as a function of greater experience with the Act: Markwart reports that legal representation progressively increased in British Columbia from 38 percent in the first *YOA* year (1984) to 80 percent by the fourth *YOA* year (1988).[172] Otherwise, it is widely agreed that the degree of legal representation has substantially increased in every Canadian jurisdiction under the *YOA*, and particularly so in non-metropolitan courts.

---

[169] Moyer and Carrington (1985) acknowledge that this latter statement was not an exact paraphrase of s. 3 (1) (6) *YOA*.

[170] Moyer, *supra*, note 150.

[171] Milner, *supra*, note 149.

[172] Markwart, *A Description of the Application of Dispositions Under the Young Offenders Act in British Columbia* (Ottawa: Canadian Centre for Justice Statistics, 1989).

The introduction of defence counsel into the juvenile justice process is associated with court delays and longer hearings[173] and, as discussed earlier, there is some evidence of increased delays under the *YOA*. Based on detailed court observations and file data obtained in Vancouver, Edmonton, Winnipeg, Toronto and Montreal for the NSFJC project, Carrington & Moyer conducted an impressive statistical analysis and concluded:

> In all five juvenile courts, there is clear evidence that legal representation (versus none), or representation by legal aid or privately retained counsel versus duty counsel or a public defender, increases the number of hearings and the number of courtroom minutes, even when antecedent factors such as case seriousness and complexity are held constant. . . Thus, we are forced to conclude that *other* factors associated with legal representation for the juvenile defendant are largely responsible for the increased workload. Possibilities suggested by the literature, but which we were unable to test, include procedural adjournments involved in getting a lawyer, manipulation of the system by defence counsel for purposes of delay, "judge-shopping", etc., or increased courtroom activity by defence and/or prosecutor other than that which was identified by our plea and pre-dispositional processing variables.[174]

Whether court delays are inherently negative is challenged by some defence counsel in the United States:

> . . . (D)elay in final resolution of a case can be good for a youth who can use the time to show job or school accomplishment and the ability to stay out of trouble. The youth who can do this may be able to avoid any negative sanction beyond arrest and court appearance.[175]

Generally, however, the view is that court delays are negative, not only for youths, but also in terms of increased costs, the effectiveness of the trial process, the confidence of the public and of other parties such as victims who are directly involved in the process, and the effectiveness of sentences imposed.[176]

Another perspective on the role of defence counsel is provided in the Hanscomb study mentioned earlier. Judges who responded to this survey overwhelmingly approved of the presence of defence counsel and supported a more active role for them in youth court proceedings. Yet, according to Hanscomb, defence counsel under the *YOA* are not functioning as most judges before whom they appear expect they should. She claims that her analysis left her wondering:

> . . . what, precisely, Defence counsel are doing on behalf of their clients. Since the rate of guilty pleas is about 90%, Defence counsel are not defending young

---

[173] Carrington and Moyer, "Legal Representation and Workload in Canadian Juvenile Courts" (Paper presented to the Annual Meeting of the American Society for Criminology, Chicago, November 1988), pp. 621–38.

[174] *Ibid*, at pp. 624-25.

[175] Mahoney, "Time and Process in Juvenile Court", *The Justice Journal*, Vol. 10, No. 1 (1985), pp. 37-55, at p. 43.

[176] Corrado and Markwart, *supra*, note 167.

offenders at trial. These results suggest that, in the opinions of the responding Judges, Defence counsel are also failing to be effective advocates at disposition hearings. They do not use character witnesses, statements by their own clients, factual evidence about the client's needs and circumstances or detailed disposition plans. Unfortunately, it appears that many young offenders are "represented" in name only at disposition hearings.[177]

Again, Hanscomb asserts that relying on the probation officers' pre-disposition reports to provide the judge with appropriate information is not always in their client's best interests. Unlike defence counsel, probation officers under the *YOA* are not committed to the client's wishes or best interests. This issue is discussed in greater detail in Chapter 6, in which the lawyers interviewed present a more varied and complex view than Hanscomb does of their role in general and of the utility of the predisposition report to their clients. Several defence counsel, though, do support the hypothesis that the defence counsel's role has not really changed under the *YOA* because the judicial process is still dominated by Welfare Model-oriented judges and their reliance on probation officers. In certain urban youth courts such as Vancouver and Montreal, defence counsel appear to have altered their role very little: a more adversarial role was already evident in Vancouver before the *YOA*, while in Montreal defence counsel appeared to retain more of an advocate function.

A rather confused and incomplete picture of the role of defence counsel under the *YOA* has emerged from the limited research available. Because of the Justice Model principles and provisions of the *YOA*, there can be little doubt that defence counsel are intended to play a crucial role in the reformed juvenile justice system. There is some evidence that their presence, as expected, has resulted in greater court delays and more and longer hearings. Yet, it is not at all clear exactly how their enhanced role has benefited youths charged and processed under the *YOA*, especially given the analysis and explanations of increased custody rates presented in Chapter 5. As will also be discussed in the section below on the judiciary, the adversarial process seems to facilitate more punitive sentencing, even though this outcome was not necessarily intended by the *YOA*.

How the increased presence and enhanced role of defence counsel under the *YOA* may have benefited youth and society at large is a vital question. The adversarial process, and the key role defence counsel play in that process, are, of course, integral to a Justice Model approach. While there was much complaint about the *potential* of abuses of legal rights under the *JDA* Welfare Model, there has been little in the way of systematic research to establish that these abuses actually occurred to any significant degree. Moreover, as Hackler has pointed out, it was changes in practices, not the law, which, by the late 1970s, avoided most of

---

[177] Hanscomb, *The Dynamics in Youth Court: A Report on a Survey of Youth Court Judges on Matters Affecting Disposition* (LL.M. Thesis, University of Toronto, 1988).

these abuses.[178] Further, removal of two key elements of the Welfare Model which likely led to the major abuses — that is, indefinite sentencing and status offences — did not necessitate the introduction of the very formalized, adversarial system of the *YOA*. On the other hand, even if, for the sake of argument, it is accepted that procedural abuses under the *JDA* were not widespread, the very presence of defence counsel offers a far better guarantee that abuses of legal rights will not occur. It is likely, as well, that abuses of legal rights under the *YOA* do, in fact, occur less frequently than under the *JDA*, even though this has yet to be systematically documented.

The Impact of the *YOA* on the Role of the Probation Officer: Diminished Influence as Officers of the Court

The *JDA* established the wide-ranging functions of the (then) novel probation officer role in order to implement the equally broad goals of the Welfare Model. Probation officers were continuously involved from the beginning to the end of the juvenile justice system process. In key provinces such as Quebec and British Columbia, they conducted pre-court social investigations which were crucial to the decision about whether to proceed with a charge or not. In these inquiries, probation officers relied on their formal and informal relationships with police, educators, social workers, health officials and the friends and family of the accused youth. Probation officers routinely attended court hearings and acted both as guardian and advocate, as well as officers of the court. In the latter capacity, they could even find themselves carrying out such prosecutional functions as speaking to issues like detention or release after arrest or, as was particularly the case in Manitoba, actually conducting uncontested cases through the court process.[179] Following a finding of delinquency, probation officers produced the critically important pre-disposition reports which, again, involved extensive information gathering about all aspects of a delinquent's life in order to recommend a sentence that was in the "best interest" of a youth. Usually, the recommendation and sentence included a period of probation during which a delinquent had to meet certain specific conditions — notably regular visits with a probation officer, but also others such as attending school, obeying curfews and avoiding specific friends and locations. If the probation officer believed that any of these conditions were not being followed, the officer could initiate a new court hearing to address the non-compliance. This new hearing provided the probation officer with considerable control over a delinquent, especially because it could be initiated by arrest and detention, followed by the possible imposition of a more severe sentence.

---

[178] Hackler, "The Impact of the Young Offenders Act" (1987) (29) (2) Can. J. Crim., pp. 205-210.

[179] Bala and Corrado, *Juvenile Justice in Canada: A Comparative Study* (Ottawa: Ministry of Solicitor General Canada, 1985).

In the informal proceedings that characterized juvenile courts for most of the history of the *JDA*, the views of the supervising probation officer appeared to be extremely influential in judges' decisions. There were few due process protections that limited the types of evidence and recommendations that probation officers provided judges. In addition, their influence was augmented because their routine contact with police and judges created a mutual dependence among those professionals.

The wardship provisions of the *JDA* also allowed delinquents to be directly entered as wards of the child welfare system, which meant probation officers acted as the liaison with their social worker counterparts in recommending a mutually agreed upon disposition to juvenile court judges. This relationship, in effect, allowed probation officers and social workers to work closely together to link the program resources of their respective departments or systems (if separate). This link was evident in the NSFJC project file data, which demonstrated that, while varying considerably by province, a substantial proportion of juvenile court cases involved child welfare wardships.[180] Most importantly, from the social worker's perspective, probation officers had the coercive power that they lacked in dealing with "troublesome" youth. In turn, probation officers could work through social workers to access the welfare institutions and other related child welfare community programs they felt were necessary for their probation clients to function within the community.

The *JDA* facilitated similar reciprocal relationships between probation officers and mental health workers and educators. Provincial child welfare, mental health and education legislation contained provisions that linked their "problem cases" to the juvenile justice system. Behaviourally disruptive or "acting out" youth and school truants, for example, could be charged and brought before a juvenile court judge under truancy and unmanageability provisions of provincial legislation. And a coercive sentence could be imposed as long as the presiding judge deemed it in the "best interest" of the delinquent. It was this enormous latitude allowed probation officers and judges that led to some of the fundamental criticisms of the Welfare model. To reiterate, the *JDA* stigmatized youth not only for committing crimes but also for being either sexually immoral, impoverished, neglected, abused, learning disabled, mentally disordered, immature or with some similar combination of social and health problems. To compound this injustice, it was eventually argued that it was really punishment rather than rehabilitation that was frequently dispensed in the youth's best interests. Finally, youth were being subjected to this coercion and punishment without full guarantees of due process.

The role of the probation officer began to change in certain provinces before proclamation of the *YOA*, but in different directions. In British Columbia, for example, Justice Model principles were introduced in the 1970s which began to narrow the types of decision-making, including sentencing recommendations. Crown counsel (rather than the police), for example, determined whether a charge

---

[180] *Ibid.*

would be formally laid, and defence counsel were increasingly defending youth in court hearings in the Vancouver Juvenile Court. British Columbia provincial Corrections policy also limited probation officers in recommending custody dispositions; only when all other less intrusive options had been exhausted were probation officers to recommend custody, and only in the most serious cases requiring "containment" for the protection of the public.[181] Also, status offences such as truancy and unmanageability were removed from provincial legislation. Though not explicitly stated, the net effect of British Columbia's provincial policy was to narrow the jurisdiction of probation officers and the youth correctional system to criminal offences and thereby to diminish the formal overlapping of inter-relationships with child welfare and other non-justice agencies.

In contrast, the 1977 Quebec *Youth Protection Act*[182] instituted an extensive Welfare Model approach for youth in need. The probation officer's role at the intake stage was replaced by a multi-disciplinary intervention assessment team (including probation officers) which would decide whether to divert youth, assign them to specific programs available in the social service centres or to prosecute. The radical changes introduced in Quebec have been discussed in detail elsewhere,[183] and in Chapter 7. Suffice to say, there is no doubt that the direction of change in traditional probation officer functions in Quebec was expansionary or more inclusive of the varied needs and problems of youth.[184]

Interestingly, probation officers as a professional group were not generally opposed to the *YOA*. In the 1982 NSFJC survey, probation officers, along with defence counsel, were the most supportive of the new Act, although they were critical of several aspects. There was, for example, probation officer disapproval of opening court hearings to the public and of the provision for dismissal of the charge when there had been only partial compliance with an alternative measure. A slight majority disapproved of the destruction of records provisions. There was also some opposition among probation officers in Ontario to the minimum age limit. Probation officers in Alberta and British Columbia were opposed to the increase in the maximum age to age 18. Further, the three-year maximum disposition length was not supported by two-thirds of the probation officers. As

---

[181] Markwart, "Youth Containment in British Columbia", paper presented to the Canadian Sociology and Anthropology Association, Learned Societies Conference, Halifax, Nova Scotia, 1981.

[182] S.Q. 1977, c. 20.

[183] See, Trépanier, J. "The Quebec Youth Protection Act: Institutionalized Diversion", in Corrado, LeBlanc and Trépanier, eds., *Current Issues in Juvenile Justice* (Toronto: Butterworths, 1982) and LeBlanc and Beaumont, "The Quebec Perspective on the Young Offenders Act: Implementation Before Adoption" in Hudson, Hornick and Burrows, eds., *Justice and the Young Offender in Canada* (Toronto: Wall and Thompson, 1988).

[184] Bala and Corrado, *supra*, note 179.

expected, there were some variations by province in the amount of support; however, these differences were generally not substantial.[185]

Why probation officers, notwithstanding these concerns, were generally supportive of the new Act can only be addressed speculatively, because the analyses of the NSFJC data have not included any complete explanations. In one analysis, it was evident that probation officers were supportive of Welfare Model principles, yet they also were not completely opposed to Justice Model principles. In effect, these two models were not seen as mutually exclusive.[186] The *YOA*, as has been stated several times already, includes principles from both models; consequently, it may be that many probation officers believed that the Act would be flexible enough to protect youth from procedural abuse while still allowing them to help address their clients' ''special needs'' or rehabilitation. It is also possible that the large proportion of probation officers who opposed the three-year maximum disposition length believed that ''getting tough'' with violent and recidivist juveniles, rather than gambling that they might be rehabilitated, was the most appropriate sentencing option. Without information about what is being recommended in predisposition reports, it is not possible to determine whether this Crime Control perspective of many probation officers may be behind the increase in custody rates under the *YOA*. Alternatively, it is possible that probation officers have observed that judges have become more Crime Control oriented and that probation officers are simply tailoring their recommendations accordingly. It is equally plausible that if custody is being recommended more frequently, it is because probation officers believe that (especially through open custody) it is easier to access treatment resources. The former *JDA* option of direct placement to child welfare and mental health facilities or programs is, of course, not available under the *YOA*. For youth who are seen as needing some form of controlled setting, even if for their own good — i.e., to protect them from injury or abuse resulting from prostitution or drug involvement — open custody may be seen as the only viable option. Still, while it is clear that custodial committals have increased under the *YOA* in most provinces, it is not clear whether probation officers are in fact directly recommending these dispositions or whether judges are imposing more frequent custodial dispositions on their own initiative.

The impact of the *YOA* on the probation officer's role has therefore depended, to some degree, on the direction of change during the transition period leading up to the implementation of the *YOA* in 1984. The impact has been considerable in several provinces. Even in British Columbia, where, as noted above, there had already been a significant shift toward Justice Model principles and a narrowing of

---

[185] Moyer and Carrington, *The Attitudes of Canadian Juvenile Justice Professionals Towards the Young Offenders Act* (Ottawa: Ministry of Solicitor General Canada, 1985).

[186] Corrado, Kueneman, LeBlanc and Linden, ''Treatment or Justice: An Analysis of Attitudes Toward Juvenile Justice in Canada'', *Anals de Vaucresson*, Vol. 2, 1986.

jurisdiction, the probation officer's function has been narrowed further. For example, prior to the *YOA*, provincial legislation in British Columbia required Crown counsel to refer every *Criminal Code* or federal statute case against a young person to a probation officer for a pre-court inquiry (social investigation) to assess whether the youth should be diverted or prosecuted. This, of course, accorded probation officers enormous influence in this crucial gate-keeping function. With the proclamation of the *YOA*, however, and partly in response to due process-related concerns that these mandatory enquiries could no longer be suitable under the Justice Model reforms of the *YOA*,[187] this provincial legislation was amended so that enquiries would only be carried out at the (discretionary) request of Crown counsel. Obviously, this seemingly minor change greatly diminished probation officers' involvement in cases and, consequently, their influence in processing decisions (while enhancing the role of Crown counsel).

In contrast, in those jurisdictions which had little or nothing in the way of diversion programs under the *JDA* — the Atlantic provinces, Saskatchewan and Alberta, for example — the implementation of alternative measures programs and the involvement of probation officers in screening, organizing and supervising programs has enhanced their role in this "front end"of the system. The shift in organizational responsibility for youth correctional services from social service to correctional departments in provinces such as Alberta and Prince Edward Island has led to a shift in both the type and orientation of probation personnel, from a child welfare to a correctional and more Crime Control orientation. On the other hand, probation officers in Ontario and Nova Scotia (with their split jurisdictions), who formerly dealt with 16- and 17-year-olds in an adult correctional context, now find themselves administering or involved in the more welfare-like aspects of the *YOA* (for example, open custody, medical and psychological reports).

Notwithstanding these variable impacts of the *YOA* across provinces, it can be said that the role of the probation officer has been substantially changed in three key respects under the *YOA*: enforcement and control; inter-relationships with and access to other agency resources; and in crucial court decisions. In each respect, their role has been diminished.

Unlike under the *JDA*, probation officers under the *YOA* can no longer simply return a client to court in relatively informal circumstances for further disposition by the court, whether for enforcement purposes or whether this is in the youth's best interests. Under the due process provisions of the *YOA*, enforcement of a breach of a community disposition requires the formal laying of a new charge (section 26) and proof beyond a reasonable doubt, with a guaranteed right to

---

[187] The argument was that these social investigations, ostensibly conducted for the purpose of diversion eligibility, were being carried out in cases that would obviously be prosecuted (for example, robbery); therefore, continuing with this process could be seen as an inappropriate and "back door" means of obtaining social history information.

counsel. As well, a review of a community disposition for reasons other than non-compliance (section 32) cannot result in a more onerous alteration of the original disposition (except with the consent of the young person). As a result, the probation officer's capacity to control and enforce has been sharply diminished, while a greater responsibility for the conduct of these cases has been shifted to Crown and defence counsel, with all the delay and limitations that this new process entails.

As a result of the formal severance in law, through the abandonment of the former *JDA* wardship committal provisions, of the relationship between the child welfare and juvenile justice systems and the consequent reorganization of services in several provinces, probation officers in many provinces do not have the same degree of ready access to child welfare programs and community services they formerly had under the *JDA*. Now, probation officers and the youth court can only access these types of services if the young offender satisfies the criteria of applicable child welfare legislation, which varies by province and which is subject to the administrative policies and discretion of (and resources available to) child welfare departments. This can arise — but not necessarily so (for example, Quebec) — regardless of how youth correctional and child welfare services are organized. For example, in British Columbia, where there are separate child welfare and correctional ministries, it has been observed that under the *YOA* there has been a greater reluctance on the part of child welfare authorities to provide child welfare services to young offenders.[188] Even in provinces such as Ontario (Phase I) and Saskatchewan, where child welfare and youth correctional services are administered by the same department, difficulties still arise in securing child welfare services for young offenders. As well, because the age for which adolescents are eligible for child welfare services is (under) 16 years in most provinces — British Columbia and Quebec being notable exceptions — 16- and 17-year-old young offenders are normally unable to receive these services. As a result of these changes in the child welfare/young offender service interface, probation officers may look (again) to the welfare-like open custody as the most (and perhaps only) viable sentencing recommendation.

With the due process and adversarial system of the *YOA* enhancing the roles of Crown and defence counsel in crucial decisions (for example, in bail/detention, disposition) it was inevitable that the role and influence of others, at least to some degree, must accordingly diminish. In this more formalized and adult-like criminal process, the probation officer — while often still playing a vital role, particularly in custodial decisions because pre-disposition reports are mandatory — must take more of a back seat to Crown and defence counsel, reacting to and providing information or recommendations only when directed by the court. This diminished role is reflected in the apparent reduced attendance of probation

---

[188] Markwart, *A Description of the Application of Dispositions Under the Young Offenders Act in the Province of British Columbia* (Ottawa: Canadian Centre for Justice Statistics, 1989).

officers in court when these critical decisions are being made. For example, even though policy in British Columbia requires a probation officer to attend court at all first appearances, show cause (for detention) and dispositional hearings, there has been an erosion of this requirement in practice under the *YOA*.[189] In Manitoba and Alberta, it is no longer the practice for probation officers to routinely attend youth court. In the Edmonton youth court, Milner has observed how probation officers under the *YOA* have been displaced in a process in which legal issues take precedence over social welfare concerns.[190] Still, it is evident that there are some provincial variations in the impact of the *YOA* on certain aspects of the probation officer's role. For example, in several areas of Ontario probation officers attend court (Phase I) less routinely than they did under the *JDA*, but there has been a substantial province-wide increase in the volume of pre-disposition reports ordered.[191] While British Columbia probation officers also attend court less routinely than they did under the *JDA*, there has, in contrast, been (taking into account the change in the maximum age) a decrease in the volume of pre-disposition reports ordered in that province.[192] It is possible that this variable impact could be the result of differences in the way other key actors carry out their roles. For example, there may be an increased reliance on pre-disposition hearings in Ontario as a result of the apparent inadequacies of the defence counsels' representations at disposition,[193] whereas the same circumstances may not arise in British Columbia. On the other hand, the reduced reliance on pre-disposition reports in British Columbia may be largely attributable to the fact that, whereas probation officers formerly obtained social history information on every *JDA* case, they no longer do so under the *YOA*.[194]

Key aspects of the probation officer's role remain, however, in providing information for judges through pre-disposition reports (PDR's) and in maintaining their probation supervision function. The Hanscomb study included feedback from Ontario judges about the information-providing role of probation officers in Phase I courts (see Table 11). Although there is little discrepancy between what role these Ontario judges think probation officers should play and what role they observe them playing, the judges' responses in Table 11 nonetheless reveal a lack of consensus about the probation officer's role in youth court. The majority of responding judges appear to favour a Justice Model function where probation

---

[189] *Ibid.*

[190] Milner, *supra*, note 149.

[191] Moyer, *A Description of the Application of Dispositions Under the Young Offenders Act by the Ministry of Community and Social Services of Ontario* (Toronto: Department of Justice, 1989).

[192] Markwart, *supra*, note 188.

[193] Hanscomb, *supra*, note 177.

[194] Note, however, that there obviously must be consistency across provinces with respect to ordering pre-disposition reports prior to a committal to custody, since this is an essentially mandatory requirement under the Act.

TABLE 11

Judges' Responses to the Role Probation Officers Play and Should Play in Youth Court[1]

	DOES PLAY		SHOULD PLAY	
Neutral Role	31	(64%)	28	(58.3%)
Correctional Role	7	(14.2%)	7	(14.5%)
Best Interests Role	11	(22%)	13	(27%)
Total	49[2]	(100%)	49[2]	(100%)

[1] From Hanscomb, *The Dynamics in Youth Court: A Report on a Survey of Youth Court Judges on Matters Affecting Disposition*, Master of Laws Thesis, University of Toronto, Toronto, 1988.
[2] 19 judges were not included because of mixed responses which could not be coded.

officers are philosophically neutral in conducting themselves as officers of the court, only reporting "the facts relevant to disposition".[195] A small proportion of the responding judges supported the more Crime Control-oriented function of the probation officer assessing the risk posed to the protection of society by a young offender. Approximately one-quarter of the responding judges indicated they saw probation officers as continuing to act in their once traditional *JDA* or welfare role, i.e., in the best interests of the young offender. Despite the variation in judges' perceptions of the role of the probation officer, the judges in Hanscomb's survey were "very happy" with the content and quality of the PDR's they read, while 95 percent felt the amount of information included was "adequate".[196]

Since the *YOA*, it appears that the probation officers — in contrast to the police or Crown counsel, for example — have stirred the least controversy and public complaint about the new Act and their consequently changed roles in the reformed juvenile justice system. It may be that probation officers are genuinely satisfied with their functions or, alternatively, that their voices and influence within the new juvenile justice system have diminished in accordance with their reduced roles. In our informal discussions with probation officers across the country, however, many have been critical of several aspects of the new system, including their own diminished roles, the enhanced roles and performance of Crown and defence counsel, court delays, difficulties accessing appropriate resources and heavy case-loads.

It seems that probation officers may be less critical of the *YOA* than other professional groups because, while holding divergent views, they nonetheless generally approve of the Act. In a survey of 79 British Columbia probation officers, Cosgrove found that different and sometimes conflicting opinions about

---

[195] Hanscomb, *supra*, note 177.
[196] *Ibid.*

the *YOA* are held by probation officers.[197] For example, approximately two-thirds approved of the *YOA*'s more formal nature, including the clarification of roles and the Act's ability to encourage more consistent practices. As well, approximately one-half approved of the *YOA*'s emphasis on legal rights.

In contrast, Cosgrove's survey also found that approximately 70 percent of the probation officers were critical of the complex nature of the *YOA*, particularly as these relate to court delays. Also, approximately 50 percent did not approve of the increased presence of defence counsel under the *YOA* since, as examples, these lawyers may not always act in the best interests of the youths they represent, youths may learn how to manipulate the court system, and defence counsel had contributed to an erosion of the probation officer's own professional role in the youth court system.

In spite of these divergent and conflicting views, Cosgrove found that a preponderance of the probation officers who had worked under both the *JDA* and *YOA* preferred the *YOA* — 57 percent preferred the *YOA*, only 18 percent preferred the *JDA*, and 25 percent did not respond to this question. It may be that these probation officers prefer the *YOA* for genuine philosophical reasons. It is likely, however, that the clarification and diminution of the role of the probation officer in British Columbia, in light of the heavy case-loads these professionals carry, may be a welcome outcome of the *YOA* for many. It seems apparent, however, that these probation officers are confused in their reaction to the *YOA*. Their responses suggest that while the majority embrace the principle of more entrenched legal rights, they simultaneously resent some of the outcomes of the implementation of these rights — for example, court delays and diminished professional influence.

Impact of the *YOA* on Role of the Judiciary: Circumscribed Roles but Retention of Sentencing Discretion

The *JDA* allowed judges enormous discretion in defining their roles. For much of the history of that Act, judges shed their long-standing common law tradition of neutrality in the adversarial criminal justice process. The Welfare Model *JDA* was revolutionary in the way it radically redefined the role of judges. They were to conduct themselves in the manner of a doctor or father figure seeking, first, to diagnose the conditions and circumstances that caused the young person before the court to become delinquent and, second, to proffer a wise and caring remedy or rehabilitative sentence, albeit firm and disciplinary where necessary. Proceedings were informal and loosely structured to provide the juvenile court judge with the latitude to gather the information necessary to decide what was in the ''best interest'' of the young person. Judges routinely adopted an inquisitorial role toward the youth, parents, social workers and probation officers.

---

[197] Cosgrove, *An Exploratory Study of the Implementation of the Custody and Review Provisions of the Young Offenders Act in British Columbia*, (M.A. (Criminology) thesis, Simon Fraser University, Burnaby, B.C., 1991).

Clearly, judges had unprecedented authority under the *JDA*, yet their role had already changed to a substantial degree, at least in urban courts, prior to the implementation of the *YOA*. As has been stated several times, provincial authorities in certain provinces such as Quebec and British Columbia undertook fundamental changes in their juvenile justice systems by the mid-1970s. As well, the evolution of case law and, generally, the wider acceptance of concerns about the rights of young offenders in the later years of the *JDA*, led to an increasing degree of procedural regularity in the juvenile courts. These changes affected judicial roles in varying degrees and in different ways. Generally, however, these early Justice Model-related reforms contributed to more formalized and circumscribed judicial practices such that their role in juvenile court became akin to their role in the adult criminal justice system. In non-metropolitan areas, judges were more likely to continue to conduct their courts according to traditional *JDA* norms, partly because case-loads and resources remained limited. It was in the urban courts where new corrections programs and Legal Aid programs for the provision of defence counsel were largely concentrated and publicly visible. In contrast, judges in small cities and towns, and in the less populated provinces and territories, who were not engaged full-time as juvenile court judges held irregular and relatively infrequent juvenile court hearings, and therefore did not face the same organizational and policy imperatives of their urban colleagues. These variations were still evident just prior to the passage of the *YOA*.[198]

In keeping with their traditional role as neutral parties independent of the legislative and executive arms of government, judges, as a professional group,[199] did not publicly engage in any concerted criticisms of the proposed *YOA* (although they were informally and privately consulted in the formulation of the Act). The 1982 NSFJC survey of judges revealed that they stood between police and Crown counsel, who were the least supportive, and defence counsel and probation officers, who were the most supportive of the new Act. The provincial variations were, however, considerable. Judges in British Columbia, for example, were markedly less accepting of the "least possible interference principle" and less favourable to the "special guarantees" of rights principle than judges in Ontario and Quebec. Judges' views of these principles also varied according to location and urbanization: judges from cities of more than 100,000 population were much more likely to be supportive than judges working in smaller communities.[200] This is not a surprising result given that judges in non-metropolitan courts tended to operate in a much less formalized manner and therefore would likely be most affected by the new Act.

---

[198] Bala and Corrado, *Juvenile Justice in Canada: A Comparative Study* (Ottawa: Ministry of Solicitor General Canada, 1985).

[199] A small number of individual judges have, however, voiced public criticisms of the *YOA* before and after implementation.

[200] Moyer and Carrington, *supra*, note 185.

Since the implementation of the *YOA*, the judiciary has not been visibly and systematically involved in the bureaucratic and political process in advocating amendments (although some degree of informal and confidential consultation does, in fact, occur). A few judges are willing to state their individual critical views publicly. More typically, judges have expressed their views through academic channels, including scholarly publications[201] and participation in survey research and seminars. Judges may, as well, be critical of legislation through case decisions. This occurred, for example, with several appellate court decisions which have been critical of the great disparity in the youth versus adult sentencing options facing a judge hearing an application to transfer a youth charged with murder to adult court. Despite these individual criticisms of specific aspects of the Act, few judges appear to support a return to the traditional Welfare Model juvenile justice system. In effect, there appears to be a consensus that the *JDA* Welfare Model needed to be replaced, but there seems to be at least some ambivalence about its Justice Model substitute.

Given this mixed view of the *YOA* among judges, fundamental provincial organizational and policy variations, and the limited research available, it is difficult to generalize about how the new Act has affected the role of judges. Some general observations may, however, be made. At the pre-adjudication stages of youth court proceedings, significant due process changes such as the increased presence of defence counsel, the application of adult bail laws and restrictions on the admissibility of statements have introduced far more formality and procedural regularity. This has created a more adversarial process, with attendant increases in court delays, trials and case backlogs. As well, the *YOA* no longer permits judges to transfer young offenders to adult court on their own initiative (i.e., without application by Crown counsel), an infrequent practice under the *JDA* in most provinces. Nevertheless, this change seems, in part, to account for a decline in the volume of transfers to adult court, particularly in Manitoba. As a result of these due process changes, it can be generally said that the roles of youth court judges in pre-adjudication proceedings have been altered and circumscribed, particularly in non-metropolitan courts.

This observation about the narrowing of judicial discretion at the pre-adjudication stage of proceedings presupposes that the more formalized procedures required by the *YOA* are always or usually observed. This may not, however, necessarily be the case. In her study of the Edmonton youth court, Milner found, for example, that there was no difference under the *YOA* from the informal bail hearing practices of the *JDA*.[202] She also found statutory requirements, such as explaining a young person's right to counsel when the youth was not represented and explaining charges to the young person, that were widely ignored. Milner's study was, however, conducted fairly early (1985) after proclamation of the new

---

[201] For example, see Thomson, "Commentary on the Young Offenders Act" (1983) (7) (2) Prov. Judges J. pp. 27-34.

[202] Milner, *supra*, note 190.

legislation, and it obviously cannot be said that these findings necessarily remain the case in the court studied or in other Canadian youth courts.

In contrast to the narrowing of judicial authority at the pre-adjudication stage, the role of youth court judges, generally speaking, has been substantially enhanced at the sentencing phase of court proceedings. Judges continue to have very broad discretion to order pre-disposition reports, although there appear to be substantial variations in judicial practices by provinces. For example, as noted earlier, the relative volume of pre-disposition reports under the *YOA* in British Columbia has diminished when compared to the *JDA*,[203] but in Ontario the volume has substantially increased.[204] As well, *YOA* judges now have explicit authority and wide latitude to order medical and psychological reports. While *YOA* judges no longer have the authority to directly commit a young offender to the care of provincial child welfare authorities — a change which has significantly affected several provinces — they now have more varied and explicit authority to impose community-based dispositions (larger fines, community and victim service, compensation and so on).

The greatest enhancements of judges' roles have, however, occurred with respect to their authority to impose custodial dispositions and to exercise direct control over the administration of these dispositions. Under the *YOA*, judges now determine the length of the custodial disposition (rather than impose indefinite terms), they decide the level of custody (open or secure) and they decide, by way of the review provisions, whether a young offender committed to custody should be transferred between levels of custody or released early from custody (and on what terms). All of these changes amount to a direct transfer of powers from correctional administrators to judges in all provinces, except British Columbia, where, under the *JDA*, definite sentences and judicially authorized early release were the universal practices. This new judicial authority goes far beyond what is even available to judges in the adult system. For example, judges in the adult system do not decide the level of custody once a prison sentence is imposed, nor do they act as a custodial releasing authority. Although it could be argued that the legislated considerations and offence criteria *YOA* judges must consider before imposing a custodial disposition have circumscribed their capacity to impose these dispositions, these apparent limitations (as will be discussed in Chapter 5) are hardly restrictive. Indeed, these statutory restrictions seem to have had little or no effect, and may even unwittingly encourage the use of custody by setting such low standards.

By transferring some key sentencing administration powers from correctional authorities to youth court judges, the *YOA* has obviously also transferred the exercise of discretion — which was so broad and so roundly criticized under the *JDA* — to judges. While it cannot be said, by any means, that the sentencing discretion accorded judges under the *YOA* nearly approaches what was given to

---

[203] Markwart, *supra*, note 188.

[204] Moyer, *supra*, note 191.

correctional administrators under the *JDA*, it nonetheless remains, as will be argued in Chapter 5, very broad. This, along with the lack of clear guidance from appellate court sentencing decisions[205] and the confused "mixed model" approach taken in the *YOA*'s Declaration of Principle, arguably continues to encourage differences in the treatment of young offenders, varying with many factors, such as the type and availability of dispositional services, but also with the personal ideologies of judges.

There is some evidence that there has been considerable variation in how judges have responded to their enhanced sentencing roles. Table 12, derived from the Youth Court Survey, describes the proportions of most significant decisions[206] by type of disposition in youth court cases in 1989–90 for all provinces, (except Ontario,[207] which does not report to the survey).

This table indicates that there is some variation in the proportions of cases committed to custody; for example, the proportion of young offenders committed to custody ranges by province from approximately one-fifth to one-third of cases. There is also considerable variation in the sub-types of custodial and non-custodial dispositions. Secure custody dispositions outnumber open custody dispositions in four provinces, but in five provinces the inverse is the case. For example, in Quebec 58 percent of custodial dispositions are to secure custody, but in Nova Scotia only 27 percent are committed to secure custody. As well, there are great differences in the per capita rates of incarceration across provinces. For example, Ontario's per capita rate of use of custody is nearly double that of British Columbia even though, as noted earlier, the latter province has a substantially higher crime rate.[208] There are also considerable differences in the types of non-

---

[205] Young, "Appellate Court Sentencing Principles" in Beaulieu, ed., *Young Offender Dispositions: Perspectives on Principles and Practice*. (Toronto: Wall and Thompson, 1989).

[206] To account for multiple dispositions in one case only, the "most significant" disposition is coded; for example, if a youth is committed to secure custody to be followed by probation, the case disposition would be coded only as a secure custody disposition. Significance is coded in the order in which these dispositions appear in the table.

[207] Data respecting the use of custody in Ontario are discussed in Chapter 5. Data concerning the use of non-custodial dispositions in Ontario are available but are *not* comparable to the data in Table 12. These data indicate that, of all non-custodial dispositions (only) in 1989–90, 62.5 percent were probation orders, 12.1 percent were community service orders, 8.0 percent restitution/compensation orders, 10.8 percent fines, and 6.6 percent absolute discharges (Kennewell et al., 1990).

[208] Derived from data provided by the British Columbia Ministry of the Solicitor General and Ontario's Ministries of Correctional Services and Community and Social Services (1989–90). Data are based on the rate per 10,000 population of 12- to 17-year-olds and include both pre- and post-dispositional custody. It is

TABLE 12

Most Significant Dispositions Imposed in Youth Court Cases, by Province,[1]
1989–90

Province	Custodial Dispositions			Non-Custodial Dispositions						
	Secure	Open	Sub-Total	Probation	Fine	Compensatory[2]	CSO[3]	Discharge	Other[4]	Sub-Total
Newfoundland	13.6%	11.1%	24.7%	61.3%	7.3%	1.1%	1.0%	4.3%	0.5%	75.3%
P.E.I.	20.4%	13.9%	34.3%	54.1%	7.1%	0.1%	2.7%	0.1%	0.4%	65.7%
Nova Scotia	7.3%	19.5%	26.9%	53.5%	11.1%	0.4%	4.2%	2.4%	1.6%	73.1%
New Brunswick	18.3%	14.2%	32.6%	59.2%	4.2%	0.5%	0.6%	1.6%	1.3%	67.4%
Quebec	18.8%	13.2%	31.9%	46.0%	11.0%	1.5%	7.0%	1.8%	0.7%	68.1%
Manitoba	11.3%	13.5%	24.8%	43.7%	13.2%	1.9%	10.0%	2.7%	3.6%	75.2%
Saskatchewan	9.9%	16.2%	26.1%	52.4%	7.1%	0.5%	6.7%	4.5%	2.7%	73.9%
Alberta	10.2%	11.3%	21.5%	33.5%	21.4%	1.5%	15.1%	5.9%	1.2%	78.5%
British Columbia	9.3%	14.4%	23.7%	59.6%	10.4%	0.5%	1.8%	3.5%	0.6%	76.3%

SOURCE: Youth Court Survey, Canadian Centre for Justice Statistics, Statistics Canada, 1989–90.

[1] Ontario does not report to the Youth Court Survey.
[2] Compensatory includes monetary compensation, restitution, payment to an innocent purchaser and compensation in kind.
[3] CSO means community service orders.
[4] Other includes detention for treatment, prohibition/seizure/forfeiture and miscellaneous orders such as essays and apologies.

custodial dispositions imposed among provinces, particularly in the proportions of probation and fine dispositions (notably in Alberta).[209]

The problem with these data, of course, is that the apparent differences in disposition practices could be related to a wide variety of factors beyond simple variation in judicial attitudes. These could include the volume and type of cases appearing in the youth court, which can be significantly affected by the extent of police screening and formal alternative measures; the organization and type of services available respecting alternatives to custody and open versus secure custodial services; and other factors. For example, the relatively high proportion of cases committed to custody in Quebec[210] may arise because that province extensively screens out minor cases to its diversion system, leaving only the more serious cases for the youth court to deal with. This observation seems to be substantiated by the finding that youth court cases in Quebec have nearly double the number of charges per case than any other province.[211] Several of these factors are discussed in more detail in Chapter 5.

Statistical indices aside, there are also qualitative studies which have attempted to examine the impact of the *YOA* on judicial decision-making and which suggest variations by province and amongst individual judges. In Alberta, *Gabor et al.* interviewed 13 of the 15 full-time Family and Youth Division judges to assess the impact of the Act after its first year. These interviews led to the conclusion that:

---

also known there are wide differences among other provinces, but these data are not presently publicly available.

[209] The coding of multiple case dispositions according to most significant type can, however, significantly suppress the apparent frequency of use of certain types of non-custodial dispositions. For example, a case disposition involving a community service order made in combination with a probation order — a frequent occurrence in many provinces — would only be coded as a probation disposition, thereby obscuring the frequency of use of community service orders. To illustrate these differences, when all dispositions are counted (i.e., not only the most significant) community service orders account for 19 percent of dispositions in British Columbia (Markwart, 1989).

[210] A high proportion of youth court cases committed to custody does not necessarily translate into a high volume of custody committals or a high incarceration rate (per 10,000 young persons). Incarceration rates will vary according to, for example, the volume of youth court cases appearing (which in turn are affected by screening practices), sentence length, court review practices, etc. For example, although Quebec has a high proportion of court cases resulting in custodial committals its per capita rate of incarceration is among the lowest in the country.

[211] Statistics Canada, "Youth Court Statistics, Preliminary Data: 1989-90 Highlights" (1990) (10 (13) *Juristat Services Bulletin* (Ottawa: Canadian Centre for Justice Statistics).

> . . . most judges continue to be treatment-oriented, as they were under the *Juvenile Delinquents Act*. However, the judges are concerned about the decreased quality of services for young offenders since the advent of the *YOA*. The emphasis on the rights of young offenders in the *YOA* has not had a major impact on the courts, because the judges feel that rights were generally being respected under the *JDA*. Nevertheless, there has apparently been a significant increase in legal representation, which seems to present more advantages to lawyers than to young offenders. Unless the justice system is able to respond to the major principles of the *YOA* in a more balanced way, some of the best features of the old system may be lost without corresponding gains from the new legislation.[212]

Consistent with the treatment orientation of custodial facilities established in that province under the *JDA*, most of these Alberta youth court judges viewed custody more in terms of treatment than punishment, yet the latter was seen as increasing in secure custody facilities. Punitiveness was also seen to vary, depending on the type of rehabilitative programs available at a specific facility; most judges felt such programs were inadequate. The authors asserted that, primarily as a result of fiscal restraint policies: "Alberta has chosen to implement a [juvenile justice] system which places minimal importance on the 'special needs' provisions of the Act, and which can only deliver the 'accountability' provisions."[213] Most Alberta judges consequently expressed concern that, without more treatment resources, the presence of defence counsel and other due process protections would not offset these *YOA*-related structural or organizational changes in the juvenile justice system which, intentional or not, had shifted the orientation of the system away from rehabilitation. In fact, the stated policy intention of the Alberta Department of the Solicitor General was to continue the emphasis on individual needs and rehabilitation which characterized the operation of custodial and placement facilities by the Department of Social Services and Community Health under the *JDA*.[214] It is not yet apparent whether treatment resources will be more forthcoming from the Conservative government of Don Getty if and when fiscal restraint in Alberta is eased. It is not yet evident to what extent fiscal restraint, rather than the *YOA*-induced changes in youth corrections, explains the apparent decline in treatment resources perceived by most of the Alberta judges. According to the Gabor *et al.* interviews, it does not appear that these judges had clearly shifted to either Justice Model or Crime Control Model sentencing principles following the first year of the implementation of the *YOA*, but some change was still evident: nearly half (6) of the 13 judges indicated that

---

[212] Gabor, Greene, and McCormick, "The Young Offenders Act: The Alberta Youth Court Experience in the First Year" (1986) (5) (2) Can. J. Fam. L. pp. 301-19 at p. 301.

[213] *Ibid.* at p. 318.

[214] Mason, "Implementing the Young Offenders Act: An Alberta Perspective" in Hudson, Hornick and Burrows, eds., *Justice and the Young Offender in Canada* (Toronto: Wall and Thompson, 1988).

"they had changed their attitudes to place more emphasis on young offenders taking responsibility for their actions.[215]

A similar view about the inadequacy of treatment resources was expressed by many of the Ontario judges in the Hanscomb study. Approximately half (52 percent) of the judges found alcohol/drug therapy programs, and remedial education and vocational training either unavailable or inadequate, while 42 percent found psychiatric counselling similarly wanting.[216] Hanscomb maintains that inadequate treatment resources and, to a lesser extent, inadequate community service and probation services, might contribute to an increased use of custodial sentences in Ontario.

Unlike most of the Alberta judges, Hanscomb found that her sample of Ontario judges perceived "a great change in their approach to sentencing under the YOA".[217] The focus no longer is the offender but the offence and, instead of individualized sentencing, a more tariff-like approach has become established in these Ontario youth courts. Three-quarters of these judges indicated that they placed greater weight on "punishment or accountability" under the YOA than under the JDA, while 98 percent indicated that deterrence to the individual was a "very" or "quite" important consideration in sentencing. Hanscomb claims further that a significant number of judges believe that these goals, along with the "protection of society", can be accomplished by custodial dispositions.

The apparent differences in perceptions between the Alberta and Ontario judges suggest considerable variability in the impact of the YOA on the judiciary, although it should be noted that, since these two studies were conducted in the first (Alberta) versus the third (Ontario) years of the new Act, some of the differences may be attributed to Ontario judges' increased experience with the YOA, the waning influence of the residual effects of the JDA and the evolution of case law. For example, as discussed in Chapter 5, it is apparent that there has been an increased reliance on custody over time in most provinces, including Alberta and Ontario, as experience with the new Act has increased.

Variability among individual youth court judges was, however, very evident at a three-day seminar on the YOA held in late 1988 which was sponsored by the Youth and Family Court Committee of the Canadian Association of Provincial Court Judges. Senior Judge Lucien Beaulieu from Toronto organized the conference and invited not only youth court judges from across Canada, but also appellate court judges. Several research papers were delivered [by academics and other researchers] on various controversial YOA issues, but the major focus was on dispositions under the new Act.[218] Professor Anthony Doob conducted a

---

[215] Gabor, Greene and McCormick, *supra*, note 212.
[216] Hanscomb, *The Dynamics in Youth Court: A Report on a Survey of Youth Court Judges on Matters Affecting Disposition.* (LL.M. thesis, University of Toronto, 1988).
[217] *Ibid.*
[218] Beaulieu, ed., *Young Offender Dispositions: Perspective on Principles and Practice* (Toronto: Wall and Thompson, 1989).

simulation at the conference where judges were asked how they would sentence individuals in several young offender cases and why. The sentencing variation for identical cases was substantial, as were the sentencing philosophies or rationales. For example, in one case of assault causing bodily harm, the severity of the disposition selected by the judges ranged from a community disposition (probation or a fine) to 12 months' secure custody. As well, "there was enormous variation in the relative importance given to the various principles/purposes of sentencing."[219]

In his summarizing chapter of a book based on the papers delivered at the conference, Doob addressed the sentencing disparity issue and related issues. Both the questions and issues raised, and the various responses, were largely based on Doob's observations about what judges and other participants said about the crucial issue of rendering dispositions under the YOA. Some of these issues have been discussed in Chapter 2 by Bala; however, they are re-iterated here because Doob provides his own perspective about the YOA. Several general factors emerged to explain why controversies exist about the judicial role under the Act. First, the difficult task of interpreting and balancing the various YOA principles and goals inevitably results in conflicting values and purposes in sentencing. Second, most judges find that rendering dispositions for young offenders is more difficult and stressful than adult sentences because of the developmental differences and consideration of needs routinely involved in young offender dispositions. Third, as judges who have to administer the promises of the YOA, they are limited in fulfilling them because of financial restraints or inadequate programs, and insufficient research and feedback about which types of sentences are effective. Compounding these problems are both the public concern that sentences for young offenders, especially violent young offenders, are too lenient, and the public's misunderstanding and ignorance of the complexity of YOA. While it is not evident to what extent this negative public reaction affects judges, it does add to the media controversy and confusion about the Act.

This confusion, to a considerable degree, is a reflection of the inability to clearly interpret and categorize the YOA philosophy in a manner similar to the straightforward philosophy of the Welfare Model embodied in the JDA — i.e., the YOA does not provide clear guidance as to its apparent objectives. While judges at the conference agreed that the two statutes are decidedly different, they disagreed about the degree to which the YOA is a Justice Model. Judge Omar Archambault, who played a key role in drafting the Act, vigorously rejected characterizing the YOA in Justice Model terms. Yet several judges argued:

> . . . there are 'hints' enough to suggest that the YOA philosophy is 'offence' in its orientation and that dispositions should be assessed largely in terms of offence seriousness and handed down in such a way that disposition severity is proportional

---

[219] Doob, "Dispositions Under the Young Offenders Act: Issues without Answers?" in Beaulieu, ed., *Young Offender Dispositions: Perspectives on Principles and Practice* (Toronto: Wall and Thompson, 1989).

to the seriousness of the offence. Examples that are offered to support this view are that transfers are allowed only for certain types of offences, that dispositions are supposed to be no more serious than sentences for comparable offences for adults, that the maximum length of dispositions under the *YOA* depends on the offence of conviction.[220]

Archambault and other judges, while admitting that offence is relatively more important under the *YOA* than the *JDA*, maintain that it is completely misleading to conclude that sentencing severity under the *YOA* should simply be proportional to the seriousness of the harm inflicted. This principle is the keystone to the "just desserts" model and important for the punishment and deterrence principles of the closely related Crime Control Model. Yet the *YOA* does identify the protection of society from illegal behaviour as one key principle, and emphasizes the responsibility and accountability of young offenders. This, together with the ambiguity of and minimal reference to the "special needs" principle, may have led some judges to shift their sentencing rationale towards incapacitation, punishment and deterrence.

A major difficulty in interpreting sentencing rationales, again, is in deciding whether the focus is on the offender or the offence. Sentencing disparities would tend to be greater with an offender focus because individuals vary in numerous ways. However, these disparities should, because of greater definitional commonalites, be less when the offence is the focus. There did not appear to be a consensus among the conference judges about the appropriate focus. The *YOA* principles are ambiguously connected, and it has been argued that the appellate courts have not yet signalled clear sentencing directions for young offenders.[221] Consequently, youth court judges appear to be guided more by their own personal views. In group and individual discussions, Doob observed that judges discussed whether punishment resulted in deterrence; whether the costs of protecting society from non-serious or violent offences was worth the social and financial costs of custodial sentences; whether these sentences should be based, at least partly, on a prediction of future offending; and whether youth court dispositions should avoid altogether considerations of incapacitation and general deterrence. These judges also discussed the problems of administering the *YOA*, especially given the wide variation in resources inter- and intra-provincially, and of unintended consequences, such as unwarranted sentencing disparities.

There was also no consensus among these conference judges about the use of custody under the *YOA*. There was even disagreement about the usefulness of comparing custody rates between the new Act and the *JDA*. Definitional problems involving, for example, the "open" and "secure" *YOA* custody options, preclude a simple comparison (in some provinces). It was also not clear to the judges whether the apparent increase in custody rates, particularly open custody, should be regarded as a punitive trend; the alternative perspective is that this may be

---

[220] *Ibid.* at p. 197.
[221] Young, *supra*, note 205.

reflective of a rehabilitative trend — i.e., treatment program are more likely to be available in open custody facilities, which are not so onerous as traditional training schools. Local factors involving customs or traditional views about the use of custody were also seen as being possibly more important than judges' responses to the *YOA*. A more fundamental issue was raised about whether custody dispositions were inherently "bad" — whether "short, sharp shocks" might be effective in achieving individual deterrence. Another question asked by some of these judges was whether, because of the increased maximum age, more youth were appearing before them with "verifiable criminal records". Two related points were that police might be processing more serious cases under the *YOA* because of their perception of an increased likelihood of a custodial sentence and that "non-criminal" type offenders who cannot be controlled in child welfare and other social control systems are being pushed into the youth court. Another explanation was that judicial custodial reviews, as mandated by the Act, were not routinely and effectively taking place; therefore, too many young offenders were inappropriately remaining in custody.

Many of these concerns about custody were reiterated in the judges' discussions about transferring alleged young offenders to adult criminal courts. The central issue, again, focused on the lack of clear direction provided by the key *YOA* principles. Bala and Lilles maintained that section 16 of the *YOA* allowed at least three approaches to judicial interpretations of the appropriate transfer criteria — protection of society, the young person's needs and a combination of these two principles.[222] In the absence of more direct guidance from the Supreme Court of Canada, or Parliament, the substantial interprovincial variations in the number of transfers are likely to continue (see Chapter 2).

In summarizing the discussions among judges about their own experience and the research presented at the judicial conference, Doob maintained that:

> The more basic problem, however, is that there is a lack of consensus on the importance of various factors. 'Age,' for example, seems to be given different weight depending on the judge/province/Court of Appeal. In other words, the interpretive philosophy of the judge or the appellate court in the province may be of greater importance than the particular facts of the case.[223]

As was the situation with other key juvenile justice professionals described in this chapter, a confused image emerges about the impact of the *YOA* on the role of judges. The limited research suggests that there is considerable variation. The Ontario judges in the Hanscomb study appear to have adjusted differently than the Alberta judges in the Gabor *et al.* study although these differences may, in part, be attributable to the Ontario judges' lengthier experiences with the new Act at the time the Hanscomb study was conducted. According to the Winnipeg youth court

---

[222] Bala and Lilles, "Transfer to Adult Court: The Most Serious Disposition", in Beaulieu, ed., *Young Offenders Dispositions: Perspectives on Principles and Practice* (Toronto: Wall and Thompson, 1989).

[223] Doob, *supra* note 219, at p. 217.

lawyers included in the Linden *et al.* study (see Chapter 6), judges vary substantially within the same court, an unsurprising observation which likely applies to many youth courts across Canada. While the judges who attended the 1988 judicial conference in Montreal were not randomly selected, they did represent a broad range of provinces and they too differed on their perceptions of their role under the *YOA*. Despite these differences, Doob maintained that:

> Most judges appear to take the view that there is no need to change s. 3 (the 'Declaration of Principle') of the *YOA*. They see it as an improvement over the *JDA*, indicating that it gives individual judges scope to deal with almost any case. Indeed, there appear to be few judges who believe that they personally need any additional guidance.[224]

If Doob's assessment is valid, it may explain why judges have not become a major interest group seeking to replace or amend the *YOA*. While judges generally are reluctant to involve themselves in the political process through their representative provincial and national organizations, the more likely reason they have avoided this route is that they have retained their powerful position in the juvenile justice system under the *YOA* and are reluctant to see major changes. While the due process changes of the *YOA* have circumscribed (at least in non-metropolitan areas) the more informal practices of judges in the various pre-disposition stages of youth court proceedings, judges retain wide discretion in imposing dispositions. Put another way, the "scope" that Doob describes *YOA* judges as having simply means they have broad discretion. Apparently, many judges would be reluctant to have any "additional guidance" since this would narrow their broad discretion and therefore circumscribe their roles. It should also be said that the apparent differences among judges in sentencing practices, as Doob's case examples suggest, are likely little different than what occurred under the *JDA*. The obvious difference, of course, is that sentencing disparities were, in effect, an intended outcome of a *JDA* Welfare Model which focussed on the treatment needs of individuals, whereas continued sentencing disparities under the *YOA* fly in the face of one of the explicit goals of this new Justice Model legislation; i.e., greater uniformity of treatment of young offenders, including sentencing and processing.

Conclusion

The story of the evolution and implementation of the *YOA* is one of both compromise and consensus-seeking. From it Canada's new Modified Justice Model approach to juvenile crime has emerged. It is also a story of incrementalism in the gradual shift along the continuum from the pure Welfare Model of the *JDA* toward the Justice Model. Recently, as well, there has been discernable movement further along the continuum by incorporating elements of the Crime Control Model.

The first signal of a Canadian shift away from the pure Welfare Model of the *JDA* came from the 1965 Juvenile Delinquency Committee with its proposals for a

---

[224] *Ibid.* at p. 202.

mixed model of "front end" justice processing, coupled with the retention of welfare-like dispositional measures — a kind of "rights and treatment" model. However, as a result of interest group opposition and federal/provincial political disputes about costs and jurisdiction, the statute that was eventually to emerge was delayed nearly 20 years. This proved to be a delay long enough so that, in the intervening years, the emergence of increasingly critical criminological and legal research battered Welfare Model proponents into submission. This created the vacuum that would be filled by Justice Model advocates and consequently transformed national juvenile justice policy to a "rights and responsibility" orientation. Since proclamation of the new *Act*, the movement along the continuum, largely fueled by public concerns about an (apparent) increasing rate of violent juvenile crime, has continued with actual and proposed amendments which have been almost exclusively Crime Control in nature.

For those who argue that the *YOA* is not a (albeit modified) Justice Model,[225] the evidence concerning its complementation is clearly to the contrary. In response to the new Act, there has been a decided organizational shift toward services being delivered under the auspices of correctional departments and, importantly, in the severance of the relationship between juvenile justice and child welfare services in law, organizationally, and operationally.

Although their performance has been criticized, the roles of defence and Crown counsel have clearly been substantially enhanced in the more adversarial processes established by the new Act. Increased court delays and backlogs have been one apparent consequence. With a greater array of dispositions and the new capacities to determine the length of custody, type of custody and release from custody, as well as the great "scope" judges retain in imposing dispositions, their roles have also been enhanced. With this re-alignment and enhancement of roles and powers among these legally trained personnel, the roles and powers of other key juvenile justice system actors have also been affected. Police roles and powers have been both enhanced and diminished, depending upon which aspect of policing is examined. But other key actors who were formerly charged with the responsibility for implementing the ideals of the *JDA* Welfare Model — i.e., probation officers, correctional authorities and child welfare authorities — now seem to have substantially reduced roles and influence in the new system.

As we stated at the outset, the *YOA* is more or less a pure Justice Model at the "front end" of the juvenile justice process (i.e., pre-adjudication). It is at the "back end" — or in sentencing — where the confusion and debate about what the *YOA* really is has arisen. One test of how far along the Justice/Crime Control continuum Canada's new juvenile justice legislation has moved can be found in the extent of use of custodial dispositions. This is a matter which is discussed in detail in the next chapter. Put succinctly, however, the evidence of a substantially

---

[225] For example, Archambault, "Young Offenders Act: Philosophy and Principles" in Silverman and Teevan, eds., *Crime and Canadian Society* (Toronto: Butterworths, 1986).

increasing reliance on custody in most provinces makes a convincing case that the *YOA* has been interpreted and applied in a manner that is in keeping with the increased prominence of punishment, deterrence and incapacitation one would expect from Justice/Crime Control legislation.

CHAPTER 5

CUSTODIAL SANCTIONS UNDER THE
YOUNG OFFENDERS ACT

Alan Markwart[1]

INTRODUCTION

The use of custody has always been at the heart of the debate about how society should respond to the problem of juvenile crime. It was, for example, concern expressed by the "child savers" movement[2] about the inappropriateness of incarcerating juvenile offenders in adult penal institutions that, in no small part, prompted juvenile justice reform efforts in North America during the 19th and early 20th centuries. In Canada, these reform efforts[3] culminated in the enactment of the federal *Juvenile Delinquents Act*[4] (*JDA*) in 1908, which continued in force until it was repealed and replaced by the *Young Offenders Act*[5] (*YOA*) in 1984.

The *JDA* established a separate juvenile court with its own distinct philosophy and body of law and, of course, separate facilities (from adults) for the confinement of juvenile offenders. Like similar Welfare Model juvenile justice legislation enacted in the United States at about the same time, the *JDA* established a *parens patriae*, highly interventionist and treatment-oriented philosophy for the juvenile courts. A young person who offended against federal criminal or provincial statutes, or was found delinquent for a status offence, was to be treated "not as a criminal, but as a misdirected and misguided child, and one needing aid, encouragement, help, and assistance".[6]

---

[1] Alan Markwart is a Program Analyst with the British Columbia Ministry of Attorney General. The opinions expressed are the author's and do not reflect the views of the British Columbia Ministry of Attorney General.

[2] Platt, *The Child Savers: The Invention of Delinquency* (Chicago: University of Chicago Press, 1977).

[3] See, for example Leon, "The Development of Canadian Juvenile Justice: A Background for Reform" (1977) 15(1) Osgoode Hall L.J., pp. 71–106.

[4] S.C. 1908, c. 40.

[5] S.C. 1980-81-82-83, c. 110 [now R.S.C. 1985, c. Y-1].

[6] *Supra*, note 4, s. 38.

Young persons in conflict with the law were not considered "offenders", but were found to be in a "condition of delinquency";[7] i.e., the offence was not regarded as a single incident in the young person's life, but rather as symptomatic of his state of being. Help (rehabilitation) then was required to ameliorate the social (familial) conditions and personal defects that brought about this dysfunctional state of being. The way in which juvenile institutions were characterized under the Act illustrates the rehabilitative ideal underlining the legislation: delinquents were not committed to "jails" or even to "custody", but rather to helpful-sounding "industrial schools" or "juvenile reformatories". Later, these became commonly known as "training schools" or, more euphemistically in one province, as "youth development centres".

The vast discretion accorded the juvenile court and correctional administrators,[8] in pursuit of the best interests of the child, was key to the rehabilitative goal of the *JDA*. Since treatment needs would, regardless of the nature of the delinquency, necessarily vary among individuals, the Act provided for dispositions for an indefinite period — including indefinite committals to training schools — and permitted administrators to determine at what point termination of the disposition or release from the training school should occur. Since all measures imposed were for the "child's own good"[9] and industrial schools were intended to rehabilitate, there was little need for concern about substantive legal rights and procedural safeguards for the child, or for limitations on committals to training schools.[10]

As with the development of the *JDA*, it was again concern expressed about the use of custody that, in part, initiated the more recent juvenile justice reform efforts in Canada in the 1960s and 1970s that culminated in the passage of the *YOA* in the House of Commons in 1982 and its eventual proclamation in 1984. The more than 20-year process leading to the implementation of the Act began with the appointment of a committee by the federal Department of Justice in 1961 to inquire into juvenile delinquency in Canada. The appointment of the committee was triggered by a growing concern about a burgeoning adult penitentiary population; its task was to prevent further increases in the adult prison population by recommending ways of making the juvenile justice system more effective. The committee's report was critical of the inadequacies of Canadian training schools. While it

---

[7] *Supra*, note 4, s. 2.

[8] "Correctional administrators" is used here and throughout this chapter as a generic description of those responsible for the administration of juvenile dispositions. Under the *JDA*, juvenile dispositions were, in most provinces, administered by provincial child welfare departments. While this still remains the case in some provinces (for example, Quebec), the majority of provinces have now changed to correctional administrations (see Chapter 4).

[9] *Supra*, note 4, s. 20.

[10] The only explicit limitation on committals to training schools under the *JDA* was for children under 12 years of age (s. 25).

pointed to recent and "alarming" increases in juvenile crime and warned of even more alarming increases to come, the committee nonetheless endorsed the principle that committals to institutions should be used as a last resort for juvenile offenders and that this should be reflected in legislation;[11] i.e., institutionalization as a remedy for juvenile crime was implicitly rejected.[12]

The Department of Justice committee report was followed by an era of activist concern about civil and minority rights in Canada and the United States. It became apparent that the vast discretion accorded the juvenile courts and program administrators afforded the potential for, and perhaps the reality of, abuse of the rights of juveniles. The deprivation of liberty was, after all, the most serious sanction society could impose on juveniles who, given their state of immaturity, were regarded as especially vulnerable to the abuse of the power of the state. As well, academic critiques of the justice system filtered down and influenced the thinking of legislators, bureaucrats and practitioners. In this regard, labelling theory argued that the juvenile justice system could actually foster juvenile delinquency.[13] The notion of juvenile institutions as little more than "schools for crime" became a near truism and seeped into the public consciousness.[14] Further, reviews of empirical studies of the outcomes of treatment programs, especially institutional treatment, questioned their effectiveness.[15] Hence, the very foundations of the *JDA* Welfare Model — the benevolence of the juvenile justice system generally and the assumption of the effectiveness of rehabilitation efforts — were seriously challenged. A need then arose to save delinquents from the very system originally designed to save them from the perils of a life of crime.

Given the unique nature of the Canadian constitutional arrangements for the administration of justice and the time-consuming federal/provincial process required for the evolution of new law, it was left to some provinces, through provincial law and administrative changes, to take the initiative in implementing juvenile justice reforms.[16] These provincial initiatives focused on the use of

---

[11] Department of Justice, *Juvenile Delinquency in Canada: The Report of the Department of Justice Committee.* (Ottawa: Queen's Printer, 1965).

[12] Although it could be argued that the *JDA* did not discourage committals to training schools, its primary original intent was to divert those who may have been institutionalized to probation supervision in the community. See Leon (1977).

[13] Becker, *Outsiders* (Glencoe, Ill: Free Press, 1963); Lemert, *Human Deviance, Social Problems and Social Control* (Englewood Cliffs, N.J.: Prentice-Hall, 1969).

[14] Corrado, "Introduction," in Corrado, LeBlanc and Trepanier, eds., *Current Issues in Juvenile Justice* (Toronto: Butterworths, 1983), pp. 1–27.

[15] See, for example, Martinson, "What Works? Questions and Answers About Prison Reform" (1974) 35(1) *The Public Interest*, 22–54.

[16] Osborne, "Juvenile Justice Policy in Canada: The Transfer of the Initiative" (1979) 2(1) Can.J.Fam.L., pp. 7–32.

custody. In the early 1970s, for example, British Columbia abolished dispositional secure custody for juvenile offenders altogether. When secure custody was
re-introduced in that province in 1977, it was done so in a manner completely at
variance with the Welfare Model philosophy of the *JDA*: sentences were definite,
restrictive legal sentencing criteria were introduced, the number of young offenders in custody were to be limited to a small "hard-core" population and young
offenders were no longer placed in "training schools" with a rehabilitative goal
but rather in "containment centres" whose purpose was the protection of
society.[17] Other provinces, albeit in much less dramatic ways, also introduced
restrictions on the use of training schools in the 1970s.[18] Ontario, for example,
limited training school committals to children 12 years or older who had committed an offence for which an adult would be liable to imprisonment. Further, as
a result of the development of community-based programs, the training school
population in that province was more than halved between 1970 and 1980.[19]

These early provincial initiatives respecting the use of custody were eventually
incorporated, in some form or another, in the *YOA*, which largely (but not
exclusively) reflects a "Justice Model" approach to the problem of juvenile
crime. The philosophy and substantive law of the *YOA* are a radical departure
from the *JDA*. Rehabilitation is no longer the over-riding concern of the juvenile
court, but rather just one of several considerations, and arguably a subordinate
one. The great discretion formerly accorded the judiciary and program administrators has been limited by a new philosophy established by the Act's Declaration of Principle, provisions for definite sentencing, specific legal criteria and
other considerations which circumscribe custodial sentencing decisions, judicial
specification of the level (open or secure) of custody, and judicial review of
custodial dispositions for the purpose of early release. As well, other factors,
including the changes in offence and age jurisdiction, the guarantees of legal
representation and due process, the provincial organization and administrative
definition of custody, the juvenile justice system interface with the child welfare
and mental health systems and cost-sharing considerations have all affected the
use and nature of custodial programs for young offenders. These changes will all
be discussed in this chapter.

---

[17] MacDonald, "Juvenile Training Schools and Juvenile Justice Policy in British
Columbia" (1978) 19(3) Can. J. Crim., pp. 418–26; Markwart, "Youth
Containment in British Columbia" (1981) 5(2) *B.C. Journal of Special Educa-
tion*, pp. 279–92.

[18] Osborne, "Juvenile Justice Policy in Canada: The Transfer of the Initiative"
(1979) 2(1) Can. J. Fam. L., pp. 7–32.

[19] Lescheid and Jaffe, "Implementing the Young Offenders Act in Ontario:
Critical Issues and Challenges for the Future" in Hudson, Hornick and
Burrows, eds. *Justice and the Young Offender in Canada* (Toronto: Wall and
Thompson, 1988).

To begin, however, we will address in the next section a crucial issue — how the change from the Welfare Model of the *JDA* to the "modified Justice Model"[20] of the *YOA* has apparently affected the rate of incarceration[21] of young offenders. The empirical evidence presented in this forthcoming section will reveal a strong and consistent trend across most Canadian provinces of substantially increased use of custody under the *YOA*. These findings beg a question that should be posed from the outset: is this trend a positive or negative outcome of the new Act? In this regard, the writer believes that substantially increasing rates of incarceration for offences which are overwhelmingly non-violent in nature is an unproductive and undesirable (and, perhaps, unintended) by-product of the new legislation. Some, however, have suggested that increasing rates of incarceration are not necessarily undesirable.[22]

While it is obvious that incarceration is a necessary and justifiable social protection measure to incapacitate (albeit temporarily) or denounce a limited number of violent young offenders and very repetitive property offenders, there is little to otherwise justify the imposition of custody as an effective instrument of long-term social protection. For example, in a recent 18-year follow-up of 180 delinquent boys committed to the Ontario training school system during the 1970s, Hundleby *et al.* found that a very high proportion of the training school graduates were serious enough recidivists as adults to be committed to either adult provincial jails or the federal penitentiary system — approximately 80 percent had been incarcerated as adults; one-quarter had received federal penitentiary sentences of more than two years.[23]

A detailed discussion of the considerable research and relative advantages and disadvantages of incarceration is obviously beyond the scope of this chapter. Briefly, however, the imposition of a custodial sentence is most often justified on the grounds of deterrence but, even in a modified Justice Model system like the *YOA*, can also (ironically) be justified at times on the ground of rehabilitation. Lescheid *et al.* discuss the research on the effectiveness of deterrence and rehabilitation (treatment) in Chapter 7.

While it is simplistic to say that deterrence (or punishment) is ineffective, a general conclusion that can be reached from the research literature is that the

---

[20] See Chapter 1.

[21] As pre-adjudication and pre-sentence (remand) custody is a complex area in its own right, this chapter is limited to a discussion of dispositional (sentenced) custody only. Dispositional custody represents the vast majority (more than 80 percent) of juvenile custody in Canada.

[22] Doob, "Dispositions Under the Young Offenders Act: Issues Without Answers?" in Beaulieu, ed., *Young Offender Dispositions: Perspective on Principles and Practice* (Toronto: Wall and Thompson, 1989).

[23] Hundleby, Keating and Hooper, "A Follow-Up of Ontario Training School Boys" (paper presented to a symposium given at the Ontario Psychological Association, February 16, 1990).

effectiveness of punishment does improve to some degree as the certainty of apprehension, conviction and swift punishment increases, although increasing the severity of punishment appears to make little difference. Certain apprehension in a democratic society, and swift and certain punishment in a *YOA* system fraught with lengthly court delays[24] is, however, very unlikely to be achieved. While the debate about the effectiveness of treatment since Martinson's pronouncement that "nothing works"[25] have been ongoing and still inconclusive, more recent reviews of the research suggest that these efforts — notably community treatment interventions — can be more successful than many formerly believed.[26]

Even if it is conceded (which it is not), for the sake of argument, that incarceration for deterrent purposes is no less effective than community-based interventions, then obviously the inverse also is true, i.e., community interventions are no less effective than incarceration. Given this, the debate then really turns on other issues such as humaneness, respect for liberties, and costs. In this regard, the degree of victimization and exploitation that can arise in juvenile institutions is well known;[27] incarceration is, of course, the maximum degree of restraint on civil liberties in a democratic society; and juvenile institutions are inordinately expensive, comprising approximately 80–90 percent of expenditures on juvenile correctional interventions in Canada.[28]

All of this, of course, is to say that the writer believes that the restrained use of carefully targeted community intervention programs — avoiding a widening of the net — is the preferred course for non-violent young offenders and that the advent of deterrence[29] and consequent rising rates of incarceration under the *YOA* can hardly be justified on social protection or other grounds.

---

[24] Corrado and Markwart, "The Prices of Rights and Responsibilites: An Examination of the Impacts of the Young Offenders Act in British Columbia" (1988), 7(1) Can.J.Fam.L., pp. 93–115.

[25] Martinson, *supra*, note 15.

[26] See Chapter 7 and Gendreau and Ross, "Revivication of Rehabilitation: Evidence from the 1980's" (1987) 13(2) Just.Q., pp. 349–407.

[27] Bartollas, Clemens, Miller and Dinitz, *Juvenile Victimization: The Institutional Paradox* (New York: John Wiley and Sons, 1976); Feld, *Neutralizing Inmate Violence: Juvenile Offenders in Institutions* (Cambridge, Mass.: Ballinger, 1978).

[28] Morrison, Untitled paper presented to a conference on Young Offender Dispositions in Montreal, November 30 to December 5, 1988.

[29] Markwart and Corrado, "Is the Young Offenders Act More Punitive?" in Beaulieu, ed., *Young Offender Dispositions: Perspectives on Principles and Practice* (Toronto: Wall and Thompson, 1989).

THE INCREASED RELIANCE ON JUVENILE INCARCERATION

While no public polls have been taken, it is probably safe to say that most of the public who have received some information from the media and who therefore have formed impressions would suggest that the *YOA* is "soft" on juvenile crime. These impressions no doubt have been created by complaints and notorious cases that have gained the attention of the media (particularly in Ontario) on a number of matters: the concern about juvenile murderers and the three-year limit on custody, youth gangs, the incapacity to charge offending children under 12 years of age and police complaints about street-wise delinquents escaping consequences as a result of procedural/legal constraints. It is also probably safe to say that this sentiment is equally shared by many who work in the juvenile justice system itself, particularly the police and prosecutors. The empirical evidence, however, is quite to the contrary: the *YOA* appears to be considerably more punitive than its predecessor and is much more akin to the Criminal Code in sentencing outcomes than the *JDA*. Early warnings that the new Act might amount to little more than a "mini-Criminal Code for kids" appear to have had some foundation.

Determining whether the implementation of the *YOA* has been associated with an increased reliance on incarceration when compared to the *JDA* is not a simple task, nor one which can produce unequivocal answers. Unfortunately, most provinces do not have reliable and comparable pre-post-*YOA* data. These data problems are further confounded by changes in the provincial organization of services and differences in the operational definitions of custody across provinces, as well as a lack of specific age-year data to account for the effects of the implementation of the uniform maximum age (UMA) of 18 years in 1985.[30] Moreover, as has been previously pointed out by Markwart and Corrado,[31] one would expect that the effects of the *YOA* on the use of custody might well vary across provinces, given that research has found that juvenile justice system practices substantially varied across provinces under the *JDA*.[32] One would therefore expect different reference points for comparative purposes. Notwithstanding these limitations, there is strong evidence from three major provinces — British Columbia, Manitoba and Ontario   that the *YOA* has been associated with very substantial increases in the use of custody when compared to the *JDA*.

---

[30] The UMA, to be discussed later, resulted in an influx of 16 and/or 17 year olds into the new *YOA* system in eight provinces. In those provinces where admissions to custody are not recorded by age, it is therefore very difficult to determine whether any increases in custodial use are attributable to the change in age jurisdiction or to changes in sentencing patterns.

[31] Markwart and Corrado, *supra*, note 29.

[32] Bala and Corrado, *Juvenile Justice in Canada: A Comparative Study* (Ottawa: Ministry of the Solicitor General of Canada, 1985).

Additionally, there is a trend in the custody data which supports the inference that this has also been the case in several other provinces.[33] The following represents an update and elaboration of these data, which permits an analysis of longer term — six- to seven -year — trends.

Corrado and Markwart initially reported that, after controlling for the effects of the UMA in British Columbia by excluding 17-year-olds from the data,[34] the number of admissions to (open and secure) custody increased by 85 percent between the last *JDA* year (1983–84) and the third year of the *YOA*.[35] They also found that the ratio of sentenced custody admissions to probation supervision admissions for the same age group had changed considerably: from 1:8.3, or one custody admission for every 8.3 probation admissions under the *JDA*, to 1:4.0 in the third year of the *YOA*, i.e., in relation to the use of probation, custodial sanctions were used far more (twice as) frequently under the *YOA* as they were under the *JDA*. These increases could not, they argue, have been attributable to the British Columbia courts adopting a ''get tough'' approach toward crime generally. If so, it would be expected that the rate of incarceration for both adult and young offenders would increase, but during the same period of time, and again controlling for the effects of the UMA, adult admissions to provincial correctional centres actually decreased by 12 percent.

Markwart and Corrado later updated these data to include the fourth *YOA* year (1987–88) and found that custodial admissions had only decreased slightly from the preceding (peak) *YOA* year.[36] Table 1 presents an update of these data to include the 1990–91 fiscal year so that a full seven years of *YOA* data is captured.

This table indicates that admissions to sentenced custody remained fairly constant in the fifth *YOA* year and then rose again in the sixth and seventh *YOA* years; by 1990–91, the volume of admissions was 88 percent greater than the final *JDA* year. Moreover, the ratio of custodial to probation admissions had dramatically changed from one custodial admission per 8.3 probation admissions in the last *JDA* year to one per 4.1 probation admissions in the seventh *YOA* year. A 1989 analysis of the volume of admissions to probation supervision in British Columbia, again controlling for the effects of the UMA, suggests also that probation supervision is, in both absolute and relative terms, less frequently relied on under the *YOA* than it was under the *JDA*.[37] These increases in custody

---

[33] Markwart and Corrado, *supra*, note 29.

[34] In British Columbia, the maximum age under the *JDA* was (under) seventeen-years-old.

[35] Corrado and Markwart, ''The Prices of Rights and Responsibilities: An Examination of the Impacts of the Young Offenders Act in British Columbia'' (1988) 7(1) Can.J.Fam.L., pp. 93–115.

[36] Markwart and Corrado, *supra*, note 29.

[37] Markwart, *A Description of the Application of Dispositions Under the Young Offenders Act in the Province of British Columbia* (Ottawa: Statistics Canada, Canadian Centre for Justice Statistics, 1989).

TABLE 1

Admissions to Sentenced Custody and to Probation
of Young Offenders Under 17 Years
in British Columbia
83–84 to 88–89

	Sentenced Custody	Probation Supervision	Ratio
1983–84 (*JDA*)	355	2,961	1:8.3
1984–85 (*YOA*)	346	2,369	1:6.8
1985–86	515	2,472	1:4.8
1986–87	655	2,601	1:4.0
1987–88	614	2,394	1:3.9
1988–89	607	2,353	1:3.9
1989–90	653	2,544	1:3.9
1990–91	667	2,757	1:4.1

Source: Adapted from Offender File System, British Columbia Corrections Branch, Ministry of the Solicitor General.

occurred in the face of a declining adolescent population over the same period of time — i.e., the rate of incarceration rose by an even greater degree — while the volume of adjudicated criminal cases rose by less than eight percent between 1984–85 and 1987–88.[38]

The evidence from British Columbia seems unequivocal. As Markwart and Corrado have stated:

> These are important data, not only because they are precise pre- and post-*YOA* statistics that control for the effects of the UMA, but also because British Columbia did not change the organization or nature of youth dispositional resources when the *YOA* was implemented, i.e., custodial services remained under the auspices of the same government department and under the *JDA* (administratively determined) levels of open and secure custody already had been established by the province. Further, definite sentencing and judicial review of custodial dispositions for the purpose of early release had already been established under the *JDA* in British Columbia. This suggests that it is something about the sentencing philosophy and law established by the *YOA* that may account for this substantially increased reliance on incarceration.[39]

---

[38] *Ibid*. The data in this 1989 analysis include violent, property and other *Criminal Code* offences, but exclude "other federal statute offences" due to inconsistences in the data collection methodology across all years for this particular category of offences.

[39] Markwart and Corrado, *supra*, note 29, at p. 9.

The same authors have also reported that Manitoba, which was not affected by the UMA because the maximum age under the *JDA* was already (under) 18 years in that province, has also experienced dramatic increases in custody under the *YOA* when compared to the *JDA*.[40] Like British Columbia, the average daily sentenced population peaked in the third *YOA* year at 223, a volume 148 percent greater than the population of only 90 reported in the last *JDA* year. This custody population, again like British Columbia, declined slightly in 1987–88. Data for 1988–89 and 1989–90 indicates the daily sentenced population again declined modestly, to averages of 191 and 179 respectively, but the populations in these years were still double the population of the final *JDA* year.[41] The trends in these correctional data for Manitoba have also been corroborated by independent court committal data for the city of Winnipeg: Latimer found that the volume of custody committals from the Winnipeg youth court increased by 152 percent between 1983 (*JDA*) and 1985 (*YOA*).[42]

Manitoba officials have attributed these very substantial increases to the use of open custody and to an increased number of older adolescents being committed to custody. In this latter regard, the Manitoba data is confounded, to some degree, by a substantial reduction under the *YOA* in the volume of young offenders transferred to adult court; i.e., these older adolescents are now being retained in the youth system rather than being transferred and dealt with by the adult court. This change, however, can only account for some of the increases in the use of custody in Manitoba; if the decrease in transfers to adult court is controlled for, the increase in custody committals arising from the Winnipeg youth court remain substantial.[43] It has been observed, however, that this change in the number of transfers could be construed as evidence of harsher sentencing practices brought about by the *YOA*. That is, since the adequacy of the *YOA* to deal with a young offender is one of the primary considerations in determining whether to transfer to adult court, the tougher sanctions available under the *YOA* may have affected the volume of transfers to adult court.[44] With respect to the increases in open custody in Manitoba, it appears that this is, in part at least, related to internal systemic changes vis-à-vis the relationship between child welfare and youth justice services, which were administratively separated by the province after the implementation of the *YOA*.

It is notable that these increases in custody in British Columbia and Manitoba have had a decided impact on a disadvantaged minority group, the Native Indian adolescent. For example, Native youth comprise almost one-half of the custodial population in Manitoba. While Native youth comprise a substantially lesser

---

[40] Markwart and Corrado, *supra*, note 29.

[41] Information courtesy of the Manitoba Department of Justice.

[42] Latimer, *Winnipeg Youth Courts and the Young Offenders Act* (Winnipeg: Manitoba Attorney General, 1986).

[43] Latimer, *supra*, note 42.

[44] Markwart and Corrado, *supra*, note 29.

proportion of custodial admissions in British Columbia — approximately 20 percent — pre- and post-*YOA* comparisons indicate that admissions of Native youth have increased at double the rate of non-Native admissions in that province.[45]

Since Ontario has established separate systems of courts and correctional services for young offenders between the ages of 12 and 15 years and for 16- and 17-year-olds, it is possible to compare custodial data over time which is uncontaminated by the effects of the UMA. Lescheid and Jaffe have presented data on *JDA* and *YOA* dispositions for 12- to 15-year-olds in southwestern Ontario from 1983 to 1986, and found a 120 percent increase in committals to secure and open custody under the *YOA* when compared to committals to the care of Children's Aid Societies or to training schools under the *JDA*.[46] Comparisons of child welfare committals under the *JDA* with *YOA* open custody committals are, however, fraught with definitional difficulties, given the different legal and administrative means by which, for example, a group home placement could be achieved under both Acts. *YOA* secure custody and *JDA* training school committals can, however, be fairly compared; in this regard, Lescheid and Jaffe's data indicates a 67 percent increase from 1983 to 1986.

Markwart and Corrado conducted a similar analysis for the entire province of Ontario from 1983–84 to 1987–88.[47] These data are replicated in Table 2 and extended to include the fifth *YOA* year.

Table 2 indicates there have been very substantial increases in *YOA* secure custody committals in Ontario when compared to *JDA* training school committals. Moreover, even if the problematic comparison of child welfare committals in Ontario with open custody is ignored, the volume of committals to open custody has more than doubled in Ontario since the Act was implemented in 1984. As well, the trend in custody committals is the same as the trend established in both British Columbia and Manitoba; i.e., there were sharp increases in committals to custody from the first to the third *YOA* years, but thereafter custodial committals levelled off.

It should be noted that the information presented in Table 2 is court data describing the number of young persons committed to custody, but if one examines the average daily population of 12- to 15-year-olds in custody in Ontario the same trend of sharply escalating use of custody is not evident;[48] in fact, the

---

[45] Markwart, *supra*, note 37.
[46] Lescheid and Jaffe, "Implementing the Young Offenders Act in Ontario: Critical Issues and Challenges for the Future" in Hudson, Hornick and Burrows, eds., *Justice and the Young Offender in Canada* (Toronto: Wall and Thompson, 1988).
[47] Markwart and Corrado, *supra*, note 29.
[48] Note, however, that this is not the case with the British Columbia and Manitoba data. There were marked increases in both committals and average daily populations.

TABLE 2

Dispositions of Offenders in the Ontario Youth
Court (12–15 years), Persons Charged
With Federal Offences, 1983–84 to 1988–89

	Children's Aid Society	Open Custody	Secure Custody/ Training School	Total
1983–84 (*JDA*)	334	–	597	931
1984–85 (*YOA*)	9	775	701	1,476
1985–86	–	1,065	948	2,013
1986–87	–	1,579	1,019	2,598
1987–88	–	1,614	944	2,558
1988–89	–	1,594	1,003	2,597

Source: Ontario Ministry of Attorney General.

average daily population in secure custody under the *YOA* has been less than *JDA* training school levels. The discrepancy between these data would be explained by reductions under the *YOA* in the average length of stay in custody; while there are not comparable statistics available for Ontario, it is commonly accepted that the (judicially determined) length of stay in secure custody under the *YOA* is substantially less than was the (administratively determined) length of stay in training schools under the *JDA*. In short, it appears that more young persons have been committed to custody in Ontario under the *YOA*, however they have been staying in custody for shorter periods of time. Whether this mitigates the degree of concern about the extent of custody use in Ontario depends on one's perspective. If, for example, one is concerned about costs and the management of a youth custody system, then a fairly constant average daily population is obviously no cause for concern. If, however, one is concerned about individuals and the potential negative effects of incarceration, then increases in the number of persons committed to custody would be cause for concern.

The data presented above is restricted to the young offender population unaffected by the implementation of the uniform maximum age in 1985. There is also some evidence, however, that this older (UMA) population of adolescents is dealt with more harshly under the *YOA* than it formerly was as adults under the *Criminal Code*.[49] In this regard, it has been reported that the average daily population of 17-year-olds in custody in British Columbia under the *YOA* is 44 percent higher than it was when this population was dealt with as adults under the

---

[49] R.S.C. 1970, c. C-34 [now R.S.C. 1985, c. C-46].

Criminal Code.[50] In Ontario, the Ministry of Correctional Services, which is responsible for 16- and 17-year-old young offenders, has reported that the average sentence length to secure custody for this age group nearly doubled under the *YOA* when compared to sentences imposed on the same age group when they were formerly dealt with in the adult court system.[51] These changes should not be particularly surprising, since differences in earned remission, which is applicable to adult jail sentences but is not available under the *YOA*, could alone account for substantial increases in average daily populations. Increased sentence lengths could be explained by the fact that many in this older adolescent group now may appear in youth court as repeat offenders, therefore attracting lengthier sentences, rather than appearing as ''first'' (adult) offenders in adult court and attracting a mitigated sentence.

There is, therefore, strong evidence of substantial increases in the use of custody in the only three provinces in Canada where there is comparable pre- and post-*YOA* data available which can control for the effects of the UMA. It is interesting to note that the pattern of change over the six-year *JDA/YOA* period is the same in all three provinces: a rise in the use of custody to a peak in the third *YOA* year and then a levelling off. It has previously been hypothesized that if the *YOA* has prompted an increased use of custody compared to the *JDA*, then increases under the *YOA* should become evident over time since the rate of use of custody would, in part, be initially constrained by the residual effects of the *JDA*.[52] The full effects of the *YOA* would not then, it is argued, be brought to bear immediately in the first year of the Act but rather would be realized in later years as the courts became more familiar with the new law (and as case law evolved). This is clearly the pattern demonstrated in British Columbia, Manitoba and Ontario. This hypothesis may be tested by examining rates of use of custody from the implementation of the *YOA* in 1984 and beyond; if correct, the hypothesis would predict a trend of increasing rates of use of custody in the later years of the *YOA* when compared to the first *YOA* year.

Table 3 presents data, derived from the Youth Court Survey,[53] which describes

---

[50] Corrado and Markwart, *supra*, note 35.

[51] Ontario Ministry of Correctional Services, *Annual Report* of the Ontario Ministry of Correctional Services (Toronto, Ministry of Correctional Services, 1986).

[52] Markwart and Corrado, ''Is the Young Offenders Act More Punitive?'' in Beaulieu, ed., *Young Offender Dispositions: Perspectives on Principles and Practice* (Toronto: Wall and Thompson, 1989).

[53] Statistics Canada, Canadian Centre for Justice Statistics, *Youth Court Statistics*, 1984/85 to 1989/90. Throughout this chapter, reference to the Youth Court Survey, unless otherwise specified, refers to published data for the six *YOA* years from 1984/85 to 1989/90. In some instances, however, unpublished special run data will be referenced. The data refers to ''most significant disposition''; for example, a case committed to open custody followed by

the proportions of cases with guilty findings committed to secure and open custody (combined) in eight provinces during the first six years of the *YOA*. As the UMA was implemented in 1985–86, the effects of this change are controlled by holding the age groups constant for each province across all years; i.e., the UMA population (16- and/or 17-years-old) is excluded from each province affected (all but Quebec and Manitoba). Data for only eight provinces are presented since Ontario does not report to the Youth Court Survey and the number of custody committals in Prince Edward Island is so few that the data is easily skewed by small changes in volume.

The right-hand column of Table 3 describes the percentage of change in the proportion of cases committed to custody between 1984–85 and 1989–90. To illustrate how these data should be interpreted, the proportion of cases committed to custody in Manitoba increased from 13.9 percent in 1984–85 to 25.2 percent in 1989/90. This is not a mere 11.3 percent increase; the proportion of cases committed to custody nearly doubled during that time period, and therefore the increase in the relative use of custody is actually 81 percent.[54]

The data in Table 3 substantially confirm the hypothesis described earlier. In six of the eight provinces, there are, controlling for the effects of the UMA, substantial increases in the use of custody from 1984–85 to 1989–90, ranging from a "low" 50 percent increase in Newfoundland to a 109 percent increase in British Columbia. These court data also corroborate the British Columbia and Manitoba correctional data presented earlier. Referring back to Table 2, Ontario experienced a 76 percent increase in total custody committals from the first *YOA* year to 1989–90. Put together, then, there is a demonstrable pattern of substantial increases in total custody in seven of the nine provinces.

Of the seven provinces displaying substantial increases, five follow the same pattern of sharp increases between the first and third *YOA* years followed by a levelling off in the last two years; Nova Scotia and New Brunswick did not experience very substantial increases until the fourth and fifth years of the new Act. Importantly, the only two provinces which have not apparently experienced marked increases in custody — Quebec and Saskatchewan — displayed, by far, the highest proportions of committals to custody in the first *YOA* year. It is almost as if the proportion of committals could not go higher in these two provinces; in effect, the other six provinces "caught up" with Quebec and Saskatchewan by the fifth *YOA* year. Further, while the proportion of cases committed to custody in Quebec changed very little over this period of time, there was a significant shift

---

probation is reported as having open custody as the most significant disposition, and so forth.

[54] Proportions, rather than actual volumes, are used as a result of concerns about whether the Youth Court Survey represents a complete census of youth court cases. Some degree of under-reporting is known to occur in some jurisdictions. Proportions are a means of controlling for under-reporting. Nonetheless, an analysis of volumes rather than proportions indicates the same trends.

TABLE 5

Proportions of Cases With Guilty Findings Committed to (Secure and Open) Custody,
Controlling for the Effects of the UMA, by Selected Provinces, Fiscal Years 1984–85 to 1989–90

Province	Proportions of Cases Committed to Custody						
	1984–85	1985–86	1986–87	1987–88	1988–89	1989–90	% Change 1984–85 to 1989–90
Newfoundland (Age 12 to 16)	14.4	18.7	24.2	20.8	21.3	24.1	+ 67%
Nova Scotia (Age 12 to 15)	12.7	13.6	15.9	16.8	22.7	22.7	+ 79%
New Brunswick (Age 12 to 15)	20.8	22.3	21.2	27.5	29.2	31.3	+ 50%
Quebec (Age 12 to 17)	28.9	27.2	29.3	30.9	30.8	32.1	+ 11%
Manitoba (Age 12 to 17)	13.9	20.5	25.1	22.7	27.7	25.2	+ 81%
Saskatchewan (Age 12 to 15)	25.2	26.2	22.7	26.3	24.5	25.7	+ 2%
Alberta (Age 12 to 15)	10.3	13.8	19.5	18.5	18.1	18.9	+ 83%
British Columbia (Age 12 to 16)	11.2	15.9	19.8	22.0	21.6	23.4	+109%

Source: Adapted from Statistics Canada, Canadian Centre for Justice Statistics, Youth Court Survey.

toward imposing a more punitive type of custody — secure rather than open custody — in that province after the first *YOA* year.[55]

These data respecting total committals to custody — open and secure combined — are separated in Tables 4 and 5 to facilitate a comparison of trends in the proportions of cases committed to open versus secure custody. With respect to secure custody, five of the seven identified provinces (including Ontario, Table 2) which experienced marked increases in total custody also experienced increases in secure custody. In all of these provinces, the increases in secure custody were substantial — ranging from 34 to 78 percent. Manitoba only experienced a 34 percent increase in secure custody, but this modest change was achieved at great expense: a 156 percent increase in the proportion of cases committed to open custody. (And, as will be discussed later, it should be noted that the distinction between open and secure custody in Manitoba is quite blurred.) New Brunswick, which experienced a marked increase in total custody, actually experienced a modest (13 percent) decrease in secure custody between 1984–85 and 1989–90 but, like Manitoba, this was only accomplished by a corresponding increase of 227 percent in open custody.

With respect to open custody (Tables 5 and 2), every one of the seven provinces reporting an increase in total custody also reported very substantial increases — ranging from 87 to 227 percent — in the proportion of cases committed to open custody between 1984–85 and 1989–90.[56]

Let us now summarize the findings arising from the data described earlier. First, there have been, controlling for the effects of the UMA, very marked increases in the use of custody from the *JDA* to the *YOA* in the only three provinces where there is comparable pre- and post-*YOA* data available. Second, the pattern of changes in these three provinces is very similar. Third, seven of nine provinces (including Ontario) have, again controlling for the effects of the UMA, experienced substantial increases in committals to custody under the *YOA* over a six-year period, and there, again, are similar patterns in these increases. Fourth, the patterns of increases in these provinces supports the hypothesis presented. Fifth, and ignoring *JDA/YOA* comparisons, as time has passed and there has been greater experience with the new Act, accompanying increases have been seen in the use of custodial dispositions in seven of nine provinces. Sixth, the only two provinces where there has been no apparent increase in custody during the first six years of the *YOA* were those that began with relatively high rates of committals to custody in the first year. Finally, there is no evidence that the *YOA* has been

---

[55] Markwart and Corrado, ''Is the Young Offenders Act More Punitive?'' in Beaulieu, ed., *Young Offender Dispositions: Perspectives on Principles and Practice* (Toronto: Wall and Thompson, 1989).

[56] Only Quebec reported a decrease — 34 percent — in open custody, but this was offset by increases in secure custody. The Quebec data is confounded by an effective reversal in the distribution of open versus secure committals after the first *YOA* year.

Proportions of Cases With Guilty Findings Committed to Secure Custody,
Controlling for the Effects of the UMA, by Selected Provinces Fiscal Years 1984–85 to 1989–90

Province	Proportions of Cases Committed to Custody							% Change 1984–85 to 1989–90
	1984–85	1985–86	1986–87	1987–88	1988–89	1989–90		
Newfoundland (Age 12 to 16)	7.9	11.7	14.5	11.5	11.5	11.9+		+ 51%
Nova Scotia (Age 12 to 15)	2.9	1.1	1.7	1.9	4.6	2.3		– 21%
New Brunswick (Age 12 to 15)	15.3	16.0	11.2	14.4	11.1	13.3		– 13%
Quebec (Age 12 to 17)	8.8	16.1	17.6	18.5	19.3	18.8		+114%
Manitoba (Age 12 to 17)	8.5	10.5	10.6	9.4	10.9	11.4		+ 34%
Saskatchewan (Age 12 to 15)	11.3	14.6	9.4	9.9	8.6	7.7		– 32%
Alberta (Age 12 to 15)	4.1	4.3	7.0	6.0	6.2	7.3		+ 78%
British Columbia (Age 12 to 16)	5.0	9.4	9.6	9.6	7.5	8.4		+ 68%

Source: Adapted from Statistics Canada, Canadian Centre for Justice Statistics, Youth Court Survey.

TABLE 5

Proportions of Cases With Guilty Findings Committed to Open Custody,
Controlling for the Effects of the UMA, by Selected Provinces, Fiscal Years 1984–85 to 1989–90

Province	Proportions of Cases Committed to Custody						% Change 1984–85 to 1989–90
	1984–85	1985–86	1986–87	1987–88	1988–89	1989–90	
Newfoundland (Age 12 to 16)	6.5	7.0	9.7	9.3	9.8	12.2	+ 88%
Nova Scotia (Age 12 to 15)	9.7	12.5	14.2	14.9	18.1	20.4	+110%
New Brunswick (Age 12 to 15)	5.5	6.3	10.0	13.1	18.1	18.0	+227%
Quebec (Age 12 to 17)	20.1	11.1	11.7	12.4	11.5	13.3	− 34%
Manitoba (Age 12 to 17)	5.4	10.0	14.5	13.3	16.8	13.8	+156%
Saskatchewan (Age 12 to 15)	13.9	11.6	13.3	16.4	15.9	18.0	+ 29%
Alberta (Age 12 to 15)	6.2	9.5	12.5	12.5	11.9	11.6	+ 87%
British Columbia (Age 12 to 16)	6.2	6.5	10.7	12.4	14.1	15.0	+137%

Source: Adapted from Statistics Canada, Canadian Centre for Justice Statistics, Youth Court Survey.

associated with decreases in committals to custody in any province when compared to the *JDA*.

It is important to note that these trends toward an increasing reliance on custody in seven of nine provinces have been consistent across provinces with very different systems of service delivery. These differing systems range from the child welfare orientation of the Nova Scotia and Ontario (under 16 years) to the far more correctionally oriented systems of British Columbia and Alberta, where young offender services are separated from child welfare services. This suggests there is a common factor at play which over-rides organizational and service delivery variables. The common factor to all, of course, is the *YOA* itself. It should also be noted that these increases in custody are not evidently associated with socioeconomic or population factors: the changes occurred during a period of an expansionary economy, declining unemployment rates and a diminishing (general) adolescent population.

It is difficult to arrive at any other conclusion but that the implementation of the *YOA* has apparently been associated with a substantially increased reliance on incarceration. Whether this was the intended social policy outcome of the Act is not clear. On the one hand, federal documents expressly state that the imposition of custody under the new Act was intended to be "exercised with the utmost restraint".[57] This intended restraint on custody is reflected, in part, through some of the Act's principles — special needs, mitigated accountability and minimal interference with freedom — and through several substantive legal provisions, such as sentencing criteria and the right to counsel.

On the other hand, transcripts of the debates when the proposed Act was before the House of Commons in 1982 suggest that a tougher approach to juvenile crime may well have been intended. For example, in response to complaints about the *JDA* being "soft" on juvenile crime, then-solicitor general Robert Kaplan stated:

> . . . we are attempting with this legislation to toughen the kiddie-court image of the juvenile court and to make it a place where a young person will be punished and held accountable to society for what he has done.[58]

It is tempting to dismiss such talk of getting tough on juvenile crime, when made by a politician in a political forum, as merely political rhetoric intended to placate conservative interest groups and not an expression of political or parliamentary intent *per se*. There is, however, much more than simple rhetoric here. The emphasis in the principles of the Act on responsibility, accountability and protection of society lend clear support to the crime control notions of deterrence and incapacitation. Moreover, and contrary to the above-noted expression of federal intent, the sentencing regime established by the Act is not one that,

---

[57] Solicitor General of Canada, *The Young Offenders Act, 1982: Highlights* (Ottawa: Supply and Services Canada, 1982).

[58] House of Commons, *Minutes of the Proceedings and Evidence of the Standing Committee on Justice and Legal Affairs*, First Session of the Thirty-Second Parliament (Ottawa: House of Commons, March 23, 1982).

practically speaking, results in — or even could result in — custody being imposed with "utmost restraint".

Whether this apparent increased reliance on incarceration was intended or simply naively unintended is perhaps a moot point. Intent aside, this outcome should not have been unexpected. As Corrado points out in chapter 3, where roughly similar "justice model" approaches to juvenile crime were enacted in the United States, the outcomes were also increased rates of incarceration.

The following sections of this chapter will examine in detail the philosophical and substantive legal changes brought about by the new Act and how these may have affected the rate of use of and nature of custody for young offenders.

THE PHILOSOPHY OF THE ACT

The philosophical underpinnings of the *YOA* are established by section 3 of the Act, which is characterized in the singular as a "Declaration of Principle" but which, in fact, is a set of several different principles. These principles, which are not prioritized and are often seemingly inconsistent with one another, are to be somehow rationalized into a coherent philosophy which is intended to serve as a framework to guide decisions about young offenders, particularly sentencing decisions.

The lack of prioritization, the inconsistencies and the many qualifications of the principles have unfortunately left many who have to work with the Act in confusion. On the one hand, conservative crime control principles of deterrence and incapacitation, which obviously would encourage an increased reliance on custody, are included in the Declaration: young offenders should "bear responsibility for their contraventions"; they require "supervision, discipline and control"; and society "must . . . be afforded the necessary protection from illegal behaviour". At the same time, however, the Declaration includes other principles which are obviously intended to balance these principles and therefore limit harsh sentencing practices: young offenders are not to be "held accountable or suffer the same consequences . . . as adults"; they have "special guarantees of rights and freedoms"; they have a "right to the least possible interference with freedom"; and they should be "removed from parental supervision only when (other) measures . . . are inappropriate". Rehabilitation is not mentioned in the Declaration (nor in any part of the Act except a passing reference in s. 35) but still treatment considerations are alluded to in the Declaration with its references to the "special needs" of young offenders and the requirement for "guidance and assistance" for young offenders. In some cases, these often incompatible principles are included in the same propositional statement. For example, in rather tortured diction, young offenders are asserted to have "a right to the least possible interference with freedom that is consistent with the protection of society, having regard to the needs of young persons and the interests of their families".

The Declaration of Principle, and appellate court sentencing decisions that flow from this philosophy, have been the subject of analysis from several commentators. In support, Bala has argued that the "ambivalence" and "underlying philosophical inconsistencies and tensions" of the Declaration reflect "an honest attempt to achieve an appropriate balance for dealing with a complex social problem . . . (and) . . . the very complex nature of youthful criminality".[59] While this argument has a certain appeal, few commentators have been quite so generous. The philosophy of the *YOA* has been subject to criticism from the outset: while generally supportive of the Act as a whole, the Canadian Bar Association expressed concern about its philosophical inconsistencies when the Act was before the House of Commons.[60] Reid and Reitsma-Street have described four theoretical models of juvenile justice: the Crime control, Justice, Welfare and Community Change Models.[61] As a result of an analysis which included independent ratings of the principles enunciated in the Declaration, they concluded that the *YOA* reflects *all four* theoretical models. Their results indicate, however, that there is a greater combined emphasis on the Crime Control and Justice Models and a lesser combined emphasis on the Welfare and Community Change Models. Young, in a comprehensive analysis of appellate court sentencing decisions, and noting that the Declaration has not been immune to criticism from the courts themselves, has commented that the "principles . . . are vastly over-inclusive and they suggest a distinct lack of legislative resolve in deciding which principles are truly operational".[62] This philosophical ambivalance and apparent lack of legislative resolve may, in an exercise in accommodation that is typically Canadian, reflect a political interest: the *YOA* may be regarded as a masterful document that accommodates and offers appeal to a divergent range of interest groups and philosophies — law and order advocates, civil libertarians and professional treatment constituencies.[63] In short, the Act attempts to be "all things to all people".

This new and ambivalent juvenile justice philosophy has had important ramifications on appellate court and day-to-day youth court sentencing decisions. Unlike the *JDA*, where the needs and welfare of the child were the dominant concern, there has been a definite shift in the importance, given the various factors to be weighed in sentencing: there is a much greater emphasis on the offence

---

[59] Bala, "The Young Offenders Act: A Legal Framework" in Hudson, Hernick and Burrows, eds., *Justice and the Young Offender in Canada* (Toronto: Wall and Thompson, 1988), p. 15.

[60] House of Commons, 1982 *Minutes, supra*, note 58, 59.

[61] Reid and Reitsma-Street, "Assumptions and Implications of New Canadian Legislation for Young Offenders" (1984) 7(1) Can.Crim.Forum, pp. 1–19.

[62] Young, "Appellate Court Sentencing Principles" in Beaulieu, ed., *Young Offender Dispositions: Perspectives on Principles and Practice* (Toronto: Wall and Thompson, 1989), p. 70.

[63] Corrado and Markwart, "The Prices of Rights and Responsibilities: An Examination of the Impacts of the Young Offenders Act in British Columbia" (1988) 7(1) Can.J.Fam.L., pp. 93–115.

(rather than the offender), on the responsibility of the young offender and on the protection of society.[64] Rehabilitation has been relegated to secondary status as it has been in the adult system.[65] It has also been observed that there are many similarities between the Declaration of Principle and the body of case law developed for young adult offenders — those who were 16 years of age or more in most provinces — prior to the proclamation of the *YOA*,[66] but these principles are now being applied to young offenders in the 12- to 15-year-old range.

This is not to say that the Act has established a philosophy that is Draconian in nature. The appellate courts have attempted to strike a moderate balance between the often competing principles, and an individualized sentencing framework which weighs a variety of considerations has been established.[67] But what is important to note is that the *YOA* has changed the sentencing framework for juvenile offenders so that the principles of general and individual deterrence — factors which obviously encourage a greater reliance on custody — have been given a place in sentencing that was not the case under *JDA*.[68] General deterrence, which was not a consideration under the *JDA*, has been held by several provincial appellate courts to be a valid sentencing consideration under the *YOA*.[69] More importantly, several provincial appellate courts have held that individual deterrence — including the "short, sharp shock" — is also a legitimate factor to be weighed in sentencing.[70] This is not to say that individual deterrence played no role in day-to-day sentencing in the juvenile courts under the *JDA* — of course, it did — but rather that individual deterrence is now "out in the open" as a legitimate sentencing consideration and is accorded far greater weight.

It is easy to see how this change in emphasis could have a pronounced effect on sentencing outcomes. Many cases that come before the courts — particularly repeat property offenders — are exercises in "marginal decision-making"; i.e., cases which could attract either a community or a custodial disposition, depending upon a variety of factors and considerations such as the nature and history of previous offences, the resources available to the court, but also the philosophical framework in which the court operates.[71] The increased emphasis under the *YOA* on individual deterrence may push some of these marginal cases "over the edge" so that a short custodial disposition, rather than a community disposition, is the result.

---

[64] Trepanier, "Principles and Goals Guiding the Choice of Dispositions Under the YOA" in Beaulieu, ed., *Young Offender Dispositions: Perspectives on Principles and Practice* (Toronto: Wall and Thompson, 1989).

[65] Young, *supra*, note 62.

[66] Platt, *Young Offenders Law in Canada* (Toronto: Butterworths, 1989).

[67] Bala, *supra*, note 59.

[68] Markwart and Corrado, *supra*, note 55.

[69] Bala, *supra*, note 59; Young, *supra*, note 62.

[70] See: Trepanier, *supra*, note 64. Young, *supra*, note 62. Platt, *supra*, note 66. Markwart and Corrado, *supra*, note 52.

[71] Markwart and Corrado, *supra*, note 52.

Aside from appellate court decisions and the apparent increased reliance on custody discussed earlier, there is further evidence that this new emphasis on deterrence has had a significant impact on the attitudes and consequently the sentencing practices of youth court judges. Gabor *et al.*, in a 1985 survey of 13 of the 15 full-time youth court judges in Alberta, found that just under one-half indicated that under the *YOA* they had changed their attitudes to place more emphasis on young offenders taking responsibility for their actions.[72] In a more extensive and recent survey of 67 Ontario youth court judges, Hanscomb found that 98 percent indicated that individual deterrence was a "very" or "quite" important consideration in sentencing, and 73 percent indicated "punishment or accountability" was a very or quite important factor.[73] More revealing, of the 59 judges who were also judges under the *JDA*, 75 percent indicated they placed more emphasis on punishment or accountability under the *YOA*, while 42 percent placed a greater emphasis on general deterrence. Further evidence is found not only in the frequency of committals to custody, but in the length of those sentences. In this regard, one would expect that a greater emphasis on individual deterrence would likely result in a frequent use of "short, sharp shock" types of secure custody sentences. This has proved to be the case: the 1988–89 Youth Court Survey indicates that short lengths, ranging from one day to three months, comprise more than one-half of all sentences to secure custody in seven of the nine provinces which report data.[74] Further, and as will be discussed later, the escalating rate of use of custody in most provinces has coincided with diminishing average sentence lengths; i.e., the increasing frequency of short, sharp shock types of sentences has reduced the (overall) average sentence length.

While the *YOA* has brought about an increased emphasis on deterrence, rehabilitative concerns have by no means been rejected under the *YOA*. For example, in her survey of Ontario youth court judges, Hanscomb found that 97 percent still considered rehabilitation to be a very or quite important consideration in sentencing.[75] The conflicting principles of the Declaration and the consequent uncertainty arising from this "mixed model" approach to juvenile justice which legitimizes both deterrent and treatment considerations in sentencing "may afford a convenient rationalization for incarceration on either ground".[76] It may also result in confusion and disparities in sentencing. For example, Doob reports that

---

[72] Gabor, Greene and McCormick, "The Young Offenders Act: The Alberta Youth Court Experience in the First Year" (1986) 5(2) Can.J.Fam.L., pp. 93–115.

[73] Hanscomb, "The Dynamics in Youth Court: A Report on a Survey of Youth Court Judges on Matters Affecting Disposition" (LL.M. Thesis, University of Toronto, 1988).

[74] The Youth Court Survey does not, however, report aggregated sentence lengths arising from consecutive sentences.

[75] Hanscomb, *supra*, note 73.

[76] Corrado and Markwart, *supra*, note 63.

simulation cases presented to a conference of youth court and appellate court judges from across Canada in 1988 resulted in quite varied dispositions and observes "enormous variation" in the relative importance given to the various principles/purposes of sentencing.[77]

CHANGES IN JURISDICTION

Age Jurisdiction

The precise extent of the effect of the increase in the minimum age, from seven years under the *JDA* to 12 years under the *YOA*, has had on the use of custody across Canada is not known, but it can be established as minimal. Children under 12 years comprised only 1.6 percent of the persons reported to be found delinquent by *JDA* courts in 1983.[78] In British Columbia, the change in minimum age had no effect at all since there were no children under 12 years sentenced to custody in the last *JDA* year.[79]

In contrast, however, the implementation of the uniform maximum age (UMA) of (under) 18 years has had a dramatic effect on the size of the youth custody population and the operation of facilities in those eight provinces — i.e., except Quebec and Manitoba — where the maximum age moved from either 17 years (British Columbia, Newfoundland) or 16 years (the remaining provinces). The magnitude of these changes can be captured by examining committals to custody by age year. For example, 1988–89 Youth Court Survey data indicate that the one-year age increase in British Columbia and Newfoundland resulted in, respectively, 67 percent and 37 percent increases in committals to secure custody beyond what would have arisen if the maximum age had remained the same as the *JDA*. In the five remaining provinces which underwent a two-year increase in the maximum age jurisdiction, four experienced increases in cases committed to secure custody ranging from 223 to 300 percent, while Prince Edward Island's increase was 146 percent.[80] Similar effects are evident in Ontario and for open custody.

---

[77] Doob, "Dispositions Under the Young Offenders Act: Issues Without Answers?" in Beaulieu, ed., *Young Offender Dispositions: Perspectives on Principles and Practice* (Toronto: Wall and Thompson, 1989).

[78] Statistics Canada, Canadian Centre for Justice Statistics, *Juvenile Delinquents, 1983* (Ottawa: Supply and Services Canada, 1984).

[79] Corrado and Markwart, "The Prices of Rights and Responsibilities: An Examination of the Impacts of the Young Offenders Act in British Columbia" (1988) 7(1) Can.J.Fam.L., pp. 93–115.

[80] These figures are obtained by comparing the volume of committals of the pre-UMA age group against those for the post-UMA age group for each province. Ontario does not report to the survey.

Because the *YOA* requires that young offenders in custody be held separate and apart from adult offenders, seven of the eight provinces affected by the UMA — Newfoundland being the exception — were required to use former adult jails, or separate sections of those jails, to accommodate the great influx of young offenders when the UMA was implemented in 1985. Since that time, British Columbia, Alberta, Saskatchewan, Prince Edward Island, Nova Scotia and Newfoundland have constructed new (or re-constructed) and expensive youth secure custody centres. The use of former adult correctional facilities, however, still continues today in British Columbia, Ontario and New Brunswick.

There was no aspect of the *YOA* that was more strongly resisted by the provinces than the selection of a UMA age of 18 years, something which did not occur until Third Reading of the proposed legislation in the House of Commons. While all political parties, interest groups and provinces were in agreement that a UMA was desirable — and otherwise necessary, given the pending implementation of the equality rights provisions of the *Canadian Charter of Rights and Freedoms* in 1984[81] — six of the eight provinces affected (Saskatchewan and Prince Edward Island being the exceptions) objected to the age jurisdiction of 18 years, primarily on the grounds of costs.[82] These provincial concerns about costs have been realized. As noted above, new and expensive secure facilities have already been built in several provinces, and further major projects are planned for British Columbia and New Brunswick. Operational costs have risen sharply as a result of the far richer staffing ratios required in juvenile facilities compared to adult facilities. These additional costs have literally totalled in the hundreds of millions of dollars over the short life of the *YOA*: in 1988–89 alone, the federal government's contribution to cost-sharing, approximately 90 percent of which was for custodial operations, amounted to $160 million; this amount represents less than one-half of actual provincial expenditures on custody.

Robert Kaplan, then the Solicitor General and responsible for guiding the *YOA* through Parliament, justified the UMA and its acknowledged cost implications with a kind of modernized child saver's argument: his greater confidence in the youth justice system to rehabilitate this older adolescent group of offenders. It is interesting that the federal government was fully aware that a UMA of 18 years would result in significantly greater costs to both the federal and provincial governments and that this expensive decision was made in the midst of the worst recession since the Depression of the 1930s. Kaplan acknowledged that he was not under pressure from Quebec and Manitoba — which already had established 18 years as the age jurisdiction under the *JDA* — to keep the age at 18: he simply

---

[81] Part I of the *Constitution Act, 1982*, being Schedule B of the *Canada Act 1982* (U.K.), 1982, c. 11.

[82] House of Commons, *Minutes of the Proceedings and Evidence of the Standing Committee on Justice and Legal Affairs*, First Session of the Thirty-Second Parliament (Ottawa: House of Commons, 1980–81–82).

thought it was "right", the "proper way".[83] This is clearly an example of the triumph of ideology over fiscal considerations and hardly supports the view of some[84] that the fiscal crisis of the capitalist state is necessarily a critical ingredient in shaping justice and correctional policy.

While Kaplan's argument that older adolescents will benefit from inclusion in the youth justice system is an empirically testable proposition, it has yet to be tested. As noted earlier, there is some evidence from British Columbia and Ontario that offenders in the 16- and 17-year-old age group are actually being dealt with more harshly under the *YOA* than they formerly were when they were prosecuted as adults under the *Criminal Code*.

The argument of saving these older adolescent offenders from the undesirable influences of more mature, sophisticated adult offenders can be reversed: younger adolescent offenders are now (in most provinces) subject to the new negative influences of an older and more sophisticated adolescent offender group, which, as noted earlier, now comprises the majority of the youth custody population. In fact, the age range in youth custody centres has been extended well beyond the 12- to 17-year-old group since many young offenders may be sentenced at 17 years (or older) to substantial terms of custody. Hence, the age range really extends from 12 to 21 years, and a substantial proportion of "young offenders" in custody are 18 years of age or older. This wide age range may well have adverse affects on younger residents: previous research has indicated that the likelihood of victimization and violence in juvenile correctional institutions increases when an age span between residents exists and when less delinquent youths are placed with more seasoned delinquents.[85]

Ontario and Nova Scotia have administratively addressed the UMA by establishing "split jurisdictions", wherein child welfare departments have continued to be responsible for 12- to 15-year-old young offenders and correctional departments have assumed responsibility for the 16- and 17-year-olds. This has been the source of much criticism in Ontario. While these two-tiered systems may have arisen as much or more for internal political and organizational reasons than for philosophical or programmatic purposes, a major advantage of this administrative arrangement is the separation of younger and older adolescents. In other provinces, separation of these populations can be achieved by the establishment of separate institutions (or sections thereof). In some provinces, however, where small population size and/or geographic considerations come into play, such separation is much less feasible. As a result, several program administrators have observed that, because of this numerical dominance of the older adolescent group, the climate of youth institutions has been altered such that there are now more

---

[83] House of Commons, Minutes, *supra*, note 82.

[84] For example, Scull, *Decarceration: Community Treatment and the Deviant —
A Radical View* (Englewood Cliffs, N.J.: Prentice-Hall, 1977).

[85] Bartollas, Clemens, Miller and Dinitz, *Juvenile Victimization: The Institutional
Paradox* (New York: John Wiley and Sons, 1976).

''prison-like'' concerns; i.e., security and control and protective custody problems, as well as a reduced capacity to devote attention and resources to the younger adolescent group.

One advantage of the expanded youth custody system brought about by the UMA (and the open custody provisions) is that some provinces have been able to decentralize their custodial resources to a greater degree so that more young offenders may be held in custody in or nearer their home communitities. A potentially offsetting disadvantage here, however, is the greater attractiveness of such a system: the greater local availability of custodial facilities may act as an incentive to use them more frequently.

Corrado and Markwart have hypothesized that the marked increase in custody committals in British Columbia among young offenders under 17 years of age may, in part, be explained by the UMA ''fostering a more conservative climate in the youth court'' and consequently inadvertently altering sentencing patterns for this younger offender group.[86] This, they suggest, may have come about because of the greater numbers appearing in youth court and because the greater reliance on incarceration of 17-year-olds may have had a ''disinhibiting effect on any reluctance to impose custodial sanctions generally''; i.e., with the younger adolescent group. While this hypothesis cannot be completely dismissed, it seems apparent that this is not a necessary condition for increased rates of custody under the *YOA*. In this regard, the data presented earlier indicates that there were substantial increases in the use of custody among UMA — controlled age groups in Manitoba, Ontario and Nova Scotia. Manitoba, however, was not affected by the UMA, while Ontario and Nova Scotia have established separate court systems for the 12- to 15-year-old and the 16- and 17-year-old age groups. In short, custody rates increased in each of these provinces, even though there was not an increased volume of older adolescents brought into their respective court systems.

The effects of the UMA is an area fertile for research. Whether older adolescents, as Kaplan suggested, have benefited from being included in the youth justice system and whether these benefits (if any) have outweighed unintended and undesirable consequences (if any) are questions that remain to be answered by empirical studies.

Offence Jurisdiction

Under the *JDA*, the juvenile court had jurisdiction over *Criminal Code* and other federal statute matters, provincial statute and municipal bylaw infractions, and status offences created under the *JDA* itself or by provincial statute. In contrast, the jurisdiction of the *YOA* is limited to *Criminal Code* and other federal statute offences only; there are no status offences in the *YOA*, while mechanisms for the prosecution and disposition of provincial and municipal statute matters are left to provincial legislation.

---

[86] Corrado and Markwart, ''The Prices of Rights and Responsibilities: An Examination of the Impacts of the Young Offenders Act in British Columbia'' (1988) 7(1) Can.J.Fam.L., pp. 93–115.

It would appear that this narrowing of offence jurisdiction has had little effect on the use of custody. Under the *JDA*, provincial and municipal statute matters (including offences such as unmanageability and truancy) comprised a substantial proportion of the matters taken before the juvenile court, but these resulted in few institutional committals. In 1983, these offences comprised only 1.9 percent of the charges disposed of by way of a committal to an institution and 4.6 percent of charges resulting in a committal to the "care of the province". Similarly, the abolition of the *JDA* status offence of "sexual immorality or any similar form of vice" had little effect since this offence accounted for less than 0.1 percent of *JDA* charges in 1983 and less than one-quarter of these charges resulted in institutional committals.[87]

The narrowed jurisdiction of the *YOA* does not mean that young persons are no longer, or less frequently, committed to custody for provincial or municipal matters, or for status offences. Most provinces have enacted special legislation to enable the prosecution of these offences (or otherwise utilize adult legislation) and which provide for the imposition of custody. These provisions vary across the provinces: for example, in British Columbia and Ontario (under 16 years) a committal to custody can only be imposed in narrow circumstances for specified offences and to a maximum of 30 days, whereas in Nova Scotia and New Brunswick six-month penalties can be imposed.[88]

Similarly, it remains entirely within the jurisdictional competence of the provinces to enact status offences such as unmanageability or truancy, although few provinces have retained these offences. This does not mean, however, that non-criminal children and adolescents are no longer institutionalized in functionally secure (or open) facilities. Rather, in accordance with what Cohen describes as "transinstitutionalism",[89] unmanageable children still are often institutionalized by the state, but by different social/legal mechanisms. Transinstitutionalism refers to the phenomenon where deviants, especially juveniles, are re-labelled and re-processed through alternative mechanisms of social control to the criminal justice process, but nonetheless are institutionalized. The status offence of unmanageability is an example in point. Once a provincial statute offence in many provinces and hence able to be prosecuted under the *JDA*, this offence is now virtually non-existent (as a result of provincial initiatives, not the *YOA*). There are, of course, still unmanageable children in Canada, and they are

---

[87] Statistics Canada, *supra*, note 80.

[88] *Young Offenders (British Columbia) Act*, S.B.C. 1984, c. 30; *Provincial Offences Act*, R.S.O. 1980, c. 400 [now R.S.O. 1990, c. P-33]; *Young Persons Summary Proceedings Act*, S.N.S. 1985, c. 11 [now R.S.N.S. 1989, c. 509]; *Provincial Offences Procedure Act*, S.N.B. 1987, c. P-22.1. See also, Wilson (1990) for a thorough analysis of the disparate provincial legislation enacted by different provinces.

[89] Cohen, *Visions of Social Control: Crime, Punishment and Classification* (Newark, N.J.: Basil Blackwell, 1985).

still institutionalized by the state. In this regard, the child welfare statutes of every province, except for British Columbia, enable, in some fashion or another, the apprehension of a child who is "beyond control" or whose parents are "unable" to exercise appropriate control. The ultimate consequence of such a child welfare apprehension may be a "placement" in a "child care" facility, which in some provinces includes functionally secure institutions. The nature of these facilities varies widely across the country: for example, there are no locked-door child care resources in British Columbia, whereas children in need of protection in Quebec may and often are placed in secure (or open) "re-adaptation" centres which also house young offenders committed to secure (or open) custody under the *YOA*. Similarly, unmanageable children or adolescents may be psychiatrically re-labelled as "conduct disorders" or "adolescent adjustment reaction" and, pursuant to provincial mental health authority, involuntarily committed to open or closed mental health treatment facilities. Simply put, then, status offences such as unmanageability may now (if available at all) be rarely prosecuted in Canada, but unmanageable children still can be (varying by province) institutionalized by alternative civil mechanisms of social control.

Transinstitutionalism may, however, not only affect non-criminal juveniles, but also juveniles charged with or convicted of criminal offences, because many juvenile offenders are "multi-problem" youth who may be dealt with, either independently or in combination, by the criminal justice, child welfare or mental health social control mechanisms. There can be a high degree of social service system overlap in this regard: for example, in a case tracking of 2,339 juveniles charged under the *YOA* in Alberta, Thompson found that 47 percent had been previously assigned child welfare status and 18 percent had been on the caseload of mental health services.[90] These alternative systems of social control may exert a considerable influence on the juvenile justice system — and the frequency of use of "official" custody — depending upon the law, philosophy of intervention, and extent and types of resources available to the child welfare and mental health systems in each province. It is, however, difficult to trace these effects. As Cohen puts it:

> These forms of de- and re-labelling are extremely difficult to demonstrate empirically. It is already clear, however, that a probable outcome of this blurring . . . is the creation of a hidden custodial system, under welfare or psychiatric sponsorship, which official delinquency statistics simply ignore.[91]

The creation of hidden (or unofficial) custodial systems may, for example, explain why the official delinquency statistics for Quebec — which has a highly interventionist child welfare system that extensively uses secure institutions —

---

[90] Thompson, "The Young Offender, Child Welfare and Mental Health Caseload Communalities" (1988) 30(2) Can.J.Crim. pp. 135–44.

[91] Cohen, *supra*, note 89, at p. 62.

report a very low per capita rate of young offender incarceration in that province.[92] As well, given that the child welfare and mental health systems vary considerably across the provinces and therefore may have differential effects on the official use of custody within those provinces, it is unwise to engage in simple cross-provincial comparisons of official youth incarceration rates.[93]

Child Welfare Jurisdiction

The *YOA* has formally severed the relationship between the criminal court for young offenders and provincial child welfare systems. In a kind of diversion to the child welfare system at the dispositional level, the *JDA* court could commit a delinquent to the charge of a Children's Aid Society or the superintendent of Child Welfare Services, which then could (but not necessarily would) result in administrative placement in a residential or institutional resource. No similar provision is available under the *YOA*, and this has significantly affected the administration and nature — and possibly the extent of use — of custody.

The divorce from child welfare encouraged by the *YOA* — along with the Justice Model orientation of the Act and the UMA — has affected the provincial organizational responsibility for custody (and other dispositions). Under the *JDA*, child welfare departments were responsible for the administration of training school facilities in seven of the ten provinces. Under the *YOA*, youth custody centres are now exclusively administered by the same provincial government departments responsible for adult correctional facilities in five provinces, while

---

[92] Although Quebec has, as noted earlier, a high proportion of *YOA* committals to custody, the province's per capita rate of incarceration is low. These per capita rates of incarceration are calculated on the basis of average daily custody population. Unfortunately, provincial per capita rate data have not been made available by the provinces for publication. The relatively high proportion of *YOA* court committals in Quebec is likely due to the extensive use of alternative measures; i.e., since there are relatively fewer young offenders appearing in court, a high proportion of those relatively more serious offenders who do appear are committed to custody. Additionally, however, it is suggested here that the interventionist child welfare system in Quebec essentially diverts away many who might otherwise be processed and committed through the young offender system; hence, a low per capita rate of incarceration. Whether processed through the child welfare or young offender streams, however, young persons end up in the same integrated service delivery system; hence official custody statistics may obscure the real rate of institutionalization of young persons. Generally, the Quebec system is unique in Canada and therefore merits special examination.

[93] This observation does not invalidate the conclusions drawn from the data presented earlier; this was an analysis of the use of custody within, not across, provinces over time.

Ontario and Nova Scotia have "two-tiered" administrative systems in which the second tier (for those 16 years of age or older) of custodial services is administered by correctional authorities. Even in Saskatchewan and Newfoundland, where child welfare departments remain responsible for young offender services, there are separate administrative branches for young offenders; also, the child welfare and young offender populations are largely separated at the operational level.[94]

This shift toward correctional administrations can, as opposed to the more rehabilitative orientation of child welfare administrations, lead to an approach more akin to an adult correctional model, which tends to place far greater emphasis on the justice imperatives of containment and control and the enforcement of court orders.[95] As well, the richness of staffing ratios, the qualifications of staff, and the extent of professional support services tend to be less in facilities operated by correctional authorities.

The separation of young offender and child welfare services can, given the high degree of overlap among the populations they serve, lead to disputes between those organizations about their respective responsibilities and consequently "gaps" in service to young offenders. It has, for example, been observed in British Columbia that there has been a greater reluctance to make child welfare services available to young offenders than there was under the *JDA*, and that the *YOA* has "aggravated uncertainties about the interface between young offender and child welfare services";[96] program administrators in other provinces where there are separate child welfare and young offender administrations have also noted similar concerns (personal communication). Provinces which have fully (for example, Quebec) or largely (for example, Nova Scotia, 12 to 15 years) integrated young offender/child welfare administrations do not, however, appear to have experienced similar problems.

It has been suggested that the increased use of custody in some provinces may simply reflect a shift from the child welfare system to the juvenile justice system of cases that under the *JDA* were formerly dealt with in child welfare facilities, with no net increase in the level of institutionalization arising from both social control systems[97] — a kind of reverse transinstitutionalism. It can also be argued that the open custody provisions — which will be discussed in detail later — really

---

[94] See Chapter 4 for further discussion.

[95] For example, see Hackler, Garapon, and Knight, "Locking Up Juveniles in Canada: Some Comparisons with France" (1988) 13(3) Can.J.Crim., pp. 477–89.

[96] Corrado and Markwart, *supra*, note 86; Markwart, *A Description of the Application of Dispositions Under the Young Offenders Act in the Province of British Columbia* (Ottawa: Statistics Canada, Canadian Centre for Justice Statistics, 1989).

[97] Doob, "Dispositions Under the Young Offenders Act: Issues Without Answers?" in Beaulieu, ed., *Young Offender Dispositions: Perspectives on Principles and Practice* (Toronto: Wall and Thompson, 1989).

can be construed as a kind of surrogate child welfare disposition. While these arguments have some merit — particularly with respect to open custody — and require careful study province by province, they fail to take into account the escalation of sanctions that can arise — for example, administrative transfers from open to secure custody, prosecutions of escapes and consequent lengthening and severity of sentences — when these welfare-like interventions are administered and enforced directly by the juvenile justice system.

CONDITIONS FOR CUSTODY

The *YOA* sets out specific circumstances and conditions that must be satisfied before the court can impose a custodial disposition and also sets limits on the length of the disposition. These include an absolute right to counsel, the require-ment to have a pre-disposition report prepared, offence and legal criteria which limit and guide custodial sentencing conditions, prerequisites to be satisfied before intermittent custody may be imposed, and limitations on the length of custody. While these provisions are intended to circumscribe sentencing decisions and theoretically limit the use of custody, they in fact establish only very mild constraints on custody and may, in some circumstances, inadvertently encourage the use of custody.

Right to Counsel

Section 11 *YOA* is an example of one of the "special guarantees" of the rights of young persons (section 3) since it provides the accused the absolute right to counsel once charged and appearing before the court. Under the *JDA*, juveniles were represented by counsel in the majority of cases in metropolitan centres, but far less so in non-metropolitan centres.[98] It is widely agreed that the *YOA* has resulted in a substantial increase in the degree of legal representation, particularly in non-metropolitan areas. For example, in British Columbia the proportion of young persons pleading or found guilty who were represented by counsel increased from 58 percent in the first *YOA* year to 80 percent by the fourth *YOA* year.[99] In Ontario, it has been estimated that 75 percent of young offenders are represented by counsel under the *YOA*[100] and that there has been a substantial increase in legal representation in non-metropolitan courts when compared to the *JDA*.[101]

---

[98] Bala and Corrado, *Juvenile Justice in Canada: A Comparative Study* (Ottawa: Ministry of the Solicitor General of Canada, 1988).

[99] Markwart, *supra*, note 96.

[100] Hanscomb, "The Dynamics of Youth Court: A Report on a Survey of Youth Court Judges on Matters Affecting Disposition" (LL.M. Thesis, University of Toronto, 1988).

[101] Moyer, *A Description of the Application of Dispositions Under the Young Offenders Act by the Ministry of Community and Social Services of Ontario* (Ottawa: Department of Justice Canada, 1989).

There is an implied theory in the *YOA* that the weight of the criminal justice process and the potential heavy hand of the state in depriving the accused of their liberty will be balanced by rights and due process guarantees, including legal representation. A defence counsel's role is not just limited, of course, to trial proceedings; counsel also can play a vital role at disposition hearings. The trend toward an increased use of custody suggests, however, that the increased degree of legal representation under the *YOA* has not been successful in limiting the use of custody. For example, British Columbia has experienced very substantial increases in the use of custody even though 94 percent of the young offenders committed to custody in 1987–88 were represented by counsel; there is, in fact, a strong positive correlation between an increasing degree of legal representation and increasing rates of incarceration in that province.[102] This has led to speculation that "an enhanced degree of legal representation, insofar as it heightens the adversarial and criminal nature of the process, may inadvertently foster a climate that enhances the likelihood of incarceration.[103]

It has also been suggested that defence counsel are not adequately fulfilling their roles under the *YOA*. In this regard, Hanscomb,[104] on the basis of the observations and opinions of youth court judges reported in her survey, found that the vast majority of defence counsel plead their clients guilty and fail to provide effective assistance at disposition. These judges report that only infrequently do defence counsel in Ontario call character witnesses, offer statements from the accused to explain the offence, introduce independent evidence about their client's needs and circumstances or present detailed dispositional plans to the court. As well, it should be noted that, generally speaking, there are very few defence counsel who specialize in or have extensive experience with young offender cases. This is especially important, given the unique body of law for young offenders and, in particular, the need for defence counsel to be familiar with an often complex array of alternative programs that could be available to their clients.

Pre-Disposition Reports

Subsection 24(2) *YOA* requires the court to consider a pre-disposition report before making a committal to custody. Although the 1986 amendments to the Act created a provision that permits the pre-disposition report to be dispensed with, this rarely occurs in practice. While (in some provinces) the pre-disposition report may include a description of the circumstances of the offence and the young offender's account of and explanation of the offence — as well as the results of an interview with the victim — the report nonetheless is focused on the young offender and his personal and social history, and most often includes general

---

[102] Markwart, *supra*, note 96.
[103] Corrado and Markwart, *supra*, note 86, at p. 113.
[104] Hanscomb, *supra*, note 100.

recommendations for disposition. In this, the pre-disposition report is an instrument to ensure individualization in sentencing by taking into account the unique circumstances and needs of the offender.

Pre-disposition reports in Ontario youth courts generally enjoy the confidence of judges as to the accuracy of their contents and can be very influential in sentencing decisions,[105] and this is likely the case throughout the country. While these reports can be vital in recommending a dispositional plan that identifies alternatives to custody, they may, in some cases, be potentially harmful to the defence insofar as they may be used as a tool by the court to assess the need to protect society from the offender.[106]

The great emphasis in the report on the personal situation of the young offender — as examples, the "relationship between the young person and his parents and the degree of control and influence" the parents exercise, or the youth's "school attendance and performance"[107] — may also bring to light information which has little relationship to the offence, yet may, because the young person has "problems", encourage a more onerous disposition than would normally be the case for the offence in question.[108] In this regard, the criminal justice process can sometimes be used as a vehicle for "helping" these young persons by imposing greater controls (for example, strict probation orders), apparently helpful residential situations (open custody) or greater treatment intervention than would arise with offenders charged with similar offences but who do not have similar problems. Such cases clearly demonstrate that Welfare Model notions have not, by any means, been abandoned under the *YOA*. Whether such helpful interventions are in fact helpful is, of course, open to question and will vary with the case. There are dangers, however, in coupling these helpful interventions with the criminal justice process where the enforcement mechanisms of that process may come crashing down on the young offender who is to be helped yet does not wish to cooperate with that help. "System reactors" — or young persons with family/social problems who are essentially unmanageable, yet still minor offenders — typify this dilemma. Strict controls may be imposed as conditions of probation (for example, curfews, school attendance and so forth) in the young person's best interest even though the offence was minor, but then, as a result of breaches[109] and escapes from subsequent committals to open custody,[110] the eventual result may

---

[105] Hanscomb, *supra*, note 100.

[106] Hanscomb, *supra*, note 100.

[107] *Young Offenders Act*, R.S.C. 1985, c. Y-1, s. 14.

[108] It, of course, works in the reverse as well; that is, mitigating circumstances may be identified in cases which would normally attract a more severe disposition.

[109] In British Columbia, for example, section 26 breaches accounted for 29 percent of admissions to (open and secure) custody in 1989–90.

[110] Hackler *et al.*, *supra*, note 95, have also commented on the preoccupation with enforcement in Alberta.

be a term in secure custody. These types of cases are illustrative of the practical difficulties inherent in the mixed model — Welfare and Punishment — approach of the *YOA*.

Exactly what role the pre-disposition reports of probation officers have played in the escalating rates of custody in most provinces is somewhat unclear. Some facts are, however, known: custody rates have been increasing; the law requires pre-disposition reports to be prepared before a committal to custody can be ordered; and there is a high degree of concurrence between pre-disposition report recommendations and judicial decisions under the *YOA* in British Columbia[111] and Ontario,[112] and likely other provinces. This suggests that probation officers may have played an instrumental role in rising incarceration rates, but whether they have been taking a lead in this regard, merely anticipating judicial decisions in their recommendations, or have been affected by other intra- or extra-organizational factors, is entirely unclear. This is an area which requires further research.

Sentencing Criteria

The Declaration of Principle (section 3) and sections 24 and 24.1 *YOA* establish criteria which must be established before custody may be imposed. While intended to constrain the use of custody, these criteria, in fact, establish low standards and offer little in the way of real limitations on the use of custody.

While the Declaration accords young persons "the right to the least possible interference with freedom", the potential effectiveness of this principle in limiting the use of custody is — aside from the offsetting principle of responsibility and accountability — substantially watered down since this right is not absolute: the least possible interference with freedom must be "consistent with the protection of society, having regard to the needs of young persons and the interests of their families".[113] Hence, in a single proposition there are three themes — minimal interference, the protection of society, and the welfare of the young offender — that are so conflicting that the likelihood of this prinicple operating as a meaningful constraint on the imposition of custody is obviously undermined.

In a similar vein, subsection 24(1) *YOA* requires the court to establish that a committal to custody is "necessary for the protection of society", but again this is qualified: "having regard to the seriousness of the offence and the circumstances in which it was committed and having regard to the needs and circumstances of the young person". The criterion of the "protection of society" also suffers a distinct lack of clarity of meaning. Arguably, the protection of society may be achieved by quite different means — by incapacitative custodial sentences, by deterrent

---

[111] Markwart, *supra*, note 96.

[112] Moyer, *A Description of the Application of Dispositions Under the Young Offenders Act by the Ministry of Community and Social Services of Ontario* (Ottawa: Department of Justice Canada, 1989).

[113] *Supra*, note 107, s. 3.

custodial sentences or by responding to "special needs" by way of a committal to open custody. Therefore, this criterion does not necessarily support a minimal use of custody.

There is empirical evidence available which supports the view that the protection of society criterion of subsection 24(1) has been ineffective in terms of constraining the use of custody. When the Act was first proclaimed, this criterion was applicable to secure custody committals, but not open custody committals. In response to provincial concerns about the open custody provisions "widening the net" of custody, and in an effort to constrain the use of open custody, this criterion was also made applicable to open custody committals by virtue of amendments to the Act proclaimed on September 1, 1986.[114] Given this, one can examine the rates of use of custody before (i.e., 1984/85 and 1985–86) and after (i.e., 1987–88 and onward) this amendment to assess the impact of this change. If the amendment was to have its intended effect, one would expect that the use of open custody would reduce or, at minimum, would stop accelerating. One would certainly not expect that open custody committals would increase at a greater rate than secure custody, yet this is what has occurred. Between 1985–86 and 1988–89, open custody admissions increased by 41 percent in British Columbia, whereas secure custody admissions increased by only 5 percent in the same period of time.[115] Table 2 indicates that, employing the same comparisons, open custody committals increased in Ontario by 52 percent, while secure custody increased by only 8 percent. The Youth Court Survey reports that in 1985–86 open custody committals comprised 7.0 percent of dispositions, but comprised 9.7 percent of dispositions in 1988–89 — a 39 percent increase; in contrast, secure custody committals increased by only 6 percent.[116] On a province by province basis, Table 5 indicates that every province except Quebec experienced a substantial increase in the proportion of cases committed to open custody from 1985–86 to 1989–90. These data clearly suggest that the protection of society amendment in 1986 has not constrained the use of open custody; by implication, it could be argued that this same criterion has been equally ineffective in constraining the use of secure custody from the outset of the *YOA*.

Section 24.1 *YOA* sets out minimum offence qualifications which must be satisfied before the court can make a committal to secure custody. While these criteria, which vary by age, are obviously intended to limit the use of secure custody, they are — when tested against the day-to-day reality of common offences committed by delinquents — of little consequence. As Markwart and Corrado have observed:

---

[114] *Supra*, note 107, s. 24(1) [rep. and sub. R.S.C. 1985, c. 24 (2nd Supp.), s. 17].

[115] Markwart, *A Description of the Application of Dispositions Under the Young Offenders Act in the Province of British Columbia* (Ottawa: Statistics Canada, Canadian Centre for Justice Statistics, 1989).

[116] Statistics Canada, *Youth Court Statistics: Preliminary Data.* (Ottawa: Canadian Centre for Justice Statistics, 1985–86 and 1988–89).

A young offender, fourteen years of age or older, for example, only needs to commit an indictable offence for which an adult would be liable to five years imprisonment or more to attract a secure custody disposition. In real terms, this means that a juvenile could (but, of course, rarely does) attract a secure custody disposition for committing, on first offence, the most common of juvenile offences — e.g. breaking and entering, or theft or possession of stolen property over $1,000, etc. Similarly, even with the somewhat more restrictive offence criteria for young offenders under fourteen years of age, a secure custody disposition can be attracted for a first offence breaking and entering (of a dwelling house). There are, of course, no similar age and offence criteria restraining the use of open custody. While these criteria serve the purpose of curtailing committals to secure (but not open) custody for summary conviction matters (except s. 26 *YOA* offences), these very low standards may send out an unintended message. Rather than imposing exacting restrictions consistent with the principle of least interference, Parliament seems to be saying the opposite, i.e. a committal to custody for a first offence conviction on the most common of juvenile offences is something that can at least be contemplated. Such low standards may then, rather than restrain the use of custody, unwittingly encourage it.[117]

Sentence Length

With the removal of the *JDA* provisions for indefinite sentences, youth courts now fix definite lengths on disposition. The maximum period for custodial dispositions under the *YOA* has been increasingly lengthened in its short history. When the original *YOA* Bill was introduced into Parliament, there was a maximum length of two years custody, but this was extended to three years at Third Reading. The 1986 amendments to the Act created a provision that enables the imposition of consecutive custodial sentences beyond three years (albeit in rare circumstances). At the time of writing, Bill C-12 (formerly C-58) has been passed by the House of Commons and is before the Senate. This Bill proposes amendments to the Act so that a young person convicted of murder in youth court may be committed to three years' custody, followed by two years (less a day) of (parole-like) "conditional supervision". There is, however, a "gating" provision which will enable the court, in specified circumstances, to extend custody to five years less a day.

Although there has been much concern about the inadequacy of sentence lengths for murder, the limitations on sentence length in the *YOA* are (again) hardly restrictive. Presently, a young offender may receive a maximum two-year custody disposition for an indictable offence and three years for an indictable offence for which an adult would be liable to life imprisonment. Practically speaking, this means a young offender theoretically could receive two years of custody for a first offence shoplifting (proceeded by way of indictment) or of three years for a first breaking and entering of a dwelling house — again, the most common of offences and a very low standard. As well, the "short" maximum of three years' custody can be construed as a fairly onerous disposition: bearing in

---

[117] Markwart and Corrado, "Is the Young Offenders Act More Punitive?" in Beaulieu, ed., *Young Offender Dispositions: Perspectives on Principles and Practice* (Toronto: Wall and Thompson, 1989), p. 21.

mind the absence of remission and assuming the young person is not released early on judicial review, three years' custody translates into the equivalent of four and one-half to nine years of imprisonment for an adult, depending upon whether parole is granted to the adult or not.

Subsection 20(7) *YOA* provides that a young offender may not receive a disposition that "results in a punishment that is greater than the maximum punishment that would be applicable to an adult who has committed the same offence."[118] While this provision is further circumscribed by the three-year limit, it in practical terms simply means a young person may receive equal punishment for lesser offences. For example, a young person may, like an adult, still theoretically be committed to custody for six months for a summary conviction matter. In such cases, however, a young person could, in the end result, still serve a longer term than an adult since adults are virtually automatically granted reductions in sentence for remission, but young offenders do not similarly have custodial sentences automatically reduced on judicial review.[119] For example, in British Columbia available statistics indicate that young offenders committed to custody, on average, serve more than 80 percent of the original sentence imposed, whereas imprisoned adult offenders, with remission and parole, would serve less than two-thirds of the original sentence.[120]

Lengthy sentences are, however, very uncommon: the Youth Court Survey indicates that sentences in excess of two years comprised less than 0.1 percent of all custodial sentences in 1989–90.[121] As noted earlier, short deterrent custodial sentences of three months or less are the most common. There has, in fact, been a trend in most provinces toward decreasing sentence lengths under the *YOA* since it was initially proclaimed: the Youth Court Survey reports that, in total, the median sentence to secure custody declined from 150 to 90 days between 1984–85 and 1988–89, whereas the median open custody sentence length fell to 90 days from 180 days.[122] Table 6 describes the median sentence length for both open and secure custody for each of the eight provinces reporting to the Youth Court Survey over the five-year *YOA* period from 1984–85 to 1988–89. With respect to secure custody, Quebec and the four Western provinces experienced consistent and substantial reductions in sentence length from the first *YOA*, but there is no consistent pattern for the three reporting Atlantic provinces. With respect to open custody, every province but Saskatchewan has experienced marked decreases in average sentence lengths since the first *YOA* year. This trend of diminishing

---

[118] *Supra*, note 107, s. 20(7).

[119] Cosgrove (1991), for example, has found that judicial reviews of custodial dispositions (ss. 28, 29 *YOA*) are infrequently used in British Columbia; this she attributes to the formal, intricate and confusing nature of the review provisions.

[120] Markwart, *supra*, note 115.

[121] These data do not, however, account for consecutive sentences.

[122] Statistics Canada, *Sentencing in Youth Courts*. (Ottawa: Canadian Centre for Justice Statistics, 1990).

sentence lengths, coupled with an increasing frequency of committals to custody discussed earlier, is consistent with the earlier argument that individual deterrence — the "short, sharp shock" — has assumed much greater importance under the *YOA*.

There are, however, substantial variations in median sentence lengths between provinces. For example, Table 6 indicates that in 1988–89 the median length for secure custody ranged from a low of 51 days in British Columbia to a high of 150 days in Manitoba, whereas open custody ranged from a low of 45 days in British Columbia to a high of 120 days in Quebec and Manitoba. There is not a consistent pattern across provinces in the relationship between median sentence lengths for secure and open custody. Of the eight provinces for which data is available for 1988–89, open custody attracts a substantially greater median sentence length than does secure custody in three provinces, but in three provinces the median lengths are the same for both types of custody, and in two provinces the median length for secure custody is greater than open custody.

As the *JDA* provided for indefinite committals to training schools, a comparison of sentence lengths under the *JDA* and *YOA* cannot be made, except in British Columbia, where definite sentencing was the universal practice under the *JDA*. Data from British Columbia indicates that the aggregate sentence length to custody in the last *JDA* year was 120 days, but by 1989–90 this had been reduced to 84 days, a 30 percent decrease.[123] As well, and as noted earlier, it is widely accepted in Ontario that the (administratively determined) length of stay in training schools under the *JDA* was substantially longer than the (judicially determined) length of stay under the *YOA*. This is likely also the case in other provinces.

These differences are consonant with the different philosophical orientations of the two Acts. Lengthier stays under the *JDA*, with its emphasis on the offender and his treatment needs, are to be expected, whereas shorter stays under the *YOA* — with its far greater emphasis on the offence and "just proportionality" (punishment) — are equally unsurprising.

It has been suggested by some commentators[124] that the fact that judges now decide the length of custodial sentences under the *YOA* has led to an increase in the frequency of committals to custody. This, the argument goes, has arisen because under the *JDA* the length of training school committals was decided by administrators: judges, intending only a short stay, could have been reluctant to make a committal to a training school since it was not certain that a short stay would in fact be the result. In effect, the change to determinate sentencing under the *YOA* disinhibited the imposition of custody *vis-à-vis* short sentences. While this is a possibility, the explanation does not, for example, explain why there have been such substantial increases in custodial committals in British Columbia, a province where determinate sentencing was already the practice prior to the *YOA*.

---

[123] Markwart, *supra*, note 96.

[124] For example, Kennewell, Colfex, and Bala "Young Offenders" in, *The State of the Child in Ontario* (in press).

TABLE 6

Average (Median) Custodial Sentence (in Days)
Length by Type of
Custody, by Province, Fiscal Year
1984–85 to 1988–89

	Secure Custody					Open Custody				
	84–85	85–86	86–87	87–88	88–89	84–85	85–86	86–87	87–88	88–89
Newfoundland	30	60	60	30	60	120	90	90	60	60
Nova Scotia	90	60	60	90	60	180	90	60	60	60
New Brunswick	90	120	90	60	90	180	180	180	90	90
Quebec	180	180	120	120	90	210	180	180	180	120
Manitoba	300	180	180	120	150	270	180	120	120	120
Saskatchewan	90	120	90	66	60	90	120	90	90	90
Alberta	180	90	90	90	60	180	90	90	90	90
B.C.	90	60	60	60	51	120	90	90	60	45

Source: Adapted from Statistics Canada, Canadian Centre for Justice Statistics, Youth Court Survey.

It could be argued that the trend toward shorter custodial sentences under the *YOA* substantially mitigates concerns about the parallel trend to the increasing frequency of committals to custody. For example, is it "better" or "worse" to have one in every ten young offenders committed to custody for six months each, or to have two of every ten committed for three months each (resulting in no difference in the average daily custodial population)? The answer to this question turns on several considerations: the effectiveness of custodial sentences, concerns about deprivation of liberty regardless of length and the negative effects of incarceration, costs and so forth, which have been briefly discussed earlier. The trend to shorter sentence lengths is, in the writer's opinion, somewhat of a mitigating factor but not a substantial one: if one believes that the use of custody (no matter the length) should be limited to the fewest *individuals* necessary, then an increased frequency of committals to custody remains cause for substantial concern.

Intermittent Custody

The *YOA* provides for intermittent custody, but the court may not impose such a disposition unless the prosecutor makes available to the court a report from the provincial director that indicates that a place of intermittent custody is available.[125] British Columbia has a blanket policy which prohibits the use of intermittent custody — insofar as the provincial director always reports that facilities are not available — which has been upheld by the British Columbia Court of Appeal.[126] While other provinces do not have such stringent policies, intermittent custody is nonetheless uncommonly made available to the youth court by administrators and cannot be imposed unless it is made available. One of the primary reasons for limiting the availability of intermittent custody by provincial directors is the administrative complications it creates *vis-à-vis* overcrowding or available bedspace on weekends. This is an example of how administrative discretion can be a useful tool in limiting the use of custody.

OPEN AND SECURE CUSTODY

One of the more unique aspects of the *YOA* is the distinction between open and secure custody. Section 24.1 provides that where the youth court commits a young offender to custody it must, subject to qualifying offence criteria for secure custody committals, specify whether the committal is to be to open or to secure custody. The court also controls any further placement of the young person. If the initial committal is to secure custody, a transfer to open custody may only be achieved by judicial review under sections 28 or 29.[127] A young offender initially

---

[125] *Supra*, note 107, s. 24.4(2) [rep. and sub. R.S.C. 1985, c. 24 (2nd Supp.), s. 17].

[126] *R. v. G. (D.F.)* (1986), 29 C.C.C. (3d) 451 (B.C.C.A.).

[127] Section 30 permits the establishment of review boards as well, but only Newfoundland has tried (but now abandoned) this mechanism.

committed to open custody may be administratively transferred to secure custody, but only for a time-limited period (15 days) when the criteria of subsection 24.2(9) are satisfied; i.e., escape, escape attempt or to ensure the ''safety of the young person or the safety of others''. Otherwise, a young offender in open custody may only be subsequently placed in secure custody by the court, and only then if a disposition is made on a new (escape or other) charge.

The open and secure custody concept represents a radical departure from traditional juvenile (and present adult correctional) practice wherein the courts would commit delinquents to training schools and administrators would thereafter decide upon the type (or security level) of placement. In many ways, these provisions are consistent with the stated and unstated Justice Model principles of the Act, including due process, limitations on administrative discretion (or potential abuse of the same), the right to the least interference with freedom and the protection of society. For example, by enabling the courts to decide upon the level of custody and making a form of custody available (open) that is (theoretically) less restrictive, the principle of least interference with freedom can be implemented. Similarly, by having the judiciary decide on secure custody and removing the capacity for administrators to place offenders in a less restrictive level of security, the courts can ensure that the principle of the protection of society is fully respected.

The open and secure custody provisions have elicited a great deal of debate between (and among) provincial administrators, the federal government, the judiciary and interest groups. Most provinces (with the notable exception of Quebec) have lobbied for repeal and a return to a ''single level'' of custody; i.e., administrative discretion. The debate has arisen not merely because the current provisions reflect a fundamental distrust of administrative decision-making, but as a result of several concerns: the definition of custody, provincial implementation and variation, judicial ''misclassification'', program and case management concerns and the widening of the net of custody.[128]

Secure custody is defined in subsection 24.1(1) *YOA* in conceptual terms as a ''place or facility . . . for the secure containment or restraint of young persons'', whereas open custody is defined by giving examples of facilities: ''a community residential centre, group home, child care institution, or forest or wilderness camp, or any other like place or facility''. One of the difficulties with these definitions is finding the line of demarcation, in operational terms, between open and secure custody. To illustrate this problem, one can take a completely unlocked community residential facility and progressively add security features to it, asking the questions: When does this ''open'' facility become ''secure''? When a ''quiet room'' is installed? Alarms? Locked room doors? Unbreakable

---

[128] For a synopsis of the background and issues pertaining to open and secure custody, see Canada, Department of Justice. *The Young Offenders Act: Proposals for Amendment*. (Consultation Document) (Ottawa: Department of Justice, 1989).

windows? Locked perimeter doors? Exterior fencing? In practical terms, there are not *two* levels of custody, but in fact *many* levels of custody. As well, security may be achieved not only by physical measures but also by staffing levels, isolation (for example, camps) or program regulations governing privileges, freedom of movement and access to and by the community. While the distinction between a detention centre and a group home may on its face seem clear, this is not necessarily the case. For example, an intensively staffed group home with one-on-one workers may be just as secure (and personally intrusive) as a detention centre. It is also entirely unclear as to whether open and secure custody youth may be lawfully mixed in the same facility.

There is little in the way of appellate court guidance as to the distinction between open and secure custody. Courts in Nova Scotia and Prince Edward Island have invalidated provincial designations of open custody facilities on the grounds that they did not satisfy the characteristics of open custody contemplated by the Act, but these were extreme cases where portions of functionally secure adult jails were being used for open custody. [129] In contrast, the Manitoba Court of Appeal upheld the open custody designation of a facility with extensive physical security features, including electronically controlled double locking doors, on the grounds that the facility fell within the definition of a "child care institution". [130]

As a result of the unclear distinction between open and secure custody, a "patchwork of differing operational definitions across the provinces" has developed:

> The provinces do, of course, employ traditional detention centre types of facilities for secure custody, but British Columbia and Ontario have camps (or sections thereof) that are designated as secure custody, while Ontario has intensively staffed group homes that are secure custody resources. Open custody is particularly muddled. British Columbia, Manitoba and Quebec have designated open facilities (or sections thereof) that employ traditional security barriers. Quebec has several multi-purpose facilities that are co-designated secure, open, and temporary detention and which, at the same time, accept child welfare placements. Some provinces (e.g. Manitoba, Ontario) have "custody homes" — essentially foster homes — as part of their open custody systems, but others (e.g. British Columbia, New Brunswick) do not. Open custody in Manitoba ranges from these custody homes to a congregate facility with electronically controlled double locking doors, whereas a major secure facility in that province is not a locked facility. British Columbia has (largely) open custody camps but, unlike other provinces, very little in the way of open custody group homes. Further, some provinces (British Columbia, Ontario) make frequent use of probation orders with residential conditions, whereas others do not. British Columbia's extensive use of probation residence, which is nearly equivalent in size to its open custody system, commonly results in placements in

---

[129] *(Re) F. (L.H.)* (1985), 24 C.C.C. (3d) 152, 57 Nfld. & P.E.I.R. 44, 170 A.P.R. 44 (P.E.I.S.C.); B.(D.), Re (1986), 27 C.C.C. (3d) 468, 72 N.S.R. (2d) 354, 173 A.P.R. 354 (N.S. S.C.).

[130] *R. v. F.(C.)*, [1985] 2 W.W.R. 379, 30 Man. R. (2d) 297, 16 C.C.C. (3d) 258 (C.A.).

camps and community residential centres, which in any other province would be designated open custody. Ontario has group homes that house open custody, probation orders and child welfare youth in the same multi-purpose residence.[131]

The great variation in the provincial implementation of open and secure custody begs questions about the equality of treatment of young offenders before the law. An open custody committal in Newfoundland or New Brunswick, for example, can only result in placement in a truly "open" setting — a group home, foster home or community residential centre — but in British Columbia, Manitoba, Quebec and Nova Scotia (over 16 years) it can (but not always does) result in placement in facilities which have and employ functionally secure features. Conversely, a secure custody committal in provinces such as Alberta, Saskatchewan and New Brunswick can only result in placement in detention-centre-like facilities, yet in provinces such as British Columbia, Manitoba and Ontario, less secure settings — camps, group homes, open residential centres — comprise parts of their secure custody systems.

These very different operational definitions of open and secure custody across the provinces renders inter-provincial comparisons of rates of use of custody reported in official delinquency statistics essentially meaningless.[132] Certainly, one could not compare open custody rates across provinces, nor secure custody rates, given overlapping definitions. Nor is it feasible to compare total custody rates, given the variations in the use of probation residence across the provinces and the great similarities between probation residence in one province and open custody in another (or even within the same province).[133]

The distribution of secure versus open custody committals varies considerably across the provinces: for example, the Youth Court Survey indicates that in 1988–89 secure custody committals ranged from a low of 29 percent of all custody committals in Nova Scotia to a high of 63 percent in Quebec.[134] These variations could be attributed to a variety of factors — screening systems, the interface between the child welfare and juvenile justice systems, differing types of offenders and so on. The ratio of open and secure custody committals may, however, be equally affected by the judiciary having regard to the types of facilities and programs available within a province for each type of custody. Since these vary across provinces, so may the types of custody committals.

---

[131] Markwart and Corrado, *supra*, note 117, at p. 23.

[132] Markwart and Corrado, *supra*, note 117.

[133] The difficulties in comparing inter-provincial rates of custody does not undermine the conclusions drawn from the data presented earlier for increasing rates of custody, as these were comparisons over time *within*, not across provinces.

[134] These are court committals of cases. The actual distribution in open and secure custody on any given day may, however, vary considerably for a variety of reasons; i.e., administrative transfers from open to secure custody, judicial reviews, escape charges arising subsequently, temporary releases and so forth.

Provincial variations in the implementation of open and secure custody systems are not only simply attributable to the vagueness of the definitions of custody found in the *YOA*, but also to other factors. There can, for example, be philosophical differences across the provinces in the degree of emphasis placed on the "open" or the "custody" aspects of the oxymoronic "open custody". More mundane and practical considerations, however, have also influenced systems. In some provinces, the open and secure custody systems established under the *YOA* represent, in part, administrative adaptations of existing *JDA* structures to the new law. The systems established in some provinces may (as well) be construed as administrative adaptations to judicial misclassification of young offenders to either level of custody. "Judicial misclassification" refers to, from an administrator's perspective, the court committing a young offender to open custody who "should" be in the more controlled environment of a secure custody setting because of concerns about escape or behaviour management, and vice versa. To accommodate these concerns, some provinces have established a range of security levels within each type of custody so that the open custody system has some bed space that employs secure features and some secure custody bed space that has open characteristics. As a result, we find, for example, that young offenders in British Columbia and Ontario who are committed to open custody may be administratively placed in a camp setting, but then young offenders committed to secure custody can also be administratively placed in a similar camp setting. What this essentially amounts to is an administrative re-classification of the original judicial determination of the level of custody.

Judicial misclassification, and judicial control over the level of custody generally, have generated a number of concerns among many program administrators.[135] A placement in open custody, while on the face of it a less intrusive and therefore more beneficent sanction than secure custody, may, in the end result, prove to be detrimental to the young offender if he is not "suited" to the lesser constraints of an open custody environment. He may not be able to be behaviourally managed within the open custody setting or escape, with the result that he experiences failures and an "escalation of sanctions" arising from disciplinary transfers to secure custody or longer sentences for escapes. Such "inappropriate" youth may also prove to be very disruptive and compromise the effectiveness of open custody programs. Conversely, young offenders may be committed to secure custody programs more on the basis of the nature of the offence — particularly if the offence is a serious one — rather than on security risk and the needs of the young offender. As a result, secure custody may be imposed when it is not in fact required for security or behavioural management purposes. Similarly, the time-consuming nature of the rather complex judicial review process required to transfer a young person from secure to open custody may prevent timely transfers or, in the case of short, secure sentences — which, as

---

[135] These are generally outlined in a 1989 federal government consultation document (Department of Justice Canada, 1989).

noted earlier, comprise the majority of sentences — obviate the possibility of transfer altogether. Flexibility in placement, it is argued, is required to take into account the needs and changeability of young offenders. In these concerns of program administrators — and generally in the debate about whether judicial or administrative determination of the level of custody is more appropriate — it can be seen that there is a continuing struggle between the Justice and Welfare Models: between a more offence- and due process-oriented system of decision-making versus a more individualized and needs-based system.

A variety of factors may contribute to judicial misclassification. There may not, in some cases, be adequate information available to the court at the dispositional hearing for the court to make a better informed decision about which level of custody is appropriate. With first committals to custody in particular, "inappropriate" judicial decisions may simply reflect the reality that the capacity to predict how a young offender will respond to an open or a secure environment is very limited. As well, there may be a lack of awareness of and concern about the nature of custody resources available and the implications and importance of the secure/open decision on the part of judges (and community-oriented probation officers who may make recommendations). Judicial misclassification may, however, also result from a philosophical and practical confusion about the very purposes of secure versus open custody. In this regard, the legislation is silent about the purposes of the two types of custody, and little in the way of appellate court case law has developed to give the youth courts guidance in their decisions. There are many uncertainties here. Is secure custody primarily intended as an incapacitive sentence intended to contain violent offenders and to therefore ensure public safety? Should secure custody also be used for those who are likely to abscond from open custody, regardless of the less serious nature of offence, or should the court be bound by the "jump principle" and justice principles, and therefore be obliged to employ open custody first? Are open and secure custody "equivalent" in penal (or deterrent) terms, or should secure custody be regarded as a more "severe" sanction and therefore as greater punishment? These questions, like the philosophically confused Declaration of Principle, evoke different thematic concerns: public protection, deterrence and individualization of sentencing according to the unique circumstances of the offenders. And like the Declaration, as Doob has pointed out,[136] opposing answers to these questions seem to be emerging.

The open custody provisions have also been accused of "widening the net" of custody. It was in direct response to these concerns, in an effort to constrain the use of custody, that the "protection of society" criteria of section 24 was made applicable to open custody in 1986; as discussed earlier, however, the evidence suggests this change has had no effect on committals. Two somewhat similar

---

[136] Doob, "Dispositions Under the Young Offenders Act: Issues Without Answers?" in Beaulieu, ed., *Young Offender Dispositions: Perspectives on Principles and Practice* (Toronto: Wall and Thompson, 1989).

arguments have been advanced to explain why open custody may have widened the net of custody: the child welfare nature of open custody and the "soft" nature of the sanction.[137]

It has been observed that the open and secure custody provisions represent a compromise between the Justice and Welfare Models.[138] By including references to child welfare-like examples of "group homes" and "child care institutions" in the definition of open custody, it is clear that the Act envisages, and perhaps encourages, a welfare response by the youth court. In this sense, open custody may be regarded as a surrogate for the former *JDA* capacity of the court to commit a delinquent to the care of child welfare authorities. The welfare-like aspects of open custody raise further questions about the sentencing principles to be employed by youth courts. Should, for example, open custody be used to address the "needs" of young offenders even though the offence at issue, the offence history of the young person and the justice principle of proportionality suggest that custody would not otherwise be imposed in the absence of those "needs"? While it can be said that the appellate courts have consistently commented that custody should not be used as a substitute for child welfare wardship, the courts have nonetheless also not hestitated to impose a custodial term on the grounds that the juvenile is "out of control" if child welfare authorities have not already intervened in the case.[139] Given that a large proportion of young offenders also have been dealt with by child welfare authorities,[140] the potential to attract child welfare cases to open custody is great, but will vary according to the availability and nature of child welfare resources, the willingness of child welfare authorities to intervene or not and the orientation of the sentencing judge.[141]

It should also be noted that the maximum age of child welfare jurisdiction varies considerably across Canada. In Prince Edward Island, New Brunswick, Quebec, Manitoba and British Columbia, the maximum age jurisdiction is either 18 or 19 years — that is, consonant with the age jurisdiction of the *YOA* — but in the remaining provinces, the age is under 16 years. The availability of open

---

[137] Corrado and Markwart, "The Prices of Rights and Responsibilites: An Examination of the Impacts of the Young Offenders Act in British Columbia" (1988) 7(1) Can.J.Fam. L., pp. 93–115.

[138] Caputo and Bracken "Custodial Disposition and the Young Offenders Act" in Hudson, Hornick and Burrows, eds., *Justice and the Young Offender in Canada* (Toronto: Wall and Thompson, 1988).

[139] Young, "Appellate Court Sentencing Principles" in Beaulieu, ed., *Young Offender Dispositions: Perspectives on Principles and Practice* (Toronto: Wall and Thompson, 1989).

[140] Thompson, "The Young Offender, Child Welfare and Mental Health Caseload Communalities" (1988) 30(2) Can.J.Crim., pp. 135–44.

[141] Markwart and Corrado, "Is the Young Offenders Act More Punitive?" in Beaulieu, ed., Young Offender Dispositions: *Perspectives on Principles and Practice* (Toronto: Wall and Thompson, 1989).

custody in the latter provinces can then be construed as an extension of (imposed) child welfare-like services — through a criminal court — to an age group not formerly eligible for such services. This may create an incentive to process troubled teenagers through the juvenile justice system as a means of accessing these new services or to use open custody when child welfare alternatives are not available, consequently widening the net of social control.

Open custody may also widen the net simply because it appears attractive on its face in the minds of decision-makers. In contrast to the more ominous-sounding committal to "secure custody" or "youth detention centre" or "containment centre", it is "only" a committal to open custody and, after all, it is "open". It may only result in a placement in a "group home" or "forest camp". One can easily conjure images of happy lads experiencing the wonders of nature in a camp setting or under the watchful tutelage of helpful supervisors in a community residence (even though the reality may be quite different). This may be a "good and helpful" thing to do to for a young offender, or at least "not a bad thing". It is easy to see, then, how the attractiveness of this measure could affect the "in/out" decision in "marginal" or borderline cases appearing before the youth courts. There is a danger also that "open custody" may obscure the reality that such a committal still involves the deprivation of liberty and, in many provinces, may result in a placement that is not as "open" as one might expect.

While many program administrators from across the country have expressed concern about open custody widening the custodial net, it should be noted that there is very little in the way of empirical evidence to verify that it is open custody *per se* which is responsible. While there is strong evidence that the use of custody has measurably and substantially increased under the *YOA* in most provinces, these increases have been apparent in *both* open and secure custody in several provinces, although, as noted earlier, there have been greater increases, and more consistently so across provinces, in open custody than there have been in secure custody. While it is possible that there are different factors at work to account for the increases in the two types of custody — welfare and deterrence, for example — it is also possible that there are common factors affecting both types (for example, increased accountability).

TYPES OF OFFENDERS

Most young offenders committed to custody in Canada are not violent offenders. In fact, few are, as illustrated in Table 7 which presents Youth Court Survey data describing the types of offences precipitating open and secure custody dispositions in 1987–88.[142] Table 7 indicates that violent offences accounted for only 15 percent and 12 percent of secure and open custody dispositions respectively. This actually overstates the proportion of violent offenders, as the classification

[142] Data breakdowns of this nature for later *YOA* years were not available at the time of writing.

TABLE 7

Young Offender Dispositions[1]
to Secure and Open Custody
By Most Serious Offence Type
1987–88, Canada[2]

	Secure Custody	Open Custody
Violent Offences	14.8%	12.4%
Property Offences	56.1%	62.4%
Other Criminal Code	17.7%	11.7%
Drug Offences	3.0%	2.7%
YOA Offences	8.4%	10.8%

Source: Adapted from Statistics Canada, Canadian Centre for Justice Statistics, Youth Court Survey.

[1] Total dispositions is the unit of measure; i.e., where both a secure and open custody disposition arises from the same case, both are counted.

[2] Data for Ontario, P.E.I. and the Northwest Territories were not reported to the Survey.

scheme used to define "violent" offences here includes common assaults, which may be quite minor cases. Separate data for the Ontario youth custody population (Phase I, under 16 years) indicate a somewhat higher proportion of admissions are for violent offences — 23.6 percent of the secure custody population and 17.5 percent of the open custody population in 1987–88.[143] In British Columbia, correctional data indicate only 13.6 percent of secure and 13.0 percent of open custody admissions in 1988–89 were for violent offences.[144]

As Table 7 indicates, property offences account, by far, for the largest proportions of dispositions to custody — 56 percent and 62 percent of secure and open custody dispositions respectively. As well, status-like offences account for almost as many dispositions to custody as violent offences do. In this regard,

[143] Moyer, *A Description of the Application of Dispositions Under the Young Offenders Act by the Ministry of Community and Social Services of Ontario* (Ottawa: Department of Justice Canada, 1989).

[144] Markwart, *A Description of the Application of Dispositions Under the Young Offenders Act in the Province of British Columbia* (Ottawa: Statistics Canada, Canadian Centre for Justice Statistics).

"*YOA* offences" in Table 7 refer to section 26 *YOA* breaches of non-custodial dispositions. These are offences for behaviour — for example, curfew violations, failure to report to a probation officer and so forth — which in any other context would not be criminal in nature.

These data are disturbing. It is obvious that the greater reliance on custody under the *YOA* is not attributable to a response to violent juvenile crime, but rather primarily to property offenders.

While few young offenders are committed to custody for violent offences, most are, however, recidivists. In this regard, an analysis of Youth Court Survey data for 1988–89 indicates that 70 percent of young offenders ordered to serve secure custody and two-thirds of those committed to open custody are recidivists, albeit some of these are for breaches which, by definition, are recidivist offences.[145] As well, this same analysis indicates recidivist offenders are three times more likely than first-time offenders to be ordered to custody. Recidivist offenders cannot, of course, be dismissed as inconsequential, but these are exactly the types of cases discussed earlier — the repeat property offender — that are "marginal" in nature; i.e., which could or could not be committed to custody, but may be pushed over the edge into custody as a result of the more punitive orientation of the Act.

COST SHARING

Under the *JDA*, the federal government engaged in cost-sharing of provincial dispositional programs respecting juvenile court committals to the care of child welfare authorities or to training schools, but did not share in the costs of other community-based dispositions such as probation, community service or attendance programs. This federal cost-sharing arose because of the inter-relationship and overlap of these *JDA* dispositions with provincial child welfare systems and the federal government's commitment to cost-sharing of child welfare programs under the Canada Assistance Plan (CAP). *JDA* community-based programs were not able to be cost-shared under CAP because they were considered correctional services, which CAP specifically excludes.[146]

With the elimination of *JDA* child welfare committals, a new federal/provincial cost-sharing agreement was negotiated for the *YOA*. This agreement is complex but, with respect to dispositional services, it amounts to a continuation of federal cost-sharing of custodial services, but only shares in the incremental or additional costs of community-based correctional programs arising from the *YOA* (primarily, but not exclusively, brought about by the UMA). The net result is that the federal

---

[145] Statistics Canada, *Recidivists in Youth Courts: An Examination of Repeat Young Offenders Convicted in 1988–89* (Ottawa, Canadian Centre for Justice Statistics, 1990).

[146] Coflin, "The Federal Government's Role in Implementing the Young Offenders Act" in Hudson, Hornick and Burrows, eds., *Justice and the Young Offender in Canada* (Toronto: Wall and Thompson, 1988).

government provides the provinces with approximately 50 percent of the costs of dispositional custodial services, but with a substantially lesser proportion of community-based corrrectional services. In 1988–89 federal *YOA* cost-sharing contributions totalled very nearly $160 million, of which approximately 90 percent was for custodial services.

Why the provinces would enter into such an agreement is understandable. Institutional services were previously cost-shared under the *JDA* and, given that these expensive resources comprise the vast majority of dispositional expenditures, it served provincial fiscal interests to seek a continuation of cost-sharing of custodial services. Why, however, the federal government would agree to these cost-sharing arrangements is unclear. Historical precedent, easing federal/provincial tensions and softening the financial blow of the UMA to the provinces are obvious explanations, and perhaps the only explanations. It is puzzling, however, that the federal government would, as a matter of social policy, agree to these arrangements. While it cannot be said that the federal/provincial cost-sharing agreement directly encourages the use of custody, it certainly does not actively promote the development of community-based alternatives to custody. These Canadian financial arrangements stand in sharp contrast to initiatives taken in several American states where state governments provide county governments financial incentives to deinstitutionalize and to develop community-based alternatives. If the Canadian federal government had been truly committed to a social policy of deinstitutionalization, it would have similarly insisted on a formula that provided strong and continuing financial incentives to develop community-based alternatives to custody and reduced or little funding of custody itself.

It seems that the opportunity for a change in social and fiscal policy is now lost. The original five-year cost-sharing agreement expired in 1989. This enabled the federal government, as a fiscal restraint measure, to freeze cost-sharing contributions to the provinces at 1988–89 expenditure levels. Therefore, any additional young offender service expenditures required of provincial governments as a result of inflation or the implementation of new alternative programs will not be cost-shared, and the federal portion of young offender program financing will gradually diminish over the years. With high volumes of young offenders already in costly custodial centres, it will require a far greater economic and political commitment on the part of the provinces to reduce the reliance on incarceration.

CONCLUSION

When the *YOA* was introduced into the House of Commons in 1982, it was hailed by the opposition Conservative Party as the first major social justice bill to come before the House in over three decades. This has hardly proved to be the case. There is strong evidence that the implementation of the *YOA* has led to a substantially greater reliance on custody than the *JDA* and, at the least, consistent evidence across most provinces that there has been an increasing reliance on custody during the short life of the Act.

A number of possible explanations for this have been explored in this chapter: the increased emphasis on the justice principles of protection of society and, in particular, deterrence; the philosophical ambivalence and consequent "mixed model" approach of the Act; the uniform maximum age; sentencing criteria that ostensibly restrict the use of custody but which set very low standards and may therefore inadvertently encourage the use of custody; the Justice Model approach creating a more criminalized process; inter-relationships between the youth justice and child welfare systems; the open and secure custody provisions; the greater local availability of custodial resources; and federal/provincial cost-sharing of program resources.

There is some evidence beyond simple custody committal statistics — judicial surveys, case law and sentence lengths, for example — which supports the view that some of these factors have, indeed, been at work. Nonetheless, the supporting evidence is, if available at all, still not strong enough to precisely identify which factors have contributed, and to what degree, to increased custody rates. Just as Bala has argued that there is no single solution to the complex problem of juvenile delinquency,[147] it is likely that there is no simple answer, no single element, to be found in the complex provisions of the *YOA* — and in the implementation of the Act by the provinces — that can be identified. It is more reasonable to suggest that there are many contributing factors. Much more research is needed.

The evidence suggests that far too many young offenders in Canada are committed to custody for non-violent offences. Whether these rising rates of incarceration are an inherent by-product of the (modified) Justice Model of the *YOA* is not at all clear. As Corrado discusses in Chapter 3, while the passage of juvenile justice legislation that is rooted in Justice Model principles is associated with rising incarceration rates in several American states, the recent evidence from Britian suggests that this is not necessarily an inevitable consequence of Modified Justice Model legislation. Given this, it would seem premature, and perhaps simplistic, to propose repeal of the *YOA* altogether and restoration of Welfare Model legislation. A course of action involving less dramatic, yet still bold initiatives is worth trying. In this regard, a simpler, clearer and more consistent philosophical framework which asserts the need for societal protection from violent crime, yet emphasizes principles of restraint and de-institutionalization for non-violent offences, would be helpful. This, along with clear and strict sentencing criteria which stipulated that custody should only be imposed for non-violent offences as a measure of last resort, and only after all feasible alternatives to custody have been exhausted, would provide much clearer guidance to the courts. Of course, these alternatives to custody would have to be available. To address this issue, the federal government could restore and re-arrange cost-sharing in such a manner that the preponderance of funds are re-directed to community-based alternatives, rather than to custodial programs. Space does not

---

[147] See Chapter 2.

permit a discussion of other complex measures that could be considered (for example, open/secure custody or improved linkages with child welfare systems). If, however, Canada is to adopt and to remain serious about a social policy of decarceration, the status quo is obviously not acceptable.

PART II

SELECTED ISSUES IN JUVENILE JUSTICE IN CANADA

Chapter 6

The Effectiveness of Juvenile Justice in Quebec: A Natural Experiment in Implementing Formal Diversion and a Justice Model[1]

Marc Le Blanc
Hélène Beaumont

In many regards, Quebec has always been something of a special province in Canada. This also holds true for the nature of juvenile justice in Quebec. As this chapter will point out, many of the features of the *Young Offenders Act*[2] were implemented in Quebec before the law was adopted by the federal government. Between 1979 and 1984, Quebec was the theatre for a natural experiment in juvenile justice: formal diversion was implemented, due process was accentuated and the scope of judicial discretion was restricted. In this chapter, we will address the question of recidivism and how these changes modified the flow and the output of the juvenile justice system.

The federal *Juvenile Delinquents Act*[3] was passed in 1908 and remained more or less unchanged until 1982. One of the features of that Act was a definition of delinquency that overlapped the fields of criminality and child protection. Although Quebec did not pass its first youth protection law until 1951, radical changes were made to it during the seventies. A law for the protection of abused children was enacted in 1974; in 1977, a new *Youth Protection Act*[4] (hereafter

---

[1] Data used in this chapter were gathered for research commissioned by the Ministry of the Solicitor General of Canada and by a grant from the Conseil Québécois de la Recherche Sociale.

[2] R.S.C. 1985, c. Y-1.

[3] S.C. 1908, c. 40.

[4] S.Q. 1977, c. 20.

referred to as *YPA*) was passed and was implemented in 1979. This new Act radically changed the situation with its new philosophy — an important element of which was a clear distinction between protection and delinquency. It introduced a formal diversion from the juvenile justice system under the responsibility of welfare services — the Youth Protection Director (hereafter referred to as YPD) could now propose alternative voluntary measures to court processing. Under the 1977 *YPA*, children in need of protection were classified in two groups: those who experienced a situation that endangered their security and development (s. 39 lists situations of danger such as sexual or physical abuse, negligence and so on) and those who committed an infraction to an existing law (s. 40 enumerates federal, provincial and other statutory laws). This chapter is about the youth process under s. 40, an article which implies the *JDA* was applied only to delinquency cases not diverted by the YPD. Under the *YPA*, the YPD had the responsibility for screening cases that should or should not go to court and could propose diversion or voluntary measures to youths either under s. 39 or 40. Because of this situation, from 1979 to 1984 Quebec experimented with diversion prior to this being made formally possible under the *YOA*.

It is now possible to evaluate the effects of these changes on recidivism for youths committing an infraction to the *Criminal Code*[5] or other statutory law and to illustrate the potential impact of the *YOA* diversion mechanism in other provinces. In 1981, two years after the implementation of the *YPA*, a study was commissioned on the functioning of the Montreal juvenile court and of the Youth Protection Director, who was responsible for diversion; this research was carried out as part of the National Study of the Functioning of the Juvenile Courts in Canada, sponsored by the Ministry of the Solicitor General of Canada.[6] This sample of over 900 juvenile delinquents was followed until 1988 to gather information on recidivism in youths under and over 18 years of age.[7] With these

[5] R.S.C. 1985, c. C-46.

[6] For a description of the research project, see Caplan, *Planning Report: National Study of the Functioning of the Juvenile Court, Canada Legislation on Young Offenders* (Ottawa: Ministry of the Solicitor General, 1981). For project results, see Marceau and Le Blanc, "Description du Tribunal de Jeunesse de Montréal", Groupe de Recherche sur l'Inadaptation Juvénile, Université de Montréal, Montréal, 1980; Marceau, Le Blanc, La combe and Trudeau-Le Blanc, "La Cueillette des Données Auprès des Tribunaux de la Jeunesse du Québec", Groupe de Recherche sur l'Inadaptation Juvénile, Université de Montréal, Montréal, 1982; Le Blanc and Beaumont, "Déscription du Fonctionnement du Tribunal de la Jeunesse de Montréal Entre mai 1981 et avril 1982", Consultation, Évaluation et Recherche sur l'Inadaptation Juvénile, Montréal, 1985.

[7] Le Blanc and Beaumont, "L'Efficacité des Mesures pour Jeunes Délinquants Adoptées à Montréal en 1981, une Étude Longitudinale", Groupe de Recherche sur l'Inadaptation Psycho-Sociale à l'Enfance, Université de Montréal, Montréal, 1989.

data, we can measure the effectiveness of decisions taken by welfare agents and judges under conditions similar to the legislative context introduced by the *YOA* and allow at least a speculative description of what has been happening in different jurisdictions since the implementation of the *YOA* in 1984.

In this chapter, the impact of the Quebec *YPA* will be studied in two main sections: the first is concerned with formal welfare-based diversion, and the second with the functioning of juvenile courts. In each of these sections, the legislative and functional changes introduced by the *YPA*, data on recidivism in youths under and over 18 years of age and a discussion of the possible effects of the changes introduced by the *YOA* are presented.

FORMAL WELFARE-BASED DIVERSION

The *YPA* introduced many changes, including the definition of the rights of children, the distinction between delinquency and protection, the principle of minimal intervention, precise definitions of motives for protection and formalization of court procedures. We cannot review all of the changes implemented, but we can, from a juvenile justice system point of view, study the major innovation that was installed: a formal diversion mechanism that was welfare-based. Under the *YPA*, diversion became the sole responsibility of social services agencies; justice system personnel, particularly Crown prosecutors, lost to welfare services the control of that type of discretionary decision. Before commenting on the *YOA*, we will describe the legislative and administrative changes that were implemented and the measure of their usefulness in terms of their impact on recidivism.

Legislative and Functional Changes

The 1977 changes concerning diversion, which were implemented in 1979, and which preceded the adoption of the *YOA* in 1982 and its implementation in 1984, are examined first. These important changes concerned the limits imposed on judicial action and the modifications of the traditional roles of officials in the juvenile justice system.

The Limits Imposed on Judicial Action

The *YPA* imposed many limits on judicial action. Three major limitations should be mentioned that are directly relevant to diversion: lower and upper age limits, a priority for diversion and restrictions on the use of the *JDA*.

The *JDA* and the *YPA* applied in principle to all children under 18 years of age in Quebec. The *YOA* confirmed the upper age limit adopted by Quebec, but went on to set the new minimum age for criminal responsibility at 12 years of age, falling between 7 in the *JDA* and 14 in Quebec's *YPA*. The Charbonneau Commission[8] suggested 12 and 18 as appropriate minimum and maximum ages,

---

[8] Charbonneau, *Rapport de la Commission Parlementaire Spéciale sur la Protection de la Jeunesse* (Québec: Assemblée Nationale du Québec, 1982).

and a survey conducted among a representative sample of social and legal practitioners during the summer of 1982 showed that the provisions of the *YOA* governing minimum and maximum ages met with general approval.[9]

During the 1960s and 1970s, several diversion programs were begun in the United States following the President's Commission on Law Enforcement and Administration of Justice.[10] Diversion doctrine was hotly debated and publicized among Canadian specialists during the 1970s. Bill C-192, dating from 1970 and intended to replace the *JDA*, already proposed diversion after referral to the Juvenile Court. The doctrine of diversion had a major impact on Quebec's new *YPA*, which coordinated social and legal interventions according to the situation and the needs of the young persons, whether they were children in danger or delinquents. Recognizing that children have a number of rights, particularly the right to be kept in their natural environment, the *YPA* pursued an objective of diversion by limiting the court's intervention to cases where absolutely necessary to protect the child or society and by promoting instead the use of voluntary measures.

Consistent with these principles, the *YPA* proposed a mechanism for screening cases to be brought before the court. It stated that the court could only be referred to when a voluntary agreement could not be reached in the case of a child whose safety or development was considered to be compromised, or one who was suspected of an infraction to a law or regulation in effect in Quebec. In exceptional cases that called for court intervention because the parents and/or the children were not cooperative, the *YPA* attempted to ensure the best possible coordination of the various laws likely to apply. If a child was charged with breaking a law or regulation in effect in Quebec, the applicable provisions would differ depending on whether it was a federal criminal law or only a provincial statute, the latter including also municipal by-laws. With federal laws, the *JDA* applied; with provincial statutes, the *Summary Convictions Act*[11] *(SCA)* applied, insofar as it was not incompatible with the *YPA*. In protection cases, the *YPA* applied, and the

---

[9] See Le Blanc, "La Loi sur les Jeunes Contrevenants et les Intervenants du Système de Justice pour Mineurs au Québec" (1984) 21 *Annales de Vaucresson* pp. 67–92. Le Blanc, "L'Opinion des Juges, Avocats de la Défense et Procureurs de la Couronne sur le Système de Justice pour Mineurs et la Loi sur les Jeunes Contrevenants" (1984) 14(2) Revue de Droit 591–624; Le Blanc, "Les Policiers, la Loi sur les Jeunes Contrevenants et le Système de Justice pour Mineurs" (1984) XVII(1) Criminologie 91–116; Le Blanc, "Les Agents de Relations Humaines des CSS, la Loi sur les Jeunes Contrevenants et le Système de Justice pour Mineurs" (1984) 33 (2–3) *Service Sociale* pp. 323–56.
[10] President's Commission on Law Enforcement and Administration of Justice, *The Challenge of Crime in Free Society* (Washington, D.C.: U.S. Government Printing Office, 1967).
[11] S.R.Q. 1964, c. 35.

court was to be referred to only if the submission of the facts justified intervention by the court.

The *YPA* sought to restrict, as much as possible, application of the *JDA* and to give priority to Quebec law. The restrictions placed on the *JDA* were provided for in s. 39 of the *JDA*,[12] which stated that provisions of a provincial statute intended for the protection or benefit of children could be used instead of the *JDA*, except in the instance of an indictable offence under the *Criminal Code* and on condition that such action was in the best interest of the child.

In 1982, there were few social and legal practitioners in Quebec who did not support the principle of limiting legal intervention, as revealed in a survey.[13] Four out of five supported the main conditions proposed in the *YOA* for applying alternative measures (restitution, conciliation and so on). According to the 1982 Charbonneau Commission, practitioners not only supported, but also extensively practiced, diversion.

By introducing alternative measures, the *YOA* recognized the principle of diversion and at the same time eliminated the problems of coordination between the *YPA* and the *JDA*. Alternative measures, like the voluntary measures in the *YPA*, could be proposed to an adolescent, recognizing that he/she had committed an infraction of the *Criminal Code* or a federal statute, provided that the Crown prosecutor was satisfied of sufficient proof of the offence. The *YOA* also eliminated coordination problems between the federal and provincial acts by making only infractions of the *Criminal Code* and federal statutes punishable, thus confirming Quebec's approach to the *YPA* that clearly distinguished between protection and delinquency. However, these problems did not affect a large number of youths, as shown in a 1981 study in which only 19 percent of the sample had simultaneously a protection file and a conviction for a criminal or other infraction.[14] And, as seen in the next section, the *YOA* restored the traditional role of the Crown prosecutor which had been given to the YPD by the *YPA*.

Changes in the Roles of Officials in the Juvenile Justice System

The police, Crown prosecutors and social service agents, in that order, traditionally played an important role in the juvenile justice system as screening agents before a court appearance could happen. The *YPA* dramatically changed their roles by altering that sequence; social services agents would, under the *YPA*, screen in between the policeman and the Crown prosecutor.

Under *YPA*, the YPD played a major role in screening cases to be submitted to the court. A YPD was to be named in each of the social services centres (as set up under the provincial health and social services act) by the centres' administrative councils after they had consulted organizations working in that area. In this way,

---

[12] *Supra*, note 3.

[13] Leblanc, *supra*, note 6.

[14] Le Blanc and Beaumont, *supra*, note 6.

there was at least one YPD in each of the health and social service regions of the province. The YPD came under the authority of each centre's director-general. The *YPA* gave this director-general a certain number of responsibilities that he/she could, in turn, delegate in writing, in whole or in part, to a person or establishment or organization recognized by Quebec's government. The delegate was responsible primarily for defending rights, promoting interests and improving a minor's living conditions. These responsibilities, as set out in s. 33 of the *YPA*,[15] were as follows:

- to analyse the situation of any child whose safety or development could be considered as compromised (as defined in s. 38)[16] and who was charged with committing an infraction of a law or regulation in effect in Quebec;
- to take emergency measures as required by the situation, provided such measures did not exceed 24 hours in duration, without a court order;
- to decide on the orientation of the child or to participate in this decision with a person appointed by the Minister of Justice;
- to take charge of any child whose safety or development was compromised or who was charged with committing an infraction of a law or regulation in effect in Quebec, and to propose and see to the application of voluntary measures, when the parents gave their consent, or when the child was over 14 years of age;
- to see to the execution of measures ordered by the court.

The YPD could not refer cases of children under 14 years to the court simply because they had committed an infraction of a law or regulation in effect in Quebec. The YPD had the sole responsibility of deciding which children over 14 years of age would be referred to court. However, some of the provisions of the Act were challenged in court. In 1981, a Supreme Court of Canada ruling declared "*ultra vires*, that is, beyond the scope of the legislature" the provisions that prevented a person, such as a victim, from bringing a matter of delinquency before the juvenile court when the YPD and the person appointed by the justice minister refused to take legal action (*A.G. Que. v. Lechasseur*).[17] The provincial law did provide access, albeit limited, to the juvenile court to parents and to children 14 years of age and over who did not agree with a decision of the YPD.

The YPD's screening responsibilities left unchanged the discretionary role of the police officer in charging an adolescent suspected of committing a crime. The police of the Montreal urban community had a long tradition of using their

---

[15] *Supra*, note 4.

[16] *Ibid.*

[17] [1981] S.C.R. 253, 63 C.C.C. (2d) 301, 28 C.R. (3d) 44, 128 D.L.R. (3d) 739, 38 N.R. 516, 25 R.F.L. (2d) 1.

discretionary powers concerning young delinquents and diverting them from a court appearance. Since the creation of its Youth Division in 1967, and until the implementation of the *YPA*, an average 33 percent of cases were diverted. The number of diverted cases increased at the end of the 1970s;[18] in 1981, at the time of this study, 46 percent of the cases were diverted by police officers.[19] Their decision criteria were the seriousness of the crime, the age of the delinquent, the past criminal record and the source of the complaint. These criteria were revealed in a study of the files[20] and confirmed in an interview study in 1982.[21]

Like the *YOA*, the *YPA* had no specific provisions concerning the way the police should handle juvenile delinquents, except that they should refer all cases directly to the YPD instead of to the Crown prosecutor. In a survey of police officers' practices in 1982, it was shown that Montreal policemen behaved in accordance with the provision of the *YOA*.[22] This procedure was not well accepted by policemen, as stated in the 1982 Charbonneau report. However, in a survey of a large sample of Montreal policemen in 1982,[23] 75 percent agreed to alternative measures as they should be applied in the context of the *YOA*. They were particularly satisfied that the provision of the *YOA* reinstated the role the Crown prosecutor had lost with the *YPA*.

Before the *YPA* came into effect, Crown prosecutors received requests to begin legal proceedings directly from the police. Office staff completed the complaints after checking the evidence and the regulation, and sent the parents written notice by way of a copy of the hearing notice.[24] Through this procedure, 94 percent of the cases handled by the Crown prosecutor were referred to juvenile court before the implementation of the *YPA*.[25] This role was withdrawn after the *YPA* came into effect. However, when a juvenile delinquent came before the court under the *YPA*, a lawyer, representing the prosecutor-general, was always assigned to the hearings, where he/she was responsible for the defence of the victim's point of view. It is evident that all judicial personnel — judges, Crown prosecutors and defence lawyers — were against these changes.[26]

---

[18] Le Blanc, "Quebec Youth Protection Act and the Doctrines of Decriminalization, Due Process, Diversion and Deinstitutionalization", paper presented to the 5th Canadian Conference on Applied Criminology, University of Ottawa, Department of Criminology, Ottawa, 1982.

[19] *Ibid.*

[20] Le Blanc, "La Réaction Sociale à la Délinquance Juvénile: Une Analyse Stigmatique" (1971) IV Acta Crim. 113–92.

[21] Le Blanc, "L'Opinion des Juges", *supra*, note 9.

[22] *Ibid.*

[23] Le Blanc, "La Loi sur les Jeunes Contrevenants", *supra*, note 9.

[24] Marceau and Le Blanc, *supra*, note 6.

[25] Trepanier and Gagnon, "La Déjudiciarisation à la Cour du Bien-Être Social de Montréal", Université de Montréal, École de Criminologie, Montréal, 1984.

[26] Charbonneau, *supra*, note 8.

The new *YPA*, with its goal of diversion, contained a mechanism designed to provide an initial analysis of all cases of children suspected of being in danger or of having committed an offence. At this preliminary stage, agreement from parents and adolescents to the implementation of voluntary measures was strongly encouraged, and only those cases where court intervention appeared necessary continued along within the system. Since all protection and delinquency cases were, in principle, to be first submitted to this screening process, the role that was formerly played by the Crown prosecutor's office was considerably reduced. The YPD had taken over this vital function.

Thus, the police officer notified the YPD of all infractions. The YPD would analyse the cases with the help of a Justice Minister appointee and decide on the possibility of applying voluntary measures. If such measures did not appear to be appropriate, the YPD filed a complaint with the court through the Crown prosecutor's office. This diversion mechanism was harshly criticized for it did not respect the fundamental principles of Canadian criminal law and because of the practical problems discussed at length by the 1982 Charbonneau Commission. On one hand, it was argued that the mechanism failed to respect the basic rights and principles of criminal law (for example, the right to be presumed innocent, the necessity to establish sufficiency of proof and so on). On the other hand, this mechanism gave rise to a large number of practical problems. Occasionally, a YPD would request that proceedings be started without sufficient proof of an infraction, or he/she would apply voluntary measures to adolescents later found not guilty by the court.

After the Charbonneau Commission reviewed the *YPA*'s formal diversion mechanism and proposed that the Crown prosecutor receive all requests to start proceedings from police or other referring agencies or individuals, and after analysing the sufficiency of the proof, the most serious charges under specific sections of the *Criminal Code* were forwarded directly to the court. The Charbonneau Commission proposed a list of offences, and the regulations adopted by the Government of Quebec (Ruling, 787-84)[27] confirmed that list for the implementation of alternative measures available through the *YOA*. On the basis of the Charbonneau review, for municipal and provincial infractions, minors are referred to the YPD, who considers the possibility of applying alternative measures. This is the mechanism that has prevailed since the *YOA* came into effect.

Not only did the existence of the YPD produce legal and practical difficulties, it also faced some functional problems.[28] Screening was a two-step process: based

---

[27] *Ibid.*

[28] The functioning of the Montreal YPD is described by Le Blanc and Beaumont, "Description du Fonctionnement du Tribunal de la Jeunesse de Montréal", Consultation, Évaluation et Recherche sur l'Inadaptation Juvénile, Montréal, 1985; and Leclerc, "Le Choix des Mesures de Déjudiciarisation des Practiciens à la Direction de la Protection de la Jeunesse de Montréal", mémoire de maîtrise inédit, École de Criminologie, Université de Montréal, Montréal, 1986.

on the police officer's report and the control of existing files, a welfare officer would classify the case as minor or serious. Minor cases would be sent to the minimal intervention unit; if the initial diagnosis was confirmed by interviewing the adolescent and the parents, voluntary measures were negotiated. Serious cases were sent to another unit for a more in-depth evaluation and probably a reference to court. There was always the potential for transferring the case to the other unit if the initial assignment was wrong. The YPD had relatively adequate personnel for screening responsibilities and developed an instrument to guide these decisions; that is, a clinical guide was developed and circulated to all practitioners.[29]

The minimal intervention services component was relatively undeveloped, at least at the beginning of the implementation of the *YPA*. At the time of the 1982 study, there were many such alternative programs operating as restitution, community work, victim conciliation and others. However, these programs did not have a sufficient number of places to satisfy the demand, and as a result 61 percent of the cases were closed. No action was taken by the YPD beyond discussing the situation with the adolescent and his or her parents in a formal meeting at the YPD's office. This interview was supposed to be only a component of the evaluation required of the YPD for each case.

In a survey of social welfare agents in 1982,[30] they were described in the following manner: 87 percent of the personnel of the YPD had a university diploma in social and human sciences; workers had an average of nine years of experience working in the social services. They were treatment-oriented. They would do an average of three or four evaluations a week, each taking five to six hours. For the most part, they would gather information on the family, delinquency, friends and schooling, and their decision would be influenced by the seriousness of the offence, the circumstances of the crime, the existence of prior offences and the will of the adolescent to change.

Effectiveness of Formal Welfare-based Diversion in 1981

Between the implementation of the *YPA* in 1979 and the implementation of the *YOA* in 1984, Quebec was the theatre of a natural experiment with a mechanism of formal welfare-based diversion. Diversion, by definition, is a screening process by which cases are not transmitted to an upper level of the juvenile justice system. In Quebec, it is a formal welfare-based diversion mechanism in the sense that the *YOA* creates a social agency, the YPD, to make these decisions under specific rules as an agency located between police and juvenile court to which all

---

[29] Table Centrale de Consultation et de Concertation, "Evaluation-Orientation des Jeunes Contrevenants", Table Centrale de Consultation et de Concertation, Loi sur la Protection de la Jeunesse, Québec, 1980.

[30] Le Blanc, "L'Opinion des Juges, Avocats de la Défense et Procureurs de la Couronne sur le Système de Justice pour Mineurs et la Loi sur les Jeunes Contrevenants" (1984) 14(2) Revue de Droit 591–64.

delinquency cases had to be referred. However, the mechanism of diversion implemented in Quebec was different from the justice-controlled diversion programs described in the American and Canadian literature.[31]

Palmer and Lewis distinguished four of these types of diversion programs situated at four major processing points in the juvenile justice system: (1) police setting, diversion in lieu of arrest; (2) police setting, diversion in lieu of referral to court; (3) probation intake setting, diversion in lieu of petition to court; and (4) court setting, alternative measures in lieu of traditional sentences like fine, probation or incarceration.[32] The Quebec diversion mechanism falls in between types 2 and 3 of these programs, since decisions were not made by the traditional agents of the justice system, policemen and probation officers. The Quebec mechanism was also very different from other programs because it was formal, compulsory and noncoercive and because it was not related to traditional services in the juvenile justice system. Like American youth service bureaus (YSBs), it was positioned between police and court, but it differed because the decision to refer to the YPD was compulsory. Policemen had to refer all cases to the YPD. In a YSB, such referrals are optional. Not only was it compulsory, this mechanism was defined by law and involved a new administrative agency that had nothing to do with traditional juvenile justice agencies (such as probation). Finally, it was different because it was clearly noncoercive in the following manner. The adolescent accused of a crime had to recognize that he had committed an offence, and that he had the opportunity to choose between a voluntary measure and a referral to court. He also had to be informed of the nature of the voluntary measure that could be proposed.

Existing evaluations of diversion programs do not show the results that the advocates of this type of measure expected; that is, a clear advantage to diversion over traditional court processing in reducing recidivism, stigma and so on.[33] For example, in the Palmer and Lewis study, on a six-month follow-up, the difference in recidivism was only 6 percent, 25 percent for diversion versus 31 percent for court processing.[34] In the Rappaport study, the advantage of diversion wears away

---

[31] See Moyer, *La Déjudiciarisation dans le Système Judiciare pour les Jeunes et ses Répercussions sur les Enfants: Recension de la Documentation* (Ottawa: Ministry of the Solicitor General, 1980).

[32] Palmer and Lewis, *An Evaluation of Juvenile Diversion* (Cambridge: Oelgeschlager, Gunn and Hain, 1980).

[33] President's Commission on Law Enforcement and Administration of Justice, *The Challenge of Crime in Free Society* (Washington, D.C.: U.S. Government Printing Office, 1967); Lemert, ''Diversion in Juvenile Justice: What Has Been Wrong'' (1981) 18(1) *Journal of Research in Crime and Delinquency* pp. 35–45.

[34] Palmer and Lewis, *supra*, note 32.

with time.[35] Let us see if the *YPA* diversion mechanism performs at the same level. Even if the practitioners think that they are doing much better than these rates, they are estimating the *YPA* recidivism rate at around 15 percent (see the Charbonneau report).

A representative sample of 919 adolescent boys was drawn from the cases referred to the YPD for an infraction of law during the winter of 1981.[36] This sample consisted of all the cases referred to the YPD in a certain number of days. It was built in the following way: all boys (421) who appeared in court for a new infraction during the months of June and July 1981 were studied; 498 subjects were then added by including all boys who were referred to the YPD on the same days the first group of boys were referred to court. In terms of age, sex and offence distribution, this sample compares closely with Statistics Canada data on young delinquents in the region of Montreal and for Quebec as a whole for the year 1981.

Of the 919 boys sampled in Montreal, 54 percent were diverted, while 46 percent were brought to court. This distribution is comparable to Quebec statistics as a whole for the same period; depending on the region, about 50 percent of the cases were diverted.[37] Since the *YOA* was implemented, there has not been a major shift in these figures. Figures for 1986 and 1987 show that 43 percent of the cases were diverted in Quebec; equivalent data are not available for Montreal, but the proportions are usually higher there.[38] During that period, police diversion was around 25 percent for Quebec and around 40 percent in Montreal.[39] In fact, the presence or the absence of the YPD did not significantly affect the flow of cases; neither did the fact that before the *YOA* it was the YPD who made the diversion decision, while it is the Crown prosecutor who has that responsibility now.

Let us now look at the comparison of outcomes between diversion and court

---

[35] Rappaport, "Public Policy and the Dilemmas of Diversion" in Corrado, Le Blanc and Trépanier, eds., *Current Issues in Juvenile Justice* (Toronto: Butterworths, 1983).

[36] For research design, see Marceau, Le Blanc, Lacomb and Trudeau-Le Blanc, "La Cueillette des Données Auprès des Tribunaux de la Jeunesse du Québec", Groupe de Researche sur l'Inadaptation Juvénile, Université de Montréal, Montréal, 1982; and Le Blanc and Beaumont, "L'Efficacité des Mesures pour Jeunes Délinquants Adoptées à Montréal en 1981, un Étude Longitudinale", Groupe de Recherche sur l'Inadaptation Psycho-Sociale à l'Énface, Université de Montréal, Montréal, 1989.

[37] Charbonneau, *Rapport de la Commission Parlementaire Spéciale sur la Protection de la Jeunesse* (Québec: Assemblée Nationale du Québec, 1982).

[38] Ministère de la Justice du Québec, *Application du Programme de Mesures de Rechange au Québec* (Québec: Ministry of Justice, 1987).

[39] Fréchette and Le Blanc, *Délinquances et Delinquants* (Chicoutimi, Qué.: Gaétan Morin, 1987).

referral.[40] Recidivism was defined in two ways in this study: juvenile recidivism, any new conviction after the decision studied in 1981 but happening before 18 years of age; adult recidivism, any new conviction after the age of 18. The average follow-up period was three years. As shown in Table 1, there is no statistically significant difference between cases diverted and referred to court: the percentages of juvenile recidivism are 15 percent and 19 percent respectively, and their adult counterparts are 44 percent and 50 percent. Le Blanc and Beaumont also show that there is no difference in the nature of adult recidivism: frequency, nature, variety and seriousness of new convictions do not statistically distinguish the two groups. Only age of onset distinguishes these groups; the boys diverted show a statistically significant later onset of first adult conviction (20.3 years of age versus 19.6 years of age).

Since the outcome of formal welfare-based diversion is not significantly different from traditional juvenile justice measures, every knowledgeable observer would think that this result is the fault of the selection process. Perhaps the YPD did not select less serious cases for diversion on the basis of criminal and personal characteristics of the adolescent, as would have been expected. Le Blanc and Beaumont show that this was not the case. The diverted boys were most often younger, aged 14 and 15, and in school; they had, less often, prior convictions and an accepted protection request. Not only were they different in these personal characteristics, but the nature of the crimes of which they were accused is different; they were less often involved in personal crimes (6 percent versus 20 percent), more often involved in infractions to provincial statutes and municipal by-laws (28 percent versus 19 percent), and when they were involved in property crimes, it was less often for breaking and entering (22 percent versus 36 percent).

Palmer and Lewis used a research design with a matched comparison group and did not find a very large difference between diversion and court referral.[41] Even when controlling statistically for the characteristics mentioned above, there was no difference in adult recidivism between the boys diverted and the boys referred to court.[42] Adolescents with the same age, the same school and criminal antecedent status, and who have committed the same type of crime, do not show statistically significant differences in adult recidivism, whether they are diverted or referred to court. But if one eliminates all the worst risks from the sample of diverted cases — that is, taking out all older adolescents who were not in school, who had prior convictions and a protection file and who had committed a more serious offence — there would be a clear advantage for diversion over court referrals. Recidivism drops to 29 percent, and the X^2 is statistically significant (39.66, df $= 1$, p $<.0001$). These results mean that if the YPD had done a better

---

[40] For a complete analysis, see Le Blanc and Beaumont, *supra*, note 36.

[41] Palmer and Lewis, *supra*, note 32.

[42] These data are not presented here, but are available from Marc Le Blanc; See also results of the logistic regression in Le Blanc and Beaumont, *supra*, note 36.

Table 1

Diversion and Court Referral and Juvenile and Adult Recidivism

	Court referrals		Diverted cases		Total		chi square
	N	%	N	%	N	%	
Juvenile recidivism							
Adult	341	81	423	84.9	764	83.1	$X^2 = 2.53$
Presence	80	19	75	15.1	155	16.9	df = 1
Total	421	100	498	100	919	100	p = .11
Adult recidivism							
Absence	210	49.9	279	56	489	53.2	$X^2 = 3.21$
Presence	211	50.1	219	44	430	46.8	df = 1
Total	421	100	498	100	919	100	p = .07

job at selecting cases for diversion, the effectiveness of the screening mechanism would look much better; but it also means that for the same cases, diversion or referral would give virtually the same results. The best risk would do as well as either measure, and it would be the same for the worst risk. We have also confirmed Rappaport's result[43] that the effect wears away with time, with findings of juvenile recidivism of below 20 percent and adult recidivism of over 40 percent.

The *YOA* renders possible the use of alternative measures of many kinds. The two main categories of these measures are closing the file or adoption of a compensatory measure (restitution, community work, victim conciliation). It is expected that a precise intervention, a compensatory measure, should be more efficient than non-intervention, closing the file, but the literature is not very informative on this subject.[44] In the Quebec natural experiment with formal welfare-based diversion, it was possible to address the question of the relative effectiveness of these two major types of alternative voluntary measures.

Table 2 shows that neither for juvenile recidivism nor for adult recidivism is there an advantage in proposing a compensatory measure; juvenile recidivism varies between 12 percent and 8 percent respectively for closing the file and applying a compensatory measure, while adult recidivism stands at 42 percent and 38 percent. These two groups are equivalent in terms of many personal and criminal characteristics.[45] Schur was right when he proposed non-intervention.[46] Non-intervention is less intrusive for the adolescent and less costly for society (personnel do not have to be hired to maintain these measures), and it is not less efficient in terms of recidivism, as we have seen. Le Blanc and Beaumont have also shown, first, that the quality of recidivism (frequency, nature, violence, variety and so on) does not distinguish the two types of alternative measures and, secondly, that personal and criminal variables do not interact with the independent variable, types of alternative measures, and the dependent variable, adult recidivism.[47]

Implications for the *YOA*

Compared with the situation under the *YPA*, the *YOA* introduced two major changes but left unchanged other features of the Quebec diversion mechanism. The Crown prosecutor became the screening agent, after the police officer had exercised his discretion. And, the new law set precise conditions under which

---

[43] Rappaport, *supra*, note 35.

[44] See Moyer, *supra*, note 31; Palmer and Lewis, *supra*, note 32; Rappaport, *supra*, note 35.

[45] Le Blanc and Beaumont, *supra*, note 36.

[46] Schur, *Radical Non-Intervention. Rethinking the Delinquency Problem* (Englewood Cliffs, N.J.: Prentice Hall, 1973).

[47] Le Blanc and Beaumont, *supra*, note 36.

Table 2

Non-Intervention and Compensatory Measures with Juvenile and Adult Recidivism

	Closing the file		Compensatory measures		Total	
	N	%	N	%	N	%
Juvenile recidivism						
Adult	246	88.5	66	91.67	312	89.14
Presence	32	11.5	6	8.3	38	10.86
Total	278	100	72	100	350	100
Adult recidivism						
Absence	161	57.9	47	62.28	208	59.43
Presence	117	42.1	25	37.72	142	40.57
Total	278	100	72	100	350	100

alternative measures could be used. However, the implementation of the *YOA* did not affect the quantity of diversion at the police level: data cited above show that the level of police diversion did not change significantly since the *YOA* came into force. Also, the YPD is still doing the screening before court appearances, except for serious crimes and in cases of recidivism after a first court conviction. Overall, these changes did not significantly affect the flow of cases in the Quebec juvenile justice system.

Official juvenile delinquency in the middle of the eighties was at about the same level as in the middle of the seventies.[48] The police were still diverting about one-third of the cases; before and after the implementation of the *YOA*, about half of these cases were diverted under the *YPA* by the YPD. Since the *YOA*, the diversion process has been applied by a combination of decisions of the Crown prosecutors and the YPD (the statistics of the Ministry of Justice of Quebec for 1986 and 1987 are at the same level for police diversion and YPD diversion). Whether the YPD or Crown prosecutors are the screening agents, the same level of diversion is attained in Quebec. We can conclude that when the objective is diversion, a welfare-based mechanism will produce the same level of diverted cases as a justice-controlled mechanism, a situation such as we have now and had before the implementation of the *YPA* in Quebec. The new diversion mechanism has the virtue of being legally sound, but it is not more or less efficient in attaining the objective of diverting a large number of delinquents.

The data presented in this chapter apply to the natural experiment with formal welfare diversion in Quebec before the *YOA* was implemented. Data from this experiment show that diverted cases are not less recidivist than court-referred cases. However, an *a posteriori* selection of the good risks show that YPD agents could have made diversion look better than court referral, but then this significantly lower recidivism rate would not be the result of the nature of the intervention, diversion or court referral, but a consequence of the nature of the cases. Younger adolescents still in school, without prior convictions and committing minor offences, will have a low recidivism rate under any type of measure. Because of these conclusions, it cannot be expected that diversion under the *YOA* will show better results than those observed under the *YPA*.

The advocates of diversion from juvenile court would argue that the Quebec diversion mechanism has three advantages: (1) it fosters the development of new measures like restitution, community work and victim conciliation; (2) it avoids official stigma; and (3) it increases the responsibility of the adolescent for his or her delinquent acts. The *YPA* was clearly instrumental in achieving the first objective. However, if the other two objectives were attained by diversion, one would expect that recidivism should be lower for the adolescents who received such compensatory measures, and non-intervention should show a higher rate of recidivism than these compensatory measures are achieving. That is not the case

---

[48] See the data presented by Fréchette and Le Blanc, *Délinquances et Délinquants* (Chicoutimi, Qué.: Gaétan Morin, 1987).

in this data: recidivism was not different between these possibilities, even controlling for the personal and criminal characteristics of the adolescent. Because of this conclusion, we expect that the YOA will further encourage the development of compensatory measures, and that is what seems to be going on. However, the usefulness of these compensatory measures is doubtful, and it cannot be expected that they will lower the recidivism rate of the adolescents who receive them. Why is our society accepting such a social and economic cost when the outcome is not better? Non-intervention offers the minimum of cost with the same level of recidivism. Some would argue that compensatory measures have a value for victims, that they may have a deterrent effect, that their application is necessary for reasons of social symbolism and that they contribute to the education of the adolescent. All these functions of compensatory measures are still to be demonstrated with empirical data.

FUNCTIONING OF JUVENILE COURT

The YPA did not only introduce diversion, but also included some provisions that had a profound impact on the functioning of the juvenile court. Juvenile court procedures became more formal and adversarial. Between 1975 and 1984, a justice model was shaping the functioning of the Quebec juvenile courts before the similar changes that the YOA would introduce. It is well documented that the JDA was not characterized by a high level of due process,[49] while the YOA is recognized as having implemented a greater degree of formality.[50] These tendencies were very different from the trend that we have just described for pre-court processing when the welfare model was implemented. In the courts, a formal processing model highly comparable to those used in adult courts was implemented. In this section, adopting the same outline as in the previous section, the changes introduced by the YPA pertaining to the functioning of the juvenile court are reviewed. The legislative and functional changes, comments on the effectiveness of the measures ordered by the judges and on the implication of the natural experiment for the YOA are presented.

Legislative and Functional Changes

Two types of changes were introduced by the YPA: the emphasis on due process, and the separation of the responsibility for the decision from its execution. Due process was reinforced by the YPA through specific prescriptions of legal pro-

---

[49] See Corrado, Introduction to Corrado, Le Blanc and Trépanier, eds., *Current Issues in Juvenile Justice* (Toronto: Butterworths, 1983); and Bala and Corrado, ''Juvenile Justice in Canada: A Comparative Study'' (Ottawa: Ministry of the Solicitor General, Research Division, 1985).

[50] See Solicitor General of Canada, 1982. *Young Offenders Act, 1982.* Highlights, Ottawa: Ministry of Supply and Services.

cedures, as in the *YOA*; in addition, childrens' rights were explicitly defined. The *YPA*, while leaving decision-making to the judge, gave responsibility for the execution of the measures he or she ordered to the YPD. The judge, for example, could decide to order a placement in an institution after receiving a pre-disposition report, but the YPD had to choose which institution was most appropriate. Unlike under the *JDA*, the judge no longer had authority concerning the execution of the measure ordered. Once again, Quebec was preceding the *YOA*, and in these significant respects the *YPA* went even further than the *YOA*.

Due Process

The introduction of features of a justice model in Quebec extended the constitutional protection of due process rights to juveniles not only in cases involving charges of criminal conduct but also to cases involving issues of dependency, neglect or moral turpitude. The *JDA*'s *parens patriae* model of justice was replaced in Quebec by a justice model with the application of the *YPA* in the seventies. With the 1973 introduction of an extensive legal aid defence into the juvenile court of Montreal, and the implementation of the *YPA* in 1979, Quebec witnessed a progressive strengthening of juvenile court procedures. This tendency reflected a general concern for due process in North American juvenile justice. In fact, there were numerous court decisions in the United States and in Canada that favoured more formal procedures in juvenile courts. Due process rights were introduced by Chapter 2 of the *YPA*, which defined children's rights. Three of these rights had a major impact on due process: the right to consult an advocate, to appeal and to be heard. These prescriptions introduced by the *YPA* were later taken up by the *YOA*.

Because of these rights and because of the universal availability of legal aid for young persons in Quebec, a more adversarial atmosphere characterized the functioning of the juvenile court. Facts and procedure were more frequently contested by defence lawyers, and Crown prosecutors became more active in court. By the beginning of the eighties, procedures in the Montreal juvenile court were much like those in an adult court.[51] There were, for example, six full-time legal aid lawyers in the juvenile court of Montreal. This number had increased to ten by 1981. These lawyers, however, represented only 60 to 70 percent of the adolescents brought to court under the *YPA*, while the others were represented by lawyers in private practice with legal aid certificates. In these more formal proceedings, there were more adjournments, and the time between the reference to court and the decision became much longer; comparable data from Marceau and

---

[51] See descriptions of Marceau and Le Blanc, "Description du Tribunal de la Jeunesse de Montréal", Groupe de Recherche sur l'Inadaptation Juvénile, Université de Montréal, Montréal, 1980; and Le Blanc and Beaumont, "Description du Fonctionnement du Tribunal de la Jeunesse de Montréal Entre mai 1981 et avril 1982", Consultation, Évaluation et Recherche sur l'Inadaptation Juvénile, Montréal, 1985.

Le Blanc, and Le Blanc and Leduc showed that the number of hearings in cases of placement in an institution increased from two to four months, and that the interval between reference to court and decision increased by one month.[52]

The introduction of legal aid and the formalization of the procedures had the following impact. In the Montreal juvenile court, there were no acquittals in 1973–1974, while the percentage of acquittals stood at 0.7 percent in 1979.[53] However, these changes did not increase significantly the number of transfers to adult court that are also rare in Quebec — usually less than ten cases a year. In our study of the Montreal juvenile court in 1981, for example, only two out of 454 adolescents were transfered to an adult court.[54]

The National Study on the Functioning of Juvenile Courts showed that in the Montreal court,[55] minors were accompanied by a lawyer for almost all criminal charges and at the vast majority of their hearings. In most cases, parents were informed of the arrest, detention, charging and appearance of their adolescent before the court. However, not more than half the parents were present at the hearings. A survey carried out during the summer of 1982 among practitioners from the social services and the judiciary indicated that they accepted and supported legal representation for minors at all stages of the proceedings.[56] They did not, however, accept that an adult should take the place of a lawyer if the adolescent did not have one. This opinion was shared by over 90 percent of those surveyed, the only exception being police officers, 65 percent of whom agreed. This study also revealed virtual unanimity on the question of notifying parents at the time of arrest and of the beginning of procedures in court; once again, police officers were alone in seeing less need for such action.

In short, the *YPA* meant that minors' and parents' rights were significantly respected, even before the *YOA* came into effect. Moreover, it was noted in 1981

---

[52] See Marceau and Le Blanc, *ibid.*, and Le Blanc and Leduc, "L'Entrée a Boscoville. Recherche Évaluation de Boscoville", Rapport Technique No. 12, Groupe de Recherche sur l'Inadaptation Juvénile, Université de Montréal, Montréal, 1976.

[53] Le Blanc, "Quebec Youth Protection Act and the Doctrine of Decriminalization, Due Process, Diversion and Deinstitutionalism", paper presented to the 5th Canadian Congress on Applied Criminology, University of Ottawa, Department of Criminology, Ottawa, 1982.

[54] Le Blanc and Beaumont, "Description du Fonctionnement de Tribunaux de la Jeunesse de Montréal Entre mai 1981 et avril 1982", Consultation, Évaluation et Recherche sur l'Inadaptation Juvénile, Montréal, 1985.

[55] *Ibid.*

[56] Le Blanc, "Les Agents de Relations Humaines des CSS, la Loi sur les Jeunes Contrevenants et le Système de Justice pour Mineurs" (1984) 33 (2–3) *Service Social* pp. 323–56.

that social and, if necessary, psychological evaluations were common practice.[57] These reports were being prepared even before the *YOA* gave them explicit legislative recognition; the reports were normally circulated among judges, defence lawyers and Crown prosecutors, although their authors rarely appeared in court.

The data of Marceau and Le Blanc[58] and of Le Blanc and Beaumont[59] also showed that there were three procedures that were not explicitly observeable in the Montreal juvenile court before the *YOA* was implemented: establishment of jurisdiction, reading of the charge and registration of the plea. Our observations showed that the initial hearing seemed informal at first glance, but that the judge would ensure that the adolescent was informed of his rights and that he was represented by a lawyer. Generally, the defence lawyer would renounce the reading of the charge but the judge would ensure that the adolescent understood the content of the accusation. Overall, the three procedures mentioned above were followed in spirit, if not in the letter of the law. The *YOA* would require the judiciary to pay particular attention to these procedures and to render more explicit the process of charging the youth, ensuring that he or she understood the charge and understood the right to counsel provided by the state.

According to a 1981 study,[60] juvenile justice was administered slowly, but was seldom contested. There were generally two months between the first and the last hearing, and each adolescent had to be present in court for two or three hearings, each lasting around 15 minutes. There were changes in pleas: for example, 13 percent changed their plea from not guilty to guilty. Trials were rare, but if there was a trial, proceedings were formal. Seven percent of the adolescents in the sample had a trial. Guilty pleas usually occurred after a few adjournments. Dismissing formal charges and merely warning the juvenile was also rare.[61]

From observations of the functioning of the Montreal juvenile court in 1981, 80 percent of the sample were found to have had a hearing during which pre-trial detention was discussed; 42 percent had been detained during the study, but 44 percent were detained for one day or less and 18 percent were detained for more than one month.[62] A long detention was seldom imposed between the committal of the crime and the decision, even before the *YOA*. The spirit of the *YOA* was already being respected, as detention was only used for serious offences alleged to have been committed by a chronic delinquent without adequate community resources.

---

[57] Le Blanc and Beaumont, *supra*, note 51.

[58] Marceau and Le Blanc, *supra*, note 51.

[59] Le Blanc and Beaumont, *supra*, note 51.

[60] *Ibid.*

[61] Le Blanc, "Les Policies, la Loi sur Les Jeunes Contrevenants et le Système de Justice pour Mineurs" (1984) XVII (1) Criminologie 91–116.

[62] Le Blanc and Beaumont, *supra*, note 54.

It can be concluded from these observations that as early as the beginning of the 1980s Quebec generally conducted legal proceedings in a formal way.[63] All the categories of those in the juvenile justice system indicated support for the increased respect for due process; more than 60 percent of the police officers, social service agents, lawyers, prosecutors and judges were very supportive of the status quo in 1982.[64] In the beginning of the eighties, due process was already implemented in Quebec, and the introduction of *YOA* in 1984 made no significant difference.

Separating Decisions and the Execution of Measures

The second major change introduced by the *YPA* was a modification of the responsibility of the judges. Under the *YPA*, judges could no longer decide exact punitive measures, but only their general nature. As well, it was no longer their responsibility to supervise the execution of the measure ordered. Whenever a case came before the juvenile court for disposition under the *JDA*, the judge took one or more of the several courses of action set out, in rather general terms, in section 20 of the federal act. When acting under the *YPA*, the judge could order the execution of various measures set out in the provincial law and listed in sections 54 and 91, some of which were rather general and others which were more specific. Also, judges had to render their decisions in writing and state the reasons for their decisions. The major change was that the power of the supervision of the execution of the measure ordered was taken away from the judge. Section 92 of the *YPA* stated that "where the Court orders the carrying out of a measure with regard to a child, it shall entrust the case of the child to the director [YPD].[65] The payment of fines, however, was not supervised by the YPD.

As for the carrying out of these measures, Quebec law provided that the Social Affairs Minister would automatically act as provincial secretary for the purposes of s. 21 of the *JDA*. The Minister could thus order that children who were committed under s. 20 to a children's aid society, a superintendent or an industrial school be dealt with under the laws of the province. The *YPA* stipulated that except in the case of a fine, whenever the court ordered execution of a measure concerning a minor, the YPD would see that it was carried out by choosing the most appropriate resource. It was also stated that "every decision or order of the Court is executory as soon as it is rendered" and that "any person contemplated in it must comply therewith without delay" (s. 93).[66] Sanctions were stated in case of non-compliance.

---

[63] For a description of the functioning of small courts in non-metropolitan areas, see Le Blanc and Beaumont, *supra*, note 54.

[64] Le Blanc, *supra*, note 56.

[65] S.Q. 1977, c. 20.

[66] *Ibid*.

The court could revise or modify the measures adopted under the *JDA*, according to section 20(3), (4) of this law. The *YPA* also stated that the YPD, the parents of the child, or the child himself, if 14 years of age or over, could ask the court to revise its decision or order in light of new information. Court decisions and orders could also be appealed under the *JDA* and the *YPA*, and an appeal under the provincial law was not as exceptional as one under the old federal law.

The *YOA* confirmed the separation between decisions and the execution of punitive measures. Youth court judges sitting under the *YOA* can order that an adolescent be placed in custody, the type of which, open or secure, they have to stipulate. However, as had been the case with Quebec's old *YPA*, it is up to the provincial director to determine the facility; even within the categories of open and secure custody, there is substantial variation in the environment and type of control. The *YOA* allows changes in the type of custody, but a youth cannot be transferred to a more secure facility without the court's consent. In comparison, custody under the *YPA* had to be re-examined by the court one year from the date of the court's decision, at which time a progress report on the adolescent's behaviour was required.

As found in a 1982 inquiry, the principle of separating decisions and the execution of measures introduced in the *YPA* and confirmed by the *YOA* was far from universally accepted by officials in the juvenile justice system.[67] Whereas the vast majority of social and legal practitioners agreed to the *YOA* requirement of submitting a pre-sentence report, social practitioners would have preferred a greater role in making this decision, while their legal counterparts would have liked to retain total control of that aspect of the process of decision-making. Virtually all the judges and all the prosecutors agreed that judges should decide whether custody should be open or secure; less than half of social services agents were of the same opinion. However, neither social nor legal practitioners were overwhelmingly in favour of the provincial director deciding on the appropriate place of custody. This is the type of distinction between making the decision and executing the decision that was introduced by the *YPA*.

Effectiveness of Court Decisions in 1981

Functional and legal changes in the Quebec juvenile justice system were described above. These changes created a more formal justice system. To evaluate the impact of these changes, one would need to compare the effectiveness of court decisions under the *JDA*, which was applied until 1979, and under the *YPA*, which was in force between 1979 and 1984. Data which would allow a thorough comparison of these two situations do not exist. However, Le Blanc and Beaumont made a rough comparison of these two periods using the 1981 sample of cases referred to court and a sample of wards of the court recruited in the

---

[67] Le Blanc, *supra*, note 59.

seventies.[68] They concluded that there was not much difference in recidivism in these two samples, either in terms of participation, frequency, nature of offences, variety, duration, onset and seriousness of offence. From these data, one is inclined to conclude that neither informal nor formal juvenile justice make a difference in terms of recidivism.

Before such a tentative conclusion can be accepted, however, a certain number of in-depth studies should be referred to. In Canada, prior to the 1981 studies, there was little research on the functioning of juvenile courts. The two studies in that domain were concerned only with decision-making and the factors that supported the decisions of juvenile court judges.[69] Even with a more comprehensive literature review, no study could be found comparing recidivism rates for the whole spectrum of court decisions. Existing studies compared types of probation with placements in institutions[70] or treatment in the community with treatment in institutions.[71] A recently completed study of the Montreal juvenile court and the follow-up, however, give an opportunity to address the question of the comparative effectiveness of the measures ordered by judges in terms of reducing recidivism.

Le Blanc and Beaumont observed 27 categories of decisions that were ordered by the judges of the Montreal juvenile court under the *JDA* and *YPA* during the study period in 1981.[72] The fine category came first, constituting 24 percent of the decisions, probation second, constituting 20 percent, and placement in a treatment institution third, constituting 13 percent of the adolescents for whom a judge ordered such a decision. These 27 categories of decisions could be classified under

---

[68] From the study reported by Le Blanc and Fréchette, *Male Criminal Activity from Childhood Through Youth: Multilevel and Developmental Perspectives* (New York: Springer-Verlag, 1989).

[69] See Le Blanc, "La Réaction Sociale à la Délinquance Juvénile: Une Analyse Stigmatique" (1971) IV Acta Crim. 113–92; and Kueneman and Linden, "Factors Affecting Dispositions in the Winnipeg Juvenile Court" in Corrado, Le Blanc and Trépanier, eds., *Current Issues in Juvenile Justice* (Toronto: Butterworths, 1983) pp. 219–35.

[70] Wooldredge, "Differentiating the Effects of Juvenile Court Sentences on Eliminating Recidivism" (1988) 25(3) *Journal of Research in Crime and Delinquency* pp. 264–300.

[71] See Sechrest, White and Brown, *The Rehabilitation of Criminal Offenders* (Washington, D.C.: National Academy of Sciences, 1979); and Murray and Cox, *Beyond Probation: Juvenile Corrections and the Chronic Delinquent* (Beverly Hills, Calif.: Sage Publications, 1979).

[72] Le Blanc and Beaumont, "L'Efficacité des Mesures pour Jeunes Délinquants Adoptées à Montréal en 1981, une Étude Longitudinale" Groupe de Recherche sur l'Inadaptation Psycho-Sociale à l'Enface, Université de Montréal, Montréal, 1989.

four main types: *no intervention* for 25 percent of the cases (in order of importance: suspended sentence, adjournment *sine die*); *fines* for 29 percent (this type includes fines, for 82 percent, but also other compensatory measures, such as restitution and community work, and other combinations of these measures); *probation* for 24 percent (82 percent of these decisions involved only probation, while 18 percent combined probation with one of the preceding measures); and, finally, 22 percent of the adolescents were *placed in an institution* of some kind for various periods of time (detention, treatment and other). Of these youths, 44 percent were the subject of only one measure; others received an average of 2.55 orders between the ages of 14 and 18.

Table 3 reports adult recidivism for each of these four types of measures in regard to the last decision taken for each juvenile boy. In this sample, 53 percent of the male adolescents recidivated after 18 years of age. Recidivism increased with the severity of the sentence in the following order: fine, 42 percent; probation, 50 percent; and placement in care, 69 percent. But the decision not to intervene had a level of recidivism just over the overall average, 55 percent, which is rather surprising. The observed level of adult recidivism for each type of order is quite consistent with what we would normally expect, except for non-intervention. The youths subject to this type of order should recidivate less because they should have committed less serious offences and should be better adapted. This result can be interpreted as some sort of decision error by the judges.

In sum, the formalization of juvenile court procedures does not seem to have had a significant impact. Overall, the new juvenile justice system does not seem to have been any more effective than the old one despite two important considerations: (1) data revealed that the well-known concordance between severity of sentence and level of recidivism still holds true; and (2) the movement in Quebec has been toward non-intervention and lighter sentences for juveniles.

What, then, is the significance of the provisions in the *YOA* relating to due process and the separation of judicial decisions from their execution — provisions for which the *YPA* paved the way? It is the well-known concordance between the severity of the sentence and the level of recidivism. And what is the significance of the Quebec natural experiment in implementing due process and separating the decision and its execution on the *YOA* adopted in 1982?

Implications for the *YOA*

We have seen that Quebec had in a real sense implemented most of the *YOA* provisions concerning due process and decisions prior to the *YOA* coming into force. Since 1984, other provinces have complied with the requirements of the *YOA*. Can they expect a more effective juvenile justice system? No, but the Quebec experiment has taught an important lesson. These provisions, rather surprisingly, failed to improve the juvenile justice system. They did not lower the recidivism rates because they were not implemented with more care. From past studies of decision-making in juvenile courts, we know that variables such as prior

Table 3

Adult Recidivism and Court Ordered Measures

Recidivism	Non-intervention	Fine	Probation	Placement in care	Total
Absence	41	62	44	25	172
	45.1%	57.9%	50%	30.9%	46.9%
Presence	50	45	44	56	195
	54.9%	42.1%	50%	69.1%	53.1%
Total	91	107	82	81	367
	24.8%	29.2%	24%	22.1%	100%

convictions are associated with more severe decisions and with a higher recidivism rate. Studies in the United States[73] and in Canada[74] have shown that specific personal and criminal characteristics of adolescents and specific events of the juvenile justice process have a significant impact on the nature of the decision and on the probability of recidivism. Not only do the characteristics of the youth matter a great deal; some traits of the decision-maker are also significant.[75]

How to improve decision-making in the juvenile courts may be a more appropriate question than the question of how to ensure more effective punitive measures. Perhaps the state should improve the quality of these measures. It should also be concerned, however, with the quality of the decisions. In a recent study of judges' decisions,[76] it has been shown that the gaps between the recidivism rate of each type of decision could be widened if male adolescents with certain characteristics were excluded from certain of these measures. Using certain characteristics systematically such as age, prior delinquency and so on, judges could lower the recidivism rate for types of decisions such as non-intervention, fines and probation. A sentencing guide would be a helpful instrument to achieve the maximum effectiveness of each decision, a strategy supported by the Canadian Sentencing Commission.[77] Why can we not expect the judiciary to seriously consider such an alternative to the existing situation and to systematically experiment with it?

[73] See Bortner, "Process and Discretion in Juvenile Court: An Analysis of Legal Factors and Socioeconomic Variables" (Ann Arbor, Mich.: University Microfilms International, 1978); Cohen, "Conferring the Delinquent Label: The Relative Importance of Social Characteristics and Legal Factors in the Processing of Juvenile Offenders" (Ann Arbor, Mich.: University Microfilms International, 1974). Gottfredson, and Gottfredson, *Decision Making in Criminal Justice: Toward a Rational Exercise of Discretion* (Cambridge: Ballinger, 1980); Terry, "Discrimination in the Handling of Juvenile Offenders by Social Control Agencies" (1967) 4(2) *Journal of Research in Crime and Delinquency* pp. 218–30; Thornberry, "Race, Socioeconomic Status and Sentencing in the Juvenile Court" (1973) 64(1) *Journal of Criminal Law and Criminology* pp. 90–8; Wooldredge, *supra*, note 70.

[74] See Beaumont, "Les Critères de Décision des Juges du Tribinal de la Jeunesse de Montréal", mémoire de maitrise inédit, Université de Montréal, Montréal, 1984; Kuneman and Linden, "Factors Affecting Dispositions in the Winnipeg Juvenile Court" in Corrado, Le Blanc and Trépanier, eds., *Current Issues in Juvenile Justice* (Toronto: Butterworths, 1983) pp. 219–35; Le Blanc, *supra*, note 71; Trépanier, "Événements Judiciaires et Récidive chez les Adolescents Délinquants", Mémoire de maitrise inédit, Université de Montréal, Montréal, 1969.

[75] Gottfredson and Gottfredson, *supra*, note 73.
[76] Le Blanc and Beaumont, *supra*, note 72.
[77] Canadian Sentencing Commission, *Sentencing Reform: A Canadian Approach* (Ottawa: Supply and Service Canada, 1987).

CONCLUSION: THE PROFESSIONALIZATION OF JUVENILE JUSTICE

It is clear that Quebec had, in effect, implemented many *YOA* provisions before its adoption — particularly in establishing formal diversion, implementing due process and limiting the responsibilities of judges in the execution of their decisions — and that these important changes did not substantially modify the effectiveness of the juvenile justice system. In light of this, some possible explanations for these changes and the argument that they reflect a professionalization of the juvenile justice system will be discussed.

To explain changes in the justice system, four factors are usually stressed in the literature: public opinion,[78] moral entrepreneurship;[79] judicial decisions;[80] and organizational conflicts.[81] We will argue that professionalization explains why Quebec preceded Canada in its legislative juvenile justice changes. This professionalization, however, was incomplete. It did not address the question of the systematization of the decisions in the juvenile justice system through decision guidelines.

Public opinion cannot be considered the main, or even an important, factor in support of the legislative changes in Quebec in 1977. A study of press clippings shows that there was little public involvement in the discussion of legislative changes, yet after the *YPA* was adopted the reaction of the public was generally negative.[82] Moreover, three years after the *YPA* was in force — in 1982 — public opinion was one of the main reasons why the government set in place a commission of inquiry for the revision of that legislation — the 1982 Charbonneau Commission.

Nor did any moral entrepreneur of significance show up during the discussion of the forthcoming *YPA*. However, one cabinet minister must be mentioned, a

---

[78] See Pound, ''The Limits of Effective Legal Action'', 22nd Annual Report of the Pennsylvania Bar Association, Philadelphia, Penn., 1916, p. 221; and Dicey, *Law and Public Opinion in England* (London: MacMillan and Co., 1952.

[79] Platt, *The Child Savers: The Invention of Delinquency* (Chicago: University of Chicago Press, 1969).

[80] Rubin, ''Retain the Juvenile Court? Legislative Developments, Reform Directives, and the Call for Abolition'' (1979) 25(3) *Crime and Delinquency* 281–98.

[81] Hagan and Leon, ''Rediscovering Delinquency: Social History, Political Ideology and the Sociology of Law'' (1977) 42 *American Sociological Review* pp. 587–98.

[82] Ducasse, ''Synthèse des Remarques et des Amendements Présentés Lors de l'Étude Article par Article des Projets de Loi 24 et 10'' (Québec: Assemblée Nationale du Québec, Commission Parlementaire Spéciale sur la Protection de la Jeunesse, 1982).

psychiatrist responsible for the deinstitutionalization of the largest psychiatric hospital in Quebec. This psychiatrist sponsored Bill 24 and was supported by several ministers and deputies of the Parti Québécois, as well as by members of the opposition, all of whom had worked for welfare or medical services departments. An analysis of comments during the discussion of Bill 24 and of the papers submitted to the National Assembly revealed that they came almost exclusively from professional groups.[83]

During the discussion of the *YPA* Bill and before this period, there were no Appeal Court or Supreme Court decisions in Canada that could have significantly influenced the bill's content. Had there been, other provinces or the Government of Canada would have had to modify their laws concerning children. Quebec passed its legislation without this kind of encouragement.

Organizational conflicts were not a major source of change; they were the consequence of the adoption of the *YPA*. Traditionally in Quebec, the Department of Justice had jurisdiction over the police and the courts and the Department of Social Affairs had the task of furnishing the required service. This division of labour worked satisfactorily for many years. As we have seen earlier, the *YPA* changed this distribution of labour in two ways: by introducing diversion measures which stood between police and the court, and by separating decisions and their execution. The world of justice (police officers, lawyers, prosecutors and judges) was obviously unwilling to accept these changes and contested their validity before the courts — and in many other ways. Consequently, a Quebec parliamentary commission — the 1982 Charbonneau Commission — was set in place to find a compromise that solved this conflict; this compromise was implemented after the adoption of the *YOA*.

If public opinion, moral entrepreneurship, judicial decisions and organizational conflicts were not the main factors that led to the legislative changes in 1977 in Quebec, then the most important factor was the professionalization of juvenile justice and of the social services system. Quebec reform was not in any sense an expression of social or economic instrumentalities. Rather, it was institutional and political in nature. It was a negotiated order just as the control of delinquency was in the United States between 1640 and 1981.[84]

It must be remembered that in Quebec during the sixties and the seventies there was a massive increase in the number of university-trained people who created new services and took over others traditionally administered by religious services agencies. For example, in 1972 in the Montreal juvenile court there were rarely any defence lawyers, but a decade later there were ten legal aid lawyers, and many others from the private practice. In 1973, only 21 percent of probation officers

[83] Charbonneau, *Rapport de la Commission Parlementaire sur la Protection de la Jeunesse* (Québec: Assemblée Nationale du Québec, 1982).
[84] Sutton, *Stubborn Children: Controlling Delinquency in the United States, 1640–1981* (Berkeley: University of California Press, 1988).

were university trained; this proportion rose to 87 percent by 1982.[85] The situation was similar for child care workers and other professionals who had to deal directly or indirectly with the juvenile justice system. Not only did the qualifications of personnel increase, the number of services also rose. For example, the readaptation centres had, in 1975, only a few treatment programs based in the community (group home, day care centre and so on), but in 1985 there were more than 100 of these programs throughout Quebec.[86]

As a consequence of this explosion, the discussion about how the juvenile justice system was to be structured by a new law became a matter of debate between experts. It was a professional debate, if we refer to analyses of the written statements to parliamentary commissions.[87] A new doctrine was discussed — minimal intervention — implying five objectives: decriminalization, diversion, respect for rights, involvement of the community and deinstitutionalization. Even at the political level, scientific theories and facts were cited, and treatment evaluations and experimental treatments were referred to. The nature of this professional discussion is illustrated by the 1982 Charbonneau Report.

Comprehensive discussion on juvenile justice system reconstruction took place in interministerial meetings, colloquiums and other forums. This centred on principles and structures debate and was encouraged by an intensive implementation program, particularly through information dissemination and training. (This implementation program is described in Le Blanc and Beaumont).[88] But this program never reached the day-to-day decision-making level; that is, the criteria for a systematic decision process by a police officer, a Crown prosecutor, a social service agent, a judge and a child care worker. In that sense, the professional debate was incomplete; it did not systematize decision-making. Except for the

---

[85] Le Blanc, ''L'Opinion des Juges, Avocats de la Défense et Procureurs de la Courrone sur le Système de Justice pour Mineurs et la Loi sur les Jeunes Contrevenants'' (1984) 14(2) Revue de Droit 591–624.

[86] Le Blanc and Beaumont, *La Réadaptation dans la Communauté au Québec: Inventaire des Programmes*, Recherche 40 (Québec: Les Publications du Québec, Commission d'Enquête sur les Services de Santé et les Services Sociaux, 1987).

[87] For example, Ducasse, ''Synthèse des Remarques et des Amendements Présentés lors de l'Étude Article par Article des Projets de Loi 24 et 10'' (Québec: Assemblé Nationale du Québec, Commission Parlementaire Spéciale sur la Protection de la Jeunesse, 1982); and Chalin and Suppa, ''Document Synthèse des Mémoires des Personnes et Organisimes (Volet Délinquance)'' (Québec: Assemblée Nationale du Québec, Annexe III au Rapport de la Commission Parlementaire Spéciale sur la Protection de la Jeunesse, 1982).

[88] Le Blanc and Beaumont, ''The Quebec Perspective on the Young Offender Act, Implementation Before Adoption'' in Hudson, Hornick and Burrows, eds., *Justice and the Young Offender in Canada* (Toronto: Wall and Thompson, 1988).

social services agents involved in diversion and the list of offences not to be diverted by Crown prosecutors, no decision guideline was prepared for the police officer or for the judges. The decision guideline for social services agents was not compulsory; it was only a recommendation for Crown prosecutors.

It is important to reform legislation and administrative structures, to develop new programs and to educate personnel involved with youth, as Quebec did in its juvenile justice system. But, it is also necessary to conceive, to experiment with and to improve decision guides. Without this reformation, decisions may be not only discretionary, they may clearly be inadequate. The task that awaits is to find which punitive measure is the most appropriate for which type of adolescent, what Fréchette and Le Blanc have called the differential approach. To improve the qualitative matching of types of measures with types of adolescents, more research on decision-making and on the effectiveness of each punitive measure is necessary. Because of the specific features of the Canadian juvenile justice system, reliance cannot be placed on American research. The Government of Canada and the governments of each of the provinces will have to invest in this type of research to improve the quality of the service the juvenile justice system offers.

CHAPTER 7

ADVOCATE OR GUARDIAN: THE ROLE OF DEFENCE COUNSEL IN YOUTH JUSTICE[1]

Heather A. Milne
Rick Linden
Rod Kueneman

INTRODUCTION

At the time of its implementation, the *Young Offenders Act*[2] was described by one of its drafters as being "among the most significant social legislation enacted by the Parliament of Canada during the last few years".[3] This legislation was the result of more than 20 years of political and legal debate over the inadequacies of the *Juvenile Delinquents Act*[4] and represented Parliament's response to criticism that had been directed toward the juvenile justice system.

The incorporation of the philosophical and procedural changes required by the Act has provoked a diverse response from the legal and social science communities. Much of this response has focused on the shift of philosophical orientation underlying the principles of the legislation. The Act's Declaration of Principles[5] represents an explicit attempt to depart from the traditional *parens patriae* philosophy and to incorporate a due process model of juvenile justice. Theoretically, at least, the nature of the relationship between the state and the child is

---

[1] This research was supported by the contributions program of the Ministry of the Solicitor General. The views expressed in this paper are not necessarily those of the Ministry.
[2] R.S.C. 1985, c. Y-1.
[3] Archambault, "Young Offenders Act: Philosophy and Principles" (1983) 7(2) Prov. Judges J. p. 3.
[4] R.S.C. 1970, c. J-3.
[5] *Supra*, note 2, s. 3.

changed. The principles are not a preamble to the legislation, but are critical to the subsequent interpretation of the entire Act.[6] The implications of this shift are significant.

Section 11 of the *Young Offenders Act*,[7] establishing the right to counsel, is a good example of the move toward a due process model and away from the exercise of other procedural rights. Prior to 1967, legal representation of children in delinquency proceedings was rare. In a proceeding where the interests of the state and the accused were assumed to be identical, counsel was not seen as necessary.[8] The proceedings were informal and intended to be rehabilitative and non-punitive; there seemed to be little place for lawyers acting in a traditional adversarial role. The structure and content of the proceedings were more compatible with the objectives of social workers and probation officers. Dispositions relied more upon their assessment of the juvenile's behaviour and recommendations than upon strictly legal considerations.[9]

The *Young Offenders Act* does not assume that the child's interests are identical to those of the state. Therefore, legal representation is necessary to ensure that the interests of the child are represented. By establishing the right to retain and to instruct counsel, the state has acknowledged the necessity for independent representation of the child's interests in court. Under the *YOA*, the presence of defence counsel has the potential to become a more prominent and influential factor in determining the direction and outcome of juvenile proceedings.[10] Under these circumstances, understanding the nature and role of defence counsel becomes important.

While it has been argued by legal practitioners that the legislation defines the role of counsel as that of an advocate representing the interests of the youth, as defined by the youth, the debate as to whether this is the appropriate role

---

[6] Bala and Lilles, *Young Offenders Act, Annotated* (Ottawa: Solicitor General of Canada and the Canadian Government Publishing Centre in cooperation with Richard De Boo Publishers, 1984).

[7] *Supra*, note 2.

[8] Dickens, "Representing the Child in Courts" in Baxter and Eberts, eds., *The Child and the Courts* (Toronto: Carswell, 1978).

[9] Costello, "Ethical Issues in Representing Juvenile Clients: A Review of the IJA–ABA Standards on Representing Private Parties" (1980) 10 (Summer) N.M.L.Rev. 255–78.

[10] Little research has been done on the actual impact of lawyers on case outcome. In a recent study, Carrington and Moyer (forthcoming) cite several U.S. studies which show that lawyers have little impact on *PLGA* or adjudication. Their own research using data collected prior to the implementation of the *YOA* found that the overall effect of legal representation on overall conviction rates in five Canadian cities was small. Those differences which do exist are due to the greater use of not guilty pleas in cases where the juvenile was represented by counsel.

continues. The controversy is due, in part, to ambiguity with regard to the principles of the legislation. If the young person is to be held responsible and accountable for his or her actions, he/she is also entitled to all the procedural safeguards afforded to adults. Contradictions emerge because the Declaration of Principles, s. 3 of the *YOA*, emphasize supervision, discipline and control while simultaneously recognizing the special needs of young persons requiring guidance and assistance.[11] The result of this contradiction has been observed in Manitoba, where in two decisions the right of a young person to retain and to instruct independent counsel was questioned by judges still operating under a treatment model of juvenile justice.[12]

Also contributing to the problem of role definition were significant provincial disparities in administering juvenile justice which evolved under the *Juvenile Delinquents Act*. While enacted as federal legislation, the administration of juvenile justice, correctional and other social services provided in the *JDA* were the responsibility of each provincial government.[13] The nature of the juvenile justice process has been largely determined by the interaction of federal and provincial legislation and its implementation by local agencies and institutions which often differ from one another in orientation and practice.[14]

For many years, attempts at the federal level to revise or to replace the outdated and inadequate aspects of the *JDA* were not successful. Subsequently, the provinces, operating autonomously, introduced legislative and procedural changes that created considerable disparity in the structure and administration of juvenile justice. The result "was a juvenile justice system which, despite the uniformity provided by the *Juvenile Delinquents Act*, evolved markedly over the years into a highly complex system characterized by very significant geographical variation".[15] One type of variation was in the role of defence counsel.

RESEARCH ON THE ROLE OF LAWYERS IN JUVENILE COURT

During the last 15 years, there has been a notable increase in the number of lawyers acting on behalf of juveniles. However, only a limited body of empirical

---

[11] Bala and Lilles, *supra*, note 6.

[12] *R. v. H. (R.J.N.)* (1985), 36 Man. R. (2d) 202, 22 C.C.C. (3d) 114 (*sub nom.* *R. v. H.*), 19 C.R.R. 68 (C.A.). As discussed below, the effect of these two decisions was reversed by Parliamentary action in 1986.

[13] See Bala and Corrado, *Juvenile Justice in Canada: A Comparative Study* (Ottawa: Solicitor General of Canada, 1985). Corrado, Kueneman, LeBlanc *et al*, "Treatment of Justice: An Analysis of Attitudes Toward Juvenile Justice in Canada", paper presented to the International Seminar on Juvenile Delinquency, Vaucresson, France, May 1985.

[14] Bala and Corrado, *supra*, note 12.

[15] *Ibid.*, at p. 1.

research specifically addresses the issue of the role of the defence lawyer in juvenile proceedings.[16] Contributions to this topic have largely been made by members of the legal profession, and typically take the form of legal opinion rather than empirical research.

Defence Counsel Role Types

Opinion varies about whether or not a single role is appropriate for the lawyer acting in juvenile proceedings. Some lawyers suggest that a combination of roles is required in order to provide effective representation. The type of role adopted will depend on the type and stage of the proceeding, as well as on the capacity of the child.[17]

Although the terminology used to describe counsel's role may vary according to the type and context of the dispute, there are essentially two representational stances that counsel may assume when defending a juvenile client in delinquency proceedings. These are the roles of the advocate and the guardian. Each role describes the lawyer's task "in terms of increasing or decreasing emphasis on the elements of traditional advocacy, and in terms of various degrees of movement toward the 'treatment' or 'conciliatory' functions of the youth court."[18]

The advocate has the primary objective of winning an acquittal or a reduction of charges or, if there is a conviction, of reducing the severity of the sentence . Of major concern are the "protection of the client, observance of proper procedures, arguing technical questions of law, testing of evidence, representation of the *child's* wishes and rigorous promotion of the child's strict legal rights."[19]

The advocate would review the case and give the client recommendations. Any disagreement between the lawyer's recommendations and the client's preference would result in a cooperative effort to re-evaluate those preferences.[20] This common position would be argued before the court to the extent that the evidence permits. However, if a conflict between the lawyer and the client is evident, "it would be the lawyer's duty to represent the *child's* position with zeal."[21]

---

[16] Catton, "Children in the Courts: A Selected Empirical Review" (1978) 1 J. Fam. L.; Thomson, "Commentary on the Young Offenders Act" (1983) 7 Prov. Judges J. 27–34.

[17] Treadwell, "The Lawyer in Juvenile Court Dispositional Proceedings: Advocate, Social Worker, or Otherwise" (1965–67) 16–17(3) Juv. Ct. Judges J. 109–15; Leon, *Legal Representation of Children in Selected Court Proceedings: The Capacity of Children to Retain Legal Counsel* (Toronto: University of Toronto, Centre for Urban and Community Studies and the Child in the City Programme, 1978); McHale, "The Proper Role of the Lawyer as Legal Representative of the Child" (1980) 18(2) Alta. L. Rev. 216–36.

[18] *Ibid.*, McHale, at p. 219.

[19] *Ibid.*

[20] Leon, *supra*, note 17.

[21] *Ibid.*, at p. 42.

The guardian possesses more of a "helping" or "social work" character.[22] Theoretically, this role resembles the functions performed by the guardian *ad litem* in a civil proceeding, where the child is represented either by the parents or by another relative, or by a friend or a person appointed by the court.

Historically, the common law allowed for representation because it was assumed that children, as a result of their incapacity to make contracts and instruct counsel, were under a legal disability, similar to an adult who is determined insane. At common law, children could generally only engage in legal action through a competent adult who made decisions on their behalf.[23]

Adopting similar principles in the context of delinquency proceedings, the lawyer as guardian acts as a "surrogate parent" who independently identifies and then advocates to the court a judgment made in the child's best interests.[24] The objective of the guardian lawyer is not necessarily to achieve the result which the child desires, but one that reflects the lawyer's view of the best interests of the child.[25] In determining the client's best interests, the lawyer operates on the basis of the treatment philosophy or child welfare model and recommends what the child "needs" in order to be successfully "rehabilitated".

Under these circumstances, the lawyer would determine whether to take into account the juvenile's expressed desires, and if so, how much emphasis to place on them. The factor distinguishing the guardian role from others is that it is "the *lawyer's view* as informed by expert opinion or otherwise, that is the position placed before the court".[26] It is the lawyer's function to accurately "present the true needs of the child, and thereby, establish the 'best interest' tests as a suitable formulation for insuring a child's welfare",[27] although in appropriate cases this might involve entering a not guilty plea and having a trial.

The lawyer may pursue a strategy or advocate to the court a disposition to which the juvenile objects.[28] Where there appears to be a conflict between the lawyer and the client regarding the determination of best interests, the lawyer's viewpoint would be considered over that of the juvenile's by the court.

The rationale underlying the guardian role for defence counsel is that juveniles are perceived to have a lack of or limited capacity to identify and to effectively

---

[22] Leon, *supra*, note 17; Dickens, Representing the Child in the Courts" in Baxter and Eberts, eds., *The Child and the Courts* (Toronto: Carswell, 1978); McHale, *supra*, note 20.

[23] Maczko, "Some Problems with Acting for Children" (1979) 2 Can. J. Fam. L. p. 267.

[24] Costello, "Ethical Issues in Representing Juvenile Clients: A Review of the IJA–ABA Standards Representing Private Parties" (1980) 10 N.M.L.Rev. 255–78.

[25] Leon, *supra*, note 17; McHale, *supra*, note 17.

[26] Leon, *supra*, note 17, at p. 43.

[27] *Ibid.*

[28] Costello, *supra*, note 24.

communicate their own best interests. For this reason, the guardian role was recommended for lawyers defending cases where the client is very young and does not have an appointed guardian, or where there is a perceived conflict of interest between the parent and the child which prevents the lawyer from seeking instructions from the parent.[29]

There is no consensus in the legal literature as to which of these role types is most appropriate. Criticism has been directed toward the guardian role because it does not adhere to the goals and objectives delineated by law. While it is more "psychologically attractive" to have lawyers present in the court in order to interpret and to aid in the rehabilitative process, some argue this was not what the law intended.[30]

It has been suggested that the guardian role is based on the assumption that the juvenile client is in need of social services in order to be deterred from future involvement or, ideally, rehabilitated, regardless of whether the charges are technically proven.[31] Protection of the child may also be a consideration. For example, a lawyer acting in the guardian role may not try to have a child released on bail if it is likely that child will immediately return to life on the streets as a prostitute. The advocate, on the other hand, would follow the child's wishes in a bail hearing.

The guardian role requires the lawyer to perform functions that are essentially judicial in nature. If the lawyer assumes that the juvenile will ultimately benefit by receiving care or treatment rather than by being acquitted, the decision-making function is transferred from the judge to defence counsel. Critics say that adherence to this role creates a situation in which the lawyer usurps the judge's role and creates an informal atmosphere where legal safeguards are not considered necessary for the protection of the rights of the client.

Proponents of the advocate role base their argument on the premise that the legal system has conferred a variety of rights and powers upon children under the age of majority and, as a reflection of moral autonomy, entitles them to make certain decisions regarding their own lives.[32] As such, youths are entitled to direct the course of their attorney's actions.

This view was supported by the Sub-Committee of the Law Society of Upper Canada on Representation of Children. Its 1981 report on the representation of children explicitly supported the traditional advocate role of counsel in youth court. Further, the Committee suggested that it was not appropriate in a quasi-criminal proceeding for counsel to argue for what he/she considers to be in the

---

[29] *Ibid.*

[30] *Ibid.*

[31] Ferster, Courtless and Snethan, "The Juvenile Justice System: In Search of the Role of Counsel" (1971) 39 Fordham L. Rev. 375; Costello, *supra*, note 24.

[32] Guggenheim, "The Right to be Represented but Not Heard: Reflections on Legal Representation for Children" (1984) 50(1) N.Y.U. L. Rev. 76–155.

child's best interests, unless this accords with the child's instructions.[33]

Those who are opposed to the incorporation of a strict advocate role suggest that the apparent failure of the treatment philosophy of the court and the informality of procedure does not warrant the use of legal technicalities to get their clients "off", if help or treatment is needed. In its most extreme form, this argument perceives delinquency as an illness requiring treatment in order that the person may return to a state of normalcy. As such, there is little difference between a child who is physically ill as opposed to behaviourally or emotionally "sick". Therefore, the child should not be encouraged to deceive the doctor or the judge.[34]

It is argued by some proponents of the guardian role that counsel should not be guided by the child's instructions or counsel's opinion as to the child's best interests, but by the wishes of the parent.[35] To support their position, proponents of this role point to the decision of the United States Supreme Court,[36] which acknowledged that a child should not be deprived of the right to counsel due to financial limitation of their family resources. While *Gault* is often viewed as an affirmation of the rights of juveniles to legal counsel, it may be interpreted as an affirmation of the right of a family to be free from undue state interference, and of the rights of parents to make decisions regarding their children's needs without inappropriate state interference.

The Manitoba Court of Appeal rejected the traditional advocate role and maintained that "the appropriate practice is for the lawyer to receive instructions from the guardian, next friend or guardian *ad litem* rather than from the youthful offender."[37] In *R. v. W. (W.W.)*,[38] it was held that despite the explicit right to retain and instruct counsel, in s. 11(1) of the *Young Offenders Act*, it "was not intended to replace the traditional mechanisms for the lawyer to receive his instructions . . ." and that a 12-year-old child cannot be expected to ". . . shoulder the adult responsibilities" involved in decisions regarding his defence. It should be noted that in 1986 Parliament amended the *YOA*, section 11(1),[39] in

---

[33] Bala and Lilles, *Young Offenders Act, Annotated* (Ottawa: Solicitor General of Canada and the Canadian Government Publishing Centre in cooperation with Richard De Boo Publishers, 1984).

[34] Bala, Lilles and Thomson, *Canadian Children's Law: Cases, Notes and Materials* (Toronto: Butterworths, 1982).

[35] Goldstein, Freud and Solnit, *Before the Best Interests of the Child* (New York: Free Press, 1979).

[36] *Re Gault*, 387 U.S. 1, 18 L. 2d 527, 87 S. Ct. 1428 (1967).

[37] *R. v. W. (W.W.)*, [1984] 6 W.W.R. 477, 29 Man. R. (2d) 77 (C.A.) *per* Matas and O'Sullivan JJ.A.; *R. v. H. (R.J.N.)* (1985), 36 Man. R. (2d) 202, 22 C.C.C. 114 (*sub nom. R. v. H.*), 19 C.R.R. 68 (C.A.).

[38] *Ibid.*

[39] [rep. and sub. R.S.C. 1985, c. 24 (2nd Supp.), s. 9].

order to provide youths with the right "to exercise that right personally", clearly reversing the Manitoba Court of Appeal's decisions.

The Effects of Organizational Variables on Role Types

Research focusing on the extra-legal factors affecting role definition indicate that the philosophy and structure of the court as well as the expectations of other court personnel are significant determinants of the role adopted by counsel.[40] The findings suggest that methods of representation vary considerably depending on the organization of the particular court. Consequently, determining the perspective of an organization may allow predictions to be made regarding the existence of particular role "types".[41]

Research has examined the effect of court orientation on the structural organization and the roles of key participants in the juvenile court. Stapleton and Teitelbaum studied the differences in style of representation, procedure and case outcome in two juvenile courts in the United States. Working with the assumption that the structural features of the organization influence the form and manner of the actor's behaviour, they hypothesized that the role of defence counsel is largely determined by the environment in which the lawyer operates. In a structural comparison, Stapleton and Teitelbaum reported that the two courts differed significantly in orientation and procedure to the extent that they could be considered "distinct systems".[42]

The orientation of the two courts was reflected in their organizational structure. The court which was defined as "traditional" in orientation did not have a prosecutor present during the proceedings, combined the three stages of arraignment, adjudication and disposition into a single hearing and did not keep a transcript of the proceedings. In the court that reflected a "legalistic" model, the state's attorney appeared at all stages of the proceedings, which were separated into three stages, and transcripts were taken at each hearing.

The researchers found that the court procedure and the role of the lawyers were affected by the type of model operating in each court. To analyse the prevalence of particular role types, the number of contested cases and the use of guilty pleas served as indicators of "adversariness". The findings indicated that the court defined as "traditional" in orientation had fewer contested cases and that the incidence of adversarial defences was reduced.

The court defined as "legalistic" in orientation had a significantly larger number and type of motions, which indicated a greater willingness of defence

---

[40] Catton, "Children in the Courts: A Selected Empirical Review" (1978) 1 J. Fam. L.; Stapleton and Teitelbaum, *In Defense of Youth: A Study of the Role of Counsel in American Juvenile Courts* (New York: Russell Sage Foundation, 1972).

[41] Thomson, "Commentary on the Young Offenders Act" (1983) 7 Prov. Judges J. 27–34.

[42] Stapleton and Teitelbaum, *supra*, note 40.

counsel to use legal remedies in the conduct of their cases. They found that this court granted more favourable (less severe) dispositions because of counsel's request for dismissal, as opposed to the "traditional" court model, where leniency was initiated by the court rather than by defence counsel. The researchers concluded that it was the organization of the "legalistic" court which allowed lawyers to ". . . apply different criteria in deciding how to handle cases — criteria both universalistic and more suited to the maintenance of an adversarial posture."[43]

In another study comparing two British juvenile courts, Anderson reported that the two courts differed in their approach to the court process as well as in their attitudes toward the interpretation of the governing legislation.[44] These differences were exhibited in the sentencing policy of the two courts. While cases coming before the courts were similar in terms of the age of the juvenile and the distribution and incidence of offence types, one court used a wider, more severe range of dispositions than the other.

Explaining the effect of court orientation or context on the role of defence counsel, Anderson found that where the court emphasized "culpability" and closely adhered to a legal model, the lawyer was accorded a relatively high status, and the lawyer's contribution was considered more relevant than that of the social worker. However, the lawyer's role was not deemed as effective or as necessary in a court which emphasized the social or psychological needs of the offender and placed less emphasis on the offence.

Related to the definition and analysis of the role of defence counsel, research has also focused on the factors contributing to role conflict. One source of conflict has been attributed to the pressures created by different participants in the proceedings expecting lawyers to perform opposing roles in court.[45] Trained as advocates, lawyers experienced conflict due to the informality of the juvenile court and the necessity of modifying their role to that of a social worker.[46] Erickson reported that role conflict was evident as a result of contradictory "intra-role" expectations expressed by judges and social workers.[47] Expectations also varied according to whether the lawyer was retained privately or worked as a government-paid duty counsel. According to the judges and social workers in the study, privately retained lawyers were expected to be more legalistic than duty counsel.

---

[43] *Ibid.*, at p. 149.

[44] Anderson, *Representation in the Juvenile Court* (London: Routledge and Kegan Paul, 1978).

[45] Dootjes, Erickson and Fox, "Defence Council in Juvenile Court: A Variety of Roles" (1972) 14 Can. J. Crim. & Corr. 132; Catton, *supra*, note 16.

[46] Dootjes, Erickson and Fox, *supra*, note 45.

[47] Erickson, "The Defence Lawyer's Role in Juvenile Court: An Empirical Investigation into Judges' and Social Workers' Points of View" (1974) 24 U.T.L.J. 126.

THE RESEARCH PROBLEM

The role the lawyer is expected to play in the juvenile justice system remains a controversial issue. This problem reflects a broader ambiguity with respect to the relationship between the child and the state. Under the *Juvenile Delinquents Act*, at least in theory, the interests of the child and the state were regarded as identical. A cooperative relationship existed where the protection of the child's interests through legal representation was not necessary. With the incorporation of the legalistic philosophy in the *Young Offenders Act*, there may be significant changes required regarding the role of defence counsel.

The opposing perspectives and philosophies regarding the nature of the relationship between the child and the state, as well as that of the lawyer and client, are encompassed within the advocate and guardian role types.

Research that has addressed the issue of role, using a variety of methods including court observation and records,[48] survey questionnaires and interviews,[49] has applied the advocate and guardian role typology.

Using data collected through participant observation and file analysis, Platt and his colleagues concluded that the role of public defender incorporated the "child-saving ethic" of the social worker with the lawyer's "craft of advocacy".[50] Research conducted by Cayton also explained the differing attitudes of defence lawyers toward their role in terms of advocate versus the traditional "rehabilitative" role types.[51]

Dootjes *et al.* concluded that the lawyers in Juvenile Court combined the legalistic as well as the *amicus curiae* roles.[52] They reported that lawyers experienced confusion as a result of conflict between individual role perceptions and their perceptions of the expectations of other court participants. They concluded that their findings supported previous research which suggested that defence counsel in juvenile court were likely to develop orientations that coincided with particular situations and their own individual predispositions.

These findings suggest that the distinct role types of advocate and guardian were identifiable. Further, the findings confirmed that there was a considerable

---

[48] See Stapleton, Vaughan and Teitelbaum, *supra*, note 40. Anderson, *supra*, note 44. Parker, Casburn and Turnbull, *Receiving Juvenile Justice: Adolescents and State Care and Control* (Oxford: Basil Blackwell, 1981).

[49] See Platt, Schechter and Tiffany, "In Defense of Youth: A Case of the Public Defender in Juvenile Court" (1968) 43 (April) Ind. L.J. 619–40. Brennan and Khinduka, "Role Expectations of Social Workers and Lawyers in the Juvenile Court" (1971) 17 Crim. Delinq. 191–201. Dootjes, Erickson and Fox, *supra*, note 45.

[50] Platt, Schecter and Tiffany, *supra*, note 49.

[51] Cayton, "Relationships of the Probation Officer and the Defense Attorney After Gault" (1970) 34(1) Fed. Prob.

[52] Dootjes, Erickson and Fox, *supra*, note 45.

degree of role ambiguity.[53] The confusion experienced by lawyers in the fulfil-
ment of either role type was attributed to the influence of organizational variables
associated with the orientation of the court as well as conflicting perceptions of the
expectations of other important participants within the system.[54]

However, Farrington has criticized much of this research on methodological
grounds.[55] He noted that most of the research used small, unrepresentative
samples, had failed to report tests of statistical significance, had failed to control
the extraneous variables and had subsequently failed to eliminate many alternative
explanations of the observed effects.

To provide baseline data for an assessment of the impact of the *Young
Offenders Act*, the Solicitor General funded the National Study on the Functioning
of Juvenile Court. This study was carried out in 1982, prior to the implementation
of the Act. Data were collected in Halifax, Montreal, Toronto, Winnipeg,
Edmonton, Vancouver, Kamloops and rural sites in Quebec and Alberta.[56]

Analysis of the data describing the functioning of the juvenile justice system at
each of the study sites revealed significant ideological, structural and procedural
variations among provincial jurisdictions.[57] A comparison of the major stages of
the court process showed that while all of the courts operated within the statutory
framework of the *Juvenile Delinquents Act*, the procedure with which young
offenders were handled in each province varied considerably.[58]

The extent to which the provinces varied in terms of philosophy, structure and
procedure in the processing of young offenders reflected the response of the
provinces to federal legislation. The majority of administrative matters came
under provincial legislation and were implemented by local agencies and institutions which were distinctive in their philosophies and practices.[59] The interaction
of these levels of legislation and the way in which they became incorporated into
the existing structure and organization determined the precise nature of the court
process in each province.

---

[53] Platt, Schecter and Tiffany, *supra*, note 49.

[54] See Brennan and Khinduka, *supra*, note 49; Stapleton, Vaughan and
Teitelbaum, *supra*, note 40; Erickson, *supra*, note 47; Catton, *supra*, note 40;
Anderson, *supra*, note 44; Parker, Casburn and Turnbull, *supra*, note 48.

[55] Farrington, *Juvenile Justice in England and Canada* (Ottawa: Solicitor General
of Canada, 1979).

[56] Ministry of the Solicitor General, "National Study on the Functioning of
Juvenile Court" (Ottawa: Ministry of the Solicitor General, 1982).

[57] Bala and Corrado, *Juvenile Justice in Canada: A Comparative Study* (Ottawa:
Ministry of the Solicitor General, 1985); Corrado, Kueneman, LeBlanc and
Linden, "Treatment of Justice: An Analysis of Attitudes Toward Juvenile
Justice in Canada", paper presented to the International Seminar on Juvenile
Delinquency, Vaucresson, France, May 1985.

[58] Bala and Corrado, *supra*, note 57.

[59] *Ibid.*

In practice, the formal process as prescribed by the legislation and the informal process as implemented by the court organization in response to legislative change are often contradictory in the establishment of procedures and goals. Therefore, in assessing the roles of court personnel, attention must be focused on the interaction of the formal legislative structure and the court's informal processes, which influence the operation of the court organization.

The purpose of this study was to examine the role perception of defence counsel. Incorporating an organizational perspective, the study concentrated on the variation among defence counsel regarding the perception of appropriate roles and the utilization of informal rules and procedure that may vary among provinces. The research also addressed several related questions, including:

1. How do defence counsel perceive their role in the system?
2. Do jurisdictions vary in terms of lawyers' perceptions of appropriate roles?
3. What factors affect their perceptions?
    A. Attitudes toward the causes of delinquency?
    B. Attitudes toward the objectives of the court?
4. Do perceptions of defence counsel toward their role have an effect on the handling of juvenile cases or decision-making?

Using data collected as part of a National Study on the Functioning of Juvenile Court in 1982,[60] the analysis combines observational data from six principal urban study sties, with data obtained from a survey administered to a sample of defence counsel.

The questionnaire was administered to a sample of "key actors", including judges, Crown counsel/attorneys/agents, defence counsel, and probation and police officers in Nova Scotia, Quebec, Ontario, Manitoba, Alberta and British Columbia. The survey was designed to measure attitudes toward objectives of the court; provisions of the *YOA*; legal representation in the juvenile court; police handling of juvenile offenders; the juvenile court and the community; and the structure of the juvenile justice system and decision-making in juvenile court. A related objective was to see if attitudes toward the legislation varied according to the role of the key actor and the jurisdiction.

Characteristics of the Defence Counsel Sample

In five of the six sites, a total sample of 244 defence counsel was drawn from those appearing in juvenile court during the observation phase of this study. With the exception of Quebec, where the survey attempted to include a wider range of public defenders and lawyers, the defence sample was composed of urban lawyers who had appeared as retained representatives or as duty counsel.

---

[60] Kueneman, Linden and Michaud, "National Study on the Functioning of the Juvenile Court: Descriptive Site Report for Winnipeg Site" (Ottawa: Ministry of the Solicitor General, 1984).

The response rate of defence lawyers was the lowest of all the key actor groups, at 48 percent, and varied from 38 percent in British Columbia to 59 percent in Manitoba. While this is an adequate response rate, there are no available data to assess the representativeness of the responding defence counsel. The low response rate might be attributed to the fact that many of those in the defence sample may have had limited experiece with juvenile matters and may not have been in a position to respond to the survey items. In addition, lawyers who were used to billing for their time and who had busy schedules may have been reluctant to respond to the questionnaire.

The study confirmed that juvenile court serves as a means of training inexperienced defence lawyers. The findings indicated that almost two-thirds of the lawyers were under the age of 35 and over 50 percent had practised law for less than five years. Most spent a relatively small proportion of their time in Juvenile Court.

With regard to the percentage of workload constituting juvenile matters, the study reported that

> With one exception, 80% or more of defence counsel in the sample worked in juvenile court less than 20% of their time. One third of the Quebec respondents worked 30% or more of their time in juvenile court . . . while counsel from Nova Scotia, Alberta, British Columbia had minimal contact with the court, 75% spent less than 10% of their time on juvenile matters.[61]

Conceptualization and Operationalization of the Variables

The first stage of the research involved a descriptive analysis of the attitudinal data obtained from the survey questionnaire. The first research question pertained to the way in which the sample of defence counsel perceived their role in the juvenile justice system.

Several questions were formulated which related to the identification of the perceptions of lawyers toward their role and the variation of these perceptions across jurisdictions. Additional questions addressed role-related issues such as attitudes toward the nature of delinquency and the objectives of the court. The final questions concerned the effect of role perceptions on attitudes toward the handling of juvenile cases and the decision-making process.

The perception of role was measured using two sections of the questionnaire. The first section, the Philosophy of the *Young Offenders Act*, was designed to measure the attitudes of defence counsel towards statute's of the new Declaration of Principle, though the *YOA* was not yet in force at the time of the study.[62] Due to the significance of the principles section and the expectation that responses to these items would be indicators of the values and assumptions that contribute to

---

[61] Moyer and Carrington, *The Attitude of Canadian Juvenile Justice Professionals Towards the Young Offenders Act*, Programs Branch User Report (Ottawa: Ministry of the Solicitor General, 1985) p. A.5.

[62] *Young Offenders Act*, R.S.C. 1985, c. Y-1, ss. 3(1), (2).

the formulation of the role of defence counsel, this section of the questionnaire was used in differentiating role types.

A second section of the questionnaire, concerning Legal Representation in Juvenile Court, was also used. As a direct measure of defence counsel attitudes toward legal representation of youths, the items dealt with the importance and quality of representation as well as the appropriate conduct of lawyers acting on behalf of young offenders. Of particular importance and interest were items that specifically measured the attitudes of the sample toward the appropriate conduct of the lawyer. The content of these items refers to the fundamental legal assumptions and rationale underlying the lawyer-client relationship in the Juvenile Court context.

The literature suggests the defence counsel will either perceive their appropriate role in juvenile court as that of an advocate or a guardian. The advocate will act in a legalistic fashion and will try to minimize the involvement of the juvenile with the legal system and its remedies. The guardian, on the other hand, will act in the best long-term interests of the juvenile client, even though this may conflict with the client's short-term preferences. The literature also suggests that the type of role adopted by defence lawyers will be related to the structure and practice of the particular court within which the lawyer practices.

This research examines the responses given by our sample of lawyers to see if they hold consistent sets of attitudes toward the law and their representation of juveniles fitting the advocate-guardian distinction. If lawyers can be categorized in this way, we will see if provincial differences in court practice and structure[63] are associated with differences in the type of role which is perceived as appropriate by the respondents.

RESEARCH FINDINGS

The statistical technique used to determine if attitudes cluster together in distinct categories such as advocate and guardian is called factor analysis. If claims in the literature are to be supported by these data, two factors corresponding to these categories should emerge from the analysis.

The 1982 National Study

The previous findings were *not* supported by our analysis, in that factors did not emerge categorizing lawyers into two clear groups. While the results of the factor analysis are too complex and technical to be presented here,[64] Table 1 illustrates how the views of lawyers did not have the degree of internal consistency suggested by previous research. This table shows the relationship between two of

---

[63] Bala and Corrado, *supra*, note 57.

[64] Complete results are available in Milne, *The Role of Counsel in Canadian Youth Court* (M.A. thesis, University of Manitoba, 1987).

the questions used in the factor analysis. The first of these questions asked the extent to which lawyers agreed with the statement:

> In their dealings with the juvenile justice system, young persons should have the right to the least possible interference with their freedoms.

The second question asked the lawyers the extent to which they agreed with the statement:

> In plea bargaining, the defence counsel should give precedence to negotiating in the long term interests rather than for the short term satisfaction of the juvenile client.

Those lawyers who would be considered advocates should be the most likely to agree strongly with the first of these questions, as it represents a very legalistic point of view. On the other hand, those lawyers who would be considered guardians should be the most likely to agree with the second question, as it suggests that the long-term interests of the youth should prevail, even if this means interference in freedoms. The relationship between these questions should be negative — those who agree with one should disagree with the other if there is consistency in their attitudes.

The results shown in Table 1, however, do not show any consistency as a relatively even distribution of responses across the categories is shown. The failure of the analysis to show clear factors suggests that the advocate-guardian typology does not represent an adequate description of defence attitudes toward their role. The actual picture is far more complex and confusing. Because of these results, the original research question concerning the impact of differences in court structure and practice on perception of role was no longer a valid one. In fact, while there were some differences among the sites in response to particular questions, these differences were not consistent and in many cases were the opposite of those predicted.[65]

We are left with the finding that relationships predicted by the previous literature did not appear in our data. This raises a number of questions. First, why were our findings different from those previously reported? Could the difference be due to methodological problems such as the low response rate (48 percent) or to the fact that many of our respondents did not have a great deal of juvenile court experience? More interestingly, if the research findings are valid, how do lawyers cope with the fact that their attitudes toward the practice of juvenile law do not appear consistent? While in adult court lawyers appear to have a clear mandate to achieve the result which minimizes the restriction of the freedom of their client, do they approach youth justice with conflicting goals?

The 1986 Manitoba Study

To answer these questions, a second research project was carried out on the role perception of defence lawyers. This study was carried out in 1986, two years after the implementation of the *Young Offenders Act*, with its more legalistic orienta-

---

[65] *Ibid.*

Table 1

Relationship of Least Interference with Plea-Bargaining

INTERESTS IN PLEA-BARGAINING

Count Row PCT Col PCT		Strongly Agree	Agree	Mildly Agree	Mildly Disagree	Disagree	Strongly Disagree
SUPPORT FOR LEAST INTERFERENCE	STRONGLY AGREE	20.0	8.6	4.1	34.5	14.3	26.3
	AGREE	17.8	24.1	28.6	24.1	37.1	31.6
	MILDLY AGREE	15.6	24.1	26.5	3.4	17.1	21.1
	MILDLY DISAGREE	17.8	8.6	18.4	20.7	14.3	
	DISAGREE	22.2	25.9	18.4	10.3	11.4	10.5
	STRONGLY DISAGREE	6.7	8.6	4.1	6.9	5.7	10.5
Total		45 100.0	58 100.0	49 100.0	29 100.0	35 100.0	19 100.0

235

tion. The research was undertaken in Winnipeg and consisted of interviews with 15 lawyers who were the most frequent defence counsel in youth court.

The lawyers interviewed had between ten months and 15 years of practice, with average experience of 6.5 years. The percentage of their case-load involving youth court ranged from 5 percent for some members of the private bar to 98 percent for legal aid lawyers. An average of one-third (33.7 percent) of their case-load was made up of juvenile matters. The vast majority of their work was done through legal aid certificates. Only two lawyers stated they were privately retained as counsel on a substantial basis.

In this study, lawyers were asked open-ended rather than structured questions. Thus, in trying to determine the perception of role, counsel were asked, ''How would you describe your function as defence counsel in Youth Court?''. Responses to this question were very diverse. Once again, it was not possible to place lawyers clearly in advocate and guardian categories.

Rather than describing the role of counsel by categorizing responses according to limited typology, therefore, a more accurate procedure may be to conceptualize the notion of role on a continuum or scale. On either end of the continuum are strict advocates and guardians. In between these opposites are the majority of lawyers whose role or approach may vary depending on both the legal and extra-legal circumstances in each case.

A modified typology was developed which enabled the categorization and identification of responses while also reflecting the diversity with which lawyers perceived their role. This provided a basis for comparing responses according to a typology similar to the one initially proposed. Although the role distinctions developed in the modified typology represent some improvement over the original advocate-guardian role types, they should not be interpreted as consistent distinct types. The interview results suggest that the ability of defence lawyers to adopt or adhere to a consistent role type is affected by several interpersonal and organizational constraints. On the basis of the revised typology, four lawyers were identified as strict advocates, four lawyers as ''moderate'' advocates; six lawyers combined the advocate and guardian roles, and one lawyer adhered to a guardian role type.

Lawyers who adhered to a strict advocate role when acting as defence counsel in youth court characteristically made reference to legalistic criteria or principles that formulated the guidelines for their position. In describing their role, these lawyers typically referred to their desire to ensure the fairness and impartiality of the trial proceedings. They wished to see that their clients' rights were protected through adherence to the rules of evidence and procedure. Also, they invariably sought to win either an acquittal or an unconditional discharge; but if this proved impossible and their client was convicted, then at the sentencing stage they tried to secure a disposition that caused the least interference with their client's liberty. In other words, the primary focus of their role was to address the legal interests of their client.

There were several types of responses that were indicative of or reflected the tendency toward the advocate role type. In reference to the nature and purpose of this role, the following two comments from the interviews clearly typified the attitude of the strict advocate. One lawyer said that:

> My main concern is not the treatment. If I can get this kid acquitted on a technicality, even if he needs the treatment, forget about that. I mean, it's the win. You want to get this kid off or you want the most lenient sentence.

Another respondent stated:

> I'm not trying to be cynical. I see the role as a positive one, being a lawyer for kids because they have rights, too. They have the right to beat charges.

Of the 15 lawyers interviewed, four were classified within the strict advocate role type.

Several lawyers perceived themselves as advocates, but differed slightly from the strict advocates in the nature of their role. While the role of the strict advocate was influenced by the legal variables of the case, lawyers who adhered to a "moderate" advocate role commented that their attitude was affected by factors including the age and maturity of the offender and whether or not the client was a first or repeat offender.

These lawyers admitted that they tended to be less adversarial with younger first-time offenders than with older clients who had been extensively involved with the system. This position was justified with a perception of the offence committed by the younger client as an "acting out" behaviour attributed to social and family problems. Conversely, the older client was perceived to have made conscious decisions to adopt a criminal lifestyle, and would receive representation more like that afforded an adult.

Generally, these lawyers were more paternalistic than the strict advocate when dealing on a personal level with their younger clients and admitted that they had a tendency to lecture them. The strict advocates also admitted that they played a more educative role when their clients were young offenders. However, they still conceptualized and handled their criminal and youth court cases in a similar manner.

Lawyers who perceived themselves as advocates generally acknowledged that the disposition process was tempered by extra-legal considerations. A characteristic that distinguished the "strict" from the "moderate" advocate role type, however, was the attitude toward the nature and purpose of the sentencing process and the function of counsel at the sentencing stage. The lawyers who perceived their role as that of the strict advocate did not differentiate between the trial and disposition stages in terms of their role or purpose. Both stages were considered to be part of the adversarial process in which the lawyer's function was to act in the best legal interests of clients by securing a dismissal or acquittal or, in the case of conviction, obtaining the least restrictive disposition. In this sense, these lawyers perceived their role to be the same, regardless of whether they were representing an adult or a youth.

The strict advocates felt that child welfare considerations should be introduced by probation services and the youth court judges. They did not feel it part of their function to decide on the relevance of the child welfare concerns to the case. Furthermore, these concerns did not influence the way in which the client was to be represented. As one lawyer stated:

> I make decisions with my client in mind and the general state of the law, rather than my personal feelings. There are judges to make decisions as to what will and won't happen, as well as other professionals with skills that I don't have whose input the court will consider.

As noted earlier, the lawyers who adhered to what has been labelled a moderate advocate approach differed in their attitude toward adult and youth clients — and differed, as well, in responses to younger and older juvenile clients. The paternalistic attitude with which these lawyers treated their young first offenders was also reflected in their attitude toward their role at the sentencing stage. They felt a degree of responsibility to decide on the importance or relevance of the child welfare concerns which affected the representation of the case. For example, some lawyers mentioned that in circumstances where the recommended disposition was not the least restrictive, given the facts of the case, but provided some form of treatment, they might advise their clients to accept the dispositions. They admitted that they have persuaded clients to accept more restrictive dispositions, especially in cases where the offenders have been very young. However, this type of compromise is only considered in cases where the difference, in terms of severity, between the recommended disposition and the least restrictive disposition has been minimal. As one lawyer explained:

> You don't sell out your client just because you're social work-oriented. Generally, you try to get the most lenient sentence while taking child welfare concerns into account. But if custody was needed, I might not fight as hard against it in the strict adversarial sense.

While lawyers who adopted a child welfare orientation asserted that this decision constituted a legitimate aspect of their role, the moderate advocate expressed a reluctance to suggest that this behaviour was entirely appropriate. One lawyer "hated to admit" to persuading a client to accept a potentially more restrictive disposition. This lawyer comments that the "role shouldn't be that of a parent" but adds, "I just can't help it with some of these kids." Another lawyer explained:

> In a lot of cases, you compromise. You relax the adversarial role when the predisposition report indicates a bad home environment. You try and reach a disposition that you can live with. For example, instead of a fine, which is appropriate, you accept probation, which may be better in terms of child welfare interests than a fine. So, unfortunately, I would tend to lean that way.

With reference to securing the most lenient disposition, another respondent concluded:

> The most lenient disposition is not always the best. In some cases, the kid needs something, sometimes supervised probation.

The attitude that child welfare concerns intrude upon what lawyers feel proper, rather than being an integral part of the defence role, is a general characteristic distinguishing the advocate from the guardian. Lawyers oriented toward the latter end of the continuum perceived that because of the nature of their clientele and the youth justice system child welfare concerns formed a legitimate aspect of their role.

Unlike the advocate role types, lawyers who adhered to either the guardian or a combination of the advocate/guardian role types expressed difficulty separating their personal values and opinions about the best interests of the welfare of their client from their legal interests. Moreover, for the lawyers who had developed a child welfare approach in dealing with clients, the separation of legal and moral interests was not perceived as a valid approach to representing youths. While a few lawyers conceded that their approach may not be consistent with that delineated by the *YOA*, they maintained that one set of interests should not be ignored for the sake of the other.

Similar to the "moderate" advocate, but to a greater degree, lawyers who maintained the role of guardian indicated that their attitudes toward the causes of delinquency affected their role. For these lawyers, delinquency was more directly attributed to a deprived social and family background which resulted in the youth committing an offence. Their attitude toward delinquency, combined with the notion of reduced responsibility, produced a different perception about their role. One lawyer remarked:

> Kids get in trouble because of problems with cultural and family background, and you can't ignore that aspect of the problem in the court process.

Another noted that:

> When you're dealing with a 13-year-old, first offender charged with Break and Enter, I'm not saying that the court is blind to that — but they will deal with it strictly adversarially, and I think that maybe we should be looking behind the act of the child and looking at what's going on elsewhere.

The lawyers who adopted a social welfare orientation differed significantly from the advocates. While the "moderate" advocates acknowledged that child welfare considerations influenced the sentencing process, the social welfare role lawyer placed less emphasis on securing the least restrictive disposition in attempts to reconcile welfare and legal interests.

According to these lawyers, the ideal disposition satisfied both sets of interests. Further, they maintained that in the majority of cases the court was able to address the issue of treatment and rehabilitation without exceeding what they felt constituted a reasonable disposition according to the law. One lawyer suggested that working with juveniles allowed for a more "imaginative" response to the development of their role. Subsequently, the ability to address the legal and moral interests was attributed to the flexibility of both the role of counsel and the youth court. This lawyer continued by commenting that:

> In some cases, a severe intervention with the client's liberty may be consistent with the client's best interests. Whereas in criminal court there are hardly ever cases where a long period of secure custody is going to benefit an adult.

Conversely, lawyers who adhered to an advocate approach adamantly opposed the incorporation of the moral or child welfare interests as part of their role as counsel. In reference to the function of an advocate, one lawyer commented that:

> I'm a 100 percent advocate. I'm not an expert in anything other than the law. That's my job. They have other people with other training to look after the social welfare interests.

Another stated:

> I don't want to play a social worker role. That's not my function. There are probation officers and social workers out there. I don't want them to play lawyer and I don't want to play their role.

Of the lawyers interviewed, only one expressed an orientation that could be placed on the extreme guardian end of the continuum. In philosophy and practice, this lawyer had developed an entirely different and unique opinion regarding the nature and objectives of juvenile justice. Opposed to the intended change toward a criminal justice model and philosophy underlying the *Young Offenders Act*, this respondent maintained an orientation toward the role of counsel similar to that idealized under the *Juvenile Delinquency Act*.

This lawyer preferred to practice in conjunction with the child's parents and appreciated the ongoing exchange with probation services. This attitude was directly related to the respondent's opinion regarding the occurence of delinquency. Similar to the explanation related by other lawyers, the interviewee stated that delinquent acts were spontaneous occurrences frequently committed by irresponsible children who were not "streetwise" criminals. In describing this approach, the lawyer commented that:

> My attitude to the practice of law is not adversarial. I am aware of the legal issues and the fact that I am a lawyer, but I am concerned with rehabilitation. I do take the role of the stern parent.

In the majority of the interviews, the question about least possible interference in the sentencing of young offenders was the subject area precipitating broader discussion on the issue of role conflict. In fact, it became evident over the course of the interviews that the conflict of legal versus moral interests associated with the notion of least interference, in part, formed the basis of the controversy about the role of counsel.

As noted earlier, the provision related to the right to the least possible interference and legal rights principle[66] marked a significant departure from the *parens patriae* philosophy characteristic of the former legislation.[67] It would appear that the intent of the provision was to initiate a shift toward a legalistic philosophy.

---

[66] *Young Offenders Act*, R.S.C. 1985, c. Y-1, ss. 3(1)(*e*), (*f*), (*g*).

[67] Bala and Lilles, *Young Offenders Act, Annotated* (Ottawa: Solicitor General of Canada and the Canadian Government Publishing Centre in cooperation with Richard De Boo Publishers, 1984).

It was anticipated that the attitudes toward this provision would vary according to the tendency of lawyers to adhere to a particular orientation. However, regardless of role perception and description, the lawyers stated that in the majority of cases they supported the right to least interference.

In addition, there were lawyers who stated that under specific circumstances they would consider a more restrictive disposition. Contary to expectations, this view was not limited to the lawyers who expressed a guardian orientation, but was also mentioned by those who have been described as moderate advocates. For example, in the case of a transfer hearing, some lawyers were of the opinion that although their client may receive a less restrictive sentence from a criminal court than from a youth court they would advise them against the transfer.[68] These lawyers explained that, in the best legal and welfare interests of the client, it would be better to remain in youth court. In terms of the legal interests, a successful transfer would result in the client accumulating a criminal record. Further, any sentence served in an adult facility was not considered in the best interests of the client. One lawyer, who questioned the legitimacy of always seeking the most lenient disposition, stated that:

> The quality of the facility in terms of what's available for potential treatment and what the client is doing in that time should be considered along with the length or quantity of time.

However, other lawyers, typically those who were classified as strict advocates, maintained that in the case of a transfer where there was a good possibility of the client serving a shorter sentence if transferred, they would accept the transfer and secure the sentence that least interferes with their client's liberty.

For some lawyers, the entire issue concerning the conflict of interests between the child welfare and criminal justice philosophies created considerable degrees of confusion over their role. Three of the lawyers explicitly stated that they were confused about their role in defending young offenders. Typically, these lawyers were less experienced or had developed a combination of advocate-guardian role types with a tendency toward a child welfare approach. In attempting to address these concerns one lawyer mentioned that:

> The confusion arises from the need of the young offenders and perhaps the need of counsel to take a more human role. You need to get involved in a personal way with the clients so that you don't feel like a machine, giving advice, taking instructions and firing it back to the court.

---

[68] In cases involving the most serious offences, particularly homicide, transferred youth would always receive more severe sanctions in adult court. However, older youths facing less serious charges, like robbery, might actually receive a shorter sentence, for they would be viewed as "youthful" offenders. In most provinces, these "less serious" cases would not be the subject of transfer applications, but in Manitoba, such cases are not infrequently transferred, especially with older youths.

Another explained that:

> There is a conflict. I am torn sometimes, but most times I think the adversarial role and the philosophy of the Act is probably the right one.

A third commented:

> I have doubts about what I should be doing. Doubts about knowing, in reality, what I'm doing is not really what is in the best interests of my client.

Those lawyers who had perceived themselves strictly as advocates did not express any sense of personal confusion regarding their role. Characteristically, they maintained a more traditional lawyer-client relationship as well as a definite separation between the legal and child welfare interests. As one stated:

> I know what's right and wrong, legally, maybe not for the kid's welfare, but that's not my function. I'm not here to rehabilitate you, I'm here to get you off. I don't suffer from moral dilemmas. I know what I'm supposed to do and I do it.

Another commented that:

> I think that the whole area presents far too much of a problem, far too many conflicts for lawyers. The best way to resolve those conflicts is to treat the process as being adversarial, the trial process as the trial process, the sentencing process as the sentencing process, both of which are adversarial, the trial more so. In sentencing, you try to get the best result for the client, bearing in mind the overall reasonableness of what you're doing and your ability to persuade the judge. I try to be objective. It is necessary to set your personal values aside and to perform your function as a courtroom lawyer, not someone who is harassed by their personal emotions or feelings so that it interferes with your role.

Typically, this type of response was expressed by senior lawyers with more experience in both criminal and youth court. It was not surprising, therefore, that they attributed the confusion expressed by some lawyers to their lack of experience. When asked if they thought there was a possibility of a maturation process among lawyers that may have an effect on the attitude toward their role, they agreed that with experience, younger lawyers who have developed a welfare orientation would likely "drift toward a legalistic approach".

When this question was posed to the less experience lawyers or lawyers who differed in approach from the advocates, the responses varied considerably. Some lawyers agreed that it was possible that their attitude would change over time. One lawyer admitted that there had been a change in attitude, but did not consider it to be a positive one. The lawyer remarked that:

> I was probably more of a caring type when I first started practicing law. As a senior lawyer, I would probably not do as good of a job for a client as I would have two years out of law school when I really cared and knew them.

Other lawyers mentioned that while experience had an effect on role perception, other factors including their personality type and the size of their practice also affected the approach to their role. One lawyer explained that a larger practise necessitated a shift toward a more adversarial orientation. This respondent added:

> Unfortunately, I don't have too much time for the more human aspects of law.

In addition, two lawyers attributed their perception of their role to the type of articling experience they had received as junior lawyers and not to maturation of the profession. As one lawyer explained:

> I had this attitude toward my role from the start of my career. I articled with a senior criminal lawyer who taught me that this is the way you do it. Everything is cut and dried.

Most of the lawyers were willing to defend their position or attitude regarding their role. Some of those who adhered to a strict advocate role type were very critical of lawyers who mixed the function of defence lawyer with that of social worker. For example, one lawyer stated that:

> Young lawyers that don't fight as hard as they should because they're concerned with the long-term benefits are making a mistake. You can't be a lawyer and a social worker; you can't mix the two.

With reference to the welfare orientation, another lawyer commented:

> If you want him [the client] to confess, take him to a priest. I'm not a priest. I think that's improper for a lawyer to do, that's not a lawyer's function at all.

Another respondent concluded that in the attempt to address both sets of interests a lawyer starts to make decisions about clients and cases which make practicing criminal law very difficult.

In defence of their position, a few welfare-oriented lawyers criticized the advocate approach as being totally impersonal and reflecting more of an interest in the business aspect of practise in that it costs too much in time and money to use a welfare approach. In addition, the strict advocate attitude was considered by some to be "too black and white". One lawyer concluded, "I hope I'm never to the stage where things don't bother me and the facts of the case don't offend me."

As noted earlier, one lawyer expressed the opinion that lawyers with less experience and cynicism are better able to represent young offenders. However, some lawyers disagreed and suggested that lawyers who adopt a child welfare approach to their role are placing their clients at a disadvantage and as a result youths are not receiving as competent representation as they should. This opinion was expressed by one lawyer who suggested that senior lawyers are better equipped to represent young offenders because "Juvenile law is much more technical than criminal law. There is much more you can do, in a legal sense, for a juvenile than for an adult", implying that experienced lawyers are better able to test the legal "loopholes" than junior lawyers.

Other lawyers attributed the sense of confusion they experienced about their role to the type of clientele they represented. As indicated earlier, some lawyers clearly distinguished between their juvenile and adult clients in terms of approach and treatment. In some cases, this attitude subsequently affected their attitudes toward their role as counsel and the objectives of the sentencing process. In explaining the difference in the lawyer-client relationship when the client is a juvenile, one lawyer remarked, "You're not just their mouthpiece, but also a friend." Another stated that because:

You're advising them [clients] on aspects other than legal aspects; a lot of the time it's a lawyer–social worker–parent type of role. I don't know how you can be a mouthpiece for a 12-year-old kid who has never been through the court process and has no idea as to what's going on. I don't think that the mouthpiece role will give the kid an appreciation for what the system is all about.

For a few lawyers, frustration with the youth justice system was attributed to fundamental procedural and structural or organizational differences between criminal and youth court proceedings. As one respondent explained:

It's a different setting. People who come here [youth court] have to recognize that there are different rules here.

Many lawyers remarked that despite the substantial philosophical and procedural changes encompassed within the *Young Offenders Act*, the legislation has had a negligible impact on the actual operation of the court.

For example, several lawyers mentioned that, despite changes in the provisions governing judicial interim release, securing bail under the new legislation had become more difficult. In an attempt to reduce the incidence of pre-trial detention, the provisions of the *Criminal Code* governing judicial interim release or bail reform provisions[69] were applied to proceedings under the *Young Offenders Act*.[70] However, some lawyers maintained that there was still considerable disparity between criminal and youth court with respect to the frequency with which interim releases were granted. Comparing two cases with the same charges in criminal and youth court, one lawyer recalled that despite the fact that the adult client had a more damaging prior record than the youth client, the adult was released on bail while the youth spent three months in pre-trial detention.

Most lawyers attributed the problems associated with securing judicial interim release to the belief that the majority of youth court judges continued to apply a *parens patriae* approach to youth justice. Judges were criticized as being paternalistic and were said by some lawyers to be using pre-trial detention as a means of punishment or behaviour modification, or to deal with child welfare concerns. One lawyer stated that:

They [judges] use it [pre-trial detention] as a sword. Now we've got you here, you're going to see what it's like to spend some time in jail. It's an archaic method of strap and whip to scare juveniles.

Another concluded that:

The legal tests for bail are the same for both courts, but judges are quicker to say that a kid will get re-involved so they detain them.

A third lawyer noted that an indication that judges were adhering to a child welfare philosophy in their approach to pre-trial detention was the frequency with which

---

[69] *Criminal Code*, R.S.C. 1985, c. C-46, s. 515.

[70] Latimer, *Winnipeg Youth Court and the Young Offenders Act* (Ottawa: Office of the Attorney General, 1986).

they stated that they wouldn't release the accused unless the parent was present or there was proof of accommodation. The lawyer commented that in adult court this was not required in order to grant release on bail.

In addition to this explanation, two lawyers also attributed the problems associated with pre-trial detention to a failure on the part of Child and Family Services to provide adequate placements for homeless youths. As a result, despite their eligibility for bail based on the legal criteria, youths are being detained due to a lack of accommodation. Commenting on this problem, one lawyer agreed that while it was a legitimate consideration of the court as to whether a youth has accommodation, it should be the responsibility of the system to provide the placements in order that they are not denied bail. Another lawyer commented:

> Child and Family Services has not been as diligent in utilizing the resources that might have been available.

In addition to the comments pertaining to the difficulty of securing judicial interim release, a few lawyers mentioned that when a youth is released, the bail conditions imposed are often more stringent than those that an accused would receive in criminal court and are used, in fact, to modify or control the youth's behaviour. In the opinion of one lawyer, the imposition of conditions that are unreasonable and irrelevant to the offence, including school attendance, securing employment and obeying house rules, ". . . set youths up for failure" in that non-compliance is likely and could result in pre-trial incarceration and further charges.

The comments in reference to judicial interim release, pre-trial detention and bail conditions were substantiated by the findings of the report on Winnipeg Youth Court and the *Young Offenders Act*.[71] According to the report, youth were detained prior to trial more frequently than adults and for longer periods of time. In addition, bail conditions appeared to ". . . be the rule rather than the exception . . ." and were not, ". . . limited to ensuring attendance at trial or ensuring that the accused does not interfere with the administration of justice prior to trial."[72]

Several lawyers also suggested that there was a notable difference between the operation of the criminal and youth court at the trial stage. Most lawyers attributed this difference to the preoccupation of some judges with child welfare concerns. Some lawyers maintained that despite their arguments based on the legal aspects or facts of the case, they were at the "mercy of a particular judge" who may be child welfare-oriented. In reference to the trial process in youth court, one respondent remarked:

> It's supposed to be adversarial but you don't get the same reception of legal arguments. There is an underlying attitude of resolving the dispute in order to address the "real" needs.

Another stated that:

> You don't get the same hearing because of judges who have their own philosophy and they don't want fancy lawyers arguing a case . . . You're not treated the same. They [judges] don't like trials, and they don't like a young offender to beat a charge.

---

[71] *Ibid.*
[72] *Ibid.*, at pp. 37–41.

A few lawyers were critical of judges for their lack of experience and familiarity with the rules of evidence and procedure. One lawyer commented that, as a result, the rules were not as stringently enforced in youth court as in criminal court. Another lawyer stated that there was no appreciation for the principle of beyond reasonable doubt and that there was an underlying attitude with some judges that ". . . even if they do [improperly] convict, it's probably for the best, we're here to help them [youths]." Similarly, it was noted that the "standard of proof" appeared to be lower in youth court than in criminal court and that "Defences that work in the ordinary court will not work in youth court." However, this was not attributed so much to inexperienced judges but to their attitude regarding ". . . teaching youth a lesson, and not letting them get away with anything".

Lawyers also attributed the disparity in the trial process of the two courts to factors other than the orientation of the particular judge. For example, one lawyer explained that:

> In the context of the court and the legislation, judges are put in the position that if they grant an acquittal on a technicality that they're teaching kids that they can get away with this type of behaviour and then there are ways of beating the system.

Two lawyers disagreed with the opinion that there was a discernible difference in the trial processes. One of these lawyers maintained that:

> I'm not satisfied with every judge out there [youth court] or in adult division, but I go out there to put in a case just as I would anywhere else. I think that when I go there to do a trial, the judges know that I'm coming to work, not to fool around and not treat it as 'kiddie court'. This is business, this is the trial process.

Several lawyers mentioned that when comparing cases with similar circumstances, dispositions in youth court are notably more severe than those in criminal court. In reference to the disposition process, one lawyer commented:

> Youth clients with a record get hammered in youth court. Yet, if they appear in adult court in front of a judge who knows their record they will get a much more lenient sentence than the last youth offence, even though the same record is before the judge, almost without exception. They [judges] really aren't fair in terms of sentencing juveniles.

Other lawyers agreed with this observation but stated that this occurrence also varied according to offence category. These lawyers also suggested that the variation in terms of the severity of disposition between offences was more acute in youth court compared to adult court. Others agreed that while dispositions under the *Young Offenders Act* remain excessive they represent an improvement over the situation that existed under the previous legislation. Another lawyer felt that the new legislation had not changed the types of dispositions. He stated that:

> There is not practical difference between the *YOA* and the *JDA*. The average sentence is about the same, except that it's couched in different language. The language has changed, but not the effect.

The comments related to the severity of dispositions in youth court were, in part, substantiated by Latimer.[73] She concluded that, "Probation and community services were used proportionately more often by youth courts while custody and monetary penalties are used proportionately more often by adult courts." While the report did not speculate about possible discrepancies in the way dispositions were imposed, it was stated that: "Some of the dispositions, however, are not meeting the statutory requirements for their imposition."[74]

Ironically, explanations as to why disparities existed in sentencing between criminal and youth court were similar to those which explained why there were no differences in sentencing under the *JDA* and *YOA*. Most of the lawyers who commented on the severity of youth court dispositions compared to those in criminal court were also critical of youth court judges who were perceived to be inexperienced in dealing with criminal law issues and who lacked knowledge in appropriate sentencing procedure. These lawyers also expressed the opinion that many judges continued to apply a *parens patriae* approach to sentencing. Similarly, it was suggested that because of the emphasis placed on rehabilitation in the youth justice system as well as the predominance of the child welfare philosophy, there were few differences in the type and severity of dispositions between the new legislation and the *Juvenile Delinquents Act*. As one lawyer commented, "The judges look at themselves as social workers."

According to several lawyers, the influence of the *parens patriae* approach to sentencing was exhibited on the part of some judges by the continued reliance on the opinions and recommendations of probation officers who are perceived as an impartial third party. However, several lawyers expressed the view that the pre-disposition[75] reports quite often contain inadmissible evidence in the form of inflammatory statements and hearsay reflecting the bias of the particular probation officer. When asked about the responsibility of the judge to eliminate inadmissible evidence one lawyer stated:

> Right, that's one of their [judges'] little fictions. Quite frankly, a lot of the judges wouldn't know what was inadmissible if it hit them in the face.

The contents of the pre-disposition report become particularly effective in persuading judges who have either directly or indirectly exhibited their pre-disposition toward a child welfare philosophy. Several lawyers stated that in the majority of cases the judges concurred with the disposition recommended in the report. One lawyer was convinced that:

> In some instances, judges make decisions as to disposition based on the pre-disposition report before counsel has even made submissions.

---

[73] *Ibid.*

[74] *Ibid.*, at p. 64.

[75] Section 14(1), *Young Offenders Act* requires that the youth court consider a pre-disposition report prior to making an order of committal to custody. Reports may also be ordered in other cases at the discretion of the court.

Another commented that:

> If the Crown concurs with the pre-disposition report, it's basically two against one.

Several lawyers felt that the combination of circumstances pertaining to the orientation of the judge and the lack of control defence counsel has over the information submitted to the court, as well as the limited ability to mitigate the potentially damaging contents of the pre-disposition report creates a social welfare bias in youth court. Expressing a sense of frustration, one lawyer concluded:

> Sometimes it seems like these decisions are coming from away out in left field. It's not just dispositions: in the trial process, they're too quick to convict.

In explaining the attitude of the judges with respect to sentencing, one lawyer commented:

> They think it's for the good of these kids to give them a short shot in the youth centre.

Similarly, another lawyer maintained that the emphasis on responsibility intended by the legislation has been interpreted, by some judges, as "government sanctioned deterrence" which has been equated with custody. This rationale justifies the notion of a "short, sharp shock" of incarceration in order to deter juveniles.

Two lawyers, however, were not opposed to the role played by pre-disposition reports in the sentencing of youth. One remarked:

> There is a lot of information before the judge from the pre-disposition report. Some defence counsel are uneasy because hearsay and inflammatory remarks are included. But I think that the reports are useful to the defence. The judge gets the idea that he's dealing with a person who is not just a case, but a human being.

Another lawyer, who had himself requested pre-disposition reports for his clients, did not consider that probation officers were a "hindrance" and was not pleased that their role had been reduced under the *YOA*.

Despite the criticism directed at the youth court judges and the social welfare agencies, all of the lawyers interviewed recognized that addressing child welfare considerations at the disposition stage was a legitimate concern of the court. The controversy emerges regarding the extent to which these concerns should be emphasized as well as the degree to which the welfare philosophy pervades the other stages of the process.

The continued emphasis placed on the *parens patriae* philosophy with its history of inconsistent treatment of juveniles was perceived by most lawyers as a primary reason for the difficulty in determining an appropriate role. The perceived imbalance between legal and welfare interests provoked a feeling of futility and frustration on the part of several respondents. In fact, one lawyer suggested that the presence of counsel only preserved the "appearance of justice". He commented:

> The majority of times the defence counsel role is limited because the judges and probation officers take over. I will still play the role of an advocate, but I am constrained because I know that the probation officer still carries a very strong club

and so does the judge . . . To me, it's the same as adult court, but I know there are certain lines, because my role is not as strong as it is in the Safety Building [Criminal Court] . . . It's a harder hill to climb in youth court than criminal court.

Other lawyers believed that their role was constrained because of the conflicting expectations of some judges. These lawyers expressed frustration with the demands and expectations placed on them because judges believed that part of their role was similar to the function of the probation officer, social worker or, in some instances, the parents. One lawyer maintained that:

Some judges have the perception and expectation that lawyers should act like social workers. They perceive that as part of the adversarial role. For example, one judge asked if the child was in need of protection because he had received information that the kid was out of control. He said that we all have a duty under the *Child Welfare Act* to report to the appropriate agency, when a child is in need of protection.

Similarly, another lawyer remarked that "Some judges will put you in a position to decide on long-term solutions, but that's not my role".

In addition, there were lawyers who suggested that the nature of the *Young Offenders Act* was such that in recognizing the "special needs" of the youth the legislation has, simultaneously, ". . . opened the door to child welfare". This has had both positive and negative effects on their role. Some lawyers suggested that, ". . . the *YOA* is a compromised document and intends to be. The system has to have, for some kids, a heart." Another lawyer agreed that ". . . there is room to consider child welfare". Others maintained that:

The legislation is confused, it doesn't know what it wants to do. It's a criminal process but recognized, in a covered or cloaked method, the child welfare concerns. It's not a proper balance.

While some lawyers considered this recognition as beneficial to their role, others perceived it as a source of role conflict.

Conversely, when asked how the legislation has affected their role, some lawyers maintained that the *YOA* has clarified their role as well as the role of other key actors in the system and believed that this was a desirable development. One lawyer remarked:

It has defined our role better. It has helped our role because now we know what we have to do and who we are accountable to. It has made it nice for lawyers because it's back to being nice and legalistic and rigid, which is what lawyers love.

Another lawyer expressed the view that the legislation had established the role of counsel as adhering to the traditional advocate role. He commented that:

That's maybe one way in which the *YOA* has changed things. You can be more adversarial with people who interfere like probation officers, judges and Crown attorneys.

Similarly, another lawyer added, "I feel more like a lawyer now because the *YOA* has firmed things up in terms of process".

Toward the end of the interview, some lawyers were asked if there was anything they considered to be unique with respect to their role as lawyers for youths. In response, most lawyers did not mention that there was anything particularly unique about their role, with the exception that in dealing with young persons the lawyer is required to assume a more educative role than would be expected with adult clients. However, one lawyer maintained that acting as counsel for young people was "emotionally draining" and ". . . difficult if you are a caring type . . . because . . . clients are more dependent upon their lawyer as a friend."

Lawyers were also asked to describe the ideal role type as well as the most difficult aspect of their role. The responses varied in relation to the way in which the lawyers initially perceived and described their role. Generally, lawyers who perceived themselves as advocates maintained that this was the ideal role type.

Lawyers who were identified as moderate advocates disagreed. These lawyers felt that the ideal role type incorporated more of a balance between the child welfare and legal approach. One lawyer suggested that ideally a junior lawyer who adhered to a welfare approach should act as counsel, while a senior lawyer should supervise and advise on the legal aspects of the case. In this way, both sets of interests are addressed by the appropriate person.

Similarly, lawyers who perceived themselves as adhering to either a guardian or a combination of guardian-advocate approach maintained that this was the ideal role type. However, one lawyer mentioned that under ideal circumstances the input from the social welfare agencies would not be "automatic" so as to present a "barrier" to the role of counsel, but that counsel would have more control over the emphasis placed on the child welfare considerations.

In addition, one lawyer seriously questioned the legitimacy of the youth court as the appropriate organization or structure for dealing with essentially behavioural or social welfare problems. This lawyer favoured "community-based justice" over the present youth justice system. When asked what would constitute the ideal model, this lawyer suggested that defence counsel and Crown attorneys would not be involved in dealing with young offenders. Reflecting on the youth justice system, this lawyer remarked: "The real question is whether we ought to be having a youth court."

In response to the question regarding the most difficult aspect of representing young persons, most lawyers mentioned problems that were related to the nature of the clientele. Several lawyers expressed difficulty in accepting or receiving instructions from their young clients. The reluctance on the part of these lawyers to accept instructions was partly correlated with their perceptions regarding the competence and ability of their clients to give appropriate instructions. Some lawyers, who perceived their clients as "streetwise", did not have difficulty regarding legal competence. Other lawyers were not as confident of their clients' capacity to understand the express themselves adequately. These lawyers implied that their clients did not instruct them, in the strict sense, but were inclined to "go along with" their lawyers' advice.

Finally, in relation to the continued predominance of the child welfare philosophy in youth justice, a few lawyers commented that they found it difficult to balance or "juggle" all of the interests that influenced the court process. One lawyer commented that it was difficult to ". . . know when and how to restrain personal and emotional involvement with a case".

SUMMARY AND CONCLUSION

The enactment of the *YOA* introduced fundamental changes to the nature of the relationship between the child, the state and the defence lawyer. The incorporation of philosophical and procedural changes required by the Act marked a departure from the doctrine of *parens patriae*. The Act also provided for independent representation of the adolescents in youth in court. Due to the theoretical and practical effect the legislative changes had on the role of the defence lawyer in youth court, it became important to examine and attempt to clarify the role of counsel in youth justice.

Based on survey data collected as part of a National Study on the Functioning of Juvenile Court in 1982 and interview data from defence counsel in the Manitoba Youth Court in 1986, this research examined the perception of defence counsel toward their role in the youth justice system. The results of these analyses did not support those of previous research. Due to the degree of inconsistency in the attitudinal data, confirmed in the interview data, it was not easy to differentiate the perceptions of lawyers toward their role, according to the advocate-guardian typology, as initially predicted. These findings support the conclusion that the lawyers who participated in these studies did not perceive of or adhere to a consistent role type.

Contrary to previous research which identified two polar ideal role types (traditional advocate and guardian), the results of the present studies indicate that this polarity does not exist among the lawyers who participated in the survey and interviews. The survey findings did not facilitate the distinction between the two ideal types as indicated in the literature. Further, the analysis of the interview data confirmed and provided elaboration of the survey results. This analysis identified four role types, which included the original two types of advocate-guardian but revealed additional types of moderate advocate and advocate-guardian.

The reasons for the variation in perceived role types were attributed to the extent to which these lawyers were influenced by legal and extra-legal factors. Lawyers who perceived themselves as traditional advocates maintained that there was little difference between representing youths and adults. Their role was influenced and determined by their interpretation of the evidence or legal facts of the case. In contrast, lawyers who adhered to a combination of advocate and guardian role types admitted that they were often influenced by the extra-legal factors of a case. Variables including the age, maturity of the youth and personal attitudes about the causes of delinquency and toward serving the interests of the client affected their role.

Whether these results represent the development of a new typology or simply embellish the existing framework is a question which requires additional research.

The findings of these studies indicated that there was sufficient inconsistency evident in the attitudinal and interview data to conclude that many lawyers did not adhere to a particular typology, and that the existing typology was inadequate in explaining the results. Further, the modified typology applied in the second study simplified the categorization of responses. However, it did not provide a sufficiently accurate framework to account for the wide range of diversity and inconsistency in responses. Finally, the objectives of the two studies were to identify and examine the role of defence counsel based on the existence of a typology which had been established by previous research. To that end, these research findings were unable to confirm the existence of a consistent perception of role type which would support that typology.

In attempting to identify and describe the role of defence counsel in the youth justice system, this research has shown the diverse factors affecting the attitudes and perceptions of lawyers. The findings suggest that the role of defence counsel in youth justice is a function of an interaction of subjective and organizational factors which may not be consistent over time or circumstances, and cannot be categorized in terms of consistent role types.

CHAPTER 8

TREATMENT ISSUES AND YOUNG OFFENDERS: AN EMPIRICALLY DERIVED VISION OF JUVENILE JUSTICE POLICY

Alan W. Leschied
Peter G. Jaffe
Don Andrews
Paul Gendreau

INTRODUCTION

The Juvenile Court was developed at the turn of this century to promote change in the lives of youths who found themselves in conflict with their communities. It was believed that youths were fundamentally different from adults in terms of the reasons why they violated the law, and of their responsiveness to rehabilitative efforts. This tenet of youth justice has been challenged by the *Young Offenders Act*[1] *(YOA)*. This chapter will explore the philosophical incompatibility of the justice and crime control provisions of the *YOA* with rehabilitation. The effectiveness of deterrence and treatment are explored, and challenges to the seeming incongruity of treatment within a framework of civil rights protection and public safety are answered. This chapter strongly emphasizes the incompatibility of the *YOA* with actual knowledge of effective interventions with young offenders.

TREATMENT AS THE HISTORICAL PREROGATIVE IN CANADIAN JUVENILE JUSTICE

Historical Review

The *Juvenile Delinquents Act*[2] *(JDA)* was enacted in 1908 and set an agenda in Canada for children in conflict with the law, providing that they were to be dealt

---

[1] R.S.C. 1985, c. Y-1.
[2] S.C. 1908, c. 40, s. 1.

with, not as offenders, but as misguided children in need of guidance and assistance. This *parens patriae* concept followed closely on the approaches adopted in both Great Britain and the United States about the same time.[3]

In Canada, the movement to develop the *JDA* had its greatest supporters in the Province of Ontario. Led by J.J. Kelso, the movement referred to as the "child-savers", put forth an agenda which suggested that many of this country's young persons were suffering at the hands of their families and their society. This movement focused principally on the needs of children and adolescents who, prior to the enactment of the *JDA*, could be imprisoned in adult penitentiaries and jails. There were other notable developments occurring at that time in Canada. For example, there was enormous immigration of Europeans to Canada; immigrant children were frequently placed in indentured servitude and denied access to education. Legislation, not only in Ontario but also in other provinces, was developed to provide for the protection and advancement of the needs of young persons, such as publicly funded compulsory education and the establishment of child protection agencies. It was within this climate that the "state of delinquency" concept, the essential basis of the *JDA*, was formulated.

The child-saving movement has been seriously criticized by many modern commentators.[4] This movement is frequently described as naive and overly indulgent in its identification with offenders rather than having a concern about the protection of victims. However, present-day commentators choose to regard the child-saving movement, there is little doubt about the imprint it has made on juvenile justice in Canada. The proliferation of social services grew largely out of the child-saving movement and, for better or worse, young persons were provided with specialized services, both in the community and in institutions such as industrial schools.

There are numerous hallmarks of the *JDA* which, again in the present climate, may seem hopelessly naive and repressive. For example, under the *JDA*, judges were not required to provide dispositions that were commensurate with the nature of the offence, but rather imposed dispositions in accordance with their views of the "best interests" of delinquents. Indeterminate sentencing meant that non-judicial officials determined the length of stay in places of juvenile incarceration. There was little consistency between provinces, and the legislation allowed for individual interpretation by judges as to what constituted the best interests of the child before the court.

It is important, however, to note that serious attempts at providing theoretically sound intervention did not begin to emerge in Canada until the late 1960s. Indeed, it was only in the early 1960s that the United States began to develop a serious

---

[3] Leschied, "Balancing Rights and Needs: Addressing the Dilemma's Canadian Juvenile Justice" (1987) 6(2) Can. J. Crim, pp. 369–75.

[4] For example, Shireman and Reamer, *Rehabilitating Juvenile Justice* (New York: Columbia University Press, 1986).

attitude toward effective intervention.[5] However, no sooner had Canada seriously embraced the cause of juvenile justice than several extremely noteworthy publications appeared in the American literature which decried the abuses and injustices perpetrated on young offenders, and castigated mental health professionals for their lack of effectiveness in reducing crime.[6] During the latter 1960s and early 1970s, there were two extremely important judgments in the United States Supreme Court which curtailed the intrusiveness of the juvenile court. These two cases, *Gault*[7] and *Winship*,[8] were hallmarks for justice reform.[9] These rulings established that the legal rights of young persons were similar to adults and signalled the beginning of the end for liberal interpretations of juvenile delinquency laws. Coincidentally, reports of pessimistic outcomes with respect to treatment intervention also signalled the need for a conservative revolution in American juvenile justice. Canada was not far behind in attempting a reconceptualization of its own policy toward young offenders.

It is difficult to separate the evolution of juvenile justice from other political developments of the time. The late 1960s saw the emergence of civil rights and due process, reflected in *Gault* and *Winship*. The 1970s in the United States saw the emergence of a *new conservative agenda* embracing many social issues. Specific to criminal justice, there was the rise in the so-called "get tough" movement which was a harbinger for increasing incarceration rates, not only for adults, but also for juveniles.[10] Certainly, this conservative agenda reached Canada in the early 1980s and coincided with a reformulation by Canadian policy-makers of the concept of juvenile justice.

In Canada, ideology influenced the development of new Canadian juvenile justice policy in several ways. First, there was the conservative agenda of wishing to see greater accountability and responsibility placed upon young persons for their behaviour. This movement was a considerable departure from the expressions of the *JDA* which suggested that young persons should be seen as being in need of guidance and assistance, not as criminals. Secondly, the increasing emphasis in Canada on legal rights, as reflected and reinforced by the *Canadian Charter of Rights and Freedoms* of 1982,[11] echoed the decisions of the American

---

[5] Bartollas, *Correctional Treatment. Theory and Practice* (Englewood Clifts, N.J.: Prentice-Hall, 1985).

[6] Martinson, "What Works? Questions and Answers About Prison Reform" (1974) 35 *Public Interest* pp. 22–54.

[7] 387 U.S. 1 (1967).

[8] 397 U.S. 358 (1970).

[9] Wald, "Pretrial Detention for Juveniles" in Rosenheim, ed., *Pursuing Justice for the Child* (Chicago: University of Chicago Press, 1984).

[10] Krisberg, Schwartz, Litsky *et al.*, "The Watershed of Juvenile Justice Reform" (1986) 32 Crim. Delinq. pp. 15–38.

[11] Part I of the *Constitution Act, 1982*, being Schedule B of the *Canada Act 1982* (U.K.), 1982, c. 11.

Supreme Court as it pertained to juveniles of the late 1960s. The recognition of the importance of due process was firmly embedded in the Declaration of Principle of the *YOA*.[12] In addition, young persons had a right to be protected from unwanted intrusion of the state, even though motivation for such intrusion was often rationalized by correctional and child welfare officials as being in the best interests of the young person.[13]

Cullen, Golden and Cullen suggest that the repeal of earlier treatment-oriented juvenile justice legislation in the United States was propelled by the belief that there was "unfettered discretion" underlying individualized treatment of juveniles.[14] This resulted in arbitrary, and on occasion, discriminatory, judicial sentencing practices which placed youths under the unfettered control of correctional personnel. In Canada, similar allegations had been made that, despite the well-intentioned actions of child-savers, their responses actually resulted in discrimination against youths of lower socioeconomic status and other disadvantaged young persons.[15] It has been further argued by Allen that the move to emphasize legal rights and due process for juveniles was more reactive than proactive.[16] Shireman and Reamer suggest that use of greater punishment and deterrence in the context of equitable sentencing was an unevaluated concept of controlling youth crime.[17] In many respects, the Canadian revolution of juvenile justice in the 1980s mimicked American reforms of the late 1960s and early 1970s.

The *Young Offenders Act* and Treatment

The statement of philosophy found in s. 3 of the *YOA*[18] has a curious sort of contradiction. The primary issues addressed in the Declaration of Principle suggest that:

1. young persons are to be held accountable and responsible for this behaviour;
2. they are to be afforded rights equal to those enjoyed by adults and in some situations are entitled to special legal protections; and
3. young persons are viewed as having special needs.

---

[12] *Supra*, note 1, s. 3.
[13] McConville and Bala, Children's Rights: For or Against Treatment'' (1985) 33 *Children's Mental Health* pp. 1–5.
[14] Cullen, Golden and Cullen, ''Is Child-Saving Dead? Attitudes Toward Juvenile Rehabilitation in Illinois'' (1984) 11 J. Crim. Just. pp. 1–13.
[15] West, *Young Offenders and the State: A Canadian Perspective on Delinquency* (Toronto: Butterworths, 1984).
[16] Allen, *The Decline of the Rehabilitative Ideal* (New Haven, Conn.: Yale University Press, 1981).
[17] Shireman and Reamer, *Rehabilitatin Juvenile Justice* (New York: Columbia Press, 1986).
[18] *Supra*, note 1.

It has been argued that, in many respects, the *YOA* Declaration of Principle attempts to be all things to all people.[19] At first glance, due process, accountability and rehabilitation all seem to be included within the statement of philosophy of the legislation. In defending the legislation from arguments that the *YOA* has not encouraged rehabilitation, a federal official, Mary Anne Kirvan, outlined the number of sections in the legislation that actually encouraged assessment and rehabilitation.[20] These statements, by a Ministry of Justice official, were contradicted by George Thomson,[21] a former Youth Court judge and senior provincial government official who observed that the Declaration of Principle "betrays some inconsistency or at least ambivalence" about the approaches which should be taken toward young offenders.

While in both the public media and professional literature there has been an extensive debate on the emphasis that the *YOA* places on treatment, there have been empirical findings, both through attitude surveys and data related to disposition, that has served to highlight the decreasing emphasis given the rehabilitation and treatment of young offenders under actual *YOA* implementation. Reid and Reitsma-Street,[22] addressed some of the critical issues related to the theoretical basis of the *YOA* Declaration of Principle. These researchers not only provided one of the first theoretical analyses of the *YOA*, but also asked a group of criminology students how they felt judges would interpret the legislation within the context of what seemed to be competing criminology theories. These findings, reported by Reid and Reitsma-Street, and elaborated upon by Reid,[23] suggested that crime control provisions and justice provisions with respect to equitable sentencing were incompatible with a rehabilitative response of the court; the former two aspects of the law would be emphasized over and above the special needs aspects of the law.

In an attempt to address this issue of judicial interpretation of the *YOA*, Hanscomb surveyed the attitudes of 67 Family Court judges in Ontario about their

---

[19] Leschied, "Balancing Rights and Needs: Addressing the Dilemma, in Canadian Juvenile Justice" (1987) 6(2) Can. J. Fam. L. pp. 369–75.

[20] Kirvan, "Commentary on the Young Offenders Act for Treatment and Rehabilitation" in Staff, ed., *Learning Disabilities and the Young Offender: Arrest to Disposition* (Ottawa. Canadian Association for Children and Adults with Learning Disabilities, 1986).

[21] Thomson, "Commentary on the Young Offenders Act" (1983) 7(2) Prov. Judges J. pp. 27–29. See Chapter 2 for a fuller discussion of the *YOA*'s Declaration of Principle.

[22] Reid and Reitsma-Street, "Assumptions and Implications of New Canadian Legislation for Young Offenders" (1984) 7 Can. Crim. Forum pp. 1–19.

[23] Reid, "The Juvenile Justice 'Revolution' in Canada: The Creation and Development of New Legislation for Young Offenders" (1986) 8(1) Can. Crim. Forum pp. 1–14.

perceptions of the law's emphasis on rehabilitation.[24] Overwhelmingly, the judges surveyed reported that in deciding disposition they found themselves having to emphasize deterrence and punishment to a greater extent than treatment or rehabilitation. Two notable quotes from judges in Hanscomb's study illustrate this swing away from rehabilitation: "I hope that I haven't changed. The system is forcing more punishment! I predicted that more kids would be jailed under the YOA rather than less as was promised. I was right! Incarceration has been up an astounding amount."[25] A fellow judge noted: "I don't like to, but I must give rehabilitation less emphasis under the YOA."[26]

Two fundamental provisions of the YOA are incompatible with the provision of treatment to young offenders. This first is the principle of determinate sentencing based on a "justice model". The second is the due process requirement that the young persons consent to detention for the purposes of treatment.

Justice Model Sentencing: An Impediment to Treatment/ Rehabilitation

It is apparent to the authors that the Declaration of Principle and sentencing provision of the YOA are premised on the justice model. Courts are expected to impose a determinate sentence, commensurate with the seriousness of the offence and the chronicity of the offender. Responding to the offence is fundamental to the justice model of sentencing. This model is not unique to the YOA, as it has been the hallmark of much criminal justice revisionism during recent times. Fundamentally, this attitude of "fair" justice assumes that all persons who commit crimes must be dealt with in a fair and similar manner, and that the individual circumstances of the offender must take a back seat to the actual offence that has been committed. Taking into account the individual circumstances of the offender is seen as discriminatory, other than considering the record of prior offences. In addition, fundamental to the justice model is the emphasis given to determinacy in sentencing, which requires the court to decide upon the length and terms of sentences, as opposed to leaving this to non-judicial officials. It will be recalled that under the JDA non-judicial officials were the "gatekeepers" of the many decisions made for juveniles who were committed either to a training school or placed on probation under the JDA; these officials released a juvenile from training school if there was a change in the youth's behaviour or in circumstances of the juvenile's life. In theory, juveniles remained wards of the province until their 21st birthday, long after they had graduated into the community from their training school placement, and could be returned to training school by non-judicial officials without the need for another hearing.

---

[24] Hanscomb, "The Dynamics of Disposition in Youth Court: A Report on the Survey of Youth Court Matters Affecting Disposition," LL.M. thesis, University of Toronto, 1988.

[25] *Ibid.*, at p. 41.

[26] *Ibid.*

Civil Rights Protection—Consent to Treatment

In addition to the concept of "fairness" in sentencing, the justice model is premised on a belief that detention for treatment should not be ordered by a judge without the youth's consent to such a disposition being made. Under the *JDA*, it was incumbent upon the Juvenile Court judge to make a determination of the young person's needs, based upon individual circumstances and those of the child's family. Once identified, it was further incumbent upon the judge to act upon the identified needs through a particular disposition. The judge was largely responsible for possessing knowledge of services in the community and, with the support of social service providers, made an appropriate placement within the range of available services.

The drafters of the *YOA* evidently felt that such latitude, exercised by a judge, held the potential for contravening a young person's civil rights. For example, under the *JDA* a young person convicted of a very minor offence could end up placed in a psychiatric facility for a prolonged period of time, based on an assessment of therapeutic needs rather than a response to the criminal offence.

In an effort to move away from the potential for civil rights abuse, the legislators included Section 22(1)(*i*) in the *YOA*,[27] which requires that, prior to an order being made for "detention for treatment", the young person and the proposed treatment facility must both consent, and the parents must as well, though the court may dispense with their consent.

Of the many topics that have been the subject of debate since the *YOA*'s proclamation, the consent to treatment section has produced the most controversy, along with the transfer provisions, the perceived inadequacy of the three-year maximum sentences, the minimum age provision and custody increases. Leschied and Hyatt[28] and Leschied and Jaffe[29] have identified numerous reasons why seeking the consent of the young person is an inappropriate means of providing the most effective intervention for a young person. Briefly, young persons with significant emotional distress who hold an anti-social orientation are not in the best position to appreciate their own need for treatment by providing consent. In one informal survey of 40 Canadian Youth Court judges, at least 80 percent felt that they should be able to order treatment without consent, provided this was indicated by an assessment of a mental health professional.[30] Based upon the important findings of Grisso and Vierling in the United States, young persons who have committed crimes and appear before the court in need of treatment may

---

[27] R.S.C. 1985, c. Y-1.
[28] Leschied and Hyatt, "Perspectives: Section 22(1), Consent to Treatment Section of the Young Offenders Act" (1986) 29(4) Can. J. Crim pp. 69–78.
[29] Leschied and Jaffe, "Impact of the Young Offenders Act on Court Dispositions: A Comparative Analysis" (1987) 29(4) Can. J. Crim. pp. 421–30.
[30] *Ibid.*

not themselves be in the best position to provide the degree of insight required to make the kind of commitment to treatment that is asked of them.[31]

Punishment Versus Treatment

The drafters of the *YOA* seem to have had an idealized belief in the compatibility of treatment with a justice model of sentencing and civil rights protection. In practice, dispositions from most jurisdictions in Canada have shown that the *YOA* has been interpreted as a punishment-focused piece of legislation, resulting in alarming increases in the use of custody. Hence, as articulated on a number of occasions, accountability and responsibility provisions of the *YOA* have been a pseudonym for punishment, which has manifested itself in increasing custodial rates.[32]

A prime objective of criminal law is to reduce crime, and one would assume that the drafters of the *YOA* had this outcome as their intent. It is the argument of this chapter that the *YOA* denigrates the importance of treatment, and it thus seems to have been a naive belief of the ability of a deterrent-focused philosophy to reduce crime. The following section shows that the literature to date actually repudiates the idea that deterrence-based legislation reduces crime rates. A critical issue is whether the *YOA* is attempting to reduce youth crime, or whether the justice model of sentencing and civil rights protection are seen as ends in themselves.

Deterrence

Deterrence is a simplistic premise of criminal justice philosophy. It promotes the belief that a sentence from the court that is commensurate with the offender's criminal behaviour will have the effect of producing within the offender and others the belief that increasing punishment will follow should their behaviour not be curtailed, and hence further crimes are less likely to be committed. Deterrence requires several factors to be in place for it to follow along the classical lines of thought in the psychological concept of punishment. First, the punishment needs to be meaningful to the individual as a means of suppressing subsequent behaviour. Second, timing is important; the response of the court should be closely tied to the time of the offending behaviour. Third, subsequent responses

---

[31] Grisso and Vierling, "Minor's Consent to Treatment: A Developmental Perspective" (1978) 9 *Professional Psychology* pp. 412–17.

[32] See Leschied and Jaffe, *supra*, note 29. Ministry of Community Services, *Young Offenders Act: The Second Year* (Winnipeg: Manitoba Ministry of Community Services, 1986). Gabor, Green and McCormick, "The Young Offenders Act: The Alberta Youth Court Experience in the First Year" (1986) 5(2) Can. J. Fam. L. pp. 301-19.

Corrado and Markwart, "Prices of Rights and Responsibilities: An Examination of the Impact of the YOA in British Columbia" (1989) 7(1) Can. J. Fam. L. pp. 93–115.

from the court need to escalate at a rate coincidental with the behaviour, such that some predictability is set in place. Further, the individual must engage in a rational thought process concluding with reasonable accuracy that punishment will follow the commission an offence.

Data from the *YOA* would suggest that, if deterrence were ever to be effective, it cannot be effective within the current juvenile justice system. First, predictability of response in the court is not always possible due to the variability in sentencing between judges.[33] Second, as elaborated by Corrado and Markwart extensive delays now occur routinely in youth courts.[34] In one Ontario jurisdiction, Judge Felstiner indicated that there was a 200 percent increase in the delay of deciding disposition under the *YOA* compared to the *JDA*.[35]

More fundamentally, one has to question the soundness of a justice system that is rooted in the principle of deterrence. The authors are aware of a number of recent reviews of the deterrence literature which would suggest that on no occasion has there been a published account of a study where deterrence has shown its effectiveness in either reducing or suppressing youth crime. In many respects, drafters of legislation who promote the importance of deterrence in juvenile justice philosophy are guilty of naiveté in believing that such a system of "fairness" in punishment can be effective in suppressing youth crime; two recent studies demonstrate the fallacy of this view.

The first is a report of deterrence by Schneider and Ervin who, while noting the *negative* effects of deterrence in suppressing youth crime, suggest that self-perception may have much to do with decision-making with respect to the committal of subsequent crimes. They state the following: "The results from this study clearly suggest that punishment-oriented policies may set in motion unintended effects on self-image or other values that culminate in more crimes being committed."[36]

In a second study in the same vein, Keane, Gillis and Hagan elaborate on the complexities of youth crime by suggesting that deterrence also has differential effects based upon gender. In their study on marijuana use, males tend to challenge the predictability of deterrence and suppression by actually amplifying their drug use in response to increased predictability of punishment, while females tend to be more compliant with increasing predictability of a punishing response for drug use.[37]

---

[33] Nunes, "Judges' Sentences Vary Widely in Study of Young Offender Cases" (July 13, 1989) *The Globe and Mail*, Toronto p. 4.

[34] Corrado and Markwart, *supra*, note 32.

[35] Felstiner, "Some Observations of Practice and Procedures Under the Young Offenders Act" (1986) *Social Work Review*.

[36] Schneider and Ervin, "Deterrence and Juvenile Crimes: Examining the Behavioural Assumptions of Public Policy", paper presented to the 40th Annual Meeting of the American Society of Criminology, Chicago, 1988.

[37] Keane, Gillis and Hagen, "Police Encounters With Juveniles and the Deter-

What these two studies suggest is that individual differences need to be accounted for in considering the impact of any juvenile justice philosophy. In addition, not only does the literature seem to cast doubts on deterrence as a basis for the juvenile justice system, but it is an extremely expensive means of service delivery.[38] One federal Ministry of Justice official has noted that the provinces spend 80 to 90 percent of their young offender federal funding budget on custody.[39] While custody, policing and court costs continue to escalate, there seems to be further disillusionment with a separate system for juveniles. It is an ironic outcome, therefore, that while deterrence-based legislation has proven to be expensive and ineffective, frustrations with the increase in youth crime have led to a call for further incarceration.[40]

The Status of Effective Treatment

No debate in criminal justice has consumed as much rhetoric or pages in journals as has the issue of effective treatment. Concerns regarding treatment outcomes in the human services began during the late 1950s. This issue did not become focused in criminal justice until Martinson's declaration in 1974 of "nothing works".[41] Since that time, numerous authors have reviewed studies and provided conclusions with respect to notions of effectiveness. As identified by Allen (1985), many of the commentaries on the effectiveness of treatment seem to be laden with more heated rhetoric than actual appreciation of the complexity of the issue.[42] Indeed, as has been argued, pronouncements with respect to what works seem to be dictated more by political orientation than by actual appreciation of the literature.

While Martinson set into motion the American debate in the early 1970s, Canada had its own "Martinson" in child psychiatrist Dr. Jalal Shamsie, who made the Canadian equivalent of the "nothing works" pronouncement by suggesting that "our treatments do not work; where do we go from here?"[43] It is important, therefore, in reviewing the place of treatment in Canadian juvenile

---

rence and Amplification of Delinquency", paper presented to the 40th Annual Meeting of the American Society of Criminology, Chicago, 1988.

[38] Gendreau and Ross, "Correctional Potency: Treatment and Deterrence on Trial" in Roesch and Corrado, eds., *Evaluation and Criminal Justice Policy* (Beverly Hills: Sage Publications, 1981).

[39] Morrison, "Commentary on Issues Related to Custody", paper presented to the Advanced Judicial Seminar, Montreal, 1988.

[40] Gendreau and Lescheid, "A Commentary on Doing 'Justice' in Canada", unpublished, 1989.

[41] Martinson, R. "What Works? Questions and Answers About Prison Reform" (1974) 35 Public Interest pp. 22 to 54.

[42] Allen, *The Decline f the Rehabilitative Ideal* (New Haven, Conn.: Yale University Press, 1981).

[43] Shamsie, "Antisocial Adolescents: Our Treatments Do Not Work — Where Do We Go From Here?" (1981) 26 *Canadian Journal of Psychiatry* pp. 357–64.

justice, to understand the most recent developments in the debate on effective intervention.

Misconceptions of the Effectiveness Debate: Anti-Rehabilitation Rhetoric

Human service professionals from social work, clinical sociology, education, child care, recreation, psychology and psychiatry have been leaders in the search for effective delinquency prevention and correctional programs. Human service professionals work under the assumption that it is worthwhile to attempt to prevent crime and to reduce criminal recidivism in just, ethical, humane and efficient ways. Overall, they feel that their efforts may reduce victimization in the community, reduce the costs of justice processing and improve the chances of a higher quality of life for those who cease to be offenders.

Criticism of human service professionals has questioned the naiveté of their work. The vision of anti-rehabilitation scholars has yielded a long list of the ways in which human service professionals *really* are self-serving — if not evil — agents of the socially powerful, given to mere "tinkering", conforming in a ritualistic manner to criminology's positivistic past. Moreover, a conservative public and social science "*knows*" that rehabilitation lets criminals off too easily, just as a liberal public and social science "*knows*" that rehabilitation is really punishment in disguise.

Anti-rehabilitation scholars, however, must rely on more than polemics when they promote punishment. Rather, they must deal with a research literature that, from the earliest of the systematic reviews of correctional effectiveness, consistently has revealed that a majority (or near majority) of evaluations have supported rehabilitative programming. Not repeating summaries detailed elsewhere,[44] the *fact* is that every review of controlled studies of rehabilitation from Kirby[45] through Gendreau and Ross[46] to Lab and Whitehead[47] has found that at least 40

---

[44] See, for example, Andrews, "Some Criminological Sources of Anti-Rehabilitation Bias in the Report of the Canadian Sentencing Commission" (1990) 6 Can. J. Crim. 511–524; Andrews, Bonta and Hoge, "Classification for Effective Rehabilitation: Rediscovering Psychology" (1990) 17 *Criminal Justice and Behaviour* pp. 19–52; Andrews, Zinger Hoge *et al.* "Does Correction Treatment Work? A Clinically Relevant and Psychologically Informed Meta-analysis" (1989) 28(3) Criminology pp. 369–404.

[45] Kirby, "Measuring Effects of Treatment of Criminals and Delinquents" (1954) 38 *Sociology and Social Research* pp. 368–74.

[46] Gendreau and Ross, "Effectiveness of Correctional Treatment: Bibliotherapy for Cynics" (1979) 25 Crim. Delinq. 463–89.
Also, Gendreau and Ross, "Revivification of Rehabilitation: Evidence from the 1980s" (1987) 4 Just. Q. 349–407.

[47] Lab and Whitehead, *An Analysis of Juvenile Correctional Treatment* (1988) 34 Crim. Delinq. 60–83.

percent and up to 80 percent of controlled studies of correctional services reported some evidence of positive effects of service in terms of reducing reoffending.

Moreover, there is considerable consistency in the literature regarding what works and what doesn't. Correctional services that target criminogenic need (for example, antisocial thinking rather than self-esteem) and employ appropriate modes of influence (behavioural counselling rather than non-directive counselling) with higher (as opposed to lower) risk cases are more effective than dispositions that do not involve receipt of such services, and more effective in terms of reducing recidivism than correctional services that are inappropriate with regard to need, style of service and risk.

Anti-rehabilitation criminologists had to generate a wide variety of knowledge destruction techniques in order to dismiss this evidence. As so well described by Gottfredson, the "knowledge destruction" techniques were diverse:

1. *Contaminate the treatment.* Anti-rehabilitation reviews suggest some ambiguity regarding what *really* caused the effect, despite the adequacy of the research design. For a rational empiricist, the identification of reasonable alternative "causes" provides the stimulus for additional research that might even result in a still stronger effect. For anti-rehabilitation reviewers, it is sufficient to note the absurdity of claiming effectiveness when the *true* cause of reduced recidivism remains unknown.[48]

2. *Stress the criterion problem.* There being no single perfect measure of recidivism, anti-rehabilitation scholars feel free to dismiss all evidence of apparent effectiveness. After all, a one-year follow-up period is not a two-year follow-up, and a measure of arrests is not a measure of convictions, and any official measure of recidivism is not a self-report or victim report of recidivism.

3. *Assert that massive efforts have failed.* Here the critic shakes his or her head, and somewhat sadly reminds us that we all know that "nothing works". It is wishful thinking to believe that additional research is going to uncover a magic key that has somehow been overlooked for 150 years.[49]

4. *Appeal to faulty theory.* Here the critic asserts that the evidence must be flawed because we know that the medical model and models that emphasize non-offence-related characteristics are wrong. This underscores a very interesting distinction between rational empiricism and "rehabilitation critics". Rational empiricists think that a theory may be flawed when research fails to

---

[48] Gottfredson, "Treatment Destruction Techniques" (1979) 16 C.D. *Journal of Research in Crime and Delinquency* pp. 39–54.

[49] Walker, S. *Sense and Nonsense About Crime: A Policy Guide* (Pacific Grove, Calif.: Brooks/Code, 1989).

confirm theoretically derived hypotheses, while the rehabilitation critics reject positive evidence when they think the theory is wrong.

5. *Seek universals.* When a treatment program has been found to be effective with some types of offenders under specified circumstances, it may be rejected because it doesn't work for everyone under all circumstances. Anti-rehabilitation types have difficulty with moderator variables because of the complexity of offender characteristics and their implications for treatment.

6. *Coercive treatment is immoral.* "Because anything compared with nothing will always be greater than nothing, it will always be possible to prove that all treatment programs in criminal justice involve more social control than does absolute freedom."[50] Of course, this principle also applies to "just" punishment. Just punishment will always involve more punishment and social control than does absolute freedom. Lest any reader think that we are exaggerating, let them take a look at the *Young Offender Act.*[51] This Act is very much a product of rhetoric that has minimized the contribution of rehabilitation to lowered recidivism, and established a system in which young people in conflict with the law are represented by lawyers who "protects" kids from rehabilitation while ensuring that their clients receive just punishment. Perhaps rather than argue the obvious, we should get on with the task of ensuring that treatment is decent, humane, fair, just *and* effective.

7. *The ultimate knowledge destruction technique.* We must remember that studies that report positively on treatment "are based upon the conclusions of the authors of the reports, themselves".[52] Of course, so are the reports that reach negative conclusions. All reports have authors, but some opponents of rational empirical approach are above all of that, because their knowledge is derived not from the ritual of "testing, testing" but from a morally superior vision!

Human service professionals with a positive attitude toward rehabilitation are not above criticism from either within or outside their professional communities. Indeed, a defining element of a community of rational empiricists is a respect for evidence so strong that unsparing criticism is the rule and predictive accuracy the ultimate standard. Of course, the values of rational empiricism and ideology are sometimes in conflict, and we all must draw upon our visions. Human service professionals, however, may best realize that some of their social scientist critics

---

[50] Gottfredson, *supra*, note 48, at p. 53.

[51] Leschied, "Balancing Rights and Needs: Addressing the Dilemma in Canadian Juvenile Justice" (1987) 6(2) Can. J. Fam. L. 369–75.

[52] Bailey, quoted in Gottfredson, *supra*, note 48, at p. 53.

are explicitly anti-rehabilitation. Direct service workers must be prepared to contribute even in environments where collegues argue against individual differences and effective treatment. Becoming able to distinguish between knowledge construction and applications of the techniques of knowledge destruction may be a useful part of this preparation.

General Assessment of the Literature

The number of English-language reports on controlled evaluations of correctional interventions with young offenders is fast approaching 500. "Controlled evaluations" refer to those that include some type of control or comparison condition. For all of the anti-rehabilitation rhetoric noted above, it is now clear that the average effect of "treatment" is the reduction of recidivism, to at least a mild degree. Even some of the most sceptical of the current scholars now agree with the fact. Indeed, in 1979, even the most notorious of the critics of rehabilitation, Martinson, acknowledged that some programs were effective.[53]

The most comprehensive review completed to date is that by Mark Lipsey.[54] He found that 64 percent (285) of 443 studies found differences in recidivism that favoured treatment over comparison conditions. This box score, favourable to treatment, is consistent with the previously mentioned fact that the earlier reviews had found at least 40 percent, and up to 80 percent, of the studies supporting treatment.

On average, according to Lipsey, the treatment effect was equivalent to a reduction in the rate of recidivism from 50 percent to 45 percent, compared to unspecified court processing (or a 10 percent (5/50) reduction).[55] This positive but very modest effect was an underestimate in view of the well-known unreliability in the assessment of recidivism (the offences of many who re-offend go undetected.) Lipsey estimated that the average effect of treatment more accurately represented a reduction from 50 percent to 40 percent (or a 20 percent (10/50) reduction).

Estimates of the overall average effect of treatment (corrected or uncorrected for unreliability), however, do not recognize that methodological and treatment variables may be contributing to variation around the mean effect. In other words, are some types of studies and some types of treatment associated with variation in the magnitude and direction of effects on recidivism?

Appropriately, Lipsey adopted a very conservative approach to determining the effect of type of treatment on recidivism. He insisted that any contributions of

[53] For example, Lab and Whitehead, *supra*, note 47. Martinsen, B. "New Findings: New Views: A Note of Caution Regarding Prison Reform" (1979), 7 Hofstra L. Rev. 243–58.
[54] Lipsey, "The Efficacy of Intervention For Juvenile Delinquency: Results From 400 Studies", paper presented to the 41st Annual Meeting of the American Society of Criminology, Reno, Nev., 1989.
[55] *Ibid.*

treatment variables to reduced recidivism would be considered only if evident after controls were introduced.

Clinically Relevant Treatment and Meta-Analysis

Clinical relevance in treatment and meta-analysis[56] is highlighted by making
1. an analytic distinction between the judicial disposition and the treatment services which may be delivered within the context of the disposition, and 2. distinctions between treatment services according to their clinical appropriateness. These distinctions are developed following an overview of the studies examined.

Andrews and colleagues[57] concentrated on 80 studies of correctional treatment that yielded 154 treatment-control comparisons. Forty-five of the studies were from Whitehead and Lab, who compiled an impressively complete sample of studies of juvenile correctional treatment published between 1975 and 1984.[58] The remaining studies were ones that Andrews and colleagues had in hand at the time of the review. The latter set included some studies of adult offenders.

Each of the 154 treatment-control comparisons was conducted on a binary measure of recidivism. Binary measures of recidivism are scored "0" or "1", where "1" indicates that the criteria for recidivism has been met, and "0" indicates that recidivism has not been observed. The criteria for recidivism involve scoring reoffending in terms of "none-some" or "less-more". For example, Kraus reported that 78 young people subjected to regular court processing and with unspecified intervention had a recidivism rate of 41 percent (32/78) compared to a rate of 27 percent for young people exposed only to police cautioning and released without a court appearance.[59] That relationship between "treatment" and recidivism may be summarized by the phi coefficient (a type of correlation coefficient). The phi coefficient is -1.5, with the negative sign $(-)$ indicating that more processing was associated with greater recidivism.

Overall, the average phi coefficient was .10 (N = 154, SD = .23). This positive but modest average effect size estimate is consistent with the findings of other meta-analyses.[60] The clinical relevance hypotheses, however, suggests that some approaches to treatment are better than others.

---

[56] Meta-analysis represents a more sophisticated review of the treatment literature than qualitative reviews. Meta-analysis quantifies aspects of each study (i.e., sample size, type of treatment etc.) and statistically analyzes aggregate efforts of treatment effectiveness mindful of outcome, client group etc.

[57] Andrews, "Some Criminological Sources of Anti-Rehabilitation Bias in the Report of the Canadian Sentencing Commission" (1990) Can. J. Crim. 511–24; Andrews, Bonta and Hoge, *supra*, note 44.

[58] Whitehead and Lab, "A Meta-analysis of Juvenile Correctional Treatment" (1989) 26 *Journal of Research in Crime and Delinquency* pp. 276–95.

[59] Kraus, "Police Caution of Juvenile Offenders: A Research Note" (1981) 14 *Australian and New Zealand Journal of Criminology* pp. 91–94.

[60] Lipsey, *supra*, note 54.

The Criminal Sanction Hypothesis: Andrews and colleagues hypothesized that criminal sanctioning (imposing a penalty), without the delivery of correctional treatment services, would be only minimally related to a reduction of recidivism. This hypothesis reflected the view that variations in the type and severity of criminal sanctions would have no systematic effects on criminogenic need areas such as those identified in reviews of theory and research on young offender profiles (that is, antisocial attitudes, delinquent companions, family process, school success and so forth). Fundamentally, theory associated with criminal justice processing deterrence and just desserts does not represent a well-developed social psychology of delinquency, and hence no real effect on reducing recidivism.

Of the 154 treatment comparisons, 30 offenders were assigned to the criminal sanction set. These cases involved front-end variation in the type of severity of processing including: court processing versus police cautioning; probation versus informal adjustment; probation versus open custody; secure versus open custody and probation versus secure custody. Two comparisons involved completors versus noncompletors or restitution programs. None of the comparisons involved variation in the duration of custody dispositions.

The Appropriate Correctional Treatment Hypothesis: The delivery of correctional treatment services was hypothesized to be of value, in particular when those services were clinically appropriate. Clinically appropriate treatment was defined as treatment that approximated the following conditions: (1) treatment services are delivered to higher (as opposed to lower) risk cases; (2) criminogenic needs are targeted (for example, procriminal attitudes rather than self-esteem); and (3) styles and modes of treatment are employed that are capable of influencing criminogenic need and are matched to the learning styles of offenders (for example, cognitive behavioural and social learning approaches rather than relationship-based and insight-oriented counseling).

In fact, few studies differentiated clients according to risk, and not many studies were clear on the criminogenic need areas that were being targeted in treatment. Moreover, many studies did not describe the specifics of the style and mode of service employed. Thus, the major criterion governing assignment to "appropriate correctional treatment service" proved to be the simple designation of a program as "behavioural": 70 percent (38/54) of the 54 "appropriate" treatments were behavioural. Additional treatments in the "appropriate" set were those clearly delivered to higher risk cases, structured programs that were specific and appropriate regarding criminogenic need (for example, targeting criminal thinking) and a small set of treatments involving appropriate matching according to responsivity systems such as interpersonal maturity level.

Thirty-eight treatments were coded "inappropriate" because they employed deterrence methods (for example, the "scared straight" program of taking juvenile offenders to visit adults in prison) nondirective client-centred/psychodynamic approaches, non-behavioural milieu approaches, intensive non-behavioural group interaction or mismatched cases with treatment. Finally, 32 comparisons clearly involved the delivery of some treatment service, but it was unclear whether that treatment was appropriate or inappropriate according to the clinical principles of effective service.

The results reported by Andrews and colleagues generally supported their hypotheses.[61] First, the ineffectiveness of the criminal sanctions hypothesis was supported. In fact, the effect of sanctions was negative, with more processing associated with slightly increased recidivism rates. This finding is mildly consistent with labelling theory and inconsistent with deterrence theory. If the type and severity of formal justice system processing has any effect on recidivism, it appears to be that "less" is better than "more".

Second, the value of the delivery of rehabilitative service hypothesis was supported at various levels of effectiveness, depending upon how much confidence one is willing to place upon the coding of treatment appropriateness. If one rejects deterrence-treatment distinctions, the overall evidence suggests that treatment is effective to at least a very modest degree. If the deterrence-treatment distinction is accepted, the average effect of undifferentiated treatment was clearly greater and more positive than that of criminal sanctioning without the delivery of treatment services. Additionally, behavioural treatments had a substantially greater average effect on recidivism than did not-behavioural treatments. With confidence in the full coding of type of treatment, the average effects of both appropriate and unspecified treatment were significantly greater than the effects of inappropriate treatment and criminal processing without treatment. Results for appropriate treatment represent an average reduction in recidivism of over 50 percent, findings consistent with Lipsey.[62] The evidence favourable to rehabilitation withstands controls for quality of the research design, sample size, length of follow-up, and ratings of therapeutic integrity. Indeed, under higher integrity conditions, the effects of inappropriate treatment are particularly negative, while the effects of appropriate treatment are particularly positive.

Confidence in the effect of appropriate treatment extends to tests conducted prior to and in the 1980s, to studies of young offenders and to programs offered in the community and in residential settings. In regard to custody, there was a mild but detectable tendency for the effects of inappropriate treatment to be particularly negative within custody settings, and for effects for clinically relevant service to be particularly positive in community settings.

The latter findings, in combination with the mean negative effect of criminal sanctions, led Andrews and colleagues to conclude that they had initially underestimated the negative effect of custody. They are now much more willing to say that research findings affirm a widely shared belief that custody is best viewed as

---

[61] Andrews, *supra*, note 57; and Andrews, Bonta and Hage, *supra*, note 44.

[62] Lipsey, "Juvenile Delinquency Treatment: A Meta-analytic Inquiry into the Variability of Effects", paper prepared for the Research Synthesis Committee of the Russell Sage Foundation, Beverly Hills, Calif., 1990.

the last resort. Moreover, it is particularly important that the clinical appropriateness of service be ensured in residential settings.

In concrete terms, what does clinically appropriate service look like? Summarizing the studies by Andrews and colleagues, the programs consistent with the principles of effective service were not at all mysterious. They included several variations of progress of short-term behavioural/systems family counselling in which family process is targeted for change; structured one-on-one paraprofessional programs in which the helpers were encouraged to be active and provide direct assistance; specialized academic programming; intensive, structured skill-training; and even behaviourally oriented individual counselling, group counselling and structured milieu (token economy) systems.

In summary, the evidence strongly suggests that the delivery of clinically relevant treatment service is a promising route to reduced recidivism. Whatever the social role of punishment, there is simply no evidence that reliance on just desserts or deterrence-based sanctioning will result in substantial reductions in recidivism. Rather, the promise of reduced recidivism resides in delivering appropriate correctional rehabilitative services to young people at risk. This may be accomplished in ethical and humane ways under a variety of conditions of just processing by the courts.

The federal government has endorsed the existence of a youth justice system separate from an adult system which is clearly premised on the belief; that, developmentally, youths are fundamentally different than adults. There is apparent appreciation of fundamental differences, and of the potential for change in the antisocial behaviour of youthful offenders. However, many of the specific provisions of the *YOA* and its rhetoric would not seem to support this fundamental belief. In many respects, encouragement for greater treatment in the young offender system is swimming against the strong tide of belief in punishment and due process within the court system.

Hence, there are two specific questions that challenge those who find themselves in the position of maintaining a belief in a rehabilitative Youth Court. The first relates to the place of treatment in a society that places a great emphasis on civil liberties. The second is the importance of addressing the issue related to how integral a right to treatment should be, given the prevailing pessimism whenever treatment or rehabilitation is mentioned as a part of the Youth Court process. This chapter concludes with responses to these two critical issues.

Treatment and Civil Libertarianism

McConville and Bala note that in the current climate many lawyers view their role in representing young persons is to assist the child who does *not want* to receive treatment in asserting his or her legal rights, which includes the right not to be subject to unwanted medical treatment, unless the legal capacity to make the decision is lacking.[63]

---

[63] McConville and Bala, "Children's Rights: For or Against Treatment" (1985)

What seems to have evolved is a rather one-sided argument where lawyers see their role as contesting enforced treatment. However, the other side of the disposition equation is that, while arguing against the promotion of treatment, what lawyers may indeed be doing is promoting the use of dispositions that provide greater use of incapacitation (i.e., custody), which does not possess the promise of providing programmes that may bring about behavioural change.[64] Some suggest that without an appropriate intervention being provided for some young offenders, these young people may face a future of ongoing involvement in criminal careers and a higher likelihood of future arrest and incarceration.[65] What civil liberties advocates need to be aware of is that, by not promoting the most effective intervention for a given young person, they may be actually helping to "sentence" their youthful client in the future to a longer period of incarceration, or at least, future court involvement. In other words, as spelled out by Skibinski and Koszuth, by subverting the importance of individualized treatment within the Youth Court, one impact may be the enhancement of future increased criminalization within the juvenile court process.[66] It therefore appears that "get tough" policies may espouse the rhetoric of deterrence, but will accomplish nothing more than retribution . . . it is not inconsistent with the constitutionalist philosophy that a child has a right to available treatment.[67]

Effective Treatment

The second major question that those who believe in rehabilitation must address again is derived from the Hudson *et al.* comment that there are "dubious benefits" of whatever "enforced" treatment programs can be offered through the Youth Court system.[68]

It is truly remarkable how long an afterlife the "nothing works" philosophy has had on policy makers. This chapter has given some idea as to what the rhetoric has been like with respect to the debate on effective intervention. The debate, now almost two decades old, has been mean-spirited and as has been noted as promoting nothing less than *knowledge destruction* by some antagonists of the

---

33 *Children's Mental Health* pp. 1–5. See also Chapter 7 on lawyers' attitudes to their role in representing young persons.

64 Leschied, Jaffe and Austin "From Treatment to Custody", unpublished, 1989.

65 Leschied, Austin and Jaffe, "Impact of the Young Offenders Act on Recidivision Rates of Special Needs Youth" (1998) 20(3) *Canadian Journal of Behavioural Science* pp. 315–22; Leschied, Austin and Jaffe, "Toward the Development of Risk Assessment in Young Offender Recidivism", unpublished, 1989.

66 Skibinski and Koszuth, "Getting Tough with Juvenile Offenders: Ignoring the Best Interests of the Child" (1986) 37(5) Juv. Fam. Ct. J. 43–50.

67 *Ibid*, at p. 48.

68 Hudson, Hornick and Burrows, eds., *Justice and the Young Offender in Canada* (Toronto: Wall and Thompson, 1988).

rehabilitative movement.[69] Hence, setting much of this rhetoric aside, it is important in the context of this chapter on treatment and young offenders to acknowledge the most current review of what effective intervention means. Gendreau and Ross have reviewed much of the intervention literature since 1980 and have found that, somewhat surprisingly, while pessimism seems to be on the rise in criminal justice, there continues to be a strong literature pointing to what works in rehabilitative intervention.[70] In addition, Andrews, Zinger, et al. have shown that, utilizing a sophisticated statistical approach to evaluating the available literature, there is enough knowledge about effective intervention to erase the suspicions of those who denigrate the importance of treatment and rehabilitation.[71] With this issue laid to rest, it is time to show how treatment within the Youth Court can be promoted without sacrificing the civil liberties of young people or the need to protect society. Clearly, by not promoting the most effective intervention to reduce criminality among young persons, the state may be accused of promoting criminality.

---

[69] Andrews and Wormith, "Personality and Crime: Knowledge Destruction and Construction in Criminology" (1989) 6 Just. Q. 289–309.

[70] Gendreau and Ross, "Revivication of Rehabilitation: Evidence From the 1980s" (1987) 4 Just. Q. 349–407.

[71] Andrews, Zinger, Hoge *et al.*, "Does Correction Treatment Work? A Clinically Relevant and Psychologically Informed Meta-Analysis" (1989) 28(3) Criminology pp. 369–404.

GLOSSARY

Accountability: Accountability (or responsibility), is the principle that a young person who violates the criminal law should be held accountable to society for his or her wrong, and should receive a sanction for the contravention. As articulated in s. 3(1)(*a*) of the *YOA*, the accountability of young persons should ordinarily be more limited than that of adults, and must be balanced against meeting their "special needs". Notwithstanding the principle of accountability, there are situations where it may be appropriate to take no formal measures against a young person who has violated the criminal law (s. 3(1)(*d*)).

Adult Court: A young person who is charged with a very serious offence may be transferred under s. 16 of the *YOA* to "adult court" for trial, and possible sentencing, rather than being dealt with in youth court under the *YOA*. The adult court may be a Provincial Court or a "superior court" (which operate under such names as the Alberta Court of Queen's Bench, the British Columbia Supreme Court or the Ontario Court of Justice (General Division)). Technically, the adult court is referred to in the *YOA* as the "ordinary court".

Adversarial: The adversarial model of the justice system is based on the prosecution and defence acting as opponents in presenting a legal matter before a judge. In juvenile justice, lawyers who assume an adversarial role behave in a manner historically more associated with adult court.

Advocate: To act on behalf of a person in the promotion of their interests. In the case of juvenile justice, a legal advocate (lawyer) acts on behalf of a young person charged with an offence by representing that youth's interests as determined by the advocate acting on the instructions of his or her client.

Alternative Measures: A program of diversion from youth court for dealing with young persons, typically charged with relatively first minor offences. A participating youth receives no formal record, and may be rquired to do something such as to give an apology to the victim, write an essay related to the offence, or do community service work. See s. 4 of the *YOA*.

Anti-rehabilitation: A term used to convey a lack of belief in the principles of rehabilitation in lowering recidivism.

Canadian Charter of Rights and Freedoms (1982): Fundamental constitutional document that guarantees due process and equality rights. Permits exclusion of evidence obtained in violation of Charter rights. No rights are absolute as they are subject to "such reasonable limits as can be demonstrably justified in a free and democratic society."

Children and Young Persons Act: Enacted in 1967, the Act retained rehabilitative objectives of the Welfare Model, but with the protection of legal rights.

Clinically Relevant Treatment: Describes treatment programs that target specific factors in a young person's treatment history that are related to the causes of crime, as recommended by a psychologist, psychiatrist, or other therapist.

Corporatist Model: Emphasis on the diversion of young offenders, both from the formulized juvenile justice system and from custody. An administrative system is constructed to achieve this purpose.

Crime Control Model: Emphasizes incarceration of offenders, particularly repetitive and violent offenders, with objectives of both punishment and societal protection.

Criminogenic: A description used for certain factors in a person's history which suggest that person may have an antisocial orientation.

Crown: The Crown (or Crown Attorney or prosecutor) has responsibility for the presentation of the case for the state in a criminal case, including a young offender's case. Many Crown prosecutors are government staff lawyers, but they may also be lawyers in private practice acting as "part-time" Crowns. In and relatively inexperienced lawyers or articling students often handle these cases. Under the *JDA*, it was common for police officers to present the Crown's case, but this practice has largely ceased.

  In theory, the Crown prosecutor is not expected to "win" a case, but rather to present evidence in a fair fashion, and ensure that justice is done.

Custody: The most severe sentence that may be imposed under the *YOA* is to order that a young person be placed in "custody", which involves residence in a special facility. Youth courts may sentence youths to a term in "open custody" which may be a group home, or wilderness camp or similar facility; young offenders may also be sentenced to "secure custody" which involves more security and restraint. There is substantial variation between and within provinces in types of facilities so that, for example, some secure custody facilities are a portion of an adult correctional institute, while others are treatment-oriented facilities based on small residential "cottages". See s. 24.1 of the *YOA*.

Deterrence: A theory of criminology which suggests that the presence of a punishment will decrease the probability of reoffending.

Disposition: The sentence imposed by a youth court under s. 20 of the *YOA* after a finding of guilt is technically known as a "disposition", in distinction to the adult term "sentence".

Disposition Review: A disposition imposed on a young offender may be reduced in length or severity as a result of a "disposition review" under ss. 28 to 32 of the *YOA*. Young offenders in custody are not entitled to parole or sentence remission, but are eligible to apply for disposition review, which involves a decision by a youth court judge that early release on probation is appropriate. Some reviews require court hearings, but if all parties agree, there may be a "paper review" by a judge, without a formal hearing.

Diversion: The concept that some young persons who have committed offences should not be subject to formal youth court sanction, but rather should be "diverted" from the system. "Alternative measures" (see above) is the type of formal diversion authorized by the *YOA*. Diversion may also include police decisions not to lay charges.

Due Process: The idea that individuals who are subject to coercive state intervention in their lives are entitled to a range of legal protections, including the right to legal representation, and to a fair hearing before an impartial arbiter. The trend towards recognition of due process in Canadian society was reflected in and reinforced by the introduction of the *Canadian Charter of Rights and Freedoms* in 1982, as well as by provisions of the *YOA*.

Formal Welfare-Based Diversion: A social agency created by law for the diversion of cases and operating under specific rules. This agency is located between police and juvenile court; all delinquency cases were to be referred to it.

Industrial School — see Training School.

Janus Justice System: Mixed model construct, employed by U.S. scholars Faust and Brantingham (1979) and Bortner (1988), to describe changes among the diverse juvenile justice systems in that country.

Justice Model: Focuses on due process and the assignment of punishment proportionate to the crime.

Justice-Controlled Diversion: A traditional agency of the juvenile justice system that is responsible for diversion (such as police, probation, court).

Juvenile Delinquents Act (JDA): Canadian legislation enacted in 1908 and repealed by the *Young Offenders Act* in 1984 to deal with children between the ages of 7 and 18 (with minimum and maximum varying somewhat depending on the province). Juveniles who violated federal, provincial or municipal laws, or who were guilty of "sexual immorality or a similar form of vice" could "adjudged delinquent". The *JDA* placed less emphasis on "due process" (see above) than the *YOA* and had a *parens patriae* philosophy (see below).

Meta-Analysis: A statistical means of reviewing outcome literature which codes the process and outcome characteristics described in research.

Modified Justice Model: Retains many of the features of the Justice Model, but has been altered in some respects to reflect welfare concerns.

Need: A characteristic considered a risk factor which, however, upon the demonstration of a reduction in that factor, lowers the probability for recidivism.

Neo-Classical Philosophy: The belief that adolescents willfully engage in criminal behaviour and therefore should be held responsible and accountable for their actions.

Non-Intervention: A decision by the court such as a suspended sentence, an adjournment *sine die*.

"Nothing Works": An expression that is frequently found in rehabilitation literature which refers to an article by Robert Martinson in the early 1970s conclusively stating that rehabilitation does not lower recidivism.

Open Custody: A category of residential youth correctional facility such as a group home, wilderness camp or other similar place of "custody". (See Custody above and s. 24.1(1) of the *YOA*)

Ordinary Court: The technical term for Adult Court (see above).

Parens Patriae: Literally a Latin expression for "father (or parent) of the country", used to describe the stated philosophy of the *Juvenile Delinquents Acts*. A "paternalistic" philosophy emphasizing treating the child not as an offender, but as a "misguided child, requiring help, guidance and supervision".

Placement In Care: Placement in an institution of some kind (open, closed, group home) for various periods of time and different objectives, such as detention or treatment.

Positivist Philosophy: The belief that children and adolescents engage in deviant and criminal behaviour due to problems involving their families, peers, education, poverty, cultural values, and other factors affecting their socialization.

Pre-disposition Report (PDR): A report prepared to assist a youth court judge in deciding what disposition to impose on a young offencer convicted of an offence. It is usually prepared by a "probation officer" or "youth court worker".

Recidivism: Committing a new criminal offence after a decision by a judge or a YPD.

Reformatory: See Training School.

Rehabilitation: A means of intervention which suggests a person's antisocial behaviour can be amenable to change and the likelihood of reoffending reduced.

Responsivity: A description of young persons' typical style or mode of interaction.

Risk: A factor that has been empirically determined to differentiate youths who are likely to become offenders and those who are not offenders.

Secure Custody: A category of residential youth correctional facility involving more restraint on the liberty of young offenders than "open" custody. (See Custody above and s. 24.1(1) of the *YOA*)

Status Offences: Offences that only juveniles and not adults can be convicted of, such as truancy and sexual immorality. The *JDA* had status offences, but the *YOA* does not. Some provinces continue to have status offences in their statutes.

Training School (also called Industrial School or Reformatory): Under the *Juvenile Delinquents Act* the most severe sentence that could be imposed was placement in a "training school". These institutions were roughly the equivalent to secure custody under the *YOA*, though in most province commitment was for an indefinite term, with release (prior to age 21) at the discretion of correctional authorities.

Transfer: A young person charged with a very serious offence may be "transferred" to the adult court for trial and, if convicted, sentenced there. Transfer only occurs after a hearing in youth court. Transfer can result in a much longer sentence than the youth court may impose. The sentence may be served in the adult correctional system. See *YOA*, s. 16, as amended by Bill C-12.

Welfare Model: Concerned primarily with the rehabilitation of offenders. Reflected in the *JDA*.

YPD (Youth Protection Director): The agency created by Quebec's *Youth Protection Act* to screen protection and delinquency cases before a reference to court.

Young Offender: A Young Person (see below) after conviction or pleading guilty to a charge dealt with under the *YOA*.

Young Offenders Act (YOA): The federal legislation enacted in 1984 to replace the *Juvenile Delinquents Act* (see above).

Young Person: A person between the ages of 12 and 17, as of the date of the alleged offence.

Young Persons in Conflict with the Law Act (1975): Continued the trend away from the Welfare Model by emphasizing the legal rights of juveniles as well as the new theme of responsibility of young persons for criminal behaviour.

Youth Court: The court in which young persons charged under the *YOA* are dealt with. Each province or territory designates a court as the "youth court". In some jurisdictions youth court judges also have responsibility for domestic matters and sit as Family Court judges, while in others they are Provincial Court judges with responsibility for adults charged with criminal offences.

REFERENCES

Allen, F.A. *The Decline of the Rehabilitative Ideal*. New Haven: Yale University Press, 1981.

Anderson, R. *Representation in the Juvenile Court*. London: Routeledge & Kegan Paul, 1978.

Andrews, D.A. "Some Criminological Sources of Anti-rehabilitation Bias in the Report of the Canadian Sentencing Commission" (1990) Can. J. Crim. pp. 511–24.

Andrews, D.A. and Wormith, J.S. "Personality and Crime: Knowledge Destruction and Construction in Criminology" (1989) 6 Just. Q. pp. 289–309.

Andrews, D.A., Bonta, J. and Hoge, R.D. "Classification for Effective Rehabilitation: Rediscovering Psychology (1990) 17 *Criminal Justice and Behaviour* pp. 19–52.

Andrews, D.A., Zinger, I., Hoge, R.D., Bonta, J., Gendreau, P. and Cullen, F.T. "Does Correction Treatment Work? A Clinically Relevant and Psychologically Informed Meta-analysis" (1989) 28(3), *Criminology*, pp. 369–404.

Answers?" in Beaulieu, L.A., ed. *Young Offender Dispositions: Perspectives and Practice*. Toronto: Wall and Thompson, 1989.

Archambault, O. "Young Offenders Act: Philosophy and Principles" (1983) 7(2) Prov. Judges J. pp. 1–7.

Archambault, O. "Young Offenders Act: Philosophy and Principles" in Silverman, R.A. and Teevan, J.J. Jr., eds. *Crime in Canadian Society*, 3rd ed. Toronto: Butterworths, 1986.

Asquith, S. *Children and Justice: Decision-Making in Children's Hearings and Juvenile Courts*. Edinburgh: University of Edinburgh Press, 1983.

Asquith, S. "Justice, Retribution and Children" in Morris, A. and Giller, H., eds. *Providing Criminal Justice for Children*. London: Edward Arnold, 1983.

Bagley, G. " 'Oh, What a Good Boy Am I': Killer Angels Chose When Friends Die." *Medical Post*, December 8, 1987.

Bailey, W.C. "Correctional Outcome: An Evaluation of 100 Reports" (1966) (59) (2) J. Crim. Law, Criminal and Pol. Science, pp. 155-60.

Bala, N. "The Young Offenders Act: A Legal Framework". In Hudson J., Hornick J., and Burrows, B., eds. *Justice and the Young Offender in Canada*. Toronto: Wall and Thompson, 1988.

Bala, N. "The Young Offenders Act: A New Era in Juvenile Justice". In Landau, B., ed., *Children's Rights in the Practice of Family Law*. Toronto: Carswell, 1986.

Bala, N. and Clarke, K.L. *The Child and the Law*. Toronto: McGraw-Hill Ryerson, 1981.

Bala, N. and Corrado, R.R. *Juvenile Justice in Canada: Comparative Study*. Ottawa: Ministry of Solicitor General Canada, 1985.

Bala, N. and Lilles, H. *Young Offenders Act, Annotated*. Ottawa: Solicitor General of Canada and the Canadian Government Publishing Centre in cooperation with Richard De Boo Publishers, 1984.

Bala, N., Lilles, H. and Thomson, G. *Canadian Children's Law: Cases, Notes and Materials*. Toronto: Butterworths, 1982.

Bartollas, C. *Correctional Treatment: Theory and Practice*. Englewood Cliffs, N.J: Prentice-Hall.

Bartollas, C., Miller, S.J. and Dinitz, S. *Juvenile Victimization: The Institutional Paradox*. New York: John Wiley and Sons, 1976.

Beaulieu, L.A. *Young Offender Dispositions: Perspectives on Principles and Practice*. Toronto: Wall and Thompson, 1989.

Beaumont, H. "Les Critères de Décision des Juges du Tribunal de la Jeunesse de Montréal". Mémoire de maitrise inédit, Université de Montréal, École de Criminologie, Montréal, 1984.

Becker, H.S. *Outsiders: Studies in the Sociology of Deviance*. New York: Free Press, 1963.

Becker, H.S. Book Review of A. Cicourel's *The Social Organization of Juvenile Justice*. (1968) 160 *Science* p. 644.

Bennett, J.F. "Concerns About the Young Offenders Act" (1985) 8(4) Prov. Judges J., pp. 17–18.

Black Committee. *Report of the Children and Young Persons Review Group*. Belfast: H.M.S.O., 1979.

Bortner, A. *Inside a Juvenile Court: The Tarnished Ideal of Individualized Justice*. New York, New York University Press, 1982.

Bortner, M.A. *Delinquency and Justice: An Age of Crisis*. Toronto: McGraw-Hill, 1988.

Bortner, M.A. "Process and Discretion in Juvenile Court: An Analysis of Legal Factors and Socioeconomic Variables". Ann Arbor, Mich.: University Microfilms International, 1978.

Bottoms, A.E. "Justice for Juveniles Seventy-Five Years On" in Howath, D., ed. *Seventy-Five Years of Law at Sheffield 1909–1984*, the Edward Bramley Lectures 1984. Sheffield: University of Sheffield Press, 1984, pp. 95–116.

Bottoms, A.E. "Neglected Features of Contemporary Penal Systems" in Garland, D., and Young, P., eds. *The Power to Punish*. London: Heinemann, 1983.

Bottoms, A.E. "On the Decriminalization of the English Juvenile Courts" in Hood, R., ed. *Crime, Criminology and Public Policy*, London: Heinemann, 1974.

Brennan, W.C. and Khinduka, S.K. "Role Expectations of Social Workers and Lawyers in the Juvenile Court" (1971) 17 (April) Crim. Delinq. pp. 191–201.

Brodeur. "Some Comments on Sentencing Guidelines." In Beaulieu, ed., *Young Offender Dispositions*. Toronto: Wall and Thompson, 1989.

Burney, E. *Sentencing Young People*, Aldershot, England: Gower, 1985.

Burney, E. "All Things to All Men: Justifying Custody Under the 1982 Act" (1985) (May) Crim. L. Rev. 284–93.

Canadian Council on Children and Youth. *Brief in Response to Bill C-58: Proposed Amendments to the Young Offenders Act*. Ottawa: Canadian Council on Children and Youth, 1990.

Canadian Press. "Poll Finds Draw on Special Court for the Young." *Victoria Times-Colonist*, January 6, 1992.

Canadian Sentencing Commission. *Sentencing Reform: A Canadian Approach*. Ottawa: Minister of Supply and Services Canada, 1987.

Caplan, A. "Planning Report: National Study of the Functioning of the Juvenile Court, Canada Legislation on Young Offenders". Ottawa: Ministry of the Solicitor General, Research Division, 1981.

Caputo, T. and Bracken, D.C. "Custodial Dispositions and the Young Offenders Act". In Hudson J., Hornick J.P. and Burrows, B.A., eds. *Justice and the Young Offender in Canada*. Toronto: Wall and Thompson, 1988.

Caputo, T.C. "The Young Offenders Act: Children's Rights, Children's Wrongs" (1987) 13 (2) *Can. Pub. Pol.*, pp. 125-43.

Carrington, P.J. and Moyer, S. "The Effect of Defence Counsel on Plea and Outcome in Juvenile Court" (1990) 32 (3), Can. J. Crim., pp. 621-38.

Catton, K. "Children in the Courts: A Selected Empirical Review" (1978) 1 Can. J. Fam. L.

Cawson, P. and Martell, M. *Children Referred to Closed Units*. Research Report No. 5. London: H.M.S.O., D.H.S.S., 1979.

Cayton, C.E. "Relationships of the Probation Officer and the Defense Attorney after Gault" (1970) 34(1) Fed. Prob.

Chalin, J. and Suppa, M. "Document Synthèse des Mémoires des Personnes et Organismes (Volet Délinquance)". Les mémoires soumis à l'Annexe III au rapport de la Commission Parlementaire Spéciale sur la Protection de la Jeunesse. Québec: Assemblée Nationale du Québec, 1982.

Charbonneau, J.P. *Rapport de la Commission Parlementaire Spéciale sur la Protection de la Jeunesse*. Québec: Assemblée Nationale du Québec, 1982.

Chesney-Lind, M. "Girls in Jail" 34(2) *Crime and Deliquency* pp. 150–68.

Chesney-Lind, M. "Judicial Enforcement of the Female Sex Role: The Family Court and the Female Delinquent" (1972) 8(2) *Issues in Criminology* pp. 51–69.

Cicourel, A. *The Social Organization of Juvenile Justice*. London: John Wiley and Sons, 1968.

Clarke, J. "Whose Justice? The Politics of Juvenile Control" (1985) 13 Int'l. J. Soc. Law pp. 407–21.

Coflin, J. "The Federal Government's Role in Implementing the Young Offenders Act". In Hudson, J., Hornick, J.P. and Burrows B.A., eds., *Justice and the Young Offender in Canada*. Toronto: Wall and Thompson, 1988.

Cohen, L. "Conferring the Delinquent Label: The Relative Importance of Social Characteristics and Legal Factors in the Processing of Juvenile Offenders". Ann Arbor, Mich.: University Microfilms International, 1974.

Cohen, S. *Folk Devils and Moral Panics* 2nd ed. London: Martin Robertson, 1980.

Cohen, S. *Visions of Social Control: Crime, Punishment and Classification*. Newark: Basil Blackwell, 1985.

Commission Canadienne de la Détermination de la Peine. *Réformer la Sentence, une Approche Canadienne*. Rapport de la Commission Canadienne sur la Détermination de la Peine. Ottawa: Ministère des Approvisionnements et Services Canada, 1987.

Corrado, R.R. Introduction to Corrado, R., Le Blanc, M. and Trépanier, J. *Current Issues in Juvenile Justice*. Toronto: Butterworths, 1983.

Corrado, R.R. and Markwart, A. "Is the Young Offenders Act More Punitive?" in Beaulieu, L.A., ed. *Young Offender Dispositions: Perspectives and Practices*. Toronto: Wall and Thompson, 1989, pp. 7–26.

Corrado, R.R. and Markwart, A. "The Prices of Rights and Responsibilities: An Examination of the Impacts of the Young Offenders Act in British Columbia" (1988), 7(1) pp. 93–115.

Corrado, R.R., Kueneman, R., LeBlanc, M. and Linden, R. *Treatment or Justice: An Analysis of Attitudes Toward Juvenile Justice in Canada*. Paper presented to the International Seminar on Juvenile Delinquency, Vaucresson, France, May 1985.

Corrado, R.R., and Markwart, A. "The Prices of Rights and Responsibilities: An Examination of the Impacts of the Young Offenders Act in British Columbia" (1988) 7 (1) Can. J. Fam. Law, pp. 93–115.

Cosgrove, D. "An Exploratory Study of the Implementation of the Custody Review Provisions of the Young Offenders Act in British Columbia". Master of Arts thesis, Simon Fraser University, Burnaby, British Columbia, 1991.

Costello, J.C. "Ethical Issues in Representing Juvenile Clients: A Review of the IJA-ABA Standards on Representing Private Parties" (1980) 10 (Summer) N. M. L. Rev. pp. 255–278.

Cousineau, D.F. and Veevers, J.F. "Juvenile Justice: An Analysis of the Young Offenders Act". In Boydell, C.L., Grindstaff, C.F. and Whitehead, P.C., eds., *Deviant Behaviour and Societal Reaction*. Toronto: Holt, Rinehart and Winston, 1972.

Cullen, F.T., Golden K.M. and Cullen, J.B. "Is Child-Saving Dead? Attitudes Toward Juvenile Rehabilitation in Illinois" (1984) 11 J. Crim. Just. pp. 1–13.

Currie, D. "The Transformation of Juvenile Justice in Canada: A Study of Bill C-61". In Maclean, B.D., ed., *The Political Economy of Crime*. Scarborough: Prentice-Hall, 1986.

Department of Justice. *Custody and Review Provisions of the Young Offenders Act*, Consultation Document. Ottawa: Department of Justice, 1991.

Department of Justice. *Juvenile Delinquency in Canada: The Report of the Department of Justice Committee*. Ottawa: Queen's Printer, 1965.

Department of Justice. *The Young Offenders Act: Proposals for Amendment*, Consultation Document. Ottawa: Department of Justice, 1989.

Dicey, A. *Law and Public Opinion in England*. London: Macmillan and Co., 1952.

Dickens, B.M. "Representing the Child in the Courts". Baxter, I. and Eberts, M., eds. *The Child and the Courts*. Toronto: Carswell, 1978.

Dingwell, W. "The Impact of the Young Offenders Act on Policing in Two Suburban Communities". Unpublished Paper, Simon Fraser University, Burnaby, B.C., 1987.

Donzelot, J. *Policing of Families*. London: Hutchinson, 1979.

Doob, A.N. "Dispositions Under the Young Offenders Act: Issues Without Answers?" In Beaulieu, L.A., ed. *Young Offender Dispositions: Perspectives on Principles and Practice*. Toronto: Wall and Thompson, 1989.

Doob, A.N. and Roberts, J.V. *Crime and the Official Response to Crime: The View of the Canadian Public*. Ottawa: Department of Justice, 1982.

Dootjes, I., Erickson, P. and Fox, R.G. "Defence Councel in Juvenile Court: A Variety of Roles" (1972) 14 Can. J. Crim. & Corr. p. 132.

Ducasse, R. "Dossier de Presse sur la Loi 24". Annexe III au Rapport de la Commission Parlementaire Spéciale sur la Protection de la Jeunesse. Québec: Assemblée Nationale du Québec, 1982.

Ducasse, R. "Synthèse des Remarques et des Amendements Présentés lors de l'Étude Article par Article des Projets de Loi 24 et 10". Québec: Assemblée Nationale du Québec, Commission Parlementaire Spéciale sur la Protection de la Jeunesse, 1982.

Ekstedt, J.W. "History of Juvenile Containment in British Columbia". In Corrado, R.R., LeBlanc, M. and Trepanier, J., eds., *Current Issues in Juvenile Justice*. Toronto: Butterworths, 1982.

Elliot, D.S. and Huizinga, D. *The Relationship Between Delinquent Behavior and ADM Problems*. National Youth Survey Project Report No. 28. Boulder, Col.: Behavioral Research Institute, 1984.

Emerson, R.M. *Judging Delinquents: Contexts and Process in Juvenile Courtroom*. Chicago: Aldine, 1969.

Erickson, P. "The Defence Lawyer's Role in Juvenile Court: An Empirical Investigation into Judge's and Social Workers' Points of View" (1974) 24 U.T.L.J. p. 126.

Farrington, D. "England and Wales" in Klein, M., ed. *Western Systems of Juvenile Justice*. Beverly Hills, Calif.: Sage Publications, 1984.

Farrington, D. and Bennet, T. "Police Cautioning of Juveniles in London" (1981) *British Journal of Criminology* pp. 123–35.

Farrington, D.P. *Juvenile Justice in England and Canada*. Ottawa: Ministry of the Solicitor General, 1979.

Feld, B. (1984) "Criminalizing Juvenile Justice: Rules of Procedure for the Juvenile Court" (1984) 69(2) Minn. L. Rev. pp. 141–276.

Feld, B. (1987) "The Juvenile Court Meets the Principal of the Office: Legislative Changes in Juvenile Waiver Statutes" 78(3) *Journal of Criminal Law and Criminology* pp. 471–533.

Feld, B.C. *Neutralizing Inmate Violence: Juvenile Offenders in Institutions*. Cambridge, Mass.: Ballinger, 1978.

Felstiner, J. "Some Observations of Practice and Procedures Under the Young Offenders Act" (1986) *Social Work Review*.

Ferster, E.Z., Courtless, T.F. and Snethan, E.N. "The Juvenile Justice System: In Search of the Role of Counsel" (1971) 39 Fordham L. Rev. p. 375.

Foucault, M. *Discipline and Punish: The Birth of Prison*. London: Allen Lane, 1977.

Fréchette, M. and Le Blanc, M. *Délinquances et Délinquants*. Chicoutimi, Qué.: Gaétan Morin, 1987.

Gabor, P., Greene, J. and McCormick, P. "The Young Offenders Act: The Alberta Youth Court Experience in the First Year" (1986) 5(2) Can. J. Fam. L. pp. 301–19.

Garland, D. *Punishment and Welfare: A History of Penal Strategies*. Aldershot, England: Gower, 1985.

Gendreau, P. and Leschied, A.W. "A Commentary on 'Doing Justice' in Canada: How Juvenile Justice Legislation Increases Incarceration, Encourages Criminality and Promotes Public Notions of Injustice, Process and Data 1984–1989." Unpublished, 1989.

Gendreau, P. and Ross, R.R. "Correctional Potency: Treatment and Deterrence on Trial". In R. Roesch, and Corrado R.R., eds. *Evaluation and Criminal Justice Policy*. Beverly Hills: Sage Publications, 1981.

Gendreau, P. and Ross, R.R. "Effectiveness of Correctional Treatment: Bibliotherapy for Cynics" (1979) 25 Crim. Delinq. pp. 463–89.

Gendreau, P. and Ross, R.R. "Revivification of Rehabilitation: Evidence from the 1980s. (1987) 4 Just. Q. pp. 349–407.

Goldstein, J., Freud, A. and Solnit, A.J. *Before the Best Interests of the Child*. New York: Free Press/Division of MacMillan, 1979.

Gottfredson, M.R. "Treatment Destruction Techniques" (1979) 16 *Journal of Research in Crime and Delinquency* pp. 39–54.

Gottfredson, M.R. and Gottfredson, D.M. *Decision Making in Criminal Justice: Toward a Rational Exercise of Discretion*. Cambridge: Ballinger, 1980.

Grisso, T. and Vierling, T. "Minor's Consent to Treatment: A Developmental Perspective" (1978) 9 *Professional Psychology* 412-17.

Guggenheim, M. "The Right to be Represented but not Heard: Reflections on Legal Representation for Children" (1984) 50(1) N.Y. U. L. Rev. pp. 76–155.

Hackler, J. "The Impact of the Young Offenders Act" (1987) 29 (2) Can. J. Crim., pp. 205–10.

Hackler, J. and Cossins, D., Police Screening Patterns in Five Western Canadian Cities: Looking at Data in a Different Way. Discussion Paper 20. Edmonton: University of Alberta, Centre for Criminology Research.

Hackler, J. and Garapon, A. *Stealing Conflicts in Juvenile Justice: Contrasting France and Canada*. Discussion Paper 8. Edmonton: University of Alberta, Centre for Criminology Research, 1986.

Hackler, J., Garapon, C.F., and Knight. K. "Locking Up Juveniles in Canada: Some Comparisons with France" (1987) 13(3) Can. J. Crim. pp. 477–89.

Hackler, J.C. *The Great Stumble Forward: The Reinvention of Youthful Crime*. Toronto: Methuen, 1978.

Hackler, J.C. "The Contribution of Unsung Roles to the Real RatherFaust, F. and Brantingham, P.J. *Juvenile Justice Philosophy: Readings, Cases and Comments*, 2nd ed. Criminal Justice Series. St. Paul Minn.: West Publishing Co., 1980.

Hagan, J. and Leon, J. "Rediscovering Delinquency: Social History, Political Ideology, and the Sociology of Law" (1977) 42 (3) *Am. Soc. Rev.*, pp. 587–98.

Hall, S., Critcher, C., Jefferson, T., Clarke, J. and Roberts, B. *Policing the Crisis*. London: MacMillan, 1978.

Hamparian, D.M. *Youth in Adult Courts: Between Two Worlds*. Washington, D.C.: Department of Justice, 1981.

Hamparian, D.M. and Martin, D. *The Violent Few: A Study of Dangerous Juvenile Offenders*. Lexington, Mass.: Lexington Books, 1978.

Hamparian, D.M., Davis, J.M., Jacobson, J.M. *The Young Criminal Years of the Violent Few*. in Schwartz, I.M., ed. *(In) Justice for Juveniles*. Lexington, Mass.: Lexington Books, 1984.

Hamparian, D.M., Esetep, L.K., Muntan, S.M. *et al. Major Issues in Juvenile Justice Information and Training: Between Two Worlds*. Washington, D.C.: U.S. Government Printing Office, 1982.

Hanscomb, D.K. "The Dynamics of Disposition in Youth Court: A Report on the Survey of Youth Court Matters Affecting Disposition". LL.M. thesis, University of Toronto, Toronto, 1988.

Harris, R. and Webb, D. *Welfare, Power and Juvenile Justice: The Social Control of Delinquent Youth*. London: Tavistock, 1987.

Harris, R.J. "Towards Just Welfare" (1985) 25(1) *British Journal of Criminology*. 31–45.

Havemann, P. "From Child Saving to Child Blaming: The Political Economy of the Young Offenders Act, 1908-1984". In Brickey, S. and Comack, E., eds., *The Social Basis of the Law*. Toronto: Garamond Press, 1986.

Home Office, CYPA 1969. *Observations on the 11th Report from the Expenditure Committee*, Cmrd 6494. London: H.M.S.O., 1976.

House of Commons. *Debates*. First Session of the Thirty-Second Parliament. Ottawa: House of Commons, 1980-81-82.

House of Commons. *Minutes of the Proceedings and Evidence of the Standing Committee on Justice and Legal Affairs*. First Session of the Thirty-Second Parliament. Ottawa: House of Commons, 1980–81–82.

Hudson, J., Hornick, J.P. and Burrows, B.A., eds. *Justice and the Young Offender in Canada*: Toronto: Wall and Thompson, 1988.

Huizingar, D. and Elliot, D.S. "Juvenile Offenders: Prevalence, Offender Incidence and Arrest Rates by Race" (1987) 33(2) *Crime and Delinquency* pp. 206–23.

Hundleby, J.D., Keating, L. and Hooper, C.L. "A Follow-Up of Ontario Training School Boys". Paper presented to a symposium given at the Ontario Psychological Association, February 16, 1990.

Ignatieff, M. "State, Civil Society, and Total Institutions: A Critique of Recent Social Histories of Punishment" in Tonry, M. and Morris, N., eds. *Crime and Justice*. Chicago: Chicago University Press, 1981.

Institute for Judicial Administration and the American Bar Association. *Juvenile Justice Standards Project*. Cambridge, Mass: Ballinger, 1971.

Jaffe, P.G. and Leschied, A.W. "Beyond Custody: The Case for Treatment and Rehabilitation Initiatives with Young Offenders". In Beaulieu, L., ed. *Proceedings from the Advanced Judicial Seminar on Young Offenders*. Toronto: Wall and Thompson, 1989.

Kaye, M. "There Oughta Be a Law" (1990) 15 (11), *Can. Liv.*, pp. 83-89.

Keane, C., Gillis, A.R. and Hagen, J. Police Encounters with Juveniles and the Deterrence and Amplification of Delinquency: The Importance of Guidance and Orientation to Risk. Paper presented to the 40th Annual Meeting of the American Society of Criminology, Chicago, 1988.

Kennewell, J., Colfer, P. and Bala, N. *et al.* "Young Offenders". In Barnhorst and Johnson, eds., *The State of the Child in Ontario*. Toronto: Oxford University Press, 1991.

King, J.L. *A Comparative Analysis of Juvenile Codes*. Washington, D.C.: Government Printing Office, 1979. Prepared by the Community Research Forum, University of Illinois.

Kirby, B.C. "Measuring Effects of Treatment of Criminals and Delinquents" (1954) 38 *Sociology and Social Research* pp.368–74.

Kirvan, M.A. "Commentary on the Young Offenders Act for Treatment and Rehabilitation". In Staff, H., ed. *Learning Disabilities and the Young Offender: Arrest to Disposition*. Ottawa: The Canadian Association for Children and Adults with Learning Disabilities, 1986.

Klein, M. *Western Systems of Juvenile Justice*. Beverly Hills, Calif.: Sage Publications, 1984.

Komar, R.N. and Platt, P. *Young Offender Service*. Toronto: Butterworths, 1984.

Kraus, S. "Police Caution of Juvenile Offenders: A Research Note" (1981) 14 *Australian and New Zealand Journal of Criminology* pp. 91–4.

Krisberg, B. (1991) "Juvenile Justice: The Vision and Constant Star" in Schwartz, I. and Gilgun, J., eds. *Rethinking Child Welfare*. Lincoln, Nebr.: University of Nebraska Press.

Krisberg, B., Lisky, P. and Schwartz, I. *The Watershed of Juvenile Justice Reform*. Minneapolis, Minn.: Unversity of Minnesota, Hubert H. Humphrey Institute of Public Affairs, 1985.

Krisberg, B., Litsky P. and Schwartz, I. "Youth Confinement: Justice by Geography" (1984) 21(2) *Crime and Delinquency*: pp. 153–81.

Krisberg, B., Schwartz, J.M., Litsky, P. and Austin, J. "The Watershed of Juvenile Justice Reform" (1986) 32 (1) Crim. Delinq., pp. 5–38.

Kueneman, R. and Linden, R. "Factors Affecting Dispositions in the Winnipeg Juvenile Court. In Corrado, R., Le Blanc, M. and Trépanier, J. *Current Issues in Juvenile Justice*. Toronto: Butterworths, 1983, pp. 219-35.

Kueneman, R., Linden, R. and Michaud, V. *National Study on the Functioning of the Juvenile Court: Descriptive Site Report for Winnipeg Site*. Ottawa: Ministry of the Solicitor General, 1984.

Lab, S.P. and Whitehead, J.T. "An Analysis of Juvenile Correctional Treatment" (1988) 34 Crim. Delinq. 60–83.

Laprairie, C. "The Young Offenders Act and Aboriginal Youth." In Hudson, J., Hornick, J. and Burrows, B., eds., *Justice and the Young Offender in Canada*. Toronto: Wall and Thompson, 1988.

Latimer, C.A. *Winnipeg Youth Courts and the Young Offenders Act*. Ottawa: Ministry of the Attorney General, Research, Planning and Evaluation Branch, 1986.

Law Society of Upper Canada, Professional Conduct Committee, *Subcommittee Report on the Legal Representation of Children*. Toronto: Law Society of Upper Canada, 1981.

Le Blanc, M. "L'Opinion des Juges, Avocats de la Défense et Procureurs de la Couronne sur le Système de Justice pour Mineurs et la Loi sur les Jeunes Contrevenants" (1984) 14(2) Revue de Droit pp. 591–624.

Le Blanc, M. "La Loi sur les Jeunes Contrevenants et les Intervenants du Système de Justice pour Mineurs au Québec" (1984) 21 *Annales de Vaucresson* pp. 67–92.

Le Blanc, M. "La Réaction Sociale à la Délinquance Juvénile: Une Analyse Stigmatique" (1971) IV Acta Crim. pp. 113-92.

Le Blanc, M. "Les Agents de Relations Humaines des CSS, la Loi sur les Jeunes Contrevenants et le Système de Justice pour Mineurs" (1984) 33 (2-3) *Service Sociale* pp. 323–56.

Le Blanc, M. "Les Policiers, la Loi sur les Jeunes Contrevenants et le Système de Justice pour Mineurs" (1984) XVII(1) Criminologie pp. 91–116.

Le Blanc, M. "Quebec Youth Protection Act and the Doctrines of Decriminalization, Due Process, Diversion and Deinstitutionalization". Paper submitted to the 5th *Canadian Conference on Applied Criminology*, University of Ottawa, Department of Criminology, Ottawa, 1982.

Le Blanc, M. and Beaumont, H. "Description du Fonctionnement du Tribunal de la Jeunesse de Montréal Entre mai 1981 et avril 1982. Consultation, Évaluation et Recherche sur l'Inadaptation Juvénile, Montréal, 1985.

Le Blanc, M. and Beaumont, H. "L'efficacité des Mesures pour Jeunes Délinquants Adoptées à Montréal en 1981, une Étude Longitudinale". Groupe de Recherche sur l'Inadaptation Psycho-Sociale a l'Enfance, Université de Montreal, Montréal, 1989.

Le Blanc, M. and Beaumont, H. "The Quebec Perspective on the Young Offenders Act: Implementation before Adoption. In Hudson, J., Hornick, J.P. and Burrows, B.B. *Justice and the Young Offender in Canada*. Toronto, Wall & Thompson, 1988.

Le Blanc, M. and Fréchette, M. *Male Criminal Activity from Childhood through Youth: Multilevel and Developmental Perspectives*. New York, Springer-Verlag, 1989.

Le Blanc, M. and Leduc, R. "Recherche Évaluation de Boscoville, Rapport Technique no. 12". Groupe de Recherche sur l'Inadaptation Juvénile, Université de Montréal, Montréal, 1976.

Le Blanc, M., Beaumont, H. *La Réadaptation dans la Communauté au Québec: Inventaire des Programmes* Québec: Les Publications du Québec, Recherche 40, Commission d'Enquête sur les Services de Santé et les Services Sociaux, 1987.

Leclerc, L. "Le Choix des Mesures de Déjudiciarisation des Praticiens à la Direction de la Protection de la Jeunesse de Montréal". Mémoire de maîtrise inédit, Université de Montréal, École de Criminologie, Montréal, 1986.

Lemert, E.M. *Human Deviance, Social Problems and Social Control*. Englewood Cliffs, NJ: Prentice-Hall, 1967.

Lemert, E.M. *Instead of Court: Diversion in Juvenile Justice*. Chevy Chase, Md: National Institute of Mental Health, Center for the Studies of Crime and Delinquency, 1971.

Lemert, E.W. "Diversion in Juvenile Justice: What Has Been Wrong" (1981) 18(1) *Journal of Research in Crime and Delinquency* pp. 35–45.

Leon, J.S. *Legal Representation of Children in Selected Court Proceedings: The Capacity of Children to Retain Legal Counsel*. Toronto: University of Toronto, Centre for Urban & Community Studies and the Child in the City Programme, 1978.

Leon, J.S. "New and Old Themes in Canadian Juvenile Justice: The Origins of Delinquency Legislation and the Prospects for Recognition of Children's Rights". In Berkeley, H., Gaffield, C. and West, W.G., eds., *Children's Rights: Legal and Educational Issues*. Toronto: The Ontario Institute for Studies in Education, 1978.

Leon, J.S. "The Development of Canadian Juvenile Justice: A Background for Reform" (1977) 15 (1), *Osgoode L.J.*, pp. 71–106.

Leschied, A. and Vark, L. "A Summary of Literature Related to the Young Offenders Act." In *Assessing Outcome of Special Needs Young Offenders*. London: Family Court Clinic, 1989.

Leschied, A.W. Jaffe, P.G. and Austin, G.W. "From Treatment to Custody: Examining a Shift in Dispositions from the Juvenile Delinquents Act to the Young Offenders Act". Unpublished, 1989.

Leschied, A.W. "Balancing Rights and Needs: Addressing the Dilemma in Canadian Juvenile Justice" (1987) 6(2) Can. J. Fam. L. 369–75.

Leschied, A.W. and Hyatt, C. "Perspectives: Section 22(1), Consent to Treatment under the Young Offenders Act" (1986) 29(4) Can. J. Crim. 421–30.

Leschied, A.W. and Jaffe, P.G. "Impact of the Young Offenders Act on Court Dispositions: A Comparative Analysis" (1987) 29(4) Can. J. Crim. 421–30.

Leschied, A.W. and Jaffe, P.G. "Implementing the Young Offenders Act in Ontario: Critical Issues and Challenges for the Future". In Hudson J., Hornick J. and Burrows B., eds. *Justice and the Young Offender in Canada*. Toronto: Wall and Thompson, 1988.

Leschied, A.W. and Jaffe, P.G. "Implications of the Consent to Treatment Section of the Young Offenders Act: A Case Study " (1986) 27(3) *Canadian Psychology* pp. 312–313.

Leschied, A.W., Austin, G.A. and Jaffe, P.G. "Impact of the Young Offenders Act on Recidivism Rates of Special Needs Youth: Clinical and Policy Implications" (1988) 20(3) *Canadian Journal of Behavioural Science* pp. 315–22.

Leschied, A.W., Austin, G.A. and Jaffe, P.G. "Toward the Development of Risk Assessment in Young Offender Recidivism: A Necessary Concept in Juvenile Justice Policy". Unpublished, 1989.

Lipsey, M.W. "Juvenile Delinquency Treatment: A Meta-analytic Inquiry into the Variability of Effects". Paper prepared for the Research Synthesis Committee of the Russell Sage Foundation, 1990.

Lipsey, M.W. "The Efficacy of Intervention for Juvenile Delinquency: Results from 400 Studies". Paper presented at the 41st Annual Meeting of the American Society of Criminology, Reno, Nev., 1989.

Lipton, D.R., Martinson, R. and Wilks, J. *The Effectiveness of Correctional Treatment: A Survey of Treatment Evaluation*. New York: Praeger, 1975.

MacDonald, J.A. "Critique of Bill C-192: The Young Offenders Act" (1971) 13 (1) Can. J. Crim. and Corr., pp. 166–80.

MacDonald, J.A. "Juvenile Training Schools and Juvenile Justice Policy in British Columbia" (1978) 20 (3) Can. J. Crim., pp. 418-36.

Maczko, F. "Some Problems with Acting for Children" (1979) 2 Can. J. Fam. L. p. 267.

Mahoney, A. "Time and Process in Juvenile Court" (1985) Justice Journal 10(1), pp. 37–55.

Manitoba Ministry of Community Services. *Young Offenders Act: The Second Year*. Winnipeg, Manitoba: Manitoba Ministry of Community Services, 1986.

Marceau, B. and Le Blanc, M. "Description du Tribunal de la Jeunesse de Montréal. Groupe de Recherche sur l'Inadaptation Juvénile, Université de Montréal, Montréal, 1980.

Marceau, B., Le Blanc, M., Lacombe, P. and Trudeau-Le Blanc, P. "La Cueillette des Données auprès des Tribunaux de la Jeunesse du Québec: Rapport Technique et Annexes". Groupe de Recherche sur l'Inadaptation Juvénile, Université de Montréal, Montréal, 1982.

Markwart, A. *A Description of the Application of Dispositions Under the Young Offenders Act in the Province of British Columbia*. Ottawa: Statistics Canada, Canadian Centre for Justice Statistics, 1989.

Markwart, A. "Crown Counsel Services in British Columbia". In Markwart, A., *A Description of the Youth Justice Process Under the Young Offenders Act*. Ottawa: Canadian Centre for Justice Statistics, 1986.

Markwart, A. "Youth Containment in British Columbia" (1981) 5(2) *B.C. Journal of Special Education* pp. 279–92.

Markwart, A. "Youth Containment in British Columbia". Paper presented to the Canadian Sociology and Anthropology Association, Learned Societies Conference, Halifax, Nova Scotia, May 1981.

Markwart, A. and Corrado R.R. "Is the Young Offenders Act More Punitive?" In Beaulieu, L., ed. *Young Offender Dispositions: Perspectives on Principles and Practice*. Toronto: Wall and Thompson, 1989.

Martin, F.M., Fox, S. and Murray, K. *Children Out of Court*. Edinburgh: Scottish Academic Press, 1981.

Martinson, R. New Findings, New Views: A Note of Caution Regarding Prison Reform" (1979) 7 Hofstra L. Rev. 243–58.

Martinson, R. "California Research at the Crossroads" (1976) 22 Crim. Delinq. 178–191.

Martinson, R. "What Works? Questions and Answers about Prison Reform (1974) 35 (1) *The Public Interest*, pp. 22–54.

Martinson, R. and Palm, T. *Rehabilitation, Recidivism and Research*. Haskensack, NJ: National Council on Crime and Delinquency, 1976.

Mason, B. "Implementing the Young Offenders Act: An Alberta Perspective. In Hudson, J., Hornick, J.J., and Burrows, B.A., eds., *Justice and the Young Offender in Canada*. Toronto: Wall and Thompson, 1988.

Matza, D. *Delinquency and Drift*. New York: John Wiley and Sons, 1964.

McCabe, S. and Treital, P. *Juvenile Justice in the United Kingdom: Comparisions and Suggestions for Change*. London: New Approaches to Juvenile Crime, 1983.

McConville, B.T. and Bala, N.M. "Children's Rights: For or Against Treatment" (1985) 33 *Children's Mental Health* pp. 1–5.

McHale, M.J. "The Proper Role of the Lawyer as Legal Representative of the Child" (1980) 18(2) Alta. L.Rev. pp. 216–36.

McKelvy, J.G. "Removing Runaways from the Justice System: The Experience in Washington State" in Decker, S., ed. *Juvenile Justice Policy: Analyzing Trends and Outcomes*. Beverly Hills, Calif.: Sage Publications, 1984.

Millham, S. *Juvenile Justice and Child Care in England*. Ann Arbor, Mich. Center for the Study of Youth Policy, 1991.

Milne, H. *The Role of Counsel in Canadian Youth Court*. M.A. thesis, University of Manitoba, 1987.

Milner, T. "The New Juvenile Justice: The Impact of the Young Offenders Act in the Edmonton Juvenile Court". Ph.D. thesis (Department of Sociology), University of Alberta, 1991.

Ministry of the Solicitor General. "National Study on the Functioning of Juvenile Court". Ottawa: Ministry of the Solicitor General, 1982.

Ministère de la Justice du Québec. "Application du Programme de Mesures de Rechange au Québec". Gouvernement du Québec: Ministère de la Justice, Direction Générale des Affaires Criminelles et Pénales, Direction du Secteur de la Jeunesse, 1987.

Morris, A. "Revolution in the Juvenile Court". (1989) (September) Crim. L. Rev. pp. 529–39.

Morris, A. and Giller, H. *Understanding Juvenile Justice*. London: Groom Helm, 1987.

Morris, A. and Giller, H. "Juvenile Justice and Social Work in Great Britian" in Parker, H. ed. *Social Work and the Courts*. London: Edward Arnold, 1978, pp. 8–33.

Morrison, B. Untitled paper presented to a conference on Young Offender Dispositions in Montreal, November 30 to December 5, 1988.

Morrison, B. "Commentary on Issues Related to Custody." Paper presented to the Advanced Judicial Seminar, Montreal, 1988.

Moyer, S. *A Description of the Application of Dispositions Under the Young Offenders Act by the Ministry of Community and Social Services of Ontario*. Ottawa: Department of Justice Canada, 1989.

Moyer, S. *Diversion from the Juvenile Justice System and Its Impact on Children: A Review of the Literature*. Ottawa: Ministry of the Solicitor General, 1980.

Moyer, S. *La Déjudiciarisation dans le Système Judiciaire pour les Jeunes et ses Répercussions sur les Enfants: Recension de la Documentation*. Ottawa: Ministère du Solliciteur Général, Division de la Recherche, 1980.

Moyer, S. and Carrington, P., *The Attitude of Canadian Juvenile Justice Professionals Towards the Young Offenders Act*, Programs Branch User Report. Ottawa: Ministry of the Solicitor General, 1985.

Murray, C.A. and Cox, L.A. *Beyond Probation: Juvenile Corrections and the Chronic Delinquent*. Beverly Hills, Calif.: Sage Publications, 1979.

National Advisory Commission on Criminal Justice Standards and Goals. Police Standard 9.5. Washington, D.C.: U.S. Government Printing Office, 1973.

Nunes, J. "Judges' Sentences Vary Widely in Study of Young Offender Cases". *The Globe and Mail*, Toronto, July 13, 1989, p. 4.

Olsen-Raymer, G. "National Juvenile Justice Policy: Myth or Reality?" In Decker, S., ed., *Juvenile Justice Policy: Analyzing Trends and Outcomes*. Beverley Hills: Sage Publications, 1984.

Ontario Ministry of Correctional Services. *Annual Report of the Ontario Ministry of Correctional Services*. Toronto: Ministry of Correctional Services, 1986.

Ontario Social Development Council. *Proceedings of the Conference on YOA Dispositions: Challenges and Choices*. Toronto: Ontario Social Development Council, 1987.

Osborne, J.A. "Juvenile Justice Policy in Canada: The Transfer of the Initiative" (1979) 2(1) Can. J. Fam. L. pp. 7–32.

Outerbridge, W.R. "The Tyranny of Treatment . . .?" (1968) 10 (2), Can. J. Corr., pp. 378–87.

Palmer, T. *Correctional Intervention and Research.* Lexington, Mass.: Lexington Books, 1978.

Palmer, T. and Lewis, R.V. *An Evaluation of Juvenile Diversion.* Cambridge: Oelgeschlager, Gunn & Hain, 1980.

Parker, H., Casburn, M. and Turnbull, D. *Receiving Juvenile Justice: Adolescents and State Care and Control.* Oxford: Basil Blackwell, 1981.

Paternoster, R. and Bynum, T. "The Justice Model as Ideology: A Critical Look at the Impetus for Sentencing Reform" (1982) 6 *Contemporary Crisis* pp. 7–24.

Platt, A., Schechter, H. and Tiffany, P. "In Defence of Youth: A Case of the Public Defender in Juvenile Court" (1968) 43 Ind. L.J. pp. 619–40.

Platt, A.M. *The Child Savers: The Invention of Delinquency.* Chicago: University of Chicago Press, 1977.

Platt, P. *Young Offenders Law in Canada.* Toronto: Butterworths, 1989.

Pound, R. "The Limits of Effective Legal Action". 22 Annual Report of the Pennsylvania Bar Association, Philadelphia, Penn., 1916, p. 221.

Pratt, J. "A Comparative Analysis of Two Different Systems of Juvenile Justice: Some Implications for England and Wales". Unpublished paper, Institute of Criminology: Cambridge University, 1985.

Pratt, J. "A Revisionist History of Intermediate Treatment" (1987) 17 *British Journal of Social Work.* pp. 417–36.

Pratt, J. "Corporatism: The Third Model of Juvenile Justice" (1989) 29(3) *British Journal of Criminology* pp. 236–53.

Pratt, J. "Crime, Time, Youth and Punishment" (1990) *Contemporary Crisis* pp. 219–42.

Pratt, J. "Juvenile Justice, Social Work and Social Control. The Need for Positive Thinking" (1985) 15 *British Journal of Social Work.* pp. 1–25.

President's Commission on Law Enforcement and Administration of Justice. *The Challenge of Crime in Free Society.* Washington, D.C.: U.S. Government Printing Office, 1967.

President's Commission on Law Enforcement and Administration of Justice. *Task Force Report: Juvenile Delinquency and Youth Crime.* Washington: U.S. Government Printing Office, 1967.

Rappaport, J. "Public Policy and the Dilemmas of Diversion". In Corrado, R., Le Blanc, M. and Trépanier, J. *Current Issues in Juvenile Justice.* Toronto: Butterworths, 1983.

Reid, S.A. "The Juvenile Justice 'Revolution' in Canada: The Creation and Development of New Legislation for Young Offenders" (1986) 8(1) Can. Crim. Forum 1–14.

Reid, S.A. and Reitsma-Street, M. "Assumptions and Implications of New Canadian Legislation for Young Offenders" (1984) 7(1) Can. Crim. Forum pp. 334–52. Also (1984) 7 Can. Crim. Forum pp. 1–19.

Reynolds, F. *A Lack of Principles*. Oxford: Oxford University Department of Social and Administrative Studies, 1985.

Reynolds, F. "Magistrates' Justifications for Making Custodial Orders on Juvenile Offenders" (1985) (May) Crim. L. Rev. 244–98.

Ross, R.R. and Gendreau, P. *Effective Correctional Treatment*. Toronto: Butterworths, 1980.

Rothman, D. *Conscience and Convenience*. Boston: Little Brown, 1980.

Rubin, M.T. "Juvenile Justice Policy, Practice, and Law" in Goodyear, *Juvenile Justice Policy: Analyzing Trends and Outcomes*. Santa Monica, Calif., 1979.

Rubin, M.T., "Retain the Juvenile Court? Legislative Developments, Reform Directives, and the Call for Abolition" (1979) 25(3) pp. 281–98. *Crime and Delinquency*.

Rubin, M.T. "The Emergence of Prosecutor Dominance of the Juvenile Court Intake Process" (1980) 26(3) *Crime and Delinquency* pp. 299–318.

Rutherford, A. *Growing Out of Crime*. Harmondsworth: Penguin, 1986.

Rutherford, A. Speech cited in *NARCO News Digest*. London: National Association for the Care and Resettlement of Offenders, 1982, p. 2.

Rutherford, A. "A Statute Backfires: The Excalation of Youth Incarceration in England during the 1970s" in Doing, J.W. ed. *Criminal Corrections: Ideals and Realities*. Toronto: Lextington Books, 1983.

Ryant, J.C. and Heinrich, C. "Youth Court Committees in Manitoba". In Hudson, J., Hornick, J.J. and Burrows, B.A., eds. *Justice and the Young Offender in Canada*. Toronto: Wall and Thompson, 1988.

Sarri, R. *Under lock and Key: Juveniles in Jail and Detention*. Ann Arbor, Mich.: University of Michigan, National Assessment of Juvenile Corrections, 1974.

Sarri, R. and Hasenfeld, Y. *Brought to Justice? Juveniles, The Courts, and The Law*. Ann Arbor, Mich.: University of Michigan, National Assessment of Juvenile Corrections, 1976.

Schneider, A.L. and Ervin, L. "Deterrence and Juvenile Crimes: Examining the Behavioural Assumptions of Public Policy." Paper presented to the 40th Annual Meeting of the American Society of Criminology, Chicago, 1988.

Schur, E.M. *Radical Nonintervention: Rethinking the Delinquency Problem*. Englewood Cliffs, NJ: Prentice-Hall, 1973.

Schwartz, I.M. *(In) Justice for Juveniles: Rethinking the Best Interests of the Child*. Lextington, Mass: Lexington Books, 1989.

Schwartz, I.M. Reinvesting *Youth Corrections Resources: A Tale of Three States*. Minneapolis, Minn.: Humphrey Institute, Center for the Study of Youth Policy, 1987.

Scull, A.T. *Decarceration: Community Treatment and the Deviant — A Radical View*. Englewood Clifs, NJ: Prentice-Hall, 1977.

Scull, A.T. "Madness and Segregative Control: The Rise of the Insane Asylum" (1977) 24 *Social Problems*. pp. 337–50.

Sechrest, L., White, S.O. and Brown, G.D. *The Rehabilitation of Criminal Offenders*. Washington, D.C.: National Academy of Sciences, 1979.

Senate of Canada. *Proceedings of the Standing Senate Committee on Legal and Constitutional Affairs*. First Session of the Thirty-Second Parliament. Hull, Quebec: Canadian Government Publishing Centre, 1980-81-82.

Shamsie, S.J., "Antisocial Adolescents: All Treatments Do Not Work. Where Do We Go From Here?" (1981) 26 *Canadian Journal of Psychiatry* 357–64.

Shireman, C.H. and Reamer, F.G. *Rehabilitating Juvenile Justice*. New York: Columbia University Press, 1986.

Silberman, C.E. *Criminal Violence, Criminal Justice*. New York: Vintage Books, 1978.

Silverman, R.A. "Trends in Canadian Youth Homicide: Some Unanticipated Consequences of a Change in Law." (1990) 32 (4), Can. J. Crim., pp. 651–66.

Skibinski, G.J. and Koszuth, A.M.I. "Getting Tough with Juvenile Offenders: Ignoring the Best Interests of the Child" (1986) 37(5) Juv. Fam. Ct. J. pp. 43–50.

Solicitor General Canada. *Highlights of the Proposed New Legislation for Young Offenders*. Ottawa: Queen's Printer, 1979.

Solicitor General Canada. *Legislative Proposals to Replace the Young Offenders Act*. Unpublished, Ottawa, 1979.

Solicitor General Canada. *Young Offenders Act, 1982, Highlights*. Ottawa: Minister of Supply and Services Canada, 1982.

Solicitor General Canada. *Young Persons in Conflict with the Law*. Ottawa: Ministry of the Solicitor General, 1975.

Spitzer, S. "Toward a Marxian Theory of Deviance" (1975) 22 (June) *Social Problems* pp. 638–51.

Stapleton, V., Aday, D.P. and Ito, J. "An Empirical Typology of American Metropolitan Juvenile Courts" (1982) 88 *American Journal of Sociology* pp. 549–64.

Stapleton, V.W. and Teitelbaum, L.E. *In Defense of Youth: A Study of the Role of Counsel in American Juvenile Courts*. New York: Russell Sage Foundation, 1972.

Statistics Canada, Canadian Centre for Justice Statistics. *Juvenile Delinquents, 1983*. Ottawa: Supply and Services Canada, 1984.

Statistics Canada. "Dispositions under the Young Offenders Act" (1991) 11(5) *Juristat Services Bulletin*. Ottawa: Canadian Centre for Justice Statistics.

Statistics Canada. "Homicide in Canada" (1990) 10 (14) *Juristat Services Bulletin*. Ottawa: Canadian Centre for Justice Statistics.

Statistics Canada. "National Summary of Alternative Measures Services for Young Persons" (1990) 10 (11) *Juristat Services Bulletin*. Ottawa: Canadian Centre for Justice Statistics.

Statistics Canada. "Processing Time in Youth Courts" (1991) 11(4) *Juristat Services Bulletin*. Ottawa: Canadian Centre for Justice Statistics.

Statistics Canada. "Recidivists in Youth Court: An Examination of Repeat Young Offenders Convicted in 1988–89" (1990) 10(8). *Juristat Service Bulletin*, Ottawa, Canadian Centre for Justice.

Statistics Canada. "Sentencing in Youth Courts: 1984–85 to 1988–89" (1990) 10(1) *Juristat Service Bulletin*, 10(1). Ottawa, Canadian Centre for Justice Statistics.

Statistics Canada. *Uniform Crime Reports*. Ottawa: Canadian Centre for Justice Statistics, 1980, 1982, 1983, 1984, 1985, 1986, 1987, 1988.

Statistics Canada. "Violent Crime in Canada" (1990) 10 (15) *Juristat Services Bulletin*. Ottawa: Canadian Centre for Justice Statistics.

Statistics Canada. "Violent Offence Cases Heard in Youth Courts, 1990-1991" (1991) 11(16) *Juristat Services Bulletin*. Ottawa: Canadian Centre for Justice Statistics.

Statistics Canada. "Violent Offences by Young Offenders, 1986-87 to 1988-89" (1990) 10 (5) *Juristat Services Bulletin*. Ottawa: Canadian Centre for Justice Statistics.

Statistics Canada. *Youth Court Statistics, Preliminary Data*. Ottawa: Canadian Centre for Justice Statistics, 1984–85, 1985–86, 1986–87, 1987–88, 1988–89, 1989–90.

Statistics Canada. "Youth Court Statistics, Preliminary Data: 1989-90 Highlights" (1990) 10 (13) *Juristat Services Bulletin*. Ottawa: Canadian Centre for Justice Statistics.

Statistics Canada. "Youth Crime in Canada, 1986-88" (1990) 10 (2) *Juristat Services Bulletin*. Ottawa: Canadian Centre for Justice Statistics.

Sutton, J.R. *Stubborn Children: Controlling Delinquency in the United States, 1640–1981*. Berkeley, Calif.: University of California Press, 1988.

Table Centrale de Consultation et de Concertation. "Évaluation-Orientation des Jeunes Contrevenants". Québec: Table Centrale de Consultation et de Concertation, Loi sur la Protection de la Jeunesse, 1980.

Taylor, I. *Law and Order: Arguments for Socialism*. London: MacMillan, 1981.

Taylor, I. "Moral Enterprise, Moral Panic and Law and Order Campaigns" in Rosenberg, M.M., Stebbins, R.A. and Turowetz, A. *The Sociology of Deviance* New York: St. Martin's Press, 1982.

Terry, R.M. "Discrimination in the Handling of Juvenile Offenders by Social Control Agencies" (1967) 4(2) pp. 218–30. *Journal of Research in Crime and Delinquency*.

Thompson, A.H. "The Young Offender, Child Welfare and Mental Health Caseload Communalities" 1988 30(2) Can. J. Crim. pp. 135–44.

Thomson, G.M. "Commentary on the Young Offenders Act" (1983) 7 (2) Prov. Judges J. pp. 27–34.

Thornberry, T.P. "Race, Socioeconomic Status and Sentencing in the Juvenile Court" (1973) 64(1) *Journal of Criminal Law and Criminology*, pp. 90–98.

Treadwell, W.M. "The Lawyer in Juvenile Court Dispositional Proceedings: Advocate, Social Worker, or Otherwise" (1965–67) 16–17 Juv. Ct. Judges J. pp. 109–15.

Trepanier, J. "Principles and Goals Guiding the Choice of Dispositions Under the YOA". In Beaulieu, L., ed. *Young Offender Dispositions: Perspectives on Principles and Practice*. Toronto: Wall and Thompson, 1989.

Trépanier, J. "The Quebec Youth Protection Act: Institutionalized Diversion". In Corrado, R.R., LeBlanc, M. and Trepanier, J., eds., *Current Issues in Juvenile Justice*. Toronto: Butterworths, 1982.

Trépanier, J. "Trends in Juvenile Justice: Washington State". In Corrado, R.R., LeBlanc, M., and Trepanier, J., eds., *Current Issues in Juvenile Justice*. Toronto: Butterworths, 1982.

Trépanier, J. "Événements Judiciaires et Récidive chez les Adolescents Délinquants". Mémoire de maitrise inédit, Université de Montréal, Département de Criminologie, Montréal, 1969.

Trépanier, J. and Gagnon, R. "La Déjudiciarisation à la Cour du Bien-Être Social de Montréal". Université de Montréal, École de Criminologie, 1984.

Tutt, N. and Giller, H. *The Criminal Justice Act 1982*. Lancaster U.K.: Information Systems, 1983.

Tutt, N. and Giller, H. "Police Cautioning of Juveniles: The Practice of Diversity" (1983) (September) Crim. L. Rev. 587–95.

U.S. Department of Justice. *Major Issues in Juvenile Justice Information and Training*. Washington, D.C.: U.S. Government Printing Office, 1982.

Vinter, R.D. *Time Out: A National Study of Juvenile Correction Programs*. Ann Arbor, Mich.: University of Michigan Press, 1976.

Vogel, R.H. and Robinson, B.G. *Bill C-61, The Young Offenders Act: Submission to the Standing Senate Committee on Constitutional and Legal Affairs*. Victoria: Ministry of Attorney General, 1982.

Vold, G. and Bernard, T. *Theoretical Criminology*. New York: Oxford University Press, 1979.

Wald, P.M. Pretrial Detention for Juveniles. In Rosenheim, M.K. ed. *Pursuing Justice for the Child*. Chicago: University of Chicago Press, 1984.

Walker, S. *Sense and Nonsense About Crime: A Policy Guide*. Pacific Grove, Calif. Brooks/Cole, 1989.

Weiler, R. and Ward, B. "The Voluntary Sector Response to the Young Offenders Act". In Hudson, J., Hornick, J.J. and Burrows, B.A., eds. *Justice and the Young Offender in Canada*. Toronto: Wall and Thompson, 1988.

West, W.G. *Young Offenders and the State: A Canadian Perspective on Delinquency*. Toronto: Butterworths, 1984.

Whitehead, P. and MacMillan, J. "Checks or Blank Cheque?" (1985) 32 *Probation* 87–9.

Whitehead, and Lab, "A Meta-analysis of Juvenile Correctional Treatment" (1989) 26 *Journal of Research in Crime and Delinquency* pp. 276–95.

Wilson, J. and Herrnstein, R. *Crime & Human Nature*. New York: Simon and Schuster, 1985.

Wilson, J.Q. *Thinking About Crime*. New York: Vintage Books, 1975.

Wilson, L. "Changes to Federal Jurisdiction Over Young Offenders: The Provincial Response" (1990) 8(2) Can. J. Fam. L. pp. 342–3.

Wilson, L.C. *Juvenile Courts in Canada*. Toronto: Carswell, 1982.

Wilson, L.C. "Changes to Federal Jurisdiction Over Young Offenders: The Provincial Response" (1990) 8(2) Can. J. Fam. L. pp. 303–43.

Witmer, H. and Tufts, A. *The Effectiveness of Delinquency Prevention Programs*. Washington: U.S. Department of Health, Education and Welfare, Government Printing Office, 1954.

Wooldredge J.D. "Differentiating the Effects of Juvenile Court Sentences on Eliminating Recidivism" (1988) 25(3) *Journal of Research in Crime and Delinquency* pp. 264–300.

Young, A. "Appellate Court Sentencing Principles". In Beaulieu L., ed., *Young Offender Dispositions: Perspectives on Principles and Practice*. Toronto: Wall and Thompson, 1989.

Zimring, F.E. "Pursuing Juvenile Justice: Comments on Some Recent Reform Proposals" (1978) 53 J. of Urb. L. pp. 631–45.

van den Haag, E. *Punishing Criminals*. New York: Basic Books, 1975.